Best Books for Middle School and Junior High Readers

Recent Titles in the
Children's and Young Adult Literature Reference Series
Catherine Barr, Series Editor

A to Zoo: Subject Access to Children's Picture Books
Carolyn W. Lima and John A. Lima

Best Books for Children: Preschool Through Grade 6
Catherine Barr and John T. Gillespie

Books Kids Will Sit Still For 3
Judy Freeman

The Newbery/Printz Companion
John T. Gillespie and Corinne J. Naden

Classic Teenplots
John T. Gillespie and Corinne J. Naden

Best Books for Middle School and Junior High Readers

Supplement to the First Edition

Grades 6-9

John T. Gillespie
Catherine Barr

Children's and Young Adult Literature Reference Series
Catherine Barr, Series Editor

LIBRARIES UNLIMITED
A Member of the Greenwood Publishing Group

Westport, Connecticut • London

Library of Congress Cataloging-in-Publication Data

Gillespie, John Thomas, 1928-
  Best books for middle school and junior high readers : grades 6–9. Supplement to the first edition /
by John T. Gillespie and Catherine Barr.
      p. cm. — (Children's and young adult literature reference)
  Includes bibliographical references and indexes.
  ISBN 1-59158-411-6 (alk. paper)
  1. Middle school students—Books and reading—United States. 2. Junior high school students—Books
and reading—United States. 3. Preteens—Books and reading—United States. 4. Teenagers—Books and
reading—United States. 5. Children's literature—Bibliography. 6. Young adult literature—Bibliography.
7. Middle school libraries—United States—Book lists. 8. Junior high school libraries—United States—
Book lists. I. Barr, Catherine, 1951– II. Title.
  Z1037.G482 2004 Suppl.
  028.5'35—dc22   2006031033

British Library Cataloguing in Publication Data is available.

Library of Congress Catalog Card Number: 2006031033
ISBN: 1-59158-411-6

Libraries Unlimited, 88 Post Road West, Westport, CT 06881
A Member of the Greenwood Publishing Group, Inc.
www.lu.com

Printed in the United States of America

The paper used in this book complies with the
Permanent Paper Standard issued by the National
Information Standards Organization (Z39.48–1984).

10 9 8 7 6 5 4 3 2 1

Contents

Literary History and Criticism

Language and Communication

Biography, Memoirs, Etc.

The Arts and Entertainment

History and Geography

Physical and Applied Sciences

Major Subjects Arranged Alphabetically

Preface

Best Books for Middle School and Junior High Readers is intended to supply information on books recommended for readers in grades 6 through 9 or roughly ages 11 through 16. The companion volumes *Best Books for Children* and *Best Books for High School Readers* contain books recommended for preschool through grade 6 and grades 9 through 12, respectively.

As every librarian knows, reading levels are elastic. There is no such thing, for example, as a seventh-grade book. Instead there are only seventh-grade readers who, in their diversity, can represent a wide range of reading abilities and interests. This bibliography contains a liberal selection of entries that, one hopes, will accommodate readers in these grades and make allowance for their great range of tastes and reading competencies. By the ninth grade, a percentage of the books read should be at the adult level. Keeping this in mind, about one fifth of the entries in this volume are adult books suitable for young adult readers (they are designated by reading level grades of 6–12, 7–12, and 8–12 within the entries). At the other end of the spectrum, there are also many titles that are suitable for readers below the sixth grade (indicated by grade level designations such as 4–7, 4–8, 4–9, 5–7, and 5–8 within the entries).

In selecting books for inclusion, deciding on their arrangement, and collecting the information supplied on each, it was the editors' intention to reflect the current needs and interests of young readers while keeping in mind the latest trends and curricular emphases in today's schools.

General Scope and Criteria for Inclusion

This supplement covers a two-year period, picking up from *Best Books for Middle School and Junior High Readers,* which was published in 2004, and including recommended titles published through mid-2006. Of the 2989 titles listed in this supplement, 2816 are individually numbered entries and 173 are cited within the annotations as additional recommended titles by the same author.

For most fiction and nonfiction, a minimum of two recommendations were required from the current reviewing sources consulted for a title to be considered for listing. However, there were a number of necessary exceptions. For example, in some reviewing journals only a few representative titles from extensive nonfiction series are reviewed even though others in the series will also be recommended. In such cases a single favorable review was enough for inclusion. This also held true for some of the adult titles suitable for young adult readers where, it has been found, reviewing journals tend to be less inclusive than with juvenile titles. Again, depending on the strength of the review, a single positive one was sufficient for inclusion. As well as favorable reviews, additional criteria such as availability, up-to-dateness, accuracy, usefulness, and relevance were considered.

Excluded from this bibliography are general reference works, such as dictionaries and encyclopedias, except for a few single-volume works that are so heavily illustrated and attractive that they can also be used in the general circulation collection. Also excluded are professional books for librarians and teachers and mass market series books.

Some arbitrary decisions were made concerning placement of books under specific subjects. For example, books of experiments and projects in general science are placed under "Physical and Applied Sciences—Experiments and Projects," whereas books of experiments and projects on a specific branch of science (e.g., physics) appear under that branch. It is hoped that use of the many "see" and "see also" references in the Subject/Grade Level Index will help guide the user in this regard.

The graphic novels section includes contemporary graphic novels, many with elements of fantasy and/or science fiction. However, books presenting classics in a graphic novel format will be found in the appropriate location for that classic.

Arrangement

In the Table of Contents, subjects are arranged by the order in which they appear in the book. Following the Table of Contents is a listing of Major Subjects Arranged Alphabetically, which provides entry numbers as well as page numbers for easy access. Following the main body of the text, there are three indexes. The Author Index cites authors and editors, titles, and entry numbers (joint authors and editors are listed separately). The Title Index gives the book's entry number. Works of fiction in both of these indexes are indicated by (F) following the entry number. Finally, an extensive Subject/Grade Level Index lists entry numbers under hundreds of subject headings with specific grade-level suitability given for each entry. The following codes are used to identify general grade levels:

IJ (Intermediate-Junior High) suitable for upper elementary and lower middle school

J (Junior High) suitable for middle school and junior high

JS (Junior-Senior High) suitable for junior high and senior high

Entries

A typical entry contains the following information where applicable: (1) author, joint author, or editor; (2) title and subtitle; (3) specific grade levels given in parentheses; (4) adapter or translator; (5) indication of illustrations; (6) series title; (7) publication date; (8) publisher and price of hardbound edition (LB = library binding); (9) International Standard Book Number (ISBN) of hardbound edition; (10) paperback publisher (paper) and price (if no publisher is listed it is the same as the hardbound edition); (11) ISBN of paperback edition; (12) annotation; (13) review citations; (14) Dewey Decimal classification number.

Review Citations

Review citations guide you to more-detailed information about each of the books listed. The periodical sources identified are:

Booklist (BL)
Bulletin of the Center for Children's Books (BCCB)
Horn Book (HB)
Horn Book Guide (HBG)
Library Media Connection (LMC)
School Library Journal (SLJ)
VOYA (Voice of Youth Advocates) (VOYA)

Acknowledgments

Many thanks to Barbara Ittner of Libraries Unlimited and to Don Amerman, Christine McNaull, and Julie Miller for all their help with this volume.

John Gillespie
Catherine Barr

Literary Forms

Fiction

Adventure and Survival Stories

1 Alexander, Lloyd. *The Xanadu Adventure* (5–8). 2005, Button $16.99 (0-525-47371-8). 160pp. Vesper Holly, accompanied by friends and guardians, sets off for Asia Minor to search for an artifact in the ancient city of Troy but soon finds herself in the clutches of her nemesis, Dr. Desmond Helvitius. (Rev: BL 2/1/05*; SLJ 2/05)

2 Allende, Isabel. *Kingdom of the Golden Dragon* (7–12). 2004, HarperCollins $19.99 (0-06-058942-6). 448pp. Yetis, high in the Himalayas, help 16-year-old Alexander in his fight against American corporate villains in this sequel to *City of the Beasts*. (Rev: BL 2/15/04; SLJ 4/04)

3 Bledsoe, Lucy Jane. *The Antarctic Scoop* (4–7). 2003, Holiday House $16.95 (0-8234-1792-1). 168pp. In this fast-paced adventure story, 12-year-old Victoria, a shy girl with ambitious dreams, wins a trip to Antarctica but discovers during her travels that the real goal of the contest sponsor is to develop and exploit the icy continent. (Rev: BL 1/1–15/04; SLJ 1/04)

4 Hart, J. V. *Capt. Hook: The Adventures of a Notorious Youth* (7–10). 2005, HarperCollins LB $16.89 (0-06-000221-2). 352pp. The story of Captain Hook's youth follows his lonely childhood, time at Eton, difficult life aboard a slave ship, and dreams of a Neverland. (Rev: BL 7/05; SLJ 10/05)

5 Hobbs, Will. *Leaving Protection* (7–12). 2004, HarperCollins $15.99 (0-688-17475-2). 192pp. An exciting novel about a 16-year-old boy, his work on an Alaskan salmon trawler, and the secret plans of its skipper. (Rev: BL 3/1/04; SLJ 4/04)

6 Hunt, L. J. *The Abernathy Boys* (5–7). 2004, HarperCollins LB $16.89 (0-06-029259-8). 208pp. Young Bud and Temple Abernathy survive an eventful journey through the desert in this fictionalized version of a real expedition in the early 20th century. (Rev: BL 1/1–15/04; SLJ 3/04)

7 Jaramillo, Ann. *La Línea* (5–8). 2006, Roaring Brook $16.95 (1-59643-154-7). 144pp. Miguel, 15, and his sister Elena, 13, survive a terrifying journey across the border (la linea) from Mexico to California to join their parents. (Rev: BL 3/15/06*; SLJ 4/06; VOYA 4/06)

8 Korman, Gordon. *Chasing the Falconers* (4–7). 2005, Scholastic paper $5.99 (0-439-65136-0). 144pp. In this fast-paced adventure, Aiden and Meg Falconer must evade pursuers as they work to gather evidence that will prove their parents' innocence of treason. (Rev: BL 5/15/05; SLJ 8/05)

9 McFadden, Deanna. *Robinson Crusoe: Retold from the Daniel Defoe Original* (4–7). Series: Classic Starts. 2006, Sterling $4.95 (1-4027-2664-3). 160pp. The 1719 original text is retold in brief, accessible sentences that portray Crusoe and Friday as equals. (Rev: BL 2/15/06)

10 McKernan, Victoria. *Shackleton's Stowaway* (6–9). 2005, Knopf LB $17.99 (0-375-92691-7). 336pp. In this fictionalized account, the 1914–1916 Antarctic expedition of Ernest Shackleton is chronicled through the eyes of 18-year-old stowaway Perce Blackborow. (Rev: BCCB 2/05; BL 2/15/05; SLJ 2/05; VOYA 4/05)

11 MacPhail, Catherine. *Underworld* (7–10). 2005, Bloomsbury $16.95 (1-58234-997-5). 288pp. Five British teens with very different personalities find themselves trapped in a cave on a remote Scottish island; adding to their predicament is their fear of a giant worm reputed to inhabit the caves. (Rev: BL 7/05; SLJ 7/05; VOYA 8/05)

12 Meyer, L. A. *Under the Jolly Roger: Being an Account of the Further Nautical Adventures of Jacky Faber* (7–10). 2005, Harcourt $17.00 (0-15-205345-X). 528pp. In this volume full of adventure, plucky 15-year-old Jacky Faber — last seen in *Bloody Jack* (2002) and *Curse of the Blue Tattoo* (2004) — travels from Boston to England in 1804 in search of her true love but ends up taking control of a British warship. (Rev: BL 8/05; SLJ 9/05; VOYA 8/05)

13 Moodie, Craig. *The Sea Singer* (5–8). 2005, Roaring Brook $16.95 (1-59643-050-8). 176pp. Upset that his father left him behind, 12-year-old Finn stows away on Leif Eriksson's ship, which will follow his father's route to Vineland. (Rev: BL 8/05; SLJ 8/05; VOYA 2/06)

14 Napoli, Donna Jo. *North* (4–7). 2004, Greenwillow $15.99 (0-06-057987-0). 352pp. Twelve-year-old Alvin, an African American boy fascinated by explorer Matthew Henson, sets off for the Arctic and, with the help of several adults along the way, makes the long and complex journey safely. (Rev: BL 3/1/04; SLJ 5/04)

15 Nordin, Sofia. *In the Wild* (4–7). Trans. from Swedish by Maria Lundin. 2005, Groundwood $15.95 (0-88899-648-9). 119pp. Set in Sweden, this is an adventure story featuring 6th-grade outcast Amanda and bully Philip, who become lost and must rely on their own resources to survive. (Rev: SLJ 10/05)

16 Paulsen, Gary. *Brian's Hunt* (6–10). Series: Brian's Saga. 2003, Random LB $17.99 (0-385-90882-2). 144pp. Brian rescues a wounded dog and embarks on a hunt for a rogue bear that has savagely killed and partially eaten two of Brian's Cree friends. (Rev: BCCB 2/04; BL 1/1–15/04; SLJ 12/03)

17 Reiche, Dietlof. *Ghost Ship* (5–8). Trans. by John Brownjohn. 2005, Scholastic $16.95 (0-439-59704-8). 336pp. A suspenseful adventure featuring ghosts, piracy, buried treasure, and romance between 12-year-old Vicki and a boy on vacation in her seaside town. (Rev: BL 5/15/05; SLJ 8/05)

18 Shahan, Sherry. *Death Mountain* (5–8). 2005, Peachtree $15.95 (1-56145-353-6). 178pp. In this gripping thriller, 14-year-old Erin uses her survival skills to rescue her new friend Mae and navigate their way through a mountain wilderness to safety. (Rev: SLJ 11/05; VOYA 2/06)

19 Smith, Roland. *Cryptid Hunters* (5–8). 2005, Hyperion $15.99 (0-7868-5161-9). 352pp. Thirteen-year-old twins Marty and Grace find themselves in an action-packed adventure in the Congo. (Rev: BL 2/1/05; SLJ 5/05)

20 Taylor, Theodore. *Ice Drift* (4–7). 2005, Harcourt $16.00 (0-15-205081-7). 240pp. Inuit brothers Alika, 14, and Sulu, 10, struggle to survive over the months that they are trapped on an ice floe that is slowly floating south in the Greenland Strait. (Rev: BL 2/1/05; SLJ 1/05)

21 Torrey, Michele. *Voyage of Ice* (4–7). Series: Chronicle of Courage. 2004, Knopf LB $17.99 (0-375-92381-0). 192pp. In 1851, 15-year-old Nick signs on as a hand aboard the whaler *Sea Hawk* and soon discovers unexpected hardships, including struggling to survive in the Arctic. (Rev: BL 5/15/04; SLJ 7/04)

22 Withers, Pam. *Camp Wild* (7–9). Series: Orca Currents. 2005, Orca paper $7.95 (1-55143-361-3). 104pp. For reluctant readers, this is the story of 14-year-old Wilf, who must learn to work with others to succeed in his escape from summer camp. (Rev: SLJ 10/05; VOYA 10/05)

23 Wizowaty, Suzi. *A Tour of Evil* (5–8). 2005, Philomel $10.99 (0-399-24251-1). Evil lurks in a cathedral in northern France in this novel involving an 11-year-old orphan, Alma, who discovers a plot to kidnap children. (Rev: BL 5/15/05; SLJ 8/05)

Animal Stories

24 Bain, Terry. *You Are a Dog (Life Through the Eyes of Man's Best Friend)* (8–12). Illus. 2004, Harmony $16.00 (1-4000-5242-4). 159pp. A humorous dog's-eye view of the world. (Rev: SLJ 1/05)

25 Ghent, Natale. *No Small Thing* (5–8). 2005, Candlewick $15.00 (0-7636-2422-5). 256pp. Nathaniel and his siblings struggle to keep their horse while their single mother struggles to keep her family afloat. (Rev: BL 3/1/05; SLJ 4/05)

26 Morgan, Clay. *The Boy Who Spoke Dog* (5–8). 2003, Dutton $15.99 (0-525-47159-6). 166pp. Marooned on an island dominated by two warring dog packs, Jack, a young cabin boy, feels very much alone until he develops a friendship with a border collie named Moxie. (Rev: BL 1/1–15/04; SLJ 1/04; VOYA 6/04)

Classics

Europe

GREAT BRITAIN AND IRELAND

27 Carroll, Lewis. *Alice's Adventures in Wonderland* (5–12). 2003, Simply Read $29.95 (1-894965-00-0). 136pp. Interesting illustrations by Ghiuselev that interpret incidents and characters in a different way highlight this new edition of an old classic. (Rev: BL 2/1/04; SLJ 6/04)

28 Stevenson, Robert Louis. *Treasure Island* (5–9). Adapted and illus. by Tim Hamilton. Series: Puffin Graphics. 2005, Puffin paper $9.99 (0-142-40470-5). 176pp. Robert Louis Stevenson's adventure classic springs to life in this striking graphic novel adaptation that remains faithful to the original text. (Rev: SLJ 11/05)

29 Willard, Nancy, and John Milton. *The Tale of Paradise Lost: Based on the Poem by John Milton* (6–12). 2004, Simon & Schuster $17.95 (0-689-85097-2). 160pp. This prose retelling of Milton's immortal "Paradise Lost" traces the story of Adam and Eve's expulsion from the Garden of Eden and the fall of Satan from God's grace. (Rev: BL 10/1/04; HB 11/12/04; SLJ 1/05)

United States

30 Camfield, Gregg, ed. *Mark Twain* (6–9). Series: Stories for Young People. 2005, Sterling LB $14.95 (1-4027-1178-6). 80pp. A collection of five stories by Mark Twain, plus a brief biography and glossary notes. (Rev: SLJ 10/05)

31 London, Jack. *The Call of the Wild: The Graphic Novel* (6–9). Ed. by Neil Kleid. Series: Puffin Graphics. 2006, Penguin paper $9.99 (0-14-240571-X). 176pp. Jack London's classic tale in graphic format. (Rev: BL 4/1/06; SLJ 3/06)

32 Poe, Edgar Allan. *Edgar Allan Poe's Tales of Mystery and Madness* (7–12). Trans. by Stephen Soenkson. 2004, Simon & Schuster $17.95 (0-689-84837-4). 144pp. Striking artwork brings to life four of Edgar Allan Poe's classic mystery tales, presented here in abridged form. (Rev: BL 10/15/04*; SLJ 10/04)

33 Poe, Edgar Allan. *Tales of Terror* (6–9). Illus. by Michael McCurdy. 2005, Knopf LB $17.99 (0-375-93305-0). 96pp. Six of Poe's most famous tales are introduced by discussion of Poe's life and work and accompanied by dramatic illustrations and a CD of four of the shorter tales. (Rev: BL 8/05; VOYA 12/05)

34 Twain, Mark. *Graphic Classics: Mark Twain* (7–10). Illus. Series: Graphic Classics. 2004, Eureka paper $9.95 (0-9712464-8-3). 144pp. Various artists offer diverse graphic novel treatments of Twain stories including "A Ghost Story," "Advice to Little Girls," and "The Mysterious Stranger." (Rev: SLJ 3/04)

Contemporary Life and Problems

General and Miscellaneous

35 Anderson, Jodi Lynn. *Peaches* (8–11). 2005, HarperCollins LB $16.89 (0-06-073306-3). 320pp. Three teenage girls from diverse backgrounds forge lasting bonds during a summer picking peaches in a Georgia orchard. (Rev: BL 10/1/05; SLJ 8/05; VOYA 2/06)

36 Ashton, Victoria. *Confessions of a Teen Nanny* (8–12). 2005, HarperCollins LB $16.89 (0-06-077524-6). 198pp. Hired as a temporary nanny for an 8-year-old child prodigy, 16-year-old Adrienne finds herself being manipulated by her charge's older sister. (Rev: BL 8/05; SLJ 7/05)

37 Banks, Kate. *Friends of the Heart/Amici del Cuore* (6–9). 2005, Farrar $16.00 (0-374-32455-7). 144pp. Lucrezia looks back a few years to the idyllic summer she and her childhood friend spent an idyllic summer in a seaside Italian village until tragedy struck. (Rev: BL 12/1/05)

38 Bateson, Catherine. *Stranded in Boringsville* (5–8). 2005, Holiday House $16.95 (0-8234-1969-X). 138pp. Twelve-year-old Rain's life is turned upside down when she and her mother move from cosmopolitan Melbourne to a small Australian town in the middle of nowhere; but she finds a good friend in her neighbor Daniel. (Rev: BL 12/1/05; SLJ 2/06; VOYA 2/06)

39 Bauer, Joan. *Best Foot Forward* (6–9). 2005, Penguin $16.99 (0-399-23474-8). 192pp. In this funny sequel to *Rules of the Road* (1998), 17-year-old Jenna finds it difficult to juggle her high school studies, her alcoholic father, her declining grandmother, and her part-time job at the shoe store, where she has been appointed a supervisor. (Rev: BCCB 6/05; BL 5/1/05; HB 5–6/05; SLJ 6/05; VOYA 6/05)

40 Bell, Joanne. *Breaking Trail* (5–7). 2005, Groundwood $15.95 (0-88899-630-6); paper $6.95 (0-88899-662-4). 135pp. Becky's dreams of training a dog team to participate in the Junior Quest fade when her father grows increasingly depressed, but a sled trip back to the family's cabin offers a chance to make those dreams come true. (Rev: SLJ 10/05)

41 Blacker, Terence. *Boy2Girl* (6–9). 2005, Farrar $16.00 (0-374-30926-4). 304pp. After the death of his mother, American-born Sam is sent to London to live with relatives; on a dare from his cousin, Sam shows up for his first day of school dressed as a girl. (Rev: BCCB 3/05; BL 3/1/05; SLJ 3/05; VOYA 4/05)

42 Bodett, Tom. *Norman Tuttle on the Last Frontier: A Novel in Stories* (8–10). 2004, Knopf LB $17.99 (0-679-99031-3). 208pp. In this coming-of-age story presented in interconnected episodes, klutzy Alaskan teenager Norman Tuttle experiences many firsts — first job, first date, first hunting expedition — and his relationship with his father evolves. (Rev: BL 12/1/04; SLJ 12/04; VOYA 12/04)

43 Boles, Philana Marie. *Little Divas* (5–8). 2006, HarperCollins LB $16.89 (0-06-073300-4). 176pp. Twelve-year-old Cass is facing a lot of change in her life: her parents' divorce, living with her father, a new friend, a first kiss, and perhaps a new school. (Rev: BL 4/1/06; SLJ 1/06)

44 Bonners, Susan. *The Vanishing Point* (5–8). 2005, Farrar $16.00 (0-374-38081-3). 336pp. Kate, a quiet girl who is spending the summer at the beach with family friends who have a daughter about her age, concentrates on her interest in art and a mystery about a painting. (Rev: BL 9/1/05; SLJ 10/05)

45 Brian, Kate. *Megan Meade's Guide to the McGowan Boys* (8–11). 2005, Simon & Schuster $14.95 (1-4169-0030-6). 272pp. Megan does not want to move to South Korea with her military parents and chooses instead to stay with the McGowans, a family with seven sons, requiring adjustments all round. (Rev: BL 9/15/05; SLJ 11/05; VOYA 12/05)

46 Brugman, Alyssa. *Being Bindy* (6–9). 2006, Delacorte LB $17.99 (0-385-90315-4). 199pp. Since Bindy's best friend dumped her, the Australian 8th-grader's domestic and social life has gone from bad to worse. (Rev: SLJ 3/06*; VOYA 4/06)

47 Brugman, Alyssa. *Finding Grace* (6–12). 2004, Dell LB $17.99 (0-385-90142-9). 240pp. College-bound Rachel is hired to care for a brain-injured woman named Grace and in the process learns some valuable lessons about both Grace and herself. (Rev: BL 9/15/04; SLJ 11/04; VOYA 12/04)

48 Byrd, Sandra. *Island Girl* (5–8). Series: Friends for a Season. 2005, Bethany House paper $9.99 (0-7642-0020-8). 125pp. Confused by changes in her family situation, 13-year-old Meg spends a summer with her grandparents on an Oregon island where she meets and befriends Tia. (Rev: BL 10/1/05)

49 Cabot, Meg. *Teen Idol* (7–11). 2004, Harper-Collins LB $16.89 (0-06-009617-9). 304pp. Jenny Greenley, a junior at an Indiana high school, acts as a student guide for teen idol Luke Striker who comes to the school to do undercover research for an upcoming role. (Rev: BL 10/1/04; SLJ 8/04; VOYA 10/04)

50 Caletti, Deb. *Wild Roses* (7–10). 2005, Simon & Schuster $15.95 (0-689-86766-2). 296pp. Seventeen-year-old Cassie finds life with her stepfather — an unstable violinist and composer — difficult at the best of times, but things go from bad to worse when she falls for one of his music students. (Rev: BCCB 10/05; BL 10/1/05; SLJ 11/05*; VOYA 12/05)

51 Clements, Andrew. *The Report Card* (4–7). 2004, Simon & Schuster $15.95 (0-689-84515-4). 176pp. Nora, a bright 5th-grader, deliberately gets low grades in a bid to boost her friend Stephen's self-esteem, but her plans backfire. (Rev: BL 2/15/04; SLJ 3/04)

52 Clinton, Cathryn. *Simeon's Fire* (4–7). 2005, Candlewick $15.99 (0-7636-2707-0). 128pp. Simeon, a young Amish farm boy, struggles with guilt and fear after he witnesses the torching of his family's barn by two men who threaten to exact revenge if he tells what he's seen. (Rev: BL 11/1/05; SLJ 12/05)

53 Cole, Stephen. *Thieves Like Us* (8–11). 2006, Bloomsbury $16.95 (1-58234-653-4). 352pp. Jonah Wish, a member of a gang of teenage thieves, finds himself questioning the morality of certain activities. (Rev: BL 4/1/06)

54 Collins, Yvonne, and Sandy Rideout. *Introducing Vivien Leigh Reid: Daughter of the Diva* (7–10). 2005, St. Martin's $11.95 (0-312-33837-6). 240pp. Sent to Ireland to spend the summer on the set of her actress mother's latest film, 15-year-old Leigh Reid wins a bit part in the movie, develops a crush on a costar, and finally begins to build a meaningful relationship with her mom. (Rev: BL 6/1–15/05; SLJ 9/05)

55 Collins, Yvonne, and Sandy Rideout. *Now Starring Vivien Leigh Reid: Diva in Training* (8–12). 2006, Griffin paper $9.95 (0-312-33839-2). 242pp. In this sequel to the witty *Introducing Vivien Leigh Reid: Daughter of the Diva* (2005), 16-year-old Leigh lands a role in a soap opera and initially adopts a prima donna attitude that threatens her friendships and her job. (Rev: SLJ 1/06; VOYA 4/06)

56 Cooney, Caroline B. *Hit the Road* (6–9). 2006, Delacorte LB $17.99 (0-385-90174-7). 176pp. When Brit's parents leave the 16-year-old with her grandmother, they have no idea the brand-new driver will be setting off on a road trip to get the elderly woman and her two friends to their 65th college reunion. (Rev: BL 3/15/06*)

57 Craft, Elizabeth, and Sarah Fein. *Bass Ackwards and Belly Up* (8–11). 2006, Little, Brown $16.99 (0-316-05793-2). 416pp. Harper starts a trend among her friends when she pretends she has rejected college (it was the other way round) to stay home and write; the novel follows the four girls through their adventures as aspiring author, aspiring actress, backpacking European tourist, and college freshman/aspiring ski champion. (Rev: BL 4/1/06)

58 Cummings, Priscilla. *Red Kayak* (6–9). 2004, Penguin $15.99 (0-525-47317-3). 192pp. Brady's longtime friendship with J.T. and Digger is tested after a childish prank results in the death of a neighbor's child. (Rev: BL 9/1/04; SLJ 9/04; VOYA 10/04)

59 Cummings, Priscilla. *What Mr. Mattero Did* (6–9). 2005, Dutton $16.99 (0-525-47621-0). 192pp. Three 7th-grade girls thoughtlessly accuse their music teacher of inappropriate behavior and are overwhelmed by the consequences. (Rev: BL 7/05; SLJ 8/05)

60 Czech, Jan M. *Grace Happens* (8–11). 2005, Viking $15.99 (0-670-05962-5). 160pp. Grace, 15-year-old daughter of movie star Constance Meredith, looks forward to a quiet summer on Martha's Vineyard, away from the buzz that usually surrounds her mom, but it turns out to be a much more rewarding summer than she imagined and she discovers not only her father but her grandmother. (Rev: BL 5/1/05; SLJ 7/05)

61 de Guzman, Michael. *The Bamboozlers* (5–8). 2005, Farrar $16.00 (0-374-30512-9). 167pp. Twelve-year-old Albert Rosegarden is in for the adventure of his life when he accompanies his ex-con grandfather on a trip to Seattle. (Rev: HB 11–12/05; SLJ 12/05)

62 Doyle, Brian. *Boy O' Boy* (6–8). 2004, Douglas & McIntyre $18.95 (0-88899-588-1). 162pp. In Ottawa, Ontario, as World War II is nearing its end, young Martin O'Boy is struggling to cope with a dysfunctional home life and an unwelcome sexual advance by the church organist. (Rev: BL 4/1/04; HB 3–4/04; SLJ 2/04)

63 DuPrau, Jeanne. *Car Trouble* (7–10). 2005, Greenwillow LB $16.89 (0-06-073674-7). 288pp. Seventeen-year-old Duff Pringle has various car and people adventures on the road from Virginia to a promised job in California. (Rev: BL 8/05; SLJ 10/05; VOYA 10/05)

64 Durkee, Sarah. *The Fruit Bowl Project* (5–8). 2006, Delacorte LB $17.99 (0-385-90310-3). 160pp. Both an entertaining novel and an inspiration for a writing class, this is the story of a rock star, Nick Thompson, who challenges each member of an 8th-grade writing workshop to write a story or poem containing seven common elements. (Rev: BL 12/1/05; HB 3–4/06; SLJ 1/06; VOYA 4/06)

65 Fogelin, Adrian. *The Big Nothing* (7–9). 2004, Peachtree $14.95 (1-56145-326-9). 224pp. Thirteen-year-old Justin has a miserable home life and generally feels abandoned until neighbor Jemmie starts paying attention to him and he discovers he has a talent for playing the piano; this novel shares a setting and some with characters with *Crossing Jordan* (2000) and *My Brother's Hero* (2002). (Rev: BL 12/15/04; SLJ 12/04)

66 Frank, Lucy. *Lucky Stars* (4–7). 2005, Simon & Schuster $16.95 (0-689-85933-3). 304pp. Kira, a talented singer with a feisty character, arrives in New York City to find that her father has plans that don't fit in with her own. (Rev: BL 5/15/05; SLJ 7/05)

67 Fredericks, Mariah. *Crunch Time* (8–11). 2006, Simon & Schuster $15.95 (0-689-86938-X). 336pp. Four members of a private SAT study group — who have formed emotional attachments as they study — find themselves under suspicion of cheating. (Rev: BL 1/1–15/06; SLJ 1/06; VOYA 12/05)

68 Friesen, Gayle. *The Isabel Factor* (7–10). 2005, Kids Can $16.95 (1-55337-737-0). 256pp. Anna's best friend Zoe breaks her arm and, for the first time in years, Anna finds herself running her own life. (Rev: BL 9/1/05; SLJ 11/05)

69 Gallo, Donald R. *First Crossing: Stories About Teen Immigrants* (7–10). 2005, Candlewick $16.99 (0-7636-2249-4). 240pp. A collection of compelling and diverse stories about contemporary immigration to the United States and the situations of newly arrived teens. (Rev: BL 11/15/04; SLJ 10/04)

70 German, Carol. *A Midsummer Night's Dork* (4–7). 2004, HarperCollins $15.99 (0-06-050718-7). 224pp. In this sequel to *Dork on the Run* (2002), 6th-grader Jerry's class puts on an Elizabethan fair and Jerry has to stand up to another bully, even if it means making a fool of himself. (Rev: BL 2/1/04; SLJ 3/04)

71 Gilbert, Sheri. *The Legacy of Gloria Russell* (4–7). 2004, Knopf LB $17.99 (0-375-92823-5). 224pp. After his friend Gloria dies, Billy James, 12, ignores adult warnings and approaches the hermit called Satan. (Rev: BL 5/1/04; SLJ 4/04)

72 Givner, Joan. *Ellen Fremedon* (5–7). 2004, Groundwood $15.95 (0-88899-557-1). 176pp. When her family seeks to block a proposed housing development, 12-year-old Ellen Fremedon, an aspiring novelist, must set aside her summer project to cope with the repercussions. (Rev: BL 11/15/04)

73 Givner, Joan. *Ellen Fremedon, Journalist* (5–7). 2005, Groundwood $15.95 (0-88899-668-3). 192pp. In this appealing sequel to *Ellen Fremedon* (2004), young Ellen uncovers some shocking stories when she starts a newspaper in quiet Partridge Cove. (Rev: BL 11/1/05; SLJ 2/06)

74 Goldschmidt, Judy. *The Secret Blog of Raisin Rodriguez* (6–9). 2005, Penguin $12.99 (1-59514-018-2). 208pp. Uprooted from her familiar life in California and trying to adjust to her new digs in Philadelphia, 13-year-old Raisin Rodriguez keeps old friends up to date on what's happening in her life through a frank blog that she does not intend to become public. (Rev: BCCB 5/05; BL 3/1/05; SLJ 5/05)

75 Gonzalez, Julie. *Wings* (8–11). 2005, Delacorte LB $17.99 (0-385-90253-0). 176pp. A suspenseful story in which Ben is convinced he will someday sprout wings and take to the sky despite evidence to the contrary. (Rev: BCCB 4/05; BL 3/15/05; SLJ 8/05; VOYA 4/05)

76 Halpern, Sue. *Introducing . . . Sasha Abramowitz* (5–8). 2005, Farrar $17.00 (0-374-38432-0). 288pp. Eleven-year-old Sasha Marie Curie Abramowitz longs more than anything for a normal life, but her family circumstances — including a brother with Tourette's — make that seem to be an unattainable goal. (Rev: BL 10/1/05; SLJ 12/05; VOYA 12/05)

77 Han, Jenny. *Shug* (5–8). 2006, Simon & Schuster $14.95 (1-4169-0942-7). 256pp. Annemarie Wilcox, a 7th-grader better known as Shug, faces numerous challenges in addition to the usual middle-school problems: a gorgeous older sister, squabbling parents, a fight with her best friend, and a crush on Mark that doesn't seem to be reciprocated. (Rev: BL 2/15/06)

78 Herrera, Juan Felipe. *Cinnamon Girl: Letters Found Inside a Cereal Box* (6–9). 2005, HarperCollins LB $16.89 (0-06-057985-4). 176pp. In free verse, 13-year-old Yolanda struggles to cope with the impact of 9/11 and the uncertainties in her life that this shock has revived. (Rev: BL 8/05; SLJ 11/05)

79 Hiaasen, Carl. *Flush* (5–8). 2005, Knopf LB $18.99 (0-375-92182-6). 272pp. Noah Underwood and his younger sister Abbey set out to prove their father was justified in sinking a floating casino because it was polluting. (Rev: BL 8/05; SLJ 9/05)

80 High, Linda Oatman. *Sister Slam and the Poetic Motormouth Road Trip* (8–12). 2004, Bloomsbury $16.95 (1-58234-948-7). 250pp. Laura Rose Crapper, aka Sister Slam, and her friend Twig head for New York, where they meet a handsome boy named Jake. (Rev: BL 5/1/04; SLJ 5/04)

81 Hobbs, Valerie. *Defiance* (4–7). 2005, Farrar $16.00 (0-374-30847-0). 128pp. An elderly neighbor named Pearl — and her cow — become valuable friends to 11-year-old Toby, who does not want to tell his parents that his cancer is back. (Rev: BL 8/05; SLJ 9/05)

82 Hogan, Mary. *The Serious Kiss* (7–10). 2005, HarperCollins LB $16.89 (0-06-072207-X). 256pp. Fourteen-year-old Libby's life seems to be in the hands of others — her alcoholic father, her fat mother, the unkind kids at her new school. (Rev: BCCB 3/05; BL 2/1/05; SLJ 1/05; VOYA 2/05)

83 Hurwin, Davida Wills. *Circle the Soul Softly* (7–12). 2006, HarperCollins LB $16.89 (0-06-077506-8). 169pp. Only as 10th-grader Katie becomes more attached to David does she come to realize that her difficulties adapting to "normal" life stem from abuse by her now-deceased father. (Rev: BCCB 4/06; SLJ 3/06)

84 Johnson, Angela. *Bird* (6–10). 2004, Penguin $15.99 (0-8037-2847-6). 144pp. Heartbroken when her stepfather abandons the family, 13-year-old Bird travels from Cleveland to Alabama to find him and bring him home and instead finds unexpected friendship. (Rev: BL 9/1/04; SLJ 9/04; VOYA 2/05)

85 Johnson, Maureen. *13 Little Blue Envelopes* (8–11). 2005, HarperCollins LB $16.89 (0-06-054142-3). 336pp. On a trip through Europe following instructions left to her in 13 letters written by her Aunt Peg before her death, 17-year-old Ginny learns about Peg's past and about herself. (Rev: BL 9/15/05; SLJ 10/05; VOYA 10/05)

86 Kaye, Amy. *The Real Deal: Unscripted* (7–12). 2004, Dorchester paper $5.99 (0-8439-5315-2). 208pp. Claire juggles a potential Broadway career, a romance with a teen star, and the needs of her newfound half-sister, all under the glare of reality TV cameras. (Rev: SLJ 5/04)

87 Klass, David. *Dark Angel* (8–11). 2005, Farrar $17.00 (0-374-39950-6). 320pp. Seventeen-year-old Jeff's family has hidden the existence of his older brother, a murderer who has been in jail; when Troy is released and comes home to live, Jeff's life is turned upside down. (Rev: BL 9/15/05; SLJ 10/05; VOYA 10/05)

88 Komaiko, Leah. *Malibu Carmie* (6–8). 2005, Delacorte LB $17.99 (0-385-90209-3). 256pp. When 13-year-old Carmie discovers that her depressed mom used to be an accomplished surfer, the teen plots a way to lift her mother's spirits by getting her back to the beach. (Rev: BL 3/1/05; SLJ 5/05)

89 Korman, Gordon. *Born to Rock* (7–10). 2006, Hyperion $15.99 (0-7868-0920-5). 272pp. Leo, a Young Republican with traditional values, finds himself in a totally different world when he discovers his biological father is a punk singer and joins his band in hope of getting tuition money. (Rev: BL 3/1/06)

90 Koss, Amy Goldman. *Poison Ivy* (7–10). 2006, Roaring Brook $16.95 (1-59643-118-0). 176pp. Multiple voices tell the story of the mock trial of the three bullies who have been making unpopular Ivy's life a misery. (Rev: BL 2/15/06; SLJ 3/06; VOYA 4/06)

91 Krulik, Nancy. *Love and Sk8* (7–12). 2004, Simon & Schuster paper $5.99 (0-689-87076-0). 315pp. Eighteen-year-old Angie has three passions — skateboarding, art, and getting out of her Pennsylvania mill town — until she meets Carter, grandson of the mill owner, and her class preconceptions are turned upside down. (Rev: SLJ 10/04)

92 Lasky, Kathryn. *Blood Secret* (6–10). 2004, HarperCollins LB $16.89 (0-06-000065-1). 256pp. Silent since the sudden disappearance of her mother eight years earlier, 14-year-old Jerry Luna goes to live with a great-aunt where a trunk draws her into the time of the Spanish Inquisition and long-hidden secrets about her ancestors. (Rev: BL 10/1/04; SLJ 8/04; VOYA 10/04)

93 Lenhard, Elizabeth. *Chicks with Sticks (It's a Purl Thing)* (6–9). 2005, Dutton $15.99 (0-525-47622-9). 256pp. Four Chicago high school girls from diverse backgrounds become friends when they join a class at KnitWit, a local yarn shop. (Rev: BL 10/15/05; SLJ 2/06)

94 Lockhart, E. *Fly on the Wall: How One Girl Saw Everything* (7–10). 2006, Delacorte LB $17.99 (0-385-90299-9). 184pp. Gretchen Yee's wish to be a fly on the wall of the boys' locker room comes true and in the process she gains confidence and learns a lot about boys and friendship. (Rev: BCCB 4/06; BL 7/06; HB 3–4/06; SLJ 3/06)

95 Lord, Cynthia. *Rules* (4–7). 2006, Scholastic $15.99 (0-439-44382-2). 208pp. Catherine is a likable 12-year-old struggling to cope with the family challenges posed by her younger autistic brother. (Rev: BL 2/15/06; SLJ 4/06)

96 Lyons, Kelly Starling. *Eddie's Ordeal* (5–8). Illus. 2004, Just Us Books paper $3.95 (0-940975-16-5). 85pp. When Eddie's grades slip, his father makes him quit baseball. (Rev: BL 2/1/05)

97 McNeill, J. D. *The Last Codfish* (6–9). 2005, Holt $16.95 (0-8050-7489-9). 192pp. Silent since the drowning death of his mother seven years earlier, 15-year-old Tut is drawn from his self-imposed isolation by a vivacious new neighbor girl named Alex. (Rev: BCCB 6/05; BL 4/15/05; SLJ 6/05)

98 McNicoll, Sylvia. *A Different Kind of Beauty* (7–10). 2004, Fitzhenry & Whiteside $15.95 (1-55005-059-1); paper $8.95 (1-55005-060-5). 208pp. Elizabeth, who is training a puppy as a guide dog, and Kyle, whose diabetes has left him blind, attend the same high school without knowing each other. (Rev: SLJ 8/04; VOYA 8/04)

99 Martineau, Diane. *The Wall on 7th Street* (6–8). 2005, Llewellyn paper $7.95 (0-7387-0715-5). 256pp. An unlikely friendship between a 12-year-old boy and a homeless man helps the boy deal with his parents' divorce and results in a plan to save 7th Street from the gang that has ruled there. (Rev: SLJ 1/06)

100 Mass, Wendy. *Leap Day* (8–12). 2004, Little, Brown $16.95 (0-316-53728-4). 212pp. A leap year baby tells what she does on her fourth (actually sixteenth) birthday and some of the surprises she experiences. (Rev: BL 2/15/04; HB 5–6/04; SLJ 3/04; VOYA 2/04)

101 Maynard, Joyce. *The Cloud Chamber* (6–9). 2005, Simon & Schuster $16.95 (0-689-87152-X). 288pp. In 1950s Montana, 14-year-old Nate finds a friend in his science project partner Naomi as he struggles to cope with his father's apparent suicide attempt and subsequent hospitalization, his mother's withdrawal, and the needs of his younger sister. (Rev: BL 7/05; SLJ 7/05; VOYA 2/06)

102 Murdock, Catherine Gilbert. *Dairy Queen* (6–9). 2006, Houghton $16.00 (0-618-68307-0). 288pp. Fifteen-year-old D.J., who comes from an uncommunicative family, has quietly taken over the work of the family dairy farm, but when she decides to try out for the football team she suddenly becomes the focus of attention. (Rev: BL 4/1/06; SLJ 4/06)

103 Myracle, Lauren. *Eleven* (4–7). 2004, Dutton $16.99 (0-525-47165-0). 208pp. Covering Winnie's life from her 11th birthday to her 12th, this novel reveals typical friendship and family tensions. (Rev: BL 4/15/04; SLJ 2/04)

104 Myracle, Lauren. *The Fashion Disaster That Changed My Life* (5–8). 2005, Dutton $15.99 (0-525-47222-3). 160pp. Through her diary and instant messages, Allison relates the turmoil of 7th grade, from her humiliating first-day arrival with her mother's underwear clinging to her pants to her problems making and keeping friends. (Rev: BL 9/15/05; SLJ 7/05)

105 Na, An. *Wait for Me* (8–11). 2006, Penguin $15.99 (0-399-24275-9). 176pp. Unable to meet her mother's expectations, Korean American high school senior Mina resorts to lies and plans for escape, but when Ysrael, with whom she has fallen in love, is blamed for Mina's actions she must make a difficult choice. (Rev: BL 3/15/06*)

106 Nields, Nerissa. *Plastic Angel* (7–10). 2005, Scholastic $17.95 (0-439-70913-X). 208pp. Thirteen-year-olds Randi and Gellie become friends despite their differences and form a band called Plastic Angel. (Rev: BL 8/05; SLJ 9/05; VOYA 2/06)

107 O'Connell, Tyne. *Pulling Princes* (7–10). 2004, Bloomsbury $16.95 (1-58234-957-6). 221pp. Calypso Kelly, a 15-year-old from LA, finds it difficult to fit in at her posh English boarding school. (Rev: SLJ 12/04; VOYA 4/05)

108 Ostow, Micol. *Westminster Abby* (6–9). Series: Students Across the Seven Seas. 2005, Penguin paper $6.99 (0-14-240413-6). 208pp. Sent to study in London for the summer, Abby has a great time and learns a lot about herself. (Rev: BL 8/05; SLJ 6/05)

109 Parkinson, Siobhan. *Something Invisible* (4–7). 2006, Roaring Brook $16.95 (1-59643-123-7). 160pp. Jake, a self-absorbed 11-year-old, learns a lot about family and friendship over a summer that involves tragedy. (Rev: BL 3/1/06; SLJ 4/06)

110 Pollack, Jenny. *Klepto: Best Friends, First Love, and Shoplifting* (8–11). 2006, Viking $16.99 (0-670-06061-5). 288pp. In the early 1980s, Julie Prodsky, a 14-year-old drama major at New York's High School of Performing Arts, meets cool Julie Braverman and sets out on a career of "getting" rather than buying. (Rev: BL 2/15/06; SLJ 4/06)

111 Rahlens, Holly-Jane. *Prince William, Maximilian Minsky and Me* (5–8). 2005, Candlewick $15.99 (0-7636-2704-6). 320pp. Thirteen-year-old Nelly, a brainy schoolgirl living in Berlin with her German father and American Jewish mother and totally smitten by Britain's dashing Prince William, is planning her bat mitzvah, worrying about her parents' marriage, and getting her friend Max to teach her basketball; has a glossary of German, Hebrew, and Yiddish words. (Rev: BL 11/1/05; SLJ 1/06)

112 Rallison, Janette. *Fame, Glory, and Other Things on My To-Do List* (7–10). 2005, Walker $16.95 (0-8027-8991-9). 192pp. Sixteen-year-old Jessica dreams of Hollywood stardom, but things don't look promising till Jordan, the good-looking son of an actor, moves to town. (Rev: BL 10/15/05; SLJ 11/05)

113 Rosoff, Meg. *How I Live Now* (8–11). 2004, Random LB $18.99 (0-385-90908-X). 208pp. In this riveting futuristic novel, 15-year-old New York City resident Daisy, desperate to escape her evil stepmother, goes to England to stay on her aunt's farm; there she finds friendship and a sexual relationship, but war soon intervenes. Printz Award, 2005. (Rev: BL 9/1/04*; SLJ 9/04; VOYA 12/04)

114 Rosten, Carrie. *Chloe Leiberman (Sometimes Wong)* (7–10). 2005, Delacorte LB $17.99 (0-385-90271-9). 224pp. Half Chinese and half Jewish, 17-year-old Chloe Leiberman lives for fashion, but she's not really sure what the future holds for her until she meets La Contessa, a neighbor who finally helps to give the privileged teenager's life some direction. (Rev: BL 11/15/05; SLJ 12/05)

115 Rushton, Rosie. *Friends, Enemies* (6–8). 2004, Hyperion $15.74 (0-7868-5177-5). 238pp. Four teenage girls, longtime friends, begin to have doubts about each other after a newcomer named Hannah is reluctantly accepted into their circle in this fast-paced novel set in Britain. (Rev: BL 12/15/04; SLJ 2/05)

116 Ryan, Amy Kathleen. *Shadow Falls* (6–9). 2005, Delacorte LB $17.99 (0-385-90164-X). 176pp. Devastated by the death of her beloved brother in a climbing accident, 15-year-old Annie goes to spend the summer at her grandfather's home in Wyoming's Teton Mountains; after an encounter with an old grizzly sow, she begins to come to grips with her grief and once again savor all that life has to offer. (Rev: BL 6/1–15/05; SLJ 11/05)

117 Shaw, Susan. *The Boy in the Basement* (6–9). 2004, Penguin $16.99 (0-525-47223-1). 208pp. Locked in the basement for years by his abusive father, 12-year-old Charlie one day escapes his domestic prison but finds himself totally unequipped to deal with his newfound freedom. (Rev: BL 11/15/04; SLJ 11/04; VOYA 12/04)

118 Sheldon, Dyan. *Planet Janet in Orbit* (7–10). 2005, Candlewick $15.99 (0-7636-2755-0). 304pp. Janet, a live-wire British teen first seen in *Planet Janet* (2003), has a whirlwind year involving romance, friendship, family problems, driving lessons, and school adventures, all confided to her diary. (Rev: BL 10/1/05; SLJ 11/05)

119 Shulman, Polly. *Enthusiasm* (7–10). 2006, Penguin $15.99 (0-399-24389-5). 208pp. A romantic comedy of errors featuring Jane and Ashleigh, both fans of Jane Austen, who get roles in a play at the local boys' prep school. (Rev: BL 1/1–15/06*; SLJ 3/06; VOYA 4/06)

120 Snyder, Zilpha Keatley. *The Magic Nation Thing* (4–7). 2005, Delacorte LB $17.99 (0-385-90107-0). 192pp. Abby O'Mally, 13, has the ability to read minds and find lost objects but this doesn't help her to bring her parents back together. (Rev: BL 5/1/05; SLJ 9/05)

121 Sonnenblick, Jordan. *Drums, Girls and Dangerous Pie* (6–9). 2004, Turning Tide $15.95 (0-9761030-1-X). 182pp. A moving, often funny story about 8th-grader Steven and the impact on his life and his family of his younger brother's leukemia. (Rev: BL 9/15/05; SLJ 10/04)

122 Staples, Suzanne Fisher. *Under the Persimmon Tree* (7–10). 2005, Farrar $17.00 (0-374-38025-2). 288pp. The stories of Najmal, a brave young Afghani refugee, and Nusrat, an American woman helping with a refugee school, intersect as they wait for news of their loved ones in the chaos of the 2001 Afghan War. (Rev: BL 7/05*; SLJ 7/05; VOYA 10/05)

123 Sutherland, Tui T. *This Must Be Love* (7–10). 2004, HarperCollins LB $16.89 (0-06-056476-8). 256pp. Shakespearean plots are interwoven in this tale of Helena and Hermia, best friends in a modern New Jersey high school, and the comedy of errors that is their romantic life. (Rev: BCCB 1/05; SLJ 9/04)

124 Tashjian, Janet. *Vote for Larry* (7–10). 2004, Holt $16.95 (0-8050-7201-2). 240pp. In this sequel to *The Gospel According to Larry* (2001), our young hero decides to run for president of the United States. (Rev: BL 5/1/04; HB 7–8/04; SLJ 5/04; VOYA 6/04)

125 Tracey, Rhian. *When Isla Meets Luke Meets Isla* (8–10). 2004, Bloomsbury paper $9.95 (0-7475-6344-6). 159pp. Told from alternating points of view, this is the story of troubled teens Isla and Luke — a Scottish girl who has just moved to England and a son of a newly divorced, obsessive mother — and the support and affection they give to each other. (Rev: SLJ 2/04)

126 Vega, Denise. *Click Here: (To Find Out How I Survived the Seventh Grade)* (5–7). 2005, Little, Brown $15.99 (0-316-98560-0). 211pp. Middle school is challenging enough for Erin before her private Web page, containing her diary, is posted on the school Intranet. (Rev: BL 2/15/04; SLJ 5/05)

127 Vrettos, Adrienne Maria. *Skin* (8–11). 2006, Simon & Schuster $16.95 (1-4169-0655-X). 240pp. Fourteen-year-old Donnie tells the story of his parents' unhappy marriage and his older sister's death from anorexia. (Rev: BL 3/1/06)

128 Waite, Judy. *Forbidden* (8–11). 2006, Simon & Schuster $16.95 (0-689-87642-4). 249pp. As one of the Chosen girls in the True Cause cult led by Howard, 16-year-old Elinor does not question her life until Outsider Jaime appears. (Rev: BCCB 2/06; BL 4/15/06; SLJ 3/06)

129 Whitney, Kim Ablon. *The Perfect Distance* (7–10). 2005, Knopf LB $17.99 (0-375-93243-7). 256pp. Her riding ambitions and social, monetary, and romantic pressures all come to bear on Francie Martinez, daughter of a Mexican immigrant. (Rev: BL 9/1/05; SLJ 11/05)

130 Winerip, Michael. *Adam Canfield of the Slash* (4–7). 2005, Candlewick $15.99 (0-7636-2340-7). 336pp. As editors of the *Slash*, the Harris Elementary/Middle School student newspaper, Adam and Jennifer chase scoops and tackle ethical questions. (Rev: BL 5/1/05; SLJ 3/05)

131 Woodson, Jacqueline. *Behind You* (7–12). 2004, Putnam $15.99 (0-399-23988-X). 128pp. In this sequel to *If You Come Softly* (1998), Jeremiah, though dead from a policeman's bullet, watches over the people he left behind. (Rev: BL 2/15/04; HB 5–6/04; SLJ 6/04; VOYA 6/04)

132 Wyeth, Sharon Dennis. *Orphea Proud* (7–12). 2004, Dell $15.95 (0-385-32497-9). 208pp. Seventeen-year-old Orphea, an orphan and aspiring poet, interweaves recitations of her poetry with the story of her love for Lissa, who died in a car accident only a day after their first kiss. (Rev: BL 11/1/04; SLJ 12/04; VOYA 12/04)

133 Wynne-Jones, Tim. *A Thief in the House of Memory* (7–10). 2005, Farrar $17.00 (0-374-37478-3). 224pp. Sixteen-year-old Dec can barely recall the events surrounding his mother's sudden disappearance six years earlier until the death of an intruder in the family home reawakens forgotten memories. (Rev: BCCB 5/05; BL 3/1/05; HB 5–6/05; SLJ 4/05; VOYA 6/05)

Ethnic Groups and Problems

134 Abraham, Susan Gonzales, and Denise Gonzales Abraham. *Cecilia's Year* (4–7). 2004, Cinco Puntos $16.95 (0-938317-87-3). 216pp. Inspired by the real-life story of the authors' mother, this is the story of a 14-year-old Hispanic American girl's determination to defy cultural tradition and continue her schooling in Depression-era New Mexico. (Rev: BL 1/1–15/05; SLJ 4/05)

135 Abraham, Susan Gonzales, and Denise Gonzales Abraham. *Surprising Cecilia* (6–9). Series: Latino Fiction for Young Adults. 2005, Cinco Puntos $16.95 (0-938317-96-2). 216pp. In this appealing sequel to *Cecilia's Year*, set in the Rio Grande Valley during the Depression, the title character gets a chance to move to El Paso to further her education but is given little encouragement at home to do so. (Rev: BL 11/15/05; SLJ 1/06)

136 Alegría, Malín. *Estrella's Quinceañera* (7–10). 2006, Simon & Schuster $14.95 (0-689-87809-5). 272pp. Planning for her fifteenth birthday celebration, Mexican American Estrella finds herself balancing her hopes against reality. (Rev: BL 2/15/06; SLJ 4/06)

137 Alvarez, Julia. *Finding Miracles* (8–11). 2004, Knopf LB $17.99 (0-375-82760-9). 272pp. Sixteen-year-old Milly Kaufman, rescued as a child from a strife-torn Latin American nation, is encouraged to return to her native country and learn more about her family roots. (Rev: BL 10/15/04; SLJ 10/04; VOYA 12/04)

138 Bradby, Marie. *Some Friend* (4–8). 2004, Simon & Schuster $15.95 (0-689-85615-6). 240pp. Pearl, an 11-year-old African American, relates her social problems in this moving story set against the backdrop of the civil rights movement. (Rev: BL 2/15/04; HB 3–4/04; SLJ 3/04)

139 Canales, Viola. *The Tequila Worm* (6–9). 2005, Random LB $17.99 (0-385-90905-5). 176pp. Sofia, a Mexican American girl, realizes the values of community, culture, and new experiences. (Rev: BL 10/15/05*; SLJ 2/06; VOYA 8/05)

140 Cheng, Andrea. *Honeysuckle House* (4–7). 2004, Front Street $16.95 (1-886910-99-5). 136pp. The problems of immigration and adjustment to new cultures are shown in this story of two girls of Chinese heritage, told in the girls' alternating voices. (Rev: BL 4/1/04; HB 7–8/04; SLJ 6/04)

141 Flake, Sharon G. *Who Am I Without Him?* (6–12). 2004, Hyperion $15.99 (0-7868-0693-1). Funny, moving, and truthful, these 10 short stories deal with growing up black in today's society. (Rev: BL 4/15/04*; HB 7–8/04; SLJ 5/04; VOYA 6/04)

142 Flinn, Alex. *Fade to Black* (7–10). 2005, HarperCollins LB $17.89 (0-06-056841-0). 192pp. In alternating passages, an attack on an HIV-positive Hispanic teen is recounted from the viewpoints of three principals: the victim, the alleged attacker, and a witness. (Rev: BCCB 5/05; BL 4/15/05; SLJ 5/05; VOYA 4/05)

143 Griffis, Molly Levite. *Simon Says* (6–12). 2004, Eakin Press $22.95 (1-57168-836-6). It's 1942, and 11-year-old Jewish refugee Simon, shipped from Poland to live with an American family five years earlier, is remembering his past amid signs of rising anti-Semitism in his adopted Oklahoma home; a sequel to *The Rachel Resistance* (2001) and *The Feester Filibuster* (2002). (Rev: BL 11/1/04; SLJ 1/05)

144 Herrera, Juan Felipe. *Downtown Boy* (5–8). 2005, Scholastic $16.90 (0-439-64489-5). 304pp. This poignant free-verse novel, narrated by 10-year-old Juanito, offers an unflinching look at what life was like for Chicano migrant workers and their families in 1950s California. (Rev: BL 12/15/05; SLJ 1/06; VOYA 4/06)

145 Himelblau, Linda. *The Trouble Begins* (4–8). 2005, Delacorte LB $16.99 (0-385-90288-3). 200pp. Du Nguyen, 11 years old and a refugee from Vietnam via the Philippines, initially longs for his former freedom and chafes against the expectations of his relatives and elders in America. (Rev: BCCB 12/05; HB 1–2/06; SLJ 2/06)

146 Ly, Many. *Home Is East* (4–7). 2005, Delacorte LB $17.99 (0-385-73223-6). 224pp. When Amy's mother leaves, the young Cambodian American struggles to get on with her father and to make friends and fit in when they move from Florida to San Diego. (Rev: BL 8/05)

147 McDonald, Janet. *Brother Hood* (7–12). 2004, Farrar $16.00 (0-374-30995-7). 176pp. Nate Whitely, a 16-year-old student at a prestigious boarding school, finds himself straddling two very different cultures as he seeks to remain loyal to his Harlem roots. (Rev: BL 9/1/04; SLJ 11/04; VOYA 2/05)

148 Mead, Alice. *Swimming to America* (5–8). 2005, Farrar $16.00 (0-374-38047-3). 160pp. Eighth-grader Linda comes from an immigrant family determined to forget the past in this book about fitting in and telling the truth. (Rev: BL 3/1/05; SLJ 3/05)

149 Miller-Lachmann, Lyn, ed. *Once Upon a Cuento* (6–9). 2003, Curbstone paper $15.95 (1-880684-99-3). 241pp. A diverse collection of short stories by Hispanic American authors, each preceded by editor's comments that add context. (Rev: SLJ 1/04; VOYA 12/04)

150 Mobin-Uddi, Asma. *My Name Is Bilal* (4–7). 2005, Boyds Mills $15.95 (1-59078-175-9). 32pp. When they start at a new school, Muslim Bilal and his sister Ayesha balance pride in their own heritage and their desire to blend in. (Rev: BL 8/05; SLJ 8/05)

151 Myers, Walter Dean. *Autobiography of My Dead Brother* (8–11). 2005, HarperCollins LB $16.89 (0-06-058292-8). 224pp. In this compelling novel of teenage life in contemporary Harlem, Jessie watches helplessly as his friend Rise drifts away from him, dragged down in a whirlpool of drugs and crime. (Rev: BL 6/1–15/05; SLJ 8/05; VOYA 10/05)

152 Namioka, Lensey. *Mismatch* (6–9). 2006, Random LB $17.99 (0-385-90220-4). 224pp. Despite the similarities perceived by their high school classmates, Sue Hua, a Chinese American girl, and Andy Suzuki, a Japanese American boy, face many cultural threats to their relationship. (Rev: BL 12/15/05; SLJ 3/06)

153 Nislick, June Levitt. *Zayda Was a Cowboy* (4–7). 2005, Jewish Publication Soc. paper $9.95 (0-8276-0817-9). 128pp. A Jewish grandfather tells his grandchildren about his exploits as a cowboy when he first arrived in America from Eastern Europe; an epilogue gives background and there is a glossary and a bibliography. (Rev: BL 8/05*)

154 Ortiz Cofer, Judith. *First Person Fiction: Call Me Maria* (6–9). 2004, Scholastic $16.95 (0-439-38577-6). 176pp. Fifteen-year-old Maria feels torn between two cultures when she leaves her mother in Puerto Rico and comes to the mainland United States to live with her father. (Rev: BL 12/1/04; SLJ 11/04)

155 Pagliarulo, Antonio. *A Different Kind of Heat* (7–10). 2006, Delacorte LB $9.99 (0-385-90319-7); paper $7.50 (0-385-73298-8). 192pp. Luz Cordero's anger about life in general and her brother's violent death in particular begins to abate when she finds friendship at the St. Therese Home for Boys and Girls and faces the truth. (Rev: BL 4/1/06)

156 Park, Linda Sue. *Project Mulberry* (5–8). 2005, Clarion $16.00 (0-618-47786-1). Working on a silkworm project with her friend Patrick, Korean American Julia also learns about prejudices and friendship. (Rev: BL 8/05; SLJ 5/05)

157 Singer, Marilyn, ed. *Face Relations: 11 Stories About Seeing Beyond Color* (7–12). 2004, Simon & Schuster $17.95 (0-689-85637-7). 240pp. This collection of 11 original short stories by well-known authors explores the issues of racial identity and race relations in American high schools. (Rev: BL 8/04*; SLJ 6/04; VOYA 8/04)

158 Vaught, Susan. *Stormwitch* (7–10). 2005, Bloomsbury $16.95 (1-58234-952-5). 200pp. Sixteen-year-old Ruba Cleo, transplanted in 1969 to a Mississippi Gulf Coast town from Haiti, wants to strike back at the racism and hostility she encounters by calling on the voodoo skills she learned in her native land. (Rev: BCCB 3/05; BL 2/15/05; SLJ 5/05; VOYA 2/05)

159 Wiseman, Eva. *No One Must Know* (4–7). 2004, Tundra paper $8.95 (0-88776-680-3). 208pp. Thirteen-year-old Alexandra, who's been raised as a Catholic in Canada, learns that her parents are really Jewish Holocaust survivors. (Rev: BL 1/1–15/05; SLJ 6/05)

160 Wishinsky, Frieda. *Queen of the Toilet Bowl* (7–9). Series: Orca Currents. 2005, Orca paper $7.95 (1-55143-364-8). 104pp. For reluctant readers, this is the story of high school student Renata, who immigrated to the United States from Brazil with her mother and now faces — and conquers — bullying by a classmate. (Rev: SLJ 10/05; VOYA 10/05)

Family Life and Problems

161 Abbott, Hailey. *The Bridesmaid* (6–9). 2005, Delacorte $7.95 (0-385-73220-1). 240pp. Abby Beaumont, 15-year-old daughter of parents who run a wedding planning service and jaundiced by the whole idea, watches with wry amusement as her older sister falls into the trap. (Rev: BCCB 9/05; BL 4/15/05; SLJ 4/05)

162 Adoff, Jaime. *Jimi and Me* (8–11). 2005, Hyperion $15.99 (0-7868-5214-3). 330pp. Struggling to recover from the shock of his father's brutal murder, Keith, a biracial teen who loves the music of Hendrix, moves from Brooklyn to Ohio and discovers that his father had another son, named Jimi. (Rev: BL 10/1/05; SLJ 9/05)

163 Amateau, Gigi. *Claiming Georgia Tate* (8–12). 2005, Candlewick $15.99 (0-7636-2339-3). 196pp. When her beloved and protective grandmother dies, 12-year-old Georgia Tate finds herself at the mercy of her sexually abusive father in this novel set in the 1970s. (Rev: SLJ 6/05; VOYA 6/05)

164 Amato, Mary. *The Naked Mole Rat Letters* (4–7). 2005, Holiday $16.95 (0-8234-1927-4). 266pp. Through emails and diary entries, readers learn about Frankie's fear that her father is becoming involved in a new romance. (Rev: BL 6/1–15/05; SLJ 8/05)

165 Avi, and Rachel Vail. *Never Mind! A Twin Novel* (5–7). 2004, HarperCollins $15.99 (0-06-054314-0). 208pp. Told in alternating voices, this is the well-written and entertaining story of twins Meg and Edward, who are as different as oil and water. (Rev: BL 4/1/04*; HB 5–6/04; SLJ 5/04)

166 Baptiste, Tracey. *Angel's Grace* (5–8). Illus. 2005, Simon & Schuster $15.95 (0-689-86773-5). 176pp. Thirteen-year-old Grace, who has always felt different, embarks on a search for the man she believes is her biological father. (Rev: BL 2/1/05; SLJ 3/05)

167 Bryant, Ann. *One Mom Too Many!* Book No. 1 (4–7). Series: Step-Chain. 2003, Lobster paper $3.95 (1-894222-78-4). 190pp. Sarah, 12, is not pleased to discover that both her divorced parents have found new romantic interests. (Rev: SLJ 5/04)

168 Bryant, Ann. *You Can't Fall for Your Stepsister* (4–7). Series: Step-Chain. 2003, Lobster paper $3.95 (1-894222-77-6). 190pp. Ollie, 13, thinks he may be falling in love with his stepsister Frankie, but she ends up becoming his new best friend. (Rev: SLJ 5/04)

169 Carlson, Melody. *Just Ask* (8–12). Series: Diary of a Teenage Girl. 2005, Multnomah paper $12.99 (1-59052-321-0). 183pp. A family tragedy shakes the faith of 16-year-old Kim, who's been struggling to live a Christian life. (Rev: SLJ 12/05)

170 Cassidy, Catherine. *Dizzy* (7–9). 2004, Penguin $15.99 (0-670-05936-6). Abandoned by her mother when she was only 4 years old, Dizzy is stunned when her mom shows up on the girl's 12th birthday and sweeps her off to a solstice festival in Scotland; she soon discovers her fantasies had been misguided. (Rev: BL 10/1/04; SLJ 9/04; VOYA 2/05)

171 Cassidy, Cathy. *Indigo Blue* (5–8). 2005, Viking $15.99 (0-670-05927-7). 256pp. As her family life slowly disintegrates, 11-year-old Indigo tries her best to conceal the truth from her friends at school in this realistic story set in Britain. (Rev: BL 10/1/05; SLJ 11/05)

172 Creech, Sharon. *Replay* (4–7). 2005, HarperCollins LB $16.89 (0-06-054020-6). 240pp. Twelve-year-old Leo untangles some of the secrets of his boisterous Italian American family when he finds his father's boyhood journal. (Rev: BL 9/1/05*; SLJ 9/05; VOYA 12/05)

173 Dalton, Annie, and Maria Dalton. *Invisible Threads* (8–11). 2006, Delacorte LB $17.99 (0-385-90303-0). 208pp. In alternating chapters, Carrie Ann describes her need to find her birth mother and Naomi, the birth mother, talks about her pregnancy and the decision to give her baby up. (Rev: BL 4/1/06; SLJ 4/06)

174 Deuker, Carl. *Runner* (7–10). 2005, Houghton $16.00 (0-618-54298-1). 224pp. Living on a weather-beaten sailboat on Puget Sound with his alcoholic father, high school senior Chance Taylor gets mixed up in some shady dealings to help pay the family bills. (Rev: BL 6/1–15/05; SLJ 6/05; VOYA 8/05)

175 Dowell, Frances O'Roark. *Chicken Boy* (4–7). 2005, Simon & Schuster $15.95 (0-689-85816-7). 208pp. A new friend called Henry brings some comfort into Tobin's sad life. (Rev: BL 5/15/05*; SLJ 7/05*)

176 Flinn, Alex. *Nothing to Lose* (7–12). 2004, HarperCollins $15.99 (0-06-051750-6). 288pp. At age 17, Michael returns home after being a runaway for a year to find that his mother is on trial for the murder of his abusive father. (Rev: BL 3/15/04; HB 5–6/04; SLJ 3/04; VOYA 6/04)

177 Fuqua, Jonathon Scott. *The Willoughby Spit Wonder* (6–8). 2004, Candlewick $15.99 (0-7636-1776-8). 160pp. Deeply troubled by his father's seemingly hopeless struggle against a life-threatening illness, young Carter Johnson undertakes a Herculean challenge in the hope that it will inspire his father to live. (Rev: BL 3/1/04; SLJ 4/04; VOYA 6/04)

178 Fusco, Kimberly Newton. *Tending to Grace* (7–10). 2004, Knopf LB $16.99 (0-375-92862-6). 176pp. Left with an eccentric great-aunt when her mother runs off with a boyfriend, 14-year-old Cornelia realizes in time that she and her aunt are both outcasts but together can help each other grow stronger. (Rev: BL 8/04*; SLJ 5/04; VOYA 6/04)

179 Goobie, Beth. *Something Girl* (5–8). 2005, Orca paper $7.95 (1-55143-347-8). 112pp. Fifteen-year-old Sophie tries to hide the fact that her mother is an alcoholic and her father abusive in this book for reluctant readers. (Rev: BL 7/05; SLJ 12/05)

180 Grimes, Nikki. *Dark Sons* (5–8). 2005, Hyperion $15.99 (0-7868-1888-3). 218pp. Alternating between biblical times and contemporary New York, free-verse narratives express the frustrations of Ishmael — son of Abraham, who must wander the desert with his rejected mother — and of Sam, whose father has left his mother for a young white woman. (Rev: BL 8/05*; SLJ 11/05; VOYA 10/05)

181 Hapka, Catherine. *Supernova* (4–7). Series: Star Power. 2004, Simon & Schuster paper $4.99 (0-689-86787-5). 136pp. With her album topping the pop charts, 14-year-old Star Calloway should be enjoying success, but her happiness is marred by the continuing disappearance of her family. The sequel is *Always Dreamin'* (2004). (Rev: SLJ 8/04)

182 Hicks, Betty. *Out of Order* (4–7). 2005, Roaring Brook $15.95 (1-59643-061-3). 176pp. In alternating chapters, four new stepsiblings relate the problems — and the fun — they have had adjusting to life together. (Rev: BL 9/15/05; SLJ 10/05; VOYA 12/05)

183 Hite, Sid. *The King of Slippery Falls* (6–9). 2004, Scholastic $16.95 (0-439-34257-0). 208pp. Sixteen-year-old adoptee Lewis Hinton believes he may be a descendant of French royalty, and the whole town of Slippery Falls follows the story. (Rev: BCCB 7–8/04; BL 4/15/04; SLJ 5/04; VOYA 8/04)

184 Johnson, Maureen G. *The Key to the Golden Firebird* (7–10). 2004, HarperCollins LB $16.89 (0-06-054139-3). 304pp. Devastated by the sudden death of their father, three sisters struggle to cope with their feelings about their father, each other, and the meaning of life. (Rev: BL 9/1/04*; SLJ 6/04; VOYA 6/04)

185 Kantor, Melissa. *If I Have a Wicked Stepmother, Where's My Prince?* (8–12). 2005, Hyperion $15.99 (0-7868-0960-4). 283pp. In this modern variation on the Cinderella story with lots of interesting twists, high-schooler Lucy Norton must move to New York and coexist with her stepmother and twin stepsisters. (Rev: SLJ 9/05)

186 Kearney, Meg. *The Secret of Me* (7–10). 2005, Persea Books $17.95 (0-89255-322-7). 136pp. Lizzie, 14, is disappointed that her family won't discuss her adoption with her and her obsession with this secret affects her whole life; a novel told in verse. (Rev: BCCB 1/06; SLJ 1/06)

187 Klise, Kate. *Deliver Us from Normal* (5–8). 2005, Scholastic $16.95 (0-439-52322-2). 240pp. Charles Harrisong, 11, is embarrassed by his abnormal family life in Normal, Illinois, and horrified when his parents decide to move them all to a houseboat off the Alabama coast. (Rev: BL 3/1/05; SLJ 5/05)

188 Kogler, Jennifer Anne. *Ruby Tuesday* (8–10). 2005, HarperCollins LB $16.89 (0-06-073957-6). 307pp. The world of 13-year-old Ruby Tuesday Sweet is turned upside down when her father is arrested for the murder of a bookie. (Rev: BCCB 5/05; SLJ 4/05; VOYA 8/05)

189 Krishnaswami, Uma. *Naming Maya* (5–8). 2004, Farrar $16.00 (0-374-35485-5). 192pp. On a trip to India with her mother, 12-year-old Maya learns some important lessons about herself and the real reasons for the breakup of her parents' marriage. (Rev: BL 4/1/04; HB 7–8/04; SLJ 6/04; VOYA 6/04)

190 Kwasney, Michelle D. *Baby Blue* (6–10). 2004, Holt $16.95 (0-8050-7050-8). 208pp. In this poignant first novel, 13-year-old Blue, not yet fully recovered from the death of her father, is dealt yet another blow when her older sister runs away to escape beatings at the hands of their abusive stepfather. (Rev: BCCB 4/04; BL 4/1/04; SLJ 3/04; VOYA 4/04)

191 Leavitt, Martine. *Heck, Superhero!* (7–9). 2004, Front Street $16.95 (1-886910-94-4). 172pp. In this surprisingly upbeat tale, 13-year-old talented artist Heck, left homeless after the sudden disappearance of his mentally ill mother, wanders the streets in search of her. (Rev: BL 10/1/04; SLJ 10/04)

192 Lieberg, Carolyn. *West with Hopeless* (6–9). 2004, Penguin $15.99 (0-525-47194-4). 176pp. In this appealing road-trip tale, half-sisters Carin and Hope, ten years apart in age, learn some valuable lessons about each other and people in general as they drive from Davenport, Iowa, to Reno, Nevada. (Rev: BL 8/04; SLJ 7/04; VOYA 8/04)

193 Lowenstein, Sallie. *Waiting for Eugene* (6–9). Illus. 2005, Lion Stone $19.00 (0-965-84865-5). 202pp. Twelve-year-old Sara Goldman's father suffers from mental illness and often retreats into memories of his nightmarish experiences in France during World War II. (Rev: BL 12/1/05; SLJ 11/05)

194 Lynch, Chris. *Me, Dead Dad, and Alcatraz* (6–9). 2005, HarperCollins LB $16.89 (0-06-059710-0). 240pp. Uncle Alex, who Elvin thought was dead, is out of prison and into Elvin's life in this third novel about the funny, sarcastic, nerdy teenager. (Rev: BL 9/1/05; SLJ 9/05)

195 McCord, Patricia. *Pictures in the Dark* (7–10). 2004, Bloomsbury $16.95 (1-58234-848-0). 322pp. Set in the 1950s, this is the story of two sisters, one 12 and the other 15, and how their mother gradually sank into insanity. (Rev: BL 5/15/04; HB 7–8/04; SLJ 5/04)

196 McCormick, Patricia. *My Brother's Keeper* (7–10). 2005, Hyperion $15.99 (0-7868-5173-2). 192pp. Thirteen-year-old Toby Malone idolizes his older brother Jake, but he feels powerless to help as he sees Jake falling under the spell of drugs. (Rev: BL 6/1–15/05; SLJ 8/05; VOYA 6/05)

197 McKay, Hilary. *Permanent Rose* (6–9). 2005, Simon & Schuster $15.95 (1-4169-0372-0). 240pp. This third volume of a fast-paced series about the eccentric and colorful Casson family finds all four children — Cadmium, Indigo, Saffron, and Rose — struggling with their individual crises during a hot summer in England. (Rev: BCCB 6/05; BL 5/15/05; HB 7–8/05; SLJ 6/05; VOYA 12/05)

198 Madden, Kerry. *Gentle's Holler* (5–8). 2005, Viking $15.99 (0-670-05998-6). 144pp. Livy Two, part of a large, poor family living in the North Carolina mountains, learns a lesson when her father is injured. (Rev: BL 3/1/05; SLJ 6/05)

199 Marchetta, Melina. *Saving Francesca* (8–10). 2004, Knopf LB $17.99 (0-375-92982-7). 256pp. Unhappy with life at her new Australian high school, Francesca desperately needs the help and support of her mother, who is struggling with her own battle against depression. (Rev: BL 10/1/04; SLJ 9/04; VOYA 10/04)

200 Mazer, Norma Fox. *What I Believe* (5–8). 2005, Harcourt $16.00 (0-15-201462-4). 176pp. When Vicki's father loses his job and the family's fortunes go into free fall, Vicki finds the resulting changes hard to accept and reveals in her poems and journal her coping strategies. (Rev: BL 9/15/05; SLJ 10/05)

201 Mead, Alice. *Madame Squidley and Beanie* (4–7). 2004, Farrar $16.00 (0-374-34688-7). 144pp. Ten-year-old Beanie's mother has chronic fatigue syndrome and her illness is affecting the 5th-grader's life. (Rev: BL 4/15/04; SLJ 6/04)

202 Monthei, Betty. *Looking for Normal* (5–8). 2005, HarperCollins LB $16.89 (0-06-072506-0). 192pp. Annie, 12, and her younger brother are sent to live with their grandparents after their father kills their mother and then himself; unfortunately, life does not improve as they must cope with Grandma's drinking and abuse and Grandpa's indifference. (Rev: BL 6/1–15/05; SLJ 4/05)

203 Murphy, Rita. *Looking for Lucy Buick* (8–11). 2005, Delacorte LB $17.99 (0-385-90176-3). 176pp. Adopted by the Sandoni family when she was found as an infant in the backseat of a Buick, 18-year-old Lucy sets off on a search for her true identity. (Rev: BL 10/15/05*; SLJ 11/05; VOYA 12/05)

204 Olsen, Sylvia. *White Girl* (7–10). 2005, Sono Nis paper $8.95 (1-55039-147-X). 240pp. When her mother marries a native Canadian, 15-year-old Josie feels anger at being moved to a reservation where she is taunted for being different, but she eventually works past her resentment and begins to appreciate the larger family of which she is now a part. (Rev: BCCB 9/05; BL 4/15/05*; SLJ 7/05; VOYA 6/05)

205 Peck, Robert Newton. *Bro* (7–9). 2004, HarperCollins $16.99 (0-06-052974-1). 160pp. When his parents' sudden death forces 9-year-old Tug to return to his grandfather's ranch, the scene of an earlier trauma, the boy's older brother, Bro, escapes from a prison labor camp to rescue him; a compelling story set in 1930s Florida. (Rev: BL 3/15/04; SLJ 8/04; VOYA 6/04)

206 Peters, Julie Anne. *Between Mom and Jo* (8–11). 2006, Little, Brown $16.99 (0-316-73906-5). 256pp. At the age of 14, Nick, the only student in his class to have gay parents, reviews his life with his two mothers and makes difficult decisions when they separate. (Rev: BL 3/1/06; SLJ 4/06*; VOYA 2/06)

207 Ryan, Darlene. *Rules for Life* (7–12). 2004, Orca paper $7.95 (1-55143-350-8). 163pp. Sixteen-year-old Izzy, whose mother died two years earlier, has difficulty coming to terms with her father's decision to remarry; suitable for reluctant readers. (Rev: BCCB 2/05; SLJ 3/05; VOYA 6/05)

208 Sones, Sonya. *One of Those Hideous Books Where the Mother Dies* (7–12). 2004, Simon & Schuster $15.95 (0-689-85820-5). 272pp. In this free-verse novel, a high schooler, after the death of her mother, is sent to live with her father, a famous movie actor whom she detests. (Rev: BL 5/1/04*; SLJ 8/04)

209 Sparks, Beatrice, ed. *Finding Katie: The Diary of Anonymous, a Teenager in Foster Care* (7–10). 2005, Avon paper $5.99 (0-06-050721-7). 181pp. In this angst-filled fictional diary, Katie, a teenager living on a California estate, makes it clear that money and privilege do nothing to ensure a happy life. (Rev: SLJ 10/05)

210 Stauffacher, Sue. *Harry Sue* (5–8). 2005, Knopf LB $17.99 (0-375-93274-7). 272pp. Both her parents are in prison and 11-year-old Harry Sue Clotkin acts as tough as she can in the face of a difficult life with her grandmother. (Rev: BL 5/1/05; SLJ 8/05)

211 Strauss, Linda Leopold. *Really, Truly, Everything's Fine* (5–8). 2004, Marshall Cavendish $15.95 (0-7614-5163-3). 160pp. Life changes dramatically for 14-year-old Jill Rider when her father is arrested for jewelry theft. (Rev: BL 5/15/04; SLJ 7/04)

212 Swanson, Julie A. *Going for the Record* (7–12). 2004, Eerdmans paper $8.00 (0-8028-5273-4).

223pp. High school soccer star Leah Weiczynkowski finds herself torn between family responsibilities and her sports aspirations when her father is diagnosed with terminal cancer. (Rev: BL 9/1/04*; SLJ 8/04; VOYA 10/04)

213 Thomson, John. *A Small Boat at the Bottom of the Sea* (5–7). 2005, Milkweed $16.95 (1-57131-657-4); paper $6.95 (1-57131-656-6). 148pp. Upset and angry when he's sent to spend the summer with his ex-con uncle and dying aunt on Puget Sound, 12-year-old Donovan begins to develop a closer relationship with his uncle as his vacation progresses. (Rev: SLJ 10/05; VOYA 4/06)

214 Trueman, Terry. *Cruise Control* (7–10). 2004, HarperCollins LB $16.89 (0-06-623961-3). 160pp. High school senior Paul McDaniel is a star athlete, but he's filled with rage over his brother's disabilities and his father's desertion; a companion to *Stuck in Neutral* (2000). (Rev: BCCB 11/04; BL 3/15/05; VOYA 10/04)

215 Wilson, Jacqueline. *The Illustrated Mum* (5–7). 2005, Delacorte LB $17.99 (0-385-90263-8). 224pp. Nine-year-old Dolphin and teenager Star struggle to deal with their manic-depressive mother. (Rev: BL 1/1–15/05; SLJ 3/05)

216 Woodworth, Chris. *When Ratboy Lived Next Door* (4–8). 2005, Farrar $16.00 (0-374-34677-1). 192pp. Twelve-year-old Lydia takes an instant dislike to her new neighbor Willis and his pet raccoon, but as she gains a better understanding of the family dynamics that make the boy who he is, she also gains valuable insights into her strained relationship with her mother. (Rev: BCCB 2/05; BL 1/1–15/05; SLJ 3/05)

217 Zinnen, Linda. *Holding at Third* (5–7). 2004, Dutton $15.99 (0-525-47163-4). 160pp. Matt, 13 and a baseball player, faces many problems when he and his mother move to a different town so that his brother can undergo cancer treatment. (Rev: BL 2/1/04; SLJ 2/04; VOYA 2/04)

Physical and Emotional Problems

218 Diersch, Sandra. *Ceiling Stars* (7–12). Series: SideStreets. 2004, Lorimer paper $4.99 (1-55028-834-2). 141pp. The close friendship of two high school girls is put to the test when one falls victim to mental illness and begins acting strangely; suitable for reluctant readers. (Rev: SLJ 1/05)

219 Edwards, Johanna. *The Next Big Thing* (8–12). 2005, Berkley paper $13.00 (0-425-20028-0). Kat, determined to lose weight to win the heart of her online boyfriend, lands a spot on a reality TV makeover show but finds in the end that she likes herself just the way she is. (Rev: SLJ 11/05)

220 Fensham, Elizabeth. *Helicopter Man* (6–9). 2005, Bloomsbury $15.95 (1-58234-981-9). 160pp.

Twelve-year-old Peter's journal entries reveal the difficulties of living with a single parent who is schizophrenic; set in Australia. (Rev: BL 8/05; SLJ 6/05; VOYA 6/05)

221 Forde, Catherine. *Fat Boy Swim* (6–10). 2004, Dell $15.95 (0-385-73205-8). 240pp. Fourteen-year-old Jimmy Kelly, taunted by his Glasgow schoolmates for his obesity, persuades a sympathetic soccer coach to teach him how to swim. (Rev: BL 9/1/04; SLJ 9/04)

222 Friend, Natasha. *Perfect* (6–9). 2004, Milkweed $16.95 (1-57131-652-3); paper $6.95 (1-57131-651-5). 208pp. Thirteen-year-old Isabelle Lee struggles to recover from an eating disorder that began shortly after the death of her father. (Rev: BL 1/1–15/05; SLJ 12/04)

223 Griffin, Adele. *Where I Want to Be* (7–10). 2005, Penguin $15.99 (0-399-23783-6). 160pp. In alternating chapters, teenage sisters Lily and Jane tell about their relationship and the mental illness that led to Jane's tragic death. (Rev: BCCB 3/05; BL 2/15/05*; HB 3–4/05; SLJ 4/05; VOYA 4/05)

224 Hautman, Pete. *Invisible* (7–10). 2005, Simon & Schuster $15.95 (0-689-86800-6). 160pp. It's clear to the reader from the beginning that there's something odd about the friendship between 17-year-old Doug Hanson and his only friend Andy, and the mystery unravels as Doug's state of mind deteriorates through the course of the book. (Rev: BL 6/1–15/05; SLJ 6/05; VOYA 8/05)

225 Minchin, Adele. *The Beat Goes On* (8–11). 2004, Simon & Schuster $15.95 (0-689-86611-9). 224pp. In this British novel, 15-year-old Leyla is burdened with keeping secret the fact that her cousin Emma is HIV positive. (Rev: BL 2/15/04; SLJ 3/04; VOYA 4/04)

226 Perez, Marlene. *Unexpected Development* (7–12). 2004, Roaring Brook $16.95 (1-59643-006-0). 176pp. In a series of journal entries, high school senior Megan waxes eloquent on the drawbacks of having an overdeveloped bosom. (Rev: BL 11/15/04; SLJ 10/04; VOYA 12/04)

227 Peters, Julie Anne. *Luna* (8–12). 2004, Little, Brown $16.95 (0-316-73369-5). 256pp. Regan makes great sacrifices to protect her transgender brother Liam from discovery but has reservations when Liam decides he wants to make a permanent sex change. (Rev: BL 7/04; HB 7–8/04; SLJ 5/04; VOYA 6/04)

228 Tokio, Mamelle. *More Than You Can Chew* (8–10). 2003, Tundra paper $9.95 (0-88776-639-0). 240pp. Anorexic 17-year-old Marty Black faces an uphill struggle as she begins treatment for her eating disorder but tackles it with some humor. (Rev: BL 1/1–15/04; SLJ 6/04; VOYA 8/04)

229 Trueman, Terry. *No Right Turn* (8–11). 2006, HarperCollins LB $16.89 (0-06-057492-5). 176pp.

Only when his mother gets a boyfriend with a '76 Corvette does Jordan begin to emerge from the isolation caused by his father's suicide. (Rev: BL 2/1/06; SLJ 3/06; VOYA 2/06)

Personal Problems and Growing into Maturity

230 Allen, M. E. *Gotta Get Some Bish Bash Bosh* (7–10). 2005, HarperCollins LB $16.89 (0-06-073201-6). 208pp. When he's dumped by his girlfriend Sandi, the 14-year-old narrator resolves to cultivate a brand-new image in this entertaining novel set in Britain. (Rev: BL 1/1–15/05; SLJ 4/05; VOYA 2/05)

231 Almond, David. *The Fire-Eaters* (6–8). 2004, Delacorte $15.95 (0-385-73170-1). 176pp. In 1962, 12-year-old Bobby Burns grows increasingly troubled by his father's deteriorating health, the growing threat of another world war, and his clashes at school with a cruel teacher. (Rev: BCCB 5/04; BL 3/15/04; HB 5–6/04; SLJ 5/04; VOYA 10/04)

232 Bartek, Mary. *Funerals and Fly Fishing* (4–7). 2004, Holt $16.95 (0-8050-7409-0). 160pp. A visit to the grandfather he has never met gives Brad Stanislawski new confidence to deal with the classmates at his new school. (Rev: SLJ 8/04)

233 Brashares, Ann. *Girls in Pants: The Third Summer of the Sisterhood* (8–12). Series: Sisterhood of the Traveling Pants. 2005, Delacorte LB $18.99 (0-385-90919-5). 304pp. It's summer again for the four friends and they manage to get together for a weekend before they leave for separate colleges; the pants continue their travels. (Rev: BL 12/15/04*; SLJ 1/05; VOYA 2/05)

234 Bryant, Jen. *Pieces of Georgia* (6–9). 2006, Knopf LB $17.99 (0-375-93259-3). 176pp. Thirteen-year-old Georgia McCoy describes in her journal the solace she finds in the Brandywine River Museum after the death of her mother. (Rev: BL 2/15/06; SLJ 4/06)

235 Butcher, Nancy. *Beauty* (7–12). 2005, Simon & Schuster paper $6.99 (0-689-86235-0). 166pp. A light read about Princess Tatiana Anatolia — 16-year-old daughter of an exceedingly vain queen — who finally stands up to her mother when she learns of the queen's plan to rid the kingdom of other beautiful women. (Rev: BCCB 3/05; SLJ 3/05)

236 Castellucci, Cecil. *Boy Proof* (7–10). 2005, Candlewick $15.99 (0-7636-2333-4). 208pp. Sixteen-year-old Victoria, who prefers to be known as Egg, is smart, cool, and totally in control until Max Carter enters her life and breaks the shell. (Rev: BCCB 2/05; BL 2/15/05; HB 5–6/05; SLJ 4/05; VOYA 4/05)

237 Cheshire, Simon. *Kissing Vanessa* (6–10). 2004, Delacorte LB $17.99 (0-385-90242-5). 144pp.

Kevin is foolish enough to heed his friend's advice on attracting the opposite sex in this humorous novel set in Britain. (Rev: BCCB 1/05; SLJ 10/04)

238 Clairday, Robynn. *Confessions of a Boyfriend Stealer* (8–11). 2005, Delacorte LB $9.99 (0-385-90267-0); paper $7.95 (0-385-73242-2). 240pp. In entries from a blog, 16-year-old Gen, high school junior and aspiring documentary filmmaker, describes her growing disillusion with her best friends CJ and Tasha. (Rev: BL 9/15/05; SLJ 9/05)

239 Clark, Catherine. *The Alison Rules* (7–12). 2004, HarperCollins LB $16.89 (0-06-055981-0). 272pp. Reeling from her mother's death, high school sophomore Alison retreats into herself and creates sets of rules to help her cope; the arrival of a new student called Patrick finally brings her out of her shell. (Rev: BL 10/15/04; SLJ 8/04; VOYA 12/04)

240 Clements, Bruce. *What Erika Wants* (6–9). 2005, Farrar $16.00 (0-374-32304-6). 224pp. In alternating passages, young Erika and her court-appointed lawyer chronicle the teenager's growing confidence as she faces a series of challenges in her life. (Rev: BL 10/15/05; SLJ 9/05; VOYA 12/05)

241 Cohn, Rachel. *Pop Princess* (8–12). 2004, Simon & Schuster $15.95 (0-689-85205-3). 320pp. Sixteen-year-old Wonder Blake has a wry understanding of the changes affecting her life when she is offered a recording contract. (Rev: BCCB 4/04; BL 1/1–15/04; SLJ 3/04; VOYA 8/04)

242 Coleman, Michael. *On the Run* (8–12). 2004, Dutton $15.99 (0-525-47318-1). 208pp. When 15-year-old Luke Reid runs afoul of the law once again, he's assigned to serve as a guide for a blind runner who's training for part of the annual London Marathon. (Rev: BL 6/1–15/04; SLJ 6/04; VOYA 8/04)

243 Collard, Sneed B. *Dog Sense* (5–8). 2005, Peachtree $14.95 (1-56145-351-X). 192pp. Unhappy after moving from sunny California to a small town in Montana, 13-year-old Guy Martinez finds solace in time spent with his dog, Streak, and a new-found friend named Luke. (Rev: BL 10/15/05; SLJ 11/05)

244 Crutcher, Chris. *The Sledding Hill* (7–12). 2005, HarperCollins LB $16.89 (0-06-050244-4). 230pp. Not even death can separate teenage friends Billy Bartholomew and Eddie Proffit in this thought-provoking novel that not only features author Crutcher but also a controversial novel called *Warren Peace*. (Rev: SLJ 6/05; VOYA 6/05)

245 De Alcantara, Pedro. *Befiddled* (4–7). 2005, Delacorte LB $17.99 (0-385-90281-6). 179pp. Mr. Freeman, the superintendent in her apartment building, turns out to be the person to pull 13-year-old Becky out of her dismal doldrums and lift her violin playing to its proper level. (Rev: SLJ 2/06; VOYA 4/06)

246 Delaney, Mark. *Pepperland* (8–12). 2004, Peachtree $14.95 (1-56145-317-X). 160pp. In this poignant coming-of-age novel set in 1980, 16-year-old Pamela Jean tries to cope with the pain of her mother's death from cancer. (Rev: BL 12/1/04; SLJ 11/04; VOYA 10/04)

247 de Oliveira, Eddie. *Lucky* (8–12). 2004, Scholastic paper $6.99 (0-439-54655-9). 256pp. Sam, a 19-year-old British university student, finds himself attracted to both boys and girls and struggles to discover where he fits into the overall scheme of things sexually. (Rev: BL 6/1–15/04; SLJ 6/04; VOYA 10/04)

248 Dessen, Sarah. *Just Listen* (8–11). 2006, Viking $17.99 (0-670-06105-0). 384pp. Annabel is shunned by her friends after being seen in a compromising situation with her best friend's boyfriend. (Rev: BL 3/15/06; VOYA 4/06)

249 Douglas, Lola. *True Confessions of a Hollywood Starlet* (8–10). 2005, Penguin $16.99 (1-59514-035-2). 260pp. Teen movie star Morgan Carter, on the mend from a drug overdose in Hollywood, adopts a new identity when she is sent to a midwestern high school in this credible and amusing novel. (Rev: BCCB 2/06; SLJ 12/05; VOYA 4/06)

250 Evangelista, Beth. *Gifted* (5–8). 2005, Walker $16.95 (0-8027-8994-3). 192pp. George R. Clark is gifted and colossally unpopular with most of his classmates, so he is uneasy about going on his 8th-grade science field trip without his principal-father to protect him from the bullies; funny and real. (Rev: BL 12/15/05*; SLJ 1/06)

251 Fletcher, Christine. *Tallulah Falls* (8–11). 2006, Bloomsbury $16.95 (1-58234-662-3). 304pp. At the age of 17, unhappy Tallulah (formerly known as Debbie) runs away from home looking for her older friend Maeve, who has bipolar disease and has left Oregon for Florida; on the way, Tallulah becomes stranded in Tennessee and finds a haven working in a veterinary clinic. (Rev: BL 4/1/06)

252 Fraustino, Lisa Rowe, ed. *Don't Cramp My Style: Stories About That Time of the Month* (8–12). 2004, Simon & Schuster $15.95 (0-689-85882-5). 304pp. This collection of stories about girls' menstrual periods includes fiction about different places, cultures, and times. (Rev: BL 3/1/04; HB 3–4/04; SLJ 4/04; VOYA 4/04)

253 Fredericks, Mariah. *Head Games* (7–10). 2004, Simon & Schuster $15.95 (0-689-85532-X). 272pp. After a rift with her best friend, 15-year-old Judith retreats into the world of online gaming, assuming a new identity as a male. (Rev: BL 9/15/04; SLJ 10/04; VOYA 4/05)

254 Gardner, Graham. *Inventing Elliot* (5–9). 2004, Dial $16.99 (0-8037-2964-2). 192pp. Despite efforts to avoid bullies at his new high school, 14-year-old Elliot Sutton finds himself embroiled with the Guardians, a group that metes out punishment to those it deems "losers." (Rev: BL 5/15/04; SLJ 3/04; VOYA 4/04)

255 Garfinkle, D. L. *Storky: How I Lost My Nickname and Won the Girl* (8–11). 2005, Penguin $16.99 (0-399-24284-8). 192pp. In journal entries, 14-year-old Mike Pomerantz chronicles the troubles and unexpected joys of his first year in high school. (Rev: BCCB 5/05; BL 3/15/05; SLJ 3/05)

256 Gauthier, Gail. *Happy Kid!* (6–9). 2006, Penguin $16.99 (0-399-24266-X). 240pp. Kyle starts 7th grade with a negative attitude that is sometimes lightened and sometimes reinforced by the advice in a book his mother gives him called *Happy Kid!* (Rev: BL 4/1/06)

257 Giles, Gail. *Playing in Traffic* (8–12). 2004, Roaring Brook $16.95 (1-59643-005-2). 176pp. Seventeen-year-old Matt Lathrop, a shy and geekish high school senior, is flattered when he's picked up by sexy Goth girl Skye Colby, but he soon learns she has ulterior motives; a gripping psychological thriller. (Rev: BL 9/1/04; SLJ 12/04; VOYA 12/04)

258 Goldschmidt, Judy. *Raisin Rodriguez and the Big-Time Smooch* (6–9). 2005, Penguin $12.99 (1-59514-057-3). 192pp. The sequel to *The Secret Blog of Raisin Rodriguez* (2005) follows the perky 7th-grader as she prepares for her first romantic kiss. (Rev: BL 12/15/05; SLJ 2/06)

259 Gonzalez, Gabriela, and Gaby Triana. *Backstage Pass* (6–12). 2004, HarperCollins LB $16.89 (0-06-056018-5). 224pp. Desert McGraw, 16-year-old daughter of an aging rock star, moves to Miami and longs more than anything for normalcy in her life. (Rev: BL 7/04; SLJ 8/04)

260 Gordon, Amy. *The Secret Life of a Boarding School Brat* (5–7). 2004, Holiday House $16.95 (0-8234-1779-4). 252pp. Lydia, already unhappy about her parents' divorce and her grandmother's death, becomes even more miserable at her new boarding school and chronicles her woes in her diary. (Rev: HB 7–8/04; SLJ 8/04)

261 Graham, Rosemary. *Thou Shalt Not Dump the Skater Dude and Other Commandments I Have Broken* (7–10). 2005, Viking $16.99 (0-670-06017-8). 224pp. When high school freshman Kelsey Wilcox breaks up with skateboarding champion C. J. Logan, her jilted boyfriend starts spreading lies about her. (Rev: BL 10/15/05; SLJ 1/06)

262 Grant, Vicki. *Dead-End Job* (7–12). 2005, Orca paper $7.95 (1-55143-378-8). 104pp. Frances finds her life coming apart at the seams after she meets an emotionally disturbed loner named Devin; suitable for reluctant readers. (Rev: SLJ 11/05)

263 Greene, Bette. *I've Already Forgotten Your Name, Philip Hall!* (4–7). 2004, HarperCollins $15.99 (0-06-051835-9). 176pp. A little white lie that strains her relationship with her best friend, Philip Hall, is only one of the dramas Beth Lambert must deal with in this story set in small-town Arkansas. (Rev: BL 5/1/04; HB 3–4/04; SLJ 3/04; VOYA 6/04)

264 Griffin, Adele. *My Almost Epic Summer* (7–10). 2006, Penguin $15.99 (0-399-23784-4). 176pp. Irene, 14, who is spending the summer babysitting, learns about friendship when she takes up with the beautiful and manipulative Starla. (Rev: BL 2/15/06; SLJ 4/06; VOYA 4/06)

265 Grover, Lorie Ann. *Hold Me Tight* (5–8). 2005, Simon & Schuster $16.95 (0-689-85248-7). 336pp. In this moving novel written in free verse, 10-year-old Essie faces — and deals with — her father's departure from the family, her mother's depression, a classmate's kidnapping, and sexual advances from a family friend. (Rev: BCCB 5/05; SLJ 3/05)

266 Hartinger, Brent. *The Order of the Poison Oak* (7–10). 2005, HarperCollins LB $16.89 (0-06-056731-7). 240pp. Anxious to escape the "gay kid" label, 16-year-old Russel Middlebrook and two of his friends sign up to be counselors at a summer camp for young burn victims; a sequel to *Geography Club* (2003). (Rev: BCCB 3/05; BL 1/1–15/05; SLJ 4/05; VOYA 4/05)

267 Haworth-Attard, Barbara. *Theories of Relativity* (8–11). 2005, Holt $16.95 (0-8050-7790-1). 240pp. When his mother sends him packing to make room for her latest boyfriend, 16-year-old Dylan Wallace struggles to survive on the streets without resorting to a life of crime. (Rev: BL 11/1/05; SLJ 11/05; VOYA 2/06)

268 Hemphill, Stephanie. *Things Left Unsaid* (8–12). 2005, Hyperion $16.99 (0-7868-1850-6). 272pp. In this powerful free-verse novel, good girl Sarah Lewis becomes bored with her predictable life and adopts defiant Robin's bad habits, until Robin attempts suicide and Sarah must review her priorities. (Rev: BCCB 7–8/05; BL 5/1/05; HB 5–6/05; SLJ 2/05; VOYA 10/04)

269 Hopkins, Cathy. *Mates, Dates, and Mad Mistakes* (6–9). 2004, Simon & Schuster paper $5.99 (0-689-86722-0). 224pp. Izzie is ready for some rebellion anyway, but when Josh turns up her infatuation leads her into embarrassing territory. (Rev: SLJ 10/04)

270 Hopkins, Cathy. *Mates, Dates, and Sequin Smiles* (6–9). 2004, Simon & Schuster paper $5.99 (0-689-86723-9). 208pp. The prospect of braces sends Nesta into a funk, so she joins an acting class and there meets a cute guy named Luke. (Rev: SLJ 9/04)

271 Horvath, Polly. *The Vacation* (5–7). 2005, Farrar $16.00 (0-374-30870-8). 197pp. When his parents go to Africa as missionaries, 12-year-old Henry is taken on an eye-opening, cross-country trip by his eccentric maiden aunts, Magnolia and Pigg; comedy and weirdness ensue. (Rev: BCCB 10/05; BL 6/05; HB 7–8/05; SLJ 8/05*)

272 Howe, James. *Totally Joe* (6–9). 2005, Simon & Schuster $15.95 (0-689-83957-X). 208pp. At the age of 12, Joe knows he is gay and this is reflected in his "alphabiography" (in which he must present his life from A to Z), which shows him to be a generally happy person despite some bullying. (Rev: BL 8/05; SLJ 11/05; VOYA 12/05)

273 Hughes, Mark Peter. *I Am the Wallpaper* (6–9). 2005, Delacorte LB $17.99 (0-385-90265-4). 240pp. Tired of being overshadowed by her older and prettier sister, 13-year-old Floey Packer decides it's time to give herself a radical makeover. (Rev: BCCB 9/05; BL 3/1/05; SLJ 5/05; VOYA 8/05)

274 James, Brian. *A Perfect World* (7–10). 2004, Scholastic $16.95 (0-439-67364-X). 192pp. Haunted by the suicide of her father, Lacie Johnson follows mindlessly in the footsteps of her best friend Jenna, but when she meets Benji and falls in love, she realizes that Jenna is not a real friend at all. (Rev: BL 1/1–15/05; SLJ 1/05)

275 Jellen, Michelle. *Spain or Shine* (6–9). Series: Students Across the Seven Seas. 2005, Penguin paper $6.99 (0-14-240368-7). 224pp. A semester in Spain helps to bring 16-year-old Elena Holloway out of her shell. (Rev: BL 12/1/05; SLJ 1/06)

276 Jones, Patrick. *Things Change* (8–11). 2004, Walker $16.95 (0-8027-8901-3). 224pp. Johanna, age 16, has her first boyfriend, Paul, a disturbed boy, in this novel about dating, violence, and the problems of falling in love. (Rev: BL 5/1/04; SLJ 5/04; VOYA 6/04)

277 Juby, Susan. *Alice MacLeod, Realist at Last* (8–11). 2005, HarperCollins LB $16.89 (0-06-051550-3). 320pp. It's an eventful summer for unconventional 16-year-old Alice McLeod, who breaks up with her boyfriend, gets and loses jobs, attracts three new male admirers, and sees her activist mom packed off to jail — all with dark good humor. (Rev: BL 4/15/05; HB 9–10/05; SLJ 9/05)

278 Kimmel, Elizabeth Cody. *Lily B. on the Brink of Love* (5–8). 2005, HarperCollins LB $16.89 (0-06-075543-1). 224pp. In this charming sequel to *Lily B. on the Brink of Cool* (2003), the title character, an aspiring writer and advice columnist for her school paper, needs counsel herself when she falls in love. (Rev: BL 10/1/05; SLJ 7/05)

279 Koertge, Ron. *Boy Girl Boy* (8–11). 2005, Harcourt $16.00 (0-15-205325-5). 176pp. Longtime friends Elliot, Teresa, and Larry find that their lives and their relationships change dramatically with high school graduation. (Rev: BL 9/1/05*; VOYA 12/05)

280 Koja, Kathe. *Talk* (8–11). 2005, Farrar $16.00 (0-374-37382-5). 144pp. Kit is used to acting — he is pretending to be straight, after all — and he wins the male lead in the high school play, opposite the popular Lindsay Walsh, who promptly falls for Kit. (Rev: BCCB 3/05; BL 3/15/05; HB 3–4/05; SLJ 3/05; VOYA 4/05)

281 Kyi, Tanya L. *My Time as Caz Hazard* (8–12). 2004, Orca paper $7.95 (1-55143-319-2). 103pp. Caz Hazard — who faces problems at home and at school — strikes up a friendship with Amanda and is drawn into a series of antisocial activities, one of which leads to the suicide of a classmate. (Rev: SLJ 3/05; VOYA 2/05)

282 LaRochelle, David. *Absolutely, Positively Not* (7–10). 2005, Scholastic $16.95 (0-439-59109-0). 224pp. A funny and sensitive first-person portrayal of a 16-year-old's efforts to deny his homosexuality. (Rev: BL 7/05*; SLJ 9/05; VOYA 10/05)

283 Les Becquets, Diane. *Love, Cajun Style* (8–11). 2005, Bloomsbury $16.95 (1-58234-674-7). 300pp. Romance seems to be in the air in Lucy Beauregard's Louisiana town, spicing her interest in Dewey, son of the artist who has just opened an art gallery. (Rev: BL 9/15/05*; SLJ 10/05; VOYA 10/05)

284 Levithan, David. *Marly's Ghost* (7–10). 2006, Dial $14.99 (0-8037-3063-2). 112pp. In this contemporary spin on Dickens's *A Christmas Carol*, Ben, a teenager grieving over the loss of his girlfriend to cancer, is visited by her ghost and three other spirits on the eve of Valentine's Day. (Rev: BL 11/15/05)

285 Limb, Sue. *Girl, 15, Charming but Insane* (7–9). 2004, Delacorte $15.95 (0-385-73214-7). 224pp. Fifteen-year-old Jess Jordan has grown up in Cornwall, England, content to bask in the shadow of her friend Flora, but when both girls set their sights on the same boy, Jess's unique personality begins to assert itself more forcefully. (Rev: BCCB 10/04; BL 9/15/04; SLJ 9/04; VOYA 8/04)

286 Lion, Melissa. *Swollen* (8–12). 2004, Random LB $17.99 (0-385-90876-8). 192pp. Lonely San Diego high school student Samantha, who calls herself "invisible," runs track but never wins and indulges in casual sex. (Rev: BL 10/15/04; SLJ 8/04)

287 Littman, Sarah Darer. *Confessions of a Closet Catholic* (4–7). 2005, Dutton $15.99 (0-525-47365-3). 193pp. Since she made friends with Mac, a Catholic girl, 11-year-old Justine has been questioning her Jewish faith. (Rev: SLJ 1/05)

288 Lockhart, E. *The Boyfriend List* (8–11). 2005, Delacorte LB $17.99 (0-385-90238-7). 240pp. After her disastrous social life triggers a series of panic attacks, 15-year-old Ruby consults a psychiatrist. (Rev: BCCB 3/05; BL 4/1/05; SLJ 4/05)

289 Lubar, David. *Sleeping Freshmen Never Lie* (8–11). 2005, Dutton $15.99 (0-525-47311-4). 256pp. Aspiring writer Scott Hudson chronicles the highs and lows of his freshman year in high school. (Rev: BCCB 10/05; BL 5/15/05; SLJ 7/05*; VOYA 6/05)

290 Lyon, George. *Sonny's House of Spies* (6–10). 2004, Simon & Schuster $16.95 (0-689-85168-5). 304pp. Both humorous and heartbreaking, this is the story of a 13-year-old coming of age in Alabama in the 1950s and the family secrets he uncovers. (Rev: BL 5/15/04; SLJ 8/04)

291 McKay, Hilary. *Indigo's Star* (5–8). 2004, Simon & Schuster $15.95 (0-689-86563-5). 272pp. In this sequel to *Saffy's Angel* (2002), Saffy's younger siblings — 12-year-old Indigo and 8-year-old Rose — take a stand against school bullies with the help of a lonely young American called Tom. (Rev: BL 9/15/04; SLJ 9/04*)

292 Mackler, Carolyn. *Vegan Virgin Valentine* (8–12). 2004, Candlewick $16.99 (0-7636-2155-2). 256pp. High school senior Mara Valentine, a classic overachiever, is right on schedule with her short-term goals for her future when Vivian comes to live with Mara's family. (Rev: BL 6/1–15/04; SLJ 8/04; VOYA 10/04)

293 McWilliams, Kelly. *Doormat* (6–10). 2004, Delacorte LB $17.99 (0-385-90204-2). 144pp. For much of her young life, 15-year-old Jaime has felt like a doormat, but things begin to look up when she finds a new beau, wins the lead in a school play, and helps her best friend deal with the discovery that she is pregnant. (Rev: BL 12/1/04; SLJ 9/04; VOYA 12/04)

294 Marino, Peter. *Dough Boy* (7–10). 2005, Holiday House $16.95 (0-8234-1873-1). 221pp. Fifteen-year-old Tristan, a child of divorce, is unfazed by his weight until Kelly, the health-obsessed daughter of his mother's boyfriend, starts picking on him. (Rev: BL 11/15/05; SLJ 11/05; VOYA 2/06)

295 Matthews, Andrew. *A Winter Night's Dream* (7–10). 2004, Delacorte $15.95 (0-385-73097-7). 160pp. Heeding their English teacher's advice to "go out and fall in love with someone," high school freshman Casey and senior Stewart soon have reason to question their romantic choices; a funny novel featuring fast repartee. (Rev: BL 9/1/04; SLJ 8/04; VOYA 12/04)

296 Mayall, Beth. *Mermaid Park* (8–11). 2005, Penguin $16.99 (1-59514-029-8). 256pp. To escape family turmoil, 16-year-old Amy spends the summer with a family friend in a New Jersey shore town and dreams of becoming an underwater performer at nearby Mermaid Park. (Rev: BL 10/1/05; SLJ 9/05; VOYA 8/05)

297 Mills, Claudia. *Makeovers by Marcia* (4–7). Series: West Creek Middle School. 2005, Farrar $16.00 (0-374-34654-2). 160pp. Marcia learns that beauty is more than skin deep — and that there are more important things than the school dance — when she gives makeovers to the women in a nursing home. (Rev: BL 3/1/05; SLJ 2/05)

298 Moore, Peter. *Caught in the Act* (8–11). 2005, Viking $16.99 (0-670-05990-0). 256pp. Honor student Ethan Lederer is having trouble keeping his grades up and his problems multiply when he falls for Lydia, a Goth-type who turns out to be alarmingly manipulative. (Rev: BCCB 6/05; BL 3/1/05; HB 3–4/05; SLJ 5/05; VOYA 4/05)

299 Morgan, Nicola. *Chicken Friend* (5–7). 2005, Candlewick $15.99 (0-7636-2735-6). 160pp. When her family moves to the country, Becca tries too hard to be cool and winds up in trouble in this story told from a believable pre-teen point of view. (Rev: BL 3/1/05; SLJ 4/05)

300 Moriarty, Jaclyn. *The Year of Secret Assignments* (8–12). 2004, Scholastic $16.95 (0-439-49881-3). 352pp. A rollicking year in the lives of three Australian high school girls — Lydia, Emily, and Cassie — is chronicled in their correspondence with male pen pals at a rival school. (Rev: BCCB 4/04; BL 1/1–15/04; HB 3–4/04; SLJ 3/04; VOYA 6/04)

301 Myers, Walter Dean. *Shooter* (7–12). 2004, HarperCollins $15.99 (0-06-029519-8). 224pp. Told from many viewpoints, this is the story of a high school senior who commits suicide after shooting a star football player and injuring several others. (Rev: BL 2/15/04*; HB 5–6/04; SLJ 5/04; VOYA 6/04)

302 Myracle, Lauren. *ttyl* (6–10). 2004, Abrams $15.95 (0-8109-4821-4). 224pp. This story of three 10th-graders and their lives is told through instant messages. (Rev: BL 5/15/04; SLJ 4/04; VOYA 6/04)

303 Naylor, Phyllis Reynolds. *Alice on Her Way* (7–10). 2005, Simon & Schuster $15.95 (0-689-87090-6). 336pp. Alice, now almost 16 and hoping to get her driver's license, protests the idea of attending a sex class at church, but finds to her surprise that it's interesting and informative. (Rev: BL 7/05; SLJ 5/05; VOYA 8/05)

304 Newbery, Linda. *Sisterland* (8–12). 2004, Random $15.95 (0-385-75026-9). 384pp. This powerful story of love, anger, and guilt includes many generations and countries and revolves around Hilly, a contemporary British teen who is love with a Palestinian. (Rev: BL 3/1/04; HB 3–4/04; SLJ 4/04; VOYA 4/04)

305 O'Connell, Tyne. *Dueling Princes* (7–10). Series: Calypso Chronicles. 2005, Bloomsbury $16.95 (1-58234-658-5). 250pp. In the third volume

of the series, Calypso Kelly, an American student attending a British boarding school, is dating Prince Freddie and stands an excellent chance of winning a spot on Britain's national fencing team. (Rev: BL 12/1/05; SLJ 1/06; VOYA 2/06)

306 Pascal, Francine. *The Ruling Class* (8–11). 2004, Simon & Schuster $14.95 (0-689-87332-8). 192pp. Brutally harassed by bullies at her new high school in Dallas, 16-year-old Twyla Gay briefly considers dropping out but decides instead to seek revenge. (Rev: BCCB 12/04; BL 1/1–15/05; SLJ 12/04)

307 Perkins, Lynne Rae. *Criss Cross* (6–9). 2005, Greenwillow LB $16.99 (0-06-009273-4). 368pp. In a series of intersecting vignettes, a group of young teenage friends tell about their experiences on the difficult road to adulthood in this sequel to *All Alone in the Universe* (1999). Newbery Medal, 2006. (Rev: BL 10/15/05*; SLJ 9/05; VOYA 10/05)

308 Perkins, Mitali. *Monsoon Summer* (7–12). 2004, Delacorte LB $17.99 (0-385-90147-X). 272pp. Fifteen-year-old Jazz reluctantly accompanies her mother to India for the summer, where Jazz learns some valuable lessons about her heritage and herself. (Rev: BL 6/1–15/04; SLJ 9/04)

309 Polikoff, Barbara Garland. *Why Does the Coqui Sing?* (5–8). 2004, Holiday $16.95 (0-8234-1817-0). 213pp. Thirteen-year-old Luz and her brother Rome have trouble adjusting when they move from Chicago to Puerto Rico with their mother and stepfather. (Rev: BL 5/15/04; SLJ 6/04)

310 Prinz, Yvonne. *Still There, Clare* (5–8). 2005, Raincoast paper $6.95 (1-55192-644-X). 176pp. Clare's 13th summer is a time of change: a friend moves away, her aunt begins dating her gym teacher, and she realizes it is time to give up her imaginary friend. (Rev: BL 3/1/05; SLJ 4/05)

311 Prue, Sally. *The Devil's Toenail* (7–10). 2004, Scholastic $16.95 (0-439-48634-3). 224pp. Thirteen-year-old Stevie Saunders, still trying to recover from a brutal bullying incident that left him scarred, enters a new school determined to endear himself. (Rev: BCCB 9/04; BL 4/15/04; SLJ 8/04)

312 Roberts, Laura Peyton. *The Queen of Second Place* (7–10). 2005, Delacorte LB $17.99 (0-385-90200-X). 256pp. High school student Cassie's efforts to attract hunky Kevin Matthews do not show her in a good light, but her friends and family have the sense to see her through this folly. (Rev: BL 6/1–15/05; SLJ 9/05; VOYA 12/05)

313 Sachar, Louis. *Small Steps* (5–8). 2006, Delacorte LB $18.99 (0-385-90333-2). 272pp. Two years after being released from Camp Green Lake, African American 17-year-old Armpit is home in Texas and trying to find good work, which is hard when you have a record, when X-Ray turns up with an interesting proposal; a sequel to *Holes* (1998). (Rev: BL 1/1–15/06*; SLJ 1/06; VOYA 2/06)

314 Sandoval, Lynda. *Who's Your Daddy?* (7–10). 2004, Simon & Schuster paper $6.99 (0-689-86440-X). 318pp. Sixteen-year-old Lila Moreno and her two closest friends find their search for romance hampered by the jobs their fathers hold. (Rev: SLJ 1/05; VOYA 2/05)

315 Schumacher, Julie. *The Chain Letter* (5–7). 2005, Delacorte LB $17.99 (0-385-90205-0). 195pp. Livvie, 12, throws away a chain letter, which seems to spawn a series of calamities. (Rev: SLJ 3/05)

316 Scott, Kieran. *I Was a Non-Blonde Cheerleader* (7–10). 2005, Penguin $15.99 (0-399-24279-1). 256pp. As a brunette, Annisa has a hard time fitting in at her new high school where almost everybody else is blond. (Rev: BL 1/1–15/05; SLJ 1/05; VOYA 4/05)

317 Selvadurai, Shyam. *Swimming in the Monsoon Sea* (8–11). 2005, Tundra $18.95 (0-88776-735-4). 224pp. In Sri Lanka in 1980, Amrith's expected quiet summer is enlivened by the arrival from Canada of his cousin Niresh, a boy with whom he soon falls in love but who does not share his feelings. (Rev: BL 9/15/05*; SLJ 11/05)

318 Shaw, Tucker. *Confessions of a Backup Dancer* (8–12). 2004, Simon & Schuster paper $8.99 (0-689-87075-2). 272pp. Seventeen-year-old Kelly Kimball, a talented dancer, suddenly finds herself thrust into a close relationship with pop diva Darcy Barnes; in this journal-like novel, Kelly dishes the dirt on Darcy and the diva's entourage. (Rev: BL 9/15/04; SLJ 8/04)

319 Shull, Megan. *Amazing Grace* (7–9). 2005, Hyperion $15.99 (0-7868-5690-4). 256pp. Grace escapes the pressures of being a tennis superstar by starting a new life in Alaska. (Rev: BL 9/1/05; SLJ 10/05; VOYA 2/06)

320 Siebold, Jan. *My Nights at the Improv* (4–8). 2005, Whitman $14.95 (0-8075-5630-0). 98pp. Lizzie, a shy 8th-grader whose father died two years before, learns how to speak out by eavesdropping on an improvisational theater class, in the process also learning about bullying Vanessa. (Rev: BCCB 7–8/05; SLJ 11/05)

321 Soto, Gary. *Accidental Love* (7–10). 2006, Harcourt $16.00 (0-15-205497-9). 192pp. Something clicks when 14-year-old Marisa meets wimpy Rene and she is inspired to transfer to his school, where, despite complications, she finds herself blossoming socially and academically — and enjoying her first love. (Rev: BL 1/1–15/06; SLJ 1/06; VOYA 2/06)

322 Stolls, Amy. *Palms to the Ground* (6–9). 2005, Farrar $17.00 (0-374-35731-5). 256pp. For neurotic teen Calman Pulowitz, a cross-country trip to visit his pen pal proves to be just what the doctor

ordered. (Rev: BCCB 9/05; BL 3/1/05; SLJ 5/05; VOYA 10/05)

323 Stone, Phoebe. *Sonata No. 1 for Riley Red* (5–8). 2003, Little, Brown $15.95 (0-316-99041-8). 194pp. Thirteen-year-old Rachel and three friends share their deepest secrets with one another while they are in hiding after liberating a neglected elephant in this appealing novel set in 1960s Boston. (Rev: BL 1/1–15/04; SLJ 1/04; VOYA 4/04)

324 Strasser, Todd. *Can't Get There from Here* (7–12). 2004, Simon & Schuster $15.95 (0-689-84169-8). 208pp. A teenage girl who has been thrown out by an abusive mother tries to survive on the streets of New York City. (Rev: BL 3/15/04; SLJ 3/04; VOYA 6/04)

325 Strauss, Peggy Guthart. *Getting the Boot* (8–12). Series: Students Across the Seven Seas. 2005, Penguin paper $6.99 (0-14-240414-4). 224pp. A light story about popular high school junior Kelly Brandt's summer as an exchange student in Italy. (Rev: BL 5/15/05; SLJ 8/05)

326 Summer, Jane. *Not the Only One: Lesbian and Gay Fiction for Teens* (7–12). 2004, Alyson paper $13.95 (1-55583-834-0). 224pp. This revised edition includes 10 new stories featuring gay and lesbian teens. (Rev: BL 12/15/04; VOYA 2/05)

327 Thomson, Sarah L. *The Manny* (7–10). 2005, Dutton $15.99 (0-525-47413-7). 181pp. Sixteen-year-old Justin Blakewell looks forward to a summer of sun and fun when he lands a job as a male nanny for the 4-year-old son of a wealthy couple in the Hamptons. (Rev: BCCB 9/05; SLJ 6/05; VOYA 8/05)

328 Tolan, Stephanie S. *Listen!* (4–7). 2006, HarperCollins $15.99 (0-06-057925-8). 208pp. Lonely after the death of her mother and the departure of her best friend for the summer, 12-year-old Charley finds solace in a stray dog. (Rev: BL 4/1/06)

329 Townley, Roderick. *Sky: A Novel in 3 Sets and an Encore* (7–10). 2004, Simon & Schuster $16.95 (0-689-85712-8). 272pp. Angered by his father's opposition to his interest in jazz, 15-year-old Sky runs away from home and moves in with the blind jazz pianist whose life he saved. (Rev: BL 8/04; SLJ 7/04)

330 Vail, Rachel. *If We Kiss* (7–10). 2005, HarperCollins LB $16.89 (0-06-056915-8). 272pp. Fourteen-year-old Charlie struggles with feelings of guilt after she kisses Kevin, who just happens to be her best friend's steady. (Rev: BCCB 5/05; BL 3/15/05; HB 7–8/05; SLJ 5/05)

331 Wasserman, Robin. *Lust* (8–11). Series: Seven Deadly Sins. 2005, Simon & Schuster paper $7.99 (0-689-87782-X). 240pp. In an entertaining opening volume of a soap-opera-like series, several sex-obsessed high school seniors in a small California town ruthlessly scheme to win the girl or guy of their dreams. (Rev: BL 12/1/05; SLJ 1/06)

332 Weaver, Will. *Full Service* (7–10). 2005, Farrar $17.00 (0-374-32485-9). 240pp. Paul, a sheltered Christian 15-year-old, discovers hippies, alcohol, and sex when he takes a job at a gas station in the summer of 1965. (Rev: BL 9/1/05; SLJ 11/05; VOYA 10/05)

333 Wetter, Bruce. *The Boy with the Lampshade on His Head* (5–8). 2004, Simon & Schuster $16.95 (0-689-85032-8). 304pp. Painfully shy, 11-year-old Stanley Krakow maintains a low profile but a rich inner life until he makes friends with an abused girl and finds the inner strength to be a real hero. (Rev: BL 5/1/04; SLJ 8/04)

334 Whelan, Gloria. *Listening for Lions* (6–9). 2005, HarperCollins LB $16.89 (0-06-058175-1). 208pp. Rachel, the orphaned daughter of missionary parents, gets pulled into an elaborate scheme to get her money-grubbing neighbors reinstated in the will of an ailing Englishman. (Rev: BCCB 9/05; BL 5/15/05*; HB 9–10/05; SLJ 8/05; VOYA 8/05)

335 Wilkins, Rose. *So Super Starry* (6–9). 2004, Penguin $16.99 (0-8037-3049-7). 240pp. Octavia, a 15-year-old student at an elite London school, disdains the in-crowd and has few friends, but all that begins to change after she meets Alex, the super-cute brother of a classmate. (Rev: BL 10/15/04; SLJ 12/04)

336 Williams, Julie. *Escaping Tornado Season: A Story in Poems* (7–10). 2004, HarperCollins $15.99 (0-06-008639-4). 272pp. After relocating with her mother to live with her grandparents, 14-year-old Allie becomes a friend of an Ojibwe classmate who is raped by a white teacher. (Rev: BL 3/1/04; SLJ 4/04; VOYA 4/04)

337 Withrow, Sarah. *What Gloria Wants* (7–10). 2005, Groundwood $15.95 (0-88899-628-4); paper $6.95 (0-88899-692-6). 176pp. Gloria always seems to be a step behind her best friend Shawna, so Gloria initially exults when she is first to land a boyfriend. (Rev: BCCB 11/05; BL 12/1/05; HB 1–2/06; SLJ 2/06; VOYA 12/05)

338 Wittlinger, Ellen. *Sandpiper* (8–12). 2005, Simon & Schuster $16.95 (0-689-86802-2). 240pp. Her promiscuous past has severely tarnished 16-year-old Sandpiper's reputation, but when she develops a friendship with Walker, both troubled teens begin to make some important discoveries about the ways in which the past is shaping their future. (Rev: BL 6/1–15/05; SLJ 7/05; VOYA 8/05)

339 Wolfson, Jill. *What I Call Life* (5–8). 2005, Holt $16.95 (0-8050-7669-7). 272pp. Five young girls — all refugees from troubled families — find friendship and strength during their stay in a group home run by a wise Knitting Lady. (Rev: BL 11/1/05; SLJ 9/05; VOYA 12/05)

340 Wong, Joyce Lee. *Seeing Emily* (6–9). 2005, Abrams $16.95 (0-8109-5757-4). 271pp. This appealing free-verse novel chronicles the coming of age of 16-year-old Emily Wu, a promising artist and the daughter of Chinese immigrants. (Rev: BCCB 11/05; SLJ 12/05)

341 Zeises, Lara M. *Contents Under Pressure* (6–9). 2004, Delacorte $15.95 (0-385-73047-0). 256pp. In this appealing coming-of-age novel, 14-year-old Lucy experiences dramatic changes in her life when she starts to date Tobin. (Rev: BCCB 5/04; BL 3/15/04; HB 3–4/04; SLJ 4/04; VOYA 6/04)

World Affairs and Contemporary Problems

342 Adoff, Jaime. *Names Will Never Hurt Me* (7–10). 2004, Dutton $15.99 (0-525-47175-8). 144pp. As their high school marks the first anniversary of the shooting death of a fellow student, four very different teenagers express their feelings about school, their classmates, and themselves. (Rev: BCCB 4/04; BL 4/1/04; HB 7–8/04; SLJ 4/04; VOYA 4/04)

343 Budhos, Marina. *Ask Me No Questions* (7–10). 2006, Simon & Schuster $16.95 (1-4169-0351-8). 176pp. Fourteen-year-old Nadira describes the legal and emotional upheavals her family faces as Bangladeshis living illegally in the United States. (Rev: BCCB 3/06; BL 12/15/05*; HB 3–4/06; SLJ 4/06; VOYA 2/06)

344 Cooney, Caroline B. *Code Orange* (6–9). 2005, Delacorte LB $17.99 (0-385-90277-8). 192pp. Teenage Mitty has one huge problem — he may have contracted smallpox and worries he could pass the disease on — and then he is kidnapped by terrorists who want to infect New York City. (Rev: BL 9/1/05*; SLJ 10/05; VOYA 10/05)

345 Hopkins, Ellen. *Crank* (8–12). 2004, Simon & Schuster paper $6.99 (0-689-86519-8). 544pp. In this debut novel written in verse, Hopkins introduces readers to Kristina Snow and how the high school junior became addicted to crystal meth. (Rev: BL 11/15/04; SLJ 11/04; VOYA 2/05)

346 Lewis, Richard. *The Flame Tree* (8–12). 2004, Simon & Schuster $16.95 (0-689-86333-0). 276pp. Isaac, 12-year-old son of American missionary doctors in Java, Indonesia, finds himself held hostage by Muslim fundamentalists in the days following September 11, 2001. (Rev: SLJ 10/04)

347 Lynch, Janet Nichols. *Peace Is a Four-Letter Word* (7–10). 2005, Heyday paper $9.95 (1-59714-014-7). 168pp. The carefully ordered life of high school cheerleader Emily Rankin is shattered when a history teacher inspires her to get involved in the peace movement on the eve of the Gulf War. (Rev: BL 10/1/05; SLJ 10/05)

348 Nye, Naomi Shihab. *Going Going* (7–10). 2005, Greenwillow LB $16.89 (0-06-029366-7). 233pp. Angered by the exodus of small businesses from her hometown, 16-year-old Florrie launches a grassroots campaign against the giant chain stores that she believes are responsible. (Rev: BCCB 7–8/05; BL 4/1/05; HB 7–8/05; SLJ 5/05; VOYA 10/05)

349 Stein, Tammar. *Light Years: A Novel* (8–12). 2005, Knopf $15.95 (0-375-83023-5). 272pp. Twenty-year-old Maya leaves her native Israel to attend college in Virginia, but her memories of the death of her boyfriend, killed by a suicide bomber, intrude on her new life. (Rev: BL 12/1/04; SLJ 1/05; VOYA 6/05)

350 Woods, Brenda. *Emako Blue* (7–10). 2004, Penguin $15.99 (0-399-24006-3). 128pp. After Emako, a talented singer, is mistakenly killed in a drive-by shooting in Los Angeles, her surviving friends — Eddie, Jamal, and Monterey — share their thoughts about what she meant to them. (Rev: BL 7/04; SLJ 7/04)

Fantasy

351 Abouzeid, Chris. *Anatopsis* (6–8). 2006, Dutton $16.99 (0-525-47583-4). 326pp. Princess Anatopsis, an immortal with magical powers, questions her mother's plans for her future and considers the plight of the mere mortals in her land. (Rev: BCCB 4/06; SLJ 3/06; VOYA 4/06)

352 Adlington, L. J. *The Diary of Pelly D* (8–12). 2005, Greenwillow LB $16.89 (0-06-076616-6). 288pp. While working on an excavation crew in the ruins of City Five, Tony V finds the journal of a girl named Pelly D, and her story of widescale ethnic cleansing causes the young worker to reexamine his own beliefs. (Rev: BCCB 5/05; BL 5/1/05*; HB 7–8/05; SLJ 5/05)

353 Alton, Steve. *The Firehills* (6–9). 2005, Carolrhoda $14.95 (1-57505-798-0). 192pp. Sam, Charley, and Amergin — three teens with magical powers — do battle against a group of evil fairies known as the Sidhe. (Rev: BL 10/1/05; SLJ 1/06; VOYA 10/05)

354 Andersen, Jodi. *May Bird and the Ever After* (4–7). 2005, Simon & Schuster $15.95 (0-689-86923-1). 336pp. After falling into a lake near her home, 10-year-old May Bird finds herself in Ever After, a fantasy underworld inhabited by the souls of the dead. (Rev: BL 10/15/05; SLJ 12/05; VOYA 12/05)

355 Armstrong, Alan. *Whittington* (5–8). 2005, Random LB $16.99 (0-375-92864-2). 208pp. Happy to have found a place to live, Whittington the cat

regales the other barnyard animals with tales of his famous forebears. (Rev: BL 5/15/05; SLJ 8/05*)

356 Avi. *Strange Happenings: Five Tales of Transformation* (4–7). 2006, Harcourt $15.00 (0-15-205790-0). 160pp. Shape-shifting and invisibility are among the transformations in this collection of five fantasy tales. (Rev: BL 3/15/06)

357 Baker, E. D. *Dragon's Breath* (4–7). 2003, Bloomsbury $15.95 (1-58234-858-8). In this humorous sequel to *The Frog Princess* (2002), Princess Esmeralda needs to find the ingredients for a magic potion. (Rev: BL 4/15/04; SLJ 12/03; VOYA 4/04)

358 Barker, Clive. *Days of Magic, Nights of War* (7–12). Series: Abarat. 2004, HarperCollins $24.99 (0-06-029170-2). 512pp. In the second installment in the series, Candy Quackenbush makes discoveries about herself and the islands of Abarat as she tries to stay one step ahead of the Lord of Midnight. (Rev: BL 9/1/04; SLJ 11/04)

359 Barrett, Tracy. *On Etruscan Time* (5–8). 2005, Holt $16.95 (0-8050-7569-0). 176pp. Hector, 11, finds himself struggling to rescue an Etruscan boy from execution, in this time-travel fantasy set on an archaeological dig in Italy. (Rev: BL 6/1–15/05; SLJ 7/05)

360 Barron, T. A. *The Great Tree of Avalon* (6–12). Series: Great Tree of Avalon. 2004, Penguin $19.99 (0-399-23763-1). 448pp. The fate of Avalon, which the Lady of the Lake has prophesied will be destroyed by the Dark Child, rests in the hands of two 17-year-old boys: Tamwyn and Scree. (Rev: BL 9/1/04*; SLJ 10/04)

361 Barron, T. A. *Shadows on the Stars* (7–10). Series: Great Tree of Avalon. 2005, Philomel $19.99 (0-399-23764-X). 448pp. In the year 1002 Tamwyn, Elli, and Scree set off on separate quests to conquer the evil Rhita Gawr and save Avalon in this sequel to *Child of the Dark Prophecy* (2004). (Rev: BL 9/15/05; SLJ 12/05)

362 Bass, L. G. *Sign of the Qin* (7–10). 2004, Hyperion $17.99 (0-7868-1918-9). This, the first volume of a proposed trilogy, draws on the myths and legends of China in this classic fantasy of good versus evil. (Rev: BL 4/15/04; HB 7–8/04; SLJ 4/04; VOYA 6/04)

363 Bateman, Colin. *Running with the Reservoir Pups* (4–7). 2005, Delacorte LB $17.99 (0-385-90268-9). 272pp. Eddie becomes involved with a gang of tough Belfast kids and ends up rescuing kidnapped babies from a horrible fate in this action-packed fantasy, the first installment in a trilogy. (Rev: BL 3/1/05; SLJ 1/05)

364 Batson, Wayne Thomas. *The Door Within* (4–7). 2005, Thomas Nelson $16.99 (1-4003-0659-0). 320pp. Aidan Thomas, upset by his family's sudden move from Maryland to Colorado, finds himself drawn toward another world after he discovers three ancient scrolls in the basement of his grandfather's home in this first volume of a fantasy trilogy with a strong religious base. (Rev: BL 12/1/05; SLJ 1/06)

365 Bell, Hilari. *The Wizard Test* (5–8). 2005, HarperCollins LB $16.89 (0-06-059941-3). 176pp. Fourteen-year-old Dayven is not thrilled when he learns he has magical abilities until he undergoes wizard training. (Rev: BL 2/1/05; SLJ 3/05)

366 Bennett, Holly. *The Bonemender* (6–9). 2005, Orca paper $7.95 (1-55143-336-2). 208pp. When Gabrielle, a princess and healer, falls in love with Feolan, an elf, she sees little future for the romance because of the sharp differences between their basic natures. (Rev: BL 11/1/05; SLJ 12/05; VOYA 12/05)

367 Black, Holly. *Valiant: A Modern Tale of Faerie* (8–11). 2005, Simon & Schuster $16.95 (0-689-86822-7). 320pp. In this dark fantasy featuring drugs and homeless teens in New York City, 17-year-old Val becomes involved with trolls and faeries. (Rev: BL 7/05; SLJ 6/05)

368 Blackman, Malorie. *Naughts and Crosses* (8–11). 2005, Simon & Schuster $15.95 (1-4169-0016-0). 400pp. Callum, a 15-year-old, pale-skinned Naught in a world dominated by the dark-skinned Crosses, falls in love with Sephy, daughter of the Cross politician for whom Callum's mother works. (Rev: BL 6/1–15/05*; SLJ 6/05; VOYA 8/05)

369 Bray, Libba. *A Great and Terrible Beauty* (8–12). 2003, Delacorte $16.95 (0-385-73028-4); paper $17.99 (0-385-90161-5). 403pp. In 1895 England, 16-year-old Gemma, attending a boarding school after her mother's death in India, learns to control her visions and enter a sinister world called the Realms. (Rev: BCCB 5/04; BL 3/15/04; SLJ 2/04; VOYA 4/04)

370 Brennan, Herbie. *The Purple Emperor: Faerie Wars II* (6–8). 2004, Bloomsbury $17.95 (1-58234-880-4). 400pp. In a sequel to *Faerie Wars* (2003) full of humor and adventure, Henry Atherton returns to the Faerie Realm to help royal siblings Pyrgus Malvae and Holly Blue. (Rev: BL 9/15/04; SLJ 12/04; VOYA 2/05)

371 Browne, N. M. *Basilisk* (7–11). 2004, Bloomsbury $17.95 (1-58234-876-6). A fantasy about a city in which laborers under the control of a totalitarian ruler work above ground, and the so-called degenerates are confined to dank catacombs. (Rev: BL 4/15/04*; SLJ 6/04)

372 Bruchac, Josephine. *Wabi: A Hero's Tale* (7–10). 2006, Dial $16.99 (0-8037-3098-5). 192pp. A white great horned owl named Wabi has the power to transform himself into a human being and falls in love with an Abenaki girl named Dojihla. (Rev: BL 2/15/06; SLJ 4/06*; VOYA 4/06)

373 Buffie, Margaret. *The Finder* (6–10). Series: The Watcher's Quest. 2004, Kids Can $16.95 (1-55337-671-4). 416pp. In the final volume of the trilogy, shape-changing heroine Emma Sweeny defies her training master and passes through a magical portal where she must get to four hidden power wands before they're found by the evil Eefa. (Rev: BL 10/15/04; SLJ 1/05; VOYA 2/05)

374 Bunting, Eve. *The Lambkins* (7–10). 2005, HarperCollins LB $16.89 (0-06-059907-3). 192pp. Kyle's offer to help a woman with a flat tire goes awry when she kidnaps him and shrinks him to the size of a Coke bottle. (Rev: BL 8/05; SLJ 8/05)

375 Carmody, Isobelle. *Night Gate* (5–8). Series: Gateway Trilogy. 2005, Random LB $18.99 (0-375-93016-7). 272pp. On her way to visit her comatose mother, 12-year-old Rage is transported to another world. (Rev: BL 1/1–15/05; SLJ 1/05)

376 Carroll, Lewis. *Alice Through the Looking-Glass* (4–7). Illus. 2005, Candlewick $24.99 (0-7636-2892-1). 226pp. Faithful to the original text, Oxenbury's inviting artwork will draw young readers; a companion to her award-winning *Alice's Adventures in Wonderland* (1999). (Rev: BL 12/15/05*; SLJ 12/05)

377 Clement-Davies, David. *The Telling Pool* (6–9). 2005, Abrams $19.95 (0-8109-5758-2). 384pp. In this historical fantasy set in 12th-century England, young Rhodri Falcon must defeat the evil sorceress who has cast a spell on his father. (Rev: BCCB 1/06; BL 10/1/05; SLJ 11/05; VOYA 12/05)

378 Colfer, Eoin. *The Opal Deception* (6–9). Series: Artemis Fowl. 2005, Hyperion $16.95 (0-7868-5289-5). 352pp. In the fourth volume of the series, Artemis, his mind wiped clean of memories about the fairy world, reverts to a life of crime and provides an easy target for his nemesis, Opal Koboi. (Rev: BL 5/15/05; SLJ 7/05)

379 Constable, Kate. *The Tenth Power* (7–10). Series: Chanters of Tremaris. 2006, Scholastic $16.99 (0-439-55482-9). 306pp. Mourning the loss of her nine powers of chantment, 18-year-old Calwyn returns to Antaris to discover she must go in search of the key to the mysterious tenth, healing, power. (Rev: BL 3/15/06; SLJ 3/06)

380 Constable, Kate. *The Waterless Sea* (8–11). Series: Chanters of Tremaris. 2005, Scholastic $16.95 (0-439-55480-2). 320pp. In the second volume of the trilogy, Calwyn and her friends travel to the desolate Merithuran Empire on a mission to rescue some children with magical powers. (Rev: BL 5/15/05; SLJ 8/05; VOYA 8/05)

381 Corder, Zizou. *Lionboy: The Truth* (5–8). 2005, Dial $16.99 (0-8037-2985-5). 240pp. In the final installment in the trilogy, Charlie Ashanti, reunited with his parents in Morocco, is kidnapped by the Corporacy and put on a boat bound for the Caribbean, but the boy wonder calls on his animal friends for help. (Rev: BL 10/1/05; SLJ 9/05; VOYA 12/05)

382 Cornish, D. M. *Foundling* (7–10). Illus. Series: Monster Blood Tattoo. 2006, Penguin $18.99 (0-399-24638-X). 434pp. Rossamund Bookchild, a foundling boy with a girl's name, sets off from the orphanage to his new job as a lamplighter and finds himself in a perilous world (called Half-Continent) full of monsters. (Rev: BL 4/1/06*)

383 Cowell, Cressida. *How to Train Your Dragon: By Hiccup Horrendous Haddock III: Translated from an Old Norse Legend by Cressida Cowell* (4–8). Illus. 2004, Little, Brown paper $10.95 (0-316-73737-2). 224pp. The hilarious account of the fumbling efforts of nerdy Hiccup to capture and train a dragon and to take his rightful place as the next Warrior Chief. Also use *How to Be a Pirate: By Hiccup Horrendous Haddock III* (2005). (Rev: BL 4/15/04; SLJ 7/04)

384 Crew, Gary. *The Viewer* (5–9). 2003, Lothian $16.95 (0-85091-828-6). A well-illustrated dark fantasy linked to world catastrophes caused by mankind, from religious persecution to atomic war. (Rev: SLJ 3/04)

385 Croggon, Alison. *The Naming* (7–10). 2005, Candlewick $17.99 (0-7636-2639-2). 528pp. The life of 16-year-old Maerad, a slave, changes dramatically after she meets Cadvan, who tells her of her epic destiny. (Rev: BCCB 9/05; BL 5/1/05; SLJ 10/05*; VOYA 8/05)

386 Cross, Gillian. *The Dark Ground* (6–8). 2004, Penguin $15.99 (0-525-47350-5). 272pp. Young Robert suddenly finds himself shrunk to a minute size and seemingly far from home in a landscape inhabited by bands of tiny people; the first volume in a series. (Rev: BCCB 1/05; BL 9/1/04; HB 9–10/04; SLJ 9/04)

387 Crossley-Holland, Kevin. *King of the Middle March* (6–9). 2004, Scholastic $17.95 (0-439-26600-9). 432pp. In the final volume of the trilogy that started with *The Seeing Stone* (2001), 16-year-old Arthur de Caldicot watches the disintegration of King Arthur's court in his seeing stone as he waits in Venice for the start of the Fourth Crusade. (Rev: BL 9/1/04*; SLJ 11/04)

388 Curry, Jane Louise. *The Black Canary* (5–8). 2005, Simon & Schuster $16.95 (0-689-86478-7). 288pp. Twelve-year-old James, from a biracial family of musicians, resists pressure to develop his own musical abilities until he travels back in time to Elizabethan London and discovers he is also talented. (Rev: BL 2/15/05*; SLJ 3/05)

389 Del Vecchio, Gene. *The Pearl of Anton* (7–10). 2004, Pelican $16.95 (1-58980-172-5). 256pp. In this complex, gripping fantasy, Jason inherits the Wizard's Stone when he turns 15, but the stone's

powers cannot be realized until it is joined with the Pearl of Anton, which is hidden in a mountain cave and guarded by two fearsome beasts. (Rev: BL 6/1–15/04*; VOYA 10/04)

390 DiTocco, Robyn, and Tony DiTocco. *Atlas' Revenge: Another Mad Myth Mystery* (7–12). 2005, Brainstorm $19.95 (0-9723429-2-3); paper $11.95 (0-9723429-3-1). 234pp. PJ Allen, a carefree college senior, is called upon to travel to the world of mythology to complete the legendary Twelve Labors of Hercules and solve a cryptic riddle in this fast-paced novel full of legendary characters and literary references. (Rev: SLJ 6/05)

391 Divakaruni, Chitra Banerjee. *The Mirror of Fire and Dreaming* (5–8). 2005, Roaring Brook $16.95 (1-59643-067-2). 336pp. In this sequel to *The Conch Bearer* (2003), 12-year-old Anand continues his magic studies and travels back to Moghul times, where he encounters powerful sorcerers and evil jinns. (Rev: BL 9/1/05; SLJ 12/05)

392 D'Lacey, Chris. *The Fire Within* (5–8). 2005, Scholastic $12.95 (0-439-67343-0). 340pp. A multi-layered fantasy in which British college student David Rain comes to board at the home of Liz Pennykettle and her daughter, Lucy, and discovers that the clay dragons crafted by Liz have magical properties. (Rev: SLJ 10/05)

393 *Dr. Ernest Drake's Dragonology: The Complete Book of Dragons* (5–12). Illus. 2003, Candlewick $18.99 (0-7636-2329-6). Presented as the recently discovered research of a 19th-century scientist, this richly illustrated volume presents a very realistic encyclopedia of dragon facts and figures. (Rev: BL 4/15/04; SLJ 4/04)

394 Dunkle, Clare B. *Close Kin* (6–9). Series: Hollow Kingdom. 2004, Holt $16.95 (0-8050-7497-X). 224pp. In this sequel to *The Hollow Kingdom* (2003), Kate's younger sister Emily realizes the depth of her feelings for Seylin, who has gone in search of his elfin roots, and she sets off to find him. (Rev: BL 10/1/04; SLJ 10/04; VOYA 12/04)

395 Dunkle, Clare B. *In the Coils of the Snake* (7–10). Series: Hollow Kingdom. 2005, Holt $16.95 (0-8050-7747-2). 240pp. When human girl Miranda learns she will not after all marry the new goblin king, she flees from the kingdom; this final volume in the trilogy is set 30 years after *Close Kin* (2004). (Rev: BL 1/1–15/06*; SLJ 10/05; VOYA 10/05)

396 Ewing, Lynne. *Barbarian* (8–12). Series: Sons of the Dark. 2004, Hyperion $9.99 (0-7868-1811-5). 264pp. Four gorgeous and immortal teens with magical powers escape slavery in the parallel universe of Nefandus and must deal with life in modern Los Angeles before fulfilling their destinies. (Rev: SLJ 10/04; VOYA 2/05)

397 Farland, David. *Of Mice and Magic* (5–8). Series: Ravenspell. 2005, Covenant Communications $16.95 (1-57734-918-0). 276pp. Ben's magical mouse Amber turns Ben into a mouse and together the two set out to rescue the animals from the pet store. (Rev: SLJ 1/06)

398 Farley, Terri. *Seven Tears into the Sea* (7–10). 2005, Simon & Schuster paper $6.99 (0-689-86442-6). 288pp. Working at her clairvoyant grandmother's seaside inn for the summer, 17-year-old Gwen becomes attracted to Jesse, a strange boy with secrets. (Rev: BCCB 4/05; BL 4/1/05; SLJ 6/05; VOYA 6/05)

399 Farmer, Nancy. *The Sea of Trolls* (6–9). 2004, Atheneum $17.95 (0-689-86744-1). 480pp. In this thrill-packed Viking fantasy, 11-year-old Jack must embark on a dangerous quest into troll country to save his little sister's life. (Rev: BL 11/1/04; SLJ 10/04)

400 Federici, Debbie, and Susan Vaught. *L.O.S.T* (8–12). 2004, Llewellyn paper $9.95 (0-7387-0561-6). 321pp. Fantasy and romance are intertwined in this fast-paced story about 17-year-old Bren, who is kidnapped by Jazz, 16-year-old Queen of the Witches, because she believes he is the long-prophesied Shadowalker. (Rev: SLJ 1/05)

401 Fisher, Catherine. *The Oracle Betrayed* (5–8). 2004, Greenwillow $16.99 (0-06-057157-8). 352pp. This suspenseful story set in an imaginary country that combines aspects of ancient Greece and ancient Egypt involves a young heroine, Mirany, on a dangerous quest. (Rev: BL 2/15/04; HB 3–4/04; SLJ 3/04; VOYA 4/04)

402 Fisher, Catherine. *Snow-Walker* (6–9). 2004, HarperCollins $17.99 (0-06-072474-9). 512pp. Gudrun, an evil witch and the title character of this fantasy novel that draws on Norse and Celtic legends, faces a stiff challenge from the people of Jarshold as they fight to oust her and restore the rightful rulers to the throne. (Rev: BL 9/1/04; SLJ 11/04)

403 Fisher, Catherine. *The Sphere of Secrets* (5–8). Series: Oracle Prophecies Trilogy. 2005, Greenwillow LB $17.89 (0-06-057162-4). 384pp. Alexos, introduced in *The Oracle Betrayed* (2004), embarks on a journey to the Well of Songs while his friend Mirany serves the Oracle. (Rev: BL 3/15/05; SLJ 3/05)

404 Fisk, Pauline. *The Red Judge* (7–10). 2005, Bloomsbury $16.95 (1-58234-942-8). 208pp. Haunted by grief and guilt over his involvement in his sister's accident, Zed Fitztalbot is sent to live in the Welsh home of his recently deceased grandmother in this stand-alone companion to *The Secret of Sabrina Fludde* (2002) that combines fantasy, mythology, and typical teen problems. (Rev: BL 12/1/05; SLJ 3/06)

405 Flanagan, John. *The Ruins of Gorlan* (5–8). 2005, Philomel $15.99 (0-399-24454-9). 256pp.

Will becomes an apprentice ranger and plays a key role in protecting his kingdom in this memorable first installment in a new fantasy series. (Rev: BL 6/1–15/05*; SLJ 6/05)

406 Foon, Dennis. *The Dirt Eaters* (5–10). Series: Longlight Legacy Trilogy. 2003, Annick $19.95 (1-55037-807-4); paper $9.95 (1-55037-806-6). 320pp. In this well-written first installment of a trilogy, 15-year-old Roan finds himself torn between the peaceful ways of his upbringing and a desire to avenge a murderous attack on his village. (Rev: SLJ 1/04; VOYA 2/04)

407 Forrester, Sandra. *The Witches of Sea-Dragon Bay: The Adventures of Beatrice Bailey* (5–8). 2003, Barron's paper $4.95 (0-7641-2633-4). 228pp. Another in the series starring 12-year-old apprentice witch Beatrice Bailey, likely to appeal to Harry Potter fans. (Rev: SLJ 3/04)

408 Funke, Cornelia. *Inkspell* (6–9). 2005, Scholastic $19.99 (0-439-55400-4). 672pp. In this gripping sequel to *Inkheart*, the magical process is reversed and earlier characters find themselves in a fictional world of violence. (Rev: BL 10/1/05*; SLJ 10/05; VOYA 10/05)

409 Furlong, Monica. *Colman* (4–8). 2004, Random LB $17.99 (0-375-91514-1). 288pp. In this complex, posthumous sequel to *Wise Child* (1987) and *Juniper* (1990), Juniper and her companions must battle the evil Meroot and the Gray Knight and restore harmony in the land. (Rev: BL 1/1–15/04; SLJ 2/04)

410 Gandolfi, Silvana. *Aldabra, or the Tortoise Who Loved Shakespeare* (6–12). 2004, Scholastic $16.95 (0-439-49741-8). 160pp. In this whimsical tale set in Venice, 10-year-old Elisa faces some daunting challenges when her beloved grandmother is magically transformed into a giant tortoise. (Rev: BCCB 7–8/04; BL 4/1/04; SLJ 8/04; VOYA 8/04)

411 Garcí, Laura Gallego. *The Legend of the Wandering King* (6–9). Trans. by Dan Bellm. 2005, Scholastic $16.95 (0-439-58556-2). 213pp. Jealous of the carpet weaver who has bested him in the annual poetry competition for three consecutive years, an Arabian prince orders his rival to weave a carpet that chronicles the complete history of humankind. (Rev: BL 10/15/05; SLJ 10/05)

412 Gardner, Sally. *I, Coriander* (7–10). 2005, Dial $16.99 (0-8037-3099-3). 288pp. In a fantasy full of the atmosphere of 17th-century England, Coriander is the daughter of a human father and a fairy princess. (Rev: BL 8/05; SLJ 9/05; VOYA 10/05)

413 Gilmore, Rachna. *The Sower of Tales* (6–9). 2005, Fitzhenry & Whiteside $15.95 (1-55041-945-5). 423pp. In a land where the Plainsfolk are nourished by stories, Calantha, who dreams of following in the footsteps of the Gatherer who harvests the story pods, must act to save them all. (Rev: BL 12/15/05; SLJ 1/06; VOYA 12/05)

414 Gliori, Debi. *Pure Dead Trouble* (4–7). Series: Pure Dead. 2005, Knopf LB $17.99 (0-375-93311-5). 304pp. Nanny MacLachlan plays a key role in this fourth, darker and more complex, installment in the series. (Rev: BL 10/1/05; SLJ 8/05; VOYA 8/05)

415 Gopnik, Adam. *The King in the Window* (5–8). 2005, Hyperion $19.95 (0-7868-1862-X). 416pp. Mistaken by window wraiths as their king, 11-year-old Oliver Parker struggles to resist their efforts to pull him into their world. (Rev: BL 10/1/05; SLJ 11/05; VOYA 2/06)

416 Grant, Vicki. *The Puppet Wrangler* (6–8). 2004, Orca paper $7.95 (1-55143-304-4). 212pp. A humorous, offbeat modern fantasy in which 12-year-old Telly, unfairly banished from home because of her older sister's misdeeds, finds herself befriending a live puppet from her aunt's television show. (Rev: BCCB 7–8/04; SLJ 8/04)

417 Gray, Luli. *Falcon and the Carousel of Time* (4–7). 2005, Houghton $15.00 (0-618-44895-0). 128pp. Falcon, 13, and her Aunt Emily travel back to 1903 New York City in this novel that blends elements of *Timespinners* (2003) and the two previous Falcon novels. (Rev: BL 6/1–15/05; SLJ 7/05)

418 Gruber, Michael. *The Witch's Boy* (6–9). 2005, HarperCollins LB $17.89 (0-06-076165-2). 384pp. Lump, a grotesque foundling rescued by a witch, turns against his adoptive mother after he becomes consumed with anger over his sorry state in life. (Rev: BCCB 4/05; BL 3/15/05*; SLJ 8/05)

419 Gutman, Dan. *Abner and Me* (5–8). Series: Baseball Card Adventure. 2005, HarperCollins LB $16.89 (0-06-053444-3). 176pp. Stosh and his mother travel back to visit the Battle of Gettysburg in an effort to learn more about baseball's origins. (Rev: BL 1/1–15/05)

420 Gutman, Dan. *Satch and Me* (4–7). Series: Baseball Card Adventure. 2005, HarperCollins LB $16.89 (0-06-059492-6). 173pp. Stosh travels back to 1942 to establish whether Satchel Paige was the fastest pitcher in history and learns about racial discrimination in the process. (Rev: SLJ 2/06)

421 Halam, Ann. *Siberia* (5–8). 2005, Random LB $18.99 (0-385-90885-7). 272pp. In this richly layered novel set in a future ice-covered wilderness, 13-year-old Sloe must risk her life to deliver her arrested mother's genetically engineered animal life to a safe place. (Rev: BL 6/1–15/05; SLJ 6/05)

422 Hale, Shannon. *Enna Burning* (8–11). 2004, Bloomsbury $17.95 (1-58234-889-8). 336pp. In this companion to *The Goose Girl*, Enna returns to her home in the forest and learns to wield the power of fire, but she must struggle to use that power wisely

without risking her life or those of her people. (Rev: BL 9/15/04; SLJ 9/04; VOYA 12/04)

423 Hale, Shannon. *Princess Academy* (6–9). 2005, Bloomsbury $16.95 (1-58234-993-2). 300pp. Fantasy, feminism, adventure, and romance are combined in the story of 14-year-old Miri, prize student in the Princess Academy and advocate for the miners of the stone called *under*. (Rev: BL 6/1–15/05; SLJ 8/05; VOYA 8/05)

424 Hanley, Victoria. *The Light of the Oracle* (6–9). 2005, Random LB $17.99 (0-385-75087-0). 312pp. Chosen to train in the Temple of the Oracle, Bryn, daughter of a lowly stonecutter, displays powers that pose a threat to the evil forces lurking within the temple; set in the same world as *The Seer and the Sword* (2000) and *The Healer's Keep* (2002). (Rev: BCCB 6/05; SLJ 6/05; VOYA 6/05)

425 Haptie, Charlotte. *Otto and the Flying Twins* (4–7). 2004, Holiday $17.95 (0-8234-1826-X). 304pp. In the City of Trees, Otto is shocked to discover his father is king of the magical Karmidee. The sequel is *Otto and the Bird Charmers* (2005). (Rev: BL 4/15/04; SLJ 6/04)

426 Harrison, Mette. *Mira, Mirror* (7–10). 2004, Penguin $17.99 (0-670-05923-4). 320pp. Transformed into a mirror by her adopted sister, Mira seeks help from a peasant girl in her quest to regain human form. (Rev: BL 9/1/04; SLJ 9/04; VOYA 10/04)

427 Hearn, Julie. *Sign of the Raven* (7–10). 2005, Simon & Schuster $16.95 (0-689-85734-9). 328pp. Living with his grandmother in London while his mother recovers from cancer, 12-year-old Tom finds a portal into an 18th-century world far different from his own. (Rev: BCCB 12/05; HB 1–2/06; SLJ 11/05; VOYA 10/05)

428 Hightman, Jason. *The Saint of Dragons* (6–8). 2004, Morrow $16.99 (0-06-054011-7). 304pp. Enrolled at an elite boarding school, 13-year-old Simon St. George is approached by a man claiming to be his father who asks for the boy's help in vanquishing the last surviving dragons. (Rev: BL 8/04; SLJ 9/04)

429 Hill, Laban Carrick. *Casa Azul: An Encounter with Frida Kahlo* (7–10). 2005, Watson-Guptill $15.95 (0-8230-0411-2). 150pp. In this appealing novel, two country children roaming the streets of Mexico City in search of their mother are befriended by artist Frida Kahlo and introduced to the magical world in which she dwells. (Rev: BL 10/1/05; SLJ 9/05)

430 Hill, Stuart. *The Cry of the Icemark* (8–11). 2005, Scholastic $19.95 (0-439-68626-1). 496pp. In this sprawling military fantasy, 13-year-old Thirrin succeeds her fallen father as ruler of Icemark and sets off to forge alliances with werewolves, vampires, and talking snow leopards to help her defend her tiny country. (Rev: BCCB 4/05; BL 2/15/05; SLJ 5/05; VOYA 6/05)

431 Hoeye, Michael. *No Time Like Show Time* (5–8). Series: A Hermux Tantamoq Adventure. 2004, Putnam $14.99 (0-399-23880-8). 277pp. Hermux the mouse investigates who is responsible for sending threatening letters to famous director Fluster Varmint. (Rev: SLJ 11/04)

432 Hoffman, Alice. *The Foretelling* (7–10). 2005, Little, Brown $16.99 (0-316-01018-9). 167pp. Rain, the daughter of an unaffectionate Amazon queen, questions the tribe's beliefs and customs. (Rev: BL 7/05; SLJ 10/05; VOYA 12/05)

433 Hoffman, Mary. *Stravaganza: City of Flowers* (7–10). Series: Stravaganza. 2005, Bloomsbury $17.95 (1-58234-887-1). 496pp. In the final volume of the trilogy, Sky Meadows, a 17-year-old biracial Londoner, travels back in time to 16th-century Talia, where many of the characters become involved in multilayered intrigue. (Rev: BL 3/1/05; SLJ 5/05)

434 Hoving, Isabel. *The Dream Merchant* (8–12). Trans. from Dutch by Hester Velmans. 2005, Candlewick $17.99 (0-7636-2880-8). 630pp. An action-packed, intricately plotted adventure involving three young people in time travel and a world of collective dreams called *umaya*. (Rev: SLJ 1/06; VOYA 12/05)

435 Hunter, Erin. *A Dangerous Path* (6–9). Series: Warriors. 2004, HarperCollins LB $16.89 (0-06-052564-9). 336pp. In the fifth installment in the series, Fireheart, deputy leader of ThunderClan, worries about the future of all the cats in the forest now that Tigerstar has taken over the leadership of ShadowClan. (Rev: BL 8/04)

436 Hunter, Erin. *Dawn* (6–9). Series: Warriors: The New Prophecy. 2006, HarperCollins LB $16.89 (0-06-074456-1). 352pp. In the third volume of the series, humans are encroaching further into the habitat of the four cat clans and there is pressure to unite and seek a new home. (Rev: BL 12/1/05)

437 Hunter, Erin. *Moonrise* (6–9). Series: Warriors: The New Prophecy. 2005, HarperCollins LB $16.89 (0-06-074453-7). 304pp. The cats of the StarClan take advice from a badger named Midnight and on the ensuing journey through the mountains meet a new and unusual tribe of cats. (Rev: BL 9/1/05)

438 Hunter, Erin. *Rising Storm* (6–9). Series: Warriors. 2004, HarperCollins LB $16.89 (0-06-052562-2). 336pp. In this fourth volume of the series, Fireheart the cat faces a number of daunting challenges in his new position as deputy leader of the ThunderClan. (Rev: BL 1/1–15/04; VOYA 4/04)

439 Hussey, Charmain. *The Valley of Secrets* (4–7). 2005, Simon & Schuster $16.95 (0-689-87862-1). 400pp. A detailed, multifaceted novel about an orphan who inherits his great-uncle's estate and, through his uncle's journal, learns about the plight of the Amazon Indians. (Rev: BL 3/1/05; SLJ 2/05)

440 Jacques, Brian. *High Rhulain* (5–8). Series: Redwall. 2005, Philomel $23.99 (0-399-24208-2). 384pp. In this eighteenth installment, ottermaid Tiria bravely journeys to the Green Isle to rescue otter kinsmen from evil wildcats. (Rev: BL 9/1/05; SLJ 9/05)

441 Jacques, Brian. *Rakkety Tam* (5–8). Series: Redwall. 2004, Putnam $23.99 (0-399-23725-9). 384pp. When Redwall is threatened by a murderous wolverine called Gulo the Savage, two warrior squirrels — Rakkety Tam McBurl and Wild Doogy Plumm — take action. (Rev: BL 9/15/04; SLJ 9/04)

442 Jarvis, Robin. *The Oaken Throne* (6–9). Series: Deptford Histories. 2005, Chronicle Books $17.95 (1-58717-277-1). 382pp. Ongoing battles between bats and squirrels now involve young bat Vesper and squirrel maiden Ysabelle, who must collaborate to save their worlds from darkness; a sequel to *The Alchemist's Cat* (2004). (Rev: BL 9/1/05; SLJ 2/06)

443 Jenkins, Martin. *Jonathan Swift's Gulliver* (5–8). 2005, Candlewick $19.99 (0-7636-2409-8). 144pp. A retelling of the classic tale using contemporary language and striking artwork. (Rev: BL 3/15/05; SLJ 3/05)

444 Johnson, Kathleen Jeffrie. *A Fast and Brutal Wing* (8–11). 2004, Roaring Brook $16.95 (1-59643-013-3). 192pp. In a series of e-mails, journal entries, and newspaper stories, three teens recount the mysterious and fantastic events that led to a Halloween disappearance. (Rev: BL 12/15/04; SLJ 12/04; VOYA 12/04)

445 Jones, Diana Wynne. *Unexpected Magic: Collected Stories* (5–10). 2004, Greenwillow $16.99 (0-06-055533-5). An exciting anthology of 16 tales of mystery and magic by a master of fantasy. (Rev: BL 4/15/04; SLJ 9/04)

446 Jung, Reinhardt. *Bambert's Book of Missing Stories* (5–8). Trans. from German by Anthea Bell. 2004, Knopf LB $16.99 (0-375-92997-5). 124pp. A reclusive dwarf named Bambert writes 11 tales and sends them out on hot-air balloons, hoping they will be enhanced by their finders and sent back. (Rev: SLJ 11/04)

447 Kaberbol, Lene. *The Shamer's Daughter* (6–8). 2004, Holt $16.95 (0-8050-7541-0). 230pp. Dina has inherited her mother's powers as a Shamer, able to ferret out the shameful truths that others try to hide; the 10-year-old sees her gift as a burden until she's called upon to use her powers to save her mother's life. The sequel is *The Shamer's Signet* (2005). (Rev: BL 4/15/04; HB 5–6/04; SLJ 6/04; VOYA 6/04)

448 Kerr, P. B. *The Blue Djinn of Babylon* (5–8). Series: Children of the Lamp. 2006, Scholastic

$16.99 (0-439-67021-7). 384pp. Philippa Gaunt, 12, is wrongly convicted of cheating and her twin John must rescue her in this action-packed sequel to *The Akhenatan Adventure* (2005). (Rev: BL 3/15/06; SLJ 3/06; VOYA 2/06)

449 Kurtz, Jane. *The Feverbird's Claw* (5–8). 2004, Greenwillow $15.99 (0-06-000820-2). 304pp. Secretly trained in the art of combat by her grandfather, Moralin is swept into a series of harrowing adventures when she is kidnapped by the Arkera, longtime enemies of Moralin's clan. (Rev: BL 4/15/04; SLJ 5/04; VOYA 6/04)

450 Langrish, Katherine. *Troll Mill* (5–8). 2006, HarperCollins LB $16.89 (0-06-058308-8). 288pp. In this sequel to *Troll Fell* (2004), 15-year-old Peer Ulfsson, who still worries about his cruel uncles and is increasingly involved with Hilde, must help protect a half-selkie baby from trolls and other threats. (Rev: BL 2/1/06*; SLJ 3/06; VOYA 2/06)

451 Larbalestier, Justine. *Magic or Madness* (8–11). 2005, Penguin $16.99 (1-59514-022-0). 288pp. Australian 15-year-old Reason resists the idea of magic until she is transported from her grandmother's home to New York City and finds herself tackling new realities. (Rev: BCCB 3/05; BL 3/15/05*; SLJ 3/05; VOYA 2/05)

452 Lawrence, Michael. *A Crack in the Line* (8–12). 2004, HarperCollins $15.99 (0-06-072477-3). 336pp. Still mourning his mother's death, 16-year-old Alaric discovers how to travel to an alternate reality where his mother is still alive. (Rev: BL 6/1–15/04*; SLJ 8/04)

453 Lefaucheur, Sandi. *The Secret Shelter* (6–9). 2004, Brown Barn paper $12.95 (0-9746481-4-0). 143pp. Curious to know what life was like in London during World War II, Sophie — along with two friends and a teacher — explores an old air raid shelter and finds herself back in 1940. (Rev: SLJ 1/05)

454 Le Guin, Ursula K. *Gifts* (6–10). 2004, Harcourt $17.00 (0-15-205123-6). 288pp. In this engaging fantasy, Gry and Orrec, two Uplanders with supernatural abilities, are hesitant to use their awesome powers for fear that they will cause more harm than good. (Rev: BL 8/04*; SLJ 9/04; VOYA 12/04)

455 Leonard, Elmore. *A Coyote's in the House* (5–8). 2004, HarperEntertainment $22.00 (0-06-072882-5). 149pp. A coyote named Antwan strikes up a friendship with a couple of pampered dogs from Hollywood. (Rev: BL 5/15/04*)

456 London, Dena. *Shapeshifter's Quest* (7–10). 2005, Dutton $16.99 (0-525-47310-6). 192pp. Syanthe, a shape-shifting teenager, ventures outside the forest that has always been her home on a mission to unravel the secret of the king's black magic. (Rev: BL 10/1/05; SLJ 10/05; VOYA 8/05)

457 Lowry, Lois. *Gossamer* (5–8). 2006, Houghton $16.00 (0-618-68550-2). 144pp. A spirit called Littlest One learns to mix memories that will heal people while they sleep. (Rev: BL 2/15/06)

458 Lowry, Lois. *Messenger* (6–10). 2004, Houghton $16.00 (0-618-40441-4). 176pp. In the Village where teenage Matty is a caregiver, the residents decide to build a wall to keep out undesirables in this fantasy filled with truth and symbolism. (Rev: BL 2/15/04*; HB 5–6/04; SLJ 4/04; VOYA 6/04)

459 Lyon, Steve. *The Gift Moves* (6–9). 2004, Houghton $15.00 (0-618-39128-2). 240pp. In this quiet, futuristic novel set in an America devoid of wealth and materialism, Path Down the Mountain, a weaver's apprentice, and Bird Speaks, son of the local baker, strike up a friendship. (Rev: BL 6/1–15/04; SLJ 6/04; VOYA 6/04)

460 McGann, Oisín. *The Gods and Their Machines* (8–11). 2004, Tor $19.95 (0-765-31159-3). 240pp. Fantasy and allegory are blended in this story about Chamus, a teenage Altiman fighter pilot trainee, whose denigration of the people of nearby Bartokhrin as ignorant religious fanatics is revised when a Bartokhrin girl helps him after his plane is forced to land near her home. (Rev: BL 12/15/04)

461 MacHale, D. J. *The Rivers of Zadaa* (5–8). Series: Pendragon. 2005, Simon & Schuster $14.95 (1-4169-0710-6). 405pp. Bobby Pendragon teams up with Loor to foil the villainous Saint Dane's plan to cut off the water supply to Loor's people in Zadaa. (Rev: SLJ 7/05)

462 McKillip, Patricia A. *Harrowing the Dragon* (8–12). 2005, Ace $23.95 (0-441-01360-0). 320pp. A collection of fantasy short stories featuring dragons, princesses in distress, sorcerers, shape-shifters, and more. (Rev: BL 11/1/05; SLJ 3/06)

463 McNaughton, Janet. *An Earthly Knight* (7–10). 2004, HarperCollins $15.99 (0-06-008992-X). 272pp. In this romantic fantasy, 16-year-old Jennie in Scotland falls in love with an enchanted lord and their love is so strong that it shatters a powerful curse. (Rev: BL 2/15/04; SLJ 3/04)

464 McNish, Cliff. *The Silver Child* (6–9). 2005, Carolrhoda $15.95 (1-57505-825-1). 192pp. Mysteriously drawn to a huge garbage dump known as Coldharbour, six children undergo fantastic transformations. (Rev: BCCB 4/05; BL 4/15/05; SLJ 6/05; VOYA 6/05)

465 Magrs, Paul. *The Good, the Bat, and the Ugly* (6–10). 2004, Simon & Schuster $15.95 (0-689-87019-1). 247pp. Thirteen-year-old Jason's father is suspected of murdering some puppets in this dark but humorous fantasy set in England. (Rev: BCCB 7–8/04; SLJ 7/04)

466 Marley, Louise. *Singer in the Snow* (8–11). 2005, Viking $16.99 (0-670-05965-X). 304pp. Mreen and Emle, two gifted young Singers from the ice planet of Nevya, are sent to a remote outpost where together they complement one another's powers in this follow-up to the Singers of Nevya trilogy. (Rev: BL 12/15/05; SLJ 1/06; VOYA 12/05)

467 Marsden, John. *Out of Time* (6–9). 2005, Tor $16.95 (0-765-31412-6). 128pp. In this compelling fantasy novella told in a series of vignettes, James, a troubled Australian teen, uses a time-travel machine to connect with others across time and space. (Rev: BL 11/1/05)

468 Martin, Rafe. *Birdwing* (5–8). 2005, Scholastic $16.99 (0-459-21167-0). 359pp. This appealing fantasy picks up where "The Six Swans" by the Brothers Grimm ends, chronicling the story of Ardwin, the prince who was turned into a swan and then restored to human form apart from his left arm, which remains a swan's wing. (Rev: BCCB 12/05 ; BL 11/15/05; HB 1–2/06; SLJ 12/05; VOYA 12/05)

469 Martini, Clem. *The Mob* (5–8). Series: Feather and Bone: The Crow Chronicles. 2004, Kids Can $16.95 (1-55337-574-2). 240pp. As hundreds of crows of the Kinaar clan come together for their annual socialization at the Gathering Tree, internal conflicts threaten to tear the avian family apart in this first volume in a trilogy. (Rev: BL 10/1/04; SLJ 12/04)

470 Melling, O. R. *The Hunter's Moon* (8–11). 2005, Abrams $16.95 (0-8109-5857-0). 260pp. Gwen, an American, travels to Ireland to spend a fun-packed vacation with her cousin Findabhair but soon finds herself leading a rescue effort after Findabhair is abducted by the King of the Faeries. (Rev: BCCB 4/05; BL 4/15/05*; SLJ 4/05; VOYA 6/05)

471 Meyer, Kai. *The Water Mirror* (4–7). Trans. by Elizabeth D. Crawford. Series: Dark Reflections. 2005, Simon & Schuster $15.95 (0-689-87787-0). 256pp. In an alternate Venice in danger of destruction, 14-year-old Merle, a plucky orphan, finds herself playing a central role; the first volume in a series noted for its setting. (Rev: BL 1/1–15/06; SLJ 11/05*; VOYA 12/05)

472 Molloy, Michael. *The House on Falling Star Hill* (4–8). 2004, Scholastic $16.95 (0-439-57740-3). 384pp. While spending a vacation with his grandparents in a peaceful English village, Tim discovers an alternate world called Tallis and becomes involved in the turmoil taking place there. (Rev: BL 4/15/04; SLJ 4/04)

473 Moredun, P. R. *The Dragon Conspiracy* (5–8). Series: World of Eldaterra. 2005, HarperCollins LB $17.89 (0-06-076664-6). 304pp. A complex first installment in which a British schoolboy in 1910 must battle female dragons to save both our world and the magical parallel world of Eldaterra. (Rev: BL 6/1–15/05; SLJ 10/05)

474 Morris, Gerald. *The Princess, the Crone, and the Dung-Cart Knight* (6–9). 2004, Houghton $15.00 (0-618-37823-5). 320pp. In this absorbing Arthurian fantasy, 13-year-old Sarah enlists help from others in her quest to identify those who instigated the murderous riot that took the lives of her mother and their Jewish friend. (Rev: BCCB 3/04; BL 4/15/04; HB 5–6/04; SLJ 5/04; VOYA 6/04)

475 Nix, Garth. *Drowned Wednesday* (5–8). Series: The Keys to the Kingdom. 2005, Scholastic $15.95 (0-439-70086-8). 389pp. In the third volume of the Keys to the Kingdom fantasy series, Arthur Penhaligon faces multiple challenges as he struggles to win the third key to the kingdom. (Rev: BL 7/05; SLJ 7/05; VOYA 8/05)

476 Nix, Garth. *Grim Tuesday* (5–8). Series: Keys to the Kingdom. 2004, Scholastic paper $5.99 (0-439-43655-9). 321pp. Arthur Penhaligon returns in this second installment in the series to the house that holds an alternate universe and there must challenge the evil Grim Tuesday, who threatens to destroy everything. (Rev: SLJ 8/04)

477 Nyoka, Gail. *Mella and the N'anga: An African Tale* (5–8). 2006, Sumach paper $9.95 (1-894549-49-X). 160pp. Mella, the daughter of a king in ancient Zimbabwe, with the help of the magical powers she learns from the spiritual adviser called N'anga, strives to save her father's life and realm. (Rev: BL 3/1/06)

478 Okorafor-Mbachu, Nnedi. *Zahrah the Windseeker* (5–8). 2005, Houghton $16.00 (0-618-34090-4). 320pp. In this appealing debut novel, 13-year-old Zahrah, a "dada girl" readily identifiable by her telltale vine-entwined dreadlocks, struggles to come to terms with her magical powers. (Rev: BL 11/15/05; SLJ 12/05)

479 Oppel, Kenneth. *Airborn* (6–8). 2004, HarperCollins LB $17.89 (0-06-053181-9). 368pp. Fifteen-year-old Matt Cruse, a cabin boy on the luxury airship *Aurora*, teams up with Kate, a wealthy young passenger, to search for strange winged creatures that Kate's grandfather claims to have seen flying high in the sky. (Rev: BL 6/1–15/04; HB 7–8/04; SLJ 7/04; VOYA 6/04)

480 Page, Jan. *Rewind* (7–10). 2005, Walker $16.95 (0-8027-8995-1). 224pp. When he is injured in an accident while playing drums onstage, Liam finds himself back in time watching his parents as teenagers, when they had a band whose drummer was killed. (Rev: BL 9/1/05; SLJ 11/05; VOYA 10/05)

481 Paolini, Christopher. *Eldest* (8–11). Series: Inheritance. 2005, Knopf LB $24.99 (0-375-92670-4). 704pp. Eragon continues his training as a Dragon Rider while his cousin Roran is under threat in this second installment in the trilogy. (Rev: BL 8/05; SLJ 10/05; VOYA 12/05)

482 Park, Linda Sue. *Archer's Quest* (4–7). 2006, Clarion $16.00 (0-618-59631-3). 176pp. An ancient Korean ruler suddenly appears in the New York State bedroom of 12-year-old Kevin and the two must work out how to get him back home before the Year of the Tiger ends. (Rev: BL 3/15/06)

483 Patterson, James. *Maximum Ride: The Angel Experiment* (7–9). 2005, Little, Brown $16.99 (0-316-15556-X). 422pp. An engaging tale about a group of children, part human and part bird, who escape from the lab where they were bred and now must track down one of their number who's been kidnapped. (Rev: BCCB 4/05; BL 2/1/05; SLJ 5/05; VOYA 4/06)

484 Paul, Donita K. *Dragonspell* (4–8). 2004, WaterBrook paper $12.99 (1-57856-823-4). 339pp. Fourteen-year-old Kale is the protagonist of this classic quest tale, set in the world of Amara, with Christian overtones reminiscent of C. S. Lewis. (Rev: SLJ 11/04)

485 Paulsen, Gary. *The Time Hackers* (5–8). 2005, Random LB $17.99 (0-385-90896-2). 160pp. Twelve-year-old Dorso Clayman and best friend Frank team up to find out who's been tampering with time. (Rev: BL 1/1–15/05; SLJ 1/05)

486 Paver, Michelle. *Spirit Walker* (6–9). Series: Chronicles of Ancient Darkness. 2006, HarperCollins LB $17.89 (0-06-072829-9). 368pp. Young Stone Age survivor Torak seeks a remedy for the epidemic affecting the clans and is reunited with his beloved Wolf in this sequel to *Wolf Brother* (2005). (Rev: BL 2/15/06; VOYA 2/06)

487 Peck, Dale. *The Drift House: The First Voyage* (8–11). 2005, Bloomsbury $16.95 (1-58234-969-X). 350pp. The Oakenfield siblings are sent to live with their Uncle Farley in Canada, and when their uncle's ship-like home is swept away in a flood, they enjoy a magical journey on the Sea of Time. (Rev: BL 10/1/05; SLJ 11/05; VOYA 10/05)

488 Petti, Ken, et al. *Zenda and the Gazing Ball* (4–7). Illus. 2004, Grosset & Dunlap paper $5.99 (0-448-43223-4). 128pp. On the planet of Azureblue, 12-year-old Zenda can't resist a sneak peek at the crystal gazing ball that holds her destiny, and in the process drops and breaks the ball. In the sequel, *Zenda: A New Dimension*, she travels to a parallel dimension in search of shards. (Rev: BL 5/15/04; SLJ 9/04)

489 Pierce, Tamora. *Trickster's Queen* (7–12). 2004, Random LB $19.99 (0-375-81467-1). 480pp. In this thrilling sequel to *Trickster's Choice*, Aly must call upon her magical powers to protect the Balitang children and ensure that one of them — Dove — ascends to the throne of the Copper Isles. (Rev: BCCB 10/04; BL 10/1/04; SLJ 9/04; VOYA 2/05)

490 Pierce, Tamora. *The Will of the Empress* (8–11). 2005, Scholastic $17.99 (0-439-44171-4). 550pp.

Bowing to the will of the Empress of Namorn, Sandry, accompanied by her mage friends from the Winding Circle, embarks on a perilous journey to visit her cousin, the empress; this stand-alone novel comes after the Circle of Magic and The Circle Opens quartets. (Rev: BCCB 1/06; BL 11/15/05*; HB 11–12/05; SLJ 11/05; VOYA 10/05)

491 Pratchett, Terry. *A Hat Full of Sky* (6–10). 2004, HarperCollins $16.99 (0-06-058660-5). 288pp. Witch-in-training Tiffany Aching battles a monster with help from the wee men and head witch Granny Weatherwax in the sequel to *The Wee Free Men*. (Rev: BCCB 5/04; BL 4/15/04; HB 7–8/04; SLJ 7/04; VOYA 6/04)

492 Pullman, Philip. *Lyra's Oxford* (5–8). 2003, Knopf $10.95 (0-375-82819-2). 64pp. This slim volume takes readers back to the world of Pullman's His Dark Materials trilogy, with maps, postcards, and other ephemera. (Rev: BL 2/1/04; SLJ 1/04; VOYA 6/04)

493 Randall, David. *Clovermead: In the Shadow of the Bear* (6–9). 2004, Simon & Schuster $15.95 (0-689-86639-9). 304pp. Clovermead Wickward, the 14-year-old daughter of an innkeeper, discovers uncomfortable truths about her father and herself in this challenging but compelling fantasy. (Rev: BL 7/04; SLJ 7/04; VOYA 8/04)

494 Resnick, Mike. *Lady with an Alien: An Encounter with Leonardo da Vinci* (6–9). Series: Art Encounters. 2005, Watson-Guptill $15.95 (0-8230-0323-X). 176pp. Elements of fantasy, time travel, history, art, and philosophy are all present in this novel about da Vinci and his supposed substitution of an alien for an ermine. (Rev: BL 11/1/05; SLJ 10/05)

495 Riordan, Rick. *The Lightning Thief* (6–9). Series: Percy Jackson and the Olympians. 2005, Hyperion $17.95 (0-7868-5629-7). 384pp. Perseus (aka Percy) Jackson, a New York 12-year-old with problems, has action-packed adventures after he is sent to Camp Half Blood — a summer camp for demigods — and discovers his father is Poseidon. (Rev: BL 9/15/05; SLJ 8/05*)

496 Rowling, J. K. *Harry Potter and the Half-Blood Prince* (5–12). 2005, Scholastic LB $34.99 (0-439-78677-0). 672pp. In this sixth and penultimate volume, Harry, now 16, begins mapping a strategy to defeat the evil Lord Voldemort. (Rev: BL 8/05*; SLJ 9/05; VOYA 10/05)

497 Ruby, Laura. *The Wall and the Wing* (5–8). 2006, HarperCollins LB $17.89 (0-06-075256-4). 336pp. An offbeat fantasy set in a future New York in which 12-year-old Gurl finds she can make herself invisible, a rare talent in a population where most people can fly. (Rev: BL 2/1/06; SLJ 2/06; VOYA 2/06)

498 Sabin, E. Rose. *When the Beast Ravens* (7–12). 2005, Tor $23.95 (0-765-30858-4). 288pp. In the conclusion of the trilogy set at a school for gifted sorcerers (preceding volumes are *A School for Sorcery*, 2002, and *A Perilous Power*, 2004), students and faculty struggle to solve murders on campus and drive away demons from the Dire Realm. (Rev: BL 1/1–15/05; SLJ 7/05; VOYA 8/05)

499 Seabrooke, Brenda. *Stonewolf* (5–8). 2005, Holiday $16.95 (0-8234-1848-0). 231pp. Young orphan Nicholas is taken captive by a group called the Synod but manages to escape, taking with him a sought-after secret formula. (Rev: BL 3/15/05; SLJ 3/05)

500 Sedgwick, Marcus. *The Book of Dead Days* (6–9). 2004, Random LB $17.99 (0-385-73055-1). 288pp. In the dead days between Christmas and New Year's Eve in a nameless old city, a child named Boy follows the instructions of his master, a magician who is racing against time to save himself from the devil. (Rev: BL 9/1/04*; SLJ 11/04)

501 Shinn, Sharon. *The Safe-Keeper's Secret* (7–12). 2004, Viking $16.99 (0-670-05910-2). Truth and justice are themes in this fantasy about Fiona, a girl whose family has many secrets, and Reed, a boy without an identity, who was left as a baby with Fiona's mother. (Rev: BL 4/15/04; SLJ 6/04; VOYA 6/04)

502 Shinn, Sharon. *The Truth-Teller's Tale* (7–10). 2005, Viking $16.99 (0-670-06000-3). 288pp. Twin sisters Eleda and Adele are mirror images — Eleda can neither tell nor hear a lie, while Adele can be trusted to keep secret anything she is told. (Rev: BCCB 9/05; BL 4/15/05*; SLJ 7/05; VOYA 8/05)

503 Shusterman, Neal. *Dread Locks* (6–9). Series: Dark Fusion. 2005, Dutton $15.99 (0-525-47554-0). 176pp. When Tara, with her thick golden hair and dark sunglasses, moves in next door to the family of 14-year-old Parker Baer, bad things start to happen in this novel based on the story of Medusa. (Rev: BL 6/1–15/05; SLJ 6/05; VOYA 6/05)

504 Shusterman, Neal. *Duckling Ugly* (7–10). Series: Dark Fusion. 2006, Dutton $15.99 (0-525-47585-0). 176pp. Apart from her ability to spell, Cara DeFido has no known attributes until she finds herself in a magic kingdom; her successes there prompt her to return home, however. (Rev: BL 2/1/06)

505 Shusterman, Neal. *Red Rider's Hood* (6–9). 2005, Dutton $15.99 (0-525-47562-1). 176pp. A dark variation on the Red Riding Hood story in which Red Rider, a 16-year-old boy, vows to seek revenge after a group of werewolves attack his grandmother and steal his beloved Mustang; this will appeal to reluctant readers. (Rev: BL 10/15/05; SLJ 12/05; VOYA 10/05)

506 Silberberg, Alan. *Pond Scum* (4–7). 2005, Hyperion $15.99 (0-7868-5634-3). 304pp. Ten-year-old Oliver gains a whole new appreciation for his animal neighbors after he finds a magical gem that allows him to assume the shape of various creatures. (Rev: BL 12/1/05; SLJ 11/05)

507 Singleton, Linda Joy. *Last Dance* (6–8). Series: The Seer. 2005, Llewellyn paper $5.99 (0-7387-0638-8). 241pp. Sabine goes in search of a possible cure for her desperately ill grandmother but is sidetracked by the ghost of a young girl who reportedly committed suicide. (Rev: SLJ 7/05)

508 Snyder, Zilpha Keatley. *The Unseen* (5–8). 2004, Delacorte $15.95 (0-385-73084-5). 208pp. The discovery of a magic feather, and the experiences it brings, help 12-year-old Xandra to feel less isolated and to appreciate her family more. (Rev: BL 3/1/04; SLJ 4/04)

509 Spiegler, Louise. *The Amethyst Road* (8–11). 2005, Clarion $16.00 (0-618-48572-4). 336pp. In this cautionary futuristic novel, siblings Serena and Willow, half-Gorgio and half-Yulang, struggle to survive the violence of their urban neighborhood and the ostracism caused by their mixed blood. (Rev: BL 12/1/05; SLJ 11/05; VOYA 2/06)

510 Stanley, Diane. *Bella at Midnight* (5–8). 2006, HarperCollins LB $16.89 (0-06-077574-2). 288pp. A fine retelling of the Cinderella story featuring a plucky Bella and a storytelling format. (Rev: BL 2/1/06*; SLJ 3/06*; VOYA 2/06)

511 Stewart, Sharon. *Raven Quest* (5–8). 2005, Carolrhoda LB $15.95 (1-57505-894-4). 320pp. Tok the raven seeks to restore his good name after being falsely accused of murder and sets off to find the legendary Grey Lords. (Rev: SLJ 1/06; VOYA 12/05)

512 Stroud, Jonathan. *The Golem's Eye* (7–12). Series: The Bartimaeus Trilogy. 2004, Miramax $17.95 (0-7868-1860-3). 574pp. In this sequel to *The Amulet of Samarkand*, 14-year-old Nathaniel, a magician's apprentice, joins forces with the mischievous djinni Bartimaeus to foil the evil plot of a golem. (Rev: BL 8/04; SLJ 10/04)

513 Stroud, Jonathan. *Ptolemy's Gate* (6–9). Series: Bartimaeus. 2006, Hyperion $17.95 (0-7868-1861-1). 512pp. In the concluding volume of the trilogy, 17-year-old magician Nathaniel is up to his neck in high-tension responsibilities and his faithful djinni Bartimaeus is beginning to wear down from the stress. (Rev: BL 12/15/05*; SLJ 2/06; VOYA 2/06)

514 Taylor, G. P. *Tersias the Oracle* (8–11). 2006, Penguin $17.99 (0-399-24258-9). 272pp. Tersias, a 12-year-old blind boy, and Jonah, a young thief, become embroiled in a struggle for power in this multilayered novel. (Rev: BL 3/15/06)

515 Thornton, Duncan. *The Star-Glass* (5–8). 2004, Coteau paper $10.95 (1-55050-269-7). 402pp. Tom and Jenny face new challenges in this sequel to the fantasies *Kalifax* and *Captain Jenny and the Sea of Wonders*. (Rev: SLJ 4/04; VOYA 6/04)

516 Tiernan, Cate. *A Chalice of Wind* (8–11). Series: Balefire. 2005, Penguin paper $5.99 (1-59514-045-X). 256pp. Thais discovers that she has a twin — and that she is a witch — when her father dies and she is sent to live in New Orleans. (Rev: BL 9/1/05; SLJ 8/05)

517 Tiernan, Cate. *Night's Child* (7–12). Series: Sweep. 2003, Penguin paper $6.99 (0-14-250119-0). 318pp. In this 15th installment — a double-length, stand-alone novel — Moira, 15-year-old daughter of the powerful blood witch Morgan, learns about her heritage and tackles faces danger and treachery as well as romance. (Rev: SLJ 2/04)

518 Tunnell, Michael O. *The Wishing Moon* (6–9). 2004, Penguin $17.99 (0-525-47193-6). 272pp. Struggling to survive after the death of her parents, 14-year-old Aminah is begging for alms outside the sultan's palace when the sultan's daughter throws an old oil lamp at her, not realizing the lamp's magical properties. (Rev: BL 8/04; SLJ 7/04; VOYA 6/04)

519 Ursu, Anne. *The Shadow Thieves* (5–8). 2006, Simon & Schuster $16.95 (1-4169-0587-1). 416pp. A plot to reanimate the dead using the essence of living children is foiled by cousins Charlotte and Zee in this story of heroism and mythology that ranges from the Midwest to England to Hades. (Rev: BL 3/1/06; SLJ 4/06)

520 Van Belkom, Edo. *Lone Wolf* (5–8). 2005, Tundra paper $8.95 (0-88776-741-9). 177pp. The four teen werewolves adopted by Ranger Brock in *Wolf Pack* (2004) defend their beloved woods against a corrupt developer. (Rev: SLJ 1/06; VOYA 4/06)

521 Vande Velde, Vivian. *Now You See It . . .* (5–8). 2005, Harcourt $17.00 (0-15-205311-5). 288pp. Wendy, 15, puts on a pair of sunglasses and a whole new fantasy world is revealed. (Rev: BL 1/1–15/05; SLJ 1/05)

522 Vande Velde, Vivian. *Witch Dreams* (5–8). 2005, Marshall Cavendish $15.95 (0-7614-5235-4). 128pp. Nyssa, a 16-year-old witch, seeks justice for her parents, who were murdered six years earlier. (Rev: BL 12/15/05; SLJ 11/05; VOYA 12/05)

523 Watts, Leander. *Ten Thousand Charms* (5–7). 2005, Houghton $16.00 (0-618-44897-7). 228pp. In this historical fantasy set in the 19th century, Roddy, an 11-year-old apprentice to a ropemaker in Pharaoh, New York, joins forces with a deposed European king to rescue the king's daughter from the villainous Scalander. (Rev: BCCB 5/05; SLJ 8/05; VOYA 2/06)

524 Wersba, Barbara. *Walter: The Story of a Rat* (4–7). 2005, Front Street $16.95 (1-932425-41-1). 64pp. Miss Pomeroy, a children's author, develops a

friendship with a literary rat named Walter who shares her house in this thoughtful and sophisticated book. (Rev: BCCB 2/06; BL 11/15/05; SLJ 12/05)

525 Westerfeld, Scott. *Uglies* (7–10). 2005, Simon & Schuster paper $6.99 (0-689-86538-4). 448pp. In a futuristic dystopia, 15-year-old Tally is counting the days until she turns 16 and is transformed from ugly to pretty but events threaten this happening on schedule; a thought-provoking novel about the importance of image and ethics. (Rev: BCCB 2/05; BL 3/15/05*; SLJ 3/05; VOYA 6/05)

526 Williams, Maiya. *The Golden Hour* (4–8). 2004, Abrams $16.95 (0-8109-4823-0). 272pp. Thirteen-year-old Rowan and his 11-year-old sister Nina are sent to live with two great-aunts after the death of their mother and find themselves — with their new friends Xanthe and Xavier — transported through a time portal to 1789 Paris. (Rev: BL 3/15/04; SLJ 4/04; VOYA 6/04)

527 Williams, Mark London. *Trail of Bones* (5–8). Series: Danger Boy. 2005, Candlewick $9.99 (0-7636-2154-4). 300pp. Eli, Thea, and Clyne — three characters of very different backgrounds — travel back in time from 2019 to early-19th-century America and become involved with Lewis and Clark and the plight of escaping slaves. (Rev: SLJ 7/05)

528 Wooding, Chris. *Poison* (6–9). 2005, Scholastic $16.99 (0-439-75570-0). 288pp. Poison sets out to rescue her little sister from the phaeries and faces many challenges in this rich gothic fantasy. (Rev: BL 8/05; SLJ 9/05; VOYA 12/05)

529 Wrede, Patricia C., and Caroline Stevermer. *The Grand Tour or the Purloined Coronation Regalia: Being a Revelation of Matters of High Confidentiality and Greatest Importance, Including Extracts from the Intimate Diary of a Noblewoman and the Sworn Testimony of a Lady of Quality* (6–9). 2004, Harcourt $17.00 (0-15-204616-X). 480pp. In this sequel to *Sorcery and Cecelia* (2003) set in 1817 and blending adventure, humor, fantasy, mystery, and romance, two English cousins, honeymooning in Europe with their husbands, uncover a plot by evil wizards to create a new empire. (Rev: BL 9/1/04; SLJ 11/04)

530 Wright, Randall. *The Silver Penny* (4–7). 2005, Holt $16.95 (0-8050-7391-4). 197pp. In this compelling fantasy set in the 19th century, Jacob — after breaking his leg and facing disability — receives from his great-grandfather a lucky silver penny that gives him access to a supernatural world. (Rev: BCCB 7–8/05; SLJ 8/05; VOYA 10/05)

531 Yolen, Jane, and Adam Stemple. *Pay the Piper* (6–9). 2005, Tor $16.95 (0-765-31158-5). 176pp. Fourteen-year-old Callie discovers the secret of a member of the Brass Rat when the town's children disappear on Halloween night in this lighthearted version of the Pied Piper tale. (Rev: BL 6/1–15/05; SLJ 8/05; VOYA 8/05)

532 Zahn, Timothy. *Dragon and Soldier: The Second Dragonback Adventure* (7–10). Series: Dragonback Adventure. 2004, Tor $17.95 (0-765-30125-3). 304pp. Jack Morgan, the 14-year-old symbiotic human host for a dragon warrior named Draycos, tries to find out who's behind a plot to annihilate all the members of Draycos's race; a sequel to *Dragon and Soldier* (2003). (Rev: BL 8/04)

533 Zevin, Gabrielle. *Elsewhere* (7–10). 2005, Farrar $16.00 (0-374-32091-8). 288pp. After dying of a head injury, 15-year-old Liz Hall does not adapt easily to afterlife in Elsewhere and at first spends a lot of time watching what's going on on Earth. (Rev: BL 8/05*; SLJ 10/05*)

Graphic Novels

534 *All Star Comics: Archives*, Vol. 11 (7–12). Series: Archive Editions. 2005, DC Comics $49.95 (1-4012-0403-1). 272pp. The final volume of the Archive Editions series continues the adventures of the Justice Society of America, a band of comic book superheroes that includes the Green Lantern, Flash, Wonder Woman, Atom, and Hawkman. (Rev: BL 7/05; SLJ 9/05)

535 Austen, Chuck. *Superman: The Wrath of Gog* (5–12). 2005, DC Comics paper $14.99 (1-4012-0450-3). Superman is gravely injured in a battle with Gog and returns to his boyhood home to recuperate. (Rev: SLJ 9/05)

536 Baker, Kyle. *Plastic Man: On the Lam!* (8–12). Series: Plastic Man. 2005, DC Comics paper $14.95 (1-4012-0343-4). Plastic Man's original (1940s) zany disregard for superhero conventions is revived here as the elastic hero faces his own past and the FBI amid much play with words and slapstick humor. (Rev: BL 9/15/04; SLJ 7/05)

537 Beatty, Scott. *Catwoman: The Visual Guide to the Feline Fatale* (6–12). Illus. 2004, DK $19.99 (0-7566-0383-8). 64pp. This oversize, richly illustrated book tells all about Catwoman, including where she comes from and the equipment she uses. (Rev: BL 5/15/04; SLJ 9/04)

538 Beck, C. C., et al. *The Shazam! Archives*, Vol. 4 (8–12). Illus. 2004, DC Comics $49.95 (1-4012-0160-1). 196pp. This is a collection of Captain Marvel comic strips, most dating back to 1941–1942. (Rev: BL 5/1/04)

539 Bishop, Debbie. *Black Tide: Awakening of the Key* (6–10). 2004, Angel Gate paper $19.99 (1-93243-100-4). 208pp. In this gripping graphic novel, which collects the first eight issues of an ongoing comic book series, past and present collide when Justin Braddock embarks on a mission to solve a series of international murders. (Rev: BL 4/15/04)

540 Bradbury, Ray. *The Best of Ray Bradbury: The Graphic Novel* (6–12). Illus. 2003, iBooks paper $18.95 (0-7434-7476-7). 160pp. Some of the best artists working in the graphic novels field have adapted Bradbury's works. (Rev: BL 2/1/04)

541 Cammuso, Frank. *Max Hamm, Fairy Tale Detective*, Vol. 1 (8–12). Illus. Series: Fairy Tale Detectives. 2005, Nite Owl paper $14.95 (0-9720061-4-1). 208pp. Max Hamm, a pig, is also a private eye in a cycle of pulp-novel-style stories involving fairy tale characters and much clever wordplay. (Rev: BL 8/05; SLJ 11/05) [741.5]

542 Clugston, Chynna. *Queen Bee* (5–8). Illus. 2005, Scholastic paper $8.99 (0-439-70987-3). 112pp. In this humorous graphic novel about school cliques, Haley and Alexa, two middle school students with psychokinetic powers, battle each other to become the school's most popular girl. (Rev: BL 9/15/05; SLJ 1/06; VOYA 12/05)

543 David, Peter. *Final Exam* (6–9). Illus. Series: SpyBoy. 2005, Dark Horse paper $12.95 (1-59307-017-9). 96pp. SpyBoy Alex Fleming faces off against a villainous substitute teacher who threatens to derail Alex's plans to attend his senior prom and graduate from high school. (Rev: BL 3/15/05)

544 Dixon, Chuck. *Nightwing: On the Razor's Edge* (8–12). 2005, DC Comics paper $14.99 (1-4012-0437-6). 182pp. Robin, Batman's former sidekick, now takes on the superhero identity of Nightwing and must defend himself against his foes. (Rev: SLJ 11/05)

545 Doyle, Arthur Conan. *Graphic Classics: Arthur Conan Doyle* (8–11). Ed. by Tom Pomplun. 2d ed. Illus. Series: Graphic Classics. 2005, Eureka paper $11.95 (0-9746648-5-5). 144pp. This revised edition adds several non-Holmes stories to the collection. (Rev: BL 9/15/05; SLJ 11/05; VOYA 4/06) [741.5]

546 Eisner, Will. *Will Eisner's The Spirit Archives*, Vol. 12 (8–12). Illus. 2003, DC Comics $49.95 (1-4012-0006-0). 196pp. This collection of comic strips covers the full 12-year career of the Spirit, a masked crime fighter. (Rev: BL 2/1/04)

547 Espinosa, Rod. *Neotopia Color Manga* (6–12). Series: Neotopia. 2004, Antarctic paper $9.99 (1-932453-57-1). 168pp. In the opening volume of the graphic novel series, Nalyn, a servant girl, takes over her spoiled mistress's responsibilities as grand duchess of Mathenia, but the going gets tough when Mathenia comes under attack from the evil empire of Krossos. (Rev: BL 12/1/04)

548 Fisher, Jane Smith. *WJHC: On the Air!* (4–8). Illus. 2003, Wilson Place paper $11.95 (0-9744235-0-5). 96pp. Six episodes catalog the entertaining misadventures of a diverse band of teens who launch a high school radio station. (Rev: BL 2/1/04; VOYA 12/03)

549 Friesen, Ray. *A Cheese Related Mishap and Other Stories* (5–8). Illus. 2005, Don't Eat Any Bugs paper $8.95 (0-9728177-6-X). 96pp. This collection of zany tales full of entertaining characters and situations was created by a teenage author/illustrator. (Rev: BL 11/15/05; SLJ 3/06)

550 Fujino, Moyamu. *The First King Adventure*, Vol. 1 (4–8). Trans. from Japanese by Kay Bertrand. 2004, ADV paper $9.99 (1-4139-0194-8). Prince Tiltu cannot succeed his father as king until he's made contracts with all of the spirit masters that inhabit the kingdom. (Rev: SLJ 7/05)

551 Furman, Simon. *Transformers: The Ultimate Guide* (6–12). Illus. 2004, DK $24.99 (0-7566-0314-5). 144pp. This book gives all sorts of information about the robots that have been so popular with young readers. (Rev: BL 5/15/04)

552 Gross, Allan. *Cryptozoo Crew*, vol. 1 (7–12). 2005, NBM paper $9.95 (1-56163-437-9). Wacky, pun-filled adventures starring cryptozoologist Tork Darwyn and his smart and luscious wife Tara. (Rev: BL 9/15/05; SLJ 1/06)

553 Hurd, Damon, and Tatiana Gill. *A Strange Day* (8–12). Illus. 2005, Alternative Comics paper $3.95 (1-891867-74-1). 48pp. This appealing graphic novella tells a story of instant attraction between two teens who share the same tastes in music. (Rev: BL 5/1/05)

554 Ikezawa, Satomi. *Guru Guru Pon-Chan*, Vol. 1 (5–12). Trans. from Japanese by Douglas Varenas. 2005, Del Rey paper $10.95 (0-345-48095-3). 171pp. In this whimsical shape-changing story, Ponta, a Labrador retriever puppy, nibbles on a newly invented "chit-chat" bone and turns into a human girl who comically retains doggy behavior. (Rev: SLJ 11/05)

555 Ikumi, Mia. *Tokyo Mew Mew a la Mode*, Vol. 1 (5–8). Trans. from Japanese by Yoohae Yang. 2005, TokyoPop paper $9.99 (1-59532-789-4). 197pp. In the opening volume of the Tokyo Mew Mew a la Mode series, 12-year-old Berry Shirayuki is shanghaied into a team of girl superheroes and soon finds herself doing battle with dragons and the evil Saint Rose Crusaders. (Rev: SLJ 11/05)

556 Johns, Geoff. *JSA: Black Reign* (7–12). 2005, DC Comics paper $12.99 (1-4012-0480-5). In a setting reminiscent of present-day Iraq, superhero Black Adam fights for an unpopular cause and faces strong opposition from the people he's trying to help. (Rev: SLJ 11/05)

557 Johns, Geoff, et al. *Ignition* (8–12). Illus. Series: Flash. 2005, DC Comics paper $14.95 (1-4012-0463-5). 144pp. In volume five of the series, police mechanic Wally West slowly but surely remembers

— and regains — his superhuman powers as the Flash. (Rev: BL 5/15/05) [741.5]

558 Johns, Geoff, et al. *Teen Titans: The Future Is Now* (5–8). Illus. Series: Teen Titans. 2005, DC Comics paper $9.99 (1-4012-0475-9). 224pp. In volume four of the series, the title characters return from a mission into the future to learn that Robin's father died while they were away. (Rev: BL 3/15/06) [741.5]

559 Johnson, Kim "Howard," et al. *Superman: True Brit* (8–12). Illus. 2004, DC Comics $24.95 (1-4012-0022-2). 96pp. In this British variation on the Superman legend coauthored by John Cleese, young Colin Clark, raised on an English farm, struggles to conceal his superhuman abilities. (Rev: BL 12/1/04) [741.5]

560 Kawasaki, Anton, ed. *Batman Begins: The Movie and Other Tales of the Dark Knight* (8–12). Illus. 2005, DC Comics paper $12.99 (1-4012-0440-6). 160pp. Based on the plot of the 2005 film of the same name, this graphic novel explores the origins of Batman, specifically the tragic events in Bruce Wayne's childhood that led him to become the masked crusader. (Rev: BL 9/1/05; SLJ 1/06)

561 Kelly, Joe. *Justice League Elite*, Vol. 1 (8–12). 2005, DC Comics paper $19.99 (1-4012-0481-3). Superman and other members of the Justice League clash with the rival Justice League Elite over strategies for dealing with evildoers. (Rev: BL 10/1/05; SLJ 11/05)

562 Kennedy, Mike. *Superman: Infinite City* (5–12). 2005, DC Comics $24.99 (1-4012-0067-2). 96pp. Superman and Lois become enmeshed in a power struggle in an alternate world known as Infinite City. (Rev: SLJ 9/05)

563 Kibuishi, Kazu, ed. *Flight*, Vol. 2 (7–12). Illus. 2005, Image Comics paper $24.95 (1-58240-477-1). 432pp. Volume two of the Flight anthology series features original stories by promising young artists from the world of comic books and graphic novels. (Rev: BL 6/1–15/05) [741.5]

564 Kindt, Matt. *2 Sisters* (8–12). Illus. 2004, Top Shelf paper $19.95 (1-891830-58-9). 336pp. In this graphic novel thriller, set in Europe during World War II, Elle, a volunteer ambulance driver, is recruited as a spy and dispatched on perilous missions behind enemy lines. (Rev: BL 11/1/04)

565 Knaak, Richard A. *Dragon Hunt* (7–10). Series: Warcraft Sunwell. 2005, TokyoPop paper $9.99 (1-59532-712-6). 192pp. In the first volume of a graphic novel trilogy, Kalec, a shape-changing dragon, and Anveena race to reach the all-powerful Sunwell before the villainous Dar'khan can get to it. (Rev: BL 6/1–15/05; SLJ 7/05)

566 Kobayashi, Makoto. *Sleepless Nights* (5–8). Illus. Series: What's Michael? 2005, Dark Horse paper $8.95 (1-59307-337-2). 88pp. Volume ten of the continuing adventures of the house cat who has been described as "Japan's version of Garfield, Heathcliff, and Krazy Kat all rolled into one." (Rev: BL 9/1/05)

567 Kubert, Joe. *Yossel: April 19, 1943: A Story of the Warsaw Ghetto Uprising* (8–12). Illus. 2003, iBooks $24.95 (0-7434-7516-X). In this graphic novel, Yossel and his friends fight to the death against their Nazi oppressors. (Rev: BL 2/1/04; SLJ 7/04)

568 Kyoko, Ariyoshi. *The Swan* (6–9). Illus. 2004, DC Comics paper $9.95 (1-4012-0535-6). 200pp. In this appealing shoujo — manga designed to appeal especially to girls — a young Japanese girl from a rural area seeks to realize her dreams of becoming a prima ballerina. (Rev: BL 2/15/05)

569 Lee, Na Hyeon. *Traveler of the Moon*, Vol. 1 (7–12). Trans. from Korean by Je-wa Jeong. 2005, Infinity paper $9.95 (1-59697-061-8). 176pp. In this appealing Korean manwha, Yuh-Ur, a human girl, develops a close friendship with a vampire boy named Ida. (Rev: SLJ 7/05)

570 Loeb, Jeph, et al. *Batman: Hush*, Vol. 2 (8–12). Illus. 2004, DC Comics $19.95 (1-4012-0084-2). 176pp. This is a collection of recent Batman adventures that include appearances by Joker, Riddler, and Catwoman. (Rev: BL 4/1/04)

571 Love, Courtney, and D. J. Milky. *Princess Ai: Lumination*, Vol. 2 (7–12). Trans. from Japanese by Kimiko Fujikawa and Yuki N. Johnson. 2005, TokyoPop paper $9.99 (1-59182-670-5). 185pp. In volume two of the Princess Ai series, the title character, an aspiring rock star, turns ever more angelic as her music career begins to take off. (Rev: SLJ 11/05)

572 Ma, Wing Shing. *Storm Riders: Invading Sun: Vol. 1* (8–12). Illus. 2003, ComicsOne paper $9.95 (1-58899-359-0). 128pp. Martial arts and an alternate China are featured in this graphic novel about two expert fighters who set out to find their former master named Conquer. (Rev: BL 2/1/04)

573 Matheny, Bill. *The Batman Strikes! Crime Time*, Vol. 1 (4–7). 2005, DC Comics paper $6.99 (1-4012-0509-7). Five short episodes based on the WB cartoon series feature a rejuvenated Batman and a similarly updated cast of villains. (Rev: SLJ 1/06)

574 Matoh, Sanami. *By the Sword*, Vol. 1 (6–9). Illus. 2005, ADV paper $9.99 (1-4139-0213-8). 192pp. In this first volume of a new manga series, demon hunter Asagi enlists the help of a half-breed demon girl in his quest to find the magical Moegi Sword. (Rev: BL 4/1/05; SLJ 7/05)

575 Monroe, Kevin. *El Zombo Fantasma* (7–10). Illus. 2005, Dark Horse paper $9.95 (1-59307-284-8). 88pp. In this eye-popping superhero graphic novel, Mexican wrestler El Zombo Fantasma, murdered for throwing a match, seeks to avoid eternal

damnation by becoming guardian angel to a feisty 10-year-old and tracking down his own killer. (Rev: BL 3/15/05; VOYA 8/05)

576 Moore, Alan, et al. *Alan Moore's America's Best Comics, 2004* (8–12). Illus. 2004, DC Comics paper $17.95 (1-4012-0147-4). 192pp. The author and illustrator who created imaginative comics in the 1990s is honored in this reprint of all 10 of his America's Best Comics group. (Rev: BL 3/1/04)

577 Moore, Alan, et al. *Tom Strong Collected Edition*, Vol. 3 (8–12). Illus. 2004, DC Comics $24.95 (1-4012-0282-9). 144pp. Superhero Tom Strong, the creation of legendary comic book artist Alan Moore, tackles a number of new challenges in the third volume of the Tom Strong series. (Rev: BL 9/1/04) [741.5]

578 Mowll, Joshua. *Operation Red Jericho* (8–11). Illus. Series: Guild Trilogy. 2005, Candlewick $15.99 (0-7636-2634-1). 288pp. In this first volume of a graphic novel trilogy set in the early 20th century, teens Becca and Doug MacKenzie search for their parents, who disappeared in China, and document their exciting adventures. (Rev: BL 11/15/05; SLJ 12/05)

579 Murakami, Maki. *Kanpai!* Vol. 1 (8–12). Trans. from Japanese by Christine Schilling. 2005, TokyoPop paper $9.99 (1-59532-317-1). 209pp. Yamada finds himself torn between his rigid training to be a monster guardian and his infatuation with attractive Taino Municipal Middle School classmate Nao. (Rev: SLJ 1/06)

580 Nicieza, Fabian, et al. *A Stake to the Heart* (8–12). Illus. 2004, Dark Horse paper $12.95 (1-59307-012-8). 104pp. Angel's efforts to help Buffy and Dawn cope with their parents' problems backfire in this graphic novel that precedes the events of the TV show. (Rev: BL 6/1–15/04)

581 No, Yee-Jung. *Visitor*, Vol. 1 (7–10). Trans. from Japanese by Jennifer Hahm. 2005, TokyoPop paper $9.99 (1-59532-342-2). 175pp. On her first day at a new school, Hyo-Bin attracts a number of admirers, but she rebuffs them all, fearful that they could be harmed by the magical powers she's not yet learned to control. (Rev: SLJ 9/05)

582 Park, Young-Ha. *BamBi*, Vol. 1 (8–12). Trans. from Korean by Je-wa Jeong. 2005, Infinity paper $9.95 (1-59697-011-1). 164pp. This Korean manwha, similar to Japanese manga, recounts the forbidden romance between a girl with amnesia and a handsome young man who has a swan's wing where one of his arms should be. (Rev: SLJ 7/05)

583 Pfeifer, Will. *H-E-R-O: Powers and Abilities* (8–12). 2003, DC Comics paper $9.95 (1-4012-0168-7). 144pp. The three stories in this volume deal with a mysterious device that gives its user the powers and abilities of a super being. (Rev: BL 2/1/04)

584 Raymond, Alex, and Don Moore. *Alex Raymond's Flash Gordon*, Vol. 2 (8–12). Illus. 2004, Checker paper $19.95 (0-9741664-6-4). 96pp. The second volume of the Flash Gordon series collects comic strips that first appeared in 1935 and 1936. (Rev: BL 10/1/04) [741.5]

585 Renier, Aaron. *Spiral Bound: Top Secret Summer* (4–7). Illus. 2005, Top Shelf paper $14.95 (1-891830-50-3). 180pp. This delightful graphic novel chronicles the summer adventures of the animal residents of the Town, a community with a monster in its pond. (Rev: BL 11/1/05)

586 Rocks!, Misako. *Biker Girl* (5–8). Illus. 2006, Hyperion paper $7.99 (0-78683-676-8). 112pp. Aki, a shy, bookish girl, is transformed into a superhero after finding a discarded bicycle in her grandfather's garage. (Rev: BL 3/15/06) [741.5]

587 Rodi, Rob. *Crossovers* (5–12). Illus. 2003, CrossGeneration paper $15.95 (1-931484-85-6). 160pp. This graphic novel is an entertaining look at a suburban family whose members possess a unique power. (Rev: BL 2/1/04)

588 Ru, Lee. *Witch Class*, Vol. 1 (8–12). Trans. from Korean by Je-wa Jeong. 2005, Infinity paper $9.95 (1-59697-081-2). 174pp. The opening volume in the series introduces readers to Dorothy, a young girl who agrees to become a witch. (Rev: SLJ 9/05)

589 Sacks, Adam. *Salmon Doubts* (7–10). Illus. 2004, Alternative Comics paper $14.95 (1-891867-71-7). 128pp. In this allegorical graphic novel, two young salmon — Geoff and Henry — struggle to figure out their place in the overall scheme of things. (Rev: BL 1/1–15/05; SLJ 12/04)

590 Sakai, Stan. *Usagi Yojimbo: Volume 18: Travels with Jotaro* (8–12). 2004, Dark Horse paper $15.95 (1-59307-220-1). 208pp. In the 18th volume of the series, the title character, a rabbit samurai in feudal Japan, encounters a series of adventures while traveling with Jotaro, who is Usagi's son but doesn't know it. (Rev: BL 9/15/04; SLJ 10/04)

591 Sakura, Tsukuba. *Land of the Blindfolded* (8–11). Illus. 2004, DC Comics paper $9.95 (1-4012-0524-0). 208pp. This manga designed primarily for girls tells of two Japanese high school friends (boy and girl) who become close as they decide how to use their conflicting super powers. (Rev: BL 2/15/05)

592 Schulz, Charles M. *The Complete Peanuts: 1950 to 1952* (7–12). Ed. by Gary Groth. Illus. 2004, Fantagraphics paper $28.95 (1-56097-589-X). 330pp. The first volume of a series that will eventually include the entire 50 years of this classic comic strip. (Rev: BL 4/1/04)

593 Sfar, Joann. *The Rabbi's Cat* (8–12). Illus. 2005, Pantheon $21.95 (0-375-42281-1). 152pp. The entertaining and sophisticated adventures of a talking cat who lives with a rabbi and his daughter in 1930s Algeria. (Rev: BL 7/05; SLJ 3/06) [741.5]

594 Shanower, Eric. *Sacrifice* (8–12). 2004, Image Comics $29.95 (1-58240-360-0). 224pp. In this second volume of the graphic novel series, Shanower picks up his epic retelling of the Trojan War with the return of Paris and Helen to Troy. (Rev: BL 10/15/04; SLJ 10/04) [741.5]

595 Shimizu, Aki. *Qwan*, Vol. 1 (7–12). Trans. from Japanese by Mike Kief. 2005, TokyoPop paper $9.99 (1-59532-534-4). 178pp. This compelling graphic novel follows Qwan and his friend as they embark on a magical journey to uncover Qwan's destiny. (Rev: SLJ 7/05)

596 Siu-Chong, Ken. *Round One: Fight!* (6–9). Illus. Series: Street Fighter. 2004, DDP paper $9.99 (1-932796-08-8). The opening volume in the series brings to life the characters and action of the popular video game of the same name and will appeal to reluctant readers. (Rev: SLJ 7/05)

597 Sugisaki, Yukiro. *Rizelmine* (8–12). Trans. from Japanese by Alethea Nibley and Athena Nibley. 2005, TokyoPop paper $9.99 (1-59532-901-3). 136pp. Fifteen-year-old Iwaki Tomonori rejects the advances of robot-like Rizel, who's become his bride by government decree. (Rev: SLJ 11/05)

598 Taniguchi, Tomoko. *Call Me Princess* (5–8). Trans. from Japanese by Mutsumi Masuda and C. B. Cebulski. 2003, CPM Manga paper $9.99 (1-58664-898-5). This graphic novel, set in Japan, centers on the young heroine's romantic attachments but gets a "G" rating. (Rev: SLJ 3/04)

599 Tetzner, Lisa. *The Black Brothers* (6–9). Trans. by Peter F. Neumeyer. Illus. 2004, Front Street $16.95 (1-932425-04-7). 146pp. This striking graphic novel adaptation of Lisa Tetzner's 1941 novel recounts the trials and tribulations of 13-year-old Giorgio, a young chimney sweep in 19th-century Europe whose friendship with the leader of a secret society called the Black Brothers ultimately leads him to happiness. (Rev: BL 9/1/04; SLJ 11/04; VOYA 2/05)

600 Toyoda, Minoru. *Love Roma*, Vol. 1 (8–11). Illus. 2005, Del Rey paper $10.95 (0-345-48262-X). 208pp. This delightful manga chronicles the budding romance of teenagers Hoshino and Negishi. (Rev: BL 10/15/05; SLJ 1/06)

601 Trondheim, Lewis. *Mister O* (4–8). 2004, NBM $12.95 (1-56163-382-8). 32pp. Mister O, portrayed in wordless rectangular cartoons, is a round caricature who — à la Wile E. Coyote — can't seem conquer a chasm, no matter how many successful crossings he views. (Rev: SLJ 9/04) [741.5]

602 Tsukiji, Toshihiko. *Maburaho*, Vol. 1 (8–12). Trans. from Japanese by Kay Bertrand. 2005, ADV paper $9.99 (1-4139-0293-6). 161pp. Kazuki, a hapless magician-in-training, is pursued by three female students who know that he is destined to father a child who'll become a powerful wizard. (Rev: SLJ 7/05)

603 Uslan, Michael, and Peter Snejbjerg. *Detective No. 27* (7–12). Illus. 2003, DC Comics $19.95 (1-4012-0185-7). 96pp. This story about the beginnings of Batman takes place at various times in our history including 1865, 1929, and 1939. (Rev: BL 2/1/04)

604 Von Sholly, Pete. *Dead but Not Out! Pete Von Sholly's Morbid 2* (7–12). Illus. 2005, Dark Horse paper $14.95 (1-59307-289-9). 96pp. Cheap horror movies are the target of this entertaining parody. (Rev: BL 3/15/05) [741.5]

605 Waid, Mark. *Legion of Super-Heroes: Teenage Revolution* (8–11). 2005, DC Comics paper $14.99 (1-4012-0482-1). 200pp. In this comic book vision of the future, teenage superheroes rebel against their parents' utopian government. (Rev: BL 1/1–15/06; SLJ 3/06)

606 Woo, Park Sung. *Now.* Volume 1 (6–12). Illus. 2003, ComicsOne paper $9.95 (1-58899-327-2). 200pp. Kung fu and humor are found in this fantasy about young descendants of warriors who are masters of the lost martial art of Sashinmu. (Rev: BL 2/1/04) [741.5]

607 Yoshimura, Natsuki. *Mystical Prince Yoshida-kun!* Vol. 1 (6–9). Trans. from Japanese by Kay Bertrand. 2004, ADV paper $9.99 (1-4139-0207-3). 175pp. Sixteen-year-old Yoshida, selected to succeed King Dark Fleet, embarks on a series of adventures to fulfill his destiny. (Rev: SLJ 7/05)

608 Yoshizaki, Mine. *Sgt. Frog,* Vol. 1 (8–11). Illus. 2004, TokyoPop paper $9.99 (1-59182-703-5). 192pp. In this *manga* work, a young brother and sister are dealing with an uninvited guest, an invader from another planet. (Rev: BL 3/15/04)

609 Yune, Tommy. *From the Stars* (7–12). Illus. 2003, DC Comics paper $9.95 (1-4012-0144-X). 160pp. When an alien ship crashes on earth, Roy Fokker signs up to be a test pilot and then learns a great deal about alien technology. (Rev: BL 2/1/04)

Historical Fiction and Foreign Lands

Prehistory

610 Levin, Betty. *Thorn* (7–10). 2005, Front Street $16.95 (1-932425-46-2). 168pp. Thorn, a young boy with an atrophied leg, is befriended by Willow but still feels uncomfortable and plans his escape. (Rev: BL 12/15/05; SLJ 1/06)

611 Paver, Michelle. *Wolf Brother* (6–9). 2005, HarperCollins LB $17.89 (0-06-072826-4). 304pp. In the distant prehistoric past, 12-year-old Torak

and his wolf cub companion sets off on a perilous journey to destroy a demon-possessed bear. (Rev: BCCB 2/05; BL 3/1/05; SLJ 2/05)

Ancient and Medieval History

GENERAL AND MISCELLANEOUS

612 McCaughrean, Geraldine. *Not the End of the World* (7–10). 2005, HarperCollins LB $17.89 (0-06-076031-1). 256pp. A harrowing but thought-provoking story of what it was really like aboard Noah's ark, with terrified animals and humans unhinged by their circumstances. (Rev: BL 8/05; SLJ 8/05*; VOYA 8/05)

613 Tingle, Rebecca. *Far Traveler* (7–10). 2005, Penguin $17.99 (0-399-23890-5). 240pp. In this historical novel set in 10th-century England, 16-year-old Aelfwyn flees when her uncle, West Saxon King Edward, tells her she must marry one of his allies or enter a convent. (Rev: BCCB 3/05; BL 2/1/05; SLJ 2/05; VOYA 8/05)

GREECE AND ROME

614 Lawrence, Caroline. *Gladiators from Capua* (5–8). Series: Roman Mysteries. 2005, Roaring Brook $16.95 (1-59643-074-5). 198pp. In their search for Jonathan, who may be alive after all, Flavia, Lupus, and Nubia venture into the coliseum and witness gladiator fights. (Rev: BL 12/1/05; SLJ 2/06)

615 Mitchell, Jack. *The Roman Conspiracy* (5–9). 2005, Tundra paper $8.95 (0-88776-713-3). 164pp. In this compelling historical thriller set in the Roman Empire, young Aulus Spurinna travels to Rome in a desperate attempt to protect his homeland of Etruria from military pillagers. (Rev: SLJ 11/05)

616 Rao, Sirish, and Gita Wolf. *Sophocles' Oedipus the King* (7–10). 2004, Getty $18.95 (0-89236-764-4). 29pp. This retelling of Sophocles' tragic tale of Oedipus is highlighted by the striking illustrations of Indrapromit Roy. (Rev: BL 1/1–15/05)

MIDDLE AGES

617 Cadnum, Michael. *The Dragon Throne* (7–10). 2005, Viking $16.99 (0-670-03631-5). 224pp. Edmund and Herbert, newly returned to England from the Crusades and just knighted, are ordered by Eleanor of Aquitaine to safeguard Lady Ester on a perilous pilgrimage to Rome; the third volume in a trilogy that includes *The Book of the Lion* (2000) and *The Leopard Sword* (2002). (Rev: BL 6/1–15/05; SLJ 6/05; VOYA 10/05)

618 Grant, K. M. *Blood Red Horse* (6–9). 2005, Walker $16.95 (0-8027-8960-9). 288pp. This epic historical novel chronicles the adventures of English brothers Gavin and William de Granville as they leave home to join the Third Crusade under the leadership of King Richard I. (Rev: BCCB 5/05; BL 4/1/05*; SLJ 5/05; VOYA 6/05)

619 Jinks, Catherine. *Pagan's Vows* (8–10). 2005, Candlewick $16.99 (0-7636-2021-1). 336pp. Seventeen-year-old Pagan Kidrouk, squire to Lord Roland, joins his master at the Abbey of St. Martin where they are to begin training as monks, but Pagan soon finds that he has trouble adjusting to all the rules of his new life. (Rev: BL 10/1/04; SLJ 9/04; VOYA 10/04)

620 Shulevitz, Uri. *The Travels of Benjamin of Tudela: Through Three Continents in the Twelfth Century* (4–7). Illus. 2005, Farrar $17.00 (0-374-37754-5). 48pp. Based on Benjamin's diaries, this picture book, which is incredibly detailed in both illustrations and text, tells of his perilous journey through parts of Europe, the Mediterranean, and the Middle East. (Rev: BL 3/15/05*; SLJ 4/05)

621 Thal, Lilli. *Mimus* (8–11). Trans. by John Brownjohn. 2005, Annick $19.95 (1-55037-925-9); paper $9.95 (1-55037-924-0). 398pp. Prince Florin is taken captive and made a jester when the kingdom of Vinland overpowers Moltovia in this novel of the Middle Ages. (Rev: BL 9/1/05*; SLJ 12/05*; VOYA 2/06)

622 Wright, Randall. *Hunchback* (6–9). 2004, Holt $16.95 (0-8050-7232-2). 256pp. Fourteen-year-old Hodge, a hunchbacked orphan in medieval times, dreams that one day he will be a servant to royalty, and when his dream comes true Hodge finds himself drawn into a series of intrigues and adventures. (Rev: BCCB 6/04; BL 5/1/04; SLJ 4/04; VOYA 6/04)

Africa

623 Ellis, Deborah. *The Heaven Shop* (5–8). 2004, Fitzhenry & Whiteside $16.95 (1-55041-908-0). 192pp. The AIDS epidemic has a devastating impact on the family of Binti, a 13-year-old Malawi girl. (Rev: BL 9/1/04; SLJ 10/04)

624 Glass, Linzi Alex. *The Year the Gypsies Came* (8–11). 2006, Holt $16.95 (0-8050-7999-8). 260pp. An elderly Zulu watchman turns out to be young Emily's strongest anchor in this moving story about a 12-year-old in 1960s Johannesburg, whose life is changed when a family of Australian vagabonds arrives, bringing additional tensions. (Rev: BL 3/1/06)

625 Mwangi, Meja. *The Mzungu Boy* (5–8). 2005, Groundwood $15.95 (0-88899-653-5). 160pp. In 1950s Kenya, a 12-year-old Kenyan boy becomes friendly with the white landowner's son despite both families' disapproval. (Rev: BL 8/05; SLJ 11/05)

626 Stolz, Joelle. *The Shadows of Ghadames* (6–10). 2004, Random LB $17.99 (0-385-73104-3). 128pp. In late-19th-century Libya, Malika dreads the restricted life her 12th birthday will bring, but her father's two wives defy convention and nurse a wounded man back to health within the women's community, opening new horizons for Malika. (Rev: BL 12/1/04*; SLJ 11/04)

627 Wein, Elizabeth E. *The Sunbird* (7–12). Series: The Winter Prince. 2004, Viking $16.99 (0-670-03691-9). 224pp. Telemakos, grandson of noblemen, undertakes a perilous journey to the African kingdom of Aksum to find those responsible for allowing the plague to enter the kingdom in this third volume in the saga. (Rev: BL 6/1–15/04; HB 3–4/04; SLJ 5/04; VOYA 4/04)

Asia and the Pacific

628 Clarke, Judith. *Kalpana's Dream* (6–9). 2005, Front Street $16.95 (1-932425-22-5). 164pp. A visit from her Indian great-grandmother and a school essay assignment help Australian teen Neema to make some important discoveries about who she is. (Rev: BCCB 4/05; BL 5/1/05*; HB 1–2/06; SLJ 8/05; VOYA 8/05)

629 Crew, Gary. *Troy Thompson's Excellent Poetry Book* (4–7). 2003, Kane/Miller $14.95 (1-929132-52-2). Troy Thompson, an 11-year-old Australian boy, uses different forms of poetry to express his feelings about various elements of his life, participating in a yearlong literature assignment and, we learn at the end, winning the grand prize. (Rev: SLJ 1/04)

630 Halam, Ann. *Taylor Five* (8–10). 2004, Random $15.95 (0-385-73094-2). 192pp. When rebels attack 14-year-old Taylor's home in Borneo, she must flee through the jungle with her wounded younger brother. (Rev: BL 2/15/04; SLJ 4/04)

631 Herrick, Steven. *The Simple Gift* (8–10). 2004, Simon Pulse paper $14.95 (0-689-86867-7). 205pp. In this compelling free-verse novel told in three voices, Australian 16-year-old Billy escapes an unhappy family life and takes up residence in an abandoned freight car where he finds both friendship and love. (Rev: BL 8/04; SLJ 9/04; VOYA 2/05)

632 Hoobler, Dorothy, and Thomas Hoobler. *In Darkness, Death* (7–10). 2004, Putnam $16.99 (0-399-23767-4). 208pp. Set in 18th-century Japan like the authors' previous *The Ghost in the Tokaido Inn* (1999), this novel tells how 14-year-old Seikei and his adopted father set out to discover who murdered a powerful warlord. (Rev: BL 5/1/04; SLJ 3/04; VOYA 4/04)

633 Hoobler, Dorothy, and Thomas Hoobler. *The Sword That Cut the Burning Grass* (5–8). 2005,

Philomel $10.99 (0-399-24272-4). 224pp. In this fourth book about the aspiring young samurai, Seikei tackles a challenging task involving the teenage emperor. (Rev: BL 5/1/05; SLJ 10/05)

634 Jeans, Peter. *Stoker's Bay* (8–12). 2003, Cygnet paper $13.50 (1-876268-97-2). 222pp. In Australia after World War II, Angus McCrea adjusts to life at high school, makes a friend called Kes, and falls in love with Kate, whose continuing sexual harassment by Charlie leads to tragedy. (Rev: SLJ 4/04)

635 Mah, Adeline Yen. *Chinese Cinderella and the Secret Dragon Society* (5–8). 2005, HarperCollins LB $16.89 (0-06-056735-X). 242pp. During the Japanese occupation of Shanghai in World War II, 12-year-old Ye Xian is expelled from her home after an argument with her stepmother, joins a kung fu group, and seeks to help the American side. (Rev: SLJ 1/05)

636 Place, Francois. *The Old Man Mad About Drawing* (5–8). Trans. by William Rodarmor. Illus. 2003, Godine $19.95 (1-56792-260-0). 128pp. In 19th-century Edo (now Tokyo), Tojiro, a 9-year-old orphan who sells rice cakes, becomes the assistant to a famous old artist. (Rev: BL 3/15/04*; HB 3–4/04; SLJ 5/04)

637 Sheth, Mashmira. *Koyal Dark, Mango Sweet* (8–11). 2006, Hyperion $15.99 (0-7868-3857-4). 224pp. At the age of 16, Jeeta, who lives in Mumbai (formerly Bombay), finds many of the traditions that preoccupy her mother to be old-fashioned and inappropriate. (Rev: BL 4/1/06; SLJ 4/06)

638 Stone, Jeff. *Tiger* (6–9). Series: The Ancestors. 2005, Random LB $17.99 (0-375-93071-X). 224pp. Five young warrior monk trainees survive a deadly attack on their monastery and use their martial arts skills to avenge their beloved grandmaster, who was killed in the attack. (Rev: BCCB 2/05; BL 2/15/05; SLJ 2/05)

639 Whelan, Gloria. *Chu Ju's House* (6–9). 2004, HarperCollins $15.99 (0-06-050724-1). 240pp. To save her baby sister, destined to be put up for adoption to comply with China's limits on a family's number of children, 14-year-old Chu Ju leaves home and is forced to fend for herself. (Rev: BCCB 5/04; BL 3/15/04; HB 5–6/04; SLJ 5/04; VOYA 10/04)

640 Whitesel, Cheryl Aylward. *Blue Fingers: A Ninja's Tale* (5–8). 2004, Clarion $15.00 (0-618-38139-2). 256pp. In 16th-century Japan, 12-year-old Koji is trained to become a ninja warrior. (Rev: BL 3/15/04; SLJ 3/04)

Europe and the Middle East

641 Bajoria, Paul. *The Printer's Devil* (7–10). 2005, Little, Brown $16.99 (0-316-01090-1). 382pp. Mog Winter, a 12-year-old orphan in Victorian London,

is working as a printer's apprentice when a case of mistaken identity sends the boy headlong into the violent underworld of the English capital. (Rev: BL 12/1/05; SLJ 10/05; VOYA 10/05)

642 Banks, Lynne Reid. *Tiger, Tiger* (5–8). 2005, Delacorte LB $17.99 (0-385-90264-6). 256pp. Two tiger cubs arrive in Rome destined for different fates; Brute is trained to be a killer of men in the Colosseum while Boots becomes a pet for the caesar's daughter, a decision with dangerous consequences. (Rev: BL 5/15/05; SLJ 6/05)

643 Bowler, Tim. *Firmament* (6–10). 2004, Simon & Schuster $16.95 (0-689-86161-3). 320pp. Reality and fantasy mix in this story of a 14-year-old English boy, a brilliant musician, who, because of his father's untimely death, finds his life falling apart. (Rev: BL 3/1/04; SLJ 4/04; VOYA 4/04)

644 Dhami, Narinder. *Bindi Babes* (5–8). 2004, Delacorte LB $16.99 (0-385-90214-X). 69pp. The three Bindi sisters, aged 10 to 13, still trying to cope with their mother's death when an aunt arrives from India, look for ways to get the unwelcome visitor out of their lives. (Rev: BL 9/15/04; SLJ 8/04)

645 Dhami, Narinder. *Bollywood Babes* (5–8). 2005, Delacorte LB $16.99 (0-385-90215-8). 176pp. The Bindi sisters (introduced in *Bindi Babes*) hatch a scheme involving a washed-up Bollywood star in the hopes of helping their school in this light novel set in England. (Rev: BL 3/1/05; SLJ 4/05)

646 Dowswell, Paul. *Powder Monkey: Adventures of a Young Sailor* (5–9). 2005, Bloomsbury $16.95 (1-58234-675-5). 276pp. In this stirring historical novel set in the opening years of the 19th century, 13-year-old Sam Witchall begins his career at sea as a "powder monkey," assisting the gun crews on a warship. (Rev: SLJ 11/05; VOYA 10/05)

647 Gavin, Jamila. *The Blood Stone* (7–10). 2005, Farrar $18.00 (0-374-30846-2). 352pp. In this sprawling historical fantasy set in the 17th century, 12-year-old Filipo Veroneo makes a dangerous journey from Venice to Hindustan to rescue the father he has never met, and finds help in strange quarters. (Rev: BL 12/15/05; SLJ 12/05; VOYA 12/05)

648 Gilman, Laura Anne. *Grail Quest: The Camelot Spell* (5–8). Series: Grail Quest. 2006, HarperCollins LB $14.89 (0-06-077280-8). 304pp. On the eve of King Arthur's quest for the Holy Grail, three young teens of different backgrounds — Gerard, Newt, and Ailias — must reverse a spell crippling all adults. (Rev: BL 2/1/06)

649 Harris, Robert, and Jane Yolen. *Prince Across the Water* (6–10). 2004, Penguin $18.99 (0-399-23897-2). 320pp. Thirteen-year-old Duncan shares his countrymen's pride at Bonnie Prince Charlie's struggle to reclaim the crown of England and Scotland from German-born George II, but when the boy runs away from home to join the battle, he discovers the true horrors of war. (Rev: BL 11/15/04; SLJ 12/04; VOYA 10/04)

650 Hassinger, Peter W. *Shakespeare's Daughter* (7–12). 2004, HarperCollins $15.99 (0-06-028467-6). 320pp. An assortment of historical figures make appearances, including papa, in this story about the 14-year-old daughter of William Shakespeare. (Rev: BL 3/1/04; SLJ 4/04)

651 Havill, Juanita. *Eyes Like Willy's* (6–9). 2004, HarperCollins LB $16.89 (0-688-13673-7). 135pp. Guy, who lives in Paris, and Willy, an Austrian, have been friends since they met in the summer of 1906; now they may face each other across the trenches of World War I. (Rev: BCCB 9/04; BL 3/1/04*; SLJ 7/04)

652 Hawes, Louise. *The Vanishing Point* (8–10). 2004, Houghton $17.00 (0-618-43423-2). 256pp. In this appealing historical novel that imagines the adolescence of Italian Renaissance artist Lavinia Fontana, young Vini resorts to subterfuge to get her father to let her paint in his studio. (Rev: BL 11/1/04; SLJ 12/04; VOYA 12/04)

653 Hearn, Julie. *The Minister's Daughter* (7–10). 2005, Simon & Schuster $16.95 (0-689-87690-4). 272pp. In this historical novel set against the backdrop of the English Civil Wars, a Puritan minister's daughter tries to blame her pregnancy on spells cast by the granddaughter of the village's healer. (Rev: BL 5/15/05; SLJ 6/05)

654 Holmes, Victoria. *The Horse from the Sea* (5–8). 2005, HarperCollins LB $16.89 (0-06-052029-9). 320pp. In 1588, Nora, an Irish girl, defies the English and helps a young Spanish sailor and a beautiful stallion, survivors of a shipwreck. (Rev: BL 5/15/05; SLJ 8/05)

655 Holub, Josef. *An Innocent Soldier* (8–11). Trans. by Michael Gofmann. 2005, Scholastic $16.99 (0-439-62771-0). 240pp. Pressed into Napoleon's army for the ill-fated Russian campaign, Adam, a teenage farmhand, is selected as a personal servant by Konrad, an officer from a wealthy family, and the two develop a strong friendship. (Rev: BL 11/15/05; SLJ 12/05; VOYA 2/06)

656 Hopkins, Cathy. *The Princess of Pop* (6–8). Series: Truth or Dare. 2004, Simon & Schuster paper $5.99 (0-689-87002-7). 191pp. On a dare, Becca competes in the British version of "American Idol." (Rev: SLJ 7/04)

657 Hopkins, Cathy. *White Lies and Barefaced Truths*. Book No. 1 (6–8). Series: Truth or Dare. 2004, Simon & Schuster paper $5.99 (0-689-87003-5). 176pp. A funny story in which Cat, a 14-year-old living in Cornwall, England, is kissed by the wrong boy and learns about choosing between telling the truth and diplomacy. (Rev: SLJ 7/04)

658 Ibbotson, Eva. *The Star of Kazan* (4–8). 2004, Dutton $16.99 (0-525-47347-5). 336pp. Set in the Austro-Hungarian empire, this richly detailed and very readable novel tells the story of 12-year-old Annika, who gets a rude awakening when her aristocratic mother whisks her away from her adoptive family. (Rev: BL 10/15/04*; SLJ 10/04*)

659 Kacer, Kathy. *The Night Spies* (4–7). 2003, Second Story paper $5.95 (1-896764-70-3). 197pp. Hiding from the Nazis, Gabi and her family can leave their cramped quarters only at night, but Gabi and her cousin Max manage to help the partisans. (Rev: BL 1/1–15/04; SLJ 3/04)

660 Lasky, Kathryn. *Broken Song* (5–8). 2005, Viking $15.99 (0-670-05931-5). 160pp. Reuven Bloom, a 15-year-old Jew and promising violinist, escapes from late-19th-century Russia with his baby sister, the only surviving member of his family. (Rev: BL 1/1–15/05; SLJ 3/05)

661 Lasky, Kathryn. *Dancing Through Fire* (4–7). Series: Portraits. 2005, Scholastic paper $9.99 (0-439-71009-X). 160pp. The Franco-Prussian War interrupts the dreams of 13-year-old Sylvie, a student at the Paris Opera Ballet in the 1870s. (Rev: BCCB 1/06; BL 12/1/05; SLJ 11/05)

662 Lawlor, Laurie. *Dead Reckoning* (6–9). 2005, Simon & Schuster $15.95 (0-689-86577-5). 272pp. In this compelling historical novel, 15-year-old Emmet Drake, an orphan raised by a monk, is offered a job as a page aboard the ship of his cousin Francis. (Rev: BCCB 9/05; BL 5/15/05; SLJ 8/05; VOYA 8/05)

663 Lawrence, Iain. *The Convicts* (7–10). 2005, Delacorte LB $17.99 (0-385-90109-7). 224pp. In early-19th-century London, 14-year-old Tom is cast into the streets after his father is hauled away to debtor's prison and has various adventures including being transported to Australia. (Rev: BCCB 4/05; BL 3/15/05; HB 3–4/05; SLJ 7/05)

664 MacKall, Dandi Daley. *Eva Underground* (8–11). 2006, Harcourt $17.00 (0-15-205462-6). 256pp. In 1978, Eva Lott's father moves her from her high school life in Chicago to Communist Poland, where she initially rebels but later meets a young political activist named Tomek and develops a strong affection for him and an understanding of the oppression he is fighting. (Rev: BL 3/1/06)

665 Malone, Patricia. *Lady Ilena: Way of the Warrior* (7–10). 2005, Delacorte LB $17.99 (0-385-90251-4). 224pp. In this engaging sequel to *The Legend of Lady Ilena* (2002) set in Britain in the Dark Ages, the title character triggers a war when she refuses to accept the marriage proposal of a warrior from Dun Struan. (Rev: BL 12/1/05; SLJ 12/05)

666 Marks, Graham. *Radio Radio* (8–11). 2004, Bloomsbury paper $11.99 (0-7475-5939-2). 220pp. A group of London club kids goes up against both the government and some unsavory competitors when they set up a pirate radio station. (Rev: BL 1/1–15/05; SLJ 1/05)

667 Marston, Elsa. *Figs and Fate: Stories About Growing Up in the Arab World Today* (6–9). 2005, George Braziller $22.50 (0-8076-1551-X); paper $15.95 (0-8076-1554-4). 146pp. A revealing collection of stories portraying contemporary Arab teens living in Egypt, Iraq, Lebanon, Palestine, and Syria. (Rev: BL 2/15/05; HB 5–6/05; SLJ 3/05; VOYA 10/05)

668 Meyer, Carolyn. *Marie, Dancing* (6–9). 2005, Harcourt $17.00 (0-15-205116-3). 272pp. Marie van Goethem, the girl who posed for Degas' famous *Little Dancer, Aged Fourteen* sculpture, is at the center of this moving novel about the lives of three sisters struggling to make their way in the artistic world of 19th-century Paris. (Rev: BCCB 1/06; BL 11/1/05; SLJ 11/05)

669 Meyer, Carolyn. *Patience, Princess Catherine* (6–9). 2004, Harcourt $17.00 (0-15-216544-4). 256pp. This appealing historical novel recounts the confusion surrounding the future of 15-year-old Catherine of Aragon, alone in England when she is widowed only six months after her marriage to Prince Arthur, heir to the British throne. (Rev: BL 3/15/04; SLJ 7/04)

670 Molloy, Michael. *Peter Raven Under Fire* (6–9). 2005, Scholastic $16.95 (0-439-72454-6). 512pp. A fast-paced multilayered story featuring midshipman Peter Raven, 13, who becomes embroiled in international politics during the Napoleonic Wars. (Rev: BL 8/05; SLJ 10/05; VOYA 10/05)

671 Morgan, Nicola. *Fleshmarket* (8–12). 2004, Delacorte LB $17.99 (0-385-90192-5). 208pp. In early 19th-century Edinburgh, Robbie nurtures a hatred for the doctor who operated on his dying mother as Robbie and his sister struggle to survive. (Rev: BCCB 10/04; HB 7–8/04; SLJ 9/04; VOYA 2/05)

672 Morris, Gerald. *The Lioness and Her Knight* (6–9). 2005, Houghton $16.00 (0-618-50772-8). 352pp. Lady Luneta, 16 and headstrong, travels to Camelot with her cousin Ywain and a fool named Rhience and finds adventure and romance. (Rev: BL 9/15/05; SLJ 9/05; VOYA 12/05)

673 Ortiz, Michael J. *Swan Town: The Secret Journal of Susanna Shakespeare* (7–10). 2006, Harper-Collins LB $16.89 (0-06-058127-1). 208pp. Shakespeare's teenage daughter Susanna writes in her diary about her current circumstances and her literary and acting ambitions, revealing much about Elizabethan life. (Rev: BL 2/15/06; SLJ 3/06; VOYA 2/06)

674 Pennington, Kate. *Brief Candle* (6–9). 2005, Hodder paper $12.50 (0-340-87370-1). 272pp. Fourteen-year-old Emily Brontë helps two hapless lovers in this novel set in Yorkshire and featuring the whole Brontë family. (Rev: BL 12/1/05; SLJ 11/05)

675 Priestley, Chris. *Redwulf's Curse* (6–9). Series: Tom Marlowe Adventure. 2005, Doubleday $16.99 (0-385-60695-8). 192pp. When the elderly Dr. Harker and 18-year-old Tom Marlowe travel from London to the English countryside in the early 18th century, they become swept up in intrigues surrounding the looting of the grave of Redwulf, a 7th-century East Anglian king. (Rev: BL 11/1/05; SLJ 12/05)

676 Priestley, Chris. *The White Rider* (5–8). 2005, Corgi paper $8.99 (0-440-86608-1). 192pp. In this riveting sequel to *Death and the Arrow*, 16-year-old Tom Marlowe is swept up in a series of intrigues in early-18th-century London. (Rev: BL 10/15/05)

677 Rabin, Staton. *Betsy and the Emperor* (6–9). 2004, Simon & Schuster $16.95 (0-689-85880-9). 304pp. In this engaging historical novel set on the island of St. Helena in the South Atlantic, 14-year-old Betsy Balcombe develops a friendship with the exiled Napoleon Bonaparte. (Rev: BCCB 11/04; BL 11/15/04; SLJ 11/04; VOYA 12/04)

678 Rees, Elizabeth M. *The Wedding: An Encounter with Jan van Eyck* (8–11). Series: Art Encounters. 2005, Watson-Guptill $15.95 (0-8230-0407-4). 144pp. In this novel set in 15th-century Bruges and channeling Jan van Eyck's *The Arnolfini Portrait*, 14-year-old Giovanna falls in love with a troubadour called Angelo even as her father plans her marriage to a wealthy man. (Rev: BL 9/15/05; SLJ 9/05)

679 Rinaldi, Ann. *Mutiny's Daughter* (5–7). 2004, HarperCollins $15.99 (0-06-029638-0). 224pp. Fletcher Christian, who led the mutiny on *H.M.S. Bounty*, covertly returns to England with his young half-Tahitian daughter and leaves her to live with relatives, hiding the truth about her parentage. (Rev: BL 2/15/04; SLJ 3/04; VOYA 4/04)

680 Rinaldi, Ann. *Nine Days a Queen: The Short Life and Reign of Lady Jane Grey* (6–8). 2005, HarperCollins $15.99 (0-06-054924-6). 192pp. This fictionalized first-person account of the tragically brief life of Lady Jane Grey relates the complex palace intrigues that brought the 16-year-old Jane to the throne of England for nine days. (Rev: BL 12/1/04; SLJ 3/05; VOYA 2/05)

681 Rushton, Rosie. *The Dashwood Sisters' Secrets of Love* (6–9). 2005, Hyperion $15.99 (0-7868-5136-8). 336pp. In the wake of their father's remarriage and sudden death, the three Dashwood sisters experience a humbling reversal of fortunes. (Rev: BCCB 3/05; BL 3/1/05; SLJ 4/05; VOYA 6/05)

682 *Sir Gawain and the Green Knight* (4–7). Retold by Michael Morpurgo. 2005, Candlewick $18.99 (0-7636-2519-1). 112pp. Morpurgo retells in contemporary prose the story of the Green Knight's challenge to the court of King Arthur. (Rev: BL 11/1/04*; SLJ 10/04)

683 Sturtevant, Katherine. *A True and Faithful Narrative* (6–9). 2006, Farrar $17.00 (0-374-37809-6). 256pp. In 17th-century London, 16-year-old Meg has abandoned some of her early dreams but still hopes to be a writer and not just a wife in this sequel to *At the Sign of the Star* (2000). (Rev: BL 3/1/06*)

684 Thomas, Jane Resh. *The Counterfeit Princess* (5–8). 2005, Clarion $15.00 (0-395-93870-8). 198pp. Iris, a young English girl with an uncanny resemblance to Princess Elizabeth (soon to be Elizabeth I), finds herself embroiled in intrigue in this novel set in the 16th century. (Rev: BL 11/15/05; SLJ 10/05)

685 Updale, Eleanor. *Montmorency* (6–9). 2004, Scholastic $16.95 (0-439-58035-8). 240pp. After surviving a near-fatal accident, a petty thief in Victorian London creates a double life and in the process becomes a criminal mastermind. (Rev: BCCB 4/04; BL 5/1/04; HB 3–4/04; SLJ 4/04; VOYA 6/05)

686 Vande Velde, Vivian. *The Book of Mordred* (8–11). 2005, Houghton $18.00 (0-618-50754-X). 352pp. A multilayered account of Mordred's acts, seen through the eyes of three women who know him well. (Rev: BL 9/15/05; SLJ 10/05; VOYA 10/05)

687 Wallace, Karen. *Wendy* (7–10). 2004, Simon & Schuster $16.95 (0-689-86769-7). 208pp. In this engaging story set before the events of *Peter Pan*, life in the Darling household is less than idyllic for 9-year-old Wendy and her brothers. (Rev: BCCB 3/04; BL 1/1–15/04; HB 3–4/04; SLJ 3/04; VOYA 4/04)

688 Wilson, John. *Flames of the Tiger* (5–8). 2003, Kids Can $16.95 (1-55337-618-8). 176pp. The horrors of World War II are seen through the eyes of 17-year-old Dieter, who with his younger sister is fleeing his native Germany as the war nears an end. (Rev: SLJ 1/04; VOYA 6/04) [813]

689 Woodruff, Elvira. *The Ravenmaster's Secret* (4–7). 2003, Scholastic $15.95 (0-439-28133-4). 225pp. Eleven-year-old Forrest becomes embroiled in dangerous intrigue in this story set inside the Tower of London in the early 18th century, with a glossary and historical notes appended. (Rev: BL 1/1–15/04; SLJ 1/04; VOYA 4/04)

690 Wyatt, Melissa. *Raising the Griffin* (8–12). 2004, Random LB $18.99 (0-385-90115-1). 288pp. When the people of Rovenia vote to restore their monarchy, 16-year-old Alex Varenhoff leaves Britain with his family so his father can ascend to the throne of his homeland, but the teen finds life as a prince is not all it's cracked up to be. (Rev: BCCB 2/04; BL 1/1–15/04; SLJ 2/04)

Latin America and Canada

691 Crook, Connie Brummel. *The Perilous Year* (5–7). 2003, Fitzhenry & Whiteside paper $7.95 (1-55041-818-1). 197pp. In this fast-paced sequel to *The Hungry Year* (2001), 11-year-old twins Alex and Ryan face constant challenges and adventures — including more encounters with pirates — in 18th-century Canada. (Rev: SLJ 3/04)

692 Danticat, Edwidge. *Anacaona, Golden Flower: Haiti, 1490* (5–8). Series: Royal Diaries. 2005, Scholastic $10.95 (0-439-49906-2). 208pp. In 15th-century Haiti, Anacaona, a girl of royal heritage, records her people's struggles against the Spanish explorers. (Rev: BL 5/15/05)

693 Jocelyn, Marthe. *Mable Riley: A Reliable Record of Humdrum, Peril, and Romance* (5–10). Illus. 2004, Candlewick $15.99 (0-7636-2120-X). 288pp. This is a charming, humorous diary set in 1901 by a 14-year-old girl who accompanies her sister when she becomes a teacher in Stratford, Ontario. (Rev: BL 3/1/04; HB 5–6/04; SLJ 3/04; VOYA 6/04)

694 Kositsky, Lynne. *Claire by Moonlight* (7–10). 2005, Tundra paper $9.95 (0-88776-659-5). 272pp. History and romance are interwoven in this story of 15-year-old Claire's struggle to return to Acadia with her brother and sister after their deportation in the 1750s. (Rev: BL 7/05; SLJ 10/05)

695 Major, Kevin. *Ann and Seamus* (5–9). 2003, Groundwood $16.95 (0-88899-561-X). 128pp. Based on an early-19th-century shipwreck off the coast of Newfoundland, this historical novel in verse chronicles the romance that develops between 17-year-old Ann Harvey and the Irish teenager she rescues from the ship. (Rev: BL 3/1/04; HB 3–4/04; SLJ 2/04; VOYA 4/04)

696 Mikaelsen, Ben. *Tree Girl* (7–12). 2004, HarperTempest $16.99 (0-06-009004-9). 240pp. Through the first-person narrative of Mayan teenager Gabriela Flores, the reader experiences the civil war in Guatemala. (Rev: BL 2/15/04; SLJ 4/04; VOYA 6/04)

697 Noël, Michel. *Good for Nothing* (8–11). 2004, Douglas & McIntyre $18.95 (0-88899-478-8). 256pp. In this powerful coming-of-age novel set in northern Quebec in the late 1950s and early 1960s, 15-year-old Nipishish, part Algonquin and part white, struggles to find his own identity. (Rev: BL 1/1–15/05; SLJ 1/05; VOYA 2/05)

698 Porter, Pamela. *The Crazy Man* (6–8). 2005, Douglas & McIntyre $15.95 (0-88899-694-2). 214pp. In appealing free verse, this novel set in 1960s Saskatchewan tells the story of young Emaline, who has been crippled in a farm accident and who befriends Angus, a mental patient who's been hired to help out around the farm. (Rev: BL 11/1/05; SLJ 12/05; VOYA 2/06)

699 Taylor, Joanne. *There You Are: A Novel* (4–7). 2004, Tundra paper $8.95 (0-88776-658-7). 199pp. On post-World War II Cape Breton Island, 12-year-old Jeannie lives in a remote community and longs for a friend. (Rev: SLJ 11/04)

700 Trottier, Maxine. *Sister to the Wolf* (6–9). 2004, Kids Can $16.95 (1-55337-519-X). 348pp. In this engaging historical novel, which begins in Quebec in the early 18th century, Cecile, the teenage daughter of a fur trader, buys an Indian slave to save him from further abuse. (Rev: BL 1/1–15/05; SLJ 12/04)

United States

NATIVE AMERICANS

701 Bruchac, Joseph. *Geronimo* (7–10). 2006, Scholastic $16.99 (0-439-35360-2). 384pp. Geronimo's fictional adopted grandson narrates the tragic story of Geronimo's final surrender and the subsequent treatment of his people in this well-researched novel. (Rev: BL 3/15/06; SLJ 4/06)

702 Carvell, Marlene. *Sweetgrass Basket* (7–10). 2005, Dutton $15.99 (0-525-47547-8). 160pp. Mohawk sisters Mattie and Sarah describe the abuse they endure at the Carlisle Indian Industrial School at the turn of the 20th century. (Rev: BL 8/05*; SLJ 12/05)

703 Creel, Ann Howard. *Under a Stand Still Moon* (6–10). 2005, Brown Barn paper $8.95 (0-9746481-8-3). 192pp. In this captivating story set among the ancient Anasazi of the American Southwest, a young girl uses her magical powers to preserve her people's way of life. (Rev: SLJ 11/05)

704 Erdrich, Louise. *The Game of Silence* (5–8). 2005, HarperCollins LB $16.89 (0-06-029790-5). 272pp. As 9-year-old Omakayas is coming of age, the intrusion of the European settlers increasingly impacts the Ojibwe lifestyle in this sequel to *The Birchbark House* (1999). (Rev: BL 5/15/05*; SLJ 7/05)

705 Schwartz, Virginia Frances. *Initiation* (5–8). Illus. 2003, Fitzhenry & Whiteside $16.95 (1-55005-053-2). 268pp. Kwakiuti Indian twins Nana and Nanolatch prepare to face the responsibilities of adulthood in this story set on the West Coast of North America in the 15th century. (Rev: SLJ 3/04) [813]

706 Spooner, Michael. *Last Child* (8–11). 2005, Holt $16.95 (0-8050-7739-1). 256pp. Rosalie, who is part Mandan and part Scottish American, is caught up in the conflicts between the Native Americans and the whites in 1837 North Dakota. (Rev: BL 9/1/05; SLJ 11/05; VOYA 8/05)

707 Wyss, Thelma Hatch. *Bear Dancer: The Story of a Ute Girl* (4–7). 2005, Simon & Schuster $15.95 (1-4169-0285-6). 192pp. In this fact-based historical novel, life is turned upside down for Elk Girl, a member of the Tabaguache Ute, when she is kidnapped by a rival tribe. (Rev: BL 10/15/05; SLJ 10/05)

COLONIAL PERIOD AND FRENCH AND INDIAN WARS

708 Duble, Kathleen Benner. *The Sacrifice* (6–9). 2005, Simon & Schuster $15.95 (0-689-87650-5). 224pp. Strong-minded Abigail, 10, and her older sister are accused of witchcraft in 1692 Massachusetts in this compelling novel full of social history. (Rev: BL 9/15/05*; SLJ 12/05)

709 Karr, Kathleen. *Worlds Apart* (4–7). 2005, Marshall Cavendish $15.95 (0-7614-5195-1). 196pp. In 1670 South Carolina, Christopher — a teenage settler — and Sewee Indian Asha-po become friends. (Rev: BCCB 5/05; SLJ 5/05)

710 Ketchum, Liza. *Where the Great Hawk Flies* (4–7). 2005, Clarion $16.00 (0-618-40085-0). 272pp. The Coombs family and the Tuckers have trouble getting along — even the young boys — because Mrs. Tucker is a Pequot Indian and the Coombs suffered mightily during an Indian raid seven years before. (Rev: BL 9/15/05*; SLJ 1/06)

711 Rinaldi, Ann. *The Color of Fire* (7–10). 2005, Hyperion $15.99 (0-7868-0938-8). 208pp. Based on a little-known historical event, this compelling novel chronicles what happens when false accusations unleash a storm of violence toward black people in mid-18th-century New York City. (Rev: BCCB 4/05; BL 2/1/05; SLJ 5/05; VOYA 4/05)

REVOLUTIONARY PERIOD AND THE YOUNG NATION (1775–1809)

712 Ernst, Kathleen. *Betrayal at Cross Creek* (5–10). 2004, Pleasant $10.95 (1-58485-879-6). 178pp. During the Revolutionary War, a young Scottish refugee and her grandparents are torn by conflicting loyalties. (Rev: BL 3/1/04; SLJ 5/04)

713 Meyer, L. A. *Curse of the Blue Tattoo: Being an Account of the Misadventures of Jacky Faber, Midshipman and Fine Lady* (6–9). 2004, Harcourt $17.00 (0-15-205115-5). 384pp. Forced to leave her ship after being exposed as a girl, Jacky Faber enrolls in an elite Boston girls' school but frustrates all attempts to make a lady out of her in this sequel to *Bloody Jack* (2002). (Rev: BL 5/15/04*; HB 7–8/04; SLJ 7/04; VOYA 8/04)

45

NINETEENTH CENTURY TO THE CIVIL WAR (1809–1861)

714 Cadnum, Michael. *Blood Gold* (7–12). 2004, Viking $16.99 (0-670-05884-X). 224pp. Eighteen-year-old William encounters greed, murder, and revenge in this exciting novel set during the 1849 California gold rush. (Rev: BL 5/15/04*; HB 7–8/04; SLJ 6/04)

715 LeSourd, Nancy. *The Personal Correspondence of Hannah Brown and Sarah Smith: The Underground Railroad, 1858* (4–7). 2003, Zondervan $9.99 (0-310-70350-6). 192pp. In letters to each other, two Quaker girls discuss their abolitionist ideals and become involved in helping a runaway slave. (Rev: BL 1/1–15/04)

716 Lester, Julius. *Day of Tears: A Novel in Dialogue* (6–9). 2005, Hyperion $15.99 (0-7868-0490-4). 176pp. In this heart-rending novel based on a real event and told mostly in present-tense dialogue, a slave named Emma is torn from the life she knows when her master puts her up for sale at the biggest slave auction in American history. (Rev: BCCB 7–8/05; BL 2/1/05*; HB 7–8/05; SLJ 3/05; VOYA 6/05)

717 Lester, Julius. *The Old African* (4–7). 2005, Dial $19.99 (0-8037-2564-7). 80pp. An elderly slave who never speaks uses his acute mental powers to relieve the pain of his people on a Georgia plantation. (Rev: BL 7/05*; SLJ 9/05; VOYA 12/05)

718 Moses, Shelia P. *I, Dred Scott* (8–11). 2005, Simon & Schuster $16.95 (0-689-85975-9). 112pp. In this fictionalized account, Dred Scott, born a slave, chronicles the ultimately unsuccessful 11-year legal battle to win his freedom. (Rev: BCCB 4/05; BL 3/15/05; SLJ 2/05; VOYA 4/05)

719 Prince, Bryan. *I Came as a Stranger: The Underground Railroad* (7–12). 2004, Tundra paper $15.95 (0-88776-667-6). 160pp. This account tells what happened after the runaway slaves reached Canada and contains material both about famous leaders and about ordinary people involved in the Underground Railroad. (Rev: BL 5/1/04; SLJ 6/04) [971.1]

720 Wilson, Diane Lee. *Black Storm Comin'* (7–10). 2005, Simon & Schuster $16.95 (0-689-87137-6). 304pp. Son of a white father and a freed-slave mother, 12-year-old Colton Westcott joins the Pony Express in an effort to make sure his mother and siblings finally make it to the West Coast. (Rev: BL 8/05*; SLJ 7/05; VOYA 10/05)

THE CIVIL WAR (1861–1865)

721 Durrant, Lynda. *My Last Skirt* (5–8). 2006, Clarion $16.00 (0-618-57490-5). 208pp. After migrating from Ireland to America, Jennie Hodgers, who prefers wearing pants to skirts, adopts the persona of Albert Cashier and joins the Union army in this novel based on a true story. (Rev: BL 2/15/06; SLJ 4/06*)

722 Elliott, Laura Malone. *Annie, Between the States* (7–11). 2004, HarperCollins LB $16.89 (0-06-001211-0). 496pp. As the Civil War rages around her northern Virginia home, 15-year-old Annie finds her feelings about the North-South conflict evolving. (Rev: BL 12/1/04; SLJ 11/04)

723 McMullan, Margaret. *How I Found the Strong: A Civil War Story* (5–9). 2004, Houghton $16.00 (0-618-35008-X). The Civil War changes the way a boy looks at life when it takes away his father and brother and comes close to his Mississippi home. (Rev: BL 2/15/04; SLJ 4/04; VOYA 6/04)

724 Myers, Anna. *Assassin* (7–12). 2005, Walker $16.95 (0-8027-8989-7). 212pp. The events surrounding the assassination of Abraham Lincoln are explored in this fictionalized account, narrated in alternating chapters by a teenage White House seamstress and assassin John Wilkes Booth. (Rev: SLJ 12/05; VOYA 10/05)

725 Rinaldi, Ann. *Sarah's Ground* (6–9). 2004, Simon & Schuster $15.95 (0-689-85924-4). 192pp. In this appealing Civil War novel based on a true story, 18-year-old Sarah leaves her New York home in 1861 to take a job as a caretaker at Mount Vernon, but as the war intensifies, Sarah and the rest of the staff face mounting challenges to ensure the plantation's security and neutrality. (Rev: BL 2/1/04; SLJ 5/04; VOYA 4/04)

726 Siegelson, Kim. *Trembling Earth* (7–12). 2004, Putnam $17.99 (0-399-24021-7). 176pp. This Civil War novel is told from the point of view of 12-year-old Hamp, who tracks down a runaway slave in the Okefenokee Swamp. (Rev: BL 5/15/04*; SLJ 6/04)

WESTWARD EXPANSION AND PIONEER LIFE

727 Arlington, Frances. *Prairie Whispers* (7–12). 2003, Putnam $17.99 (0-399-23975-8). During their covered wagon trip westward, Colleen switches her mother's stillborn child and gives her mother the newborn of a dying mother in a nearby wagon. (Rev: BL 5/15/04; HB 7–8/03; SLJ 5/03; VOYA 6/03)

728 Carbone, Elisa. *Last Dance on Holladay Street* (8–11). 2005, Knopf LB $17.99 (0-375-92896-0). 208pp. After the deaths of her black foster parents, 13-year-old Eva sets off to search for her birth mother and discovers she is a white prostitute; set in the late 19th century. (Rev: BCCB 6/05; BL 2/1/05; SLJ 4/05; VOYA 4/05)

729 Collier, James Lincoln. *Me and Billy* (6–9). 2004, Marshall Cavendish $15.95 (0-7614-5174-9). 192pp. In the Old West, Billy and Possum, best friends who grew up together in the same orphanage, escape and head for a legendary lake full of gold. (Rev: BL 9/15/04; SLJ 1/05)

730 Couloumbis, Audrey. *The Misadventures of Maude March, or, Trouble Rides a Fast Horse* (5–8). 2005, Random LB $17.99 (0-375-93245-3). 291pp. When their aunt and sole guardian is killed, Maude and Sally March rebel against their new foster family and set off on their own in this rollicking tale of the Old West. (Rev: SLJ 9/05)

731 Holm, Jennifer L. *Boston Jane: The Claim* (5–8). 2004, HarperCollins $15.99 (0-06-029045-5). 240pp. In the third installment in Jane's story, an old rival named Sally and a former suitor cause difficulties for Jane. (Rev: BL 3/1/04; SLJ 5/04; VOYA 4/04)

732 Karr, Katherine. *Exiled: Memoirs of a Camel* (4–8). 2004, Marshall Cavendish $15.95 (0-7614-5164-1). 240pp. This fascinating story of the U.S. Camel Corps is told from the viewpoint of Ali, an Egyptian camel drafted for service in this shortlived branch of the United States Army. (Rev: BL 5/1/04; SLJ 5/04)

733 McMullan, Kate. *My Travels with Capts. Lewis and Clark by George Shannon* (5–9). 2004, Harper-Collins LB $16.89 (0-06-008100-7). 272pp. This well-researched fictional diary of a teenager traveling on the great expedition gives readers a good sense of life at the time and an insight into the key characters. (Rev: BCCB 10/04; BL 10/15/04; HB 11–12/04; SLJ 9/04)

734 Oatman, Eric. *Cowboys on the Western Trail: The Cattle Drive Adventures of Josh McNabb and Davy Bartlett* (4–7). Illus. Series: I Am America. 2004, National Geographic paper $6.99 (0-7922-6553-X). 40pp. The excitement of a cattle drive is shown in the journals and letters of two young teen boys in this blend of fact and fiction set in 1887 and presented in an appealing magazine format. (Rev: BL 5/15/04)

735 Taylor, Theodore. *Billy the Kid* (6–9). 2005, Harcourt $17.00 (0-15-204930-4). 240pp. In this fictionalized account, author Theodore Taylor provides a different twist on the story of Old West outlaw Billy the Kid. (Rev: BCCB 9/05; BL 5/15/05; SLJ 7/05; VOYA 4/06)

736 Wolf, Allan. *New Found Land: Lewis and Clark's Voyage of Discovery* (7–12). 2004, Candlewick $18.99 (0-7636-2113-7). 500pp. Seaman the dog, here called Oolum, is the primary narrator of this verse account of the famous expedition that draws heavily on such primary source documents as letters and journals. (Rev: BL 9/04; SLJ 9/04)

RECONSTRUCTION TO WORLD WAR I (1865–1914)

737 Boling, Katharine. *January 1905* (4–7). 2004, Harcourt $16.00 (0-15-205119-8). 160pp. In alternating voices, 11-year-old mill worker Pauline and her deformed, stay-at-home twin sister Arlene describe the harsh circumstances of their early-20th-century life. (Rev: BL 5/15/04; HB 7–8/04; SLJ 7/04)

738 Clark, Clara Gillow. *Hattie on Her Way* (4–7). Series: Hattie. 2005, Candlewick $15.99 (0-7636-2286-9). 208pp. The sequel to *Hill Hawk Hattie* (2003) finds Hattie living with her grandmother after her mother's death and seeking to solve a family mystery. (Rev: BL 3/1/05; SLJ 3/05)

739 Henderson, Aileen Kilgore. *Hard Times for Jake Smith* (5–9). 2004, Milkweed $16.95 (1-57131-648-5). 192pp. Abandoned by her parents in the depths of the Great Depression, 12-year-old MaryJake disguises herself as a boy. (Rev: BL 4/15/04; SLJ 9/04)

740 Hill, Kirkpatrick. *Dancing at the Odinochka* (4–7). 2005, Simon & Schuster $15.95 (0-689-87388-3). 272pp. An atmospheric life of Erinia — daughter of a Russian father and Athabascan mother — growing up in the 1860s in what is now Alaska. (Rev: BL 8/05; SLJ 8/05)

741 Hurwitz, Johanna. *The Unsigned Valentine: And Other Events in the Life of Emma Meade* (6–9). 2006, HarperCollins LB $16.89 (0-06-056054-1). 176pp. Emma, 15, has left school to work on her family's Vermont farm in 1911 and is dismayed when her father won't allow handsome Cole Berry to court her. (Rev: BL 3/1/06)

742 Lerangis, Peter. *Smiler's Bones* (7–10). 2005, Scholastic $16.95 (0-439-34485-9). 160pp. Lerangis brings alive the sad story, based on truth, of an Inuit boy named Minik, who, with his father and four others, was brought to New York City in the late 19th century by explorer Robert Peary. (Rev: BCCB 6/05; BL 4/1/05; SLJ 6/05; VOYA 8/05)

743 Myers, Anna. *Hoggee* (5–7). 2004, Walker $16.95 (0-8027-8926-9). 182pp. Despite all his own problems, 14-year-old mule driver Howard decides to do what he can to help a deaf mute girl in this novel set in 19th-century New York State. (Rev: SLJ 11/04)

744 Napoli, Donna Jo. *The King of Mulberry Street* (6–9). 2005, Random LB $17.99 (0-385-90890-3). 224pp. In the 1890s, 9-year-old Italian Jew Beniamino travels alone by ship from Naples to New York, where he assumes the name of Dom and tries to make his way while longing for his home. (Rev: BL 8/05; SLJ 10/05; VOYA 12/05)

745 Peck, Richard. *Here Lies the Librarian* (5–8). 2006, Dial $16.99 (0-8037-3080-2). 208pp. Four young female librarians arrive in a small town in Indiana in 1914 and inspire 14-year-old Peewee McGrath to consider her future in different ways. (Rev: BL 3/1/06; SLJ 4/06*; VOYA 2/06)

746 Schmidt, Gary D. *Lizzie Bright and the Buckminster Boy* (7–12). 2004, Clarion $15.00 (0-618-43929-3). 224pp. When Turner, son of a rigid minister, moves with his family to a small town in Maine during 1912, he doesn't fit in. (Rev: BL 5/15/04*; SLJ 5/04)

747 Tal, Eve. *Double Crossing: A Jewish Immigration Story* (7–10). 2005, Cinco Puntos $16.95 (0-938317-94-6). 216pp. At the beginning of the 20th century, young Raizel and her Orthodox Jewish grandfather travel from Europe to New York only to find they are rejected by immigration officials. (Rev: BL 8/05*; SLJ 10/05; VOYA 4/06)

748 Taylor, Kim. *Bowery Girl* (8–11). 2006, Viking $16.99 (0-670-05966-8). 288pp. A realistic story about orphaned teen girls who resort to picking pockets and prostitution to survive in late-19th-century New York City. (Rev: BL 3/1/06; SLJ 3/06; VOYA 4/06)

749 Thesman, Jean. *Rising Tide* (6–9). 2003, Viking $16.99 (0-670-03656-0). 224pp. In this sequel to *A Sea So Far*, San Francisco earthquake survivor Kate Keely returns to the City by the Bay to open a linens shop in partnership with her friend Ellen Flannery. (Rev: BCCB 11/03; BL 1/1–15/04; SLJ 12/03)

750 Winthrop, Elizabeth. *Counting on Grace* (6–9). 2006, Random LB $18.99 (0-385-90878-4). 144pp. In the early 20th century, 12-year-old Grace chafes against her long hours working in the textile mill and longs to go back to school in this story based on a 1910 photograph by Lewis Hines. (Rev: BL 2/15/06; SLJ 3/06*; VOYA 4/06)

BETWEEN THE WARS AND THE GREAT DEPRESSION (1919–1941)

751 Bryant, Jen. *The Trial* (5–9). 2004, Knopf LB $16.99 (0-375-92752-2). 192pp. In this engaging historical novel told in poems, 12-year-old Katie recounts what happens to her quiet hometown when the sensational Lindbergh kidnapping trial is held in the county courthouse. (Rev: BL 5/1/04*; HB 3–4/04; SLJ 6/04)

752 Currier, Katrina Saltonstall. *Kai's Journey to Gold Mountain* (4–7). 2005, Angel Island $16.95 (0-9667352-7-7); paper $10.95 (0-9667352-4-2). 44pp. Based on the experiences of a Chinese immigrant to the United States in the 1930s, this troubling tale describes the internment of 12-year-old Kai on Angel Island in San Francisco Bay. (Rev: BL 2/15/05*)

753 Dudley, David L. *The Bicycle Man* (5–8). 2005, Clarion $16.00 (0-618-54233-7). 256pp. In this

poignant portrait of African American life in the rural South during the late 1920s, 12-year-old Carissa develops a mutually beneficial relationship with Bailey, an elderly jack-of-all-trades to whom she and her mother offer a home. (Rev: BL 11/15/05; SLJ 11/05)

754 Easton, Kelly. *Walking on Air* (6–8). 2004, Simon & Schuster $16.95 (0-689-84875-7). Traveling the 1930s revival circuit and performing as an aerialist to draw people into her father's tent shows, unhappy 12-year-old June makes some important discoveries about her birth and faith. (Rev: BCCB 7–8/04; BL 4/1/04; SLJ 7/04; VOYA 6/04)

755 Gutman, Dan. *Race for the Sky: The Kitty Hawk Diaries of Johnny Moore* (4–7). 2003, Simon & Schuster $15.95 (0-689-84554-5). 178pp. Fact and fiction are interwoven in this diary by 14-year-old John Moore, recording his firsthand observations of the Wright brothers' progress. (Rev: BL 1/1–15/04; SLJ 1/04)

756 Ingold, Jeanette. *Hitch* (8–11). 2005, Harcourt $17.00 (0-13-204747-6). 271pp. When he loses his job during the Great Depression, 17-year-old Moss Trawnley leaves home in search of his father and ends up in an interesting job with the Civilian Conservation Corps. (Rev: BCCB 9/05; BL 5/15/05; SLJ 8/05)

757 Jackson, Alison. *Rainmaker* (5–8). 2005, Boyds Mills $16.95 (1-59078-309-3). 192pp. The farmers in Pidge Martin's town hire a rainmaker in the hopes that she will save their crops in this story set in 1939 Florida. (Rev: BL 3/15/05; SLJ 4/05)

758 Kidd, Ronald. *Monkey Town: The Summer of the Scopes Trial* (6–9). 2006, Simon & Schuster $15.95 (1-4169-0572-3). 272pp. This fictionalized account of the 1925 Scopes Monkey Trial in Dayton, Tennessee, is narrated by the perceptive 15-year-old Frances Robinson, daughter of the man primarily responsible for taking the evolution test case to the courts. (Rev: BL 12/15/05; SLJ 2/06*; VOYA 2/06)

759 Kudlinski, Kathleen. *The Spirit Catchers: An Encounter with Georgia O'Keeffe* (6–9). Series: Art Encounters. 2004, Watson-Guptill $16.95 (0-8230-0408-2); paper $6.99 (0-8230-0412-0). 176pp. Fact and fiction are mixed in this story of 15-year-old Parker, a Dust Bowl refugee who finds himself on Georgia O'Keeffe's New Mexico ranch and becomes her assistant. (Rev: SLJ 10/04)

760 Wyatt, Leslie J. *Poor Is Just a Starting Place* (5–8). 2005, Holiday $16.95 (0-8234-1884-7). 196pp. In rural Kentucky during the Great Depression, 12-year-old Artie longs for a different life. (Rev: BL 6/1–15/05; SLJ 7/05)

POST WORLD WAR II UNITED STATES
(1945–)

761 Houston, Julian. *New Boy* (8–11). 2005, Houghton $16.00 (0-618-43253-1). 256pp. In the late 1950s, Rob Garrett, an African American teen from Virginia, is the first black student at a tony Connecticut prep school, where he learns about different forms of prejudice and watches civil rights developments in the South. (Rev: BL 11/15/05*; SLJ 3/06; VOYA 2/06)

762 Kadohata, Cynthia. *Kira-Kira* (6–12). 2004, Simon & Schuster $15.95 (0-689-85639-3). 256pp. Poverty, exploitation, and racial prejudice form a backdrop to this moving story of two Japanese American sisters growing up in a small Georgia town in the late 1950s and facing the older sister's death from lymphoma. Newbery Medal, 2005. (Rev: BCCB 1/04; BL 1/1–15/04; HB 3–4/04; SLJ 3/04; VOYA 8/04)

763 Levine, Ellen. *Catch a Tiger by the Toe* (5–8). 2005, Viking $15.99 (0-670-88461-8). 208pp. Jamie's world is turned upside down when her father is put in jail for refusing to reveal the names of other Communists to the House Un-American Activities Committee. (Rev: BL 3/15/05*; SLJ 6/05)

764 McDonald, Joyce. *Devil on My Heels* (7–10). 2004, Delacorte LB $17.99 (0-385-90133-X). 272pp. When 15-year-old Dove discovers that her father's migrant pickers are working under terrible conditions on the Florida farm, she is forced to choose between family loyalties and her sense of justice. (Rev: BL 5/15/04; SLJ 7/04)

765 Moses, Shelia P. *The Legend of Buddy Bush* (6–9). 2004, Simon & Schuster $15.95 (0-689-85839-6). 224pp. In this poignant, fact-based novel, 12-year-old Pattie Mae Sheals faces many challenges when her beloved Uncle Buddy is accused of the attempted rape of a white woman in 1940s North Carolina. (Rev: BCCB 4/04; BL 3/1/04; SLJ 2/04; VOYA 2/04)

766 Rodman, Mary Ann. *Yankee Girl* (4–8). 2004, Farrar $17.00 (0-374-38661-7). 224pp. In 1964, Alice's family moves from Chicago to Mississippi and 6th-grader Alice must cope not only with the stress of a new school but also with her ambivalence about the only black girl in her class; newspaper headlines introducing each chapter keep the racial violence of the time in the reader's mind. (Rev: BL 3/1/04; SLJ 4/04)

767 Smith, D. James. *The Boys of San Joaquin* (5–8). 2005, Simon & Schuster $15.95 (0-689-87606-8). 240pp. An episodic tale set in the 1950s, in which 12-year-old Paolo describes events of his life and a mystery involving a half-eaten $20 bill. (Rev: BL 3/1/05; SLJ 1/05)

Twentieth-Century Wars

WORLD WAR I

768 Morpurgo, Michael. *Private Peaceful* (7–12). 2004, Scholastic $16.95 (0-439-63648-5). 176pp. Fifteen-year-old Thomas, who lied about his age to follow his beloved older brother into combat in World War I, reflects on the life he left behind in England and the horrors of life on the front lines. (Rev: BL 10/1/04*; SLJ 11/04; VOYA 12/04)

769 Sedgwick, Marcus. *The Foreshadowing* (8–11). 2006, Random LB $18.99 (0-385-90881-4). 288pp. Plagued by premonitions about her brother, 17-year-old Sasha signs up as a nurse so that she can look for him on the grim battlefields of World War I France. (Rev: BL 4/1/06*)

770 Spillebeen, Geert. *Kipling's Choice* (7–10). Trans. by Terese Edelstein. 2005, Houghton $16.00 (0-618-43124-1). 160pp. In this fictionalized biography of John Kipling, the son of the world-famous British author uses his father's influence to get into the army despite his poor eyesight, giving the teen a chance to do battle with the "barbaric Huns" in World War I. (Rev: BCCB 6/05; BL 5/15/05; SLJ 6/05; VOYA 12/05)

WORLD WAR II AND THE HOLOCAUST

771 Bruchac, Joseph. *Code Talker* (6–9). 2005, Dial $16.99 (0-8037-2921-9). 240pp. This inspiring novel chronicles the experiences of one of the Navajo code talkers who played a crucial role in the American victory in World War II. (Rev: BCCB 2/05; BL 2/15/05*; SLJ 5/05; VOYA 4/05)

772 Cheaney, J. B. *My Friend the Enemy* (5–8). 2005, Knopf LB $17.99 (0-375-91432-3). 256pp. A friendship with a Japanese American boy tests the resolve of 11-year-old Hazel during World War II. (Rev: BL 5/15/05; SLJ 11/05)

773 Friedman, D. Dina. *Escaping into the Night* (7–10). 2006, Simon & Schuster $14.95 (1-4169-0258-9). 208pp. Based on true events, this is the story of Halina Rudowski's escape into the forest during a Nazi roundup of Jews, and her subsequent efforts to survive. (Rev: BL 1/1–15/06; SLJ 3/06; VOYA 4/06)

774 Graber, Janet. *Resistance* (7–10). 2005, Marshall Cavendish $15.95 (0-7614-5214-1). 144pp. In this suspenseful World War II novel, 15-year-old Marianne reluctantly joins her mother and brother in fighting for the French Resistance despite her fears that they will be found out by the German soldier billeted in their home. (Rev: BCCB 6/05; BL 5/15/05; SLJ 8/05)

775 Graff, Nancy Price. *Taking Wing* (5–8). 2005, Clarion $15.00 (0-618-53591-8). 224pp. A multilayered story set in 1942 Vermont and featuring 13-

year-old Gus, who, over the course of the book, learns about prejudice, and about killing and death. (Rev: BL 5/15/05*; SLJ 5/05)

776 Hostetter, Joyce Moyer. *Blue* (4–7). 2006, Boyds Mills $16.95 (1-59078-389-1). 200pp. When her father leaves for World War II, Ann Fay, the oldest of four children, struggles to keep up with the chores in their North Carolina home until polio strikes the community. (Rev: BL 2/15/06)

777 Hunter, Bernice Thurman. *The Girls They Left Behind* (7–10). 2005, Fitzhenry & Whiteside paper $9.95 (1-55041-927-7). 192pp. This coming-of-age novel, set in Toronto against the backdrop of World War II, paints a vivid portrait of what life was like for the teenage girls left behind on the home front. (Rev: BCCB 7–8/05; BL 5/15/05; SLJ 8/05; VOYA 8/05)

778 Kositsky, Lynne. *The Thought of High Windows* (8–12). 2004, Kids Can $16.95 (1-55337-621-8). 175pp. A Jewish refugee named Esther describes her experiences in France during World War II — lice and other discomforts, loneliness, longing for her family, her differences from the other refugees — and her involvement in the Resistance in this affecting novel based on true events. (Rev: HB 5–6/04; SLJ 5/04)

779 Lawrence, Iain. *B for Buster* (7–12). 2004, Delacorte LB $17.99 (0-385-90108-9). 336pp. To escape his abusive parents, 16-year-old Kak lies about his age and joins the Canadian Air Force in 1943; he soon finds himself part of a crew flying nighttime bombing raids over Germany. (Rev: BL 6/1–15/04; SLJ 7/04; VOYA 8/04)

780 Mazer, Harry. *A Boy No More* (7–9). 2004, Simon & Schuster $15.95 (0-689-85533-8). 144pp. In this poignant sequel to *A Boy at War*, Adam Pelko, who lost his father in the Japanese bombing of Pearl Harbor, moves with his mother and sister from Hawaii to California where a Japanese American friend's request presents Adam with a moral dilemma. (Rev: BL 9/1/04; SLJ 9/04)

781 Mazer, Harry. *Heroes Don't Run: A Novel of the Pacific War* (7–10). 2005, Simon & Schuster $15.95 (0-689-85534-6). 128pp. In this gripping sequel to *A Boy at War* (2001) and *A Boy No More* (2004), 17-year-old Adam Pelko lies about his age to join the U.S. Marines and fights in a climactic battle with the Japanese on Okinawa. (Rev: BL 5/15/05; SLJ 8/05; VOYA 8/05)

782 Orgel, Doris. *Daniel, Half Human: And the Good Nazi* (7–12). 2004, Simon & Schuster $17.95 (0-689-85747-0). 304pp. Daniel and Armin, best friends in Germany in the early 1930s, both admire Hitler, but their friendship is tested when Daniel learns that he is half-Jewish. (Rev: BL 9/15/04; SLJ 12/04)

783 Patneaude, David. *Thin Wood Walls* (6–10). 2004, Houghton $16.00 (0-618-34290-7). 240pp. In this poignant tale set against the backdrop of an America reeling from the Japanese attack on Pearl Harbor, Joe Hanada and his Japanese American family feel the rising tide of prejudice and are eventually sent to an internment camp in California. (Rev: BL 9/15/04; SLJ 10/04; VOYA 12/04)

784 Paulsen, Gary. *The Quilt* (5–8). 2004, Random LB $17.99 (0-385-90886-5). 96pp. Based on events from the author's life, this gentle story, set against the backdrop of World War II, chronicles a young boy's extended stay with his grandmother in Minnesota while his father is fighting in Europe. (Rev: BL 5/15/04; SLJ 5/04)

785 Salisbury, Graham. *Eyes of the Emperor* (7–10). 2005, Random LB $17.99 (0-385-90874-1). 240pp. Sixteen-year-old Eddie Okubo, a Japanese American from Hawaii, lies about his age to join the U.S. Army but is subjected to suspicion and harassment after the Japanese attack Pearl Harbor only weeks later. (Rev: BCCB 9/05; BL 5/15/05*; HB 7–8/05; SLJ 9/05; VOYA 8/05)

786 Say, Allen. *Music for Alice* (4–7). Illus. 2004, Houghton $17.00 (0-618-31118-1). 32pp. Based on a real story, this is the moving portrait of a Japanese American couple who make the best of the challenges forced upon them during World War II. (Rev: BL 2/1/04; HB 5–6/04; SLJ 4/04)

787 Weston, Elise. *The Coastwatcher* (5–8). 2005, Peachtree $14.95 (1-56145-350-1). 160pp. Vacationing on the South Carolina coast with his family in 1943, 11-year-old Hugh sees some signs that Germans are nearby and is determined to convince the doubting adults that he is right. (Rev: BL 11/1/05; SLJ 3/06)

788 Wilson, John. *Four Steps to Death* (7–9). 2005, Kids Can $16.95 (1-55337-704-4); paper $6.95 (1-55337-705-2). 207pp. The horrors of war are plain in this story of the Battle of Stalingrad in 1942, featuring 17-year-old Vasily, a Russian defending his soil; 18-year-old Conrad, a committed German tank officer; and 8-year-old Sergei, who is simply trying to survive. (Rev: SLJ 2/06; VOYA 2/06)

KOREAN, VIETNAM, AND OTHER WARS

789 Couloumbis, Audrey. *Summer's End* (7–10). 2005, Penguin $16.99 (0-399-23555-8). 192pp. Grace finds solace at her grandmother's farm after her brother burns his draft card and sparks a family feud in this thought-provoking novel set during the Vietnam War. (Rev: BL 7/05*; SLJ 6/05)

790 Dorros, Arthur. *Under the Sun* (6–9). 2004, Abrams $16.95 (0-8109-4933-4). 224pp. Thirteen-year-old Ehmet and his mother flee war-torn Sarajevo in search of refuge in Croatia; after soldiers kill his mother, the boy struggles on alone until he reaches a multiethnic orphan community. (Rev: BL 9/15/04; SLJ 12/04; VOYA 12/04)

791 Hughes, Dean. *Search and Destroy* (7–10). 2006, Simon & Schuster $16.95 (0-689-87023-X). 224pp. Rick Ward, who joined the army during the Vietnam War to escape his home life, returns from a tour of duty unable to adjust to normal life. (Rev: BL 2/1/06; SLJ 1/06; VOYA 2/06)

792 Sherlock, Patti. *Letters from Wolfie* (6–9). 2004, Penguin $16.99 (0-670-03694-3). 240pp. In a moment of patriotic fervor, 13-year-old Mark lends his beloved dog Wolfie to the U.S. Army for use in its scout program in Vietnam; Mark's struggles to get his dog back play out against the backdrop of family disagreements about the war. (Rev: BL 7/04; SLJ 6/04; VOYA 8/04)

793 Woodworth, Chris. *Georgie's Moon* (5–8). 2006, Farrar $16.00 (0-374-33306-8). 176pp. Seventh-grader Georgie Collins lives her life waiting for her father to return from Vietnam, and is unable to accept his death at first. (Rev: BL 3/1/06; SLJ 4/06)

Horror Stories and the Supernatural

794 Anderson, M. T. *The Game of Sunken Places* (5–8). 2004, Scholastic $16.95 (0-439-41660-4). 272pp. Brian and Gregory, both 13, find themselves embroiled in a dangerous and suspenseful game during a stay at the spooky mansion of Gregory's eccentric Uncle Max. (Rev: BL 4/15/04*; SLJ 9/04; VOYA 6/04)

795 Anderson, M. T. *Whales on Stilts!* (5–7). 2005, Harcourt $15.00 (0-15-205340-9). 192pp. Twelve-year-old Lily Gefelty enlists the help of two friends to foil a plan to take over the world using an army of mind-controlled whales on stilts; a fast-paced adventure full of tongue-in-cheek fun. (Rev: BL 2/15/05*; SLJ 5/05)

796 Avi. *The Book Without Words* (5–8). 2005, Hyperion $15.99 (0-7868-0829-2). 208pp. Young Sybil searches for a book that reveals the magic of alchemy in this spooky and complex story set in medieval England. (Rev: BL 3/15/05; SLJ 5/05)

797 Bode, N. E. *The Nobodies* (5–8). 2005, HarperCollins LB $16.89 (0-06-055739-7). 304pp. In this sequel to *The Anybodies* (2004), Fern and Howard are at a sinister camp for shape-shifting Anybodies. (Rev: BL 6/1–15/05; SLJ 7/05)

798 Bradman, Tony. *Voodoo Child* (4–7). Series: Tales of Terror. 2005, Egmont paper $7.50 (1-4052-1126-1). 88pp. Megan hopes a voodoo doll will get rid of her father's girlfriend. Other scary titles in this series are *Deadly Game* and *Final Cut* (both 2005). (Rev: SLJ 6/05)

799 Bruchac, Joseph. *Whisper in the Dark* (5–8). 2005, HarperCollins $15.99 (0-06-058087-9). 192pp. A frightening Native American legend seems to be coming true for 13-year-old Maddie, descended from a Narragansett chief. (Rev: BL 9/1/05; SLJ 8/05)

800 Byng, Georgia. *Molly Moon Stops the World* (5–8). 2004, HarperCollins LB $17.89 (0-06-051413-2). 384pp. Molly Moon, a girl of unusual hypnotic powers, is dispatched to California to foil a power-mad hypnotist called Primo Cell. (Rev: BL 5/1/04; SLJ 5/04)

801 Cabot, Meg. *Twilight* (7–10). Series: The Mediator. 2005, HarperCollins LB $16.89 (0-06-072468-4). 241pp. Suze, deeply in love with a ghost named Jesse, faces a real dilemma when she discovers a way to give Jesse back his life that would mean losing him as a boyfriend; the sixth installment in the series. (Rev: SLJ 2/05)

802 Cary, Kate. *Bloodline* (7–10). 2005, Penguin $16.99 (1-59514-012-3). 336pp. When Quincey Harker takes John Shaw's sister, Lily, to Transylvania to be his bride, John and his fiancée Mary realize they must save Lily from a terrible fate. (Rev: BL 9/1/05; SLJ 9/05)

803 Connor, Gina. *Dead on Town Line* (8–11). 2005, Dial $15.99 (0-8037-3021-7). 144pp. In free-verse poems, Cassie reveals the circumstances of her own murder and her relationship with other ghosts. (Rev: BL 7/05; SLJ 7/05; VOYA 6/05)

804 Delaney, Joseph. *The Last Apprentice: Revenge of the Witch* (5–8). 2005, Greenwillow LB $15.89 (0-06-076619-0). 336pp. A scary story in which young Tom, seventh son of a seventh son, takes on the job of spook and must protect the people from ghouls, boggarts, and beasties. (Rev: BL 8/05*; SLJ 11/05)

805 de Lint, Charles. *The Blue Girl* (8–11). 2004, Penguin $17.99 (0-670-05924-2). 384pp. Imogene, determined to turn over a new leaf at her new high school, strikes up an alliance with loner Maxine and meets the ghost of a former pupil, foreshadowing a struggle between an evil underworld and an inhospitable reality. (Rev: BL 11/15/04; SLJ 11/04; VOYA 12/04)

806 Dunkle, Clare B. *By These Ten Bones* (6–9). 2005, Holt $16.95 (0-8050-7496-1). 240pp. Maddie, the weaver's daughter in a medieval Scottish village, finds herself drawn to a mysterious young wood carver who has newly arrived in her town only to discover that he is in fact a werewolf. (Rev: BCCB 5/05; BL 5/1/05; SLJ 6/05; VOYA 6/05)

807 Falcone, L. M. *Walking with the Dead* (5–8). 2005, Kids Can $16.95 (1-55337-708-7). 196pp. Alex finds himself entangled in the world of Greek mythology when a mummy in his father's museum awakens to take care of some unfinished business in the underworld. (Rev: BL 3/15/05; SLJ 6/05)

808 Gonick, Larry. *Attack of the Smart Pies* (4–7). 2005, Cricket $15.95 (0-8126-2740-7). 185pp. This complex novel with graphic elements blends fantasy, horror, mystery, and humor in the story of Emma, a 12-year-old orphan who flees from her threatening foster father and finds herself in Kokonino County, land of the New Muses. (Rev: SLJ 6/05)

809 Graff, Serena. *Blackwell's Island* (4–7). 2005, Delacorte LB $16.99 (0-385-90901-2). 192pp. In early-20th-century New York, Alex and his younger sister Anna face lunatics, criminals, and ghouls. (Rev: BL 6/1–15/05; SLJ 7/05)

810 Horowitz, Anthony. *Raven's Gate* (5–8). Series: Gatekeepers. 2005, Scholastic $17.95 (0-439-67995-8). 256pp. Faced with a choice between jail and life in a remote Yorkshire village, 14-year-old Matt chooses the latter, unaware that he's about to enter a world of frightening evil. (Rev: BL 7/05*; SLJ 7/05; VOYA 10/05)

811 Ibbotson, Eva. *The Haunting of Granite Falls* (3–7). 2004, Dutton $15.99 (0-525-47192-8). 176pp. A Scottish castle imported to Texas brings many unexpected problems for the new owner and his daughter Helen. (Rev: BL 5/1/04; HB 7–8/04)

812 Keehn, Sally M. *Gnat Stokes and the Foggy Bottom Swamp Queen* (5–8). 2005, Putnam $16.99 (0-399-24287-2). 160pp. This fantasy, set in the Appalachian mountains, features a 12-year-old girl named Gnat who faces swamp creatures and spells in her quest to rescue Goodlow Pryce. (Rev: BL 3/1/05; SLJ 4/05)

813 Kehret, Peg. *Ghost's Grave* (5–8). 2005, Dutton $16.99 (0-525-46162-0). 192pp. Josh expects to be bored when he stays in his aunt's old house, but the ghost of a coal miner who died in 1903 livens things up. (Rev: BL 5/15/05; SLJ 10/05)

814 Kessler, Liz. *The Tail of Emily Windsnap* (4–7). 2004, Candlewick $15.99 (0-7636-2483-7). 224pp. Twelve-year-old Emily Windsnap, who turns into a mermaid when she gets into the water, learns the truth about her parents. (Rev: BL 5/1/04; SLJ 6/04; VOYA 6/04)

815 Koontz, Dean. *Life Expectancy* (8–12). 2004, Bantam $27.00 (0-553-80414-6). 401pp. Jimmy is stalked by a mad clown from the moment of his birth in this novel that spoofs cinematic and literary conventions. (Rev: BL 11/1/04)

816 Langrish, Katherine. *Troll Fell* (5–7). 2004, HarperCollins $15.99 (0-06-058304-5). 272pp. Sent to live with his evil twin uncles after his father's death, 12-year-old Peer Ulfsson seeks a way to foil their plan to sell children to the trolls. (Rev: BL 4/15/04*; SLJ 7/04; VOYA 6/04)

817 Lynch, Chris. *The Gravedigger's Cottage* (6–9). 2004, HarperCollins LB $16.89 (0-06-623941-9). 208pp. In this psychological thriller, 14-year-old Sylvia McLuckie experiences a series of mysterious pet deaths and observes alarming changes in her father's personality after the family moves to a seaside house known by the locals as the Gravedigger's Cottage. (Rev: BCCB 6/04; BL 5/1/04; HB 7–8/04; SLJ 7/04; VOYA 6/04)

818 Myracle, Lauren. *Rhymes with Witches* (8–11). 2005, Abrams $16.95 (0-8109-5859-7). 208pp. Invited to join a super-popular clique at her high school, Jane is at first flattered but soon discovers that she's involved in something sinister. (Rev: BCCB 5/05; BL 3/15/05; SLJ 4/05)

819 Noyes, Deborah. *Gothic! Ten Original Dark Tales* (7–10). 2005, Candlewick $15.99 (0-7636-2243-5). 256pp. Ten Gothic tales by contemporary authors embody the dark fantasy and the fairy tale aspects of the genre as well as offering supernatural horror plus humor. (Rev: BL 10/15/04; SLJ 1/05)

820 Potter, Ellen. *Olivia Kidney and the Exit Academy* (4–7). Series: Olivia Kidney. 2005, Putnam $15.99 (0-399-24162-0). 256pp. After her brother's death, Olivia and her father move into a creepy apartment building where, she discovers, people go to rehearse their deaths. (Rev: BL 3/15/05; SLJ 5/05)

821 Pratchett, Terry. *Johnny and the Dead* (5–8). Series: Johnny Maxwell. 2006, HarperCollins LB $16.89 (0-06-054189-X). 224pp. In the funny second volume of this trilogy, ghosts of the "post-senior citizens" buried in a local cemetery ask the title character to help block plans to bulldoze their final resting place. (Rev: BL 12/15/05; HB 1–2/06; SLJ 12/05; VOYA 2/06)

822 Rees, Celia. *The Soul Taker* (5–8). 2004, Hodder paper $7.95 (0-340-87817-7). 152pp. Lewis, overweight and lacking confidence, finds himself in thrall to a sinister toy maker. (Rev: BL 1/1–15/04)

823 Reiss, Kathryn. *Sweet Miss Honeywell's Revenge* (4–7). 2004, Harcourt $17.00 (0-15-216574-6). 288pp. A haunted dollhouse, a parallel story about the original owner of the antique, and the problems of blended family life are intertwined in this story about 12-year-old Zibby Thorne. (Rev: BL 5/1/04; SLJ 8/04)

824 Richardson, E. E. *Devil's Footsteps* (8–11). 2005, Delacorte LB $17.99 (0-385-90279-4). 128pp. Still troubled by his brother's disappearance at the hands of the Dark Man five years earlier, 15-year-old Bryan meets two other teens struggling with the effects of similar attacks. (Rev: BCCB 10/05; BL 5/1/05; SLJ 1/06)

825 Sage, Angie. *Book One: Magyk* (5–8). 2005, HarperCollins LB $18.89 (0-06-057732-0). 576pp. A fantasy of magic, spells, and evil forces, focusing on young Jenna, who was raised by Septimus Heap's family and who now must flee the evil Supreme Custodian. (Rev: BL 3/15/05; SLJ 4/05)

826 Sierra, Judy. *The Gruesome Guide to World Monsters* (5–8). 2005, Candlewick $17.99 (0-7636-1727-X). 64pp. A wonderfully ghoulish field guide to more than 60 monsters from world folklore, complete with Gruesomeness Ratings and Survival Tips if appropriate. (Rev: BL 9/15/05*; SLJ 9/05)

827 Sleator, William. *The Boy Who Couldn't Die* (7–10). 2004, Abrams $16.95 (0-8109-4824-9). 176pp. After his best friend dies in a plane crash, 16-year-old Ken visits a voodoo princess and has his soul removed to keep him safe — with consequences he at first enjoys but later comes to rue. (Rev: BCCB 4/04; SLJ 4/04; VOYA 6/04)

828 Stahler, David. *A Gathering of Shades* (7–10). 2005, HarperCollins LB $16.89 (0-06-052295-X). 304pp. Sixteen-year-old Aidan, who moves to rural Vermont with his mother after his father's death, discovers that his grandmother is secretly feeding ghosts with a mixture of her own blood and spring water. (Rev: BCCB 5/05; BL 5/1/05; SLJ 8/05)

829 Stine, R. L. *The Taste of Night* (6–12). Series: Dangerous Girls. 2004, HarperCollins LB $15.89 (0-06-059617-1). 240pp. Livvy, who has chosen life as a vampire, tries to bring her twin sister Destiny over to the dark side, while her twin works with equal intensity to return Livvy to human form as their father works to rid the town of vampires. (Rev: BL 9/1/04; SLJ 8/04)

830 Stoker, Bram. *Dracula* (7–12). Adapted by Gary Reed. Series: Puffin Graphics. 2006, Puffin paper $9.99 (0-14-240572-8). 176pp. A compelling graphic novel version of the famous vampire story. (Rev: SLJ 3/06)

831 Westerfeld, Scott. *The Secret Hour* (6–10). Series: Midnighters. 2004, HarperCollins LB $16.89 (0-06-051952-5). 297pp. In this exciting first volume, 15-year-old Jessica Day discovers that — like several others — she has special abilities to battle supernatural creatures. (Rev: SLJ 6/04; VOYA 4/04)

832 Westerfeld, Scott. *Touching Darkness* (6–10). Illus. Series: Midnighters. 2005, HarperCollins LB $16.89 (0-06-051955-X). 330pp. In volume two of the Midnighters series, five teens born at the stroke of midnight learn about the hidden past of their Oklahoma hometown and a frightening conspiracy that threatens them all. (Rev: SLJ 3/05)

833 Yee, Paul. *The Bone Collector's Son* (6–9). 2005, Marshall Cavendish $15.95 (0-7614-5242-7). 144pp. In early 20th-century Vancouver, Bing is ashamed of his father's occupation as shipper of bones back to China for burial in this novel that interweaves the real and supernatural worlds. (Rev:

BCCB 11/05; BL 12/1/05; HB 11–12/05; VOYA 12/05)

834 Yep, Laurence. *Tiger's Blood* (4–7). Series: Tiger's Apprentice. 2005, HarperCollins LB $16.89 (0-06-001017-7). 240pp. Tom Lee, the Chinese American boy introduced in *The Tiger's Apprentice*, enlists the aid of three friends to keep the precious phoenix egg from falling into the hands of evildoers. (Rev: BL 1/1–15/05; SLJ 2/05)

Humor

835 Acampora, Paul. *Defining Dulcie* (7–10). 2006, Dial $16.99 (0-8037-3046-2). 176pp. Dulcie may only be 16 but she knows her own mind, and when her mother moves her to California following her janitor father's death, Dulcie drives home to Connecticut and lives with her janitor grandfather. (Rev: BL 4/1/06*; SLJ 4/06*; VOYA 4/06)

836 Ardagh, Philip. *Terrible Times* (4–7). 2003, Holt $12.95 (0-8050-7156-3). 160pp. Young Eddie Dickens sails for America and encounters all sorts of zany situations in this last installment in the trilogy set in Victorian England. (Rev: BL 2/1/04; SLJ 12/03)

837 Asamiya, Kia. *Batman: Child of Dreams* (7–12). Ed. by Max Allan Collins. Illus. 2003, DC Comics $24.95 (1-563-89906-X). In this Japanese spin-off from the Batman legend, rendered in the unique *manga* style, the Dark Knight fights a Japanese enemy who is pushing a drug that supposedly grants the realization of all dreams. (Rev: BL 2/1/04)

838 Bradley, Alex. *24 Girls in 7 Days* (8–11). 2005, Dutton $15.99 (0-525-47369-6). 272pp. Dateless only two weeks before the senior prom, Jack is desperate, so desperate that two of his friends run a personal ad in the school paper in an effort to get Jack a date. (Rev: BL 1/1–15/05; SLJ 3/05; VOYA 2/05)

839 Brockmeier, Kevin. *Grooves: A Kind of Mystery* (4–7). 2006, HarperCollins LB $16.89 (0-06-073692-5). 208pp. In this funny mystery with science fiction overtones, unprepossessing 7th-grader Dwayne Ruggles finds out that the sounds coming from his blue jeans are really cries for help from imprisoned factory workers. (Rev: BL 2/1/06; SLJ 3/06)

840 Burnham, Niki. *Royally Jacked* (8–10). 2004, Simon & Schuster paper $5.99 (0-689-86668-2). 208pp. Valerie, a 15-year-old product of divorce accompanies her father to live in a castle in Europe in this lively, humorous story. (Rev: BL 3/1/04; SLJ 2/04)

841 Burnham, Niki. *Spin Control* (8–10). 2005, Simon & Schuster paper $5.99 (0-689-86669-0). 245pp. Valerie is desperately unhappy when she's forced to leave Schwerinborg and her prince boyfriend and return to Virginia, but a reunion with an old boyfriend soon eases her pain in this sequel to *Royally Jacked* (2004). (Rev: SLJ 2/05)

842 Cabot, Meg. *Princess in Pink* (7–10). Series: Princess Diaries. 2004, HarperCollins $15.99 (0-06-009610-1). In this, the fifth volume of the Princess Diaries series, Mia celebrates her 15th birthday and her pregnant mom is about to give birth. (Rev: BL 4/15/04; SLJ 8/04)

843 Cabot, Meg. *Princess in Training* (7–10). 2005, HarperCollins $16.99 (0-06-009613-6). 288pp. Princess Mia's current worries range from English and geometry, running for student council president, and her college boyfriend's expectations, to her new baby brother and the ecology of the Bay of Genovia. (Rev: BL 8/05; SLJ 6/05; VOYA 8/05)

844 Danko, Dan, and Tom Mason. *Operation Squish!* (5–8). Series: Sidekicks. 2003, Little, Brown $10.95 (0-316-16847-5); paper $4.99 (0-316-16846-7). 106pp. A parody of the comic book superhero genre, featuring superheroes with odd attributes such as Pumpkin Pete, who has the powers of a pumpkin. The book is illustrated, but is not a graphic novel. (Rev: SLJ 3/04)

845 Dent, Grace. *LBD: Live and Fabulous!* (7–10). 2005, Penguin $15.99 (0-399-24188-4). 288pp. In this engaging sequel to *LBD: It's a Girl Thing*, Les Bambinos Dangereuses Fleur, Ronnie, and Claude land free tickets to a big musical festival. (Rev: BL 3/1/05; HB 3–4/05; SLJ 3/05)

846 Dunbar, Fiona. *The Truth Cookie* (4–7). 2005, Scholastic $15.99 (0-439-74022-3). 224pp. Twelve-year-old Lulu's campaign to keep her father from marrying a supermodel gets an unexpected boost when Lulu discovers a recipe for Truth Cookies in this entertaining novel set in London. (Rev: BL 11/15/05; SLJ 12/05)

847 Ehrenhaft, Daniel. *Tell It to Naomi* (7–12). 2004, Random LB $9.99 (0-385-73129-9). 208pp. In a convoluted scheme to win the heart of his secret crush, 15-year-old Dave Rosen covertly pens a high school advice column called "Dear Naomi." (Rev: BL 9/15/04; SLJ 8/04; VOYA 8/04)

848 Ehrenhaft, Daniel. *10 Things to Do Before I Die* (8–12). 2004, Random LB $17.99 (0-385-73007-1). 224pp. Sixteen-year-old Ted Burger believes he is dying and sets out to achieve the goals his friends had urged him to experience — losing his virginity, telling the truth, robbing a bank, and more. (Rev: BL 11/1/04; SLJ 11/04)

849 Guarente, G. A. *Hook, Line and Sinker* (7–9). 2005, Penguin paper $7.99 (1-59514-011-5). 208pp. A humorous and appealing light story in which 15-year-old Fiona buys a fish every time she splits with a boyfriend, names it for the latest ex, and adds it to

her aquarium. (Rev: BCCB 7–8/05; BL 6/1–15/05; SLJ 8/05)

850 Harlen, Jonathan. *The Cockroach War* (5–7). 2004, Allen & Unwin paper $7.95 (1-74114-168-0). 204pp. When the Judges tire of their obnoxious neighbors, they consider moving, but young Toby and Emma Judge devise a plan to unleash an army of electronically controlled cockroaches to drive the unwanted neighbors away. (Rev: BL 8/04)

851 Hautman, Pete. *Godless* (7–10). 2004, Simon & Schuster $15.95 (0-689-86278-4). 208pp. Rebelling against his devoutly Catholic father, 16-year-old Jason Block and his best friend Shin create a religion of their own with the town's water tower as the deity. (Rev: BL 6/1–15/04*; HB 7–8/04; SLJ 8/04; VOYA 10/04)

852 Ives, David. *Scrib* (6–9). 2005, HarperCollins LB $16.89 (0-06-059842-5). 208pp. His spelling and grammar may leave a lot to be desired, but 16-year-old Billy Christmas enjoys an adventure-filled life as he travels the Old West writing and delivering letters. (Rev: BCCB 4/05; BL 3/1/05; SLJ 2/05; VOYA 6/05)

853 Juby, Susan. *Miss Smithers* (7–12). 2004, HarperCollins LB $16.89 (0-06-051547-3). 336pp. Told through journal articles and a zine, this is the story of Alice of *Alice, I Think* (2003) and how she enters a beauty contest in spite of her mother's opposition. (Rev: BL 5/1/04; HB 7–8/04; SLJ 10/04)

854 Limb, Sue. *Girl, (Nearly) 16: Absolute Torture* (7–10). 2005, Delacorte LB $17.99 (0-385-90245-X). 224pp. In this appealing sequel to *Girl, 15, Charming But Insane*, Jess Jordan is taken on a two-week trip to visit her long-absent father just as her romance with Fred is beginning to intensify. (Rev: BL 10/1/05; SLJ 12/05; VOYA 10/05)

855 Lowry, Brigid. *Follow the Blue* (8–12). 2004, Holiday $16.95 (0-8234-1827-8). 205pp. A delightful novel from Australia about 15-year-old Bec, who, with her two younger siblings, is left in the care of a dowdy housekeeper while her parents are away. (Rev: BL 5/1/04*; HB 7–8/04; SLJ 5/04)

856 Maguire, Gregory. *One Final Firecracker* (4–7). Series: The Hamlet Chronicles. 2005, Clarion $17.00 (0-618-27480-4). 226pp. In the final pun-filled installment in the series, the rival Tattletales and Copycats must cooperate to defend the class and the soon-to-be-wed Miss Earth from myriad threats. (Rev: SLJ 5/05)

857 Maxwell, Katie. *They Wear What Under Their Kilts?* (8–11). 2004, Dorchester paper $5.99 (0-8439-5258-X). 208pp. Emily Williams, the 16-year-old American introduced in the riotous *The Year My Life Went Down the Loo*, is off to a Scottish sheep farm on a month-long work-study program. (Rev: BL 1/1–15/04)

858 Mlynowski, Sarah. *Bras and Broomsticks* (6–9). 2005, Delacorte LB $17.99 (0-385-90218-2). 304pp. Starved for attention and troubled by her father's plans to remarry, 14-year-old Rachel Weinstein asks for help from her younger sister Miri, who's just learned she's a witch. (Rev: BL 1/1–15/05; SLJ 1/05)

859 Montgomery, Claire, and Monte Montgomery. *Hubert Invents the Wheel* (4–7). 2005, Walker $16.95 (0-8027-8990-0). 184pp. Hubert, a struggling 15-year-old inventor in ancient Sumeria, finally finds success when he invents the wheel, but things quickly spin out of control. (Rev: SLJ 11/05)

860 Naylor, Phyllis Reynolds. *Including Alice* (6–9). 2004, Simon & Schuster $15.95 (0-689-82637-0). 288pp. Alice has trouble adjusting to life with her new stepmother as well as the usual problems of a sophomore. (Rev: HB 7–8/04; SLJ 5/04; VOYA 8/04)

861 Pratchett, Terry. *Going Postal* (8–12). Series: Discworld. 2004, HarperCollins $24.95 (0-06-001313-3). 377pp. In this humorous and inventive 29th Discworld novel, career criminal Moist von Lipwig escapes hanging by accepting the job of postmaster for Ankh-Morpork, a job he intends to leave far behind as soon as he can. (Rev: BL 9/1/04; SLJ 2/05)

862 Rennison, Louise. *Away Laughing on a Fast Camel: Even More Confessions of Georgia Nicolson* (7–10). 2004, HarperCollins $15.99 (0-06-058934-5). 288pp. Georgia finds that her interest in Robby the Sex God fades fast when he goes off to New Zealand. (Rev: BL 9/1/04; SLJ 11/04; VOYA 10/04)

863 Rennison, Louise. *Then He Ate My Boy Entrancers: More Mad, Marvy Confessions of Georgia Nicolson* (7–10). 2005, HarperCollins $15.99 (0-06-058937-X). 320pp. In her sixth volume of diaries, Georgia travels to and critiques the United States as well as cataloging her usual problems at home with friends, boyfriends, siblings, and cats. (Rev: BL 8/05; SLJ 8/05; VOYA 10/05)

864 Sheldon, Dyan. *Sophie Pitt-Turnbull Discovers America* (7–10). 2005, Candlewick $15.99 (0-7636-2740-2). 192pp. Privileged English teenager Sophie is totally unprepared for what awaits her when she spends the summer in Brooklyn. (Rev: BCCB 5/05; BL 4/1/05; SLJ 6/05)

865 Shipton, Paul. *The Pig Scrolls* (6–9). 2005, Candlewick $15.99 (0-7636-2702-X). 288pp. Shipton turns ancient Greek history and mythology on its ear to create this rollicking tale of Gryllus, who is transformed into a talking pig by Circe and goes on to save the world. (Rev: BL 10/15/05; SLJ 12/05)

866 Shusterman, Neal. *The Schwa Was Here* (6–9). 2004, Penguin $15.99 (0-525-47182-0). 240pp. The virtual invisibility of 8th-grader Calvin Schwa proves profitable for newfound friend Anthony Bonano, who takes wagers on how much his new pal can get away with. (Rev: BL 12/1/04; SLJ 10/04; VOYA 10/04)

867 Smith, Greg Leitich. *Tofu and T. Rex* (5–8). 2005, Little, Brown $15.99 (0-316-77722-6). 162pp. Cousins Freddie, a militant vegan, and Hans-Peter, who sometimes slices meat at his grandfather's deli, clash when both enroll at Chicago's prestigious Peshtigo School. (Rev: SLJ 9/05)

868 Snicket, Lemony. *The Penultimate Peril* (5–8). Series: A Series of Unfortunate Events. 2005, HarperCollins $15.89 (0-06-029643-7). 360pp. In the next-to-last volume of the popular series, the Baudelaire orphans seek respite from their earlier adventures and meet up with many previous characters at the mysterious Hotel Denouement. (Rev: BL 12/1/05)

869 Spearman, Andy. *Barry, Boyhound* (4–7). 2005, Knopf LB $17.99 (0-375-93264-X). 240pp. Barry, a fairly ordinary human boy, is transformed overnight into a boyhound, and while he still looks like a boy, he now thinks more like a dog. (Rev: BL 12/1/05; SLJ 9/05)

870 Whytock, Cherry. *My Saucy Stuffed Ravioli: The Life of Angelica Cookson Potts* (6–9). Illus. 2006, Simon & Schuster $14.95 (0-689-86550-3). 176pp. Angelica Cookson Potts, the food-loving English teen who appeared in *My Cup Runneth Over* (2003) and *My Scrumptious Scottish Dumplings* (2004), is back; this time she's in Italy with family and friends and dreaming about her classmate Sydney. (Rev: BL 12/1/05; SLJ 1/06; VOYA 2/06)

871 Whytock, Cherry. *My Scrumptious Scottish Dumplings: The Life of Angelica Cookson Potts* (6–9). 2004, Simon & Schuster $14.95 (0-689-86549-X). 176pp. In this rollicking sequel to *My Cup Runneth Over* (2003), poor privileged — and unsylphlike — Angel finds herself barred from the Harrods' food halls after her Scottish-born father stages a protest against the quality of the big store's haggis. (Rev: BL 1/1–15/05; SLJ 1/05)

872 Wilkins, Rose. *So Super Stylish* (7–11). 2006, Dial $16.99 (0-8037-3064-0). 288pp. Privileged Octavia Clairbrook-Cleve, who transferred to the local school in *So Super Starry* (2004), is adjusting well to her new environment until her nemesis India Withers turns up, researching the school for her role in a movie. (Rev: BL 2/15/06; SLJ 3/06; VOYA 4/06)

873 Wood, Maryrose. *Sex Kittens and Horn Dawgs Fall in Love* (7–10). 2006, Delacorte LB $17.99 (0-385-90296-4). 192pp. To get closer to Matthew, the object of her affection, 14-year-old Felicia suggests that the two of them work together on a science fair project investigating the workings of love's "X-factor." (Rev: BL 11/15/05; SLJ 2/06)

874 Yee, Lisa. *Stanford Wong Flunks Big-Time* (4–7). 2005, Scholastic $16.99 (0-439-62247-6). 256pp. In this rollicking sequel to *Millicent Minn, Girl Genius*, Stanford Wong is upset when his parents hire Millicent, his arch-nemesis, to tutor him in English. (Rev: BL 11/15/05; SLJ 12/05)

Mysteries, Thrillers, and Spy Stories

875 Abrahams, Peter. *Down the Rabbit Hole* (7–10). Series: Echo Falls. 2005, HarperCollins LB $16.89 (0-06-073702-6). 384pp. Thirteen-year-old Ingrid Levin-Hill takes a page from her idol Sherlock Holmes and sets out to track down the murderer of an eccentric townswoman. (Rev: BCCB 4/05; BL 5/1/05*; SLJ 5/05; VOYA 6/05)

876 Allison, Jennifer. *Gilda Joyce: Psychic Investigator* (5–7). 2005, Dutton $10.99 (0-525-47375-0). 336pp. Thirteen-year-old Gilda Joyce and a new friend, Juliet, look into the suicide of Juliet's aunt in this richly layered mystery. (Rev: BL 5/1/05*; SLJ 7/05*)

877 Alphin, Elaine Marie. *The Perfect Shot* (8–12). 2005, Carolrhoda LB $16.95 (1-57505-862-6). 360pp. Brian, a high school basketball star, learns important lessons about justice, racial prejudice, and civic responsibility when his girlfriend's father is charged with the murder of his wife and two daughters and an African American teammate is arrested on trumped-up charges. (Rev: SLJ 10/05*; VOYA 12/05)

878 Altman, Steven-Elliot, et al. *The Irregulars: . . . In the Service of Sherlock Holmes* (7–12). Illus. 2005, Dark Horse paper $12.95 (1-59307-303-8). 128pp. In this suspenseful graphic novel, Holmes assigns the Baker Street Irregulars to find out who's responsible for a murder for which Dr. Watson has been charged. (Rev: BL 5/1/05)

879 Balliett, Blue. *Chasing Vermeer* (5–8). 2004, Scholastic $16.95 (0-439-37294-1). 272pp. Petra and Calder, brainy 12-year-old classmates at the University of Chicago Lab School, join forces to find out what happened to a missing Vermeer painting. (Rev: BL 4/1/04*; HB 7–8/04; SLJ 7/04)

880 Bateman, Colin. *Bring Me the Head of Oliver Plunkett* (4–7). 2005, Delacorte LB $17.99 (0-385-90269-7). 272pp. In this zany sequel to *Running with the Reservoir Pups* (2004), set in Belfast, Northern Ireland, 12-year-old Eddie deals with school, young romance, some loony adults, and a missing preserved head of a martyr. (Rev: BL 10/15/05; SLJ 11/05)

881 Bone, Ian. *Sleep Rough Tonight* (8–12). 2005, Dutton $16.99 (0-525-47373-4). 276pp. Set in Australia, this is a harrowing story about Alex, who lacks self-confidence, and his submission to a bullying older boy who takes him on an urban survival trip. (Rev: BCCB 5/05; BL 4/15/05; SLJ 5/05; VOYA 4/05)

882 Broach, Elise. *Shakespeare's Secret* (6–9). 2005, Holt $16.95 (0-8050-7387-6). 256pp. Hero, a sixth-grade misfit named for a character in a Shakespeare play, embarks on a search for a diamond with links to the Elizabethan era. (Rev: BCCB 6/05; BL 5/1/05; SLJ 6/05; VOYA 8/05)

883 Burns, Laura J., and Melinda Metz. *The Case of the Prank That Stank* (5–8). Series: Wright and Wong. 2005, Penguin $9.99 (1-59514-014-X). 192pp. Agatha Wong is a lively extrovert, while Orville — who has Asperger's syndrome — longs for peace and tranquility, but the two are close friends and together investigate a mystery. (Rev: BL 5/1/05)

884 Butcher, A. J. *Spy High: Mission One* (7–10). 2004, Little, Brown $15.95 (0-316-73759-3); paper $6.99 (0-316-73760-7). 224pp. This thriller is set in the year 2060 and deals with a group of students at a school known as Spy High who are training to become secret agents. (Rev: BL 5/1/04; SLJ 7/04)

885 Butler, Dori Hillestad. *Do You Know the Monkey Man?* (5–7). 2005, Peachtree $14.95 (1-56145-340-4). 224pp. After a psychic says that her twin sister — believed drowned 10 years before — is not dead at all, 13-year-old Samantha sets off with a friend to investigate. (Rev: BL 5/1/05; SLJ 6/05)

886 Comino, Sandra. *The Little Blue House* (4–7). 2003, Douglas & McIntyre $15.95 (0-88899-504-0). 155pp. Young Cintia and her friend Bruno investigate why an abandoned house in their small town in Argentina turns blue for one day each year in this suspenseful novel that contains some violence. (Rev: BL 2/15/04)

887 Conly, Jane Leslie. *In the Night, on Lanvale Street* (6–8). 2005, Holt $16.95 (0-8050-7464-3). 250pp. When their next-door neighbor is murdered, 13-year-old Charlie and her younger brother are swept up in a mystery that envelops the whole community. (Rev: SLJ 6/05)

888 Cree, Ronald. *Desert Blood 10pm/9c* (8–11). 2006, Simon & Schuster paper $7.99 (1-4169-1156-1). 320pp. It's not clear to Gus Gonzalez why TV star Nicolas Hernandez adopted him, and the mystery deepens as he starts to receive threats and friends begin to disappear. (Rev: BL 2/15/06; SLJ 4/06)

889 Dale, Anna. *Dawn Undercover* (4–7). 2005, Bloomsbury $16.95 (1-58234-657-7). 350pp. Although she longs to have others notice her, 11-year-old Dawn Buckle discovers that her virtual invisibility makes her an ideal spy for the S.H.H. (Strictly Hush-Hush) agency. (Rev: BL 10/15/05; SLJ 12/05)

890 DeFelice, Cynthia. *The Missing Manatee* (5–8). 2005, Farrar $16.00 (0-374-31257-5). 192pp. Skeet Waters sets out to solve the mystery of a murdered manatee he finds near his Florida home. (Rev: BL 3/1/05; SLJ 6/05)

891 Eden, Alexandra. *Holy Smoke: A Bones and Duchess Mystery* (5–7). 2004, Alien A. Knoll $16.00 (1-888310-46-4). 112pp. Ex-cop Bones Fatzinger and Verity Buscador, a 12-year-old girl with Asperger's syndrome, work together to track down the person responsible for setting fire to a local church. (Rev: BL 5/1/04)

892 Erickson, John R. *Discovery at Flint Springs* (5–8). 2004, Viking $16.99 (0-670-05946-3). 192pp. In 1927, 14-year-old Riley and his younger brother Coy join in an exciting search for archaeological sites on their Texas ranch. (Rev: BL 2/1/05; SLJ 12/04)

893 Fardell, John. *The 7 Professors of the Far North* (5–8). Illus. 2005, Penguin $14.99 (0-399-24381-X). 224pp. Three plucky British children are on a mission to rescue six elderly scientists — and the human race — and they have only three days to get to the island fortress in the middle of the Arctic Ocean. (Rev: BL 1/1–15/06; SLJ 12/05)

894 Frels, Merry Hassell. *Simmering Secrets of Weeping Mary* (4–7). 2005, Longhorn Creek paper $9.95 (0-9714358-9-8). 120pp. Twelve-year-old Duty (short for Deuteronomy) Devilrow investigates the death of her cousin Nehemiah and the mystery of her own heritage. (Rev: BL 5/1/05)

895 Gold, Maya. *Harriet the Spy, Double Agent* (4–7). Series: Harriet the Spy. 2005, Delacorte LB $17.99 (0-385-90294-8). 160pp. Harriet the Spy is back, spying on her mysterious new classmate Annie in this installment by Gold. (Rev: BL 9/1/05; SLJ 1/06)

896 Golden, Christopher, and Rick Hautala. *Throat Culture* (8–11). Series: Body of Evidence. 2005, Simon & Schuster paper $5.99 (0-689-86527-9). 247pp. College sophomore Jenna Blake investigates the mysterious illness that has stricken her father's new bride. (Rev: BL 5/1/05; SLJ 7/05)

897 Grant, Vicki. *Quid Pro Quo* (7–10). 2005, Orca $16.95 (1-55143-394-X); paper $7.95 (1-55143-370-2). 168pp. When his mother — newly graduated from law school — suddenly disappears, 13-year-old Cyril Floyd MacIntyre tries to unravel the mystery surrounding her disappearance. (Rev: SLJ 6/05)

898 Gross, Philip. *Turn to Stone* (7–10). 2005, Dial $16.99 (0-8037-3005-5). 224pp. Nick, a 16-year-old runaway, and Swan, a street performer who specializes in posing as a statue, are selected to join a special school for immobilists, but they soon realize

that the school harbors some dark secrets. (Rev: BCCB 3/05; BL 4/15/05; SLJ 8/05; VOYA 4/05)

899 Grossman, David, and Beotsi Rozenberg. *Duel* (4–7). 2004, Bloomsbury $15.95 (1-58234-930-4). 112pp. In 1966 Jerusalem, 12-year-old David turns detective to find out what happened to the valuable painting his best friend, a 70-year-old man, is accused of stealing. (Rev: BL 9/1/04; SLJ 8/04)

900 Hartinger, Brent. *The Last Chance Texaco* (6–10). 2004, HarperCollins LB $16.89 (0-06-050913-9). 240pp. When authorities threaten to close down a group foster home for troubled teens because they suspect one of its residents is responsible for a series of car fires, 15-year-old Lucy Pitt decides to track down the real culprit. (Rev: BCCB 3/04; BL 1/1–15/04; SLJ 3/04; VOYA 2/04)

901 Horowitz, Anthony. *Alex Rider: The Gadgets* (5–8). 2006, Philomel $15.99 (0-399-24486-7). 44pp. A look at all the gadgets used in the first five Alex Rider mysteries — including such wonders as a radio mouth brace, exploding ear stud, and pizza delivery assassin kit — with diagrams and details of how they were used. (Rev: BL 4/1/06; SLJ 4/06)

902 Horowitz, Anthony. *Eagle Strike* (7–12). 2004, Putnam $17.99 (0-399-23979-0). Alex Rider, the hero of many adventures, recognizes a famous Russian assassin while Alex is vacationing in France, and a new thriller begins. (Rev: BL 5/1/04; SLJ 3/04; VOYA 4/04)

903 Horowitz, Anthony. *Scorpia* (8–11). Series: Alex Rider Adventure. 2005, Penguin $17.99 (0-399-24151-5). 320pp. Teenage spy Alex Rider infiltrates a terrorist organization called Scorpia. (Rev: BL 2/1/05; SLJ 3/05; VOYA 4/05)

904 Horowitz, Anthony. *South by Southeast: A Diamond Brothers Mystery* (4–7). Series: Diamond Brothers. 2005, Philomel $16.99 (0-399-24155-8); paper $5.99 (0-14-240374-1). 148pp. Hapless private eye Tim Diamond and his brother Nick find themselves drawn into a labyrinthine mystery after a visit from a stranger. (Rev: BL 12/1/05; SLJ 12/05)

905 Horowitz, Anthony. *Three of Diamonds* (5–8). 2005, Philomel $16.99 (0-399-24157-4). 240pp. Tim and Nick succeed in solving crimes despite Tim's blunderings in these three fast-paced and entertaining mystery stories full of wordplay. (Rev: BL 5/15/05; SLJ 5/05)

906 Johnson, Henry, and Paul Hoppe. *Travis and Freddy's Adventures in Vegas* (5–8). 2006, Dutton $15.99 (0-525-47646-6). 176pp. A lighthearted, fast-paced adventure in which preteens Travis and Freddy head to Las Vegas to win enough money to save Travis's home; there they win big but soon find they have the mob at their heels. (Rev: BL 2/15/06; SLJ 4/06)

907 Karbo, Karen. *Minerva Clark Gets a Clue* (6–9). 2005, Bloomsbury $16.95 (1-58234-677-1). 224pp.

An electric shock changes 7th-grader Minerva from a self-conscious but humorous worrier into a self-confident solver of mysteries. (Rev: BL 9/15/05; SLJ 10/05)

908 Keene, Carolyn. *Where's Nancy?* (4–7). Series: Nancy Drew Super Mystery. 2005, Simon & Schuster paper $4.99 (0-4169-0034-9). 176pp. Nancy herself is missing in this first installment of a new series. (Rev: BL 5/1/05)

909 Lachtman, Ofelia Dumas. *Looking for La Única* (6–9). 2004, Arte Publico paper $9.95 (1-55885-412-6). 192pp. In the summer before her senior year at high school, Monica gets swept into a series of adventures after a treasured guitar disappears from a shop owned by family friends in this sequel to *The Summer of El Pintor* (2001). (Rev: BL 1/1–15/05)

910 Lawrence, Caroline. *The Assassins of Rome* (5–8). Series: Roman Mysteries. 2003, Millbrook LB $22.90 (0-7613-2605-7). 163pp. In this fast-paced historical thriller, Flavia Gemina and her friends Nubia, Lupus, and Jonathan travel to Rome in an attempt to foil an assassination attempt. (Rev: BL 1/1–15/04; SLJ 1/04; VOYA 2/04)

911 Machado, Ana Maria. *From Another World* (4–7). 2005, Douglas & McIntyre $15.95 (0-88899-597-0). 128pp. Spending a night in an outbuilding of an old farmhouse, Mariano and his three friends meet the ghost of a 19th-century slave girl and promise to help in this story set in Brazil. (Rev: BL 5/1/05; SLJ 6/05)

912 Madison, Bennett. *Lulu Dark Can See Through Walls* (7–10). 2005, Penguin $9.99 (1-59514-010-7). 256pp. Lulu Dark, a junior at an exclusive high school, turns detective after the theft of her purse leads to a case of stolen identity in this lighthearted mystery. (Rev: BCCB 6/05; BL 5/1/05; SLJ 6/05; VOYA 8/05)

913 Marks, Graham. *Zoo* (8–11). 2005, Bloomsbury paper $8.95 (1-58234-991-6). 272pp. A complex and suspenseful adventure story in which 17-year-old Cam escapes from kidnappers only to find that he has a mysterious chip in his arm and his parents may have been involved in his capture. (Rev: BL 9/15/05; SLJ 10/05; VOYA 8/05)

914 Mitchell, Marianne. *Firebug* (5–8). 2004, Boyds Mills $16.95 (1-59078-170-8). 164pp. Twelve-year-old Haley investigates a suspicious fire at her Uncle Jake's Arizona ranch. (Rev: BL 3/15/04; SLJ 2/04)

915 Moloney, James. *Black Taxi* (8–11). 2005, HarperCollins LB $16.89 (0-06-055938-1). 272pp. When her grandfather is sent to jail for six months, 16-year-old Rosie Sinclair is appointed caretaker of his eye-catching black Mercedes; she enlists the help of her friends — one an attractive young man — when she starts getting threatening phone calls. (Rev: BCCB 5/05; BL 3/1/05; SLJ 3/05; VOYA 8/05)

916 Oliver, Andrew. *If Photos Could Talk* (4–7). Series: A Sam and Stephanie Mystery. 2005, Adams-Pomeroy paper $12.95 (0-9661009-6-4). 259pp. Twelve-year-olds Sam and Stephanie investigate the disappearance of an elderly man in their small Wisconsin town in this well-plotted novel. (Rev: SLJ 1/06)

917 Pascal, Francine. *Fearless FBI: Kill Game* (8–11). Series: Fearless FBI. 2005, Simon & Schuster paper $7.99 (0-689-87821-4). 240pp. Despite her unreliability, the FBI invites intrepid Gaia — of the earlier Fearless series — to try their boot camp training program. (Rev: BL 8/05; SLJ 6/05)

918 Penn, Audrey. *Mystery at Blackbeard's Cove* (5–8). 2004, Tanglewood $14.95 (0-9749303-1-8). 360pp. The death of Mrs. McNemmish, a descendant of Blackbeard the pirate, sets in motion a series of adventures for four young residents of Okracoke Island. (Rev: BL 1/1–15/05)

919 Rabb, M. E. *The Chocolate Lover* (7–10). Series: Missing Persons. 2004, Penguin paper $5.99 (0-14-250042-9). 192pp. Teen orphans Samantha and Sophie Shattenberg are able to connect art stolen during the Holocaust with its missing owner. Another mystery adventure with these girls is *The Rose Queen* (2004). (Rev: BL 5/1/04; SLJ 5/04)

920 Richards, Justin. *Shadow Beast* (5–8). Series: Invisible Detectives. 2005, Putnam $10.99 (0-399-24314-3). 192pp. Parallel stories feature exciting adventures in the sewers of 1930s London and contemporary beasts that may be related. (Rev: BL 8/05; SLJ 10/05)

921 Roberts, Willo Davis. *The One Left Behind* (4–7). 2006, Simon & Schuster $16.95 (0-689-85075-1). 144pp. Mandy, an 11-year-old mourning her dead twin sister, is accidentally left home alone for the weekend and pluckily investigates when there's a break-in downstairs. (Rev: BL 4/1/06)

922 Rose, Malcolm. *Framed!* (7–10). Series: Traces. 2005, Kingfisher paper $5.95 (0-7534-5829-2). 232pp. In this futuristic mystery novel, 16-year-old Luke Harding, newly graduated from forensics training, is assigned to investigate the murder of a classmate. (Rev: BL 5/1/05; SLJ 7/05)

923 Rose, Malcolm. *Lost Bullet* (6–9). Series: Traces. 2005, Kingfisher paper $5.95 (0-7534-5830-6). 212pp. In a futuristic London, forensic investigator Luke Harding and his robotic sidekick try to find out who's responsible for the murder of a doctor and find themselves facing a cult. (Rev: BL 6/1–15/05; SLJ 7/05)

924 Schmidt, Gary. *First Boy* (7–10). 2005, Holt $16.95 (0-8050-7859-2). 208pp. With the help of kind neighbors, 14-year-old Cooper hopes to be able to live alone on his grandparents' farm, but questions about his missing parents seem linked to politics and the presidential elections. (Rev: BCCB

2/06; BL 9/15/05; HB 9–10/05; SLJ 10/05; VOYA 4/06)

925 Scrimger, Richard. *From Charlie's Point of View* (7–10). 2005, Dutton $10.99 (0-525-47374-2). 288pp. Fourteen-year-old Charlie is blind, but best friend Bernadette acts as his eyes, and together they set out to prove that Charlie's dad had nothing to do with a series of neighborhood ATM thefts. (Rev: BCCB 9/05; BL 5/1/05; SLJ 8/05)

926 Simmons, Michael. *Finding Lubchenko* (7–10). 2005, Penguin paper $16.99 (1-59514-021-2). 281pp. Evan Macalister, a 16-year-old slacker, steals high-value computer equipment from his father's business and sells it for spending cash, but he faces a moral dilemma when he discovers evidence that could clear his father of murder charges on a laptop he's stolen; a funny, offbeat novel. (Rev: BCCB 7–8/05; SLJ 6/05; VOYA 12/04)

927 Smith, Roland. *Jack's Run* (5–8). 2005, Hyperion $15.99 (0-7868-5592-4). 288pp. Last seen adapting to being in the witness protection program in *Zach's Lie* (2001), Jack and Joanne are now in danger after Joanne has blown their cover in this fast-paced, suspenseful story. (Rev: BL 8/05; SLJ 12/05; VOYA 10/05)

928 Sorrells, Walter. *Club Dread* (8–11). 2006, Dutton paper $10.99 (0-525-47618-0). 256pp. In this thrilling, action-packed sequel to *Fake I.D.* (2004), 16-year-old Chass has formed a band in San Francisco but witnesses a murder and becomes drawn into the investigation. (Rev: BL 1/1–15/06; SLJ 3/06)

929 Sorrells, Walter. *Fake I.D.* (8–11). 2005, Dutton $10.99 (0-525-47514-1). 256pp. On the run with her mother since she was a baby, 16-year-old Chastity Pureheart has only six days to find out what happened to her mother or face placement in foster care. (Rev: BL 5/1/05*; SLJ 6/05)

930 Spradlin, Michael P. *Live and Let Shop* (6–9). 2005, HarperCollins LB $16.89 (0-06-059408-X). 224pp. To avoid a term in juvenile detention, 15-year-old Rachel Buchanan is sent to Blackthorn Academy, a Pennsylvania boarding school that's not at all what it seems to be. (Rev: BCCB 3/05; BL 3/1/05; SLJ 3/05)

931 Springer, Nancy. *The Case of the Missing Marquess: An Enola Holmes Mystery* (5–8). 2006, Philomel paper $10.99 (0-399-24304-6). 224pp. Enola Holmes, the much younger sister of Sherlock and Mycroft, embarks on a search for her mother, who disappears on Enola's 14th birthday. (Rev: BL 12/1/05*; SLJ 2/06*)

932 Sternberg, Libby. *Finding the Forger* (6–9). 2004, Bancroft $19.95 (1-890862-32-0); paper $16.95 (1-890862-37-1). 192pp. Bianca Balducci, 15-year-old wannabe detective, gets caught up in the investigation of an art forgery at the local muse-

um while at the same time worrying in humorous first-person narrative about friends, boyfriends, and family. (Rev: BL 2/1/05; SLJ 4/05; VOYA 8/05)

933 Thurlo, David, and Aimée Thurlo. *The Spirit Line* (6–10). 2004, Viking $15.99 (0-670-03645-5). 224pp. Fifteen-year-old Crystal Manyfeathers solves a theft and in so doing begins to question her Navajo beliefs. (Rev: BL 5/1/04; SLJ 6/04; VOYA 6/04)

934 Trout, Richard E. *Czar of Alaska: The Cross of Charlemagne* (5–8). Series: MacGregor Family Adventure. 2005, Pelican $15.95 (1-58980-328-0). 248pp. In volume four of the series, the five MacGregors travel to Alaska to assess the environmental impact of drilling for oil and become entangled with ecoterrorists and priests seeking an ancient cross. (Rev: SLJ 12/05)

935 Updale, Eleanor. *Montmorency and the Assassins* (7–10). 2006, Scholastic $16.99 (0-439-68343-2). 416pp. Montmorency and Lord George Selwyn-Fox, plus some teen helpers, investigate bomb-planting anarchists in this Victorian mystery that ranges from London to Florence to New Jersey. (Rev: BL 3/15/06; VOYA 2/06)

936 Updale, Eleanor. *Montmorency on the Rocks: Doctor, Aristocrat, Murderer?* (6–9). 2005, Scholastic $16.95 (0-439-60676-4). 368pp. Montmorency, recovering from opium addiction, and sidekicks Lord George Fox-Selwyn and Dr. Fawcett must unravel a London bomb plot and mysterious deaths in Scotland. (Rev: BL 5/15/05; SLJ 4/05)

937 Van Draanen, Wendelin. *Sammy Keyes and the Dead Giveaway* (5–8). 2005, Knopf LB $17.99 (0-375-92350-0). 304pp. Seventh-grade sleuth Sammy tackles personal problems — should she make a confession that would exonerate her archenemy? — and community ones as she investigates abuse of eminent domain. (Rev: BL 9/1/05; SLJ 11/05)

938 Weatherly, Lee. *Missing Abby* (6–9). 2004, Random LB $17.99 (0-385-75053-6). 208pp. When she realizes she was the last person to see Abby before she disappeared, 13-year-old Emma struggles to find out what happened and in the process learns quite a bit about role-playing games and some important lessons about herself. (Rev: BL 1/1–15/05; SLJ 12/04)

939 Weltman, June. *Mystery of the Missing Candlestick* (5–8). 2004, Mayhaven $23.95 (1-878044-98-2). 216pp. Miranda, 17, and her friends Leila and Rebecca join forces to solve the mystery of a valuable antique candlestick that has been stolen from Rebecca's grandfather. (Rev: BL 5/1/04)

940 Westerfeld, Scott. *So Yesterday* (7–12). 2004, Penguin $16.99 (1-59514-000-X). 240pp. Two teenagers who help big companies identify coming trends in the consumer marketplace find themselves caught up in a mystery when their boss disappears. (Rev: BL 9/15/04; SLJ 10/04; VOYA 10/04)

941 White, Ruth. *The Search for Belle Prater* (4–7). 2005, Farrar $16.00 (0-374-30853-5). 176pp. In this sequel to *Belle Prater's Boy,* 13-year-old Woodrow and his cousin Gypsy continue to search for Woodrow's missing mother against the backdrop of mid-1950s segregation. (Rev: BL 2/15/05*; SLJ 4/05)

Romances

942 Bennett, Cherie, and Jeff Gottesfeld. *A Heart Divided* (6–10). 2004, Delacorte LB $17.99 (0-385-90039-2). 320pp. Tensions over their Tennessee high school's symbol — the Confederate flag — intrude into the romance between new student Kate from New Jersey and Jack, whose family is proud of its southern tradition. (Rev: BCCB 5/04; BL 1/1–15/04; SLJ 5/04; VOYA 4/04)

943 Coffey, Jan. *Tropical Kiss* (8–11). 2005, HarperCollins paper $5.99 (0-06-076003-6). 338pp. Morgan's summer on Aruba with her father turns out to be more fun than she expected, but the discovery that her dad may be in trouble casts a cloud over her enjoyment of a new friend and boyfriend. (Rev: SLJ 8/05)

944 Davidson, Dana. *Jason and Kyra* (7–12). 2004, Hyperion $16.99 (0-7868-1851-4). 336pp. Brainiac Kyra and basketball star Jason come from sharply different African American worlds, but when they're teamed up by for a research project, the two find they have much more in common than they could have imagined. (Rev: BL 6/1–15/04; SLJ 7/04; VOYA 6/04)

945 Friedman, Aimee. *A Novel Idea* (7–11). 2006, Simon & Schuster paper $5.99 (1-416-90785-8). 234pp. A light romantic comedy in which Norah's focus switches from her college resume to the attractive James. (Rev: SLJ 2/06)

946 Jacobs, Holly. *Pickup Lines* (8–12). 2005, Avalon $21.95 (0-8034-9704-0). 192pp. A comic romance in which teacher Mary Rosenthal and businessman Ethan Westbrook vie to win a pickup truck. (Rev: BL 4/1/05)

947 Johnson, Kathleen Jeffrie. *Dumb Love* (8–11). 2005, Roaring Brook $16.95 (1-59643-062-1). 160pp. A funny romance in which high school student Carlotta aspires both to win the heart of Pete and to write a novel. (Rev: BL 9/15/05; SLJ 11/05)

948 Kantor, Melissa. *Confessions of a Not It Girl* (7–12). 2004, Hyperion $15.99 (0-7868-1837-9). 256pp. Jan Miller has high hopes that love will come her way during her senior year in high school, but it's soon obvious that it won't be easy in this

entertaining, true-to-life romantic comedy. (Rev: BL 6/1–15/04; HB 7–8/04; SLJ 4/04; VOYA 6/04)

949 Malcolm, Jahnna N. *Mixed Messages* (6–9). Series: Love Letters. 2005, Simon & Schuster paper $5.99 (0-689-87222-4). 204pp. Jade, a high school senior, has had a crush on Zephyr Strauss for years, but when she finally writes him a love letter, it ends up in the wrong hands. (Rev: SLJ 1/05)

950 Malcolm, Jahnna N. *Perfect Strangers* (6–9). Series: Love Letters. 2005, Simon & Schuster paper $5.99 (0-689-87221-6). 217pp. There's no love lost between high school juniors Madison and Jeremy, who are running against each other for class president, until they're secretly paired up in their school's Heart-2-Heart e-mail-pal program. (Rev: SLJ 1/05)

951 Petersen, P. J., and Ivy Ruckman. *Rob and Sara.com* (7–11). 2004, Dell $15.95 (0-385-73164-7). 224pp. Rob and Sara conduct an online relationship that is always tinged with the question of whether each is really the person claimed. (Rev: BL 10/15/04; SLJ 12/04)

952 Shaw, Tucker. *The Hookup Artist* (8–12). 2006, HarperCollins LB $16.89 (0-06-075621-7). 200pp. Teens Cate and her best friend Lucas both fall for Derek when he arrives in town. (Rev: SLJ 2/06; VOYA 2/06)

Science Fiction

953 Bechard, Margaret. *Spacer and Rat* (6–9). 2005, Roaring Brook $16.95 (1-59643-058-3). 192pp. Space resident Jack revises his views about Earth "rats" when he meets Kit and her highly intelligent bot Waldo in this novel full of references to classic works and entertaining jargon. (Rev: BL 9/1/05; SLJ 11/05; VOYA 10/05)

954 Card, Orson Scott. *First Meetings: In the Enderverse* (6–12). 2003, Tor $17.95 (0-765-30873-8). 208pp. Contains the novella "Ender's Game," first published in 1977, and three other stories, one previously unpublished. (Rev: SLJ 1/04)

955 Colfer, Eoin. *The Supernaturalist* (6–9). 2004, Hyperion $16.95 (0-7868-5148-1). 272pp. In this action-packed futuristic novel, 14-year-old Cosmo Hill escapes from an orphanage and is befriended by an unlikely trio known as the Supernaturalists, who draft the teen to join them in their campaign against the invisible but deadly Parasites. (Rev: BCCB 9/04; BL 8/04; SLJ 7/04; VOYA 8/04)

956 Collins, Paul. *The Skyborn* (8–11). 2005, Tor $17.95 (0-765-31273-5). 272pp. Accepted by the Earthborn after his ship *Colony* crashed on post-holocaust Earth, 14-year-old Welkin, born a Skyborn, learns the Earthborn are in danger from the

Skyborn; a sequel to *The Earthborn* (2003). (Rev: BL 2/15/06)

957 Craig, Joe. *Jimmy Coates: Assassin?* (4–7). 2005, HarperCollins LB $16.89 (0-06-077264-6). 224pp. Thirty-five percent human and 65 percent technologically engineered assassin, 11-year-old Jimmy Coates faces external dangers and internal struggles, all with action, suspense, and humor. (Rev: BL 5/1/05; SLJ 6/05)

958 DuPrau, Jeanne. *The People of Sparks* (5–7). 2004, Random $15.95 (0-375-82824-9). 352pp. In this sequel to *The City of Ember,* Doon and Lina, plus the 400 people they have led from Ember to the surface of the Earth, seek aid from the people of Sparks. (Rev: BL 4/15/04; HB 7–8/04; SLJ 5/04)

959 Fox, Helen. *Eager* (7–9). 2004, Random $15.95 (0-385-74672-5). 288pp. In this entertaining futuristic novel, the Bell family takes on an experimental robot model to assist their beloved — but failing — robotic butler and discovers that the new addition, named Eager, has some truly amazing abilities. (Rev: BL 6/1–15/04; HB 7–8/04; SLJ 8/04)

960 Gates, Susan. *Dusk* (6–9). 2005, Penguin $16.99 (0-399-24343-7). 169pp. Along with other mutated animals, Dusk — part-girl and part-hawk — escapes from the government lab in which she's been imprisoned. (Rev: BCCB 6/05; SLJ 6/05; VOYA 6/05)

961 Gerrold, David. *Blood and Fire* (8–12). 2004, BenBella paper $14.95 (1-932100-11-3). 232pp. In this story that is a metaphor for the AIDS problem, a starship happens on another one, adrift in space, that contains blood worms, a deadly parasite. (Rev: BL 1/1–15/04)

962 Haddix, Margaret P. *Among the Brave* (4–7). Series: Shadow Children. 2004, Simon & Schuster $15.95 (0-689-85794-2). 240pp. This sequel to *Among the Barons* (2003) features Trey's efforts to rescue Luke and other third-born children. (Rev: BL 5/15/04; SLJ 6/04)

963 Haddix, Margaret P. *Among the Enemy* (5–8). Series: Shadow Children. 2005, Simon & Schuster $15.95 (0-689-85796-9). 224pp. Matthias, one of the third children illegal in his society, is mistakenly welcomed into the Population Police; there he is confused by divided loyalties. (Rev: BL 6/1–15/05; SLJ 6/05)

964 Haddix, Margaret P. *Double Identity* (5–8). 2005, Simon & Schuster $15.95 (0-689-87374-3). 224pp. In this science fiction page-turner, 12-year-old Bethany Cole, left with her aunt after her mother suffers a nervous breakdown, uncovers some shocking family secrets. (Rev: BL 10/1/05; SLJ 11/05; VOYA 10/05)

965 Hayden, Patrick Nielsen, ed. *New Skies: An Anthology of Today's Science Fiction* (7–12). 2003, Tor $19.95 (0-7653-0010-8). 288pp. Short stories that were originally published in science fiction magazines include pieces by Orson Scott Card, Philip K. Dick, and Connie Willis. (Rev: BL 1/1–15/04)

966 Luceno, James. *Dark Lord: The Rise of Darth Vader* (8–12). 2005, Del Rey $25.95 (0-345-47732-4). 336pp. Chronicles the transformation of Anakin Skywalker from disaffected, young Jedi into the ruthless Darth Vader. (Rev: BL 11/15/05)

967 Mackel, Kathy. *Alien in a Bottle* (4–8). 2004, HarperCollins LB $16.89 (0-06-029282-2). 208pp. An entertaining and action-packed novel in which 8th-grader Sean Winger, an aspiring glassblower, mistakes an alien space ship for an ornate glass bottle and becomes swept up in intergalactic intrigue. (Rev: BL 5/1/04; SLJ 4/04)

968 McNaughton, Janet. *The Secret Under My Skin* (6–9). 2005, HarperCollins LB $16.89 (0-06-008990-3). 272pp. In a future dystopia, a young woman seeks to discover what brought the world to environmental disaster and caused scientists to be discredited and sent to concentration camps. (Rev: BCCB 1/05; BL 3/1/05; HB 1–2/05; SLJ 2/05; VOYA 4/05)

969 Mosley, Walter. *47* (7–10). 2005, Little, Brown $16.99 (0-316-11035-3). 232pp. In this compelling blend of folklore, science fiction, and history, a slave named 47 is trained to take on new and important roles by a mysterious stranger who calls himself Tall John. (Rev: BCCB 6/05; BL 4/15/05; HB 7–8/05; SLJ 6/05; VOYA 6/05)

970 Oppel, Kenneth. *Skybreaker* (6–9). 2005, HarperCollins LB $17.89 (0-06-053228-9). 384pp. In this action-packed sequel to *Airborn* (2003), Matt Cruse, now an officer trainee at Airship Academy, races to locate the long-lost *Hyperion* before pirates can loot the ghost ship. (Rev: BCCB 2/06; BL 11/15/05; HB 1–2/06; SLJ 12/05; VOYA 12/05)

971 Pratchett, Terry. *Only You Can Save Mankind* (5–8). 2005, HarperCollins LB $16.89 (0-06-054186-5). 224pp. It's up to Johnny to save the aliens in a new computer game, and the situation forces him to do some thinking about the very nature of war. (Rev: BL 4/15/05*; SLJ 10/05)

972 Reed, Gary. *Mary Shelley's Frankenstein: The Graphic Novel* (7–10). Series: Puffin Graphics. 2005, Penguin paper $9.99 (0-14-240407-1). 176pp. This graphic novel adaptation accurately conveys the dominant themes of the classic. (Rev: BL 3/15/05; SLJ 9/05; VOYA 8/05)

973 Reeve, Philip. *Predator's Gold* (7–10). Series: The Hungry City Chronicles. 2004, Morrow $16.99 (0-06-072193-6). 336pp. In a future world where large cities move about and eat up smaller towns, Tom and Hester seek refuge in Anchorage, hopeful that the small city will make its way to the Dead Continent of America before it is caught and consumed by Arkangel; a sequel to *Mortal Engines* (2003). (Rev: BL 8/04; SLJ 9/04; VOYA 10/04)

974 Skurzynski, Gloria. *The Revolt* (8–12). Series: The Virtual War Chronologs. 2005, Simon & Schuster $16.95 (0-689-84265-1). 247pp. In this action-packed third volume in the series, Corgan flees to Florida to put an end to his battle with Brigand but is soon followed there by his violent enemy. (Rev: SLJ 7/05)

975 Sleator, William. *The Last Universe* (6–9). 2005, Abrams $16.95 (0-8109-5858-9). 176pp. Quantum mechanics plays a key role in the tension in this story of 14-year-old Susan who must care for her 16-year-old, wheelchair-bound brother Gary; they spend a lot of time in a maze that seems to allow travel to other dimensions. (Rev: BCCB 4/05; BL 4/15/05; SLJ 7/05; VOYA 4/05)

976 Stahler, David. *Truesight* (5–7). 2004, Harper-Collins LB $16.89 (0-06-052286-0). 168pp. A race of blind people living in a colony on a distant planet includes one teenager who discovers he can see, and he sees all sorts of flaws in the people of his community. (Rev: SLJ 3/04; VOYA 4/04)

977 Thompson, Kate. *Fourth World* (5–8). Series: Missing Link. 2005, Bloomsbury $16.95 (1-58234-650-X). 320pp. Christie and his older stepbrother Danny go from Ireland to Scotland, where they discover strange developments at Fourth World, the compound where Danny's scientist mother lives and works, in this first volume of a trilogy. (Rev: BL 5/15/05; SLJ 10/05)

978 Valentine, James. *Rule No. 2: Don't Even Think About It* (5–8). Series: Jumpman. 2006, Simon & Schuster $14.95 (0-689-87353-0). 288pp. In their second adventure full of neat gadgets and humorous cultural tidbits, Australian 13-year-olds Jules and Gen are again involved with young people from the far future. (Rev: BL 4/1/06; SLJ 3/06)

979 Waugh, Sylvia. *Who Goes Home?* (4–7). 2004, Delacorte $15.95 (0-385-72965-0). 224pp. On his 13th birthday Jacob receives the sobering news that his father is an alien from the planet Ormingat, and so is Jacob. (Rev: BL 4/15/04; HB 3–4/04; SLJ 6/04)

980 Westerfeld, Scott. *Pretties* (8–11). 2005, Simon & Schuster paper $6.99 (0-689-86539-2). 384pp. In the sequel to *Uglies* (2005), Tally enjoys her transformation into a Pretty and the accompanying hedonistic lifestyle until she is reminded of her underlying purpose and faces real danger. (Rev: BL 9/15/05; SLJ 12/05; VOYA 10/05)

981 White, Andrea. *No Child's Game: Reality TV 2083* (7–10). 2005, HarperCollins LB $16.89 (0-06-055455-X). 336pp. In this chilling look at a future in which television is used to distract the populace

from grim reality, five teens will live or die while reenacting a historic Antarctic expedition for the entertainment of the viewing audience. (Rev: BL 4/15/05; SLJ 7/05)

Sports

982 Baskin, Nora Raleigh. *Basketball (or Something Like It)* (6–9). 2005, HarperCollins LB $16.89 (0-06-059611-2). 176pp. In alternating chapters, three 6th-grade basketball players — and the basketball-loving sister of one team member — tell stories of parental interference or indifference and how these have taken away some of the fun of the game. (Rev: BCCB 3/05; BL 2/1/05; SLJ 2/05; VOYA 6/05)

983 Carter, Alden R. *Love, Football, and Other Contact Sports* (8–11). 2006, Holiday House $16.95 (0-82341-975-4). 261pp. The football team at Argyle West High School is at the center of these entertaining short stories. (Rev: BL 3/15/06*)

984 Corbett, Sue. *Free Baseball* (4–7). 2006, Dutton $15.99 (0-525-47120-0). 152pp. An endearing 11-year-old called Felix, who loves baseball and is annoyed that his mother won't tell him more about his Cuban outfielder father, is thrilled when he gets the chance to be batboy for a minor league Florida team. (Rev: BCCB 2/06; SLJ 2/06; VOYA 4/06)

985 Coy, John. *Crackback* (7–12). 2005, Scholastic $16.99 (0-4B9-69753-6). 206pp. High school football player Miles Manning faces many challenges including difficult relationships with his father and his coach, girl problems, and whether to join his teammates in using steroids. (Rev: SLJ 12/05)

986 Coy, John. *Crackback* (8–11). 2005, Scholastic $16.99 (0-439-69733-6). 208pp. Miles must deal with a new football coach, a domineering father, and friends on steroids in this novel of the troubles of adolescence. (Rev: BL 9/1/05*; VOYA 12/05)

987 Esckilsen, Erik E. *Offsides* (6–10). 2004, Houghton $15.00 (0-618-46284-8). 176pp. Tom Gray, a top-notch soccer player, is proud of his Mohawk heritage and when he moves to a new town where the school's mascot is an Indian, he refuses to play. (Rev: BL 9/1/04; SLJ 1/05; VOYA 12/04)

988 Feinstein, John. *Last Shot: A Final Four Mystery* (6–9). 2005, Knopf LB $18.99 (0-375-93168-6). 256pp. Aspiring journalists Stevie Thomas and Susan Carol Anderson win a free trip to the NCAA Final Four basketball tournament in New Orleans and discover that there's some unsavory action going on behind the scenes; cameo appearances by famous basketball personalities add to the appeal.

(Rev: BCCB 3/05; BL 2/1/05; SLJ 1/05; VOYA 2/05)

989 Fitzgerald, Dawn. *Getting in the Game* (4–7). 2005, Roaring Brook $15.95 (1-59643-044-3). 136pp. In first-person narrative, Joanna Giordano describes her difficult experiences as the only girl on a 7th-grade ice hockey team that doesn't want her, plus her problems with peers, parents, and ailing grandfather. (Rev: BCCB 9/05; BL 3/1/05; SLJ 7/05)

990 Guest, Jacqueline. *Racing Fear* (7–10). Series: SideStreets. 2004, Lorimer paper $4.99 (1-55028-838-5). 158pp. Trent and Adam are best friends and car racing buddies until an accident puts a strain on their friendship; suitable for reluctant readers. (Rev: SLJ 1/05)

991 Harkrader, L. D. *Airball: My Life in Briefs* (4–7). 2005, Roaring Brook $15.95 (1-59643-060-5). 208pp. Kirby's middle school basketball team begins to improve when their coach — whom Kirby secretly believes is his father — insists the boys practice in their underwear. (Rev: BL 9/1/05; SLJ 11/05; VOYA 10/05)

992 Haven, Paul. *Two Hot Dogs with Everything* (4–7). 2006, Random LB $17.99 (0-375-93350-6). 320pp. Danny, 11, follows many superstitious rituals each time the Sluggers play, but his efforts seem to have no effect until he chews some 108-year-old gum that belonged to the team's founder. (Rev: BL 4/1/06)

993 Levy, Elizabeth. *Tackling Dad* (5–8). 2005, HarperCollins LB $16.89 (0-06-000050-3). 144pp. Cassie, 13, has won a place on the football team but her father won't sign the consent form. (Rev: BL 9/1/05; SLJ 8/05)

994 Lupica, Mike. *Heat* (6–9). 2006, Philomel $16.99 (0-399-24301-1). 324pp. Cuban American Michael Arroyo, who has been hiding his father's death to avoid the attention of the social services, finds his Little League pitching career in jeopardy when he can't produce a birth certificate. (Rev: BL 4/1/06*; SLJ 4/06; VOYA 4/06)

995 Lupica, Mike. *Travel Team* (6–8). 2004, Penguin $16.99 (0-399-24150-7). 384pp. Twelve-year-old Danny Walker, cut from the 7th-grade basketball travel team, fights back with a team of his own. (Rev: BL 9/1/04; SLJ 11/04; VOYA 12/04)

996 Nicholson, Lorna Shultz. *Roughing* (5–8). 2005, Lorimer paper $5.50 (1-55028-858-X). 108pp. This story set in a hockey camp in Calgary, Alberta, features Josh, a boy with type 1 diabetes; Peter, a native Canadian; and Peter, a bully who plans to teach Peter a lesson. (Rev: BL 5/15/05; SLJ 9/05)

997 Nishiyama, Yuriko. *Rebound: Volume 1* (5–8). Illus. 2004, TokyoPop paper $9.99 (1-931514-02-

X). 192pp. The first volume in a manga sequel to the Harlem Beat series takes the Johnan High School basketball team to Sapporo, Japan. (Rev: BL 5/15/04)

998 Nitz, Kristin Wolden. *Defending Irene* (5–7). 2004, Peachtree $14.95 (1-56145-309-9). 185pp. When her family moves to Italy for a year, 13-year-old Irene is determined to continue playing soccer, even if it's on the boys' team. (Rev: SLJ 9/04)

999 Roberts, Kristi. *My Thirteenth Season* (5–8). 2005, Holt $15.95 (0-8050-7495-3). 144pp. When Fran, whose mother has recently died, tries to play baseball for the boys' team in her new town, she is in for a world of trouble. (Rev: BL 3/15/05*; SLJ 3/05)

1000 Rottman, S. L. *Slalom* (6–8). 2004, Penguin $16.99 (0-670-05913-7). 256pp. Seventeen-year-old Sandro, raised in the shadow of a posh ski resort by his single mother, is shaken when the handsome Italian skier who is his father turns up and reunites with his mother. (Rev: BL 9/1/04; SLJ 11/04; VOYA 10/04)

1001 Rud, Jeff. *In the Paint* (5–8). 2005, Orca paper $7.95 (1-55143-337-0). 128pp. Matt is glad to make the basketball team but soon finds there are pressures he would prefer to avoid. (Rev: BL 7/05)

1002 Strasser, Todd. *Cut Back* (7–12). Series: Impact Zone. 2004, Simon & Schuster paper $5.99 (0-689-87030-2). 320pp. In this action-packed series installment, 15-year-old Kai faces off against his nemesis, Lucas Frank, in a surfing competition; a sequel is *Take Off* (2004). (Rev: BL 7/04; SLJ 8/04)

1003 Tocher, Timothy. *Chief Sunrise, John McGraw, and Me* (6–9). 2004, Cricket $15.95 (0-8126-2711-3). 160pp. In this appealing baseball tale set in 1919, 15-year-old Hank Cobb escapes from an abusive father, joins forces with a 19-year-old baseball hopeful who claims to be a Seminole, and travels to New York in search of a career playing ball. (Rev: BCCB 7–8/04; BL 5/15/04; SLJ 9/04)

1004 Walters, Eric. *Juice* (6–9). 2005, Orca paper $7.95 (1-5514-3351-6). 112pp. Moose gets caught up in his high school football team's doping scandal in this novel for reluctant readers. (Rev: BL 9/1/05; VOYA 8/05)

1005 Withers, Pam. *Skater Stuntboys* (6–9). Series: Take It to the Xtreme. 2005, Walrus paper $6.95 (1-55285-647-X). 191pp. An action-filled novel about 15-year-olds Jake and Peter, who take jobs as skateboarding stunt doubles on the set of an extreme-sports film and find they're in the middle of a mystery. (Rev: SLJ 11/05)

Short Stories and General Anthologies

1006 Carlson, Lori Marie, ed. *Moccasin Thunder: American Indian Stories for Today* (8–11). 2005, HarperCollins LB $16.89 (0-06-623959-1). 176pp. Ten contemporary short stories feature Native American teens. (Rev: BL 8/05; SLJ 12/05*; VOYA 2/06)

1007 Cart, Michael, ed. *Face: A Journal of Contemporary Voices*, Vol. 3 (8–12). Illus. Series: Rush Hour. 2005, Delacorte LB $12.99 (0-385-90182-8); paper $9.95 (0-385-73032-2). 211pp. Our images of ourselves and others are at the heart of this collection of stories and poems that tackle a wide variety of situations. (Rev: HB 5–6/05; SLJ 7/05)

1008 Crebbin, June, ed. *Horse Tales* (4–7). 2005, Candlewick $18.99 (0-7636-2657-0). 152pp. Diverse short stories about horses, with color illustrations. (Rev: BL 9/1/05; SLJ 8/05)

1009 Davis, Donald. *Mama Learns to Drive and Other Stories: Stories of Love, Humor, and Wisdom* (4–7). 2005, August House $17.95 (0-87483-745-6). 119pp. Brief, slow-paced short stories based on his mother, who grew up in the Smoky Mountains in the 1930s, are mixed with tales about the author's own youth in the 1950s. (Rev: BL 8/05; SLJ 10/05)

1010 Editors of McSweeney's. *Noisy Outlaws, Unfriendly Blobs, and Some Other Things . . .* (4–7). Illus. 2005, McSweeney's $22.00 (1-932416-35-8). 208pp. Kid-friendly stories by well-known authors including Nick Hornby, Neil Gaiman, and Jon Scieskza. (Rev: BL 9/1/05)

1011 Estevis, Anne. *Down Garrapata Road* (6–12). 2003, Arte Publico paper $12.95 (1-55885-397-9). 128pp. In this collection of closely linked short stories, Estevis paints an appealing portrait of life in a small Mexican American community in South Texas during the 1930s and 1940s. (Rev: BL 1/1–15/04)

1012 Howe, James, ed. *13: Thirteen Stories That Capture the Agony and Ecstasy of Being Thirteen* (6–9). 2003, Simon & Schuster $16.95 (0-689-82863-2). 288pp. This collection of short stories by such popular authors as Ann Martin, Alex Sanchez, and Ellen Wittlinger beautifully captures what it means to be 13 years old. (Rev: BL 1/1–15/04; SLJ 10/03; VOYA 12/03)

1013 Jocelyn, Marthe, sel. *Secrets* (5–8). 2005, Tundra paper $8.95 (0-88776-723-0). 175pp. A collection of 12 short stories that reveal the importance of secrets. (Rev: SLJ 2/06)

1014 Kurtz, Jane, ed. *Memories of Sun: Stories of Africa and America* (6–10). 2004, Greenwillow LB $16.89 (0-06-051051-X). 160pp. In this appealing anthology of short stories and poems, contemporary African and African American authors write about their cultures. (Rev: BL 1/1–15/04; HB 1–2/04; SLJ 1/04; VOYA 2/04)

1015 Levithan, David, ed. *Where We Are, What We See: Poems, Stories, Essays, and Art from the Best Young Writers and Artists in America* (8–11). 2005, Scholastic paper $7.99 (0-439-73646-3). 272pp. Winning entries in the Scholastic Art and Writing Awards program. (Rev: BL 9/15/05; SLJ 1/06) [810]

1016 Lubar, David. *Invasion of the Road Weenies and Other Warped and Creepy Tales* (4–7). 2005, Tor $16.95 (0-765-31447-9). 192pp. Entertaining stories about how things don't always work out how you hope or expect; suitable for reluctant readers. (Rev: BL 8/05; SLJ 9/05; VOYA 10/05)

1017 Nix, Garth. *Across the Wall: A Tale of the Abhorsen and Other Stories* (7–10). 2005, HarperCollins LB $17.89 (0-06-074714-5). 320pp. In this collection of short stories, Garth offers an eclectic mix of genres and settings — only the first is related to Abhorsen — suitable for a range of readers. (Rev: BL 6/1–15/05; SLJ 11/05; VOYA 10/05)

1018 November, Sharyn, ed. *Firebirds Rising: An Anthology of Original Science Fiction and Fantasy* (7–10). 2006, Penguin $19.99 (0-14-240549-3). 512pp. Contributors to this anthology of 16 original stories include Tamora Pierce, Charles de Lint, Patricia A. McKillip, Kara Dalkey, and Tanith Lee. (Rev: BL 4/1/06; SLJ 4/06; VOYA 4/06)

1019 Oldfield, Jenny, comp. *The Kingfisher Book of Horse and Pony Stories* (4–7). Illus. 2005, Kingfisher $16.95 (0-7534-5850-0). 127pp. The special relationship between horses and humans is celebrated in this collection of 12 contemporary, fantasy, and historical short stories. (Rev: SLJ 12/05)

1020 Peck, Richard. *Past Perfect, Present Tense* (5–12). 2004, Dial $16.99 (0-8037-2998-7). 192pp. This anthology includes 11 previously published stories and two new ones, with comments on each story's inspiration and tips on writing fiction. (Rev: BL 4/1/04; HB 3–4/04; SLJ 4/04; VOYA 6/04)

1021 Pierce, Meredith Ann. *Waters Luminous and Deep: Shorter Fictions* (7–12). 2004, Viking $16.99 (0-670-03687-0). A stirring collection of fictional stories, long and short, that have water as a connecting link. (Rev: BL 4/15/04; SLJ 4/04)

1022 Pierce, Tamora, and Josepha Sherman, eds. *Young Warriors: Stories of Strength* (7–10). 2005, Random LB $19.99 (0-375-92962-2). 320pp. This collection of 15 short stories recounts the exploits of teenage warriors in such diverse settings as ancient Greece, colonial India, World War II, and the plains of Africa. (Rev: BL 10/1/05; SLJ 10/05; VOYA 10/05)

1023 Reuter, Bjarne. *The Ring of the Slave Prince* (7–12). Trans. by Tiina Nunnally. 2004, Dutton $21.99 (0-525-47146-4). 376pp. Thrilling action scenes abound in this historical adventure set on 17th-century Caribbean plantations and also on the high seas with bloodthirsty pirates. (Rev: BL 2/1/04; SLJ 4/04; VOYA 2/04)

1024 Singer, Marilyn. *Make Me Over: 11 Original Stories About Transforming Ourselves* (7–10). 2005, Dutton $16.99 (0-525-47480-3). 272pp. Teenage transformations and the importance of relationships are themes of these stories by writers including Joseph Bruchac, Margaret Peterson Haddix, and Joyce Sweeney. (Rev: BL 9/15/05; SLJ 2/06)

1025 Soto, Gary. *Help Wanted* (7–10). 2005, Harcourt $17.00 (0-15-205201-1). 224pp. In this collection of ten short stories, Soto explores the dreams and struggles of Mexican American teens living in central California. (Rev: BCCB 5/05; BL 5/1/05; HB 5–6/05; SLJ 5/05)

1026 *Sports Shorts* (4–7). 2005, Darby Creek $15.99 (1-58196-040-9). 128pp. Eight writers contribute "semi-autobiographical" tales about their sporting achievements at school, many humorously revealing failings rather than triumphs. (Rev: BL 9/1/05; SLJ 11/05)

1027 *Twice Told: Original Stories Inspired by Original Artwork* (7–10). Illus. 2006, Dutton $19.99 (0-525-46818-8). 320pp. Nine charcoal drawings by Scott Hunt were provided as inspiration to pairs of popular YA writers; the resulting short stories cover a wide range of styles and themes. (Rev: BL 2/15/06*; SLJ 4/06)

1028 *What a Song Can Do: 12 Riffs on the Power of Music* (8–10). 2004, Random LB $17.99 (0-375-92499-X). 208pp. The power of music to transform young lives is explored in this appealing collection of 12 short stories. (Rev: BL 8/04; SLJ 7/04)

Plays

General and Miscellaneous Collections

1029 Bansavage, Lisa, and L. E. McCullough, eds. *111 Shakespeare Monologues for Teens: The Ultimate Audition Book for Teens Volume V* (7–12). Series: Young Actors. 2003, Smith & Kraus paper $11.95 (1-57525-356-9). 192pp. Monologues ranging from 15 seconds to 2 minutes and chosen for the youthful speakers or topics of interest to young people are arranged in three sections: for female actors, for male actors, and for male or female; an introduction explains Shakespeare's language and rhythms. (Rev: SLJ 7/04) [808.82]

1030 Dabrowski, Kristen. *Teens Speak, Boys Ages 16 to 18: Sixty Original Character Monologues* (7–12). Series: Kids Speak. 2005, Smith & Kraus paper $11.95 (1-57525-415-8). 71pp. A collection of brief, varied monologues for teenage boys from 16 to 18. Also in the series are *Teens Speak, Boys Ages 13 to 15: Sixty Original Character Monologues*, *Teens Speak, Girls Ages 16 to 18: Sixty Original Character Monologues*, and *Teens Speak, Girls Ages 13 to 15: Sixty Original Character Monologues* (all 2005). (Rev: SLJ 7/05) [808.82]

Geographical Regions

Europe

GREAT BRITAIN AND IRELAND

1031 Cover, Arthur Byron. *Macbeth* (6–9). 2005, Penguin paper $9.99 (0-14-240409-8). 176pp. This imaginative graphic-novel adaptation transports Shakespeare's *Macbeth* to a futuristic setting in outer space. (Rev: BL 10/15/05; SLJ 3/06) [741.5]

1032 Coville, Bruce. *William Shakespeare's Hamlet* (4–8). 2004, Dial $16.99 (0-8037-2708-9). 40pp. This masterful prose retelling makes the famous play accessible to young people. (Rev: BL 5/15/04; SLJ 2/04) [822.3]

1033 McKeown, Adam, retel. *Hamlet* (5–8). Series: The Young Reader's Shakespeare. 2003, Sterling $14.95 (1-4027-0003-2). 80pp. In this appealing retelling, McKeown remains true to Shakespeare's plot line and incorporates many of the best-known lines. (Rev: SLJ 2/04) [822.3]

1034 McKeown, Adam, retel. *Macbeth* (5–10). Series: The Young Reader's Shakespeare. 2005, Sterling $14.95 (1-4027-1116-6). 96pp. This conversational prose retelling includes an introduction to the play and incorporates many of the important poetic passages. (Rev: BL 3/1/05; SLJ 5/05) [822.3]

1035 McKeown, Adam, and William Shakespeare. *Romeo and Juliet: Young Reader's Shakespeare* (5–10). 2004, Sterling $14.95 (1-4027-0004-0). 96pp. Faithful to the original, this retelling uses finely crafted prose and interweaves many of the best-known poetic stanzas. (Rev: BL 8/04; SLJ 10/04) [822.3]

United States

1036 Almond, David. *Two Plays* (5–8). 2005, Delacorte LB $14.99 (0-385-90101-1). 240pp. Grief and hope are strong themes in both the dramatization of Almond's successful novel *Skellig* and the shorter *Wild Girl, Wild Boy*. (Rev: BL 10/1/05; HB 1–2/06; SLJ 12/05)

Poetry

General and Miscellaneous Collections

1037 Asher, Sandy, ed. *On Her Way: Stories and Poems About Growing Up Girl* (4–8). 2004, Dutton $17.99 (0-525-47170-7). 224pp. Poems and stories about the difficulties of adolescence will strike a chord for many readers. (Rev: BL 2/15/04; SLJ 3/04) [810.8]

1038 Donegan, Patricia. *Haiku: Asian Arts and Crafts for Creative Kids* (4–8). Illus. 2004, Tuttle $9.95 (0-8048-3501-2). 64pp. Haiku advice and exercises follow an introduction to the verse form. (Rev: BL 3/15/04; SLJ 8/04) [372.6]

1039 Frost, Helen. *Spinning Through the Universe: A Novel in Poems from Room 214* (5–7). 2004, Farrar $16.00 (0-374-37159-8). 112pp. A variety of poetic forms — including haiku, tercelle, sonnet, pantoun, and tanka — are used in these diverse and compelling poems about the lives of a fifth-grade teacher and her students. (Rev: BL 4/1/04; SLJ 4/04) [811]

1040 Grimes, Nikki. *At Jerusalem's Gate: Poems of Easter* (5–8). 2005, Eerdmans $20.00 (0-8028-5183-5). 48pp. More than 20 poems are introduced by thoughtful paragraphs and enhanced by handsome illustrations. (Rev: BL 2/15/05; SLJ 3/05) [232.96]

1041 Grimes, Nikki. *Tai Chi Morning: Snapshots of China* (4–8). 2004, Cricket $15.95 (0-8126-2707-5). 64pp. Grimes's journal in verse describes her impressions on a tour of China. (Rev: BL 3/1/04; SLJ 5/04) [811]

1042 Grimes, Nikki. *What Is Goodbye?* (4–8). 2004, Hyperion $15.99 (0-7868-0778-4). 64pp. A brother and sister mourn the death of their older brother in poems in alternating voices. (Rev: BL 5/1/04; SLJ 6/04) [811]

1043 Haas, Jessie. *Hoofprints: Horse Poems* (8–12). 2004, Greenwillow $15.99 (0-06-053406-0). 224pp. In these sophisticated poems, the author writes about different aspects of the horse, including its prehistoric origins and the first pairing of a horse and rider. (Rev: BL 3/15/04; SLJ 3/04; VOYA 4/04) [811]

1044 Hollander, John, ed. *Animal Poems* (5–7). Series: Poetry for Young People. 2005, Sterling $14.95 (1-4027-0926-9). 48pp. A collection of classic poems (by such poets as Blake, Frost, Melville, and Yeats) accompanied by artwork and explanatory notes. (Rev: BL 4/1/05; SLJ 3/05) [808.81]

1045 Hopkins, Lee Bennett, ed. *Days to Celebrate: A Full Year of Poetry, People, Holidays, History, Fascinating Facts, and More* (4–7). 2005, Greenwillow LB $18.89 (0-06-000766-4). 112pp. A wide-ranging collection organized by month, each introduced by a calendar page that highlights important dates. (Rev: BL 1/1–15/05; SLJ 1/05) [811]

1046 Hopkins, Lee Bennett, ed. *Got Geography!* (4–7). 2006, Greenwillow LB $16.89 (0-06-055602-1). 32pp. Poems celebrate the joys of travel and the maps that guide the way. (Rev: BL 2/1/06) [811]

1047 Janeczko, Paul B., ed. *Blushing: Expressions of Love in Poems and Letters* (8–12). 2004, Scholastic $15.95 (0-439-53056-3). 112pp. All aspects of love — from the first blush of new love to the heartbreak that follows love gone wrong — are covered in this anthology that includes classic and contemporary works. (Rev: BL 1/1–15/04; SLJ 5/04; VOYA 4/04) [821.008]

1048 Janeczko, Paul B. *Worlds Afire* (4–8). 2004, Candlewick $15.99 (0-7636-2235-4). 112pp. This moving book written in verse tells, from many points of view, the story of a tragic circus fire in

1944 that killed 167 people. (Rev: BL 1/1–15/04; HB 5–6/04; SLJ 4/04; VOYA 4/04) [811]

1049 Kennedy, Caroline, ed. *A Family of Poems: My Favorite Poetry for Children* (4–7). 2005, Hyperion $19.95 (0-7868-5111-2). 144pp. This collection of poems for children includes a number of Kennedy family favorites. (Rev: BL 10/15/05; SLJ 12/05*) [811]

1050 Lewis, J. Patrick. *Heroes and She-roes: Poems of Amazing and Everyday Heroes* (4–7). 2005, Dial $16.99 (0-8037-2925-1). 40pp. Helen Keller, Rosa Parks, and Gandhi are among the courageous individuals featured in this collection of poems. (Rev: BL 1/1–15/05; SLJ 3/05) [811]

1051 Lewis, J. Patrick. *Vherses: A Celebration of Outstanding Women* (4–7). 2005, Creative $18.95 (1-56846-185-2). 32pp. The accomplishments of 14 notable and diverse women — including Emily Dickinson, Georgia O'Keeffe, and Venus and Serena Williams — are celebrated in an appealing blend of poetry and art. (Rev: BL 12/15/05) [811]

1052 Little, Jean. *I Gave My Mom a Castle* (4–7). 2004, Orca paper $7.95 (1-55143-253-6). 80pp. Gifts — expected and unexpected, rewarding and trying — are the theme of this diverse collection of prose poems. (Rev: BL 3/1/04; SLJ 4/04) [811]

1053 Lyne, Sandford, ed. *Soft Hay Will Catch You* (3–8). 2004, Simon & Schuster $17.95 (0-689-83460-8). 128pp. Poems by students are grouped by theme and reveal new perspectives on age-old worries and delights. (Rev: BL 3/15/04; SLJ 4/04) [811]

1054 McGough, Roger, ed. *Wicked Poems* (4–8). 2005, Bloomsbury paper $15.00 (0-7475-6195-8). 198pp. Misbehavior of varying degrees is displayed in this varied collection of poems accompanied by cartoons. (Rev: SLJ 1/05) [811]

1055 Mark, Jan, ed. *A Jetblack Sunrise: Poems About War and Conflict* (7–10). 2005, Hodder paper $8.99 (0-340-89379-6). 160pp. This anthology of poems explores not only the barbarity and savagery of war but also the courage, selflessness, and valor that sometimes shine through. (Rev: BL 9/1/05) [808.9]

1056 Morgenstern, Constance. *Waking Day* (4–7). Illus. 2006, North Word $17.95 (1-55971-919-2). 32pp. In a picture book for older readers, Morgenstern melds Impressionist works with lines from her own poetry. (Rev: BL 2/15/06) [811]

1057 Nye, Naomi Shihab. *A Maze Me: Poems for Girls* (8–11). 2005, Greenwillow LB $17.89 (0-06-058190-5). 128pp. In this collection of more than 70 original poems, Nye addresses a broad range of subjects that will resonate with teenage girls. (Rev: BL 1/1–15/05*; SLJ 3/05; VOYA 2/05) [811]

1058 *Once Upon a Poem: Favorite Poems That Tell Stories* (4–7). Illus. 2004, Scholastic $18.95 (0-439-

65108-5). 128pp. This appealing collection of 15 narrative poems includes offerings from Lewis Carroll, Longfellow, C. S. Lewis, Roald Dahl, Edward Lear, and Robert Service. (Rev: BL 1/1–15/05; SLJ 1/05) [811]

1059 Rowden, Justine. *Paint Me a Poem: Poems Inspired by Masterpieces of Art* (4–7). Illus. 2005, Boyds Mills $16.95 (1-59078-289-5). 32pp. Each of the 14 poems in this collection is inspired by a famous painting from the National Gallery of Art. (Rev: BL 11/1/05; SLJ 10/05) [811.54]

1060 Smith, Charles R. *Hoop Kings* (4–7). Illus. 2004, Candlewick $14.99 (0-7636-1423-8). 40pp. This celebration of basketball, presented in a blend of rap-style poetry with eye-catching photographs, focuses on 12 of the biggest stars. (Rev: BL 2/15/04; SLJ 3/04) [811]

1061 Strand, Mark, ed. *100 Great Poems of the Twentieth Century* (8–12). 2005, Norton $24.95 (0-393-05894-8). 256pp. Pulitzer Prize-winning poet Strand offers his selection of the 100 best poems of the 20th century. (Rev: BL 5/15/05) [821]

1062 Vecchione, Patrice, ed. *Revenge and Forgiveness: An Anthology of Poems* (8–12). 2004, Holt $16.95 (0-8050-7376-0). 160pp. This anthology on war, violence, and the search for peace contains poems from many lands and times. (Rev: BL 3/15/04; HB 3–4/04; SLJ 7/04; VOYA 6/04) [808.81]

Geographical Regions

Europe

GREAT BRITAIN AND IRELAND

1063 Dahl, Roald. *Vile Verses* (5–8). Illus. 2005, Viking $25.00 (0-670-06042-9). 192pp. New illustrations adorn the poems in this aptly titled collection. (Rev: BL 11/1/05; SLJ 11/05*) [811]

1064 Maynard, John, ed. *Alfred, Lord Tennyson* (5–8). Series: Poetry for Young People. 2004, Sterling $14.95 (0-8069-6612-2). 48pp. This large-format introduction to Tennyson's works includes an informative profile of the poet, selections accompanied by notes, and rich illustrations. (Rev: BL 2/15/04) [821]

1065 Noyes, Alfred. *The Highwayman* (7–10). Series: Visions in Poetry. 2005, Kids Can $16.95 (1-55337-425-8). 48pp. In this beautifully illustrated Art Deco version of Noyes's immortal poem, the title character is transformed into a motorcycle-riding thief who roams the streets of New York City, while his beloved Bess is now a voluptuous glamour girl. (Rev: BL 5/1/05; SLJ 8/05; VOYA 10/05) [821]

1066 Tennyson, Alfred Lord. *The Lady of Shalott* (5–7). 2005, Kids Can $16.95 (1-55337-874-1). 48pp. The setting of Tennyson's "The Lady of Shalott" is moved from the England of King Arthur to the streets of an early-20th-century city in this beautifully illustrated adaptation. (Rev: BL 10/1/05; SLJ 12/05) [821]

United States

1067 Carlson, Lori, ed. *Red Hot Salsa: Bilingual Poems on Being Young and Latino in the United States* (8–11). 2005, Holt $14.95 (0-8050-7616-6). Poems in Spanish and English voice issues important to teens and the joys and sorrows of straddling two cultures. (Rev: BL 8/05; SLJ 8/05*) [811]

1068 DeDonato, Collete. *City of One: Young Writers Speak to the World* (7–12). 2004, Aunt Lute Books paper $10.95 (1-879960-69-9). 239pp. In this moving collection of poetry from San Francisco-based WritersCorps, scores of young people give voice to their feelings about peace and violence. (Rev: BL 8/04; SLJ 8/04; VOYA 10/04) [810.8]

1069 Hayford, James. *Knee-Deep in Blazing Snow: Growing Up in Vermont* (4–7). 2005, Boyds Mills $17.95 (1-59078-338-7). 64pp. Hayford's simple, quiet poems evoke a simpler country life. (Rev: BL 1/1–15/06; SLJ 11/05) [811]

1070 Hollander, John, ed. *American Poetry* (4–10). Series: Poetry for Young People. 2004, Sterling $14.95 (1-4027-0517-4). 48pp. A colorful celebration of American life, containing 26 poems by well-known poets including Robert Frost, Walt Whitman, Maya Angelou, and Langston Hughes. (Rev: SLJ 8/04) [811]

1071 Hudson, Wade, ed. *Poetry from the Masters: The Pioneers* (6–12). 2003, Just Us Books paper $9.95 (0-940975-96-3). 88pp. Two-page biographical profiles introduce 11 African Americans and their works; among them are Phillis Wheatley, Paul Laurence Dunbar, Countee Cullen, Langston Hughes, and Gwendolyn Brooks. (Rev: SLJ 2/04) [811]

1072 Myers, Walter Dean. *Voices from Harlem: Poems in Many Voices* (7–10). 2004, Holiday House $16.95 (0-8234-1853-7). 96pp. In this appealing collection of 54 poems, modeled on Edgar Lee Masters's *Spoon River Anthology*, Myers speaks in the diverse voices of imagined Harlem

residents from many walks of life. (Rev: BCCB 12/04; BL 11/1/04*; HB 1–2/05; SLJ 12/04; VOYA 2/05) [811]

1073 Nelson, Marilyn. *Fortune's Bones: The Manumission Requiem* (7–12). 2005, Front Street $16.95 (1-932425-12-8). 40pp. Six poems celebrate the life of Fortune, a slave who died in 1798 but continued to serve his master, who rendered his bones and used Fortune's skeleton to teach anatomy. (Rev: BCCB 2/05; BL 11/15/04; HB 1–2/05; SLJ 12/04) [811]

1074 Roessel, David, and Arnold Rampersad, eds. *Langston Hughes* (7–10). 2006, Sterling $14.95 (1-4027-1845-4). 48pp. An illustrated picture-book-format collection of 26 poems with a useful introduction, a biography, and notes. (Rev: BL 2/1/06*) [811]

1075 Rylant, Cynthia. *Boris* (7–10). 2005, Harcourt $16.00 (0-15-205412-X). 80pp. This collection of free-verse poems celebrates the life and times of Boris, a big, gray cat adopted from a humane shelter. (Rev: BCCB 4/05; BL 2/15/05; HB 5–6/05; SLJ 4/05; VOYA 4/05) [811]

1076 Soto, Gary. *A Fire in My Hands*. Rev. ed. (6–9). 2006, Harcourt $16.00 (0-15-205564-9). 96pp. The joys and agonies of everyday life are captured in these poems, half of them new to this edition. (Rev: BL 4/1/06) [811]

Other Regions

1077 Agard, John. *Half-Caste and Other Poems* (4–7). 2005, Hodder $16.99 (0-340-89382-6). 80pp. Guyana-born Agard offers a collection of his saucy, Caribbean-flavored poetry dealing with topics such as tolerance and diversity that young people will recognize. (Rev: BL 10/15/05; SLJ 1/06) [821.9]

1078 Brand, Dionne. *Earth Magic* (4–7). 2006, Kids Can $14.95 (1-55337-706-0). 32pp. In her first collection of poetry for young people, Brand writes about life in Trinidad, the island of her birth. (Rev: BL 4/1/06) [811]

1079 Tadjo, Veronique, ed. *Talking Drums: A Selection of Poems from Africa South of the Sahara* (4–8). 2004, Bloomsbury $15.95 (1-58234-813-8). 96pp. Arranged by theme, these 75 poems — traditional and contemporary — cover a broad range of topics. (Rev: BL 3/1/04; SLJ 4/04; VOYA 4/04) [811]

Folklore and Fairy Tales

General and Miscellaneous

1080 Calhoun, Dia. *The Phoenix Dance* (4–7). 2005, Farrar $17.00 (0-374-35910-5). 272pp. Phoenix Dance, apprentice to the royal shoemaker and subject to emotional extremes, tries to find out what magic compels 12 princesses to wear out their shoes by dancing every night. (Rev: BL 12/15/05; SLJ 11/05; VOYA 10/05)

1081 Dokey, Cameron. *Sunlight and Shadow* (6–10). Series: Once Upon a Time. 2004, Simon & Schuster paper $5.99 (0-689-86999-1). 192pp. Mina — daughter of Pamina, the Queen of the Night, and of Sarastro, the Mage of the Day — falls in love with a prince called Tern and together the two face obstacles in this reworking of "The Magic Flute." (Rev: SLJ 11/04; VOYA 12/04)

1082 MacDonald, Margaret Read. *Three Minute Tales: Stories from Around the World to Tell or Read When Time Is Short* (8–12). 2004, August House $24.95 (0-87483-728-6); paper $17.95 (0-87483-729-4). 160pp. Brief tales that are easy to learn come with notes about sources and tips about effective telling. (Rev: BL 9/15/04; SLJ 10/04) [398.2]

1083 Mutén, Burleigh. *Grandfather Mountain: Stories of Gods and Heroes from Many Cultures* (4–7). Retold by Burleigh Muten. 2004, Barefoot Books $19.99 (1-84148-789-9). 80pp. Strong male protagonists are featured in folktales from England, Greece, Ireland, Japan, Mexico, New Zealand, Nigeria, and the Seneca Indians. (Rev: BL 11/15/04; SLJ 1/05) [398.2]

1084 Norman, Howard. *Between Heaven and Earth: Bird Tales from Around the World* (3–7). 2004, Harcourt $22.00 (0-15-201982-0). 96pp. Five beautifully illustrated bird-themed folktales hail from Africa, Australia, China, Norway, and Sri Lanka. (Rev: BL 11/1/04) [398.2]

1085 Oberman, Sheldon. *Solomon and the Ant* (5–8). 2006, Boyds Mills $19.95 (1-59078-307-7). 168pp. Nearly 50 traditional Jewish stories are arranged chronologically and accompanied by notes and commentary. (Rev: BL 2/1/06; SLJ 3/06) [398.2]

1086 Russell, P. Craig. *The Fairy Tales of Oscar Wilde: The Devoted Friend, The Nightingale and the Rose* (5–8). Illus. 2004, NBM $15.95 (1-56163-391-7). 32pp. Two of Oscar Wilde's fairy tales — "The Devoted Friend" and "The Nightingale and the Rose" — are presented in a rich, picture-book-size graphic novel format. (Rev: BL 8/04; SLJ 11/04) [741.5]

Geographical Regions

Africa

1087 McCall Smith, Alexander. *The Girl Who Married a Lion and Other Tales from Africa* (8–12). 2004, Pantheon $20.00 (0-375-42312-5). 208pp. Traditional tales feature characterful animals and humans. (Rev: BL 11/1/04) [398.2]

Asia and the Middle East

1088 Bedard, Michael, ed. *The Painted Wall and Other Strange Tales* (4–7). 2003, Tundra $16.95 (0-88776-652-8). 120pp. Chinese folktales collected centuries ago are full of action and the supernatural. (Rev: BL 1/1–15/04; SLJ 1/04) [398.2]

1089 Napoli, Donna Jo. *Bound* (7–12). 2004, Simon & Schuster $16.95 (0-689-86175-3). 192pp. In this multilayered and thought-provoking Cinderella tale that draws on traditional Chinese elements, Xing Xing is mistreated by her stepmother and stepsister after the death of the girl's beloved father, but she escapes the cruel foot binding inflicted on her stepsister. (Rev: BL 12/1/04*; SLJ 11/04; VOYA 2/05)

Europe

1090 Andersen, Hans Christian. *Fairy Tales* (8–12). Ed. by Jackie Wullschlager. Trans. by Tuna Nunnally. Illus. 2005, Viking $27.95 (0-670-03377-4). 438pp. A collection of new translations of 30 stories. (Rev: BL 3/15/05)

1091 Krull, Kathleen, ed. *A Pot o' Gold: A Treasury of Irish Stories, Poetry, Folklore and (of Course) Blarney* (4–8). 2004, Hyperion $16.99 (0-7868-0625-7). 192pp. This is a comprehensive collection — including riddles, blessing, and battle cries — with attractive and appropriate illustrations. (Rev: BL 2/15/04; SLJ 3/04) [820.8]

1092 Radunsky, Vladimir. *The Mighty Asparagus* (4–7). Illus. 2004, Harcourt $16.00 (0-15-216743-9). 34pp. In this entertaining version of the Russian folktale "The Enormous Turnip" with eye-catching illustrations full of artistic allusions, a gigantic stalk of asparagus sprouts in the courtyard of an Italian king. (Rev: BL 5/15/04; SLJ 7/04) [398.2]

North America

UNITED STATES

1093 Hamilton, Virginia. *The People Could Fly: The Picture Book* (3–9). 2004, Knopf LB $18.99 (0-375-92405-1). 40pp. A beautifully illustrated picture-book version of the folktale about slaves' dreams in the face of diversity. (Rev: BL 9/15/04; SLJ 4/05*) [398.2]

South and Central America

1094 Kirwan, Anna. *Lady of Palenque: Flower of Bacal, Mesoamerica, C.E. 749* (6–9). Illus. 2004, Scholastic $10.95 (0-439-40971-3). 208pp. In this gripping adventure, ShahnaK'in Yaxchel Pacal, a 13-year-old Maya princess, embarks on a dangerous journey to meet her future husband. (Rev: BL 5/15/04; SLJ 7/04)

Mythology

General and Miscellaneous

1095 Berk, Ari. *The Runes of Elfland* (7–12). 2003, Abrams $25.00 (0-8109-4612-2). 111pp. Brief stories and wonderful art highlighting the rune's significance and associations accompany each of 24 runes. (Rev: SLJ 5/04; VOYA 2/04) [398.2]

1096 Bingham, Ann. *South and Meso-American Mythology A to Z* (6–12). Series: Mythology A to Z. 2004, Facts on File $35.00 (0-8160-4889-4). 142pp. A handsome and thorough guide to the legends and folklore of early civilizations in Central and South America. (Rev: BL 10/1/04; SLJ 2/05) [398.2]

1097 Echlin, Kim. *Inanna: From the Myths of Ancient Sumer* (7–12). 2003, Groundwood $19.95 (0-88899-496-6). The stories of the powerful goddess Inanna and her adventures in love and war, based on 4,000-year-old sources. (Rev: BL 3/1/04; SLJ 3/04; VOYA 12/03) [398.2]

1098 Lynch, Patricia Ann. *Native American Mythology A to Z* (6–12). Series: Mythology A to Z. 2004, Facts on File $35.00 (0-8160-4891-6). 130pp. A handsome and thorough guide to Native American legends and folklore. (Rev: BL 10/1/04; SLJ 2/05) [398.2]

1099 Philip, Neil. *Mythology of the World* (8–12). 2004, Houghton $24.95 (0-7534-5779-2). 160pp. An excellent and thorough overview of world mythology, introducing readers to the plots and characters of myth and legend and examining the historical, cultural, and spiritual aspects of mythology. (Rev: BL 12/1/04; SLJ 10/04) [398.2]

1100 Roberts, Jeremy. *Japanese Mythology A to Z* (6–12). Illus. Series: Mythology A to Z. 2003, Facts on File $35.00 (0-8160-4871-1). 136pp. An easy-to-use alphabetically arranged volume introducing important places, practices and rituals, people, creatures, and so forth, with guidance on pronunciation. (Rev: SLJ 4/04) [299]

Classical

1101 Catran, Ken. *Voyage with Jason* (5–8). 2003, Lothian paper $10.95 (0-7344-0151-5). 208pp. A new twist on the story of Jason and the Argonauts, narrated by a youth who is part of the eventful three-year quest for the Golden Fleece and concentrating on character as well as adventure. (Rev: SLJ 4/04) [398.2]

1102 Daly, Kathleen N. *Greek and Roman Mythology A to Z*. Rev. ed. (6–12). Illus. Series: Mythology A to Z. 2003, Facts on File $35.00 (0-8160-5155-0). 146pp. A newly updated, easy-to-use volume containing more than 500 entries of differing lengths covering places, practices and rituals, people, creatures, and so forth. (Rev: BL 3/1/04; SLJ 4/04; VOYA 6/04) [292]

1103 Harris, John. *Strong Stuff: Herakles and His Labors* (4–7). 2005, Getty $16.95 (0-89236-784-9). 32pp. A lively, tongue-in-cheek account of the 12 labors of ancient Greece's mythical strongman, Herakles (known to the ancient Romans as Hercules). (Rev: BL 11/15/05; SLJ 11/05) [398.2]

1104 Hovey, Kate. *Ancient Voices* (6–10). 2004, Simon & Schuster $18.95 (0-689-83342-3). 40pp. Poems and dramatic illustrations introduce key characters of Greek myths, occasionally injecting contemporary realism. (Rev: BL 1/1–15/04; SLJ 3/04) [811]

1105 *Odysseus* (4–8). Retold by Geraldine McCaughrean. 2004, Cricket Books $15.95 (0-8126-2721-0). 128pp. Homer's dramatic story is retold in rhythmic prose. (Rev: BL 12/15/04; SLJ 12/04)

1106 Spinner, Stephanie. *Quicksilver* (8–11). 2005, Knopf LB $17.99 (0-375-92638-0). 240pp. Hermes, son of Zeus and quite a character in this incarnation, describes his participation in various well-known myths. (Rev: BCCB 4/05; BL 4/15/05; HB 3–4/05; SLJ 9/05; VOYA 4/05)

1107 Woff, Richard. *A Pocket Dictionary of Greek and Roman Gods and Goddesses* (4–8). 2003, Getty $9.95 (0-89236-706-7). 48pp. Varied reproductions from the British Museum add visual appeal to this brief who's who. (Rev: SLJ 2/04) [292.2]

Scandinavian

1108 Coville, Bruce. *Thor's Wedding Day* (4–7). 2005, Harcourt $15.00 (0-15-201455-1). 128pp. A hilarious retelling of an ancient Norse poem, in which Thor's goat boy describes how he helped Thor to retrieve his stolen magic hammer. (Rev: BL 8/05) [398.2]

1109 Daly, Kathleen N. *Norse Mythology A to Z.* Rev. ed. (6–12). Illus. Series: Mythology A to Z. 2003, Facts on File $35.00 (0-8160-5156-9). 126pp. A newly updated, easy-to-use volume containing approximately 400 entries covering places, practices and rituals, people, creatures, and so forth. (Rev: BL 3/1/04; SLJ 4/04; VOYA 6/04) [292.1]

Humor and Satire

1110 Mash, Robert. *How to Keep Dinosaurs*. Rev. ed. (7–12). Illus. 2003, Weidenfeld & Nicolson $14.99 (0-297-84347-8). 96pp. A tongue-in-cheek cleverly illustrated guide to the selection and care of your own pet prehistoric animal. (Rev: SLJ 4/04; VOYA 8/04)

Speeches, Essays, and General Literary Works

1111 Davis, Jill, ed. *Open Your Eyes: Extraordinary Experiences in Faraway Places* (8–12). 2003, Viking $16.99 (0-670-03616-1). 201pp. Ten writers, among them Lois Lowry and Harry Mazer, tell stories about how travel changed their lives. (Rev: BL 1/1–15/04; SLJ 1/04; VOYA 4/04) [910.4]

1112 *Lines in the Sand: New Writing on War and Peace* (6–10). 2003, Disinformation paper $7.95 (0-9729529-1-8). Essays, stories, memoirs, and pictures calling for peace by more than 150 children from around the world. (Rev: BL 2/1/04) [808.803]

1113 Sedaris, David. *Dress Your Family in Corduroy and Denim* (8–12). 2004, Little, Brown $24.95 (0-316-14346-4). 272pp. In this collection of 27 essays, David Sedaris mines humor from a series of incidents in his personal life, some of which were not at all funny when they happened. (Rev: SLJ 1/05) [813]

Literary History and Criticism

Fiction

Europe

Great Britain and Ireland

1114 Beahm, George. *Muggles and Magic: J. K. Rowling and the Harry Potter Phenomenon* (7–12). Illus. 2004, Hampton Roads paper $16.95 (1-57174-412-6). 393pp. An impressive collection of information about the boy-wizard, his world, and his creator, J. K. Rowling. (Rev: SLJ 2/05)

1115 Gribbin, Mary, and John Gribbin. *The Science of Philip Pullman's His Dark Materials* (6–9). 2005, Knopf LB $17.99 (0-375-93144-9). 224pp. Explore the scientific underpinning of the dominant themes found in Pullman's trilogy. (Rev: BL 8/05; SLJ 8/05) [823]

1116 Swisher, Clarice. *Understanding The Canterbury Tales* (8–12). Series: Understanding Great Literature. 2003, Gale LB $21.96 (1-56006-782-9). 128pp. Background on Chaucer and medieval life precedes discussion of the themes, characters, and literary devices found in the tales. (Rev: SLJ 1/04) [821]

United States

1117 Bernard, Catherine. *Understanding To Kill a Mockingbird* (7–10). Series: Understanding Great Literature. 2003, Gale LB $27.45 (1-56006-860-4). 112pp. Provides a biography of Harper Lee, historical background, and discussion of the plot and characters in addition to study questions and quotations from reviews and articles. (Rev: SLJ 3/04) [813]

1118 Diorio, Mary Ann L. *A Student's Guide to Nathaniel Hawthorne* (7–10). Series: Understanding Literature. 2004, Enslow LB $21.95 (0-7660-2283-8). 160pp. The plot, characters, themes, and literary devices found in Hawthorne's works are discussed, and there are details of his life and major influences. (Rev: SLJ 6/04) [813]

1119 Newman, Gerald, and Eleanor Newman Layfield. *A Student's Guide to John Steinbeck* (8–12). Series: Understanding Literature. 2004, Enslow LB $27.93 (0-7660-2259-5). 176pp. This guide examines the writer's life as well as the characters, themes, and symbolism found in his novels. (Rev: SLJ 3/05) [813]

1120 Pingelton, Timothy J. *A Student's Guide to Ernest Hemingway* (7–12). Series: Understanding Literature. 2005, Enslow LB $27.93 (0-7660-2431-8). 160pp. Introduces Hemingway's life and works, with analysis of some of his best-known writings. (Rev: SLJ 10/05) [813]

Plays and Poetry

Europe

Shakespeare

1121 Page, Philip, and Marilyn Pettit, eds. *Romeo and Juliet* (8–11). Illus. Series: Picture This! Shakespeare. 2005, Barrons paper $7.95 (0-7641-3144-3). 64pp. This attractive title uses both straight text and cartoon characters to present not only the full text of Shakespeare's tragic romance but also notes on devices and related information. (Rev: BL 3/15/05; SLJ 9/05) [745.1]

United States

1122 Borus, Audrey. *A Student's Guide to Emily Dickinson* (7–12). Series: Understanding Literature. 2005, Enslow LB $27.93 (0-7660-2285-4). 152pp. Introduces Dickinson's life and poetry, with discussion of key themes, how to analyze the poems, and a glossary of terms. (Rev: SLJ 10/05) [813]

1123 Dunkleberger, Amy. *A Student's Guide to Arthur Miller* (7–12). Series: Understanding Literature. 2005, Enslow LB $27.93 (0-7660-2432-6). 160pp. Combines biographical information and discussion of Miller's key works. (Rev: SLJ 10/05) [813]

1124 Jimerson, M. N. *Understanding The Crucible* (7–10). Series: Understanding Great Literature. 2003, Gale LB $28.70 (1-56006-996-1). 112pp. A look at the characters, plot, and historical context of the classic play, with biographical information on Arthur Miller. (Rev: SLJ 2/04)

1125 MacGowan, Christopher, ed. *Poetry for Young People: William Carlos Williams* (6–12). 2004, Sterling $14.95 (1-4027-0006-7). 48pp. Thirty-one poems by Williams plus biographical and critical material are included in this excellent collection. (Rev: BL 3/1/04) [811]

Language and Communication

Signs and Symbols

1126 Janeczko, Paul B. *Top Secret: A Handbook of Codes, Ciphers, and Secret Writing* (4–7). 2004, Candlewick $16.99 (0-7636-0971-4). 144pp. Would-be cryptographers and secret agents will enjoy this collection of tips for developing codes and covertly passing information to others. (Rev: BL 5/15/04*; SLJ 5/04) [652]

1127 Baker, Rosalie. *In a Word: 750 Words and Their Fascinating Stories and Origins* (4–8). 2003, Cobblestone $17.95 (0-8126-2710-5). 250pp. Useful for reference, this guide to the origins and meanings of words and phrases is drawn from a monthly column in *Cobblestone*. (Rev: BL 2/15/04; SLJ 4/04) [422]

1128 Casagrande, June. *Grammar Snobs Are Great Big Meanies: A Guide to Language for Fun and Spite* (8–12). 2006, Penguin paper $14.00 (0-14-303683-1). 200pp. A lighthearted review of the rules of grammar, from prepositions and split infinitives to new conventions for e-mail and text messaging. (Rev: BL 4/1/06) [428]

1129 Edwards, Wallace. *Monkey Business* (4–8). Illus. 2004, Kids Can $16.95 (1-55337-462-2). 32pp. Whimsical artwork introduces such common idioms as "opening a can of worms" and "a bull in a china shop"; readers will also enjoy looking for hidden monkeys. (Rev: BL 11/1/04; SLJ 9/04*) [423]

1130 Shields, Carol Diggory. *English, Fresh Squeezed! 40 Thirst-for-Knowledge-Quenching Poems* (4–7). Series: BrainJuice. 2005, Handprint $14.95 (1-59354-053-1). 80pp. A humorous, rhyming look at annoying grammatical and other rules of language, with appealing illustrations and useful mnemonic devices. (Rev: BL 2/15/04; HB 5–6/04; SLJ 5/05)

Writing and the Media

General and Miscellaneous

1131 Currie, Stephen, ed. *Terrorism* (7–10). Illus. Series: Writing the Critical Essay. 2005, Gale LB $20.96 (0-7377-3206-7). 111pp. Opposing viewpoints on terrorism are combined with tips for writing a succinct essay on the subject. (Rev: BL 3/1/06) [363.32]

1132 Francis, Barbara. *Other People's Words: What Plagiarism Is and How to Avoid It* (6–12). Series: Issues in Focus Today. 2005, Enslow LB $31.93 (0-7660-2525-X). 112pp. Practical suggestions about avoiding plagiarism are accompanied by examples of plagiarism through history and current instances of "borrowing" ideas and words. (Rev: SLJ 12/05)

1133 Harper, Timothy, and Elizabeth Harper. *Your Name in Print: A Teen's Guide to Publishing for Fun, Profit and Academic Success* (8–12). 2005, St. Martin's paper $13.95 (0-312-33759-0). 186pp. The Harpers (father and daughter) offer alternating how-to advice on writing and getting published in a variety of formats. (Rev: BL 9/1/05; SLJ 11/05; VOYA 8/05) [808]

1134 Harrison, David Lee. *Writing Stories* (4–8). Series: Scholastic Guides. 2004, Scholastic $16.95 (0-439-51914-4). 128pp. This straightforward guide to writing offers clear advice on plot, setting, character, and voice as well as the importance of revision and practice. (Rev: BL 11/1/04; SLJ 1/05) [808.3]

1135 Janeczko, Paul B. *Writing Winning Reports and Essays* (5–8). Series: Scholastic Guides. 2003, Scholastic LB $16.95 (0-439-28717-0); paper $7.95 (0-439-28718-9). 224pp. Suggests useful strategies for researching and writing tasks including descriptive essays, book reports, persuasive and personal essays, and social studies reports. (Rev: SLJ 1/04) [808]

1136 Otfinoski, Steven. *Extraordinary Short Story Writing* (5–8). Series: F. W. Prep. 2005, Watts LB $30.50 (0-531-16760-7). 128pp. Tips and activities reinforce the information on writing different types of stories, choosing ideas, and using available resources effectively; a sample short story offers step-by-step guidance. (Rev: SLJ 2/06) [808]

1137 Rivera, Shelia. *The Media War* (5–8). Illus. Series: World in Conflict. 2004, ABDO LB $17.95 (1-59197-418-6). 48pp. A brief overview of American journalism's impact on war from the Civil War to the U.S. invasion of Afghanistan. (Rev: BL 4/1/04) [070.1]

1138 Roy, Jennifer Rozines. *You Can Write a Story or Narrative* (4–8). Illus. Series: You Can Write! 2003, Enslow LB $17.95 (0-7660-2085-1). 64pp. Sound advice for plotting and writing a wide array of different narratives, including adventure, history, fantasy, and folklore. (Rev: SLJ 1/04; VOYA 4/04) [808]

1139 Trueit, Trudi Strain. *Keeping a Journal* (4–8). Illus. 2004, Watts LB $19.50 (0-531-12262-X). 80pp. Trueit encourages readers to keep journals, offering tips on getting started, writing prompts and exercises, a calendar of ideas, and alternatives for those who don't enjoy writing, such as scrapbooks and drawing. (Rev: BL 10/15/03; SLJ 3/05) [808]

Print and Other Media

1140 Lawrence, Colton. *Big Fat Paycheck: A Young Person's Guide to Writing for the Movies* (6–9). 2004, Random paper $8.99 (0-553-37600-4). 288pp.

Although the chances of winning that big fat paycheck may be slim, this volume offers practical advice for aspiring scriptwriters. (Rev: BCCB 5/04; BL 9/1/04; SLJ 6/04; VOYA 6/04) [808.2]

1141 Rollins, Prentis. *The Making of a Graphic Novel* (7–12). 2006, Watson-Guptill paper $19.95 (0-8230-3053-9). 168pp. One side of this "double-sided flip book" contains the text of a graphic novel called *The Resonator*; the other side holds a detailed account of the construction of this novel and the inspirations for the designs. (Rev: SLJ 3/06) [741.5]

1142 Sullivan, George. *Journalists at Risk: Reporting America's Wars* (6–9). Series: People's History. 2005, Twenty-First Century LB $26.60 (0-7613-2745-2). 128pp. A look at the historical role of journalists in reporting on U.S. wars in far-flung corners of the globe, including information on the embedded journalists covering the war in Iraq. (Rev: SLJ 12/05; VOYA 2/06)

Biography, Memoirs, Etc.

General and Miscellaneous

1143 Hatch, Robert, and William Hatch. *The Hero Project: How We Met Our Greatest Heroes and What We Learned from Them* (8–12). Illus. 2005, McGraw-Hill paper $14.95 (0-07-144904-3). 204pp. Fascinating interviews with such luminaries as Jackie Chan, Lance Armstrong, Orson Scott Card, Yo-Yo Ma, and Jimmy Carter result from the Hatch brothers' "hero project," which started when William was only 11 years old. (Rev: BL 9/15/05; SLJ 1/06) [920]

Adventurers and Explorers

Collective

1144 Atkins, Jeannine. *How High Can We Climb? The Story of Women Explorers* (5–8). 2005, Farrar $17.00 (0-374-33503-6). 224pp. Atkins celebrates the lives and achievements of 12 women adventurers and explorers in this attention-grabbing volume that unfortunately mixes fact and fiction. (Rev: BL 10/15/05; SLJ 9/05) [910]

1145 Colman, Penny. *Adventurous Women: Eight True Stories About Women Who Made a Difference* (6–9). Illus. 2006, Holt $17.95 (0-8050-7744-8). 208pp. Letters and other primary sources add to these accessible profiles of women adventurers, many of whom are not well-known. (Rev: BL 2/15/06; SLJ 3/06) [920.72]

1146 Fleming, Fergus. *Tales of Endurance and Exploration* (8–12). Illus. 2005, Grove $26.00 (0-87113-899-9). 560pp. From the well known — Marco Polo and Christopher Columbus, for example — to less-recognized adventurers, this celebration of the courage of 45 explorers is divided into three eras and accompanied by excellent black-and-white illustrations. (Rev: BL 6/1–15/05) [910]

1147 Jones, Charlotte Foltz. *Westward Ho! Explorers of the American West* (5–8). Illus. 2005, Holiday $22.95 (0-8234-1586-4). 233pp. Intriguing narrative describes the lives and adventures of 11 explorers, including Zebulon Pike and John Wesley Powell. (Rev: BL 5/1/05; SLJ 8/05) [920]

1148 Kimmel, Elizabeth Cody. *The Look-It-Up-Book of Explorers* (5–9). Illus. 2004, Random LB $17.99 (0-375-92478-7); paper $10.99 (0-375-82478-2). 128pp. Chronologically arranged spreads introduce explorers from Leif Eriksson to Robert Ballard, with maps, illustrations, and historical context. (Rev: SLJ 1/05) [920]

1149 Rooney, Frances. *Extraordinary Women Explorers* (5–8). Illus. Series: Women's Hall of Fame. 2005, Second Story paper $7.95 (1-896764-98-3). 118pp. Women endowed with curiosity and courage are celebrated in this text-dense volume. (Rev: BL 3/1/06; SLJ 12/05) [910]

Individual

ARMSTRONG, NEIL

1150 Byers, Ann. *Neil Armstrong: The First Man on the Moon* (4–7). Illus. Series: The Library of Astronaut Biographies. 2004, Rosen LB $29.25 (0-8239-4461-1). 112pp. A lively overview focusing mainly on Armstrong's education and training. (Rev: SLJ 1/05) [921]

BALBOA, VASCO NUNEZ DE

1151 Otfinoski, Steven. *Vasco Nunez de Balboa: Explorer of the Pacific* (5–8). Series: Great Explorations. 2004, Benchmark LB $20.95 (0-7614-1609-9). 79pp. After material on Balboa's early life, Otfinoski looks at the Spanish explorer's trip to the Pacific. (Rev: SLJ 3/05) [921]

CABEZA DE VACA, ALVAR NUNEZ

1152 Waldman, Stuart. *We Asked for Nothing: The Remarkable Journey of Cabeza de Vaca* (5–8). Series: A Great Explorers Book. 2003, Mikaya $19.95 (1-931414-07-6). 46pp. Drawing on the writings of Cabeza de Vaca, Waldman tells the riveting story of the Spaniard's eight years in 16th-century Texas and Mexico. (Rev: SLJ 2/04) [921]

CHAMPLAIN, SAMUEL DE

1153 Faber, Harold. *Samuel de Champlain: Explorer of Canada* (5–8). Series: Great Explorations. 2004, Benchmark LB $20.95 (0-7614-1608-0). 80pp. Drawing on Champlain's own accounts, this well-illustrated volume examines his voyages to Canada and achievements as governor of New France. (Rev: SLJ 3/05) [921]

DA GAMA, VASCO

1154 Calvert, Patricia. *Vasco da Gama: So Strong a Spirit* (5–8). Series: Great Explorations. 2004, Benchmark LB $20.95 (0-7614-1611-0). 96pp. After material on da Gama's early life, Calvert looks at the 15th-century Portuguese explorer's voyages. (Rev: SLJ 3/05) [921]

EARHART, AMELIA

1155 Van Pelt, Lori. *Amelia Earhart: The Sky's No Limit* (8–12). Series: American Heroes. 2005, Tor $21.95 (0-765-31061-9). 208pp. A brief but information-packed biography that gives lots of personal details as well as covering her passion for flying. (Rev: BL 3/1/05) [629.13]

HENSON, MATTHEW

1156 Hoena, B. A. *Matthew Henson: Arctic Adventurer* (4–7). Series: Graphic Biographies. 2005, Capstone LB $18.95 (0-7368-4634-4). 32pp. The life of the African American explorer is presented in speedy, user-friendly, classic comic book format. (Rev: BL 11/1/05) [910]

1157 Johnson, Dolores. *Onward: A Photobiography of African-American Polar Explorer Matthew Henson* (5–8). Illus. Series: National Geographic Photobiography. 2005, National Geographic LB $27.90 (0-7922-7915-8). 64pp. The extraordinary life and achievements of African American explorer Matthew Henson are beautifully documented in this volume that also discusses the racism that Henson faced. (Rev: BL 12/15/05*; SLJ 3/06*) [910]

OCHOA, ELLEN

1158 Iverson, Teresa. *Ellen Ochoa* (4–8). Series: Hispanic-American Biographies. 2005, Raintree LB $32.86 (1-4109-1299-X). 64pp. The personal and professional life of the first Hispanic American woman astronaut. (Rev: SLJ 1/06) [921]

1159 Paige, Joy. *Ellen Ochoa: The First Hispanic Woman in Space* (4–7). Illus. Series: The Library of Astronaut Biographies. 2004, Rosen LB $29.25 (0-8239-4457-3). 112pp. A lively overview focusing mainly on Ochoa's education and training. (Rev: SLJ 1/05) [921]

PIKE, ZEBULON

1160 Calvert, Patricia. *Zebulon Pike: Lost in the Rockies* (5–8). Series: Great Explorations. 2004, Benchmark LB $20.95 (0-7614-1612-9). 96pp. Presents the life and career of the army officer who explored the West and Southwest. (Rev: SLJ 3/05) [921]

PONCE DE LEON, JUAN

1161 Otfinoski, Steven. *Juan Ponce de Leon: Discoverer of Florida* (5–8). Series: Great Explorations. 2004, Benchmark LB $20.95 (0-7614-1610-2). 76pp. A well-illustrated account of the explorer's life and discoveries, dismissing the idea that he was really searching for the fountain of youth. (Rev: SLJ 3/05) [921]

RAMON, ILAN

1162 Sofer, Barbara. *Ilan Ramon: Israel's Space Hero* (4–8). 2004, Lerner LB $16.95 (1-58013-115-8); paper $6.95 (1-58013-116-6). 63pp. The story of the first Israeli astronaut, from his early life and schooling to his selection for the crew of the ill-fated Columbia space shuttle that broke apart on re-entry in 2003. (Rev: SLJ 6/04) [921]

SELKIRK, ALEXANDER

1163 Kraske, Robert. *Marooned: The Strange but True Adventures of Alexander Selkirk, the Real Robinson Crusoe* (5–8). 2005, Clarion $15.00 (0-618-56843-3). 128pp. The adventurous life of Alexander Selkirk, the Scottish navigator who served as the model for Daniel Defoe's *Robinson Crusoe*. (Rev: BL 11/15/05; SLJ 12/05) [996.1]

SHACKLETON, SIR ERNEST

1164 Riffenburgh, Beau. *Shackleton's Forgotten Expedition: The Voyage of the Nimrod* (8–12). 2004, Bloomsbury $25.95 (1-58234-488-4). 384pp. This story of Shackleton's first expedition to the Antarctic aboard the *Nimrod* underlines its significant scientific and exploratory achievements. (Rev: BL 10/15/04) [919.8]

SHEPARD, ALAN

1165 Orr, Tamra. *Alan Shepard: The First American in Space* (4–7). Illus. Series: The Library of Astronaut Biographies. 2004, Rosen LB $29.25 (0-8239-4455-7). 112pp. A lively overview focusing mainly on Shepard's education and training. (Rev: SLJ 1/05) [921]

Artists, Authors, Composers, and Entertainers

Collective

1166 Bostrom, Kathleen Long. *Winning Authors: Profiles of the Newbery Medalists* (5–10). Series: Popular Authors. 2003, Libraries Unlimited $52.00 (1-56308-877-0). 338pp. Report writers will find useful information on the authors who won this prestigious award, including quotations and material on experiences that relate to the winning books. (Rev: SLJ 6/04; VOYA 6/04) [920]

1167 De Angelis, Gina. *Motion Pictures: Making Cinema Magic* (6–10). Series: Innovators. 2004, Oliver LB $21.95 (1-881508-78-1). 144pp. Profiles eight inventors of motion picture technology, including Auguste and Louis Lumière, Lee de Forest, and Mike Todd. (Rev: BCCB 5/04; SLJ 9/04) [920]

1168 Koopmans, Andy. *Filmmakers* (7–10). Illus. Series: History Makers. 2005, Gale LB $22.96 (1-59018-598-6). 112pp. Profiles five of the world's most influential filmmakers — Alfred Hitchcock, Stanley Kubrick, Francis Ford Coppola, Spike Lee, and Peter Jackson. (Rev: BL 6/1–15/05) [920]

1169 Martin, Marvin. *Extraordinary People in Jazz* (5–9). Series: Extraordinary People. 2004, Children's Pr. LB $39.00 (0-516-22275-9). 288pp. Duke Ellington, Billie Holiday, and John Coltrane are among the jazz musicians included in this chronologically arranged volume. (Rev: SLJ 1/05) [781.65]

1170 Scieszka, Jon, ed. *Guys Write for Guys Read: Favorite Authors Write About Being Boys* (6–9). 2005, Viking $16.99 (0-670-06007-0); paper $10.99 (0-670-06027-5). 288pp. Well-known male authors and illustrators share boyhood memories in this delightful collection of stories, anecdotes, poems, drawings, and comics. (Rev: BL 4/15/05; SLJ 4/05) [810.8]

1171 Tessitore, John. *Extraordinary American Writers* (6–12). 2004, Children's Pr. LB $39.00 (0-516-

22656-8). 288pp. Writers profiled here "examined and analyzed American society in their works" and range from Benjamin Franklin to Philip Roth; biographical essays include information on important works and a brief excerpt. (Rev: SLJ 9/04) [920]

Artists and Architects

BOTTICELLI, SANDRO

1172 Connolly, Sean. *Botticelli* (4–8). Illus. Series: Lives of the Artists. 2005, World Almanac LB $22.50 (0-8368-5648-1). 48pp. A tall, slender volume full of facts about Botticelli's life and times, with many color reproductions. (Rev: BL 6/1–15/04; SLJ 3/05) [921]

CALDECOTT, RANDOLPH

1173 Hegel, Claudette. *Randolph Caldecott: An Illustrated Life* (5–9). Series: Avisson Young Adult. 2004, Avisson $27.50 (1-888105-60-7). Many of Caldecott's drawings are included in this account of the artist's life and work, with coverage of the children's award named in his honor. (Rev: BL 10/1/04; SLJ 11/04) [741.6]

CASSATT, MARY

1174 Ferrara, Cos. *Mary Cassatt: The Life and Art of a Genteel Rebel* (5–8). Illus. Series: Girls Explore, Reach for the Stars. 2005, Girls Explore $20.00 (0-9749456-3-3). 101pp. Cassatt's art, shown in small full-color reproductions, is introduced in this biography that also discusses her independence and feminist views. (Rev: BL 2/15/05) [921]

CÉZANNE, PAUL

1175 Burleigh, Robert. *Paul Cézanne: A Painter's Journey* (4–7). Illus. 2006, Abrams $17.95 (0-8109-5784-1). 32pp. A lavishly illustrated and thoughtfully written profile of Cézanne's life and art. (Rev: BL 2/15/06; SLJ 3/06) [759.4]

CHAGALL, MARC

1176 Mason, Antony. *Marc Chagall* (4–8). Illus. Series: Lives of the Artists. 2005, World Almanac LB $22.50 (0-8368-5649-X). 48pp. A tall, slender volume full of facts about Chagall's life and times, with many color reproductions. (Rev: BL 6/1–15/04; SLJ 3/05) [921]

DA VINCI, LEONARDO

1177 *Leonardo da Vinci* (5–8). Series: Lives of the Artists. 2004, World Almanac LB $29.26 (0-8368-5599-X). 48pp. Lots of facts and illustrations are included in this tall-format volume covering da Vinci's life and work. (Rev: SLJ 8/04) [921]

1178 Reed, Jennifer. *Leonardo da Vinci: Genius of Art and Science* (4–7). Illus. Series: Great Minds of Science. 2005, Enslow LB $26.60 (0-7660-2500-4). 128pp. Reed describes da Vinci's wide-ranging achievements — showing, for example, his urban planning ideas, his design for a flying machine, and his anatomical drawings — and emphasizes his originality and creativity. (Rev: SLJ 6/05) [921]

GEHRY, FRANK

1179 Lazo, Caroline Evensen. *Frank Gehry* (7–10). Series: A&E Biography. 2005, Twenty-First Century LB $27.93 (0-8225-2649-2); paper $7.95 (0-8225-3388-X). 112pp. Introduces the architect and his most famous structures, with full-color photos and reproductions. (Rev: SLJ 2/06) [921]

MICHELANGELO

1180 *Michelangelo* (5–8). Series: The Lives of the Artists. 2004, World Almanac LB $29.26 (0-8368-5600-7). 48pp. A tall, slender volume full of facts about Michelangelo's life and times, with many color reproductions. (Rev: SLJ 8/04) [921]

1181 Somervill, Barbara A. *Michelangelo: Sculptor and Painter* (6–9). Illus. Series: Signature Lives. 2005, Compass Point LB $30.60 (0-7565-0814-2). 112pp. Michelangelo comes to life in this readable biography that includes color images. (Rev: BL 8/05) [709]

MONET, CLAUDE

1182 Connolly, Sean. *Claude Monet* (4–8). Illus. Series: Lives of the Artists. 2005, World Almanac LB $22.50 (0-8368-5650-3). 48pp. A tall, slender volume full of facts about Monet's life and times, with many color reproductions. (Rev: BL 6/1–15/04; SLJ 3/05) [921]

O'KEEFFE, GEORGIA

1183 Shull, Jodie A. *Georgia O'Keeffe: Legendary American Painter* (6–8). Illus. Series: People to Know. 2004, Enslow LB $19.95 (0-7660-2104-1). 112pp. Events that tilted O'Keeffe in the direction of her artistic style are revealed in this appealing biography. (Rev: BL 11/1/04) [921]

PICASSO, PABLO

1184 Hodge, Susie, and Pablo Picasso. *Pablo Picasso* (4–8). Series: Lives of the Artists. 2004, Gareth Stevens LB $29.26 (0-8368-5606-6). 48pp. Works by the young Picasso are a feature of this well illustrated profile. (Rev: BL 6/1–15/04) [921]

1185 *Picasso: Soul on Fire* (4–7). Trans. by Rick Jacobson. 2004, Tundra Books of Northern New York $15.95 (0-88776-599-8). 32pp. Oil paintings of the Spanish-born artist, along with reproductions of some of his best-known pieces, introduce his work and brief facts about his life. (Rev: BL 11/1/04) [921]

POLITI, LEO

1186 Stalcup, Ann. *Leo Politi: Artist of the Angels* (4–9). 2004, Silver Moon $24.95 (1-893110-38-9). 104pp. The life of the American-born man who spent his formative years in Italy and returned as an adult to make his home in Los Angeles and portray the ethnic communities there in his books for children. (Rev: SLJ 4/05) [921]

RECTOR, ANNE ELIZABETH

1187 Rector, Anne Elizabeth. *Anne Elizabeth's Diary: A Young Artist's True Story* (3–7). Ed. by Kathleen Krull. Illus. 2004, Little Brown $16.95 (0-316-07204-4). 64pp. Krull's sidebars add context to this fascinating diary, started when Rector was 12 years old, that reflects the young artist's life in both text and illustrations. (Rev: BL 6/1–15/04; SLJ 9/04) [974.7]

REMBRANDT VAN RIJN

1188 Mason, Antony. *Rembrandt* (4–8). Illus. Series: Lives of the Artists. 2005, World Almanac LB $22.50 (0-8368-5651-1). 48pp. A tall, slender volume full of facts about Rembrandt's life and times, with many color reproductions. (Rev: BL 6/1–15/04; SLJ 3/05) [921]

RIVERA, DIEGO

1189 Litwin, Laura Baskes. *Diego Rivera: Legendary Mexican Painter* (7–10). Illus. Series: Latino Biography. 2005, Enslow LB $23.95 (0-7660-2486-5). 128pp. The life, art, and controversial politics of Mexican artist Diego Rivera are explored in this attractive and readable title. (Rev: BL 11/1/05; SLJ 4/06) [759.972]

SCHULZ, CHARLES

1190 Marvis, Barbara. *Charles Schulz: The Story of the Peanuts Gang* (4–8). Illus. Series: Robbie Reader. 2004, Mitchell Lane LB $16.95 (1-58415-289-3). 32pp. This photo-filled biography traces Schulz's life and his love of cartoons; it is especially suitable for reluctant readers. (Rev: BL 9/1/05)

WARHOL, ANDY

1191 Greenberg, Jan, and Sandra Jordan. *Andy Warhol, Prince of Pop* (8–12). 2004, Random LB $18.99 (0-385-73056-X). 208pp. Warhol had a successful career in commercial art before rising to fame as a pop icon; this volume covers his youth, early career, love of celebrity, and early death as well as his art and its lasting influence. (Rev: BCCB 12/04; BL 6/1–15/04*; HB 1–2/05; SLJ 11/04; VOYA 10/04) [709]

WRIGHT, FRANK LLOYD

1192 Fandel, Jennifer. *Frank Lloyd Wright* (7–12). Series: Xtraordinary Artists. 2005, Creative Education LB $21.95 (1-58341-378-2). 48pp. This well-illustrated life of the visionary architect draws on comments from his students, contemporaries, and admirers. (Rev: SLJ 12/05)

1193 Mayo, Gretchen Will. *Frank Lloyd Wright* (5–8). Series: Trailblazers of the Modern World. 2004, World Almanac LB $29.27 (0-8368-5101-3). 48pp. Report writers will find useful information on Wright's life, achievements, and lasting contributions. (Rev: SLJ 7/04) [921]

ZHANG, ANGE

1194 Zhang, Ange. *Red Land, Yellow River: A Story from the Cultural Revolution* (5–8). 2004, Groundwood $16.95 (0-88899-489-3). 56pp. In this compelling autobiography, artist Ange Zhang tells how he came of age during one of the most turbulent periods in modern Chinese history — the Cultural Revolution of the late 1960s. (Rev: BL 12/1/04*; SLJ 12/04) [921]

Authors

ALLENDE, ISABEL

1195 Main, Mary. *Isabel Allende: Award-Winning Latin American Author* (6–9). Series: Latino Biography Library. 2005, Enslow LB $31.93 (0-7660-2488-1). 128pp. An engaging life of the writer that gives readers a perspective on life in Chile and on the world affairs that have impacted Allende. (Rev: SLJ 1/06) [921]

ANDERSEN, HANS CHRISTIAN

1196 Varmer, Hjordis. *Hans Christian Andersen: His Fairy Tale Life* (4–7). Trans. by Tina Nunnally. 2005, Groundwood $19.95 (0-88899-670-X). 112pp. This large-format, lively biography presents the Danish storyteller's single-minded struggle to rise above adversity. (Rev: BL 11/1/05) [839.81]

AUSTEN, JANE

1197 Locke, Juliane. *England's Jane: The Story of Jane Austen* (8–11). Illus. 2006, Morgan Reynolds LB $26.95 (1-931798-82-6). 144pp. The parallels between Austen's life and novels are evident in this appealing biography. (Rev: BL 2/15/06; SLJ 2/06) [823]

1198 Wagner, Heather Lehr. *Jane Austen* (7–10). Series: Who Wrote That? 2003, Chelsea House LB $22.95 (0-7910-7623-7). 112pp. Details of Austen's family life and education and of the mores of the time give insight into her humorous attitude toward society and romance. (Rev: SLJ 6/04) [921]

AVI

1199 Sommers, Michael A. *Avi* (5–8). Series: The Library of Author Biographies. 2004, Rosen LB $26.50 (0-8239-4522-7). 112pp. Covers Avi's life and career as a YA author, with analysis of his work, an interview, and lists of works and awards. (Rev: SLJ 1/05) [921]

BRADBURY, RAY

1200 Mass, Wendy. *Ray Bradbury: Master of Science Fiction and Fantasy* (6–9). Illus. Series: Authors Teens Love. 2004, Enslow LB $19.95 (0-7660-2240-4). 104pp. Report writers will find ample details about Bradbury's life and career, with plot summaries of his most famous books. (Rev: BL 11/1/04; SLJ 12/04) [921]

BROOKS, GWENDOLYN

1201 Hill, Christine M. *Gwendolyn Brooks: "Poetry Is Life Distilled,"* (7–10). Illus. Series: African-American Biography Library. 2005, Enslow LB $23.95 (0-7660-2292-7). 128pp. Poet Gwendolyn

Brooks, the first African American to win the Pulitzer Prize, is profiled in accessible text with lots of photos and background information. (Rev: BL 11/1/05; SLJ 11/05) [811]

CATHER, WILLA

1202 Ling, Bettina. *Willa Cather: Author and Critic* (6–9). Series: Great Life Stories. 2003, Watts LB $29.50 (0-531-12316-2). 111pp. Sidebar features provide background information on society and politics in the late 19th and early 20th centuries, adding depth to this life of the author of *My Antonia* and other classics. (Rev: SLJ 1/04) [305.235]

CISNEROS, SANDRA

1203 Brackett, Virginia. *A Home in the Heart: The Story of Sandra Cisneros* (7–12). Series: World Writers. 2004, Morgan Reynolds LB $21.95 (1-931798-42-7). 128pp. The life and literary career of Mexican American author Sandra Cisneros. (Rev: BL 12/1/04; SLJ 3/05) [921]

CRANE, STEPHEN

1204 Kepnes, Caroline. *Stephen Crane* (5–8). Series: Classic StoryTellers. 2004, Mitchell Lane LB $19.95 (1-58415-272-9). 48pp. An introduction to Crane's life, work, and legacy, with background information on relevant historical, cultural, and economic factors. (Rev: BL 1/05; SLJ 1/05) [921]

CRUTCHER, CHRIS

1205 Summers, Michael A. *Chris Crutcher* (5–8). Series: The Library of Author Biographies. 2005, Rosen LB $26.50 (1-4042-0325-7). 112pp. An interview with Crutcher is an interesting addition to this description of the author's life — including his experiences as a novelist, educator, therapist, and child protection advocate — and his works for children. (Rev: SLJ 9/05) [921]

DAHL, ROALD

1206 Cooling, Wendy. *D Is for Dahl: A Gloriumptious A–Z Guide to the World of Roald Dahl* (5–8). 2005, Viking $15.99 (0-670-06023-2). 160pp. For Dahl fans, this is an alphabetically arranged collection of trivia about his life and writings. (Rev: BL 8/05; SLJ 10/05) [823]

DICKENS, CHARLES

1207 Caravantes, Peggy. *Best of Times: The Story of Charles Dickens* (7–10). Illus. Series: Writers of Imagination. 2005, Morgan Reynolds LB $24.95 (1-931798-68-0). 160pp. Examines the events in the author's life that led to his literary preoccupation with social injustices. (Rev: BL 8/05; SLJ 12/05) [823]

1208 Rosen, Michael. *Dickens: His Work and His World* (4–7). 2005, Candlewick $19.99 (0-7636-2752-6). 96pp. Before reviewing Dickens's major works, Rosen discusses the author's difficult childhood and the social conditions of his times. (Rev: BL 9/15/05*; SLJ 11/05*) [921]

DICKINSON, EMILY

1209 Herstek, Amy Paulson. *Emily Dickinson: Solitary and Celebrated Poet* (7–10). Series: Historical American Biographies. 2003, Enslow LB $20.95 (0-7660-1977-2). 128pp. A life of Dickinson, describing her childhood, the development of her beliefs, her love of nature, family, and friends, and her work. (Rev: SLJ 5/04; VOYA 4/04) [921]

1210 Meltzer, Milton. *Emily Dickinson* (8–11). Illus. Series: American Literary Greats. 2006, Lerner LB $31.93 (0-7613-2949-8). 128pp. Dickinson's life story is interwoven with quotes from her poetry and excerpts from primary sources including letters. (Rev: BL 2/15/06; VOYA 4/06) [811]

DINESEN, ISAK

1211 Leslie, Roger. *Isak Dinesen: Gothic Storyteller* (8–12). Illus. 2004, Morgan Reynolds LB $21.95 (1-931798-17-6). 128pp. Danish-born author Isak Dinesen, best known for *Out of Africa*, a memoir of her years spent in Kenya, is profiled in this engaging volume that emphasizes her battle with syphilis. (Rev: BL 4/1/04; SLJ 5/04) [921]

FITZGERALD, F. SCOTT

1212 Bankston, John. *F. Scott Fitzgerald* (5–8). Series: Classic StoryTellers. 2004, Mitchell Lane LB $19.95 (1-58415-249-4). 48pp. An introduction to Fitzgerald's life, work, and legacy, with background information on relevant historical, cultural, and economic factors. (Rev: BL 1/05; SLJ 1/05) [921]

1213 Boon, Kevin Alexander. *F. Scott Fitzgerald* (7–10). Series: Writers and Their Works. 2005, Benchmark LB $25.95 (0-7614-1947-0). 142pp. *The Great Gatsby* is discussed in some detail in this overview of Fitzgerald's life and works. (Rev: SLJ 3/06) [921]

FLEISCHMAN, SID

1214 Freedman, Jeri. *Sid Fleischman* (5–9). Series: The Library of Author Biographies. 2004, Rosen LB $26.50 (0-8239-4019-5). 112pp. Traces the popular, Newbery-winning author's life and looks at his works, writing process, and inspirations, concluding with an interview and reference material. (Rev: SLJ 9/04) [921]

FOX, PAULA

1215 Daniel, Susanna. *Paula Fox* (5–8). Series: The Library of Author Biographies. 2004, Rosen LB

$26.50 (0-8239-4525-1). 112pp. Covers Fox's life and career, with analysis of her work and its themes, an interview, and lists of works and awards. (Rev: SLJ 1/05) [921]

GIFF, PATRICIA REILLY

1216 Giff, Patricia Reilly. *Don't Tell the Girls: A Family Memoir* (4–7). Illus. 2005, Holiday $16.95 (0-8234-1813-8). 144pp. The author tells of the search for her family's roots that led her to Ireland. (Rev: BL 3/1/05; SLJ 7/05) [813]

HEMINGWAY, ERNEST

1217 Whiting, Jim. *Ernest Hemingway* (6–8). Series: Classic StoryTellers. 2005, Mitchell Lane LB $19.95 (1-58415-376-8). 48pp. A concise and readable introduction to the author's life and works. (Rev: SLJ 12/05)

HOMER

1218 Tracy, Kathleen. *The Life and Times of Homer* (5–8). Series: Biography from Ancient Civilizations: Legends, Folklore, and Stories of Ancient Worlds. 2004, Mitchell Lane LB $.00 (1-58415-260-5). 48pp. Drawing on ancient legends, this is a profile of ancient Greek poet and storyteller Homer. (Rev: BL 10/15/04; SLJ 12/04)

HOPKINS, LEE BENNETT

1219 Strong, Amy. *Lee Bennett Hopkins: A Children's Poet* (5–8). Series: Great Life Stories. 2003, Watts LB $29.50 (0-531-12315-4). 111pp. An inspiring biography that chronicles Hopkins's early struggles and his love for his work. (Rev: SLJ 2/04) [921]

HUGHES, LANGSTON

1220 Rummel, Jack. *Langston Hughes: Poet*. Rev. ed. (7–12). Series: Black Americans of Achievement. 2005, Chelsea House LB $23.95 (0-7910-8250-4). 108pp. A revised edition of the highly readable and well illustrated biography of the African American poet and fiction writer, containing excerpts from his writings. (Rev: SLJ 11/05) [921]

KING, STEPHEN

1221 Whitelaw, Nancy. *Dark Dreams: The Story of Stephen King* (7–10). Illus. Series: World Writers. 2005, Morgan Reynolds $26.95 (1-931798-77-X). 128pp. An inviting introduction to King and to his writing, with lots of interesting anecdotes and snippets of his work. (Rev: BL 11/15/05; VOYA 2/06) [813]

LONDON, JACK

1222 Bankston, John. *Jack London* (4–7). Illus. Series: Classic StoryTellers. 2005, Mitchell Lane LB $19.95 (1-58415-263-X). 48pp. An introduction to London's life, work, and legacy, with background information on relevant historical, cultural, and economic factors. (Rev: BL 1/05) [921]

MANZANO, JUAN FRANCISCO

1223 Engle, Margarita. *The Poet Slave of Cuba: A Biography of Juan Francisco Manzano* (7–10). 2006, Holt $16.95 (0-8050-7706-5). 184pp. This lyrical free-verse biography tells the story of the poet born into slavery in Cuba in 1797, describing his early talent with languages and how it helped him survived amazing brutality. (Rev: BL 2/15/06*; SLJ 4/06*) [811]

MELTZER, MILTON

1224 Meltzer, Milton. *Milton Meltzer: Writing Matters* (8–11). Illus. 2004, Watts LB $28.00 (0-531-12257-3). 160pp. Meltzer combines recollections of his childhood, adolescence, and working days with details of his progression as a writer. (Rev: BL 1/1–15/05; SLJ 4/05) [973.07]

MELVILLE, HERMAN

1225 Meltzer, Milton. *Herman Melville: A Biography* (8–12). Series: American Literary Greats. 2005, Twenty-First Century LB $31.93 (0-7613-2749-5). 128pp. Traces the writer's difficult life and links his struggles to passages from his works, in particular *Moby Dick*. (Rev: SLJ 1/06) [921]

MILLER, ARTHUR

1226 Andersen, Richard. *Arthur Miller* (7–10). Series: Writers and Their Works. 2005, Benchmark LB $25.95 (0-7614-1946-2). 144pp. *The Crucible* and *Death of a Salesman* are discussed in some detail in this overview of Miller's life and works. (Rev: SLJ 3/06) [921]

MONTGOMERY, L. M.

1227 Kjelle, Marylou Morano. *L. M. Montgomery* (6–9). Illus. Series: Who Wrote That? 2005, Chelsea House LB $23.95 (0-7910-8234-2). 124pp. This interesting profile shows the parallels between Montgomery and her most famous character, Anne of Green Gables. (Rev: BL 11/1/05) [813]

MORRISON, TONI

1228 Andersen, Richard. *Toni Morrison* (7–10). Series: Writers and Their Works. 2005, Benchmark LB $25.95 (0-7614-1945-4). 144pp. *Sula* and *The Bluest Eye* are discussed in some detail in this overview of Morrison's life and works. (Rev: SLJ 3/06) [921]

MOEYAERT, BART

1229 Moeyaert, Bart. *Brothers: The Oldest, the Quietest, the Realest, the Farthest, the Nicest, the Fastest, and I* (7–9). Trans. from Flemish by Wanda J. Boeke. 2005, Front Street $16.95 (1-932425-18-7). 163pp. The Belgian author offers candid and often wistful vignettes of growing up the youngest of seven brothers and the incidents that seemed of utmost importance to him. (Rev: SLJ 1/06; VOYA 4/06) [921]

MYERS, WALTER DEAN

1230 Burshtein, Karen. *Walter Dean Myers* (7–10). Series: The Library of Author Biographies. 2004, Rosen LB $26.50 (0-8239-4020-9). 112pp. A look at the life and work of the well-known author, with many quotations. (Rev: SLJ 9/04) [921]

NIXON, JOAN LOWERY

1231 Wade, Mary Dodson. *Joan Lowery Nixon: Masterful Mystery Writer* (5–8). Series: Authors Teens Love. 2004, Enslow LB $26.60 (0-7660-2194-7). 128pp. Examines Nixon's life, writings, and her focus on girls of character and strength. (Rev: SLJ 11/04) [921]

PATERSON, KATHERINE

1232 Kjelle, Marylou Morano. *Katherine Paterson* (4–7). Illus. Series: Classic StoryTellers. 2004, Mitchell Lane LB $15.95 (1-58415-268-0). 48pp. Examines the life and times of the award-winning children's author, including her work as a missionary in Japan and how religious faith informs her writing. (Rev: BL 1/1–15/05; SLJ 3/05) [921]

1233 McGinty, Alice B. *Katherine Paterson* (5–8). Series: The Library of Author Biographies. 2005, Rosen LB $26.50 (1-4042-0328-1). 112pp. An interview with Paterson is an interesting addition to this description of the author's life and works for children. (Rev: SLJ 9/05) [921]

PECK, ROBERT

1234 Peck, Robert Newton. *Weeds in Bloom: Autobiography of an Ordinary Man* (8–11). 2005, Random LB $17.99 (0-375-92801-4). 224pp. In a series of essays, Peck looks back at his life and at various important incidents and people who played a part in it. (Rev: BL 4/15/05) [813]

POE, EDGAR ALLAN

1235 Frisch, Aaron. *Edgar Allan Poe* (5–9). Photos by Tina Mucci. Series: Voices in Poetry. 2005, Cre-

ative Education LB $31.35 (1-58341-344-8). 45pp. A brief biography that adds atmospheric paintings and photographs to a chronological narrative and excerpts from Poe's works. (Rev: SLJ 3/06) [921]

1236 Peltak, Jennifer. *Edgar Allan Poe* (6–8). Series: Who Wrote That? 2003, Chelsea House LB $22.95 (0-7910-7622-9). 120pp. The dark details of Poe's personal life provide insight into the themes of his stories and poems; a well-written and attractive volume. (Rev: SLJ 6/04; VOYA 6/04) [921]

1237 Schoell, William. *Mystery and Terror: The Story of Edgar Allan Poe* (7–12). Illus. Series: Writers of Imagination. 2004, Morgan Reynolds LB $21.95 (1-931798-39-7). 128pp. Poe's unhappy childhood, marriage, and alcoholism are among the personal aspects covered in this biography that also talks about his work and his continuing need to earn enough money. (Rev: BL 10/1/04; SLJ 12/04) [921]

PULLMAN, PHILIP

1238 Yuan, Margaret Speaker. *Philip Pullman* (7–10). Illus. Series: Who Wrote That? 2005, Chelsea House LB $30.00 (0-7910-8658-5). 120pp. In addition to profiling this author of award-winning books, this biography describes his writing methods. (Rev: BL 3/15/06) [823]

SACHAR, LOUIS

1239 Greene, Meg. *Louis Sachar* (5–9). Series: The Library of Author Biographies. 2004, Rosen LB $26.50 (0-8239-4017-9). 112pp. Traces the popular, Newbery-winning author's life and looks at his works, writing process, and inspirations, concluding with an interview and reference material. (Rev: SLJ 9/04) [921]

SEUSS, DR.

1240 Cohen, Charles D. *The Seuss, the Whole Seuss, and Nothing but the Seuss* (8–12). Illus. 2004, Random $35.00 (0-375-82248-8). 400pp. This oversize, abundantly illustrated book gives a profile of the great author/illustrator and an analysis of his ideas and work. (Rev: BL 3/15/04; SLJ 6/04) [921]

SHAKESPEARE, WILLIAM

1241 Hilliam, David. *William Shakespeare: England's Greatest Playwright and Poet* (5–8). Illus. Series: Rulers, Scholars, and Artists of the Renaissance. 2005, Rosen LB $23.95 (1-4042-0318-4). 112pp. Information on Shakespeare's life and on the theater scene in 16th-century London is interwoven with quotes from the plays and poems. (Rev: BL 8/05) [822.3]

1242 Nettleton, Pamela Hill. *William Shakespeare: Playwright and Poet* (5–9). Series: Signature Lives. 2005, Compass Point $30.60 (0-7565-0816-9).

112pp. Nettleton places facts about Shakespeare's life within the context of everyday life of the time, with details about the theater and publishing. (Rev: SLJ 6/05) [921]

SPINELLI, JERRY

1243 Seidman, David. *Jerry Spinelli* (5–9). Series: The Library of Author Biographies. 2004, Rosen LB $26.50 (0-8239-4016-0). 112pp. Traces the popular, Newbery-winning author's life and looks at his works, writing process, and inspirations, concluding with an interview and reference material. (Rev: SLJ 9/04) [921]

STEINBECK, JOHN

1244 Tracy, Kathleen. *John Steinbeck* (5–8). Series: Classic StoryTellers. 2004, Mitchell Lane LB $19.95 (1-58415-271-0). 48pp. An introduction to Steinbeck's life, work, and legacy, with background information on relevant historical, cultural, and economic factors. (Rev: BL 1/05; SLJ 1/05) [921]

STINE, R. L.

1245 Parker-Rock, Michelle. *R. L. Stine: Creator of Creepy and Spooky Stories* (5–8). Series: Authors Teens Love. 2005, Enslow LB $26.60 (0-7660-2445-8). 104pp. Stine's writing career is the main focus of this biography that includes an interview. (Rev: SLJ 1/06) [921]

STOWE, HARRIET BEECHER

1246 Griskey, Michèle. *Harriet Beecher Stowe* (5–7). Series: Classic StoryTellers. 2005, Mitchell Lane LB $19.95 (1-58415-375-X). 48pp. Good historical and social context makes clear the importance of Stowe's achievements. (Rev: SLJ 11/05) [921]

TAYLOR, MILDRED

1247 Houghton, Gillian. *Mildred Taylor* (5–8). Series: The Library of Author Biographies. 2005, Rosen LB $26.50 (1-4042-0330-3). 112pp. An interview with Taylor is an interesting addition to this description of the African American author's life and writings. (Rev: SLJ 9/05) [921]

THOREAU, HENRY DAVID

1248 Hausman, Gerald, and Loretta Hausman. *A Mind with Wings: The Story of Henry David Thoreau* (6–9). Illus. 2006, Shambhala $15.95 (1-59030-228-1). 160pp. Told in a series of anecdotes, this is a lively portrayal of Thoreau's life that uses dialogue based on his own statements. (Rev: BL 3/1/06) [921]

TOLKIEN, J. R. R.

1249 Willett, Edward. *J. R. R. Tolkien: Master of Imaginary Worlds* (6–9). Illus. Series: Authors Teens Love. 2004, Enslow LB $19.95 (0-7660-2246-3). 128pp. Tolkien's interesting life will grab readers' attention, as will the quotations in the "In His Own Words" section. (Rev: BCCB 9/04; BL 11/1/04; SLJ 12/04) [921]

TWAIN, MARK

1250 Rasmussen, R. Kent. *Mark Twain for Kids: His Life and Times, 21 Activities* (4–7). Illus. Series: For Kids. 2004, Chicago Review paper $14.95 (1-55652-527-3). 160pp. An engaging biography that reveals interesting details of Twain's life and shows how many of the episodes in his books were based on his own experiences. (Rev: BL 9/15/04; SLJ 9/04) [921]

WHEATLEY, PHILLIS

1251 Kent, Deborah. *Phillis Wheatley: First Published African-American Poet* (4–7). Series: Our People. 2003, The Child's World LB $27.07 (1-59296-009-X). 32pp. The life of the 18th-century poet is outlined in this well-illustrated work that features large type and includes historical background. (Rev: SLJ 4/04) [921]

WHITE, E. B.

1252 Bernard, Catherine. *E. B. White: Spinner of Webs and Tales* (5–8). Series: Authors Teens Love. 2005, Enslow LB $26.60 (0-7660-2350-8). 104pp. An introductory chapter that gives a good overview of White's life is followed by chapters that delve into more detail plus a timeline and an excerpt from a 1969 interview that adds a more personal dimension. (Rev: BCCB 12/05; SLJ 10/05) [921]

1253 Murcia, Rebecca Thatcher. *E. B. White* (5–8). Series: Classic StoryTellers. 2004, Mitchell Lane LB $19.95 (1-58415-273-7). 48pp. An introduction to White's life, work, and legacy, with background information on relevant historical, cultural, and economic factors. (Rev: BL 1/05; SLJ 1/05) [921]

WHITMAN, WALT

1254 Kerley, Barbara. *Walt Whitman: Words for America* (4–8). 2004, Scholastic $16.95 (0-439-35791-8). 56pp. Whitman's experiences during the Civil War, including his service as a nurse to injured and dying soldiers, are highlighted in this picture-book biography. (Rev: BL 11/15/04; SLJ 11/04) [811]

WILDER, LAURA INGALLS

1255 Wilder, Laura Ingalls. *A Little House Traveler: Writings from Laura Ingalls Wilder's Journeys Across America* (5–8). 2006, HarperCollins $16.99 (0-06-072491-9). 352pp. Three of Wilder's diaries — one never before published — chronicle the Little House author's travels with her husband Almanzo and daughter Rose. (Rev: BL 12/15/05) [813]

WOOLF, VIRGINIA

1256 Brackett, Virginia. *Restless Genius: The Story of Virginia Woolf* (7–12). Series: Writers of Imagination. 2004, Morgan Reynolds LB $21.95 (1-931798-37-0). 144pp. Woolf's personal life — her relationship with Vita Sackville-West is touched on — and mental stability are the main focus of this brief, interesting biography that also discusses her writing and its influence. (Rev: BCCB 11/04; BL 10/1/04; SLJ 11/04) [921]

ZINDEL, PAUL

1257 Daniel, Susanna. *Paul Zindel* (5–8). Series: The Library of Author Biographies. 2004, Rosen LB $26.50 (0-8239-4524-3). 112pp. Covers Zindel's career as a YA author, with analysis of his work, an interview, and lists of works and awards. (Rev: SLJ 1/05) [921]

Composers

BACH, JOHANN SEBASTIAN

1258 Getzinger, Donna, and Daniel Felsenfeld. *Johann Sebastian Bach and the Art of Baroque Music* (6–12). Illus. Series: Classical Composers. 2004, Morgan Reynolds LB $23.95 (1-931798-22-2). 144pp. This biography reviews Bach's life and times, emphasizing in particular his musical education and commitment and his love for this family. (Rev: BL 6/1–15/04; SLJ 8/04) [780]

BERLIOZ, HECTOR

1259 Whiting, Jim. *The Life and Times of Hector Berlioz* (5–7). Series: Masters of Music: The World's Greatest Composers. 2004, Mitchell Lane LB $19.95 (1-58415-259-1). 48pp. A brief biography of the talented and troubled creator of the *Symphonie fantastique*. (Rev: SLJ 2/05) [921]

HANDEL, GEORGE FRIDERIC

1260 Getzinger, Donna, and Daniel Felsenfeld. *George Frideric Handel and Music for Voices* (6–10). Series: Classical Composers. 2004, Morgan Reynolds LB $23.95 (1-931798-23-0). 144pp. Han-

del's life and career are placed in historical context. (Rev: SLJ 11/04) [921]

JOPLIN, SCOTT

1261 Bankston, John. *The Life and Times of Scott Joplin* (5–7). Series: Masters of Music: The World's Greatest Composers. 2004, Mitchell Lane LB $19.95 (1-58415-270-2). 48pp. Joplin's career as a ragtime piano player and composer is documented, with coverage of his African American heritage. (Rev: SLJ 2/05) [921]

MESSIAEN, OLIVIER

1262 Bryant, Jen. *Music for the End of Time* (4–7). 2005, Eerdmans $17.00 (0-8028-5529-7). 32pp. This fictionalized picture-book biography tells how French soldier Olivier Messiaen was allowed by his captors to compose and perform music at a German prison camp. (Rev: BL 9/1/05) [921]

VIVALDI, ANTONIO

1263 Getzinger, Donna, and Daniel Felsenfeld. *Antonio Vivaldi and the Baroque Tradition* (6–10). Series: Classical Composers. 2004, Morgan Reynolds LB $23.95 (1-931798-20-6). The story of the rise and fall of this prolific composer as well as of his music world and the importance of Venice in this sphere. (Rev: BL 4/15/04; SLJ 6/04) [921]

WAGNER, RICHARD

1264 Getzinger, Donna, and Daniel Felsenfeld. *Richard Wagner and German Opera* (6–10). Series: Classical Composers. 2004, Morgan Reynolds LB $23.95 (1-931798-24-9). 144pp. A well-written, balanced biography that discusses Wagner's flaws as well as his great achievements. (Rev: SLJ 11/04) [921]

Performers (Actors, Musicians, etc.)

AILEY, ALVIN

1265 Cruz, Barbara C. *Alvin Ailey: Celebrating African-American Culture in Dance* (5–9). Series: African-American Biographies. 2004, Enslow LB $26.60 (0-7660-2293-5). 112pp. Ailey's life and contributions to dance are detailed, including a chapter on the classic "Revelations" and information on his contemporaries. (Rev: SLJ 1/05) [921]

ANDERSON, MARIAN

1266 Freedman, Russell. *The Voice That Challenged a Nation: Marian Anderson and the Struggle for Equal Rights* (4–8). 2004, Houghton $18.00 (0-618-

15976-2). 128pp. Beautifully illustrated with period photographs, this picture-book biography of the African American vocalist describes her life and the events leading up to her historic concert at the Lincoln Memorial. (Rev: BL 6/1–15/04; HB 5–6/04; SLJ 7/04) [782.1]

BALANCHINE, GEORGE

1267 Gottlieb, Robert. *George Balanchine: The Ballet Maker* (8–12). 2004, HarperCollins $19.95 (0-06-075070-7). 224pp. Balanchine's ballet talent was recognized at a young age; this biography follows his progress from St. Petersburg to New York and worldwide fame. (Rev: BL 11/1/04) [792.8]

1268 Seibert, Brian. *George Balanchine* (6–9). Illus. Series: Library of American Choreographers. 2005, Rosen LB $23.95 (0-4042-0447-4). 48pp. The life and career of the Russian-born ballet choreographer; there are no source notes. (Rev: BL 11/1/05) [792.8]

CHARLES, RAY

1269 Duggleby, John. *Uh Huh! The Story of Ray Charles* (6–12). 2005, Morgan Reynolds LB $26.95 (1-931798-65-6). 160pp. In addition to an account of Ray Charles's life and music, this volume reveals much about the social context of his times. (Rev: SLJ 10/05) [921]

DAVIS, MILES

1270 Dell, Pamela. *Miles Davis: Jazz Master* (5–8). Series: Journey to Freedom. 2005, Child's World LB $28.50 (1-59296-232-7). 40pp. An easy-to-read biography that deals frankly with the trumpeter's addiction to heroin and his difficult personality. (Rev: SLJ 8/05) [921]

DYLAN, BOB

1271 Roberts, Jeremy. *Bob Dylan: Voice of a Generation* (8–11). Illus. Series: Lerner Biographies. 2005, Lerner LB $27.93 (0-8225-1368-4). 128pp. This evenhanded biography chronicles the folk singer's transformation from Bobby Zimmerman in small-town Minnesota to cultural icon. (Rev: BL 6/1–15/05) [921]

JACKSON, MAHALIA

1272 Kramer, Barbara. *Mahalia Jackson: The Voice of Gospel and Civil Rights* (6–10). Illus. Series: African-American Biographies. 2004, Enslow LB $20.95 (0-7660-2115-7). 128pp. This biography traces the life of the singer and civil rights activist

from her childhood in New Orleans to her great successes as a gospel singer. (Rev: BL 2/15/04) [921]

KELLY, EMMETT, SR.

1273 Wilkerson, J. L. *Sad-Face Clown: Emmett Kelly* (5–8). Illus. Series: The Great Heartlanders. 2004, Acorn paper $9.95 (0-9664470-9-3). 118pp. The story of Emmett Kelly, Sr., who — as Weary Willie — became possibly the world's most famous circus clown. (Rev: SLJ 4/04) [791.3]

MA, YO-YO

1274 Chippendale, Lisa A. *Yo-Yo Ma: A Cello Superstar Brings Music to the World* (6–8). Illus. Series: People to Know. 2004, Enslow LB $19.95 (0-7660-2286-2). 112pp. Traces the life of cellist Yo-Yo Ma, from child prodigy to internationally recognized musical virtuoso. (Rev: BL 11/1/04; SLJ 2/05) [921]

MILLER, NORMA

1275 Govenar, Alan, ed. *Stompin' at the Savoy: The Story of Norma Miller* (5–8). 2006, Candlewick $16.99 (0-7636-2244-3). 56pp. The energy of Norma Miller, who was still going strong in her early 80s, infuses the pages of this brief biography, made up largely of excerpts from interviews with the legendary African American swing dancer. (Rev: BL 2/1/06; SLJ 3/06) [792.8]

PUENTE, TITO

1276 Olmstead, Mary. *Tito Puente* (4–7). Illus. Series: Hispanic-American Biographies. 2004, Raintree LB $31.36 (1-4109-0713-9). 64pp. A concise account of the life and career of Tito Puente, the popular American bandleader and percussionist who in the 1950s was nicknamed the Mambo King. (Rev: BL 2/1/05; SLJ 8/05) [784.4]

WINFREY, OPRAH

1277 Krohn, Katherine. *Oprah Winfrey* (6–9). Illus. Series: Just the Facts Biographies. 2005, Lerner LB $20.95 (0-8225-2472-4). 112pp. Simple text and clear definitions make this biography suitable for reluctant and ESL readers. (Rev: BL 4/1/05) [794.4502]

1278 Westen, Robin. *Oprah Winfrey: "I Don't Believe in Failure."* (5–8). Series: African-American Biography Library. 2005, Enslow LB $31.93 (0-7660-2462-8). 128pp. Winfrey's phenomenal rise to success in the worlds of business and entertainment is placed in social context. (Rev: SLJ 11/05) [921]

Contemporary and Historical Americans

Collective

1279 Angelo, Bonnie. *First Families: Their Lives in the White House* (8–12). Illus. 2005, Morrow $25.95 (0-06-056356-7). 352pp. A fascinating look at life in the White House for presidents and their family members. (Rev: BL 8/05) [973]

1280 Buller, Jon, et al. *Smart About the Presidents* (4–7). Series: Smart About History. 2004, Penguin paper $5.99 (0-448-43372-9). 64pp. Pertinent facts about each president are conveyed in an informative, accessible style. (Rev: BL 9/1/04; SLJ 4/05) [920]

1281 Delano, Marfé Ferguson. *American Heroes* (5–8). Illus. 2005, National Geographic LB $45.90 (0-7922-7215-3). 192pp. Fifty men and women whose heroism has helped to shape America are profiled in this attractive large-format volume. (Rev: BL 12/1/05; SLJ 2/06) [920.073]

1282 Doherty, Kieran. *Voyageurs, Lumberjacks, and Farmers: Pioneers of the Midwest* (5–8). Series: Shaping America. 2004, Oliver LB $22.95 (1-881508-54-4). 176pp. The lives and accomplishments of eight individuals — including Antoine Cadillac, Jean du Sable, and Josiah and Abigail Snelling — who played key roles in the settlement of the Midwest are placed in historical context, with discussion of the plight of Native Americans in the region. (Rev: SLJ 9/04) [920]

1283 Fradin, Dennis Brindell. *The Founders: The 39 Stories Behind the U.S. Constitution* (4–7). 2005, Walker $22.95 (0-8027-8972-2). 176pp. The 39 men who signed the Constitution are profiled in brief chapters that include information on their home states. (Rev: BL 10/15/05; SLJ 9/05) [973.3]

1284 Hughes, Chris. *The Constitutional Convention* (5–9). Series: People at the Center Of. 2005, Gale LB $23.70 (1-56711-918-2). 48pp. After an overview of the convention, this volume provides biographical information on key figures including George Washington, Benjamin Franklin, James Madison, and Alexander Hamilton. (Rev: SLJ 6/05) [920]

1285 Hutchinson, Kay Bailey. *American Heroines: The Spirited Women Who Shaped Our Country* (8–12). Illus. 2004, Morrow $24.95 (0-06-056635-3). 384pp. Hutchinson, U.S. senator from Texas, celebrates the lives of courageous American women from many walks of life, both in and out of the limelight. (Rev: BL 11/15/04) [920.72]

1286 Kallen, Stuart A. *Women of the Civil Rights Movement* (7–12). Series: Women in History. 2005, Gale LB $28.70 (1-59018-569-2). 112pp. Women who made important contributions to the U.S. civil rights movement are celebrated in chapters devoted to organizations, protests, education, voting rights, radicals, and so forth. (Rev: SLJ 11/05) [920]

1287 Langley, Wanda. *Women of the Wind: Early Women Aviators* (6–9). Illus. 2006, Morgan Reynolds LB $26.95 (1-931798-81-8). 160pp. From childhood through achievements in the air, this attractive collective biography covers nine American women flyers. (Rev: BL 2/15/06; SLJ 2/06) [629.13]

1288 Masters, Nancy Robinson. *Extraordinary Patriots of the United States of America: Colonial Times to Pre-Civil War* (5–8). Series: Extraordinary People. 2005, Children's Pr. LB $40.00 (0-516-24404-3). 288pp. Interesting 3- to 5-page profiles are arranged chronologically by year of birth. (Rev: SLJ 2/06) [920]

1289 O'Connor, Jane. *If the Walls Could Talk: Family Life at the White House* (4–7). 2004, Simon & Schuster $16.95 (0-689-86863-4). 48pp. This inside view of family life within the White House — with caricatures and interesting trivia — is similar to Judith St. George's *So You Want to Be President* (Putnam, 2000). (Rev: BL 8/04; SLJ 9/04)

1290 Orr, Tamra. *The Salem Witch Trials* (5–8). Illus. Series: People at the Center. 2004, Gale LB $18.96 (1-56711-770-8). 48pp. This collective biography introduces some of the men and women who played key roles in the Salem Witch Trials. (Rev: BL 5/15/04; SLJ 9/04) [133.4]

1291 Rappaport, Doreen. *In the Promised Land: Lives of Jewish Americans* (4–7). 2005, Harper-Collins LB $16.89 (0-06-059395-4). 32pp. A look at the lives and diverse accomplishments of 13 notable Jewish Americans, including Asser Levy, Harry Houdini, Jonas Salk, and Steven Spielberg. (Rev: BL 1/1–15/05; SLJ 5/05) [920]

1292 Rodriguez, Robert, and Tamra Orr. *Great Hispanic-Americans* (6–12). 2005, Publications Int'l LB $38.00 (1-4127-1148-7). 128pp. More than 50 Hispanic Americans from different walks of life are profiled in accessible text. (Rev: SLJ 1/06) [920]

1293 Sullivan, Otha Richard. *African American Millionaires* (5–10). Series: Black Stars. 2004, Wiley $24.95 (0-471-46928-9). 158pp. Tyra Banks and Oprah Winfrey are included here, but so are many names that may be unfamiliar to readers, such as William Alexander Leidesdorff and Annie Turnbo Malone. (Rev: SLJ 5/05) [920]

Civil and Human Rights Leaders

ADDAMS, JANE

1294 Caravantes, Peggy. *Waging Peace: The Story of Jane Addams* (5–8). 2004, Morgan Reynolds LB $21.95 (1-931798-40-0). 144pp. Covers Addams's life and achievements, with good material on her youth and the lessons she learned from her Quaker father. (Rev: SLJ 2/05) [921]

BAKER, ELLA

1295 Bohannon, Lisa Frederiksen. *Freedom Cannot Rest: Ella Baker and the Civil Rights Movement* (7–12). Illus. Series: Civil Rights Leaders. 2005, Morgan Reynolds LB $24.95 (1-931798-71-0). 176pp. A well-illustrated and evenhanded introduction to the life and accomplishments of Ella Baker, a major — but often overlooked — player in the U.S. civil rights movement. (Rev: SLJ 12/05)

BATES, DAISY

1296 Fradin, Judith Bloom, and Dennis Brindell Fradin. *The Power of One: Daisy Bates and the Little Rock Nine* (8–11). Illus. 2004, Clarion $19.00 (0-618-31556-X). 178pp. A detailed profile of Daisy Bates, who as president of the Arkansas chapter of

the NAACP played a pivotal role in the 1957 integration of Central High School in Little Rock. (Rev: BL 2/1/05; SLJ 4/05) [323]

BETHUNE, MARY MCLEOD

1297 Somervill, Barbara A. *Mary McLeod Bethune: African-American Educator* (4–7). Series: Our People. 2003, The Child's World LB $27.07 (1-59296-008-1). 32pp. A profile of the African American educator and leader, with sidebars that add historical context. (Rev: SLJ 4/04) [921]

BROWN, JOHN

1298 Reynolds, David S. *John Brown, Abolitionist: The Man Who Killed Slavery, Sparked the Civil War, and Seeded Civil Rights* (8–12). 2005, Knopf $30.00 (0-375-41188-7). 496pp. This insightful biography adds fuel to the continuing debate over what motivated the fiery abolitionist. (Rev: BL 2/1/05) [973.7]

CHAVEZ, CESAR

1299 Brown, Jonatha A. *Cesar Chavez* (5–8). Series: Trailblazers of the Modern World. 2004, World Almanac LB $29.27 (0-8368-5097-1). 48pp. Report writers will find lots of suitable information in this work that covers Chavez's life and accomplishments. (Rev: SLJ 7/04) [921]

GARVEY, MARCUS

1300 Caravantes, Peggy. *Marcus Garvey: Black Nationalist* (6–10). Series: Twentieth Century Leaders. 2004, Morgan Reynolds LB $21.95 (1-931798-14-1). 128pp. A biography of this black nationalist, Pan-Africanist, and exponent of black civil rights. (Rev: BL 2/15/04; SLJ 11/03; VOYA 6/04) [921]

1301 Schraff, Anne. *Marcus Garvey: Controversial Champion of Black Pride* (6–10). Illus. Series: African-American Biographies. 2004, Enslow LB $20.95 (0-7660-2168-8). 128pp. This is a fine biography of the controversial leader of the early 20th-century Pan-African movement with discussion of his opinions, including his separatist views on race. (Rev: BL 2/15/04) [921]

HAMER, FANNIE LOU

1302 Fiorelli, June Estep. *Fannie Lou Hamer: A Voice for Freedom* (5–10). Series: Avisson Young Adult. 2005, Avisson paper $19.95 (1-888105-62-3). 117pp. Hamer's life, including her youth, are described and placed in the context of events in the United States at the time. (Rev: SLJ 2/06) [921]

KING, CORETTA SCOTT

1303 Rhodes, Lisa Renee. *Coretta Scott King: Civil Rights Activist* (7–12). Illus. Series: Black Americans of Achievement. 2005, Chelsea House LB $23.95 (0-79108-251-2). 136pp. This revised edition of King's life adds new photographs and information boxes to the description of her childhood, education, marriage, participation in the civil rights movement, and work after her husband's assassination. (Rev: SLJ 11/05) [921]

KING, MARTIN LUTHER, JR.

1304 Hatt, Christine. *Martin Luther King Jr.* (6–9). Series: Judge for Yourself. 2004, World Almanac LB $29.26 (0-8368-5562-0). 64pp. Biographical information about King is followed by a "Judge for Yourself" section of controversial issues that should be considered. (Rev: SLJ 10/04) [921]

1305 Pastan, Amy. *Martin Luther King Jr.* (5–10). Illus. Series: DK Biography. 2004, DK LB $14.99 (0-7566-0491-5); paper $4.99 (0-7566-0342-0). 128pp. A heavily illustrated, attractive biography of King that offers broad historical background. (Rev: BL 6/1–15/04) [921]

1306 Schloredt, Valerie, and Pam Brown. *Martin Luther King Jr.* (5–10). Illus. Series: World Peacemakers. 2004, Gale LB $27.44 (1-56711-977-8). 64pp. A readable account of this civil rights leader and the times in which he lived. (Rev: BL 2/15/04; SLJ 2/94) [921]

LYON, MARITCHA RÉMOND

1307 Bolden, Tonya. *Maritcha: A Remarkable Nineteenth-Century American Girl* (4–7). Illus. 2005, Abrams $17.95 (0-8109-5045-6). 48pp. Drawing on primary sources, Bolden tells the story of Maritcha Rémond Lyon, a free black girl who succeeded in her fight to attend an all-white high school in Rhode Island in the mid-19th century. (Rev: BL 2/1/05*; SLJ 2/05) [921]

PARKS, ROSA

1308 Davis, Kenneth C. *Don't Know Much About Rosa Parks* (4–7). Series: Don't Know Much About. 2005, HarperCollins LB $15.89 (0-06-028819-1); paper $4.99 (0-06-442126-0). 128pp. A question-and-answer format, interesting sidebars, and news photographs enliven this profile of Parks, which emphasizes her long-term commitment to civil rights. (Rev: BL 2/1/05) [323]

1309 Schraff, Anne. *Rosa Parks: "Tired of Giving In,"* (4–8). Series: African-American Biography Library. 2005, Enslow LB $31.93 (0-7660-2463-6).

128pp. An accessible profile of Parks and her importance. (Rev: SLJ 10/05) [921]

RANDOLPH, A. PHILIP

1310 Miller, Calvin Craig. *A. Philip Randolph and the African-American Labor Movement* (7–10). Illus. Series: Civil Rights Leaders. 2005, Morgan Reynolds $24.95 (1-931798-50-8). 160pp. The life and achievements of the founding president of the Brotherhood of Sleeping Car Porters. (Rev: BL 2/15/05; SLJ 5/05) [323]

RUSTIN, BAYARD

1311 Miller, Calvin Craig. *No Easy Answers: Bayard Rustin and the Civil Rights Movement* (7–10). Illus. Series: Civil Rights Leaders. 2005, Morgan Reynolds LB $24.95 (1-931798-43-5). 160pp. Rustin's significant achievements in the field of civil rights are discussed along with his homosexuality, which was a large factor in his relative obscurity. (Rev: BL 2/1/05; SLJ 6/05; VOYA 8/05) [323]

TRUTH, SOJOURNER

1312 Brezina, Corona. *Sojourner Truth's "Ain't I a Woman?" Speech: A Primary Source Investigation* (6–9). Illus. Series: Great Historic Debates and Speeches. 2005, Rosen LB $29.95 (1-4042-0154-8). 64pp. A fascinating account of Truth's historic 1851 speech to the Women's Convention in Akron, Ohio; the primary sources offer insight into the words of a woman who could neither read nor write. (Rev: BL 2/15/05; SLJ 5/05) [306.3]

TURNER, NAT

1313 Bisson, Terry. *Nat Turner: Slave Revolt Leader* (6–9). Illus. Series: Black Americans of Achievement. 2004, Chelsea House LB $22.95 (0-7910-8167-2). 96pp. New illustrations, essays on related figures, and a list of Web sites enhance this new edition of a profile of Nat Turner, who led a bloody Virginia slave uprising in 1831. (Rev: BL 2/1/05) [975.5]

WOODHULL, VICTORIA

1314 Brody, Miriam. *Victoria Woodhull: Free Spirit for Women's Rights* (7–12). Series: Oxford Portraits. 2004, Oxford LB $28.00 (0-19-514367-1). 159pp. Presenting historical and social context, this biography covers the American reformer's difficult childhood and complex adult life. (Rev: SLJ 2/05) [921]

Presidents and Their Families

ADAMS, JOHN

1315 Behrman, Carol H. *John Adams* (5–8). Illus. Series: Presidential Leaders. 2003, Lerner LB $26.60 (0-8225-0820-6). 112pp. This biography provides lots of details and illustrations, covering Adams's life and career. (Rev: BL 1/1–15/04) [973.4]

1316 Feinberg, Barbara S. *John Adams* (5–8). Illus. Series: Encyclopedia of Presidents. 2003, Children's Pr. LB $33.00 (0-516-22680-0). 128pp. An informative and appealing account of Adams's life and achievements, with glossary, timeline, and lists of books and Web sites. (Rev: BL 1/1–15/04) [973.4]

ADAMS, JOHN AND ABIGAIL

1317 Ashby, Ruth. *John and Abigail Adams* (5–8). Illus. Series: Presidents and First Ladies. 2005, Gareth Stevens LB $22.50 (0-8368-5755-0). 48pp. An accessible, balanced, and attractive discussion of the Adamses and the contributions each made to their joint lives. (Rev: BL 3/1/05) [921]

BUSH, GEORGE W.

1318 Kachurek, Sandra J. *George W. Bush* (4–7). Series: United States Presidents. 2004, Enslow LB $26.60 (0-7660-2040-1). 128pp. A balanced and well-documented profile with plenty of photographs plus lists of Web sites and places to visit. (Rev: BL 9/15/04) [921]

CARTER, JIMMY

1319 Kent, Deborah. *Jimmy Carter* (4–7). Illus. Series: Encyclopedia of Presidents — Second Series. 2005, Children's Pr. LB $33.00 (0-516-22975-3). 112pp. Updated from the 1989 volume, this new, redesigned edition covers the former president's life and career and adds information about his recent work. (Rev: BL 6/1–15/05) [973.926]

CLINTON, BILL AND HILLARY

1320 Ashby, Ruth. *Bill and Hillary Rodham Clinton* (5–8). Illus. Series: Presidents and First Ladies. 2005, Gareth Stevens LB $22.50 (0-8368-5756-9). 48pp. The story of the Clintons before, during, and after Mr. Clinton's presidency; with photographs and a bibliography. (Rev: BL 3/1/05; SLJ 8/05) [921]

GRANT, ULYSSES S.

1321 Rice, Earle, Jr. *Ulysses S. Grant: Defender of the Union* (8–11). Illus. Series: Civil War Leaders. 2005, Morgan Reynolds LB $24.95 (1-931798-48-6). 176pp. A vivid portrait of Grant, who rose from humble beginnings in his native Ohio to achieve acclaim as a military leader and ascend to the highest office in the land. (Rev: BL 3/15/05; SLJ 11/05) [973.8]

HOOVER, HERBERT

1322 Ruth, Amy. *Herbert Hoover* (5–8). Series: Presidential Leaders. 2004, Lerner LB $26.60 (0-8225-0821-4). 112pp. Quotations, photographs, and informative sidebars add to the engaging text about Hoover's life and times. (Rev: SLJ 1/05) [921]

JACKSON, ANDREW

1323 Marrin, Albert. *Old Hickory: Andrew Jackson and the American People* (6–12). 2004, Penguin $30.00 (0-525-47293-2). 240pp. The life and times of a colorful president are presented in a suitably vivid biography. (Rev: BL 12/1/04; SLJ 12/04; VOYA 6/05) [921]

JEFFERSON, THOMAS

1324 Davis, Kenneth C. *Don't Know Much About Thomas Jefferson* (4–7). Series: Don't Know Much About. 2005, HarperTrophy LB $15.89 (0-06-028821-3); paper $4.99 (0-06-442128-7). 128pp. Jefferson's many accomplishments and contributions are presented in a question-and-answer format amplified by sidebar features, maps, and quotations that add context. (Rev: BL 2/1/05; SLJ 5/05) [921]

1325 Harness, Cheryl. *Thomas Jefferson* (4–7). Illus. 2004, National Geographic $17.95 (0-7922-6496-7). 48pp. Harness paints a personal portrait of Jefferson and his various roles in this picture book, enhanced by maps and eye-catching illustrations. (Rev: BL 2/1/04; SLJ 2/04) [973.4]

KENNEDY, JOHN F.

1326 Anderson, Catherine Corley. *John F. Kennedy* (5–8). Series: Presidential Leaders. 2004, Lerner LB $26.60 (0-8225-0812-5). 112pp. Quotations, photographs, and informative sidebars add to the engaging text about Kennedy's life and times. (Rev: SLJ 1/05) [921]

1327 Kaplan, Howard S. *John F. Kennedy* (5–10). Illus. Series: DK Biography. 2004, DK paper $4.99 (0-7566-0340-4). 128pp. A heavily illustrated, attractive biography of Kennedy that offers broad historical background. (Rev: BL 6/1–15/04) [921]

1328 Sommer, Shelley. *John F. Kennedy: His Life and Legacy* (5–8). Illus. 2005, HarperCollins LB $17.89 (0-06-054136-9). 160pp. This engaging biography presents a favorable profile of the 35th president's private and public lives and assesses his legacy. (Rev: BL 1/1–15/05; SLJ 10/05) [921]

LINCOLN, ABRAHAM

1329 Davis, Kenneth C. *Don't Know Much About Abraham Lincoln* (4–8). Series: Don't Know Much About. 2004, HarperCollins LB $15.89 (0-06-028820-5); paper $4.99 (0-06-442127-9). 142pp. A question-and-answer format gives easy access to key details about Lincoln's life. (Rev: BL 2/1/05; SLJ 2/04) [921]

1330 Holzer, Harold. *The President Is Shot! The Assassination of Abraham Lincoln* (5–8). Illus. 2004, Boyds Mills $17.95 (1-56397-985-3). 144pp. A riveting account of Lincoln's assassination, with archival illustrations and historical context. (Rev: BL 3/1/04*; SLJ 2/04) [973.7]

1331 Roberts, Jeremy. *Abraham Lincoln* (5–7). Series: Presidential Leaders. 2003, Lerner LB $26.60 (0-8225-0817-6). 112pp. From childhood through assassination, this is a thorough, well-illustrated, and well-organized account of Lincoln's life. (Rev: SLJ 2/04) [921]

1332 Stone, Tanya Lee. *Abraham Lincoln* (5–10). Illus. Series: DK Biography. 2005, DK $14.99 (0-7566-0833-3); paper $4.99 (0-7566-0834-1). 128pp. A heavily illustrated, attractive biography of Lincoln that offers broad historical background. (Rev: BL 6/1–15/04) [921]

MADISON, JAMES

1333 Kent, Zachary. *James Madison: Creating a Nation* (5–8). Series: America's Founding Fathers. 2004, Enslow LB $26.60 (0-7660-2180-7). 128pp. This profile of Madison focuses largely on his public life from the period leading up to the American Revolution through his presidency. (Rev: BL 6/1–15/04) [921]

MADISON, JAMES AND DOLLEY

1334 Ashby, Ruth. *James and Dolley Madison* (5–8). Illus. Series: Presidents and First Ladies. 2005, Gareth Stevens LB $22.50 (0-8368-5757-7). 48pp. An accessible, balanced, and attractive discussion of the Madisons and the contributions each made to their joint lives. (Rev: BL 3/1/05; SLJ 8/05) [921]

ROOSEVELT, ELEANOR

1335 Fleming, Candace. *Our Eleanor: A Scrapbook Look at Eleanor Roosevelt's Remarkable Life* (6–9). Illus. 2005, Simon & Schuster $19.95 (0-689-86544-9). 192pp. Archival photos, first-person accounts, direct quotes, and informative sidebars document Roosevelt's life and cover her character

and questions about her sexuality. (Rev: BL 9/1/05; SLJ 11/05*; VOYA 10/05) [973.917]

1336 Koestler-Grack, Rachel A. *The Story of Eleanor Roosevelt* (4–7). Illus. Series: Breakthrough Biographies. 2004, Chelsea House LB $14.95 (0-7910-7313-0). 32pp. This brief biography covers Roosevelt's early years as well as her later contributions to her country and to the world. (Rev: BL 3/1/04) [973917]

1337 Somervill, Barbara A. *Eleanor Roosevelt: First Lady of the World* (5–8). Illus. Series: Signature Lives: Modern America. 2005, Compass Point $22.95 (0-7565-0992-0). 112pp. An appealing biography that traces the First Lady's life and focuses on her tireless efforts to make life better for America's disadvantaged minorities. (Rev: BL 10/15/05) [973.917]

ROOSEVELT, FRANKLIN D.

1338 Allport, Alan. *Franklin Delano Roosevelt* (5–7). Series: Great American Presidents. 2003, Chelsea House LB $21.85 (0-7910-7598-2). 102pp. A concise life of the longest-serving president in U.S. history, from his childhood through his years in the White House, with a foreword by Walter Cronkite. (Rev: SLJ 4/04) [921]

ROOSEVELT, FRANKLIN D. AND ELEANOR

1339 Ashby, Ruth. *Franklin and Eleanor Roosevelt* (5–8). Illus. Series: Presidents and First Ladies. 2005, Gareth Stevens LB $22.50 (0-8368-5758-5). 48pp. An accessible, balanced, and attractive discussion of the Roosevelts and the contributions each made to their joint lives. (Rev: BL 3/1/05) [921]

ROOSEVELT, THEODORE

1340 Kelley, Alison Turnbull. *Theodore Roosevelt* (5–7). Series: Great American Presidents. 2003, Chelsea House LB $21.85 (0-7910-7606-7). 102pp. An illustrated profile of the 26th president, from his childhood through his public life and legacy. (Rev: SLJ 4/04) [921]

WASHINGTON, GEORGE

1341 Adler, David A. *George Washington: An Illustrated Biography* (5–7). 2004, Holiday House $24.95 (0-8234-1838-3). 288pp. Adler presents a balanced and well-researched biography of Washington, giving details of his character as well as information on key events of his time. (Rev: BL 9/15/04; SLJ 12/04) [973.4]

1342 Hort, Lenny. *George Washington* (5–10). Illus. Series: DK Biography. 2005, DK $14.99 (0-7566-0832-5); paper $4.99 (0-7566-0835-X). 128pp. A heavily illustrated, attractive biography of the man born in Virginia. (Rev: BL 6/1–15/04) [921]

1343 McNeese, Tim. *George Washington: America's Leader in War and Peace* (4–8). Series: Leaders of the American Revolution. 2005, Chelsea House LB $24.95 (0-7910-8619-4). 140pp. An even-handed introduction to Washington's life and contributions, presented chronologically with occasional factboxes; suitable for report writers. (Rev: SLJ 1/06) [921]

1344 Roberts, Jeremy. *George Washington* (5–7). Series: Presidential Leaders. 2003, Lerner LB $26.60 (0-8225-0818-4). 112pp. This engaging biography chronicles the life and achievements of America's first president and dispels some widely believed myths. (Rev: SLJ 2/04) [921]

WILSON, WOODROW

1345 Lukes, Bonnie L. *Woodrow Wilson and the Progressive Era* (6–10). Series: World Leaders. 2005, Morgan Reynolds LB $26.95 (1-931798-79-6). 192pp. A chronological survey of Wilson's life from birth in 1856 through his death in 1924, with discussion of his achievements in light of the global events of the time. (Rev: SLJ 2/06) [921]

WILSON, WOODROW AND EDITH

1346 Ashby, Ruth. *Woodrow and Edith Wilson* (5–8). Illus. Series: Presidents and First Ladies. 2005, Gareth Stevens LB $22.50 (0-8368-5759-3). 48pp. An accessible, balanced, and attractive discussion of the Wilsons and the contributions each made to their joint lives. (Rev: BL 3/1/05; SLJ 8/05) [921]

Other Government and Public Figures

ADAMS, SAMUEL

1347 Burgan, Michael. *Samuel Adams: Patriot and Statesman* (4–7). Illus. Series: Signature Lives (Revolutionary War Era). 2005, Compass Point LB $22.95 (0-7565-0823-1). 48pp. Profiles the man who played a key role in the tax rebellion and Boston Tea Party. (Rev: BL 4/1/05) [921]

ALLEN, ETHAN

1348 Haugen, Brenda. *Ethan Allen: Green Mountain Rebel* (4–7). Illus. Series: Signature Lives (Revolutionary War Era). 2005, Compass Point LB $22.95 (0-7565-0824-X). 48pp. Traces the life of the man who, along with Benedict Arnold, led the Green Mountain Boys in capturing Fort Ticondero-

ga from the British. (Rev: BL 4/1/05; SLJ 8/05) [921]

ARNOLD, BENEDICT

1349 Dell, Pamela. *Benedict Arnold: From Patriot to Traitor* (4–7). Illus. Series: Signature Lives (Revolutionary War Era). 2005, Compass Point LB $22.95 (0-7565-0825-8). 48pp. A well-designed and informative profile of the man who betrayed his country. (Rev: BL 4/1/05) [921]

1350 Powell, Walter L. *Benedict Arnold: Revolutionary War Hero and Traitor* (5–8). Series: Library of American Lives and Times. 2004, Rosen LB $31.95 (0-8239-6627-5). 112pp. The life of Benedict Arnold, the American patriot who switched his allegiance to the British cause. (Rev: SLJ 7/04) [921]

1351 Sonneborn, Liz. *Benedict Arnold: Hero and Traitor* (4–8). Series: Leaders of the American Revolution. 2005, Chelsea House LB $24.95 (0-7910-8617-8). 130pp. An even-handed introduction to Arnold's life, presented chronologically with occasional factboxes; suitable for report writers. (Rev: SLJ 1/06) [921]

BOOTH, EDWIN AND JOHN WILKES

1352 Giblin, James Cross. *Good Brother, Bad Brother: The Story of Edwin Booth and John Wilkes Booth* (5–8). Illus. 2005, Clarion $22.00 (0-618-09642-6). 256pp. In a compelling and highly readable narrative, Giblin reveals the alcoholism and depression that plagued the theatrical Booth family, the disagreement between the two brothers over the Civil War, and the effects of the assassination on Edwin's later life. (Rev: BL 5/1/05*; SLJ 5/05) [792.02]

BURR, AARON

1353 Melton, Buckner F. *Aaron Burr: The Rise and Fall of an American Politician* (5–8). Series: Library of American Lives and Times. 2004, Rosen LB $31.95 (0-8239-6626-7). 112pp. This engaging biography chronicles the rise and fall of the Revolutionary War hero who was later branded a traitor. (Rev: SLJ 7/04) [921]

CLINTON, HILLARY RODHAM

1354 Guernsey, JoAnn Bren. *Hillary Rodham Clinton* (5–8). Illus. 2005, Lerner LB $27.93 (0-8225-2372-8); paper $7.95 (0-8225-9613-X). 112pp. Traces Clinton's life from childhood, and covers the trials of her husband's second term in office in some detail. (Rev: BL 6/1–15/05; SLJ 7/05) [921]

1355 Gullo, Jim. *Hillary Rodham Clinton* (7–12). Series: The Importance Of. 2004, Gale LB $21.96 (1-59018-310-X). 112pp. Clinton's natural leadership abilities and achievements in office are the main focus of this balanced biography that also covers her youth, education, and law career. (Rev: SLJ 4/04) [921]

CRAZY HORSE (SIOUX CHIEF)

1356 Haugen, Brenda. *Crazy Horse: Sioux Warrior* (5–8). Series: Signature Lives. 2005, Compass Point LB $22.95 (0-7565-0999-8). 112pp. Crazy Horse's life and efforts to save his native lands and way of life are documented here. (Rev: SLJ 2/06) [921]

CUSTER, GEORGE ARMSTRONG

1357 Anderson, Paul Christopher. *George Armstrong Custer: The Indian Wars and the Battle of the Little Big Horn* (4–8). Series: The Library of American Lives and Times. 2004, Rosen LB $31.95 (0-8239-6631-3). 112pp. The importance of understanding history is emphasized in this balanced and well-illustrated look at Custer's life and stance at Little Big Horn. (Rev: SLJ 7/04) [920]

FRANKLIN, BENJAMIN

1358 Dash, Joan. *A Dangerous Engine: Benjamin Franklin, from Scientist to Diplomat* (6–10). 2006, Farrar $17.00 (0-374-30669-9). 246pp. Franklin's keen interest in science and the development of new technology is emphasized in this lively biography illustrated with pen-and-ink drawings. (Rev: BCCB 1/06; HB 3–4/06; SLJ 2/06) [921]

1359 Gaustad, Edwin S. *Benjamin Franklin: Inventing America* (7–10). Series: Oxford Portraits. 2004, Oxford LB $28.00 (0-19-515732-X). 143pp. The life and achievements of Benjamin Franklin are described using many quotations from Franklin's autobiography. (Rev: SLJ 2/05) [921]

GERONIMO

1360 Haugen, Brenda. *Geronimo: Apache Warrior* (5–8). Series: Signature Lives. 2005, Compass Point LB $22.95 (0-7565-1002-3). 112pp. Geronimo's unsuccessful efforts to secure freedom for his people are documented in this attractive book. (Rev: SLJ 2/06) [921]

HAMILTON, ALEXANDER

1361 Haugen, Brenda. *Alexander Hamilton: Founding Father and Statesman* (4–7). Illus. Series: Signature Lives (Revolutionary War Era). 2005, Compass Point LB $22.95 (0-7565-0827-4). 48pp. Traces the life of the man who became the first sec-

retary of the treasury. (Rev: BL 4/1/05; SLJ 8/05) [921]

HICKOK, WILD BILL

1362 Rosa, Joseph G. *Wild Bill Hickok: Sharpshooter and U.S. Marshal of the Wild West* (4–8). Series: The Library of American Lives and Times. 2004, Rosen LB $31.95 (0-8239-6632-1). 112pp. The importance of understanding history is emphasized in this balanced and well-illustrated look at Hickok's life. (Rev: SLJ 7/04) [921]

HOOVER, J. EDGAR

1363 Cunningham, Kevin. *J. Edgar Hoover: Controversial FBI Director* (5–8). Series: Signature Lives. 2005, Compass Point LB $22.95 (0-7565-0997-1). 112pp. This introduction to Hoover's career provides limited personal details, concentrating instead on his political ambitions and tendency to ignore ethical standards. (Rev: SLJ 1/06) [921]

HOUSTON, SAM

1364 Caravantes, Peggy. *An American in Texas: The Story of Sam Houston* (5–8). Series: Founders of the Republic. 2003, Morgan Reynolds LB $21.95 (1-931798-19-2). 144pp. A portrait of the colorful general who became the first president of the Republic of Texas. (Rev: SLJ 5/04) [921]

JACKSON, STONEWALL

1365 Brager, Bruce L. *There He Stands: The Story of Stonewall Jackson* (8–10). Illus. Series: Civil War Leaders. 2005, Morgan Reynolds LB $24.95 (1-931798-44-3). 176pp. The life and military career of Stonewall Jackson, one of the Civil War's most skilled tacticians; photographs, reproductions, and maps complement the well-written text. (Rev: SLJ 11/05) [921]

JOSEPH (NEZ PERCE CHIEF)

1366 Moulton, Candy. *Chief Joseph: Guardian of the People* (8–12). 2005, Tor $21.95 (0-765-31063-5). 240pp. The story of Chief Joseph's 1877 attempt to lead the Nez Percé tribe to safety in Canada. (Rev: BL 3/1/05) [979.50]

KENNEDY, ROBERT F.

1367 Koestler-Grack, Rachel A. *The Assassination of Robert F. Kennedy* (5–8). Series: American Moments. 2005, ABDO LB $25.65 (1-59197-931-5). 48pp. Kennedy's assassination is placed in historical context, with a brief biography and discussion of the aftermath of this tragedy. (Rev: SLJ 11/05) [921]

KERRY, JOHN

1368 Brager, Bruce L. *John Kerry: Senator from Massachusetts* (6–10). 2005, Morgan Reynolds LB $21.95 (1-931798-64-8). 128pp. Kerry's life and military service are presented along with his career in politics and unsuccessful bid for the presidency in 2004. (Rev: SLJ 8/05) [921]

LEE, ROBERT E.

1369 Rice, Earle, Jr. *Robert E. Lee: First Soldier of the Confederacy* (8–10). Illus. Series: Civil War Leaders. 2005, Morgan Reynolds LB $24.95 (1-931798-47-8). 176pp. Lee's childhood, adult life, and military career are covered; photographs, reproductions, and maps complement the well-written text. (Rev: SLJ 11/05) [921]

1370 Robertson, James I. *Robert E. Lee: Virginian Soldier, American Citizen* (7–10). Illus. 2005, Simon & Schuster $21.95 (0-689-85731-4). 176pp. A rich and even-handed portrait of Robert E. Lee, including a number of excerpts from such primary sources as letters and diaries. (Rev: BL 11/15/05; SLJ 1/06; VOYA 10/05) [973.7]

LITTLE CROW

1371 Swain, Gwenyth. *Little Crow: Leader of the Dakota* (6–12). 2004, Minnesota Historical Society $22.95 (0-87351-502-1). 112pp. Little Crow, who died in 1863, did all in his power to keep his people from war but joined them on the front lines when they chose to disregard his counsel. (Rev: BL 7/04; SLJ 7/04) [978.004]

MACARTHUR, DOUGLAS

1372 Haugen, Brenda. *Douglas MacArthur: America's General* (5–8). Series: Signature Lives. 2005, Compass Point LB $22.95 (0-7565-0994-7). 112pp. This introduction to MacArthur's career provides limited personal details but concentrates instead on his leadership abilities and military achievements. (Rev: SLJ 1/06) [921]

MORRIS, GOUVERNOR

1373 Crompton, Samuel Willard. *Gouverneur Morris: Creating a Nation* (5–8). Series: America's Founding Fathers. 2004, Enslow LB $20.95 (0-7660-2213-7). 128pp. An introduction to the life and legacy of Gouverneur Morris, who helped to edit the final draft of the Declaration of Independence. (Rev: SLJ 7/04) [973.4]

NORTON, ELEANOR HOLMES

1374 Marcovitz, Hal. *Eleanor Holmes Norton* (7–12). Series: African-American Leaders. 2003, Chelsea House LB $22.95 (0-7910-7682-2). 115pp.

Profiles the woman representing Washington, D.C. in the House of Representatives, and discusses her work on sexual harassment in the workplace. (Rev: SLJ 4/04) [921]

OBAMA, BARACK

1375 Brill, Marlene Targ. *Barack Obama: Working to Make a Difference* (5–8). Illus. Series: Gateway Biography. 2006, Lerner LB $23.93 (0-8225-3417-7). 48pp. Obama, the U.S. senator from Illinois, is profiled with details of his family life, education, and entrance to politics. (Rev: BL 3/15/06) [328.73]

PAINE, THOMAS

1376 Burgan, Michael. *Thomas Paine: Great Writer of the Revolution* (4–7). Illus. Series: Signature Lives (Revolutionary War Era). 2005, Compass Point LB $22.95 (0-7565-0830-4). 48pp. A well-designed profile of the revolutionary thinker. (Rev: BL 4/1/05) [921]

POWELL, COLIN

1377 Shichtman, Sandra H. *Colin Powell: "Have a Vision. Be Demanding."* (5–8). Series: African-American Biography Library. 2005, Enslow LB $31.93 (0-7660-2464-4). 128pp. Sandra H. Shichtman profiles former Secretary of State Colin Powell in this title from the African-American Biography Library series. (Rev: SLJ 11/05) [921]

RICE, CONDOLEEZZA

1378 Cunningham, Kevin. *Condoleezza Rice: U.S. Secretary of State* (5–8). Illus. Series: Journey to Freedom: The African American Library. 2005, Child's World LB $28.50 (1-59296-231-9). 40pp. A lavishly illustrated account of Rice's life, describing her many successes. (Rev: BL 2/1/05; SLJ 8/05) [921]

1379 Ryan, Bernard. *Condoleezza Rice: National Security Advisor and Musician* (5–8). 2003, Ferguson LB $21.95 (0-8160-5480-0). 155pp. Rice's life and career are detailed, up to the invasion of Iraq. (Rev: SLJ 5/04) [921]

SCHWARZENEGGER, ARNOLD

1380 Brandon, Karen. *Arnold Schwarzenegger* (5–8). Series: People in the News. 2004, Gale LB $28.70 (1-59018-539-0). 112pp. A thorough and appealing overview of actor-turned-governor Schwarzenegger's life and career. (Rev: BL 11/1/04; SLJ 11/04) [921]

1381 Sexton, Colleen A. *Arnold Schwarzenegger* (5–8). Series: A&E Biography. 2004, Lerner LB $27.93 (0-8225-1634-9). 112pp. This evenhanded profile, with many photographs and quotations, covers Schwarzenegger's life from his childhood in Austria to his election as governor of California and appends a list of his films. (Rev: BL 11/1/04) [921]

SCHWARZKOPF, NORMAN

1382 McNeese, Tim. *H. Norman Schwarzkopf* (6–9). Series: Great Military Leaders of the 20th Century. 2003, Chelsea House LB $22.95 (0-7910-7406-4). 124pp. Schwarzkopf's personal life and military career are explored in this admiring biography of the Persian Gulf War general. (Rev: SLJ 2/04) [921]

SUTTER, JOHN

1383 Engstrand, Iris, and Ken Owens. *John Sutter: Sutter's Fort and the California Gold Rush* (4–8). Series: The Library of American Lives and Times. 2004, Rosen LB $31.95 (0-8239-6630-5). 112pp. The importance of understanding history is emphasized in this balanced and well-illustrated look at Sutter's life. (Rev: SLJ 7/04) [921]

Miscellaneous Persons

BARTON, CLARA

1384 Koestler-Grack, Rachel A. *The Story of Clara Barton* (4–7). Illus. Series: Breakthrough Biographies. 2004, Chelsea House LB $14.95 (0-7910-7312-2). 32pp. From her childhood and early career to her founding of the American Red Cross, this profile gives personal details and historical context. (Rev: BL 3/1/04; SLJ 9/04) [361.763]

CHIPETA

1385 Krudwig, Vickie Leigh. *Searching for Chipeta: The Story of a Ute and Her People* (4–7). 2004, Fulcrum paper $12.95 (1-55591-466-7). 128pp. In the second half of the 19th century, Chipeta and her Ute husband worked tirelessly — but ultimately unsuccessfully — to forge an agreement with the U.S. government that would allow the tribe to remain in its traditional homeland. (Rev: BL 9/1/04) [921]

CRANDALL, PRUDENCE

1386 Jurmain, Suzanne. *The Forbidden Schoolhouse: The True and Dramatic Story of Prudence Crandall and Her Students* (5–8). Illus. 2005, Houghton $18.00 (0-618-47302-5). 160pp. The inspiring story of Prudence Crandall, who in the 1830s risked ostracism — and worse — from the townspeople of Canterbury, Connecticut, when she opens her academy to young African American women. (Rev: BL 10/1/05*; SLJ 11/05) [370]

GATES, HENRY LOUIS, JR.

1387 Kjelle, Marylou Morano. *Henry Louis Gates, Jr.* (6–12). Series: African-American Leaders. 2003, Chelsea House LB $22.95 (0-7910-7687-3). 111pp. A life of the influential historian and author who teaches at Harvard. (Rev: SLJ 4/04) [921]

HAYSLIP, LE LY

1388 Englar, Mary. *Le Ly Hayslip* (5–8). Series: Asian-American Biographies. 2005, Raintree LB $32.86 (1-4109-1055-5). 64pp. An interesting profile of the Vietnamese-born woman who started the East Meets West Foundation. (Rev: SLJ 3/06) [921]

KELLER, HELEN

1389 Garrett, Leslie. *Helen Keller: Biography* (5–10). Series: DK Biography. 2004, DK paper $4.99 (0-7566-0339-0). 128pp. Keller's struggles to conquer her physical disabilities and her worldwide recognition as a political activist and public speaker are covered in the usual rich DK format. (Rev: BL 6/1–15/04) [921]

WEBER, EDNAH NEW RIDER

1390 Weber, EdNah New Rider. *Rattlesnake Mesa: Stories from a Native American Childhood* (4–8). 2004, Lee & Low $18.95 (1-58430-231-3). In this poignant memoir, Weber tells of her life as a student at a government-run boarding school for Native Americans during the 1920s. (Rev: BL 12/15/04; SLJ 12/04) [921]

WEST, CORNEL

1391 Morrison, John. *Cornel West* (7–12). Series: African-American Leaders. 2003, Chelsea House LB $22.95 (0-7910-7686-5). 120pp. West's commitment to populism and improved race relations is the focus of this biography of the African American Ivy League professor. (Rev: SLJ 4/04) [921]

Science, Medicine, Industry, and Business Figures

Collective

1392 Aaseng, Nathan. *Business Builders in Broadcasting* (7–10). Series: Business Builders. 2005, Oliver LB $24.95 (1-881508-83-8). 160pp. From Morse and Marconi to Sarnoff and Rupert Murdoch, this is a useful overview of key figures in broadcasting. (Rev: SLJ 3/06) [920]

1393 Balchin, Jon. *Science: 100 Scientists Who Changed the World* (6–12). 2003, Enchanted Lion $18.95 (1-59270-017-9). 208pp. Two-page chapters introduce 100 scientists and their accomplishments, grouped by century. (Rev: SLJ 1/04) [920]

1394 Camp, Carole Ann. *American Women Inventors* (5–10). Illus. Series: Collective Biographies. 2004, Enslow LB $20.95 (0-7660-1913-6). 104pp. A collective biography of 10 important American female inventors, their lives, and their discoveries. (Rev: BL 3/1/04) [920]

1395 Cullen, Katherine. *Science, Technology, and Society: The People Behind the Science* (8–11). Illus. Series: Pioneers in Science. 2006, Chelsea House $29.95 (0-8160-5468-1). 172pp. Pioneers whose biographies appear in this volume include Marie Curie, Louis Pasteur, Guglielmo Marconi, Rachel Carson, and J. Robert Oppenheimer. (Rev: BL 4/1/06) [509]

1396 De Angelis, Gina, and David J. Bianco. *Computers: Processing the Data* (7–10). Illus. Series: Innovators. 2005, Oliver LB $24.95 (1-881508-87-0). 144pp. Profiles of computer pioneers including Charles Babbage, Steve Wozniak, and Tim Berners-Lee are accompanied by explanations of the technology involved. (Rev: BL 12/1/05; SLJ 1/06) [004]

1397 Evans, Harold. *They Made America: From the Steam Engine to the Search Engine: Two Centuries of Innovators* (8–12). Illus. 2004, Little, Brown $40.00 (0-316-27766-5). 496pp. For both browsing and research, this is an interesting and information-packed celebration of American inventiveness, focusing as much on the entrepreneurs as on the products. (Rev: BL 10/1/04) [609.2]

1398 Kent, Jacqueline C. *Business Builders in Cosmetics* (6–9). Series: Business Builders. 2004, Oliver LB $22.95 (1-881508-82-X). 160pp. Entrepreneurs including Elizabeth Arden, Max Factor, and Anita Roddick are profiled here, with a history of cosmetics dating back to Queen Nefertiti and sidebars on companies such as Clinique and Gillette. (Rev: SLJ 9/04) [920]

1399 Marshall, David, and Bruce Harper. *Wild About Flying: Dreamers, Doers, and Daredevils* (8–12). 2003, Firefly $35.00 (1-55297-849-4). 232pp. Brief biographies of key figures in the history of aviation are grouped in three categories: Dreamers, Doers, and Daredevils. (Rev: SLJ 3/04; VOYA 6/04) [920]

1400 Platt, Richard. *Eureka! Great Inventions and How They Happened* (4–8). Illus. 2003, Kingfisher $18.95 (0-7534-5580-3). 95pp. Inventors and their inventions — including the cotton gin, the smallpox vaccination, the microwave, and the Internet — are profiled in two-page spreads with many illustrations. (Rev: SLJ 3/04) [920]

1401 Shell, Barry. *Sensational Scientists: The Journeys and Discoveries of 24 Men and Women of Science* (8–11). Illus. 2006, Raincoast paper $15.95 (1-55192-727-6). 208pp. Profiles of 24 scientists associated with Canada cover a wide range of interests. (Rev: BL 2/15/06) [509]

Individual

ARCHIMEDES

1402 Gow, Mary. *Archimedes: Mathematical Genius of the Ancient World* (5–8). Illus. Series: Great Minds of Science. 2005, Enslow LB $26.60 (0-7660-2502-0). 128pp. Archimedes' mathematical discoveries are explained and placed in social, scientific, and cultural context. (Rev: SLJ 12/05) [921]

BELL, ALEXANDER GRAHAM

1403 Bankston, John. *Alexander Graham Bell and the Story of the Telephone* (5–8). Illus. Series: Uncharted, Unexplored, and Unexplained. 2004, Mitchell Lane LB $19.95 (1-58415-243-5). 48pp. As a teacher of the deaf and son of a deaf mother, Bell had a special interest in finding new and better ways to communicate. (Rev: BL 10/15/04) [921]

BENZ, KARL

1404 Bankston, John. *Karl Benz and the Single Cylinder Engine* (5–8). Illus. Series: Uncharted, Unexplored, and Unexplained. 2004, Mitchell Lane LB $19.95 (1-58415-244-3). 48pp. The first person to build a three-wheeled automobile, Benz went on to design many more-sophisticated cars. (Rev: BL 10/15/04) [921]

BOYLE, ROBERT

1405 Gow, Mary. *Robert Boyle: Pioneer of Experimental Chemistry* (6–9). Illus. Series: Great Minds of Science. 2005, Enslow LB $19.95 (0-7660-2501-2). 128pp. Pioneering 17th-century chemist Robert Boyle is profiled in this volume that will be useful for report writers. (Rev: BL 3/15/05; SLJ 6/05) [530]

BREAZEAL, CYNTHIA

1406 Brown, Jordan D. *Robo World: The Story of Robot Designer Cynthia Breazeal* (6–10). Series: Women's Adventures in Science. 2005, Watts LB $31.00 (0-531-16782-8). 108pp. An interesting biography that blends personal information with scientific facts. (Rev: SLJ 2/06) [921]

CARNEGIE, ANDREW

1407 Edge, Laura B. *Andrew Carnegie: Industrial Philanthropist* (7–10). Series: Lerner Biography. 2004, Lerner LB $25.26 (0-8225-4965-4). 128pp. The fascinating story of Carnegie's progress from poor Scottish immigrant to wealthy industrialist and generous philanthropist. (Rev: BL 6/1–15/04; SLJ 2/04) [936.2]

CHANEL, COCO

1408 Gaines, Ann. *Coco Chanel* (6–12). Series: Women in the Arts. 2003, Chelsea House LB $22.95 (0-7910-7455-2). 116pp. Introduces the life of the famous designer, attempting to distinguish between fact and Chanel's own fictions about herself. (Rev: SLJ 2/04) [921]

CHIEN-SHIUNG WU

1409 Cooperman, Stephanie H. *Chien-Shiung Wu: Pioneering Physicist and Atomic Researcher* (5–8). Illus. Series: Women Hall of Famers in Mathematics and Science. 2004, Rosen LB $29.95 (0-8239-3875-1). 112pp. This biography describes Wu's life and achievements, explaining how she found a flaw in a widely held assumption about atoms. (Rev: BL 3/1/04; SLJ 9/04) [921]

COPERNICUS

1410 Ingram, Scott. *Nicolaus Copernicus: Father of Modern Astronomy* (5–9). Series: Giants of Science. 2004, Gale LB $24.95 (1-56711-489-X). 64pp. Copernicus's life, the influences of the church, and his important contributions to science are presented in clear prose and historical context. (Rev: SLJ 6/05) [921]

CURIE, MARIE

1411 Birch, Beverley. *Marie Curie, Spanish and English* (5–8). Series: Giants of Science Bilingual. 2005, Gale LB $21.96 (1-4103-0505-8). 64pp. English and Spanish versions of this life of Curie are presented side by side, and the timeline, glossary, and index are also bilingual. (Rev: SLJ 2/06) [921]

1412 Goldsmith, Barbara. *Obsessive Genius: The Inner World of Marie Curie* (8–12). Illus. 2004, Norton $23.95 (0-393-05137-4). 320pp. Curie's personal triumphs are also covered in this account of her scientific achievements. (Rev: BL 12/1/04) [540]

1413 Healy, Nick. *Marie Curie* (6–9). Illus. Series: Genius. 2005, Creative Education LB $21.95 (1-58341-332-4). 48pp. This attractive picture-book biography will interest readers but report writers will want more documentation. (Rev: BL 2/15/06) [540]

1414 Lassieur, Allison. *Marie Curie: A Scientific Pioneer* (6–9). Series: Great Life Stories. 2003, Watts LB $29.50 (0-531-12270-0). 111pp. Curie's ability to succeed in a man's world is underlined in this well-written biography. (Rev: SLJ 1/04) [921]

1415 McClafferty, Caria Killough. *Something Out of Nothing: Marie Curie and Radium* (7–10). Illus. 2006, Farrar $18.00 (0-374-38036-8). 144pp. This readable biography examines Curie's personal life and her valuable contributions to scientific knowledge. (Rev: BL 3/1/06) [540]

DA VINCI, LEONARDO

1416 Krull, Kathleen. *Leonardo da Vinci* (5–8). Series: Giants of Science. 2005, Viking $15.99 (0-670-05920-X). 128pp. The less attractive features of da Vinci's times are covered here, along with the artist's childhood and adolescence and his development into both an artist and a scientist, drawing connections between the two disciplines and incorporating much from da Vinci's notebooks. (Rev: BL 9/1/05; SLJ 10/05*) [921]

DARWIN, CHARLES

1417 Greenberger, Robert. *Darwin and the Theory of Evolution* (5–8). Series: Primary Sources of Revolutionary Scientific Discoveries and Theories. 2005, Rosen LB $29.25 (1-4042-0306-0). 64pp. Profiles English naturalist Charles Darwin and the events that led up to his groundbreaking theory of evolution; useful for brief reports. (Rev: SLJ 11/05) [921]

1418 Lawson, Kristan. *Darwin and Evolution for Kids: His Life and Ideas with 21 Activities* (5–9). Illus. 2003, Chicago Review paper $16.95 (1-55652-502-8). 146pp. The naturalist's life and work are examined in clear, interesting text, with thorough coverage of his five-year research voyage on *H.M.S. Beagle* and the continuing controversy over his theories. (Rev: SLJ 4/04) [921]

EDISON, THOMAS ALVA

1419 Carlson, Laurie. *Thomas Edison for Kids: His Life and Ideas: 21 Activities* (4–7). Illus. 2006, Chicago Review paper $14.95 (1-55652-584-2). 160pp. Activities allow readers to try some of the inventor's experiments; the biography section covers Edison's personal life as well as his achievements and introduces some of his contemporaries. (Rev: BL 2/15/06) [621.3]

EINSTEIN, ALBERT

1420 Delano, Marfé Ferguson. *Genius: A Photobiography of Albert Einstein* (5–8). Illus. 2005, National Geographic $17.95 (0-7922-9544-7). 64pp. Photographs of the scientist's life, as well as brief explanations of his work, help to make the man and his theories more accessible to young readers; an

oversized and engaging volume. (Rev: BL 4/1/05*; SLJ 5/05) [921]

1421 Hasday, Judy L. *Albert Einstein: The Giant of 20th Century Science* (7–12). Series: Nobel Prize–Winning Scientists. 2004, Enslow LB $20.95 (0-7660-2185-8). 128pp. Report writers will find this a useful source of material on Einstein's breakthrough achievements in physics. (Rev: SLJ 4/04) [921]

1422 Lassieur, Allison. *Albert Einstein: Genius of the Twentieth Century* (5–8). Series: Great Life Stories. 2005, Watts LB $29.50 (0-531-12401-0). 127pp. In addition to placing Einstein's life (including his childhood) and contributions in historical and social context, Lassieur explains his theories and their application. (Rev: SLJ 9/05) [921]

ELION, GERTRUDE

1423 MacBain, Jennifer. *Gertrude Elion: Nobel Prize Winner in Physiology and Medicine* (5–8). Illus. Series: Women Hall of Famers in Mathematics and Science. 2004, Rosen LB $29.95 (0-8239-3876-X). 112pp. Elion, a biochemist and pharmacologist who never earned a doctorate, won a Nobel Prize for her advances in the field of chemotherapy. (Rev: BL 3/1/04; SLJ 9/04) [615]

FERMI, ENRICO

1424 Stux, Erica. *Enrico Fermi: Trailblazer in Nuclear Physics* (7–12). Illus. Series: Nobel Prize–Winning Scientists. 2004, Enslow LB $20.95 (0-7660-2177-7). 128pp. This review of the Fermi's achievements in nuclear physics offers good material for report writers. (Rev: BL 6/1–15/04; SLJ 4/04) [921]

FRANCE, DIANE

1425 Hopping, Lorraine Jean. *Bone Detective: The Story of Forensic Anthropologist Diane France* (7–10). Illus. Series: Women's Adventures in Science. 2005, Watts LB $31.00 (0-531-16776-3). 128pp. Part of the Women's Adventures in Science series, this compelling biography of Diane France traces the forensic anthropologist's life from her childhood in Colorado to her role in identifying victims of the 9/11 terrorist attacks. (Rev: BL 10/15/05; SLJ 2/06) [363.25]

FUNG, INEZ

1426 Skelton, Renee. *Forecast Earth: The Story of Climate Scientist Inez Fung* (6–10). Illus. Series: Women's Adventures in Science. 2005, Watts LB $31.00 (0-531-16777-1). 116pp. An interesting biography that blends personal information with scientific facts. (Rev: SLJ 2/06) [921]

GALILEO

1427 Hilliam, Rachel. *Galileo Galilei: Father of Modern Science* (5–8). Series: Rulers, Scholars, and Artists of the Renaissance. 2005, Rosen LB $31.95 (1-4042-0314-1). 112pp. Ford places Galileo's life and accomplishments in the context of culture and politics of the time. (Rev: SLJ 10/05) [921]

1428 Panchyk, Richard. *Galileo for Kids: His Life and Ideas* (5–9). Illus. 2005, Chicago Review paper $16.95 (1-55652-566-4). 166pp. A clearly written and well-illustrated overview of Galileo's life and scientific achievements, with excerpts from Galileo's writings and suggested activities. (Rev: SLJ 9/05) [921]

HAMMEL, HEIDI

1429 Bortz, Fred. *Beyond Jupiter: The Story of Planetary Astronomer Heidi Hammel* (6–10). Illus. Series: Women's Adventures in Science. 2005, Watts LB $31.00 (0-531-16775-5). 110pp. An interesting biography that blends personal information with scientific facts. (Rev: SLJ 2/06) [921]

HAWKING, STEPHEN

1430 Bankston, John. *Stephen Hawking: Breaking the Boundaries of Time and Space* (6–9). Series: Great Minds of Science. 2005, Enslow LB $26.60 (0-7660-2281-1). 128pp. The life and scientific career of British physicist Stephen Hawking are presented in clear and simple text. (Rev: SLJ 6/05) [921]

HUBBLE, EDWIN

1431 Kupperberg, Paul. *Hubble and the Big Bang* (6–9). Illus. Series: Primary Sources of Revolutionary Scientific Discoveries and Theories. 2005, Rosen LB $21.95 (1-4042-0307-9). 64pp. A profile of American astronomer Edwin Hubble with an easy-to-understand explanation of his theory of the expanding universe and reproductions of newspaper and journal articles. (Rev: BL 9/1/05; SLJ 11/05; VOYA 12/05) [921]

JACKSON, SHIRLEY ANN

1432 O'Connell, Diane. *Strong Force: The Story of Physicist Shirley Ann Jackson* (5–8). Series: Women's Adventures in Science. 2005, Watts LB $31.00 (0-531-16784-4). 110pp. The life and scientific career of Jackson, physicist and former chairman of the U.S. Nuclear Regulatory Commission. (Rev: SLJ 12/05) [921]

KOEHL, MIMI

1433 Parks, Deborah. *Nature's Machines: The Story of Biomechanist Mimi Koehl* (6–10). Illus. Series: Women's Adventures in Science. 2005, Watts LB $31.00 (0-531-16780-1). 118pp. An interesting biography that blends personal information with scientific facts. (Rev: SLJ 2/06) [921]

MEAD, MARGARET

1434 Horn, Geoffrey M. *Margaret Mead* (5–8). Series: Trailblazers of the Modern World. 2004, World Almanac LB $29.27 (0-8368-5099-8). 48pp. Report writers will find useful information on Mead's life, achievements, and lasting contributions. (Rev: SLJ 7/04) [921]

MENDEL, GREGOR

1435 Bankston, John. *Gregor Mendel and the Discovery of the Gene* (5–8). Illus. Series: Uncharted, Unexplored, and Unexplained. 2004, Mitchell Lane LB $19.95 (1-58415-266-4). 48pp. Profiles the 19th-century Austrian monk who discovered the laws of genetics. (Rev: BL 10/15/04; SLJ 12/04) [921]

MENDELEYEV, DMITRI

1436 Zannos, Susan. *Dmitri Mendeleev and the Periodic Table* (5–8). Series: Uncharted, Unexplored, and Unexplained. 2004, Mitchell Lane LB $.00 (1-58415-267-2). 48pp. This brief biography looks at the life of the inventor of the periodic table, focusing initially on his childhood and offering political context. (Rev: BL 10/15/04) [540]

MEXIA, YNES

1437 Anema, Durlynn. *Ynes Mexia: Botanist and Adventurer* (6–9). 2005, Morgan Reynolds $26.95 (1-931798-67-2). 144pp. Mexia is known for her adventurous spirit and her important collections of plants from North and South America, which she started in her mid-50s. (Rev: SLJ 1/06) [921]

MUIR, JOHN

1438 Lasky, Kathryn. *John Muir: America's First Environmentalist* (4–7). 2006, Candlewick $16.99 (0-76361-957-4). 32pp. Quotations from Muir's diary and double-page landscape watercolors add to the narrative about the pioneering environmentalist in this attractive picture-book biography. (Rev: BL 2/1/06; SLJ 4/06) [333.7]

NEWTON, ISAAC

1439 Boerst, William J. *Isaac Newton: Organizing the Universe* (6–10). Illus. Series: Renaissance Scientists. 2004, Morgan Reynolds LB $23.95 (1-931798-01-X). 144pp. A fine biography of Newton that includes good explanations of the laws of motion and excellent color reproductions of period paintings. (Rev: BL 2/1/04; SLJ 4/04) [921]

1440 Krull, Kathleen. *Isaac Newton* (5–8). Series: Giants of Science. 2006, Viking $15.99 (0-670-05921-8). 128pp. Newton's childhood and adult personality are highlighted in this readable biography that gives good explanations of his scientific theories. (Rev: BL 4/1/06; SLJ 3/06*) [530]

OPPENHEIMER, J. ROBERT

1441 Allman, Toney. *J. Robert Oppenheimer: Father of the Atomic Bomb* (5–9). Series: Giants of Science. 2005, Gale $24.95 (1-56711-889-5). 64pp. Controversial physicist Oppenheimer, who played a key role in the development of the atomic bomb, is profiled in readable text with lots of details for report writers. (Rev: SLJ 7/05) [921]

PASTEUR, LOUIS

1442 Ackerman, Jane. *Louis Pasteur and the Founding of Microbiology* (7–12). Illus. Series: Great Scientists. 2004, Morgan Reynolds $23.95 (1-931798-13-3). 144pp. Using his microscope, Pasteur developed the fields of immunology and microbiology and invented the pasteurization of milk. (Rev: BL 2/1/04; SLJ 4/04) [921]

PAULING, LINUS

1443 Pasachoff, Naomi. *Linus Pauling: Advancing Science, Advocating Peace* (7–12). Illus. Series: Nobel Prize–Winning Scientists. 2004, Enslow LB $20.95 (0-7660-2130-0). 128pp. Pauling's scientific errors are not dismissed in this biography that relates the Nobel prize winner's achievements in science and his campaign against nuclear weapons. (Rev: BL 6/1–15/04) [921]

RUTHERFORD, ERNEST

1444 Pasachoff, Naomi. *Ernest Rutherford: Father of Nuclear Science* (6–12). Series: Great Minds of Science. 2005, Enslow LB $26.60 (0-7660-2441-5). 128pp. The life and scientific career of the New Zealand-born physicist who helped to pave the way for the development of nuclear physics. (Rev: SLJ 8/05)

TESLA, NIKOLA

1445 Aldrich, Lisa J. *Nikola Tesla and the Taming of Electricity* (8–11). Illus. Series: Modern Scientists. 2005, Morgan Reynolds LB $24.95 (1-931798-46-X). 160pp. The life and many inventions — including radio — of the Croatian-born electrical engineer. (Rev: BL 5/1/05; SLJ 10/05; VOYA 10/05) [621.3]

TIENDA, MARTA

1446 O'Connell, Diane. *People Person: The Story of Sociologist Marta Tienda* (5–8). Series: Women's Adventures in Science. 2005, Watts LB $31.00 (0-531-16781-X). 108pp. An informative and accessible profile of sociologist Marta Tienda and her work to create opportunities for people around the world. (Rev: SLJ 12/05) [921]

VEDDER, AMY

1447 Ebersole, Rene. *Gorilla Mountain: The Story of Wildlife Biologist Amy Vedder* (5–8). Series: Women's Adventures in Science. 2005, Watts LB $31.00 (0-531-16779-8). 118pp. An informative and accessible account of Vedder's efforts to protect the endangered mountain gorillas of Rwanda. (Rev: SLJ 12/05)

WEXLER, NANCY

1448 Glimm, Adele. *Gene Hunter: The Story of Neuropsychologist Nancy Wexler* (6–10). Illus. Series: Women's Adventures in Science. 2005, Watts LB $31.00 (0-531-16778-X). 118pp. An interesting biography that blends personal information with scientific facts. (Rev: SLJ 2/06) [921]

WRIGHT, WILBUR AND ORVILLE

1449 McPherson, Stephanie Sammartino, and Joseph Sammartino Gardner. *Wilbur and Orville Wright: Taking Flight* (4–7). Illus. Series: Trailblazer Biographies. 2003, Carolrhoda LB $25.26 (1-57505-443-4). 120pp. A well-written, detailed account of the Wright brothers' landmark experiments, enlivened with period photographs and other illustrations. (Rev: SLJ 4/04) [921]

Sports Figures

Collective

1450 Hotchkiss, Ron. *The Matchless Six: The Story of Canada's First Women's Olympic Team* (5–8). Illus. 2006, Tundra $16.95 (0-88776-738-9). 200pp. Profiles the individual athletes and achievements of Canada's groundbreaking women's Olympic team of 1928. (Rev: BL 3/15/06) [796.48]

1451 Lipsyte, Robert. *Heroes of Baseball: The Men Who Made It America's Favorite Game* (4–7). Illus. 2006, Simon & Schuster $19.95 (0-689-86741-7). 96pp. As well as introducing key players of the game, this volume presents a concise history of the sport itself. (Rev: BL 2/15/06; SLJ 4/06) [796.357]

1452 Rappoport, Ken. *Ladies First: Women Athletes Who Made a Difference* (5–8). Illus. 2005, Peachtree $14.95 (1-56145-338-2). 160pp. Gymnast Nadia Comaneci and dogsled racer Susan Butcher are only two of the many women in diverse sports featured in this collective biography that also gives a brief history of women's participation in sports. (Rev: BL 5/1/05; SLJ 6/05) [920]

Automobile Racing

STEWART, TONY

1453 Leebrick, Kristal. *Tony Stewart* (4–7). Illus. Series: NASCAR Racing. 2004, Capstone LB $22.60 (0-7368-2425-1). 32pp. This profile of auto racing star Tony Stewart chronicles his meteoric rise from go-karts and midget racers to the top ranks of NASCAR. (Rev: BL 4/1/04) [790.72]

Baseball

CLEMENTE, ROBERTO

1454 Marquez, Heron. *Roberto Clemente: Baseball's Humanitarian Hero* (4–7). Illus. 2005, Carolrhoda LB $27.93 (1-57505-767-0). 112pp. The story of the ballplayer, from his birth in Puerto Rico to his death in a plane crash, with photographs. (Rev: BL 3/15/05; SLJ 5/05) [796.357]

GEHRIG, LOU

1455 Viola, Kevin. *Lou Gehrig* (4–7). Series: Sports Heroes and Legends. 2004, Lerner LB $26.60 (0-8225-5311-2). Starting with Gehrig's sad retirement and his "Luckiest Man" speech, this well-written and informative biography goes back to look at his life and successful career. (Rev: BL 9/1/04) [921]

MANTLE, MICKEY

1456 Marlin, John. *Mickey Mantle* (4–7). Series: Sports Heroes and Legends. 2004, Lerner LB $26.60 (0-8225-1796-5). A concise, well-written biography that focuses on Mantle's illustrious career. (Rev: BL 9/1/04; SLJ 11/04) [921]

MATSUI, HIDEKI

1457 Beach, Jerry. *Godzilla Takes the Bronx: The Inside Story of Hideki Matsui* (8–12). 2004, Taylor $24.95 (1-58979-113-4). 256pp. A biography of the Japanese baseball player who recently joined the Yankees. (Rev: BL 3/15/04) [921]

ROBINSON, JACKIE

1458 Robinson, Sharon. *Promises to Keep: How Jackie Robinson Changed America* (3–7). Illus. 2004, Scholastic $16.95 (0-439-42592-1). 64pp. The inspiring story of Robinson's life and his struggle to break into major league baseball is told by his daughter. (Rev: BL 2/15/04*; SLJ 3/04) [796.357]

Basketball

DUNCAN, TIM

1459 Adams, Sean. *Tim Duncan* (4–7). Illus. Series: Sports Heroes and Legends. 2004, Lerner LB $21.96 (0-8225-1793-0). 106pp. A balanced, well-crafted life of the basketball star. (Rev: BL 9/1/04) [921]

JAMES, LEBRON

1460 Morgan, David Lee. *LeBron James* (7–12). Illus. 2003, Gray & Company paper $14.95 (1-886228-74-4). 208pp. The biography of the African American basketball superstar who came from a culture of poverty and drugs to reach the peak of the sports world. (Rev: BL 2/15/04; SLJ 6/04) [921]

MING, YAO

1461 Krawiec, Richard. *Yao Ming: Gentle Giant of Basketball* (6–8). Illus. 2004, Avisson paper $19.95 (1-888105-63-1). 108pp. This story of the Chinese basketball player's path to stardom brings up interesting questions about the business and patriotic aspects of professional sports. (Rev: BL 2/15/04; SLJ 3/04) [790.323]

1462 Ming, Yao, and Ric Bucher. *Yao: A Life in Two Worlds* (8–12). Illus. 2004, Miramax $22.95 (1-4013-5214-6). 272pp. Yao Ming writes of his success in the NBA and also of the sharp contrast between the culture of his native China and that of the United States. (Rev: BL 9/1/04) [796.323]

Ice Skating and Hockey

WICKENHEISER, HAYLEY

1463 Etue, Elizabeth. *Hayley Wickenheiser: Born to Play* (4–7). Illus. 2005, Kids Can paper $6.95 (1-55337-791-5). 40pp. The story of Canadian-born Wickenheiser, a member of Canada's gold medal-winning women's ice hockey team at the Salt Lake City Olympics, who went on to become the first woman to play professional hockey. (Rev: BL 9/1/05) [921]

Tennis

ASHE, ARTHUR

1464 Cunningham, Kevin. *Arthur Ashe: Athlete and Activist* (5–8). Illus. Series: Journey to Freedom: The African American Library. 2005, Child's World LB $19.95 (1-59296-228-9). 40pp. Chronicles the Virginia-born athlete's rise to tennis stardom and his involvement in the fight against apartheid. (Rev: BL 2/1/05) [921]

Track and Field

RUDOLPH, WILMA

1465 Schraff, Anne. *Wilma Rudolph: The Greatest Woman Sprinter in History* (6–9). Series: African-American Biographies. 2004, Enslow LB $20.95 (0-7660-2291-9). 112pp. Rudolph's childhood battle with polio, pregnancy at the age of 17, and struggles to deal with racism and supporting her family make a poignant background to her athletic achievements. (Rev: SLJ 8/04) [921]

Miscellaneous Sports

ARMSTRONG, LANCE

1466 Benson, Michael. *Lance Armstrong: Cyclist* (5–8). Series: Ferguson Career Biographies. 2003, Ferguson LB $21.95 (0-8160-5479-7). 139pp. Traces the inspiring life of the great bicycle-racer through his fifth Tour de France win, with an emphasis on his perseverance and optimism. (Rev: SLJ 5/04) [796.6]

1467 Coyle, Daniel. *Lance Armstrong's War: One Man's Battle Against Fate, Fame, Love, Death, Scandal, and a Few Other Rivals on the Road to the Tour de France* (8–12). Illus. 2005, HarperCollins $25.95 (0-06-073794-3). 336pp. Traces Armstrong's winning 2004 season and reviews the daunting challenges the cyclist has had to overcome in his life. (Rev: BL 6/1–15/05) [796.6]

BECKHAM, DAVID

1468 Beckham, David. *Both Feet on the Ground: An Autobiography* (8–12). 2003, HarperCollins $24.95 (0-06-057093-8). 400pp. Full of illustrations, this biography traces Beckham's life from childhood through soccer stardom. (Rev: SLJ 1/04; VOYA 2/04) [921]

HAMILTON, BETHANY

1469 Hamilton, Bethany. *Soul Surfer: A True Story of Faith, Family, and Fighting to Get Back on the Board* (6–9). Illus. 2004, Pocket $18.00 (0-7434-9922-0). 240pp. Bethany Hamilton, the teenage surfer who lost an arm in a shark attack off Kauai in 2003, tells how her family and faith helped to sustain her and give her the courage to return to surfing. (Rev: BL 1/1–15/05) [797.1]

HAWK, TONY

1470 Peterson, Todd. *Tony Hawk: Skateboarder and Businessman* (8–11). Illus. Series: Ferguson Career Biographies. 2005, Ferguson LB $25.00 (0-8160-5893-8). 122pp. Skateboarder Tony Hawk's childhood, skating career, and business achievements are all covered in this readable volume. (Rev: BL 9/1/05) [796.22]

ROSENFELD, FANNY BOBBIE

1471 Dublin, Anne. *Bobbie Rosenfeld: The Olympian Who Could Do Everything* (5–8). 2004, Second Story paper $11.95 (1-896764-82-7). 120pp. Fanny Bobbie Rosenfeld migrated from the Ukraine to Canada in 1905, became an outstanding athlete excelling in many sports, and led the Canadian women's relay team to an Olympic gold in 1928. (Rev: BL 9/1/04) [921]

THORPE, JIM

1472 Crawford, Bill. *All American: The Rise and Fall of Jim Thorpe* (8–12). Illus. 2004, Wiley $24.95 (0-471-55732-3). 288pp. An in-depth look at the tumultuous life of the Native American athlete who triumphed on the world's playing fields but ultimately died in relative obscurity. (Rev: BL 11/15/04) [796]

World Figures

Collective

1473 Bardhan-Quallen, Sudipta. *The Mexican-American War* (5–9). Series: People at the Center Of. 2005, Gale LB $23.70 (1-56711-927-1). 48pp. After an overview of the war, this volume provides biographical information on key figures including James K. Polk, Abraham Lincoln, Santa Anna, and Zachary Taylor. (Rev: SLJ 6/05) [920]

1474 Bledsoe, Karen E. *Daredevils of the Air: Thrilling Tales of Pioneer Aviators* (7–12). Series: Avisson Young Adult. 2003, Avisson paper $19.95 (1-888105-58-5). 155pp. The Wright brothers, Eddie Rickenbacker, Bessie Coleman, and Beryl Markham are among the early flyers profiled in stories of exciting aerial exploits. (Rev: SLJ 1/04) [920]

1475 Butts, Ed. *She Dared: True Stories of Heroines, Scoundrels, and Renegades* (6–9). 2005, Tundra paper $8.95 (0-88776-718-4). 121pp. Engaging profiles of 15 diverse women who defied social norms. (Rev: BL 12/1/05; SLJ 12/05) [920.72]

1476 Chin-Lee, Cynthia. *Amelia to Zora: Twenty-Six Women Who Changed the World* (4–7). Illus. 2005, Charlesbridge $15.95 (1-57091-522-9). 32pp. Brief information on 26 remarkable and varied women (scientists, artists, athletes, inventors) along with beautiful artwork and quotations from the subjects. (Rev: BL 4/1/05*; SLJ 4/05) [920.72]

1477 Hansen, Joyce. *African Princess: The Amazing Lives of Africa's Royal Women* (4–8). 2004, Hyperion $16.99 (0-7868-5116-3). 48pp. From Hatshepsut of ancient Egypt to Princess Elizabeth of today's Togo, this volume profiles six African women of note. (Rev: BL 9/15/04; SLJ 11/04) [920]

1478 Haskins, Jim. *African Heroes* (5–8). Series: Black Stars. 2005, Wiley $24.95 (0-471-46672-7).

163pp. Profiles 27 important Africans, both contemporary and from the past, in entries of varying length. (Rev: SLJ 7/05) [920]

1479 Humphrey, Sandra McLeod. *Dare to Dream! 25 Extraordinary Lives* (4–7). 2005, Prometheus paper $14.00 (1-59102-280-0). 115pp. Twenty-five individuals — including artists, athletes, politicians, and scientists — who overcame obstacles to achieve greatness are profiled, with information on childhood and adult life. (Rev: BL 3/1/05; SLJ 6/05) [920]

1480 Hunter, Ryan Ann. *In Disguise: Stories of Real Women Spies* (5–8). Illus. 2004, Beyond Words paper $9.95 (1-58270-095-8). 133pp. Profiles 26 women who risked their lives to spy for causes in which they believed, from 1640 to the Cold War. (Rev: SLJ 8/04) [920]

1481 Kupferberg, Audrey. *The Spanish-American War* (5–9). Series: People at the Center Of. 2005, Gale LB $23.70 (1-56711-924-7). 48pp. After an overview of the war, this volume provides biographical information on key figures including Grover Cleveland, William Randolph Hearst, and Theodore Roosevelt. (Rev: SLJ 6/05) [920]

1482 Nardo, Don. *Ancient Philosophers* (7–12). Series: History Makers. 2004, Gale LB $21.96 (1-59018-281-2). 112pp. The lives and essential philosophies of Democritus, Plato, Aristotle, Buddha, and Confucius are laid out in clear text. (Rev: SLJ 6/04) [920]

1483 Phibbs, Cheryl Fisher, ed. *Pioneers of Human Rights* (8–11). Illus. Series: Profiles in History. 2005, Gale LB $27.96 (0-7377-2146-4). 240pp. Among the figures profiled in this volume are Mohandas Gandhi, Frederick Douglass, Nelson Mandela, and Eleanor Roosevelt. (Rev: BL 7/05) [323]

1484 Scandiffio, Laura. *Evil Masters: The Frightening World of Tyrants* (7–10). 2005, Annick $24.95 (1-55037-895-3); paper $12.95 (1-55037-894-5). 230pp. Nero, Ivan the Terrible, Hitler, Stalin, and Saddam Hussein are five of the seven rulers profiled; an introduction discusses personality traits and the reasons why such men are able to assume power. (Rev: SLJ 1/06) [920]

1485 Weatherly, Myra. *Women of the Sea: Ten Pirate Stories* (6–9). Illus. 2006, Morgan Reynolds LB $26.95 (1-931798-80-X). 160pp. This revised edition of a 1998 publication (*Women Pirates: Eight Stories of Adventure*) adds information on two women pirates plus source notes and additional resources. (Rev: BL 12/15/05; SLJ 4/06) [910.4]

1486 Zalben, Jane Breskin. *Paths to Peace: People Who Changed the World* (4–7). Illus. 2006, Dutton $18.99 (0-525-47734-9). 48pp. Zalben profiles 16 individuals who have devoted much of their lives to the goal of making peace a reality. (Rev: BL 1/1–15/06; SLJ 2/06) [920]

Africa

AMIN, IDI

1487 Allen, John. *Idi Amin* (6–9). Series: History's Villains. 2004, Gale LB $21.96 (1-56711-759-7). 112pp. An interesting profile of the Ugandan leader that describes the atrocities committed under his regime. (Rev: SLJ 5/04) [921]

CLEOPATRA

1488 Nardo, Don. *Cleopatra: Egypt's Last Pharaoh* (6–10). Series: The Lucent Library of Historical Eras. 2005, Gale LB $28.70 (1-59018-660-5). 112pp. Presenting many quotations from ancient writings about Cleopatra, Nardo discusses their biases plus the importance of the Egyptian leader's relationships with Julius Caesar and Marc Antony. (Rev: SLJ 11/05) [921]

MANDELA, NELSON

1489 Pogrund, Benjamin. *Nelson Mandela* (5–10). Illus. Series: World Peacemakers. 2004, Gale LB $27.44 (1-56711-978-6). 64pp. As well as a fine biography of Mandela, this book gives a concise history of apartheid in South Africa. (Rev: BL 2/15/04; SLJ 5/04) [921]

TUTANKHAMEN, KING

1490 Hawass, Zahi. *Tutankhamun: The Mystery of the Boy King* (4–7). Illus. 2005, National Geographic $17.95 (0-7922-8354-6). 64pp. The director of excavations at key Egyptian archaeological sites

offers a fascinating account of the life, death, and burial of King Tut and of new revelations about his fate. (Rev: BL 11/1/05; SLJ 10/05*) [932]

Asia and the Middle East

BIN LADEN, OSAMA

1491 Loehfelm, Bill. *Osama bin Laden* (6–12). Illus. Series: History's Villains. 2004, Gale LB $21.96 (1-56711-760-0). 112pp. Osama bin Laden, nominal leader of al-Qaeda and arguably the world's most wanted man, is profiled here, with information on his wealthy family, his youth, and the factors that led him to terrorism. (Rev: BL 7/04) [958.104]

BUDDHA

1492 Gedney, Mona. *The Life and Times of Buddha* (5–7). Series: Biography from Ancient Civilizations: Legends, Folklore, and Stories of Ancient Worlds. 2005, Mitchell Lane LB $19.95 (1-58415-342-3). 48pp. Gedney recounts what is known of the life of Siddartha Gautama, whose search for a better way of living led to the founding of Buddhism. (Rev: SLJ 9/05) [921]

GANDHI, MAHATMA

1493 Hatt, Christine. *Mahatma Gandhi* (6–9). Series: Judge for Yourself. 2004, World Almanac LB $29.26 (0-8368-5561-2). 64pp. Biographical information about Gandhi is followed by a "Judge for Yourself" section of controversial issues that should be considered. (Rev: SLJ 10/04) [921]

1494 Nicholson, Michael. *Mahatma Gandhi* (6–12). Series: World Peacemakers. 2003, Gale LB $24.95 (1-56711-976-X). 64pp. Although Gandhi's peacemaking activities are the emphasis of this slim, introductory biography, it also covers his youth. (Rev: SLJ 5/04) [921]

1495 Wilkinson, Philip. *Gandhi: The Young Protestor Who Founded a Nation* (4–7). Illus. Series: World History Biographies. 2005, National Geographic LB $27.90 (0-7922-3648-3). 64pp. Gandhi's character shines through the straightforward text and interesting anecdotes in this biography that gives historical context plus maps and photographs. (Rev: BL 6/1–15/05) [954.03]

GENGHIS KHAN

1496 Rice, Earle, Jr. *Empire in the East: The Story of Genghis Khan* (7–11). Illus. Series: World Leaders. 2005, Morgan Reynolds LB $24.95 (1-931798-62-1). 160pp. A life of Genghis Khan, who rose from obscurity to become leader of the Great Mongol Nation and ruler of vast territories that stretched from the Adriatic to the Pacific. (Rev: BL 8/05; SLJ 8/05) [950]

HUSSEIN, SADDAM

1497 Stewart, Gail B. *Saddam Hussein* (8–12). Series: Heroes and Villains. 2004, Gale LB $21.96 (1-59018-350-9). 96pp. Ending before Saddam Hussein's capture by U.S. forces, this is a portrait of a ruthless dictator and his ascent to and maintenance of power. (Rev: SLJ 4/04) [921]

NOOR, QUEEN

1498 Raatma, Lucia. *Queen Noor: American-Born Queen of Jordan* (6–9). Illus. Series: Signature Lives. 2006, Compass Point LB $30.60 (0-7565-1595-5). 112pp. The life of the American-born woman who became the queen of Jordan. (Rev: BL 4/1/06) [956.9504]

POL POT

1499 Koopmans, Andy. *Pol Pot* (8–12). Series: Heroes and Villains. 2005, Gale LB $28.70 (1-59018-596-X). 112pp. A readable biography of the leader of Cambodia's murderous Khmer Rouge guerrillas. (Rev: SLJ 9/05) [921]

RIZAL, JOSE

1500 Arruda, Suzanne Middendorf. *Freedom's Martyr: The Story of José Rizal, National Hero of the Philippines* (6–12). Series: Avisson Young Adult. 2003, Avisson paper $19.95 (1-888105-55-0). 106pp. A patriot and activist on behalf of the native peoples of the Philippines, Rizal was executed by the Spanish for treason in 1896 and remains the country's national hero. (Rev: SLJ 5/04) [921]

SUNG, KIM IL

1501 Ingram, Scott. *Kim Il Sung* (6–12). Illus. Series: History's Villains. 2004, Gale LB $21.96 (1-4103-0259-8). 112pp. Profiles North Korean dictator Kim Il Sung, who ruled his country with a brutal hand for more than 40 years. (Rev: BL 7/04; SLJ 5/04) [951.930]

ZEDONG, MAO

1502 Hatt, Christine. *Mao Zedong* (8–11). Illus. Series: Judge for Yourself. 2003, World Almanac LB $29.26 (0-8368-5536-1). 64pp. Mao's life is presented followed by two essays that present different viewpoints of his importance and accomplishments. (Rev: BL 2/1/04; SLJ 3/04) [921]

1503 Slavicek, Louise Chipley. *Mao Zedong* (6–9). Series: Great Military Leaders of the 20th Century. 2003, Chelsea House LB $22.95 (0-7910-7407-2).

116pp. Mao's beliefs, personal life, and political career are clearly described, with maps, photographs, and reproductions. (Rev: SLJ 3/04) [921]

Europe

ALEXANDER THE GREAT

1504 Adams, Simon. *Alexander: The Boy Soldier Who Conquered the World* (5–7). Series: National Geographic World History Biographies. 2005, National Geographic LB $27.90 (0-7922-3661-0). 64pp. An attractive, well-illustrated account of Alexander's life and accomplishments, with references to his less-appealing characteristics. (Rev: SLJ 9/05) [921]

ARISTOTLE

1505 Anderson, Margaret J., and Karen F. Stephenson. *Aristotle: Philosopher and Scientist* (5–8). Series: Great Minds of Science. 2004, Enslow LB $20.95 (0-7660-2096-7). 112pp. Aristotle's life, times, and contributions to philosophy and science are examined in concise text. (Rev: SLJ 7/04) [921]

ATTILA THE HUN

1506 Oliver, Marilyn Tower. *Attila the Hun* (6–10). Series: Heroes and Villains. 2005, Gale LB $28.70 (1-59018-638-9). 112pp. The softer side of Attila is revealed in this balanced and well-documented account of his youth and later achievements. (Rev: SLJ 3/06) [921]

CATHERINE THE GREAT

1507 Hatt, Christine. *Catherine the Great* (8–11). Illus. Series: Judge for Yourself. 2003, World Almanac LB $29.26 (0-8368-5535-3). 64pp. After an interesting illustrated biography of Catherine the Great, two essays present differing views on her importance. (Rev: BL 2/1/04; SLJ 4/04) [921]

1508 Whitelaw, Nancy. *Catherine the Great and the Enlightenment in Russia* (8–12). Illus. Series: European Queens. 2004, Morgan Reynolds LB $24.95 (1-931798-27-3). 160pp. The colorful life of the Russian empress from childhood in her native Germany to her pivotal role in leading her adopted country into full participation in the cultural and political life of Europe. (Rev: BL 12/15/04; SLJ 12/04) [921]

CHURCHILL, SIR WINSTON

1509 Binns, Tristan Boyer. *Winston Churchill* (5–8). Series: Great Life Stories. 2004, Watts LB $29.50 (0-531-12361-8). 127pp. The complex life of Churchill is well portrayed in this biography that covers his youth and career, triumphs and losses, and many and varied interests. (Rev: SLJ 3/05) [921]

CLEISTHENES

1510 Parton, Sarah. *Cleisthenes: Founder of Athenian Democracy* (7–10). Series: Leaders of Ancient Greece. 2004, Rosen LB $31.95 (0-8239-3826-3). 110pp. Information about Cleisthenes and his times is carefully couched in discussion of the sources used and the ways in which this material has been gathered and analyzed. (Rev: SLJ 9/04) [921]

DRAKE, SIR FRANCIS

1511 Whitfield, Peter. *Sir Francis Drake* (8–12). Illus. Series: British Library Historic Lives. 2004, New York Univ. $22.00 (0-8147-9403-3). 160pp. Drake's great naval accomplishments are balanced against less admirable activities. (Rev: BL 10/15/04) [942.05]

ELEANOR OF AQUITAINE

1512 Hilliam, David. *Eleanor of Aquitaine: The Richest Queen in Medieval Europe* (6–9). Illus. Series: Leaders of the Middle Ages. 2005, Rosen LB $23.95 (1-4042-0162-9). 112pp. A readable life of the wealthy monarch, underlining her unusual accomplishments. (Rev: BL 4/1/05; SLJ 6/05) [942.03]

ELIZABETH I, QUEEN OF ENGLAND

1513 Weatherly, Myra. *Elizabeth I: Queen of Tudor England* (6–8). Series: Signature Lives. 2005, Compass Point LB $22.95 (0-7565-0988-2). 112pp. A clearly written and well illustrated life of the fascinating queen. (Rev: SLJ 1/06) [921]

THE FRANK FAMILY

1514 Denenberg, Barry. *Shadow Life: A Portrait of Anne Frank and Her Family* (6–10). 2005, Scholastic $16.95 (0-439-41678-7). 240pp. In this engaging title from the Shadow Life series, author Barry Denenberg tells the complete story of Anne Frank and her family from their earlier life in Frankfurt to their eventual transport to Nazi concentration camps. (Rev: BL 2/1/05*; SLJ 4/05; VOYA 4/05) [940.53]

FRANK, ANNE

1515 Hermann, Spring. *Anne Frank: Hope in the Shadows of the Holocaust* (5–7). Series: Holocaust Heroes and Nazi Criminals. 2005, Enslow LB $27.93 (0-7660-2531-4). 160pp. The story of Anne Frank before, during, and after the two years she

and her family hid from the Nazis. (Rev: SLJ 11/05) [921]

1516 Poole, Josephine. *Anne Frank* (4–7). 2005, Knopf LB $19.99 (0-375-93242-9). 40pp. This picture-book biography for older readers presents Anne's story clear text and haunting illustrations. (Rev: BL 6/1–15/05*; SLJ 9/05) [921]

1517 Sawyer, Kem Knapp. *Anne Frank: A Photographic Story of a Life* (5–10). Illus. Series: DK Biography. 2004, DK LB $14.99 (0-7566-0341-2); paper $4.99 (0-7566-0490-7). 128pp. This richly illustrated biography draws on Anne's diary and accounts by her father and by Miep Gies. (Rev: BL 6/1–15/04) [921]

GEORGE III, KING

1518 Ingram, Scott. *King George III* (6–9). Series: Triangle History of the American Revolution, Revolutionary War Leaders. 2004, Gale LB $21.96 (1-56711-779-1). 104pp. This discussion of the life of the British king brings out his personality and his relationships with his own court and with the rebellious colonists across the Atlantic. (Rev: SLJ 6/04) [941]

HIMMLER, HEINRICH

1519 Worth, Richard. *Heinrich Himmler: Murderous Architect of the Holocaust* (8–11). Illus. Series: Holocaust Heroes and Nazi Criminals. 2005, Enslow LB $20.95 (0-7660-2532-2). 160pp. A profile of the career of the architect of Nazi Germany's lethally effective campaign against the Jews and other victims of the Holocaust. (Rev: BL 10/15/05; SLJ 1/06) [940.53]

HITLER, ADOLF

1520 Rice, Earle, Jr. *Adolf Hitler and Nazi Germany* (6–9). Series: World Leaders. 2005, Morgan Reynolds LB $26.95 (1-931798-78-8). 176pp. This accessible biography traces Hitler's progress from a modest childhood and uncertain adolescence through his army career, rise to power, and crafting of the German war machine. (Rev: BL 1/1–15/06; SLJ 1/06) [921]

JOHN PAUL II, POPE

1521 Behnke, Alison. *Pope John Paul II* (7–10). Illus. Series: A&E Biography. 2005, Lerner LB $27.93 (0-8225-2798-7); paper $8.95 (0-8225-3387-1). 112pp. This very human portrait of Pope John Paul II traces his life and presents the views of his critics as well as his supporters. (Rev: BL 10/1/05; SLJ 9/05) [282]

LENIN, VLADIMIR ILICH

1522 Naden, Corinne J., and Rose Blue. *Lenin* (6–10). Series: Importance Of. 2005, Gale $27.45 (1-59018-233-2). 112pp. The life and political career of Vladimir Lenin, founder of the Russian Communist Party. (Rev: BL 6/1–15/04) [921]

MACHIAVELLI, NICCOLÒ

1523 Ford, Nick. *Niccolò Machiavelli: Florentine Statesman, Playwright, and Poet* (5–8). Series: Rulers, Scholars, and Artists of the Renaissance. 2005, Rosen LB $31.95 (1-4042-0316-8). 112pp. Ford places Machiavelli's life and accomplishments in the context of culture and politics of the time. (Rev: SLJ 10/05) [921]

MARIE ANTOINETTE

1524 Lotz, Nancy, and Carlene Phillips. *Marie Antoinette and the Decline of the French Monarchy* (8–12). Illus. Series: European Queens. 2004, Morgan Reynolds LB $24.95 (1-931798-28-1). 160pp. The turbulent life of Marie Antoinette from her birth in Vienna to her death on the guillotine in October 1793. (Rev: BL 12/15/04; SLJ 12/04) [921]

MEDICI, LORENZO DE

1525 Hancock, Lee. *Lorenzo De' Medici: Florence's Great Leader and Patron of the Arts* (5–8). Series: Rulers, Scholars, and Artists of the Renaissance. 2005, Rosen LB $31.95 (1-4042-0315-X). 112pp. Ford places de Medici's life and accomplishments in the context of culture and politics of the time. (Rev: SLJ 10/05) [921]

MENGELE, JOSEF

1526 Grabowski, John F. *Josef Mengele* (8–12). Series: Heroes and Villains. 2004, Gale LB $21.96 (1-59018-425-4). 112pp. A life of the Nazi who committed atrocities during World War II but escaped to South America. (Rev: SLJ 4/04) [921]

PUTIN, VLADIMIR

1527 Streissguth, Thomas. *Vladimir Putin* (7–10). Illus. Series: A&E Biography. 2005, Lerner LB $27.93 (0-8225-2374-4); paper $7.95 (0-8225-9630-X). 112pp. Putin's professional and political life take center stage in this biography that will be useful for report writers. (Rev: BL 9/1/05) [947.086]

ROBINSON, MARY

1528 Friedman, Lita. *Mary Robinson: Fighter for Human Rights* (6–9). Series: Avisson Young Adult. 2004, Avisson paper $19.95 (1-888105-65-8). 142pp. In 1990 Robinson became the first female president of Ireland; subsequently she served as the United Nations High Commissioner for Human Rights. (Rev: SLJ 10/04) [921]

SOLON

1529 Randall, Bernard. *Solon: The Lawmaker of Athens* (7–10). Series: Leaders of Ancient Greece. 2004, Rosen LB $31.95 (0-8239-3829-8). 112pp. Information about Solon and his times is carefully introduced with discussion of the sources used and the ways in which this material has been gathered and analyzed. (Rev: SLJ 9/04) [921]

THEMISTOCLES

1530 Morris, Ian Macgregor. *Themistocles: Defender of Greece* (7–10). Series: Leaders of Ancient Greece. 2004, Rosen LB $31.95 (0-8239-3830-1). 110pp. Information about Themistocles and his times is carefully couched in discussion of the sources used and the ways in which this material has been gathered and analyzed. (Rev: SLJ 9/04) [921]

WALLENBERG, RAOUL

1531 McArthur, Debra. *Raoul Wallenberg: Rescuing Thousands from the Nazis' Grasp* (5–7). Series: Holocaust Heroes and Nazi Criminals. 2005, Enslow LB $27.93 (0-7660-2530-6). 160pp. A well-documented profile of the courageous Swedish diplomat who saved thousands of Hungarian Jews and disappeared after the end of the war. (Rev: SLJ 11/05) [921]

South and Central America, Canada, and Mexico

MENCHU, RIGOBERTA

1532 Menchú, Rigoberta, and Dante Liano. *The Girl from Chimel* (4–7). Trans. by David Unger. 2005, Groundwood $16.95 (0-88899-666-7). 56pp. Rigoberta Menchu, winner of the 1992 Nobel Peace Prize and Maya activist, tells about growing up in the Guatemalan Indian village of Chimel. (Rev: BL 11/1/05; SLJ 2/06) [868]

Miscellaneous Interesting Lives

Individual

APPELT, KATHI

1533 Appelt, Kathi. *My Father's Summers: A Daughter's Memoir* (6–12). 2004, Holt $15.95 (0-8050-7362-0). 208pp. In a series of prose poems, Appelt paints a poignant portrait of her life growing up in Houston and the pain caused by the extended absences of her father. (Rev: BCCB 7–8/04; BL 6/1–15/04; SLJ 6/04; VOYA 6/04) [813]

BAKER, ALIA MUHAMMAD

1534 Stamaty, Mark Alan. *Alia's Mission: Saving the Books of Iraq* (4–7). 2004, Knopf LB $14.99 (0-375-93217-8). 32pp. In graphic novel format, this is the inspiring story of Iraqi librarian Alia Muhammad Baker, who hid thousands of books in advance of the 2003 invasion of her country. (Rev: BL 2/1/05*; SLJ 3/05) [020]

BECKWOURTH, JAMES

1535 Gregson, Susan R. *James Beckwourth: Mountaineer, Scout, and Pioneer* (5–8). Series: Signature Lives. 2005, Compass Point LB $22.95 (0-7565-1000-7). 112pp. Beckwourth was one of the first African Americans to play a role in the exploration of the West. (Rev: SLJ 2/06) [921]

CALLAHAN, STEVEN

1536 Cefrey, Holly. *Steven Callahan: Adrift at Sea* (4–7). Series: Survivor. 2003, Children's Pr. LB $20.00 (0-516-24330-6); paper $6.95 (0-516-27868-1). 48pp. The exciting story of Callahan's survival after capsizing off Africa, plus the vivid photo-graphs, will appeal to reluctant readers. (Rev: SLJ 2/04) [921]

MACDONALD, WARREN

1537 Macdonald, Warren. *A Test of Will: One Man's Extraordinary Story of Survival* (8–12). 2004, Douglas & McIntyre paper $14.95 (1-55365-064-6). 208pp. The riveting story of Macdonald's survival after his legs were pinned under a massive rock on an island off Australia. (Rev: BL 9/15/04) [790.5]

MCGOUGH, MATTHEW

1538 McGough, Matthew. *Bat Boy: My True Life Adventures Coming of Age with the New York Yankees* (8–12). 2005, Doubleday $22.95 (0-385-51020-9). 240pp. McGough tells how a boyhood dream came true when he was selected to be a bat-boy for the New York Yankees. (Rev: BL 3/1/05; SLJ 11/05) [796.357]

MILLMAN, ISAAC

1539 Millman, Isaac. *Hidden Child* (4–7). Illus. 2005, Farrar $18.00 (0-374-33071-9). 80pp. The author relates his experiences as a child in World War II, when he was hidden in various homes in France to save him from the Nazis. (Rev: BL 6/1–15/05*; SLJ 9/05) [921]

O'GRADY, SCOTT

1540 Somervill, Barbara A. *Scott O'Grady: Behind Enemy Lines* (4–7). Series: Survivor. 2003, Children's Pr. LB $20.00 (0-516-24332-2); paper $6.95 (0-516-27871-1). 48pp. The story of O'Grady's success in escaping detection for six days after being shot down over Bosnia. (Rev: SLJ 2/04) [949.703]

RUNYAN, BRENT

1541 Runyon, Brent. *The Burn Journals* (8–12). 2004, Random LB $19.99 (0-375-82621-1). 384pp. In this powerful memoir, Runyon recounts his journey to recovery from life-threatening burns suffered in a teenage suicide attempt. (Rev: BL 6/1–15/04; SLJ 11/04) [362.28]

SWADOS, ELIZABETH

1542 Swados, Elizabeth. *My Depression: A Picture Book* (8–12). Illus. 2005, Hyperion $16.95 (1-4013-0789-2). 160pp. In a candid yet entertaining cartoon picture-book format, Swados reveals her struggles with severe depression. (Rev: BL 3/15/05) [818]

WARNER, ANDREA

1543 Warren, Andrea. *Escape from Saigon: How a Vietnam War Orphan Became an American Boy* (5–12). Illus. 2004, Farrar $17.00 (0-374-32224-4). 128pp. An inspiring account of a young Amerasian war orphan's long journey from Vietnam to a new and successful life in the United States. (Rev: BL 6/1–15/04*; SLJ 10/04) [959.704]

WEINSTEIN, LAUREN

1544 Weinstein, Lauren. *Girl Stories* (7–10). Illus. 2006, Holt paper $16.95 (0-80507-863-0). 240pp. Episodic graphic novel-format vignettes paint a vivid portrait of the author's 8th- and 9th-grade years. (Rev: BL 3/15/06; VOYA 4/06) [741.5]

WONG, LI KENG

1545 Wong, Li Keng. *Good Fortune: My Journey to Gold Mountain* (4–7). 2006, Peachtree $14.95 (1-56145-367-6). 144pp. Wong, who migrated to the United States from China with her mother and sister in 1933, writes about the challenges of adjusting to a new culture. (Rev: BL 3/1/06) [979.4]

YAN, MA

1546 Yan, Ma. *The Diary of Ma Yan: The Struggles and Hopes of a Chinese Schoolgirl* (6–9). Ed. by Pierre Haski. Trans. by He Yanping. 2005, HarperCollins LB $16.89 (0-06-076497-X). 176pp. In the pages of this heartbreaking diary, Chinese peasant girl Ma Yan writes of the hardscrabble life she and her family endured in the drought-stricken province of Ningxia. (Rev: BL 6/1–15/05; SLJ 8/05; VOYA 6/05) [921]

YU, CHUN

1547 Yu, Chun. *Little Green: Growing Up During the Chinese Cultural Revolution* (7–10). 2005, Simon & Schuster $15.95 (0-689-86943-6). 112pp. Chun Yu, who was born the year that China's Cultural Revolution began, recounts in poetry what life was like during one of the most tumultuous periods in Chinese history. (Rev: BL 1/1–15/05; SLJ 3/05; VOYA 10/05) [951.05]

ZENATTI, VALÉRIE

1548 Zenatti, Valérie. *When I Was a Soldier* (8–11). Trans. by Adriana Hunter. 2005, Bloomsbury $16.95 (1-58234-978-9). 250pp. In this compelling memoir, Valerie Zenatti, an immigrant to Israel from France, chronicles her two years of compulsory service in the Israeli army. (Rev: BCCB 7–8/05; BL 5/1/05*; SLJ 5/05) [921]

The Arts and Entertainment

Architecture and Building

General and Miscellaneous

1549 Arbogast, Joan Marie. *Buildings in Disguise: Architecture That Looks Like Animals, Food, and Other Things* (4–7). 2004, Boyds Mills $16.95 (1-59078-099-X). 48pp. Buildings in the shapes of milk bottles, elephants, wigwams, and baskets are among the wonders shown in many period and contemporary photographs. (Rev: BL 11/1/04; SLJ 1/05) [720]

1550 Pascoe, Elaine, ed. *The Pentagon* (4–7). Series: Super Structures of the World. 2003, Gale LB $23.70 (1-56711-867-4). 48pp. An architectural tour of the Pentagon, headquarters of the U.S. Department of Defense. (Rev: SLJ 4/04) [355.6]

History of Architecture

1551 Nardo, Don. *Artistry in Stone: Great Structures of Ancient Egypt* (6–10). Illus. Series: The Lucent Library of Historical Eras. 2005, Gale LB $28.70 (1-59018-661-3). 112pp. Photographs, reproductions, and film and documentary stills illustrate this well-documented examination of massive ancient Egyptian structures such as the pyramids and the Sphinx. (Rev: SLJ 11/05) [932]

Various Types of Buildings

1552 Forward, Toby. *Shakespeare's Globe: An Interactive Pop-up Theatre* (5–8). 2005, Candlewick $19.99 (0-7636-2694-5). 14pp. A large-format pop-up model of the Globe Theatre, with narrative by a Shakespeare colleague and scenes from Shakespeare's plays. (Rev: BL 5/1/05; SLJ 11/05) [792]

Painting, Sculpture, and Photography

General and Miscellaneous

1553 Aldana, Patricia, ed. *Under the Spell of the Moon: Art for Children from the World's Great Illustrators* (6–12). Trans. by Stan Dragland. 2004, Groundwood $25.00 (0-88899-559-8). 72pp. Artwork by children's book illustrators from around the world celebrates children's literature and the work of the International Board on Books for Young People. (Rev: BL 12/15/04; SLJ 1/05) [741.6]

1554 *The Art of Reading: Forty Illustrators Celebrate RIF's 40th Anniversary* (7–10). Illus. 2005, Dutton $19.99 (0-525-47484-6). 96pp. To mark Reading Is Fundamental's 40th birthday, 40 illustrators choose a favorite children's book, talk about its importance, and create an image that captures the spirit of the book; a large, attractive volume. (Rev: BL 7/05; SLJ 8/05*) [745.6]

1555 Coyne, Jennifer Tarr. *Come Look with Me: Discovering Women Artists for Children* (4–7). Illus. Series: Come Look with Me. 2005, Lickle $15.95 (1-890674-08-7). 32pp. Beautifully reproduced examples of works by women artists' are paired with brief biographical information and questions that direct the reader's attention to different aspects of art. (Rev: BL 5/1/05; SLJ 6/05) [709]

1556 Ganz, Nicholas. *Graffiti World: Street Art from Five Continents* (8–12). Ed. by Tristan Manco. Illus. 2004, Abrams $35.00 (0-8109-4979-2). 376pp. Graffiti from around the world is organized by continent and then by artist, with more than 2,000 color photos showing the common themes and wonderful inventiveness of these artists. (Rev: BL 1/1–15/05; SLJ 5/05) [751.7]

1557 Hand, John Oliver. *National Gallery of Art: Master Paintings from the Collection* (8–12). Illus.

2004, Abrams $60.00 (0-8109-5619-5). 480pp. Four hundred paintings from the National Gallery serve as the base for a satisfying review of European and American art. (Rev: BL 11/15/04) [750]

1558 Nilsen, Anna. *Art Auction Mystery* (5–8). Illus. 2005, Kingfisher $16.95 (0-7534-5842-X). 48pp. Wannabe art sleuths are challenged to find forgeries hidden in a selection of world-famous paintings. (Rev: BL 11/1/05; SLJ 1/06; VOYA 12/05) [759]

1559 Nilsen, Anna. *The Great Art Scandal: Solve the Crime, Save the Show!* (4–9). Illus. 2003, Kingfisher $16.95 (0-7534-5587-0). 48pp. Readers must solve a mystery involving an art exhibition in this comic-book-format work that introduces many famous paintings and artists. (Rev: SLJ 3/04) [759.06]

1560 Ross, Stewart. *Art and Architecture* (5–8). Series: Medieval Realms. 2004, Gale LB $27.45 (1-59018-534-X). 48pp. Romanesque, Gothic, Moorish, and Islamic art and architecture are covered in this well-organized and well-illustrated volume that includes discussions of houses of the poor as well as castles, manors, monasteries, and cathedrals. (Rev: SLJ 3/05) [720]

1561 Rubin, Susan G. *Art Against the Odds* (5–8). 2004, Crown $19.95 (0-375-82406-5). 64pp. This inspiring book explores art created in the face of adversity, such as the quilts of slaves and the graffiti painted on city walls by underprivileged teens. (Rev: BL 2/15/04; SLJ 3/04) [700]

1562 Rynck, Patrick De, ed. *How to Read a Painting: Lessons from the Old Masters* (8–12). Illus. 2004, Abrams $35.00 (0-8109-5576-8). 383pp. Introduces readers to the symbols, themes, and motifs that aid understanding of the great masters' art; two-page spreads display 150 paintings and frescoes. (Rev: BL 12/15/04) [753]

History of Art

1563 Chrisp, Peter. *Ancient Rome* (4–8). Series: History in Art. 2004, Raintree LB $29.93 (1-4109-0520-9). 48pp. A look at what art can reveal about the culture and technology of a society. (Rev: SLJ 4/05) [709]

1564 Langley, Andrew. *Ancient Greece* (4–8). Series: History in Art. 2004, Raintree LB $29.93 (1-4109-0517-9). 48pp. A look at what art can reveal about the culture and technology of a society. (Rev: SLJ 4/05) [709]

1565 Robinson, Shannon. *Cubism* (6–12). Series: Movements in Art. 2005, Creative Education LB $31.35 (1-58341-347-2). 48pp. A review of cubism from the works of Picasso and Braque through the movement's influence on sculpture and architecture, with large, clear reproductions. (Rev: SLJ 2/06)

1566 Sayre, Henry M. *Cave Paintings to Picasso: The Inside Scoop on 50 Famous Masterpieces* (3–7). Illus. 2004, Chronicle Books $22.95 (0-8118-3767-X). 96pp. This short but impressive historical overview chronicles the evolution of the visual arts from prehistoric cave paintings to the 1960s, presenting 50 major works and including historical context and information on the artist. (Rev: BL 11/1/04; SLJ 10/04) [709]

Regions

Asia and the Middle East

1567 Barber, Nicola. *Islamic Art and Culture* (5–8). Illus. Series: World Art and Culture. 2005, Raintree LB $21.95 (1-4109-1105-5). 56pp. High-quality color photographs document the architecture, sculpture, painting, pottery, music, dance, and other art forms found in the Islamic world from early times to the present. (Rev: BL 4/1/04)

1568 Bingham, Jane. *Indian Art and Culture* (5–8). Illus. Series: World Art and Culture. 2004, Raintree LB $29.99 (0-7398-6607-9). 56pp. High-quality color photographs document the architecture, sculpture, painting, pottery, music, dance, and other art forms found in India from early times to the present. Also use *Aboriginal Art and Culture* (2004). (Rev: BL 4/1/04; SLJ 2/04) [709]

1569 Hibbert, Clare. *Chinese Art and Culture* (5–8). Illus. Series: World Art and Culture. 2005, Raintree LB $21.95 (1-4109-1107-1). 56pp. High-quality color photographs document the architecture, sculpture, painting, pottery, music, dance, and other art forms found in China from early times to the present. (Rev: BL 4/1/04)

1570 Khanduri, Kamini. *Japanese Art and Culture* (5–8). Illus. Series: World Art and Culture. 2004, Raintree LB $29.99 (0-7398-6609-5). 56pp. High-quality color photographs document the architecture, sculpture, painting, pottery, music, dance, and other art forms found in Japan from early times to the present. (Rev: BL 4/1/04)

Europe

1571 Impelluso, Lucia. *Nature and Its Symbols* (8–12). Trans. by Stephen Sartarelli. Illus. 2004, J. Paul Getty Museum paper $24.95 (0-89236-772-5). 384pp. A helpful guide to the symbols found in European painters' depictions of the natural world from the 14th through the 17th centuries. (Rev: BL 12/15/04) [704.9]

North America

UNITED STATES

1572 Amaki, Amalia K., ed. *A Century of African American Art: The Paul R. Jones Collection* (8–12). Illus. 2004, Rutgers paper $29.95 (0-8135-3457-7). 288pp. The work of 66 African American artists is showcased in this attractive volume that includes profiles and commentary. (Rev: BL 2/1/05) [704.03]

1573 Bolden, Tonya. *Wake Up Our Souls: A Celebration of Black American Artists* (6–12). Illus. 2004, Abrams $24.95 (0-8109-4809-5). 128pp. Beginning with the 19th century and ending with the present, this is a beautifully illustrated history of a selection of African American artists along with short biographies and material on the social conditions under which they worked. (Rev: BL 2/15/04*) [704.03]

1574 Clee, Paul. *Photography and the Making of the American West* (6–9). 2003, Linnet LB $27.50 (0-208-02512-X). 124pp. Clee explores the photographs that documented the exploration of the West and the impact they had on Americans' perceptions. (Rev: SLJ 1/04; VOYA 4/04) [770]

1575 Curtis, Edward S., and Christopher Cardozo. *Edward S. Curtis: The Women* (8–12). Illus. 2005, Bulfinch $35.00 (0-8212-2895-1). 128pp. This stunning volume showcases 100 of photographer Edward S. Curtis's portraits of Native American women. (Rev: BL 4/1/05) [779]

1576 January, Brendan. *Native American Art and Culture* (5–8). Series: World Art and Culture. 2005, Raintree LB $31.36 (1-4109-1108-X). 56pp. Pottery, textiles, carving, painting, textiles, and architecture are all discussed, along with body art, ceremonies, songs, and dances; many color photographs are included and a list of museums is appended. (Rev: BL 4/1/04; SLJ 6/05)

1577 Panchyk, Richard. *American Folk Art for Kids: With 21 Activities* (6–12). 2004, Chicago Review paper $16.95 (1-55652-499-4). 128pp. This historical survey of American folk art is supplemented by detailed instructions for projects that readers can make for themselves. (Rev: BL 11/1/04; SLJ 11/04) [745]

1578 Sandler, Martin W. *America Through the Lens: Photographers Who Changed the Nation* (6–9). Illus. 2005, Holt $18.95 (0-8050-7367-1).

192pp. Profiles 11 American photographers whose inspiring works may have influenced how America perceives itself and its actions. (Rev: BL 9/1/05; SLJ 11/05; VOYA 8/05) [770]

1579 Slowik, Theresa J. *America's Art: Smithsonian American Art Museum* (8–12). Illus. 2006, Abrams $65.00 (0-8109-5532-6). 324pp. An oversize volume showcasing some of the best-known works in the collection of the Smithsonian American Art Museum. (Rev: BL 3/15/06) [709]

Music

Jazz and Popular Music
(Country, Rap, Rock, etc.)

1580 Marsalis, Wynton. *Jazz A B Z: An A to Z Collection of Jazz Portraits* (7–12). Illus. 2005, Candlewick $24.99 (0-7636-2135-8). 76pp. Arranged in alphabet-book format, this strikingly illustrated volume celebrates jazz and its best-known practitioners. (Rev: BL 1/1–15/06; SLJ 1/06*) [811]

Songs and Folk Songs

1581 Bates, Katharine Lee. *America the Beautiful* (4–7). 2004, Little, Brown $16.95 (0-316-73743-7). 32pp. The lyrics of this patriotic song are accompanied by striking images that underline the sentiments expressed and give additional historical emphasis. (Rev: BL 5/1/04*; SLJ 4/04) [811]

1582 Yolen, Jane. *Apple for the Teacher: Thirty Songs for Singing While You Work* (4–7). Illus. 2005, Abrams $24.95 (0-8109-4825-7). 160pp. This collection of work songs, compiled by Yolen and featuring music arrangements by her son Adam Stemple, celebrates 30 diverse occupations from astronaut to weaver. (Rev: BL 10/1/05; SLJ 10/05) [782.42]

Theater, Dance, and Other Performing Arts

General and Miscellaneous

1583 Amendola, Dana. *A Day at the New Amsterdam Theatre* (4–9). Photos by Gino Domenico. 2004, Disney $24.95 (0-7868-5438-3). 125pp. A behind-the-scenes look at a production of a musical in the renovated theater in New York City, introducing the wide variety of individuals involved. (Rev: SLJ 1/05) [792]

Dance (Ballet, Modern, etc.)

1584 Anderson, Janet. *Modern Dance* (7–12). Series: World of Dance. 2003, Chelsea House LB $22.95 (0-7910-7644-X). 115pp. Traces the history of modern dance, describing key personalities and innovations and looking at a modern dance class. (Rev: SLJ 3/04; VOYA 8/04) [792.8]

1585 Dillman, Lisa. *Ballet* (4–7). Illus. Series: Get Going! Hobbies. 2005, Heinemann LB $19.45 (1-4034-6115-5). 32pp. A useful overview of ballet that includes a history of the dance form, techniques, dress, and terminology. (Rev: BL 11/1/05) [792.8]

1586 Rinaldi, Robin. *Ballet* (7–12). Series: World of Dance. 2003, Chelsea House LB $22.95 (0-7910-7640-7). 114pp. Traces the history of ballet, describing key personalities and innovations and looking at a modern ballet class. (Rev: SLJ 3/04; VOYA 8/04) [792.8]

1587 Schorer, Suki, and School of American Ballet. *Put Your Best Foot Forward: A Young Dancer's Guide to Life* (4–8). Photos by Chris Carroll. 2005, Workman $9.95 (0-7611-3795-5). 96pp. Practical tips are combined with artistic advice in this helpful guide for young ballet dancers, written by a former principal dancer. (Rev: SLJ 3/06) [792.8]

1588 Yolen, Jane, and Heidi Stemple. *The Barefoot Book of Ballet Stories* (5–7). 2004, Barefoot Books $19.99 (1-84148-229-3). 96pp. The stories behind seven of the world's classic ballets — including "Cinderella," "The Nutcracker," "Coppelia," and "Sleeping Beauty" — are introduced by a general discussion of ballet as an art form and accompanied by production notes on each work. (Rev: BL 11/1/04; SLJ 12/04) [792.8]

Motion Pictures

1589 Clee, Paul. *Before Hollywood: From Shadow Play to the Silver Screen* (7–12). Illus. 2005, Clarion $22.00 (0-618-44533-1). 192pp. Early technologies and the reactions of early audiences are the focus of this fascinating account. (Rev: BCCB 7–8/05; HB 9–10/05; SLJ 7/05) [791.43]

1590 McCaig, Iain, et al. *Star Wars Visionaries* (7–10). Illus. 2005, Dark Horse paper $17.95 (1-59307-311-9). 128pp. Artists who worked on *The Revenge of the Sith* showcase their individual artistic styles in this gallery of Star Wars scenarios. (Rev: BL 5/15/05; SLJ 11/05) [741.5]

1591 Miller, Ron. *Special Effects: An Introduction to Movie Magic* (7–10). Illus. 2006, Lerner LB $26.60 (0-76132-918-8). 128pp. Covers both the history of special effects and the techniques used today; boxed features discuss key figures and offer career advice. (Rev: BL 3/15/06) [778.5]

1592 Vaz, Mark Cotta, et al. *The Art of The Incredibles* (8–12). Illus. 2004, Chronicle $40.00 (0-8118-4433-1). 160pp. Many illustrations enhance this look at the making of the popular animated motion picture. (Rev: BL 10/15/04) [791.43]

Radio, Television, and Video

1593 Balkin, Karen F., ed. *Reality TV* (6–12). Series: At Issue. 2004, Gale LB $27.45 (0-7377-2254-1). 75pp. The pros and cons of reality television shows are the focus of this collection of writings. (Rev: BL 2/15/04; SLJ 7/04) [791.45]

1594 Riess, Jana. *What Would Buffy Do? The Vampire Slayer as Spiritual Guide* (7–12). 2004, Jossey-Bass paper $14.00 (0-7879-6922-2). 192pp. For fans of the TV series, this is a guide to the first seven seasons with material on the show's values and characters. (Rev: BL 5/1/04) [791.45]

1595 Schieffer, Bob. *Face the Nation: My Favorite Stories from the First 50 Years of the Award-Winning News Broadcast* (8–12). Illus. 2004, Simon & Schuster $26.95 (0-7432-6585-8). 240pp. Highlights from the first 50 years of CBS's popular *Face the Nation*. (Rev: BL 9/1/04) [791.45]

Theater and Other Dramatic Forms

1596 Dunleavy, Deborah. *The Jumbo Book of Drama* (4–8). 2004, Kids Can paper $14.95 (1-55337-008-2). 208pp. Divided into Acts, this volume covers all aspects of drama and stagecraft, from body movement to lighting and props. (Rev: BL 5/1/04; SLJ 6/04) [372.66]

History and Geography

General History and Geography

Atlases, Maps, and Mapmaking

1597 Ritchie, Robert. *Historical Atlas of the Renaissance* (8–12). Illus. Series: Historical Atlas. 2004, Facts on File $35.00 (0-8160-5731-1). 192pp. Art, culture, politics, literature, science, and key figures are all covered in this chronologically organized atlas. (Rev: SLJ 2/05)

1598 Wilkinson, Philip. *The Kingfisher Student Atlas* (5–8). 2003, Kingfisher $24.95 (0-7534-5589-7). 128pp. An atlas of the earth, with detail on each area's physical characteristics and political boundaries and material on such problems as pollution and deforestation. An accompanying CD offers printable maps. (Rev: SLJ 4/04)

Paleontology

1599 Dixon, Dougal, and John Malam. *Dinosaur* (7–12). Illus. Series: DK/Google e.guides. 2004, DK $17.99 (0-7566-0761-2). 96pp. An attractive, highly illustrated yet informative overview of dinosaurs and dinosaur discoveries, with a link to a Web site that offers additional material. (Rev: BL 12/1/04) [567.9]

1600 Larson, Peter, and Kristin Donnan. *Bones Rock! Everything You Need to Know to Be a Paleontologist* (5–9). Illus. 2004, Invisible Cities paper $19.95 (1-931229-35-X). 204pp. A comprehensive, accessible guide to paleontology, describing how to dig for fossils, clean them, keep records, and develop and test theories, with interesting accounts of the authors' experiences. (Rev: SLJ 11/04) [560]

Anthropology and Evolution

1601 Naff, Clay Farris, ed. *Evolution* (7–12). Series: Exploring Science and Medical Discoveries. 2005, Gale LB $34.95 (0-7377-2823-X). 222pp. This collection of writings documents the history of theories about human origins from ancient Greece to the 20th century. (Rev: SLJ 12/05)

1602 Robertshaw, Peter, and Jill Rubalcaba. *The Early Human World* (8–12). Series: The World in Ancient Times. 2005, Oxford LB $32.95 (0-19-516157-2). 173pp. Using primary sources and good illustrations, this volume looks at the world's earliest hominids and the evidence that they evolved from more primitive primates. (Rev: SLJ 6/05; VOYA 8/04) [599]

1603 Sloan, Christopher. *The Human Story: Our Evolution from Prehistoric Ancestors to Today* (8–12). Illus. 2004, National Geographic $19.95 (0-7922-6325-1). 80pp. Using evidence from fossils and DNA, this is the history of human evolution for a period of more than 6 million years, with recent findings on the subject. (Rev: BL 3/1/04; SLJ 3/04) [599.93]

Archaeology

1604 Dean, Arlan. *Terra-Cotta Soldiers: Army of Stone* (4–7). Illus. Series: High Interest Books: Digging Up the Past. 2005, Children's Pr. LB $23.00 (0-516-25124-4); paper $6.95 (0-516-25093-0). 40pp. For reluctant readers, this is a useful introduction to one of the world's most extraordinary archaeological finds: the 8,000 terracotta warriors of China. (Rev: BL 10/15/05; SLJ 2/06) [931]

1605 Tanaka, Shelley. *Mummies: The Newest, Coolest and Creepiest from Around the World* (4–7). Illus. 2005, Abrams $16.95 (0-8109-5797-3). 48pp. Mummies from across history and around the world are on display in the colorful — and often graphic — pages of this fascinating book. (Rev: BL 12/1/05*; SLJ 12/05*) [393]

1606 Wheatley, Abigail, and Struan Reid. *The Usborne Introduction to Archaeology: Internet-Linked* (6–9). Illus. Series: Archaeology. 2005, EDC $22.95 (0-7945-0806-5). 128pp. This excellent, large-format introduction to archaeology explores the discipline itself, the various techniques used to date and preserve artifacts, and significant discoveries around the world. (Rev: BL 4/1/05) [930.1]

World History and Geography

1607 Blackwood, Gary L. *Enigmatic Events* (5–8). Illus. Series: Unsolved History. 2005, Marshall Cavendish LB $20.95 (0-7614-1889-X). 80pp. Explores some of history's most enduring mysteries — the disappearance of the dinosaurs and of the *Mary Celeste*, to name only two. (Rev: BL 3/1/06; SLJ 3/06) [904]

1608 Cawthorne, Nigel. *Military Commanders: The 100 Greatest Throughout History* (6–12). 2004, Enchanted Lion $18.95 (1-59270-029-2). 208pp. This chronology identifies the greatest military battles in world history and the men who led their forces to victory in those battles. (Rev: BL 6/1–15/04; SLJ 4/04) [355]

1609 Cox, Caroline, and Ken Albala. *Opening Up North America, 1497–1800* (6–12). Series: Discovery and Exploration. 2005, Facts on File $40.00 (0-8160-5261-1). 196pp. Chronicles the arrival of Europeans in North America and their progression across the continent, with maps, illustrations, and excerpts from primary sources. (Rev: SLJ 8/05) [973]

1610 Defries, Cheryl L. *Seven Natural Wonders of the United States and Canada* (4–7). Illus. Series: Seven Wonders of the World. 2005, Enslow LB $25.26 (0-7660-5291-5). 48pp. This tour of seven of North America's natural wonders, including the Grand Canyon, Everglades, and Niagara Falls, is extended by constantly updated links to Web sites. (Rev: SLJ 11/05) [557]

1611 De Porti, Andrea. *Explorers: The Most Exciting Voyages of Discovery — from the African Expeditions to the Lunar Landing* (8–12). Illus. 2005, Firefly $49.95 (1-55407-101-1). 174pp. Rare archival photos document the history of exploration over the past 150 years, telling 53 stories of discovery — some well-known and others more obscure. (Rev: BL 12/1/05) [910.92]

1612 Gilpin, Daniel. *Food and Clothing* (6–9). Illus. Series: History of Invention. 2004, Facts on File $35.00 (0-8160-5441-X). 96pp. A slim introductory overview of advances in food and clothing from prehistoric times to today, with maps, illustrations, and profiles of key figures. (Rev: SLJ 12/04) [973]

1613 Graham, Amy. *Seven Wonders of the Natural World* (4–7). Illus. Series: Seven Wonders of the World. 2005, Enslow LB $25.26 (0-7660-5290-7). 48pp. A tour of seven of the world's natural wonders, including Mount Everest, the Great Barrier Reef, and the Grand Canyon; the text is extended by constantly updated links to Web sites. (Rev: SLJ 11/05)

1614 Grant, Kevin Patrick. *Exploration in the Age of Empire, 1750–1953* (6–10). Series: Discovery and Exploration. 2004, Facts on File $35.00 (0-8160-5260-3). 166pp. A look at the exploration that took place during these two centuries and the underlying political and religious motivations, in clear, informative text plus photographs, illustrations, and excerpts from primary sources. (Rev: SLJ 12/04) [973]

1615 Huff, Toby. *An Age of Science and Revolutions: 1600–1800* (7–10). Illus. Series: Medieval and Early Modern World. 2005, Oxford $32.95 (0-19-517724-X). 176pp. A sweeping overview of history in both the East and West from the beginning of the 17th century through the end of the 18th century, with color photographs, maps, profiles of key figures, and so forth. (Rev: BL 10/15/05) [909]

1616 Johnston, Andrew K. *Earth from Space: Smithsonian National Air and Space Museum* (7–12). Illus. 2004, Firefly $49.95 (1-55297-820-6). 272pp. Breathtakingly detailed color images of

Earth are organized into categories such as weather, geology, and human activity. (Rev: BL 12/1/04) [525]

1617 Kyi, Tanya L. *Fires!* (6–9). Series: True Stories from the Edge. 2004, Annick $18.95 (1-55037-877-5); paper $8.95 (1-55037-876-7). 112pp. The stories behind ten of history's most horrific fires — including the Great Fire of London in 1666 and the Chernobyl nuclear plant explosion in 1986 — are recounted in this compelling title. (Rev: BL 1/1–15/05; VOYA 6/05) [363.37]

1618 Llewellyn, Claire. *Great Discoveries and Amazing Adventures: The Stories of Hidden Marvels and Lost Treasures* (4–7). Illus. 2004, Kingfisher $18.95 (0-7534-5783-0). 76pp. Important discoveries — and hoaxes — are described in inviting text, plus many illustrations, factoids, and a foreword by Robert Ballard. (Rev: SLJ 1/05) [509]

1619 Markle, Sandra. *Rescues!* (4–7). Illus. 2006, Lerner LB $25.26 (0-8225-3413-4). 88pp. Markle covers rescue efforts in 11 recent disasters (2004 to 2005), giving details of technology used and providing accounts by victims, rescuers, and eyewitnesses. (Rev: BL 4/1/06*) [363.34]

1620 Middleton, Nick. *Extremes: Surviving the World's Harshest Environments* (8–12). 2005, St. Martin's $24.95 (0-312-34266-7). 272pp. Middleton, an Oxford geography professor, describes his experiences visiting — and trying to be more than a tourist in — some of the world's most extreme climates. (Rev: BL 4/1/05) [910.4]

1621 *One People: Many Journeys* (8–12). Illus. 2005, Lonely Planet $40.00 (1-74104-600-9). 288pp. Striking photographs from around the world capture the universality of the human experience and demonstrate the wide diversity of resources. (Rev: BL 1/1–15/06) [910]

1622 Phillips, Dee, et al. *People of the World* (4–7). Illus. Series: Just the Facts. 2006, School Specialty paper $9.95 (0-7696-4257-8). 64pp. Statistics and fast facts on the countries and peoples of the world are presented on double-page spreads. (Rev: BL 4/1/06) [305.8]

1623 Scandiffio, Laura. *Escapes!* (5–9). Series: True Stories from the Edge. 2004, Annick $18.95 (1-55037-823-6); paper $7.95 (1-55037-822-8). 170pp. Ten stories of great escapes and escape attempts, from the first century B.C. to the late 1970s, with a concentration on resourcefulness and bravery. (Rev: SLJ 6/04) [904]

1624 Shapiro, Stephen. *Battle Stations! Fortifications Through the Ages* (5–8). Illus. 2005, Annick LB $19.95 (1-55037-889-9); paper $7.95 (1-55037-888-0). 32pp. A tall, slim, and very visual overview of fortifications around the world and throughout history. (Rev: BL 9/15/05) [355.7]

1625 Stefoff, Rebecca. *Exploration* (6–9). Series: World Historical Atlases. 2004, Marshall Cavendish $18.95 (0-7614-1640-4). 48pp. A brief overview of world exploration, with many clear maps, chronicling voyages of discovery from ancient times through the polar explorations of Amundsen and Shackleton. (Rev: BL 1/05) [910]

1626 Stewart, Robert, et al. *Mysteries of History* (7–12). Illus. 2003, National Geographic $29.95 (0-7922-6232-8). 192pp. Such controversial topics as Stonehenge, Napoleon's death, and Custer's Last Stand are presented with 16 others in this well-illustrated book. (Rev: BL 2/1/04) [902]

1627 Wells, Don. *The Spice Trade* (5–8). Illus. Series: Great Journeys. 2004, Weigl $26.00 (1-59036-208-X); paper $7.95 (1-59036-261-6). 32pp. Colorful illustrations and an attractive format will appeal to browsers seeking information about the spice trade; a useful timeline and links to Web sites are included. (Rev: BL 11/1/04)

1628 Wojtanik, Andrew. *Afghanistan to Zimbabwe: Country Facts That Helped Me Win the National Geographic Bee* (5–12). 2005, National Geographic LB $28.90 (0-7922-7442-3); paper $12.95 (0-7922-7981-6). 384pp. Facts and figures about the world's 192 independent countries are organized into three categories: Physical, Political, and Environmental/Economic. (Rev: SLJ 10/05; VOYA 8/05) [910]

1629 Worth, Richard. *The Great Empire of China and Marco Polo in World History* (5–8). Illus. Series: In World History. 2003, Enslow LB $20.95 (0-7660-1939-X). 112pp. Quotations from primary documents and excerpts from Polo's own writings add context to this account of his 13th-century journeys to the Far East. (Rev: SLJ 3/04) [915.04]

Ancient History

General and Miscellaneous

1630 Bowman, John S., and Maurice Isserman, eds. *Exploration in the World of the Ancients* (6–10). Series: Discovery and Exploration. 2004, Facts on File $35.00 (0-8160-5257-3). 144pp. A look at the voyages and routes of explorers from prehistoric times to the beginning of the Middle Ages. (Rev: SLJ 12/04) [973]

1631 Calvert, Patricia. *The Ancient Celts* (5–8). Series: People of the Ancient World. 2005, Watts LB $29.50 (0-531-12359-6); paper $9.95 (0-531-16845-X). 112pp. Introduces readers to the arts, religious beliefs, and society of the ancient Celts, with discussion of individual occupations and of the discoveries by archaeologists and anthropologists. (Rev: SLJ 9/05) [973]

1632 Curlee, Lynn. *Parthenon* (5–8). 2004, Simon & Schuster $17.95 (0-689-84490-5). 40pp. A beautifully composed overview of the construction and history of the temple built by the ancient Greeks to honor the goddess Athena. (Rev: BL 9/15/04*; HB 7–8/04; SLJ 6/04) [726]

1633 Fagan, Brian M., ed. *The Seventy Great Inventions of the Ancient World* (7–12). Illus. 2004, Thames & Hudson $40.00 (0-500-05130-5). 304pp. This photo-filled volume explores inventions in categories ranging from hunting and farming to artwork and communications. (Rev: BL 12/1/04) [609]

1634 Hunter, Erica C. D., and Mike Corbishley. *First Civilizations*. Rev. ed. (5–8). Illus. Series: Cultural Atlas for Young People. 2003, Facts on File $35.00 (0-8160-5149-6). 96pp. Colorful topical spreads introduce readers to the culture, geography, history, and politics of Mesopotamia, Persia, and Assyria. (Rev: SLJ 1/04) [939]

1635 Perl, Lila. *The Ancient Maya* (5–8). Series: People of the Ancient World. 2005, Watts LB $29.50 (0-531-12381-2); paper $9.95 (0-531-16848-4). 112pp. Introduces readers to the arts, religious beliefs, and society of the Maya, with discussion of individual occupations and of the discoveries by archaeologists and anthropologists. (Rev: SLJ 9/05) [973]

1636 Richardson, Hazel. *Life in Ancient Africa* (4–7). Illus. Series: Peoples of the Ancient World. 2005, Crabtree LB $23.92 (0-7787-2043-8); paper $8.95 (0-7787-2073-X). 32pp. Introduces the early civilizations of Africa, examining their arts, spiritual beliefs, government, language, and technology; color photographs, sidebars, and timelines add information and appeal. (Rev: SLJ 11/05) [973]

1637 Richardson, Hazel. *Life in Ancient Japan* (4–7). Illus. Series: Peoples of the Ancient World. 2005, Crabtree LB $23.92 (0-7787-2041-1); paper $8.95 (0-7787-2071-3). 32pp. Introduces ancient Japan's arts, spiritual beliefs, government, language, and technology; color photographs, sidebars, and timelines add information and appeal. (Rev: SLJ 11/05) [952]

1638 Richardson, Hazel. *Life in the Ancient Indus River Valley* (4–7). Illus. Series: Peoples of the Ancient World. 2005, Crabtree LB $23.92 (0-7787-2040-3); paper $8.95 (0-7787-2070-5). 32pp. Introduces life in the earliest urban civilization on the Indian subcontinent, examining the arts, spiritual beliefs, government, language, and technology; color photographs, sidebars, and timelines add information and appeal. (Rev: SLJ 11/05) [973]

1639 Richardson, Hazel. *Life of the Ancient Celts* (4–7). Illus. Series: Peoples of the Ancient World. 2005, Crabtree LB $23.92 (0-7787-2045-4); paper $8.95 (0-7787-2075-6). 32pp. Introduces the early Celtic civilization, examining arts, spiritual beliefs,

government, language, and technology; color photographs, sidebars, and timelines add information and appeal. (Rev: SLJ 11/05) [973]

1640 Schomp, Virginia. *Ancient India* (6–8). Series: People of the Ancient World. 2005, Watts LB $29.50 (0-531-12379-0). 112pp. Readable text and attractive illustrations introduce readers to ancient India and its art, culture, religion, government, agriculture, and societal levels. (Rev: SLJ 6/05) [954]

1641 Schomp, Virginia. *The Vikings* (6–8). Series: People of the Ancient World. 2005, Watts LB $29.50 (0-531-12382-0). 112pp. The culture, literature, arts, religious beliefs, and government of the Vikings are explored in readable text and attractive illustrations. (Rev: SLJ 6/05) [948]

1642 Sonneborn, Liz. *The Ancient Aztecs* (6–8). Series: People of the Ancient World. 2005, Watts LB $29.50 (0-531-12362-6). 112pp. The culture, arts, literature, religious beliefs, and government of the Aztecs are explored in readable text accompanied by attractive illustrations. (Rev: SLJ 6/05) [972]

1643 Sonneborn, Liz. *The Ancient Kushites* (5–8). Series: People of the Ancient World. 2005, Watts LB $29.50 (0-531-12380-4); paper $9.95 (0-531-16847-6). 112pp. Explores the arts, religious beliefs, and culture of Africa's ancient Kushites, who were also known as Nubians. (Rev: SLJ 9/05) [973]

1644 Stefoff, Rebecca. *The Ancient Mediterranean* (5–8). Series: World Historical Atlases. 2004, Benchmark LB $27.07 (0-7614-1641-2). 48pp. Maps, text, and illustrations give a broad overview of the cultures found in the ancient Mediterranean. Also use *The Ancient Near East* and *The Asian Empires* (both 2004). (Rev: SLJ 2/05) [930]

1645 Wells, Donald. *The Silk Road* (5–8). Series: Great Journeys. 2004, Weigl LB $.00 (1-59036-207-1). Colorful illustrations and an attractive format will appeal to browsers seeking information on this ancient trade route; a useful timeline and links to Web sites are included. (Rev: BL 11/1/04) [950]

Egypt and Mesopotamia

1646 Chrisp, Peter. *Mesopotamia: Iraq in Ancient Times* (4–7). Illus. Series: Picturing the Past. 2004, Enchanted Lion $15.95 (1-59270-024-1). 32pp. History and archaeology are the highlights of this nicely illustrated overview of Mesopotamian civilization. (Rev: BL 10/15/04; SLJ 11/04) [935]

1647 Cline, Eric H., and Jill Rubalcaba. *The Ancient Egyptian World* (5–10). Series: The World in Ancient Times. 2005, Oxford LB $32.95 (0-19-517391-0). 190pp. An overview of ancient Egyptian history and culture, with chronologically arranged chapters covering religion, medicine, clothing, arts, and so forth and introducing key figures such as

Hatshepsut, Tutankhamen, and Cleopatra. (Rev: SLJ 1/06) [932]

1648 Giblin, James Cross. *Secrets of the Sphinx* (7–12). 2004, Scholastic LB $17.95 (0-590-09847-0). 48pp. Full of interesting facts and details of archaeological discoveries, this is a handsome, well-illustrated picture-book-format account of the mysteries that still surround the Sphinx and the facts that are known. (Rev: BL 9/15/04; HB 11–12/04; SLJ 11/04) [932]

1649 Harris, Geraldine. *Ancient Egypt*. Rev. ed. (5–8). Illus. Series: Cultural Atlas for Young People. 2003, Facts on File $35.00 (0-8160-5148-8). 96pp. Colorful topical spreads introduce readers to the culture, history, and politics of ancient Egypt. (Rev: SLJ 1/04; VOYA 2/04) [932]

1650 Hawass, Zahi. *Tutankhamun and the Golden Age of the Pharaohs* (8–12). Illus. 2005, National Geographic $35.00 (0-7922-3873-7). 256pp. Companion to a traveling exhibit, this volume highlights the importance of items retrieved from Tutankhamen's tomb. (Rev: BL 6/1–15/05) [932]

1651 Kaplan, Sarah Pitt. *The Great Pyramid at Giza: Tomb of Wonders* (5–8). Series: Digging Up the Past. 2005, Children's Pr. LB $23.00 (0-516-25131-7); paper $6.95 (0-516-25095-7). 48pp. A richly illustrated survey of the important pyramid and the reasons for its creation; suitable for reluctant readers. (Rev: SLJ 2/06) [932]

1652 Nardo, Don. *Arts, Leisure, and Sport in Ancient Egypt* (6–10). Illus. Series: The Lucent Library of Historical Eras. 2005, Gale LB $28.70 (1-59018-706-7). 112pp. Photographs, reproductions, and film and documentary stills illustrate this well-documented examination of the art and leisure activities of ancient Egyptians, from music and dance to hunting and fishing. Also use *Mummies, Myth, and Magic: Religion in Ancient Egypt* (2005). (Rev: SLJ 11/05) [932]

1653 Perl, Lila. *The Ancient Egyptians* (4–7). Series: People of the Ancient World. 2004, Watts LB $29.50 (0-531-12345-6). 112pp. Pharaohs, mummy makers, farmers, and brewers are among the people presented in this overview of life in ancient Egypt. (Rev: SLJ 2/05) [930]

1654 Podany, Amanda H., and Marni McGee. *The Ancient Near Eastern World* (8–12). Series: The World in Ancient Times. 2005, Oxford LB $32.95 (0-19-516159-9). 174pp. Using primary sources and useful illustrations, this volume explores the ancient civilizations that flourished in the Fertile Crescent until the region was conquered by Alexander the Great in the 4th century B.C. (Rev: SLJ 6/05; VOYA 10/04) [935]

1655 Putnam, James. *The Ancient Egypt Pop-Up Book* (5–8). Illus. 2003, Universe $29.95 (0-7893-0985-8). Seven imaginatively designed pop-up spreads introduce ancient Egypt, including its pyramids, pharaohs, and mummies. (Rev: SLJ 3/04)

1656 Schomp, Virginia. *Ancient Mesopotamia: The Sumerians, Babylonians, and Assyrians* (5–8). Series: People of the Ancient World. 2004, Watts LB $29.50 (0-531-11818-5). 112pp. This fascinating volume covers the history and culture of the Sumerians, Babylonians, and Assyrians, looking at writing, warfare, and the daily life of people ranging from farmers and traders to warriors and nobles. (Rev: SLJ 3/05) [935]

Greece

1657 Ackroyd, Peter. *Ancient Greece* (7–12). Illus. Series: Voyages Through Time. 2005, DK $19.99 (0-7566-1368-X). 144pp. With maps, photographs, and other illustrations, this introduction to ancient Greece and its geography, history, culture, most important institutions, and key figures will be a useful volume for report writers. (Rev: BL 10/1/05; SLJ 2/06) [938]

1658 Malam, John. *Ancient Greece* (4–7). Series: Picturing the Past. 2004, Enchanted Lion $15.95 (1-59270-022-5). 32pp. This photo-filled volume uses images of ancient Greek artifacts and structures to introduce the civilization's governmental organization, religion, mythology, recreation, and theater. (Rev: BL 10/15/04; SLJ 11/04) [938]

1659 Nardo, Don. *A History of the Ancient Greeks* (8–12). Illus. Series: The Lucent Library of Historical Eras. 2004, Gale LB $21.96 (1-59018-525-0). 112pp. An excellent overview of ancient Greek history. (Rev: SLJ 1/05) [938]

1660 Powell, Anton. *Ancient Greece*. Rev. ed. (5–8). Illus. Series: Cultural Atlas for Young People. 2003, Facts on File $35.00 (0-8160-5146-1). 96pp. Colorful topical spreads introduce readers to the culture, history, and politics of ancient Greece, with information on the Olympics, daily life, and women's role. (Rev: SLJ 1/04) [938]

1661 Roberts, Jennifer T., and Tracy Barrett. *The Ancient Greek World* (7–10). Series: The World in Ancient Times. 2004, Oxford LB $32.95 (0-19-515696-X). 190pp. The authors take a lively and humorous approach to their carefully researched account of political and cultural life in ancient Greece. (Rev: SLJ 8/04) [938]

Rome

1662 Blacklock, Dyan. *The Roman Army* (5–8). 2004, Walker $17.95 (0-8027-8896-3). 48pp. The soldiers, weaponry, fighting techniques, and ingenuity of the Romans are detailed here in clear text and effective cartoon-style illustrations. (Rev: BL 3/1/04*; SLJ 4/04) [355]

1663 Corbishley, Mike. *Ancient Rome*. Rev. ed. (5–8). Illus. Series: Cultural Atlas for Young People. 2003, Facts on File $35.00 (0-8160-5147-X). 96pp. Colorful topical spreads introduce readers to the culture, history, and politics of ancient Rome, with information on architecture and major cities of the provinces. (Rev: SLJ 1/04) [937]

1664 Deem, James M. *Bodies from the Ash: Life and Death in Ancient Pompeii* (5–8). Illus. 2005, Houghton $16.00 (0-618-47308-4). 48pp. This photoessay full of vivid illustrations outlines what archaeologists have uncovered about the destruction of Pompeii when Mount Vesuvius erupted nearly 2,000 years ago. (Rev: BL 11/1/05; SLJ 12/05*) [937]

1665 Lassieur, Allison. *The Ancient Romans* (6–8). Illus. Series: People of the Ancient World. 2004, Watts LB $29.50 (0-531-12338-3); paper $9.95 (0-531-16742-9). 112pp. Government, the arts, social life — from aristocrats to slaves — and women's rights are among the topics discussed in this lively and accessible text. (Rev: BL 10/15/04; SLJ 1/05) [937]

1666 Mellor, Ronald, and Marni McGee. *The Ancient Roman World* (7–10). Illus. Series: The World in Ancient Times. 2004, Oxford LB $32.95 (0-19-515380-4). 192pp. This attractive and accessible volume introduces readers to the history, people, and culture of ancient Rome, using many quotations and illustrations. (Rev: BL 4/1/04; SLJ 7/04) [937]

1667 Nardo, Don. *The Roman Army: Instrument of Power* (8–12). Illus. Series: The Lucent Library of Historical Eras. 2003, Gale LB $27.45 (1-59018-316-9). 112pp. An interesting survey of Roman military power and tactics, with comparisons to other systems of the time and helpful diagrams of famous battles. Also in this series are *Arts, Leisure, and Entertainment: Life of the Ancient Romans* and *From Founding to Fall: A History of Rome* (both 2003). (Rev: SLJ 5/04)

1668 Nardo, Don. *A Roman Gladiator* (6–10). Series: The Working Life. 2004, Gale LB $27.45 (1-59018-480-7). 112pp. Gladiators' recruitment, training, living conditions, and status are all covered here. (Rev: SLJ 1/05) [937]

1669 Nardo, Don. *A Roman Senator* (6–9). Illus. Series: Working Life. 2004, Gale LB $21.96 (1-59018-481-5). 112pp. Black-and-white illustrations add to this account of the evolution of the Roman senate over almost 12 centuries. (Rev: BL 2/1/05) [328]

Middle Ages Through the Renaissance (500–1700)

1670 Aronson, Marc. *John Winthrop, Oliver Cromwell, and the Land of Promise* (7–10). 2004, Houghton $20.00 (0-618-18177-6). 224pp. In this fascinating historical study, Aronson explores the interrelationship between John Winthrop, 17th-century governor of the Massachusetts Bay Colony, and Oliver Cromwell, who led the successful Puritan revolt against Britain's King Charles I. (Rev: BL 6/1–15/04; HB 7–8/04; SLJ 9/04) [974.4]

1671 Barter, James. *A Medieval Knight* (6–9). Illus. Series: Working Life. 2005, Gale LB $28.70 (1-59018-580-3). 112pp. A medieval knight's life involves training, tournaments, fighting, and administration and legal duties as laid out in this thorough overview that includes relevant images and excerpts from primary sources. (Rev: SLJ 11/05) [940]

1672 Crompton, Samuel Willard. *The Third Crusade: Richard the Lionhearted vs. Saladin* (7–12). Series: Great Battles Through the Ages. 2003, Chelsea House LB $22.95 (0-7910-7437-4). 114pp. A useful survey of the First and Second Crusades is followed by details of the third campaign and portrayals of Richard and Saladin. (Rev: SLJ 5/04) [909.07]

1673 Ford, Nick. *Jerusalem Under Muslim Rule in the Eleventh Century: Christian Pilgrims Under Islamic Government* (5–9). Series: The Library of the Middle Ages. 2004, Rosen LB $29.25 (0-8239-4216-3). 64pp. Useful for report writers, this volume looks at life in Jerusalem for people of all religions, providing details from primary sources. (Rev: SLJ 8/04) [956.94]

1674 Hancock, Lee. *Saladin and the Kingdom of Jerusalem: The Muslims Recapture the Holy Land in AD 1187* (5–9). Series: The Library of the Middle Ages. 2004, Rosen LB $29.25 (0-8239-4217-1). 64pp. Useful for report writers, this volume looks at life in Jerusalem under the Crusaders, providing details from primary sources. (Rev: SLJ 8/04) [956]

1675 Hilliam, Paul. *Islamic Weapons, Warfare, and Armies: Muslim Military Operations Against the Crusaders* (5–9). Series: The Library of the Middle Ages. 2004, Rosen LB $29.25 (0-8239-4215-5). 64pp. Useful for report writers, this volume looks at the spread of Islam and the conflicts with the Crusaders. (Rev: SLJ 8/04) [355]

1676 Hinds, Kathryn. *The Church* (6–9). Series: Life in the Renaissance. 2003, Benchmark LB $20.95 (0-7614-1679-X). 95pp. Hinds describes life for men and women involved in the church, both Catholic and Protestant, during the upheavals of the Renaissance; a recipe for hot-cross buns is included. (Rev: SLJ 4/04)

1677 Hinds, Kathryn. *The Countryside* (6–9). Series: Life in the Renaissance. 2003, Benchmark LB $20.95 (0-7614-1677-3). 93pp. A handsome and detailed portrayal of life in rural Europe during the Renaissance, covering both landowners and peasants. (Rev: SLJ 4/04)

1678 Kallen, Stuart A. *A Medieval Merchant* (6–9). Illus. Series: The Working Life. 2005, Gale LB $28.70 (1-59018-581-1). 112pp. Trade routes, guilds, training, fairs, and the banking system are all covered in this thorough overview that includes relevant images and excerpts from primary sources. (Rev: SLJ 11/05) [909]

1679 MacDonald, Fiona. *Knights, Castles, and Warfare in the Middle Ages* (5–8). Series: World Almanac Library of the Middle Ages. 2005, World Almanac LB $30.00 (0-8368-5895-6). 48pp. Describes the role of knights, the equipment they used, and their lives and homes. Also use *The Plague and Medicine in the Middle Ages* (2005). (Rev: SLJ 1/06) [940.1]

1680 Martin, Alex. *Knights and Castles: Exploring History Through Art* (5–8). Illus. Series: Picture That! 2004, Two-Can $19.95 (1-58728-441-3). 64pp. Paintings serve as the vehicle to draw students into the discussion of life in Europe during the late medieval period. (Rev: BL 11/1/04; SLJ 2/05) [940.1]

1681 Padrino, Mercedes. *Cities and Towns in the Middle Ages* (5–8). Series: World Almanac Library of the Middle Ages. 2005, World Almanac LB $30.00 (0-8368-5893-X). 48pp. A look at medieval urban living — social structure, government structure, employment, education, religion, food and clothing, and so forth. Also use *Feudalism and Village Life in the Middle Ages* (2005). (Rev: SLJ 1/06) [940.1]

1682 Ross, Stewart. *Monarchs* (5–8). Illus. Series: Medieval Realms. 2004, Gale $27.45 (1-59018-535-8). 48pp. This colorfully illustrated, oversize volume explores the structure of European governments during the Middle Ages and such topics as the birth of new nations, wars, and the Crusades. (Rev: BL 10/15/04) [940.1]

1683 Thomson, Melissa, and Ruth Dean. *Women of the Renaissance* (7–12). Series: Women in History. 2004, Gale LB $27.45 (1-59018-473-4). 128pp. A look at women's lives during the Renaissance, covering such topics as work, religion, and art. (Rev: SLJ 3/05)

1684 Waldman, Nomi J. *The Italian Renaissance* (5–7). Series: Daily Life. 2004, Gale LB $30.35 (0-7377-1398-4). 48pp. In simple language, this slim volume describes Italy's rebirth, the blossoming of commerce and culture, and daily life for people of different backgrounds. (Rev: SLJ 2/05) [945]

1685 White, Pamela. *Exploration in the World of the Middle Ages, 500–1500* (6–12). Illus. Series: Discovery and Exploration. 2005, Facts on File $40.00 (0-8160-5264-6). 176pp. The expeditions of Marco Polo, the Vikings, and other explorers of the Middle Ages are chronicled in clear, informative text plus maps, illustrations, and excerpts from primary sources. (Rev: SLJ 8/05) [973]

1686 Woolf, Alex. *Education* (5–8). Series: Medieval Realms. 2004, Gale LB $27.45 (1-59018-532-3). 48pp. Discusses the forms of education available during the Middle Ages — including apprenticeships, song schools, monastic schools, universities — and who was able to enjoy them and what they learned, ending with material on the rise of humanism. (Rev: SLJ 3/05) [370]

Twentieth Century

World War I

1687 Hamilton, John. *Aircraft of World War I* (5–8). Illus. Series: World War I. 2003, ABDO LB $16.95 (1-57765-912-0). 32pp. How aircraft became a valuable military tool for the first time in World War I, and how some of the pilots became internationally famous. (Rev: SLJ 6/04) [940.4]

1688 Hamilton, John. *Battles of World War I* (5–8). Illus. Series: World War I. 2003, ABDO LB $16.95 (1-57765-913-9). 32pp. A review of key battles that took place during the three years before the United States entered the conflict in 1917, with information on key figures. (Rev: SLJ 6/04) [940.4]

1689 Hamilton, John. *Events Leading to World War I* (5–8). Illus. Series: World War I. 2003, ABDO LB $16.95 (1-57765-914-7). 32pp. An evenhanded description of events and circumstances during the years leading up to World War I in each of the countries that became involved in the conflict. (Rev: SLJ 6/04) [940.3]

1690 Myers, Walter Dean, and Bill Miles. *The Harlem Hellfighters: When Pride Met Courage* (5–8). Illus. 2006, HarperCollins LB $17.89 (0-06-001137-8). 160pp. A tribute to the World War I heroism of the 369th Infantry Regiment, which was made up entirely of African Americans. (Rev: BL 2/1/06; SLJ 4/06) [940.4]

1691 Ross, Stewart. *The Battle of the Somme* (5–8). Series: The World Wars. 2003, Raintree LB $28.56 (0-7398-5479-8). 64pp. An examination of the first Battle of the Somme in 1916, an all-out assault on entrenched German forces in northern France by British and French troops, and of the enormous carnage involved. (Rev: SLJ 5/04) [940.4]

1692 Schomp, Virginia. *World War I* (6–8). Illus. Series: Letters from the Battlefront. 2004, Marshall

Cavendish LB $20.95 (0-7614-1661-7). 96pp. History and firsthand accounts are combined into a memorable overview of World War I. (Rev: BL 4/1/04; SLJ 2/04) [940.3]

World War II and the Holocaust

1693 Altman, Linda J. *Crimes and Criminals of the Holocaust* (5–10). Illus. Series: Holocaust in History. 2004, Enslow LB $20.95 (0-7660-1995-0). 104pp. This book focuses on the end of World War II and the war crimes trials in Nuremberg as well as other cases such as that of Adolf Eichmann. (Rev: BL 5/1/04) [940.53]

1694 Altman, Linda J. *Impact of the Holocaust* (5–10). Illus. Series: Holocaust in History. 2004, Enslow LB $20.95 (0-7660-1996-9). 104pp. This book discusses the Holocaust's influence in the creation of a homeland for the Jews and a Universal Declaration of Human Rights. (Rev: BL 5/1/04) [940.53]

1695 Barr, Gary E. *Pearl Harbor* (6–8). Series: Witness to History. 2004, Heinemann LB $27.07 (1-4034-4569-9). 56pp. Eyewitness accounts add to this overview of the attack on Pearl Harbor; readers are asked to consider the lessons that have been learned from this event. Also in this series: *World War II Home Front* (2004). (Rev: SLJ 10/04) [940.54]

1696 Clive, A. Lawton. *Hiroshima* (6–12). 2004, Candlewick $18.99 (0-7636-2271-0). 48pp. This powerful photo-essay presents the history of the development and dropping of the first atom bomb, documenting with many quotations the misgivings of some of the key figures. (Rev: BL 7/04; SLJ 11/04) [940.54]

1697 Downing, David. *The Origins of the Holocaust* (7–10). Illus. Series: World Almanac Library of the Holocaust. 2005, World Almanac LB $22.50 (0-8368-5943-X). 48pp. Downing looks at the roots of anti-Semitism and the continuing persecution of the Jews over the centuries, connecting this history with the rise of the Nazi Party. (Rev: BL 10/15/05; SLJ 3/06) [940.53]

1698 Drez, Ronald J. *Remember D-Day: The Plan, the Invasion, Survivor Stories* (4–8). 2004, National Geographic $17.95 (0-7922-6666-8). 64pp. Filled with period photographs and personal stories, this large-format survey of the Allied invasion of Normandy focuses on the military operation and on the strategic planning that preceded it. (Rev: BL 7/04; SLJ 7/04) [940.54]

1699 Fuller, William, and Jack James. *Reckless Courage: The True Story of a Norwegian Boy Under Nazi Rule* (8–11). 2005, Taber Hall paper $13.95 (0-9769252-0-6). 168pp. The true story of a Norwegian boy's participation in the resistance

against his country's Nazi occupiers. (Rev: BL 9/15/05) [940.53]

1700 Hillman, Laura. *I Will Plant You a Lilac Tree: A Memoir of a Schindler's List Survivor* (8–11). 2005, Simon & Schuster $16.95 (0-689-86980-0). 256pp. In this inspiring true story of Holocaust survival, Hannelore escapes the Nazi gas chambers when her name is added to Schindler's list. (Rev: BCCB 7–8/05; BL 5/1/05*; HB 7–8/05; SLJ 9/05; VOYA 8/05) [940.5]

1701 Kacer, Kathy. *The Underground Reporters: A True Story* (5–8). Illus. 2005, Second Story $11.95 (1-896764-85-1). 156pp. Based on real events, this inspiring story tells how a newspaper, published by a group of Jewish teenagers in Budejovice, Czechoslovakia, helped to lift the spirits of the Jewish community during the years of Nazi occupation. (Rev: BL 2/15/05; SLJ 8/05) [940.53]

1702 Krinitz, Esther Nisenthal, and Bernice Steinhardt. *Memories of Survival* (6–9). Illus. 2005, Hyperion $15.99 (0-7868-5126-0). 64pp. Steinhardt adds commentary to her mother's affecting hand-embroidered panels depicting her experiences during the Holocaust. (Rev: BL 10/15/05*; SLJ 11/05*) [910]

1703 Levy, Pat. *The Home Front in World War II* (5–8). Series: The World Wars. 2003, Raintree LB $28.56 (0-7398-6065-8). 64pp. A description of life on the home front in World War II, both in the Allied countries and the Axis countries, including the bombing, refugees, and various shortages. (Rev: SLJ 5/04) [940.53]

1704 Miller, Donald L. *D-Days in the Pacific* (8–12). Illus. 2005, Simon & Schuster paper $13.00 (0-7432-6929-2). 384pp. The Allied military offensives that finally brought an end to World War II in the Pacific are described in readable text with excellent illustrations. (Rev: BL 3/15/05) [940.54]

1705 Nicholson, Dorinda Makanaonalani. *Remember World War II: Kids Who Survived Tell Their Stories* (5–8). Illus. Series: Remember. 2005, National Geographic LB $27.90 (0-7922-7191-2). 64pp. First-person accounts of World War II are given historical context plus illustrations, maps, and so forth; Madeleine Albright contributes an effective introduction. (Rev: BL 7/05; SLJ 8/05) [940.53]

1706 O'Donnell, Joe. *Japan, 1945: A U.S. Marine's Photographs from Ground Zero* (8–12). Illus. 2005, Vanderbilt $39.95 (0-8265-1467-7). 120pp. Black-and-white photographs, long kept private by the Marine Corps photographer who took them and became ill from the radiation, reveal the devastation caused by the atomic bombs dropped on Japan in 1945. (Rev: BL 3/15/05) [779]

1707 Payment, Simone. *American Women Spies of World War II* (6–9). Series: American Women at War. 2004, Rosen LB $21.95 (0-8239-4449-2).

112pp. A well-written account of the exploits of women spies — including a fashion model and entertainer Josephine Baker — during World War II. (Rev: BL 10/15/04; SLJ 12/04) [940.54]

1708 Schomp, Virginia. *World War II* (6–8). Illus. Series: Letters from the Battlefront. 2003, Marshall Cavendish LB $29.93 (0-7614-1662-5). 96pp. History and letters by men and women who served in the U.S. armed forces are combined into a memorable overview of World War II. (Rev: BL 4/1/04; SLJ 2/04) [940.54]

1709 Schroeder, Peter W., and Dagmar Schroeder-Hildebrand. *Six Million Paper Clips: The Making of a Children's Holocaust Memorial* (5–8). Illus. 2004, Kar-Ben $17.95 (1-58013-169-7); paper $7.95 (1-58013-176-X). 64pp. This is the story of a Tennessee school project in which students collected 11 million paper clips to help them grasp the magnitude of the Holocaust's human toll. (Rev: BL 1/1–15/05; SLJ 7/05) [940.53]

1710 Shapiro, Stephen, and Tina Forrester. *Hoodwinked: Deception and Resistance* (7–10). Series: Outwitting the Enemy: Stories from World War II. 2004, Annick LB $29.95 (1-55037-833-3); paper $14.95 (1-55037-832-5). 96pp. This compelling title explores some of the inventive deceptive strategies that Allied forces employed against the Axis powers. (Rev: BL 1/1–15/05; SLJ 1/05) [940.54]

1711 Soumerai, Eve Nussbaum, and Carol D. Schulz. *A Voice from the Holocaust* (6–9). Series: Voices of Twentieth-Century Conflict. 2003, Greenwood $35.00 (0-313-32358-5). 128pp. Photographs and diary entries help to tell the story of Soumerai's childhood as a privileged Jewish girl in Nazi Berlin, her years as a refugee, and her later experiences, all introduced with background information and a timeline of Nazi history. (Rev: SLJ 4/04) [940.53]

1712 Stein, R. Conrad. *The World War II D-Day Invasion* (7–10). Series: In American History. 2004, Enslow LB $20.95 (0-7660-2136-X). 128pp. This great landing in Normandy is re-created in pictures and text. (Rev: BL 3/15/04; SLJ 3/04) [940.54]

1713 van Maarsen, Jacqueline, and Carol Ann Lee. *A Friend Called Anne: One Girl's Story of War, Peace, and a Unique Friendship with Anne Frank* (5–8). 2005, Viking $15.99 (0-670-05958-7). 176pp. Anne Frank's ordinary life before the war, and how things changed once the Nazis arrived, told by Anne's childhood friend. (Rev: BL 4/1/05; SLJ 4/05) [940.53]

1714 Whiteman, Dorit Bader. *Lonek's Journey: The True Story of a Boy's Escape to Freedom* (5–8). Illus. 2005, Star Bright $15.95 (1-59572-021-9). 144pp. In this gripping true story that starts in 1939, a young Jew named Lonek survives the Nazis'

arrival in Poland, a slave labor camp in Siberia, and the long, perilous journey to Palestine. (Rev: BL 11/15/05*; SLJ 1/06) [940.53]

1715 Williams, Barbara. *World War II: Pacific* (6–8). Series: Chronicle of America's Wars. 2004, Lerner LB $27.93 (0-8225-0138-4). 96pp. The major events of the war in the Pacific theater are covered in this well-documented brief overview. (Rev: SLJ 2/05) [940.54]

Modern World History (1945–)

1716 Carlisle, Rodney P. *Iraq War* (7–10). Illus. 2005, Facts on File $35.00 (0-8160-5627-7). 176pp. Information on Iraq's history is paired with discussion of September 11 and the 2003 military incursion into Iraq. (Rev: BL 2/15/05; SLJ 4/05) [956.7044]

1717 Gallagher, Jim. *Causes of the Iraq War* (5–8). Illus. Series: Road to War. 2005, OTTN LB $22.95 (1-59556-009-4). 72pp. Explores the case put forward for the recent Iraq War, along with the views of those who oppose the conflict with good illustrations and appended material. (Rev: BL 10/15/05) [956.7044]

1718 Gunderson, Cory. *The Need for Oil* (5–8). Illus. Series: World in Conflict. 2004, ABDO LB $17.95 (1-59197-417-8). 48pp. This history of conflicts over oil includes useful statistics and will be helpful to students seeking information for reports or background context before the recent Iraq war. (Rev: BL 4/1/04; SLJ 3/04) [338.2]

1719 McArthur, Debra. *Desert Storm: The First Persian Gulf War in American History* (6–8). Series: In American History. 2004, Enslow LB $20.95 (0-7660-2149-1). 128pp. Surveys the regional history that laid the groundwork for this conflict, the war itself, and its uncertain conclusion. (Rev: SLJ 1/05) [956.7]

1720 Murdico, Suzanne J. *The Gulf War* (5–9). Illus. Series: War and Conflict in the Middle East. 2004, Rosen LB $19.95 (0-8239-4551-0). 64pp. Examines the 1991 war between Iraq and a coalition of nations. (Rev: BL 11/1/04) [956.7]

1721 Nakaya, Andrea C., ed. *Iraq* (8–12). Series: Current Controversies. 2004, Gale LB $21.96 (0-7377-2210-X); paper $14.96 (0-7377-2211-8). 202pp. Statements by key U.S. figures including President Bush and Colin Powell are included in this survey of opinions about the Iraq war. (Rev: SLJ 12/04; VOYA 6/05) [956]

1722 Richie, Jason. *Iraq and the Fall of Saddam Hussein*. Rev. ed. (8–10). Illus. 2004, Oliver LB $24.95 (1-881508-63-3). 112pp. This account traces the story of the invasion of Iraq and ends with the capture of Saddam Hussein in December 2003. (Rev: BL 5/1/04; SLJ 1/04) [956.7]

1723 Ross, Stewart. *The Collapse of Communism* (6–8). Series: Witness to History. 2004, Heinemann LB $27.07 (1-4034-4865-5); paper $8.95 (1-4034-5525-2). 56pp. Examines the forces that led to the decline of communism in the Soviet Union and Eastern Europe during the late 1980s and early 1990s, drawing on primary sources. (Rev: SLJ 1/05) [947]

1724 Sherman, Josepha. *The Cold War* (6–12). Illus. Series: Chronicle of America's Wars. 2003, Lerner LB $27.93 (0-8225-0150-3). 96pp. The half-century standoff between the United States and the Soviet Union is briefly chronicled, with coverage of the Korean and Vietnam wars, the Cuban Missile Cri-sis, and the Soviet invasion of Afghanistan. (Rev: BL 4/1/04) [909.82]

1725 Sirimarco, Elizabeth. *The Cold War* (6–9). Illus. Series: American Voices From. 2004, Benchmark LB $23.95 (0-7614-1694-3). 134pp. Primary source documents and excellent illustrations are accompanied by good introductory text and "Think about This" questions. (Rev: SLJ 2/05) [973]

1726 Stanley, George E. *America and the Cold War (1949–1969)* (5–8). Illus. Series: A Primary Source History of the United States. 2005, World Almanac LB $22.50 (0-8368-5830-1). 48pp. A simple narrative links well-chosen primary sources documenting the key events of the Cold War. Also use *America in Today's World (1969–2004)* (2005). (Rev: BL 4/1/05)

Geographical Regions

Africa

General and Miscellaneous

1727 Bangs, Richard, and Pasquale Scaturro. *Mystery of the Nile: The Epic Story of the First Descent of the World's Deadliest River* (8–12). Illus. 2005, Penguin $25.95 (0-399-15262-8). 358pp. Rapids, crocodiles, sandstorms, and armed guerrillas were only some of the perils encountered during this trip down the Nile from the highlands of Ethiopia to the Mediterranean. (Rev: BL 2/1/05; SLJ 8/05) [916.204]

1728 Beckwith, Carol, and Angela Fisher. *Faces of Africa: Thirty Years of Photography* (8–12). Illus. 2004, National Geographic $35.00 (0-7922-6830-X). 252pp. Eye-catching photographs document the traditional life of diverse African peoples. (Rev: BL 9/1/04) [305.896]

1729 Bingham, Jane. *African Art and Culture* (5–8). Illus. Series: World Art and Culture. 2004, Raintree LB $29.99 (0-7398-6606-0). 56pp. The indigenous art and culture of Africa from prehistoric times to the present are beautifully captured in this handsome and comprehensive overview. (Rev: BL 4/1/04; SLJ 2/04) [709]

1730 Bowden, Rob. *Africa* (5–8). Series: Continents of the World. 2006, World Almanac LB $32.67 (0-8368-5910-3). 64pp. Factboxes and "In Focus" articles add to this overview of the history, geography, people, culture, and so forth of the continent of Africa. (Rev: SLJ 2/06)

1731 Bowden, Rob. *The Nile* (5–7). Series: A River Journey. 2003, Raintree LB $28.56 (0-7398-6072-0). 48pp. A trip down the length of East Africa's Nile, from its source to the sea, and a look at its importance to the people who live along it and the challenge of pollution, with photographs, maps, and charts. (Rev: SLJ 3/04) [916.2]

1732 Downing, David. *Africa: Postcolonial Conflict* (6–8). Series: Troubled World. 2003, Raintree LB $28.56 (1-4109-0183-1). 64pp. Covers conflicts since the end of colonial rule in countries lying south of the Sahara apart from South Africa; factboxes, maps, and color insets defining terms and concepts add to the presentation. (Rev: SLJ 3/04) [960]

1733 Habeeb, Mark W. *Africa: Facts and Figures* (7–10). Illus. Series: Continent in the Balance: Africa. 2005, Mason Crest LB $21.95 (1-59084-817-9). 80pp. An excellent overview of the continent, including its natural features, climate, cultural diversity, history, and economy. (Rev: BL 4/1/05*) [960]

1734 Holmes, Martha, et al. *Nile* (7–12). Illus. 2004, BBC $35.00 (0-563-48713-5). 168pp. From the BBC, this is a richly illustrated guide to the history and geology of the world's longest river. (Rev: BL 11/1/04) [902]

1735 Weintraub, Aileen. *Discovering Africa's Land, People, and Wildlife* (5–8). Series: Continents of the World. 2004, Enslow LB $19.95 (0-7660-5204-4). 48pp. An introduction to the geography, history, economy, plants and animals, culture, and peoples of the continent, with discussion of the continuing need for foreign aid in many countries. (Rev: SLJ 11/04) [916]

Central and Eastern Africa

1736 Beard, Peter. *Zara's Tales: Perilous Escapades in Equatorial Africa* (8–12). Illus. 2004, Knopf $26.95 (0-679-42659-0). 176pp. In this compelling memoir, Beard talks about his many encounters — some life-threatening — with the animals of East Africa. (Rev: BL 10/15/04) [967.70]

1737 Bowden, Rob. *Kenya* (6–10). Illus. Series: Countries of the World. 2003, Facts on File $30.00 (0-8160-5384-7). 64pp. This profile of an impoverished nation gives material on physical geography, resources, population, tourism, commerce, and geography. (Rev: BL 2/1/04) [967.62]

1738 *History of Central Africa* (7–12). Illus. Series: History of Africa. 2003, Facts on File $30.00 (0-8160-5064-3). 112pp. A historical overview of the region that includes information on the Atlantic slave trade and on European colonial rule. Also use *History of East Africa* (2003). (Rev: SLJ 1/04) [967]

1739 Jansen, Hanna. *Over a Thousand Hills I Walk with You* (7–10). Trans. by Elizabeth D. Crawford. 2006, Carolrhoda $16.95 (1-57505-927-4). 344pp. The heartbreaking story of 8-year-old Jeanne, the only member of her family to survive the Rwandan genocide of 1994, is told by the girl's adoptive mother. (Rev: BL 4/1/06*) [833]

1740 Koopmans, Andy. *Rwanda* (7–10). Illus. Series: Africa. 2005, Mason Crest LB $21.95 (1-59084-812-8). 87pp. Covers the geography, history, politics, government, economy, people, and culture of Rwanda, providing a map, flag, recipes, glossary, timeline, and colorful photographs. (Rev: SLJ 3/05) [967.571]

1741 MacDonald, Joan Vos. *Tanzania* (7–10). Illus. Series: Africa. 2005, Mason Crest LB $21.95 (1-59084-813-6). 87pp. Covers the geography, history, politics, government, economy, people, and culture of Tanzania, providing a map, flag, recipes, glossary, timeline, and colorful photographs. (Rev: SLJ 3/05; VOYA 8/04) [967.8]

1742 Oghojafor, Kingsley. *Uganda* (5–8). Series: Countries of the World. 2004, Gareth Stevens LB $29.26 (0-8368-3112-8). 96pp. Introduces readers to the African country's geography, history, people, culture, and government and also takes a look at its relations with other countries and contemporary challenges. (Rev: SLJ 8/04) [967.61]

1743 Olsen, Sylvia. *The Girl with a Baby* (6–10). 2004, Sono Nis paper $7.95 (1-55039-142-9). 208pp. A biracial girl of white and Indian parents wants to stay in school and raise her baby but finds it difficult. (Rev: BL 3/15/04; SLJ 7/04)

Southern Africa

1744 Beecroft, Simon. *The Release of Nelson Mandela* (6–12). Illus. Series: Days that Changed the World. 2004, World Almanac LB $21.95 (0-8368-5571-X); paper $11.95 (0-8368-5578-7). 48pp. The significance of Mandela's release after 27 years of imprisonment is made clear through the explanation of the struggle against apartheid, with discussion of the progress South Africa has made since then. (Rev: BL 4/1/04; SLJ 7/04) [618.1]

1745 Downing, David. *Apartheid in South Africa* (7–10). Illus. Series: Witness to History. 2004, Heinemann $20.70 (1-4034-4870-1). 60pp. This brief historical survey draws on primary sources — including newspaper articles and full-color photographs — to trace apartheid's rise and fall and its impact on both the country's black and white communities. (Rev: BL 1/05) [323.168]

1746 Langley, Andrew. *Cape Town* (4–7). Illus. Series: Great Cities of the World. 2005, World Almanac LB $22.50 (0-8368-5045-9). 48pp. An informative and appealing overview of this major city, with material on its history, its economy, and what it's like to live there. (Rev: BL 4/15/04)

1747 Wooten, Jim. *We Are All the Same: A Story of a Boy's Courage and a Mother's Love* (8–12). 2004, Penguin $19.95 (1-59420-028-9). 244pp. ABC News correspondent Wooten writes movingly of Nkosi Johnson, a young South African boy born with AIDS, and his white foster mother and how together they fought the disease and the South African government's failure to acknowledge the magnitude of the AIDS problem. (Rev: BL 9/1/04) [362.196]

West Africa

1748 Alonso, Alfonso, and Carlton Ward. *The Edge of Africa: All Life Is Here* (8–12). 2003, Hylas $39.95 (1-59258-040-8). The natural history of Gabon is detailed in a series of stunning photographs of wildlife and plants, some familiar, others not. (Rev: BL 2/15/04) [590.9]

1749 Bowden, Rob, and Roy Maconachie. *Nigeria* (5–7). Series: The Changing Face Of. 2003, Raintree LB $28.56 (0-7398-6829-2). 48pp. An examination of modern-day Nigeria, with a look at the nation's past difficulties and how it may benefit from its wealth of natural resources. (Rev: SLJ 4/04) [966.9]

1750 Walker, Ida. *Nigeria* (7–10). Illus. Series: Africa. 2005, Mason Crest LB $21.95 (1-59084-811-X). 79pp. Covers the geography, history, politics, government, economy, people, and culture of Nigeria, providing a map, flag, recipes, glossary, timeline, and colorful photographs. (Rev: SLJ 3/05) [966.9]

Asia

General and Miscellaneous

1751 Bowden, Rob. *Asia* (5–8). Series: Continents of the World. 2006, World Almanac LB $32.67 (0-8368-5911-1). 64pp. Factboxes and "In Focus" articles add to this overview of the history, geography, people, culture, and so forth of the continent of Asia. (Rev: SLJ 2/06) [915]

1752 Hammond, Paula. *China and Japan* (4–8). Illus. Series: Cultures and Costumes: Symbols of Their Period. 2003, Mason Crest LB $19.95 (1-59084-436-X). 64pp. A detailed survey of the history of garments and accessories worn by people of all classes in these two Asian nations prior to the 20th century. (Rev: SLJ 3/04) [391]

1753 Kilgallon, Conor. *India and Sri Lanka* (4–8). Illus. Series: Cultures and Costumes: Symbols of Their Period. 2003, Mason Crest LB $19.95 (1-59084-443-2). 64pp. A look at the history of garments and accessories worn by all classes of people in India and Sri Lanka up to the end of the 19th century. (Rev: SLJ 3/04) [391]

1754 Kort, Michael. *Central Asian Republics* (7–12). Series: Nations in Transition. 2003, Facts on File $35.00 (0-8160-5074-0). 200pp. After a history of the region, each of the independent republics is introduced with discussion of the current challenges it faces; these include border disputes, poor environment, poor health care and quality of life, and government corruption. (Rev: SLJ 4/04)

China

1755 Barber, Nicola. *Beijing* (4–7). Illus. Series: Great Cities of the World. 2004, World Almanac LB $29.26 (0-8368-5028-9). 48pp. In addition to the usual information on history and people, this attractive volume describes living conditions and leisure time and provides maps and sidebars about contemporary environmental and political issues. (Rev: BL 4/15/04; SLJ 6/04) [951]

1756 Barter, James. *The Yangtze* (4–7). Series: Rivers of the World. 2003, Gale LB $21.96 (1-59018-370-3). 112pp. A look at China's Yangtze river, illustrated with maps and black-and-white photographs, concentrating on its exploitation and development over the past half-century. (Rev: SLJ 3/04) [951]

1757 Bingham, Jane. *Tiananmen Square: June 4, 1989* (6–8). Series: Days That Shook the World. 2004, Raintree LB $28.56 (0-7398-6649-4). 47pp. A clear, well-illustrated overview of the events in Beijing's Tiananmen Square and their legacy. (Rev: SLJ 10/04) [951.058]

1758 Bowden, Rob. *The Yangtze* (5–7). Series: A River Journey. 2003, Raintree LB $28.56 (0-7398-6074-7). 48pp. A well-illustrated trip along China's Yangtze River, concentrating on mankind's influence on the river and vice versa, with photographs, maps, and charts. (Rev: SLJ 3/04) [915.1]

1759 Malaspina, Ann. *The Chinese Revolution and Mao Zedong in World History* (5–8). Series: World History. 2004, Enslow LB $20.95 (0-7660-1935-7).

128pp. After a brief overview of Chinese history, Malaspina provides a well-researched introduction to Chinese communism under Mao Zedong, from the early days of the party in the 1920s to the post-Mao reforms of recent times. (Rev: SLJ 3/04) [951]

1760 Schomp, Virginia. *The Ancient Chinese* (4–7). Series: People of the Ancient World. 2004, Watts LB $29.50 (0-531-11817-7). 112pp. Emperors, artisans, inventors, and healers are among the people presented in this overview of life in ancient China. (Rev: SLJ 2/05) [931]

1761 Walker, Kathryn. *Shanghai* (4–7). Illus. Series: Great Cities of the World. 2005, World Almanac LB $22.50 (0-8368-5046-7). 48pp. An informative and appealing overview of this important Chinese city, with material on its history, its economy, and what it's like to live there. (Rev: BL 4/15/04)

India, Pakistan, and Bangladesh

1762 Bowden, Rob. *The Ganges* (5–7). Series: A River Journey. 2003, Raintree LB $28.56 (0-7398-6070-4). 48pp. A detailed look at India's most famous river, its importance to the people who live along it, and the challenge of pollution, with photographs, maps, and charts. (Rev: SLJ 3/04) [915.4]

1763 Downing, David. *Conflict: India vs. Pakistan* (6–8). Series: Troubled World. 2003, Raintree LB $28.56 (1-4109-0181-5). 64pp. Covers conflicts between India and Pakistan since the end of colonial rule; factboxes, maps, and color insets defining terms and concepts add to the presentation. (Rev: SLJ 3/04) [954]

1764 Guile, Melanie. *Culture in India* (4–7). Illus. Series: Culture In. 2005, Raintree LB $27.79 (1-4109-1134-9). 32pp. Customs, holidays, clothing, food, and arts and crafts are well covered in this volume that also provides basic information needed for reports and interesting sidebar features on such topics as ancestor worship and celebrities. (Rev: BL 2/15/04; SLJ 5/05) [954]

1765 Rowe, Percy, and Patience Coster. *Delhi* (4–7). Illus. Series: Great Cities of the World. 2005, World Almanac LB $22.50 (0-8368-5037-8). 48pp. An informative and appealing overview of this major Indian city, with material on its history, its economy, and what it's like to live there. (Rev: BL 4/15/04)

1766 Valliant, Doris. *Bangladesh* (8–12). Illus. Series: The Growth and Influence of Islam in the Nations of Asia and Central Asia. 2005, Mason Crest LB $25.95 (1-59084-879-9). 120pp. A well-illustrated look at Bangladesh and the importance of Islam in the country's history, politics, economy, and foreign relations. (Rev: SLJ 9/05) [954.9]

Japan

1767 Nishimura, Shigeo. *An Illustrated History of Japan* (4–7). Illus. 2005, Tuttle $19.95 (0-8048-3670-1). 64pp. Key events in Japanese history come alive in the striking tableaux of Shigeo Nishimura. (Rev: BL 10/15/05) [952]

1768 Patchett, Kaye. *The Akashi Kaikyo Bridge* (5–8). Illus. Series: Building World Landmarks. 2004, Gale LB $18.96 (1-4103-0140-0). 48pp. A concise account of the amazing construction of the bridge that links Shikoku and Honshu islands. (Rev: BL 4/1/04; SLJ 4/05)

Other Asian Countries

1769 Barber, Nicola. *Singapore* (4–7). Illus. Series: Great Cities of the World. 2005, World Almanac LB $22.50 (0-8368-5047-5). 48pp. An informative and appealing overview of one of the world's most famous cities, with material on its history, its economy, and what it's like to live there. (Rev: BL 4/15/04)

1770 Cottrell, Robert C. *Vietnam: 17th Parallel* (7–9). Illus. Series: Arbitrary Borders. 2004, Chelsea House LB $26.95 (0-7910-7834-5). 138pp. This series discusses the importance of borders in the stability (or instability) of a country; this volume looks at Vietnam and the lengthy conflict over the arbitrary division of the nation. (Rev: BL 8/04; SLJ 7/04) [959.70]

1771 Fiscus, James W. *America's War in Afghanistan* (5–9). Illus. Series: War and Conflict in the Middle East. 2004, Rosen LB $19.95 (0-8239-4552-9). 64pp. A well-organized, balanced account of the war between the United States and Afghanistan in the aftermath of the 2001 terrorist attacks on New York and Washington, D.C. (Rev: BL 11/1/04)

1772 Greenblatt, Miriam. *Afghanistan* (4–8). Series: Enchantment of the World. 2003, Children's Pr. LB $34.50 (0-516-22696-7). 144pp. A visually attractive book that covers such topics as the geography, history, government, culture, and people, with a timeline, fast facts, and a recipe. (Rev: SLJ 1/04) [958.1]

1773 Guile, Melanie. *Culture in Malaysia* (4–7). Illus. Series: Culture In. 2005, Raintree LB $27.79 (1-4109-1133-0). 32pp. Customs, holidays, clothing, food, and arts and crafts are well covered in this volume that also provides basic information needed for reports and interesting sidebar features. (Rev: SLJ 5/05)

1774 Hanson, Jennifer L. *Mongolia* (7–10). Series: Nations in Transition. 2003, Facts on File $35.00 (0-8160-5221-2). 152pp. A thorough review of Mongolia's history, geography, and culture, detail-

ing the difficulties involved in making a transition to democracy. (Rev: SLJ 5/04; VOYA 6/04) [951]

1775 Kummer, Patricia K. *Tibet* (4–8). Series: Enchantment of the World. 2003, Children's Pr. LB $34.50 (0-516-22693-2). 144pp. A visually attractive book that covers such topics as the geography, history, government, culture, and people, with a timeline, fast facts, and a recipe. (Rev: SLJ 1/04) [951]

1776 Miller, Debra A. *North Korea* (6–12). Series: The World's Hot Spots. 2004, Gale LB $22.96 (0-7377-2294-0); paper $15.96 (0-7377-2295-9). 128pp. Reprinted essays, speeches, and news articles provide a fascinating — if somewhat one-sided — overview of North Korea and its relations with the outside world. (Rev: BL 6/1–15/04; SLJ 7/04) [951.93]

1777 Miller, Raymond H. *The War in Afghanistan* (6–8). Illus. Series: American War Library: The War on Terrorism. 2004, Gale LB $21.96 (1-59018-331-2). 112pp. An account of the U.S.-led campaign to force the Taliban and al-Qaeda out of Afghanistan, the difficulties the military faced, and the resulting political reforms and efforts to rebuild the country and deal with problems such as remaining land mines. (Rev: BL 8/04) [958.10]

1778 Otfinoski, Steven. *Afghanistan* (7–12). Series: Nations in Transition. 2003, Facts on File $35.00 (0-8160-5056-2). 130pp. A thorough overview of Afghanistan presenting the current political and security problems — including healthcare needs, opium trade, and reliance on foreign funding — as well as material on the country's history, geography, people, culture, and so forth. (Rev: SLJ 4/04; VOYA 6/04) [958.1]

1779 Sheehan, Sean, and Shahrezad Samiuddin. *Pakistan* (5–9). Illus. Series: Cultures of the World. 2004, Benchmark LB $25.95 (0-7614-1787-7). 144pp. Pakistan's geography, history, economy, and people are all examined, with discussion of interesting aspects of Pakistani culture. (Rev: SLJ 2/05) [954.9]

1780 Stewart, Gail B. *Life Under the Taliban* (6–10). Series: The Way People Live. 2004, Gale LB $27.45 (1-59018-291-X). 112pp. A look at what life was like in Afghanistan under the repressive Taliban regime. (Rev: SLJ 1/05) [958.1]

1781 Taus-Bolstad, Stacy. *Pakistan in Pictures.* Rev. ed. (5–9). Illus. Series: Visual Geography. 2003, Lerner LB $27.93 (0-8225-4682-5). 80pp. This substantially revised volume covers Pakistan's history, geography, culture, and lifestyle. (Rev: SLJ 7/03) [954.9]

1782 Whitehead, Kim. *Afghanistan* (8–12). Illus. Series: The Growth and Influence of Islam in the Nations of Asia and Central Asia. 2005, Mason Crest LB $25.95 (1-59084-833-0). 136pp. A well-illustrated look at Afghanistan and the importance of Islam in the country's history, politics, economy, and foreign relations. (Rev: SLJ 9/05) [958.104]

Australia and the Pacific Islands

1783 Alter, Judy. *Discovering Australia's Land, People, and Wildlife* (5–8). Series: Continents of the World. 2004, Enslow LB $19.95 (0-7660-5207-9). 48pp. An introduction to the geography, history, economy, plants and animals, culture, and people of the continent, showing the contrast between the urban centers on the coasts and the rugged interior. (Rev: SLJ 11/04) [994]

1784 Darian-Smith, Kate. *Australia, Antarctica, and the Pacific* (5–8). Series: Continents of the World. 2006, World Almanac LB $32.67 (0-8368-5912-X). 64pp. Factboxes and "In Focus" articles add to this overview of the history, geography, people, culture, and so forth of the continents of Australia, Antarctica, and island of the Pacific. (Rev: SLJ 2/06)

1785 Vail, Martha, and John S. Bowman, eds. *Exploring the Pacific* (6–12). Illus. Series: Discovery and Exploration. 2005, Facts on File $40.00 (0-8160-5258-1). 162pp. Exploration in the Pacific, from early Polynesians onward and including such figures as Magellan and Cook, is the focus of this volume that contains clear, informative text plus maps, illustrations, and excerpts from primary sources. (Rev: SLJ 8/05) [973]

Europe

General and Miscellaneous

1786 Flint, David. *Europe* (5–8). Series: Continents of the World. 2006, World Almanac LB $32.67 (0-8368-5913-8). 64pp. Factboxes and "In Focus" articles add to this overview of the history, geography, people, culture, and so forth of the continent of Europe. (Rev: SLJ 2/06) [940]

1787 Lace, William W. *The Vatican* (7–12). Series: Building History. 2004, Gale $27.45 (1-56006-843-4). The story behind the construction of Vatican City, the centerpiece of which is St. Peter's Basilica, is told in a richly illustrated text full of interesting facts and sidebars that add context. (Rev: BL 10/1/04) [945.6]

1788 Stafford, James. *The European Union: Facts and Figures* (8–11). Illus. Series: European Union. 2006, Mason Crest LB $21.95 (1-4222-0045-0). 88pp. A useful, information-packed guide to the European Union and its origins and goals. (Rev: BL 4/1/06) [641.242]

Eastern Europe and the Balkans

1789 King, David C. *Bosnia and Herzegovina* (7–10). Illus. Series: Cultures of the World. 2005, Benchmark LB $25.95 (0-7614-1853-9). 144pp. Explores the geography, history, people, culture, and lifestyles of Bosnia and Herzegovina. (Rev: SLJ 7/05) [949.7]

1790 Nichols, Jeremy, and Emilia Trembicka-Nichols. *Poland* (7–10). Series: Countries of the World. 2005, Facts on File LB $30.00 (0-8160-6005-3). 61pp. History, geography, culture, government, and economy are all covered in this attractive overview of Poland. (Rev: SLJ 1/06) [9.4.3]

1791 Orr, Tamra. *Slovenia* (5–8). Series: Enchantment of the World. 2004, Children's Pr. LB $34.50 (0-516-24249-0). 144pp. Introduces the history, geography, people, and culture of Slovenia, with plenty of clear photographs and an emphasis on contemporary life. (Rev: BL 9/1/04; SLJ 7/04) [949.73]

1792 Otfinoski, Steven. *The Czech Republic* (7–12). Illus. Series: Nations in Transition. 2004, Facts on File $35.00 (0-8160-5083-X). 132pp. An updated edition that adds more recent events to the 1997 text about the history, people, culture, and government of the Czech Republic. (Rev: BL 12/1/04) [943.7105]

France

1793 Egendorf, Laura K., ed. *The French Revolution* (7–12). Series: Opposing Viewpoints: World History. 2004, Gale LB $33.70 (0-7377-1815-3). 240pp. Questions about the French Revolution, such as the justification for the many executions, are explored in this collection of different points of view about this turning point in French history. (Rev: BL 2/15/04; SLJ 5/04) [944]

1794 Stacey, Gill. *Paris* (4–7). Illus. 2004, World Almanac LB $29.26 (0-8368-5030-0). 48pp. This attractive introduction to Paris covers the French capital's history and examines some of its modern-day problems. (Rev: BL 4/15/04; SLJ 6/04) [944]

1795 Yuan, Margaret Speaker. *The Arc de Triomphe* (5–8). Series: Building World Landmarks. 2004, Gale LB $18.96 (1-4103-0138-9). 48pp. A concise account of the design and construction of this arch, which met financial, political, and technical difficulties. (Rev: SLJ 4/05)

Germany, Austria, and Switzerland

1796 Barber, Nicola. *Berlin* (4–7). Illus. Series: Great Cities of the World. 2005, World Almanac LB $22.50 (0-8368-5043-2). 48pp. An informative and appealing overview of one of the world's most famous cities, with material on its history, its economy, and what it's like to live there. (Rev: BL 4/15/04)

1797 Bartoletti, Susan Campbell. *Hitler Youth: Growing Up in Hitler's Shadow* (7–10). Illus. 2005, Scholastic $19.95 (0-439-35379-3). 176pp. This chilling look at the Hitler Youth movement, which at its peak boasted a membership of roughly 3.5 million boys and girls, includes excerpts from diaries, letters, oral histories, and the author's interviews with former members and resisters. (Rev: BL 4/15/05*; SLJ 6/05; VOYA 8/05) [943.086]

1798 Halleck, Elaine, ed. *Living in Nazi Germany* (8–12). Series: Exploring Cultural History. 2004, Gale LB $28.70 (0-7377-1732-7). First-person accounts excerpted from other works offer insight into life in Germany under the Nazis, from the point of view of those brutalized and of those who took part in the regime. (Rev: BL 8/04) [943.086]

1799 Levy, Debbie. *The Berlin Wall* (5–8). Series: Building World Landmarks. 2004, Gale LB $18.96 (1-4103-0137-0). 48pp. A concise account of the wall's history and its importance in the struggle between East and West; with a timeline. (Rev: SLJ 4/05)

Great Britain and Ireland

1800 Jocelyn, Marthe. *A Home for Foundlings* (7–10). Series: Lord Museum. 2005, Tundra paper $15.95 (0-88776-709-5). 128pp. A fascinating history of London's Foundling Hospital, which was opened in the 18th century to provide a home for babies whose mothers were unable to care for them and did not close until 1953. (Rev: BL 3/1/05; SLJ 6/05) [362.7]

1801 Stacey, Gill. *London* (4–8). Series: Great Cities of the World. 2003, World Almanac LB $29.26 (0-8368-5022-X). 48pp. In an appealing blend of text, photographs, quotations, and sidebar features, this volume introduces readers to some of London's history and attractions. (Rev: SLJ 1/04) [942.1]

Greece

1802 Langley, Andrew. *Athens* (4–8). Series: Great Cities of the World. 2003, World Almanac LB $29.26 (0-8368-5021-1). 48pp. An attractive introduction to the Greek capital's history, people, culture, and attractions. (Rev: SLJ 1/04) [938]

Italy

1803 Barber, Nicola. *Rome* (4–7). Illus. Series: Great Cities of the World. 2005, World Almanac LB $22.50 (0-8368-5040-8). 48pp. An informative and appealing overview of one of the world's most

famous cities, with material on its history, its economy, and what it's like to live there. (Rev: BL 4/15/04)

Russia and Other Former Soviet Republics

1804 Corrigan, Jim. *Kazakhstan* (8–12). Series: The Growth and Influence of Islam in the Nations of Asia and Central Asia. 2005, Mason Crest LB $25.95 (1-59084-882-9). 128pp. A well-illustrated look at Kazakhstan and the importance of Islam in the country's history, politics, economy, and foreign relations. (Rev: SLJ 9/05) [958]

1805 Harmon, Daniel E. *Kyrgyzstan* (8–12). Illus. Series: The Growth and Influence of Islam in the Nations of Asia and Central Asia. 2005, Mason Crest LB $25.95 (1-59084-883-7). 120pp. A well-illustrated look at Kyrgyzstan and the importance of Islam in the country's history, politics, economy, and foreign relations. (Rev: SLJ 9/05)

1806 Otfinoski, Steven. *The Baltic Republics* (7–10). Series: Nations in Transition. 2004, Facts on File LB $35.00 (0-8160-5117-8). 182pp. Introduces the Baltic republics of Estonia, Latvia, and Lithuania, and the geography, history, people, culture, religious beliefs, and economy of each. (Rev: SLJ 1/05) [947]

1807 Robbins, Gerald. *Azerbaijan* (8–12). Series: The Growth and Influence of Islam in the Nations of Asia and Central Asia. 2005, Mason Crest LB $25.95 (1-59084-878-0). 128pp. A well-illustrated look at Azerbaijan and the importance of Islam in the country's history, politics, economy, and foreign relations. (Rev: SLJ 9/05) [947]

1808 Schemann, Serge. *When the Wall Came Down* (6–9). Illus. 2006, Kingfisher $15.95 (0-7534-5994-9). 128pp. Primary sources, personal insights, and edited *New York Times* columns make this a useful account of the fall of the Berlin Wall and its impact on the whole Eastern Bloc. (Rev: BL 2/15/06) [943]

Middle East

General and Miscellaneous

1809 Broyles, Matthew. *The Six-Day War* (5–9). Illus. Series: War and Conflict in the Middle East. 2004, Rosen LB $19.95 (0-8239-4549-9). 64pp. A well-organized, balanced account of the 1973 war between Israel and its Arab neighbors Egypt, Jordan, and Syria. (Rev: BL 11/1/04; SLJ 1/05)

1810 Fiscus, James W. *The Suez Crisis* (5–9). Illus. Series: War and Conflict in the Middle East. 2004, Rosen LB $19.95 (0-8239-4550-2). 64pp. Examines the 1956 conflict over control of the canal, involving Egypt, Israel, Britain, and France. (Rev: BL 11/1/04)

Egypt

1811 Beattie, Andrew. *Cairo: A Cultural History* (8–12). Series: Cityscapes. 2004, Oxford $15.00 (0-19-517892-0). 256pp. A cultural tour of Cairo, exploring the city's ancient past and pervasively Islamic present. (Rev: BL 11/15/04) [962]

1812 Bowden, Rob, and Roy Maconachie. *Cairo* (4–7). Illus. Series: Great Cities of the World. 2005, World Almanac LB $22.50 (0-8368-5035-1). 48pp. An informative and appealing overview of one of the world's most famous cities, with material on its history, its economy, and what it's like to live there. (Rev: BL 4/15/04)

1813 Parks, Peggy J. *The Aswan High Dam* (5–8). Series: Building World Landmarks. 2004, Gale LB $18.96 (1-56711-329-X). 48pp. This is the fascinating story of the construction of the huge dam on the Nile and the immense technical and social challenges involved. (Rev: SLJ 6/04) [627]

Israel and Palestine

1814 Alger, Neil, ed. *The Palestinians and the Disputed Territories* (8–12). Series: The World's Hot Spots. 2004, Gale LB $22.96 (0-7377-1489-1); paper $15.96 (0-7377-1490-5). 144pp. Informative essays, articles, and analyses explore the history and current status of the Palestinians, emphasizing in particular the importance of Jerusalem and the role of other nations including the United States. (Rev: SLJ 6/04) [956.04]

1815 Frank, Mitch. *Understanding the Holy Land: Answering Questions About the Israeli-Palestinian Conflict* (6–9). Illus. 2005, Viking $17.99 (0-670-06032-1). 160pp. In easy-to-read question-and-answer format, author Mitch Frank provides an excellent introduction to the history of the Holy Land and the diverse factors involved in the continuing conflict between Israelis and Palestinians. (Rev: BL 3/1/05*; SLJ 3/05; VOYA 4/05) [956.9405]

1816 Gaughen, Shasta, ed. *The Arab-Israeli Conflict* (7–10). Series: Contemporary Issues Companion. 2004, Gale LB $43.15 (0-7377-1615-0); paper $28.75 (0-7377-1616-9). 160pp. After background on the long-running conflict, this volume provides opposing views about how to resolve the crisis and first-person stories of life amid turmoil. (Rev: SLJ 1/05) [956.04]

1817 Greenfeld, Howard. *A Promise Fulfilled: Theodor Herzl, Chaim Weizmann, David Ben-Gurion, and the Creation of the State of Israel* (7–10). Illus. 2005, Greenwillow LB $19.89 (0-06-051505-8). 144pp. This story of the creation of the state of Israel focuses on the contributions of three remarkable and very different men. (Rev: BL 4/15/05; SLJ 7/05) [320.54]

1818 Hayhurst, Chris. *Israel's War of Independence* (5–9). Illus. Series: War and Conflict in the Middle East. 2004, Rosen LB $19.95 (0-8239-4548-0). 64pp. An even-handed overview of Israel's struggle for independence and the ensuing years of violence, with statistics, maps, photographs, and profiles of leaders. (Rev: BL 11/1/04; SLJ 1/05) [956.04]

1819 Katz, Samuel M. *Jerusalem or Death: Palestinian Terrorism* (7–12). Illus. Series: Terrorist Dossiers. 2003, Lerner LB $26.60 (0-8225-4033-9). 72pp. This book focuses on the terrorist groups that have been active in Israel and the West Bank. (Rev: BL 3/15/04; SLJ 3/04; VOYA 4/04) [956.9]

1820 Senker, Cath. *The Arab-Israeli Conflict* (5–8). Series: Questioning History. 2004, Smart Apple Media LB $28.50 (1-58340-441-4). 64pp. A clear and balanced discussion of the history and current status of relations between Arabs and Israelis, with a timeline, glossary, and detailed index. (Rev: SLJ 2/05) [956.04]

1821 Sherman, Josepha. *Your Travel Guide to Ancient Israel* (4–8). Illus. Series: Passport to History. 2003, Lerner LB $26.60 (0-8225-3072-4). 80pp. An illustrated visit to Israel in the time of King Solomon, with description of foods, housing, clothing, customs, and notable people of that era. (Rev: SLJ 4/04) [933]

1822 *Three Wishes: Palestinian and Israeli Children Speak* (5–12). 2004, Groundwood $16.95 (0-88899-554-7). 144pp. In an evenhanded presentation that offers an introductory historical overview, 20 first-person accounts relate the experiences of Christian, Jewish, and Muslim young people during the ongoing conflict between Israelis and Palestinians. (Rev: BL 9/1/04*; SLJ 10/04) [956.04]

1823 Wingate, Katherine. *The Intifadas* (5–9). Illus. Series: War and Conflict in the Middle East. 2004, Rosen LB $19.95 (0-8239-4546-4). 64pp. An even-handed overview of the events leading up to the Palestinian uprisings, with statistics, maps, photographs, and profiles of leaders. (Rev: BL 11/1/04) [956.95]

Other Middle East Countries

1824 Al-Windawi, Thura. *Thura's Diary: My Life in Wartime Iraq* (6–12). 2004, Viking $15.99 (0-670-05886-6). 131pp. This diary was kept by a 19-year-old girl in Baghdad from the first bombings to the first days of the occupation by American forces. (Rev: BL 5/15/04; HB 7–8/04; SLJ 7/04) [956]

1825 Cinini, Mikko. *Iran* (8–12). Series: The World's Hot Spots. 2004, Gale LB $22.96 (0-7377-1723-8). 127pp. Discussion of the situation in Iran in the early 21st century is preceded by historical information. (Rev: SLJ 3/05) [955]

1826 Downing, David. *Iraq: 1968–2003* (6–8). Series: Troubled World. 2003, Raintree LB $28.56 (1-4109-0184-X). 64pp. Covers events in Iraq from the late 1960s until Saddam Hussein's removal from power, discussing factors that will remain of interest including the importance of oil; factboxes, maps, and color insets defining terms and concepts add to the presentation. (Rev: SLJ 3/04) [956.7]

1827 Graham, Amy. *Iran in the News: Past, Present, and Future* (5–8). Illus. Series: Middle East Nations in the News. 2006, Enslow LB $24.95 (1-59845-022-0). 128pp. History, culture, people, and current political issues are all covered in this readable overview of Iran that includes links to Web sites that extend the text. (Rev: BL 4/1/06) [955]

1828 Miller, Debra A. *Iraq* (6–12). Series: The World's Hot Spots. 2004, Gale LB $22.96 (0-7377-1813-7); paper $15.96 (0-7377-1814-5). 128pp. Reprinted essays, speeches, and news articles provide a fascinating overview of Iraq's history and the factors that precipitated the American-led invasion in 2003. (Rev: BL 6/1–15/04; SLJ 8/04) [956.704]

1829 Riverbend. *Baghdad Burning: Girl Blog from Iraq* (8–12). 2005, Feminist paper $14.95 (1-55861-489-3). 320pp. A young Iraqi blogger paints a grim picture of life in her country after the 2003 invasion of U.S. and allied forces. (Rev: BL 4/1/05) [956.7]

North and South America (excluding the United States)

General and Miscellaneous

1830 Ackroyd, Peter. *Cities of Blood* (7–10). Illus. Series: Voyages Through Time. 2004, DK $19.99 (0-7566-0729-9); paper $9.95 (0-7566-0758-2). 144pp. In this colorful third installment of his award-winning series (after *The Beginning* and *Escape from Earth*), Ackroyd explores the surprisingly sophisticated pre-Columbian civilizations of the Olmecs, Aztecs, Mayas, and Incas. (Rev: BL 1/05; SLJ 3/05) [972]

1831 Alter, Judy. *Discovering North America's Land, People, and Wildlife* (5–8). Series: Continents of the World. 2004, Enslow LB $19.95 (0-7660-5206-0). 48pp. An introduction to the geography, history, economy, plants and animals, culture, and people of the continent, with brief coverage of the Caribbean and Central America. (Rev: SLJ 11/04) [917]

1832 Smith, Tom. *Discovery of the Americas, 1492–1800* (6–12). Illus. Series: Discovery and Exploration. 2005, Facts on File $40.00 (0-8160-5262-X). 206pp. European exploration of the New World is the focus of this volume that contains clear, informative text plus maps, illustrations, and

excerpts from primary sources. (Rev: SLJ 8/05) [973]

North America

CANADA

1833 Cooper, John. *Season of Rage: Racial Conflict in a Small Town* (6–9). Illus. 2005, Tundra paper $9.95 (0-88776-700-1). 80pp. The arresting story of the fight to win equal treatment for blacks in the small town of Dresden, Ontario, in the 1950s. (Rev: BL 2/1/05; SLJ 7/05; VOYA 4/06) [323.1196]

1834 Garrington, Sally. *Canada* (7–10). Series: Countries of the World. 2005, Facts on File LB $30.00 (0-8160-6009-6). 61pp. History, geography, culture, government, and economy are all covered in this attractive overview of Canada. (Rev: SLJ 1/06) [971]

1835 Hughes, Susan. *Coming to Canada: Building a Life in a New Land* (6–9). Illus. Series: Wow Canada! 2005, Maple Tree $18.95 (1-897066-46-5). 112pp. From the first arrivals thousands of years ago to today's diverse immigrants, this is a fascinating overview of Canadian history that does not whitewash unhappy episodes. (Rev: BL 8/05; SLJ 11/05*) [971.004]

1836 Pang, Guek-Cheng. *Canada*. 2nd ed. (5–9). Illus. Series: Cultures of the World. 2004, Benchmark LB $25.95 (0-7614-1788-5). 144pp. History, geography, and culture are all covered in this useful volume that attempts to impart a comprehensive understanding of life in all parts of Canada. (Rev: SLJ 2/05) [971]

MEXICO

1837 Gall, Timothy L., and Susan Bevan Gall, eds. *Junior Worldmark Encyclopedia of the Mexican States* (7–12). Illus. 2004, Gale $58.00 (0-7876-9161-5). 336pp. This encyclopedia introduces readers to the 31 states of Mexico and its Federal District, providing facts and figures about the geography, history, people, government, and culture of each. (Rev: BL 12/15/04; SLJ 2/05) [972]

1838 Lewis, Elizabeth. *Mexican Art and Culture* (5–8). Illus. Series: World Art and Culture. 2004, Raintree LB $29.99 (0-7398-6610-9). 56pp. The indigenous art and culture of Mexico from prehistoric times to the present are beautifully captured in this handsome and comprehensive overview. (Rev: BL 4/1/04; SLJ 2/04) [709]

PUERTO RICO, CUBA, AND OTHER CARIBBEAN ISLANDS

1839 Carey, Charles W., Jr., ed. *Castro's Cuba* (7–12). Series: History Firsthand. 2004, Gale LB $33.70 (0-7377-1654-1); paper $22.45 (0-7377-

1655-X). 205pp. Historical documents, interviews, and newspaper and magazine articles are used in this account of Castro's takeover in Cuba and developments since then. (Rev: SLJ 11/04) [972]

1840 Fisanick, Christina. *The Bay of Pigs* (6–12). Series: At Issue in History. 2004, Gale LB $22.96 (0-7377-1989-3); paper $15.96 (0-7377-1990-7). 112pp. The failed Bay of Pigs invasion is described in an introductory overview followed by a collection of essays, speeches, and editorials that provide diverse views about the event. (Rev: BL 9/1/04) [972.910]

1841 McCarthy, Pat. *The Dominican Republic* (5–8). Illus. Series: Top Ten Countries of Recent Immigrants. 2004, Enslow LB $25.26 (0-7660-5179-X). 48pp. Information on the Dominican Republic — culture, history, climate, and people — accompanies an explanation of the reasons for migration to the United States and discussion of the contributions of this community; supported by Web links. (Rev: SLJ 3/05) [304]

1842 Sheehan, Sean, and Leslie Jermyn. *Cuba* (7–10). Illus. Series: Cultures of the World: Second Edition. 2005, Marshall Cavendish LB $25.95 (0-7614-1964-9). 144pp. A frank, balanced, and readable overview of Cuba's history, geography, economy, culture, and people. (Rev: BL 2/15/06) [972.91]

South America

1843 Calvert, Patricia. *The Ancient Inca* (5–8). Series: People of the Ancient World. 2004, Watts LB $29.50 (0-531-12358-8). 128pp. This fascinating volume covers the history and culture of the Inca people, looking at childhood and the daily life of people ranging from farmers to priests, warriors, and emperors. (Rev: SLJ 3/05) [985]

1844 Dicks, Brian. *Brazil* (6–10). Illus. Series: Countries of the World. 2003, Facts on File $30.00 (0-8160-5382-0). 64pp. A well-illustrated account that covers all important topics including present-day racial friction and economic inequality. (Rev: BL 2/1/04) [949.12]

1845 Fearns, Les, and Daisy Fearns. *Argentina* (7–10). Series: Countries of the World. 2005, Facts on File LB $30.00 (0-8160-6008-8). 61pp. History, geography, culture, government, and economy are all covered in this attractive overview of Argentina. (Rev: SLJ 1/06) [982]

1846 Somerville, Barbara. *Empire of the Inca* (7–10). Illus. Series: Great Empires of the Past. 2004, Facts on File $30.00 (0-8160-5560-2). 128pp. In addition to covering the Inca civilization, Somerville draws connections from that ancient society to contemporary culture. (Rev: BL 2/1/05) [985]

Polar Regions

1847 Anderson, Harry S. *Exploring the Polar Regions* (8–11). Illus. Series: Discovery and Exploration. 2004, Facts on File $35.00 (0-8160-5259-X). 176pp. This analytical history of polar exploration looks at the motivations behind the expeditions as well as the specifics of early and modern ventures into new terrain. (Rev: BL 1/05; SLJ 12/04) [910]

1848 Currie, Stephen. *Antarctica* (7–12). Illus. Series: Exploration and Discovery. 2004, Gale LB $21.96 (1-59018-495-5). 112pp. Currie examines early theories about what lay at the southern end of the Earth and chronicles the early-20th-century expeditions to learn more about the continent. (Rev: BL 10/15/04) [919.8]

1849 Fiennes, Ranulph. *Race to the Pole: Tragedy, Heroism, and Scott's Antarctic Quest* (8–12). 2004, Hyperion $27.95 (1-4013-0047-2). 480pp. Fiennes, a polar explorer himself, offers an in-depth account of Captain Robert Scott's ill-fated 1911–1912 expedition to the South Pole. (Rev: BL 9/15/04) [919.8]

1850 Henderson, Bruce. *True North: Peary, Cook, and the Race to the Pole* (8–12). Illus. 2005, Norton $24.95 (0-393-05791-7). 288pp. Who got to the North Pole first? Henderson offers evidence for the reader to mull over. (Rev: BL 1/1–15/05) [910]

1851 Scott, Elaine. *Poles Apart: Why Penguins and Polar Bears Will Never Be Neighbors* (4–8). Illus. 2004, Viking $17.99 (0-670-05925-0). 64pp. This fascinating overview of the two polar regions examines their physical characteristics, seasons, wildlife, magnetism, exploration, and the effects of global warming. (Rev: BL 12/1/04; SLJ 12/04) [909]

1852 Wu, Norbert, and Jim Mastro. *Under Antarctic Ice: The Photographs of Norbert Wu* (8–12). Illus. 2004, Univ. of California $39.95 (0-520-23504-5). 192pp. Life beneath the ice of Antarctica is brilliantly captured in the photographs of Norbert Wu; with a useful introduction. (Rev: BL 10/15/04) [779]

United States

General History and Geography

1853 Bockenhauer, Mark H., and Stephen F. Cunha. *Our Fifty States* (4–10). Illus. 2004, National Geographic LB $45.90 (0-7922-6992-6). 239pp. Maps of the states are accompanied by basic facts, photographs, and archival reproductions of key historical events; also includes the U.S. territories. (Rev: SLJ 1/05) [973]

1854 Brexel, Bernadette. *The Knights of Labor and the Haymarket Riot: The Fight for an Eight-Hour Workday* (5–8). Illus. Series: America's Industrial Society in the 19th Century. 2004, Rosen LB $21.25 (0-8239-4028-4). 32pp. For reluctant readers, this overview of the struggle to improve working conditions features large print and short chapters. Also use *The Populist Party: A Voice for the Farmers in an Industrial Society* (2004). (Rev: BL 4/1/04)

1855 Cole, Sheila. *To Be Young in America: Growing Up with the Country, 1776–1940* (6–9). Illus. 2005, Little, Brown $19.99 (0-316-15196-3). 160pp. Historical images and excerpts from primary sources add to the appeal of this social history of American children, which looks at topics including home, school, work, and health. (Rev: BL 9/1/05; SLJ 10/05) [973]

1856 Davenport, John C. *The Mason-Dixon Line* (6–8). Illus. Series: Arbitrary Borders. 2004, Chelsea House LB $26.95 (0-7910-7830-2). 122pp. This series examines the profound effects that artificial boundaries have had on the course of world history; this title looks at the history of the Mason-Dixon Line and the role it played in polarizing sentiments between the North and South in the years leading up to the Civil War. (Rev: BL 8/04; SLJ 9/04) [911]

1857 Edwards, Judith. *Abolitionists and Slave Resistance: Breaking the Chains of Slavery* (6–12). Series: Slavery in American History. 2004, Enslow LB $20.95 (0-7660-2155-6). 128pp. A well-written survey of the emergence and progress of the anti-slavery movement. (Rev: SLJ 8/04) [326]

1858 King, David C. *World Wars and the Modern Age* (5–8). Illus. Series: American Heritage, American Voices. 2004, Wiley paper $18.99 (0-471-44392-1). 144pp. A concise overview of the profound changes seen in the United States during the decades from 1870 to 1950, with excerpts from primary sources. (Rev: BL 2/1/05; SLJ 5/05) [973]

1859 McNeese, Tim. *The Rise and Fall of American Slavery: Freedom Denied, Freedom Gained* (6–12). Illus. Series: Slavery in American History. 2004, Enslow LB $19.95 (0-7660-2156-4). 128pp. Traces the growth of the slave trade in the American colonies, as well as the rise of the abolition movement that later pushed for an end to slavery. (Rev: BL 9/1/04; SLJ 8/04) [97]

1860 Miller, Page Putnam. *Landmarks of American Women's History* (5–8). 2004, Oxford Univ. LB $30.00 (0-19-514501-1). 143pp. Landmarks — all on the National Register of Historic Places — highlighted for their importance in women's history include Taos Pueblo, New Mexico, chosen for the strong Native American women who lived there; the Wesleyan Chapel at Seneca Falls, where the first women's rights conference was held; and the Boardinghouse at Boott Cotton Mill in Lowell, Massachusetts, home to many young women who worked in the textile industry. (Rev: SLJ 9/04) [973]

1861 Nathan, Amy. *Count on Us: American Women in the Military* (6–9). Illus. 2004, National Geographic $21.95 (0-7922-6330-8). 96pp. Nathan celebrates women's diverse contributions to the United States' military causes — from women who disguised themselves as men in the Revolutionary War to World War I nurses to women flying Black Hawk missions today. (Rev: BL 2/15/04; SLJ 3/04) [355]

1862 Sills, Leslie. *From Rags to Riches: A History of Girls' Clothing in America* (4–7). Illus. 2005, Holiday $16.95 (0-8234-1708-5). 48pp. Changes in clothing over the centuries are linked to the social mores of the time in this appealing volume. (Rev: BL 5/1/05; SLJ 8/05) [391]

1863 Stanley, George E. *The New Republic (1763–1815)* (5–8). Illus. Series: A Primary Source History of the United States. 2005, World Almanac LB $22.50 (0-8368-5825-5). 48pp. A simple narrative links well-chosen primary sources documenting the key events of the revolutionary period. (Rev: BL 4/1/05; SLJ 7/05)

1864 Tinsley, Kevin, and Phil Singer. *Milk Cartons and Dog Biscuits* (7–12). Illus. 2004, Stickman Graphics paper $19.95 (0-9675423-4-0). 216pp. People and elf-like creatures mingle in this adventure mystery about a state ranger who is searching for a runaway daughter. (Rev: BL 2/1/04)

1865 Torr, James D., ed. *Slavery* (7–12). Series: Opposing Viewpoints: World History. 2004, Gale LB $33.70 (0-7377-1705-X). 240pp. Various perspectives of slavery are presented through carefully selected primary documents; includes coverage of events leading to the Civil War. (Rev: BL 2/15/04) [306.3]

1866 Worth, Richard. *Slave Life on the Plantation: Prisons Beneath the Sun* (6–12). Illus. Series: Slavery in American History. 2004, Enslow LB $19.95 (0-7660-2152-1). 128pp. A vivid portrait of what daily life was like for slaves laboring on the vast plantations of the American South. (Rev: BL 9/1/04; SLJ 12/04) [306.3]

1867 Worth, Richard. *The Slave Trade in America: Cruel Commerce* (6–12). Series: Slavery in American History. 2004, Enslow LB $20.95 (0-7660-2151-3). 128pp. The slave trade is traced back to its origins in the days of early Romans before a more detailed survey of the American slave trade in the 17th and 18th centuries, with attention to the social and economic aspects. (Rev: SLJ 8/04) [382]

1868 Yorinks, Adrienne. *Quilt of States: Piecing Together America* (5–8). Illus. 2005, National Geographic LB $29.90 (0-7922-7286-2). 128pp. With contributions from librarians from all 50 states, this beautifully illustrated volume offers a brief story of each state's accession to the Union, along with other pertinent facts and figures. (Rev: BL 10/1/05; SLJ 12/05) [973]

Historical Periods

NATIVE AMERICANS

1869 Bial, Raymond. *The Chumash* (6–9). Illus. Series: Lifeways. 2003, Benchmark LB $23.95 (0-7614-1681-1). 126pp. A look at the history, culture, social structure, key figures, and current status of the Chumash tribe of California, with maps, drawings, and photographs. (Rev: SLJ 5/04) [973]

1870 Bial, Raymond. *The Wampanoag* (6–9). Illus. Series: Lifeways. 2003, Benchmark LB $23.95 (0-7614-1683-8). 124pp. A look at the history, culture, social structure, key figures, and current status of the Wampanoag tribe of Massachusetts, with maps, drawings, and photographs. (Rev: SLJ 5/04) [973]

1871 Birchfield, D. L. *The Trail of Tears* (4–7). Series: Landmark Events in American History. 2003, World Almanac LB $29.26 (0-8368-5381-4). 48pp. A brief account of the tragic forced removal of Native American people from their lands by the U.S. government in the mid-19th century. (Rev: SLJ 6/04) [973.04]

1872 Cornell, George L., and Gordon Henry. *Ojibwa* (8–12). Series: North American Indians Today. 2003, Mason Crest LB $22.95 (1-59084-673-7). 94pp. The contemporary status of Ojibwa Indians is emphasized in this volume that covers religion, government, and the arts. (Rev: SLJ 5/04) [973]

1873 Keoke, Emory Dean, and Kay Marie Porterfield. *Trade, Transportation, and Warfare* (7–10). Illus. Series: American Indian Contributions to the World. 2005, Facts on File $35.00 (0-8160-5395-2). 160pp. Native American accomplishments in both North and South America in the realms of transportation, trade, sports, governance, and military strategy are among the aspects highlighted here. (Rev: BL 4/1/05; SLJ 6/05) [970.004]

1874 McIntosh, Kenneth. *Apache* (8–12). Series: North American Indians Today. 2003, Mason Crest LB $22.95 (1-59084-664-8). 94pp. The contemporary status of Apache Indians is emphasized in this volume that covers religion, government, and the arts. (Rev: SLJ 5/04) [973]

1875 McIntosh, Kenneth. *Navajo* (6–9). Illus. Series: North American Indians Today. 2003, Mason Crest LB $22.95 (1-59084-672-9). 96pp. This portrait of the Navajo people offers a brief history of the tribe but focuses primarily on their present-day culture and government. (Rev: BL 4/1/04; SLJ 5/04) [979.1]

1876 McIntosh, Kenneth, and Marsha McIntosh. *Cheyenne* (8–12). Series: North American Indians Today. 2003, Mason Crest LB $22.95 (1-59084-666-4). 94pp. The contemporary status of Cheyenne

Indians is emphasized in this volume that covers religion, government, and the arts. Also use *Iroquois* (2003). (Rev: SLJ 5/04) [973]

1877 Stone, Amy M. *Creek* (4–8). Series: Native American Peoples. 2004, Gareth Stevens LB $24.67 (0-8368-4217-0). 32pp. History, tradition, and contemporary life are described with photographs, timeline, fact boxes, and activities. (Rev: SLJ 1/05) [973]

1878 Stout, Mary. *Blackfoot* (4–8). Series: Native American Peoples. 2004, Gareth Stevens LB $24.67 (0-8368-4216-2). 32pp. History, tradition, and contemporary life are described with photographs, timeline, fact boxes, and activities. (Rev: SLJ 1/05) [973]

1879 Taylor, C. J. *Peace Walker: The Legend of Hiawatha and Tekanawita* (6–9). Illus. 2004, Tundra $15.95 (0-88776-547-5). 48pp. In rhythmic prose and full-page paintings, Taylor retells the story of Hiawatha and places it in cultural context. (Rev: BL 2/15/05; SLJ 4/05) [398.2]

1880 Thompson, Linda. *The California People* (4–7). Illus. Series: Native People, Native Lands. 2003, Rourke LB $29.93 (1-58952-753-4). 48pp. One of a well-illustrated series on individual groups of native Americans, with attention to the negative impact of the arrival of European settlers. Other titles in the series include *People of the Northwest and Subarctic*, *People of the Great Basin*, *People of the Northeast Woodlands*, and *People of the Plains and Prairies* (all 2003). (Rev: SLJ 4/04) [979.4]

1881 Wood, Marion, and Brian Williams. *Ancient America*. Rev. ed. (5–8). Illus. Series: Cultural Atlas for Young People. 2003, Facts on File $35.00 (0-8160-5145-3). 96pp. Colorful topical spreads introduce readers to Native American history from the end of the Ice Age to the arrival of European explorers and conquerers. (Rev: SLJ 1/04) [970.01]

DISCOVERY AND EXPLORATION

1882 Armentrout, David, and Patricia Armentrout. *The Mayflower Compact* (4–7). 2004, Rourke $.00 (1-59515-229-6). 48pp. The reasons for the creation of this document — a political statement signed by a group of *Mayflower* passengers — are thoroughly explored in concise text, accompanied by an array of maps and illustrations. (Rev: BL 10/15/04) [974.4]

1883 Foran, Jill. *Search for the Northwest Passage* (5–8). Series: Great Journeys. 2004, Weigl LB $.00 (1-59036-205-5). Colorful illustrations and an attractive format will appeal to browsers seeking information about the search for a sea route to the West; a useful timeline and links to Web sites are included. (Rev: BL 11/1/04) [910]

1884 Warrick, Karen Clemens. *The Perilous Search for the Fabled Northwest Passage in American History* (6–9). Series: In American History. 2004, Enslow LB $26.60 (0-7660-2148-3). 128pp. Traces early efforts to find the passage as well as Amundsen's successful 1906 expedition. (Rev: SLJ 10/04) [910]

COLONIAL PERIOD AND FRENCH AND INDIAN WARS

1885 ADC, the Map People Staff. *Virginia* (4–7). Series: Life in the Thirteen Colonies. 2004, Children's Pr. LB $24.95 (0-516-24580-5). This look at colonial Virginia, including the turbulent social and political climate of the period, presents an even-handed portrait of life for both the Indians and the settlers. (Rev: BL 12/15/04)

1886 DeFord, Deborah H. *Massachusetts* (4–7). Illus. Series: Life in the Thirteen Colonies. 2004, Children's Pr. LB $35.00 (0-516-24572-4). 128pp. From the first settlers to the end of the Revolutionary War, this interesting volume covers important events and daily life of the settlers plus information on the Native Amerian tribes. (Rev: BL 12/15/04)

1887 DeFord, Deborah H. *Pennsylvania* (4–7). Illus. Series: Life in the Thirteen Colonies. 2004, Children's Pr. LB $35.00 (0-516-24577-5). 128pp. From the first settlers to the end of the Revolutionary War, this interesting volume covers important events and daily life of the settlers plus information on the Native American tribes. (Rev: BL 12/15/04)

1888 Doak, Robin. *Rhode Island* (4–7). Illus. Series: Life in the Thirteen Colonies. 2004, Children's Pr. LB $35.00 (0-516-24578-3). 128pp. From the first settlers to the end of the Revolutionary War, this interesting volume covers important events and daily life of the settlers plus information on the Native American tribes. (Rev: BL 12/15/04)

1889 Kent, Zachary. *The Mysterious Disappearance of Roanoke Colony in American History* (7–10). Illus. Series: American History. 2004, Enslow LB $20.95 (0-7660-2147-5). 128pp. A detailed account of the settlement on Roanoke Island with recent research material on the fate of the colony. (Rev: BL 3/1/04; SLJ 6/04) [975.6]

1890 McKissack, Patricia, and Fredrick McKissack. *Hard Labor: The First African Americans, 1619* (5–8). Series: Milestone Books. 2004, Simon & Schuster paper $3.99 (0-689-86149-4). 64pp. Drawing on the meager evidence available, the authors reconstruct the story of the first Africans brought to America. (Rev: BL 2/15/04; SLJ 3/04) [306.3]

1891 Paulson, Timothy J. *New York* (4–7). Illus. Series: Life in the Thirteen Colonies. 2004, Children's Pr. LB $35.00 (0-516-24575-9). 128pp. From the first settlers to the end of the Revolutionary War, this interesting volume covers important

events and daily life of the settlers plus information on the Native Amerian tribes. (Rev: BL 12/15/04)

1892 Sterngass, Jon, and Matthew Kachur. *New Jersey* (4–7). Illus. Series: Life in the Thirteen Colonies. 2004, Children's Pr. LB $35.00 (0-516-24574-0). 128pp. From the first settlers to the end of the Revolutionary War, this interesting volume covers important events and daily life of the settlers plus information on the Native Amerian tribes. (Rev: BL 12/15/04)

1893 Teitelbaum, Michael. *New Hampshire* (4–7). Illus. Series: Life in the Thirteen Colonies. 2004, Children's Pr. LB $35.00 (0-516-24573-2). 128pp. From the first settlers to the end of the Revolutionary War, this interesting volume covers important events and daily life of the settlers plus information on the Native Amerian tribes. (Rev: BL 12/15/04)

1894 Wiener, Roberta, and James R. Arnold. *Connecticut: The History of Connecticut Colony, 1633–1776* (5–8). Series: 13 Colonies. 2004, Raintree LB $31.36 (0-7398-6877-2). 64pp. A fact-filled and balanced discussion of the settlement of this area and the problems — political, social, and religious — that confronted the early European inhabitants. Also use *Delaware* and *Maryland* (both 2004). (Rev: SLJ 4/05) [974.6]

1895 Worth, Richard. *Delaware* (4–7). Illus. Series: Life in the Thirteen Colonies. 2004, Children's Pr. LB $35.00 (0-516-24569-4). 128pp. From the first settlers to the end of the Revolutionary War, this interesting volume covers important events and daily life of the settlers plus information on the Native American tribes. (Rev: BL 12/15/04)

1896 Worth, Richard. *North Carolina* (4–7). Illus. Series: Life in the Thirteen Colonies. 2004, Children's Pr. LB $35.00 (0-516-24576-7). 128pp. From the first settlers to the end of the Revolutionary War, this interesting volume covers important events and daily life of the settlers plus information on the Native Amerian tribes. (Rev: BL 12/15/04)

REVOLUTIONARY PERIOD AND THE YOUNG NATION (1775–1809)

1897 Allen, Thomas B. *George Washington, Spymaster: How the Americans Outspied the British and Won the Revolutionary War* (6–8). Illus. 2004, National Geographic $16.95 (0-7922-5126-1). 192pp. This interesting volume focuses on the general's strategic use of espionage to win America's freedom from the British, providing details about invisible ink, codes and ciphers, and secret messages. (Rev: BL 4/15/04*; SLJ 5/04) [973.3]

1898 Anderson, Dale. *The American Colonies Declare Independence* (5–8). Series: World Almanac Library of the American Revolution. 2005, World Almanac LB $30.00 (0-8368-5926-X). 48pp. Excerpts from primary sources bolster the informative, clearly written text, which is sprinkled with biographical sidebars. Also use *The Causes of the American Revolution*, *The Patriots Win the American Revolution*, and *Forming a New American Government* (all 2005). (Rev: SLJ 1/06) [973.3]

1899 Anderson, Dale. *Lexington and Concord, April 19, 1775* (5–7). Series: American Battlefields. 2004, Enchanted Lion $14.95 (1-59270-027-6). 32pp. This volume looks at the April 1775 skirmishes between American patriots and British soldiers at Lexington and Concord that marked the opening of the Revolutionary War; sidebars, illustrations, a timeline, and other features add to the narrative. (Rev: BL 11/1/04) [973]

1900 Bobrick, Benson. *Fight for Freedom: The American Revolutionary War* (5–8). 2004, Simon & Schuster $22.95 (0-689-86422-1). 96pp. Full-page illustrations face text and "Quick Facts" about topics ranging from the origins and progress of the war to the Continental Congresses, with profiles of key figures and maps. (Rev: BL 11/15/04; SLJ 11/04) [973.3]

1901 Bohannon, Lisa Frederiksen. *The American Revolution* (5–8). Series: Chronicle of America's Wars. 2003, Lerner LB $27.93 (0-8225-4717-1). 88pp. Illustrations and maps enliven this overview of the American colonies' struggle for independence, covering the two decades from the French and Indian War to the Treaty of Paris. (Rev: SLJ 3/04) [973.3]

1902 McCullough, David. *1776* (8–12). Illus. 2005, Simon & Schuster $32.00 (0-7432-2671-2). 386pp. McCullough brings to life the key events of the year 1776 for George Washington and the new young nation. (Rev: SLJ 10/05) [973]

1903 McGowen, Tom. *The Revolutionary War and George Washington's Army in American History* (7–10). Illus. Series: American History. 2004, Enslow LB $20.95 (0-7660-2143-2). 128pp. This is a readable account of all the battles in the Revolution plus a great assessment of George Washington's strengths and weaknesses. (Rev: BL 3/1/04; SLJ 3/04) [973.3]

1904 Miller, Brandon M. *Declaring Independence: Life During the American Revolution* (5–8). Series: People's History. 2005, Lerner LB $26.60 (0-8225-1275-0). 112pp. A thorough look at what life was like during the American Revolution, using primary sources. (Rev: SLJ 9/05; VOYA 6/05) [973.3]

1905 Morton, Joseph C. *The American Revolution* (7–12). Series: Greenwood Guides to Historic Events, 1500–1900. 2003, Greenwood $45.00 (0-313-31792-5). 218pp. A thorough, text-dense overview of the events leading up to the war, the war itself, and its aftermath, with profiles of key individuals. (Rev: SLJ 7/04) [973.3]

1906 Murray, Aaron R. *American Revolution Battles and Leaders* (6–12). Illus. Series: Battles and Leaders. 2004, DK $19.99 (0-7894-9888-X); paper $12.99 (0-7894-9889-8). 96pp. A richly illustrated, easily accessed source of reliable information on the battles and key figures of the Revolution. (Rev: BL 4/1/04*) [973.3]

1907 Schanzer, Rosalyn. *George vs. George: The Revolutionary War as Seen by Both Sides* (5–7). Illus. 2004, National Geographic $16.95 (0-7922-7349-4). 64pp. The two sides' differences — and commonalities — are portrayed in an appealing combination of well-written text, colorful art, and speech balloons; sensationalist aspects detract from the overall value. (Rev: BL 11/15/04; SLJ 10/04*) [973.3]

NINETEENTH CENTURY TO THE CIVIL WAR (1809–1861)

1908 Blight, David W., ed. *Passages to Freedom: The Underground Railroad in History and Memory* (8–12). Illus. 2004, Smithsonian $39.95 (1-58834-157-7). 256pp. Essays, photographs, and illustrations document the reality, rather than the myth, of the Underground Railroad; compiled on behalf of the National Underground Railroad Center in Cincinnati. (Rev: BL 7/04) [973.7]

1909 Carson, Mary Kay. *The Underground Railroad for Kids: From Slavery to Freedom* (6–9). Illus. Series: For Kids. 2005, Chicago Review paper $14.95 (1-55652-554-0). 160pp. With an engaging blend of first-person accounts and brief profiles, this is an easy-to-understand history of the Underground Railroad and the men and women who used it to escape from slavery. (Rev: BL 2/1/05; SLJ 3/05) [973.7]

1910 Currie, Stephen. *Escapes from Slavery* (5–9). Series: Great Escapes. 2003, Gale LB $27.45 (1-59018-276-6). 112pp. The stories of six of the approximately 60,000 slaves who escaped from captivity in pre-Civil War America. (Rev: SLJ 4/04) [973.7]

1911 Landau, Elaine. *Fleeing to Freedom on the Underground Railroad: The Courageous Slaves, Agents, and Conductors* (6–9). Illus. Series: People's History. 2006, Lerner LB $26.60 (0-8225-3490-8). 96pp. Anecdotes about individual contributions and quotations from primary sources add to this account of the Underground Railroad and those who created and used it; excerpts from key legislation round out this useful volume. (Rev: BL 2/1/06) [973.7]

1912 Morrison, Taylor. *Coast Mappers* (4–8). Illus. 2004, Houghton $16.00 (0-618-25408-0). 48pp. Science and biography are interwoven in this examination of the mid-19th-century mapping of the U.S. Pacific coastline. (Rev: BL 3/15/04; SLJ 5/04) [623.89]

1913 Schlesinger, Arthur M., Jr., ed. *The Election of 1860 and the Administration of Abraham Lincoln* (8–12). Series: Major Presidential Elections and the Administrations That Followed. 2003, Mason Crest LB $24.95 (1-59084-355-X). 128pp. A good source of speeches, quotations, and excerpts from public documents, with commentary, illustrations, and further reading. (Rev: SLJ 1/04) [973.7]

1914 Stewart, Mark. *The Alamo, February 23–March 6, 1836* (5–7). Illus. Series: American Battlefields. 2004, Enchanted Lion $14.95 (1-59270-026-8). 32pp. This overview of the Battle of the Alamo offers a clear account of the conflict and an examination of the developments leading up to it; sidebars, illustrations, a timeline, and other features add to the narrative. (Rev: BL 11/1/04) [976.4]

1915 Swain, Gwenyth. *Dred and Harriet Scott: A Family's Struggle for Freedom* (6–9). 2004, Borealis $22.95 (0-87351-482-3); paper $12.95 (0-87351-483-1). 102pp. The story of the Scotts' desire that their young daughters should not have to live as slaves and the lengthy court battle that they ultimately lost, a battle that brought the Civil War a step closer. (Rev: SLJ 7/04) [973.7]

CIVIL WAR (1861–1865)

1916 Armentrout, David, and Patricia Armentrout. *The Emancipation Proclamation* (4–7). Series: Documents That Shaped the Nation. 2004, Rourke $.00 (1-59515-233-4). 48pp. The reasons for the creation of this document and the results of its proclamation are thoroughly explored in concise text, accompanied by an array of maps and illustrations. (Rev: BL 10/15/04) [973.7]

1917 Armstrong, Jennifer. *Photo by Brady: A Picture of the Civil War* (6–9). Illus. 2005, Simon & Schuster $18.95 (0-689-85785-3). 160pp. This photoessay artfully uses the photographs of Mathew Brady to document Civil War history from the inauguration of Abraham Lincoln to his assassination, only days after the end of hostilities. (Rev: BL 3/15/05; SLJ 3/05; VOYA 4/05) [973.7]

1918 Ford, Carin T. *The American Civil War: An Overview* (5–8). Series: The Civil War Library. 2004, Enslow LB $23.93 (0-7660-2255-2). 48pp. This informative general overview of the war features maps, illustrations, and interesting sidebar features. Also use *Lincoln, Slavery, and the Emancipation Proclamation* (2004). (Rev: SLJ 3/05) [973.7]

1919 January, Brendan. *Gettysburg, July 1–3, 1863* (5–7). Illus. Series: American Battlefields. 2004, Enchanted Lion $14.95 (1-59270-025-X). 32pp. This overview of the Battle of Gettysburg offers a clear account of the bloody conflict and an examination of the developments leading up to it; sidebars, illustrations, a timeline, and other features add to the narrative. (Rev: BL 11/1/04) [973]

1920 Lalicki, Tom. *Grierson's Raid: A Daring Cavalry Strike Through the Heart of the Confederacy* (7–12). 2004, Farrar $18.00 (0-374-32787-4). 208pp. Lalicki recounts Union Colonel Benjamin Grierson's daring 16-day raid through the state of Mississippi in 1863. (Rev: BL 8/04; HB 7–8/04; SLJ 6/04; VOYA 8/04) [973.7]

1921 McComb, Marianne. *The Emancipation Proclamation* (4–7). Illus. Series: American Documents. 2006, National Geographic LB $23.90 (0-7922-7936-0). 40pp. The background, nature, and impact of this important document are explained clearly, with photos and illustrations plus full texts of the Emancipation Proclamation, the Fugitive Slave Law of 1850, and Constitutional Amendments XIII through XV. (Rev: BL 2/1/06; SLJ 2/06) [973.7]

1922 Murray, Aaron R. *Civil War Battles and Leaders* (6–12). Illus. Series: Battles and Leaders. 2004, DK $19.99 (0-7894-9890-1); paper $12.99 (0-7894-9891-X). 96pp. A richly illustrated, easily accessed source of reliable information on the battles and key figures of the Civil War. (Rev: BL 4/1/04*) [973.7]

1923 Schomp, Virginia. *The Civil War* (6–8). Illus. Series: Letters from the Battlefront. 2003, Marshall Cavendish LB $29.93 (0-7614-1660-9). 96pp. This collection of first-person accounts offers valuable insights into the Civil War. (Rev: BL 4/1/04; SLJ 4/04) [973.7]

1924 Stanley, George E. *The Crisis of the Union (1815–1865)* (5–8). Illus. Series: A Primary Source History of the United States. 2005, World Almanac LB $22.50 (0-8368-5826-3). 48pp. A simple narrative links well-chosen primary sources documenting the key events of the Civil War. (Rev: BL 4/1/05)

1925 Tanaka, Shelley. *A Day That Changed America: Gettysburg* (4–8). Series: A Day That Changed America. 2003, Hyperion $16.99 (0-7868-1922-7). 48pp. A brief account of the key battle, with illustrations and diagrams as well as information on Lincoln's famous speech. (Rev: SLJ 2/04; VOYA 6/04) [973.7]

WESTWARD EXPANSION AND PIONEER LIFE

1926 Dary, David. *The Oregon Trail: An American Saga* (8–12). Illus. 2004, Knopf $35.00 (0-375-41399-5). 448pp. A sweeping and very readable history of the Oregon Trail, from its early-19th-century origins through a period of obscurity to its present importance. (Rev: BL 10/15/04) [978]

1927 Galford, Ellen. *The Trail West: Exploring History Through Art* (5–8). Illus. Series: Picture That! 2004, Two-Can $19.95 (1-58728-442-1). 64pp. Paintings serve as the vehicle to draw students into the story of westward expansion. (Rev: BL 11/1/04; SLJ 2/05) [978]

1928 Isserman, Maurice. *Across America: The Lewis and Clark Expedition* (6–10). Series: Discovery and Exploration. 2004, Facts on File $35.00 (0-8160-5256-5). 180pp. A detailed look at the expedition with clear, informative text plus photographs, illustrations, and excerpts from primary sources. (Rev: SLJ 12/04) [973]

1929 Isserman, Maurice. *Exploring North America, 1800–1900* (6–12). Series: Discovery and Exploration. 2005, Facts on File $40.00 (0-8160-5263-8). 198pp. Clear text and primary sources explain the 19th-century explorations of North America by John Fremont, John Wesley Powell, and others, and put them in historical and social context. (Rev: SLJ 8/05) [973]

1930 January, Brendan. *Little Bighorn: June 25, 1876* (5–7). Series: American Battlefields. 2004, Enchanted Lion $14.95 (1-59270-028-4). 32pp. This overview of the Battle of Little Bighorn offers a clear-cut account of the bloody conflict and an examination of the developments leading up to it; sidebars, illustrations, a timeline, and other features add to the narrative. (Rev: BL 11/1/04) [973]

1931 Landau, Elaine. *The Transcontinental Railroad* (5–8). Illus. Series: Watts Library: American West. 2005, Watts LB $25.50 (0-531-12326-X). 64pp. The story behind the building of the Transcontinental Railroad, with illustrations, maps, a timeline, and sidebar features. (Rev: SLJ 12/05)

1932 MacGregor, Greg. *Lewis and Clark Revisited: A Photographer's Trail* (8–12). Ed. by Iris Tillman Hill. Illus. 2004, Univ. of Washington $50.00 (0-295-98342-6). 224pp. This book, which contains many eye-catching photographs, traces the route of the Lewis and Clark expedition in 1804–1806 and shows the route as it looks today. (Rev: BL 2/15/04) [917.804]

1933 Meltzer, Milton. *Hear That Train Whistle Blow! How the Railroad Changed the World* (5–9). Series: Landmark Books. 2004, Random LB $20.95 (0-375-91563-X). 176pp. In this fascinating historical survey full of period drawings and photographs, Meltzer examines the dramatic ways in which the railroad affected our lives and questions whether the progress achieved was worth the suffering caused. (Rev: BL 9/15/04; SLJ 10/04) [385]

1934 Rau, Margaret. *The Mail Must Go Through: The Story of the Pony Express* (7–10). Illus. Series: America's Moving Frontier. 2005, Morgan Reynolds LB $24.95 (1-931798-63-X). 176pp. A lively account of the exciting — but brief — history of the Pony Express. (Rev: BL 6/1–15/05; SLJ 10/05) [383]

1935 Schlaepfer, Gloria G. *The Louisiana Purchase* (5–8). Illus. Series: Watts Library: American West. 2005, Watts LB $25.50 (0-531-12300-6). 64pp. The story behind the Louisiana Purchase and its role in America's westward expansion, with illustrations, maps, a timeline, and sidebar features. (Rev: SLJ 12/05)

1936 Sonneborn, Liz. *The Mormon Trail* (5–8). Illus. Series: Watts Library: American West. 2005, Watts LB $25.50 (0-531-12317-0). 64pp. The story behind the westward trek of thousands of Mormons during the middle of the 19th century, with illustrations, maps, a timeline, and sidebar features. (Rev: SLJ 12/05)

1937 Sonneborn, Liz. *Women of the American West* (4–7). Illus. Series: Watts Library: American West. 2005, Watts LB $25.50 (0-531-12318-9). 64pp. Excerpts from first-person accounts offer a glimpse into what life was like for the women who helped to open the American West. (Rev: BL 10/15/05) [978]

1938 Swanson, Wayne. *Why the West Was Wild* (5–8). 2004, Annick $12.95 (1-55037-837-6); paper $12.95 (1-55037-836-8). 48pp. The excitement of the Old West is captured in this lavishly illustrated survey of the region's history during the second half of the 19th century. (Rev: BL 8/04; SLJ 6/04) [978]

1939 Uschan, Michael V. *The Transcontinental Railroad* (4–7). Series: Landmark Events in American History. 2003, World Almanac LB $29.26 (0-8368-5382-2). 48pp. In accessible language and with plenty of illustrations, this is the story of the railroad that spanned the nation. (Rev: SLJ 6/04) [385]

RECONSTRUCTION TO WORLD WAR I
(1865–1914)

1940 Bolden, Tonya. *Cause: Reconstruction America, 1863–1877* (8–11). Illus. 2005, Knopf LB $21.99 (0-375-92795-6). 128pp. Although the text is a little uneven, this is a useful, well-documented and well-illustrated survey of the turbulent years of Reconstruction and the massive challenges facing both the North and South. (Rev: BL 10/15/05; SLJ 11/05*; VOYA 12/05) [973.7]

1941 Brezina, Corona. *America's Political Scandals in the late 1800s: Boss Tweed and Tammany Hall* (5–8). Illus. Series: America's Industrial Society in the 19th Century. 2004, Rosen LB $21.25 (0-8239-4021-7). 32pp. For reluctant readers, this overview of the political scandals of the late 19th century features large print and short chapters. (Rev: BL 4/1/04)

1942 Ferrell, Claudine L. *Reconstruction* (5–10). Series: Greenwood Guides to Historic Events, 1500–1900. 2003, Greenwood $45.00 (0-313-32062-4). 220pp. Covers key individuals involved in Reconstruction and the speeches, proclamations, and other primary documents that cast light on the events of the time. (Rev: SLJ 6/04) [973.8]

1943 Greene, Meg. *Into the Land of Freedom: African Americans in Reconstruction* (5–8). Illus. Series: People's History. 2004, Lerner LB $25.26 (0-8225-4690-6). 112pp. Sepia-toned photographs and historical documents and interviews add to this portrait of the situation of African Americans during Reconstruction. (Rev: BL 2/15/04*; SLJ 5/04) [973]

1944 Jackson, Robert. *Meet Me in St. Louis: A Trip to the 1904 World's Fair* (4–7). Illus. 2004, Harper-Collins $17.99 (0-06-009267-X). 144pp. Jackson beautifully evokes the excitement surrounding the 1904 St. Louis World's Fair, which attracted nearly 20 million people, many of them key figures of the day. (Rev: BL 2/15/04; SLJ 4/04) [907]

1945 Porterfield, Jason. *Problems and Progress in American Politics: The Growth of the Democratic Party in the Late 1800s* (5–8). Illus. Series: America's Industrial Society in the 19th Century. 2004, Rosen LB $21.25 (0-8239-4026-8). 32pp. For reluctant readers, this overview of the growth of the Democratic Party features large print and short chapters. (Rev: BL 4/1/04)

1946 Sandler, Martin W. *Island of Hope: The Story of Ellis Island and the Journey to America* (5–7). Illus. 2004, Scholastic $18.95 (0-439-53082-2). 144pp. Drawing heavily on first-hand accounts, Sandler traces immigrants' progress through the processing at Ellis Island and on into the cities and farms of their new country. (Rev: BL 4/15/04; SLJ 6/04) [304.8]

1947 Schaefer, Adam R. *The Triangle Shirtwaist Factory Fire* (4–7). Series: Landmark Events in American History. 2003, World Almanac LB $29.26 (0-8368-5383-0). 48pp. An accessible account of the tragic 1911 fire in New York City, with material on the horrible working conditions and the resulting reforms in labor law. (Rev: SLJ 6/04) [974.7]

1948 Schwartz, Eric. *Crossing the Seas: Americans Form an Empire 1890–1899* (5–8). Series: How America Became America. 2005, Mason Crest LB $22.95 (1-59084-910-8). 91pp. Schwartz explores America's turn to imperialism in the final decade of the 19th century. Also use *Super Power: Americans Today* (2005). (Rev: SLJ 11/05) [973]

1949 Stanley, George E. *An Emerging World Power (1900–1929)* (5–8). Illus. Series: A Primary Source History of the United States. 2005, World Almanac LB $22.50 (0-8368-5828-X). 48pp. A simple narrative links well-chosen primary sources documenting the key events of the early 20th century. Also use *The Era of Reconstruction and Expansion (1865–1900)* and *The Great Depression and World War II (1929–1949)* (both 2005). (Rev: BL 4/1/05; SLJ 7/05)

1950 Stites, Bill. *The Republican Party in the Late 1800s: A Changing Role for American Government*

(5–8). Illus. Series: America's Industrial Society in the 19th Century. 2004, Rosen LB $21.25 (0-8239-4030-6). 32pp. For reluctant readers, this overview of the growth of the Republican Party features large print and short chapters. (Rev: BL 4/1/04)

1951 Vowell, Sarah. *Assassination Vacation* (8–12). Illus. 2005, Simon & Schuster $21.00 (0-7432-6003-1). 258pp. Author Sarah Vowell takes readers on a pilgrimage to historical sites related to the assassinations of Presidents Lincoln, Garfield, and McKinley. (Rev: SLJ 11/05)

BETWEEN THE WARS AND THE GREAT DEPRESSION (1918–1941)

1952 Callan, Jim. *America in the 1930s* (7–10). Illus. Series: Decades of American History. 2005, Facts on File $35.00 (0-8160-5638-2). 128pp. Excellent information — especially for report writers — is hampered by poor design. (Rev: BL 1/1–15/06) [973.917]

1953 Cooper, Michael L. *Dust to Eat: Drought and Depression in the 1930s* (5–8). Illus. 2004, Clarion $15.00 (0-618-15449-3). 96pp. First-person accounts and period photographs convey the hopelessness of those who were caught in the grip of the Depression and the drought in the Midwest. (Rev: BL 7/04; SLJ 9/04) [973.917]

1954 Freedman, Russell. *Children of the Great Depression* (5–8). Illus. 2005, Clarion $20.00 (0-618-44630-3). 128pp. The works of such notable photographers as Dorothea Lange and Walker Evans, moving quotations, and the accessible text of Freedman make this a memorable photoessay. (Rev: BL 12/15/05*; SLJ 12/05*) [305.23]

1955 Hill, Laban Carrick. *Harlem Stomp! A Cultural History of the Harlem Renaissance* (7–12). Illus. 2004, Little, Brown $18.95 (0-316-81411-3). 160pp. This illustrated history covers developments during the roaring 1920s and the great creations and creators of the Harlem Renaissance. (Rev: BL 2/15/04*; SLJ 1/04; VOYA 2/04) [810.9]

1956 Ruggiero, Adriane. *The Great Depression* (6–9). Illus. Series: American Voices From. 2004, Benchmark LB $23.95 (0-7614-1696-X). 116pp. Primary source documents and excellent illustrations are accompanied by good introductory text and "Think about This" questions. (Rev: SLJ 2/05) [973]

1957 Swisher, Clarice. *Women of the Roaring Twenties* (6–10). Illus. Series: Women in History. 2005, Gale LB $22.96 (1-59017-363-0). 112pp. Using primary sources, this readable volume looks at life for women from diverse backgrounds during the turbulent 1920s. (Rev: BL 2/15/06) [305.4]

1958 Yancey, Diane. *Life During the Dust Bowl* (7–12). Illus. Series: The Way People Live. 2004,

Gale LB $27.45 (1-59018-265-0). 112pp. Black-and-white photographs and excerpts from oral histories add to the narrative overview to paint a vivid portrait of the devastation caused by the Great Plains dust storms of the 1930s. (Rev: BL 8/04; SLJ 8/04) [978]

WORLD WAR II

1959 Brinkley, Douglas, ed. *The World War II Memorial: A Grateful Nation Remembers* (8–12). Illus. 2004, Smithsonian $39.95 (1-58834-210-7). 287pp. Published in conjunction with the dedication of the World War II Memorial in Washington, D.C., this striking coffee table book is loaded with photos and remembrances of the war and its lasting impact on America. (Rev: BL 9/1/04) [940.54]

POST WORLD WAR II UNITED STATES
(1945–)

1960 Feinstein, Stephen. *The 1950s: From the Korean War to Elvis* (6–9). Illus. Series: Decades of the 20th Century in Color. 2006, Enslow LB $20.95 (0-7660-2635-3). 64pp. Ample illustrations and a useful timeline make this an appealing reference to the events — cultural, scientific, and sporting — of the 1950s. (Rev: BL 4/1/06) [973.92]

1961 Gard, Carolyn. *The Attack on the Pentagon on September 11, 2001* (4–8). Series: Terrorist Attacks. 2003, Rosen LB $26.50 (0-8239-3858-1). 64pp. In addition to describing the attack itself, Gard looks at the organization of Al-Qaeda. (Rev: SLJ 2/04) [975.5]

1962 Maus, Derek C., ed. *Living Under the Threat of Nuclear War* (7–10). Series: Living Through the Cold War. 2005, Gale LB $32.45 (0-7377-2130-8). 143pp. This title examines how Americans coped with the ever-present threat of nuclear war during the half-century-long Cold War. (Rev: SLJ 10/05) [973]

1963 Schlesinger, Arthur M., Jr., ed. *The Election of 1948 and the Administration of Harry S. Truman* (8–12). Series: Major Presidential Elections and the Administrations That Followed. 2003, Mason Crest LB $24.95 (1-59084-360-6). 128pp. A good source of speeches, quotations, and excerpts from public documents, with commentary, illustrations, and further reading. Also use *The Election of 1912 and the Administration of Woodrow Wilson* and *The Election of 1960 and the Administration of John F. Kennedy* (both 2003). (Rev: SLJ 1/04) [973]

KOREAN, VIETNAM, AND GULF WARS

1964 Canwell, Diane, and Jon Sutherland. *African Americans in the Vietnam War* (5–8). Illus. Series: American Experience in Vietnam. 2005, World Almanac LB $30.00 (0-8368-5772-0). 48pp. Personal stories and full-color photographs add to the information on black Americans' contributions to the conflict and the military's efforts toward integration. Also use *American Women in the Vietnam War* (2005). (Rev: BL 2/1/05) [959.705]

1965 Caputo, Philip. *10,000 Days of Thunder: A History of the Vietnam War* (7–10). Illus. 2005, Simon & Schuster $22.95 (0-689-86231-8). 128pp. In this sweeping overview of the Vietnam War, Caputo traces the fractured country's history from the beginnings of resistance to French colonial rule to the fall of Saigon and also assesses the conflict's enduring impact on Americans. (Rev: BL 10/1/05; SLJ 11/05*; VOYA 10/05) [959.704]

1966 Carter, E. J. *The Cuban Missile Crisis* (4–8). Series: 20th Century Perspectives. 2003, Heinemann LB $27.07 (1-4034-3806-4). 48pp. A review of the 1962 crisis in which Cuba secretly installed missiles capable of carrying nuclear warheads. (Rev: SLJ 5/04) [972.9]

1967 Feldman, Ruth Tenzer. *The Korean War* (6–12). Illus. Series: Chronicle of America's Wars. 2003, Lerner LB $27.93 (0-8225-4716-3). 96pp. Explores events before, during, and after the Korean War and introduces the key individuals involved. (Rev: BL 4/1/04) [951.904]

1968 Koestler-Grack, Rachel A. *The Kent State Tragedy* (4–7). Illus. Series: American Moments. 2005, ABDO LB $17.94 (1-59197-934-X). 48pp. A concise overview of the deadly 1970 clash between National Guard troops and war protesters on the campus of Ohio's Kent State University. (Rev: BL 9/1/05; SLJ 11/05) [378.771]

1969 Mason, Andrew. *The Vietnam War: A Primary Source History* (5–8). Illus. Series: In Their Own Words. 2005, Gareth Stevens LB $19.50 (0-8368-5981-2). 48pp. Primary sources — including letters, articles, speeches, and songs — deliver the views of combatants in Vietnam and people on the home front in this well-illustrated volume. (Rev: BL 10/15/05) [959.704]

1970 Murray, Stuart. *Vietnam War* (6–9). Illus. Series: Eyewitness Books. 2005, DK LB $19.99 (0-7566-1165-2). 72pp. This photo-filled volume introduces the key events, figures, armaments, and political and social issues of the Vietnam War. (Rev: BL 9/1/05) [959.704]

Regions

MIDWEST

1971 Anderson, Reuben. *Uniquely Oklahoma* (4–7). Illus. Series: Heinemann State Studies. 2004, Heinemann LB $21.95 (1-4034-4658-X). 48pp. In addition to providing the facts necessary for report writers, this volume emphasizes the features that distinguish Oklahoma from its neighbors. (Rev: BL 10/15/03)

1972 Anderson, Reuben. *Uniquely South Dakota* (4–7). Illus. Series: Heinemann State Studies. 2004, Heinemann LB $21.95 (1-4034-4662-8). 48pp. In addition to providing the facts necessary for report writers, this volume emphasizes the features that distinguish South Dakota from its neighbors. (Rev: BL 10/15/03)

1973 Ash, Stephanie. *Uniquely Minnesota* (4–7). Series: Heinemann State Studies. 2004, Heinemann LB $27.07 (1-4034-4494-3). 48pp. In addition to providing the facts necessary for report writers, this volume emphasizes the features that distinguish Minnesota from its neighbors. (Rev: BL 4/1/04)

1974 Opat, Jamie Stockman. *Uniquely Nebraska* (4–7). Illus. Series: Heinemann State Studies. 2004, Heinemann LB $21.95 (1-4034-4649-0). 48pp. In addition to providing the facts necessary for report writers, this volume emphasizes the features that distinguish Nebraska from its neighbors. (Rev: BL 10/15/03)

1975 Redmond, Jim, and D. J. Ross. *Uniquely North Dakota* (4–7). Series: Heinemann State Studies. 2004, Heinemann LB $18.95 (1-4034-4657-1). 48pp. In addition to providing the facts necessary for report writers, this volume emphasizes the features that distinguish North Dakota from its neighbors. (Rev: BL 4/1/04)

1976 Steele, Christy Lee. *Uniquely Wisconsin* (4–7). Series: Heinemann State Studies. 2004, Heinemann LB $27.07 (1-4034-4499-4). 48pp. In addition to providing the facts necessary for report writers, this volume emphasizes the features that distinguish Wisconsin from its neighbors. (Rev: BL 4/1/04)

MOUNTAIN AND PLAINS STATES

1977 Bograd, Larry. *Uniquely Wyoming* (4–7). Illus. Series: Heinemann State Studies. 2004, Heinemann LB $21.95 (1-4034-4666-0). 48pp. In addition to providing the facts necessary for report writers, this volume emphasizes the features that distinguish Wyoming from its neighbors. (Rev: BL 10/15/03)

1978 Dumas, Bianca, and D. J. Ross. *Uniquely Utah* (4–7). Series: Heinemann State Studies. 2004, Heinemann LB $18.95 (1-4034-4663-6). 48pp. In addition to providing the facts necessary for report writers, this volume emphasizes the features that distinguish Utah from its neighbors. (Rev: BL 4/1/04)

1979 O'Connor, Rebecca K., and Dennis Myers. *Uniquely Nevada* (4–7). Illus. Series: Heinemann State Studies. 2004, Heinemann LB $21.95 (1-4034-4650-4). 48pp. In addition to providing the facts necessary for report writers, this volume

emphasizes the features that distinguish Nevada from its neighbors. (Rev: BL 10/15/03)

NORTHEASTERN AND MID-ATLANTIC STATES

1980 Attie, Alice. *Harlem on the Verge* (8–12). Illus. 2003, Quantuck Lane $35.00 (0-9714548-7-6). 120pp. After an introductory essay, this book consists of unforgettable color photographs that depict life in Manhattan's Harlem and Spanish Harlem. (Rev: BL 2/15/04) [974.7]

1981 Doak, Robin. *New Jersey* (5–8). Illus. Series: Voices from Colonial America. 2005, National Geographic LB $32.90 (0-7922-6680-3). 112pp. A compelling account of life in early New Jersey, from its initial settlement by the Dutch through the adoption of the Constitution. (Rev: BL 6/1–15/05; SLJ 1/06) [974.9]

1982 Doherty, Craig A., and Katherine M. Doherty. *Pennsylvania* (5–9). Illus. Series: The Thirteen Colonies. 2005, Facts on File LB $35.00 (0-8160-5413-4). 142pp. Traces the history of Pennsylvania from the early settlers through 1787, with discussion of the Native American culture, the Quakers, and with excerpts from primary documents, maps, and profiles of key individuals. (Rev: SLJ 8/05) [973]

1983 Doherty, Craig A., and Katherine M. Doherty. *Rhode Island* (5–9). Illus. Series: The Thirteen Colonies. 2005, Facts on File LB $35.00 (0-81605-415-0). 126pp. Traces the history of Rhode Island from the early settlers through 1787, with discussion of the Native American culture and with excerpts from primary documents, maps, and profiles of key individuals. (Rev: SLJ 8/05) [973]

1984 Melman, Peter. *Uniquely New Hampshire* (4–7). Series: Heinemann State Studies. 2004, Heinemann LB $18.95 (1-4034-4651-2). 48pp. In addition to providing the facts necessary for report writers, this volume emphasizes the features that distinguish New Hampshire from its neighbors. (Rev: BL 4/1/04)

1985 Moose, Katherine B. *Uniquely Delaware* (4–7). Series: Heinemann State Studies. 2004, Heinemann LB $18.95 (1-4034-4644-X). 48pp. In addition to providing the facts necessary for report writers, this volume emphasizes the features that distinguish Delaware from its neighbors. (Rev: BL 4/1/04)

1986 Moose, Katherine B. *Uniquely Rhode Island* (4–7). Illus. Series: Heinemann State Studies. 2004, Heinemann LB $21.95 (1-4034-4660-1). 48pp. In addition to providing the facts necessary for report writers, this volume emphasizes the features that distinguish Rhode Island from its neighbors. (Rev: BL 10/15/03)

1987 Pascoe, Elaine. *History Around You: A Unique Look at the Past, People, and Places of New York* (4–7). Illus. 2004, Gale LB $26.20 (1-4103-0490-6). 80pp. Using a news-style format with maps, charts, and illustrations, Pascoe details the history of New York State and profiles famous individuals. (Rev: SLJ 3/05) [974.7]

1988 Raabe, Emily. *Uniquely Vermont* (4–7). Illus. Series: Heinemann State Studies. 2005, Heinemann LB $21.95 (1-4034-4664-4). 48pp. In addition to providing the facts necessary for report writers, this volume emphasizes the features that distinguish Vermont from its neighbors. (Rev: BL 10/15/03)

1989 Ross, D. J. *Uniquely Maine* (4–7). Series: Heinemann State Studies. 2004, Heinemann LB $18.95 (1-4034-4655-5). 48pp. In addition to providing the facts necessary for report writers, this volume emphasizes the features that distinguish Maine from its neighbors. (Rev: BL 4/1/04)

1990 Warrick, Karen Clemens. *Independence National Historical Park* (5–8). Illus. Series: Virtual Field Trips. 2005, Enslow LB $25.26 (0-7660-5224-9). 48pp. A visit to Independence Park, using both print and related Web sites, that covers its historical importance, including Independence Hall and the Liberty Bell. (Rev: SLJ 5/05)

PACIFIC STATES

1991 Altman, Linda J. *California* (5–8). Series: Celebrate the States. 2005, Benchmark LB $25.95 (0-7614-1737-0). 143pp. This revised edition updates facts and adds information on the government and economy plus new, full-color photographs. (Rev: SLJ 3/06) [979.4]

1992 Goh, Geok Yian. *Uniquely Hawaii* (4–7). Illus. Series: Heinemann State Studies. 2004, Heinemann LB $21.95 (1-4034-4645-8). 48pp. In addition to providing the facts necessary for report writers, this volume emphasizes the features that make Hawaii unique. (Rev: BL 10/15/03)

1993 Henry, Judy. *Uniquely Alaska* (4–7). Illus. Series: Heinemann State Studies. 2005, Heinemann LB $21.95 (1-4034-4642-3). 48pp. In addition to providing the facts necessary for report writers, this volume emphasizes the features that make Alaska unique. (Rev: BL 10/15/03)

SOUTH

1994 Bredeson, Carmen, and Mary Dodson Wade. *Texas* (5–8). Series: Celebrate the States. 2005, Benchmark LB $25.95 (0-7614-1736-2). 144pp. This revised edition updates facts and adds information on the government and economy plus new, full-color photographs. (Rev: SLJ 3/06) [976.4]

1995 Coleman, Wim, and Pat Perrin. *Colonial Williamsburg* (5–8). Illus. Series: Virtual Field Trips. 2005, Enslow LB $25.26 (0-7660-5220-6). 48pp. A visit to Williamsburg, using both print and related Web sites, that covers its historical importance and its portrayal of colonial life. (Rev: SLJ 5/05)

1996 Cribben, Patrick. *Uniquely West Virginia* (4–7). Illus. Series: Heinemann State Studies. 2005, Heinemann LB $21.95 (1-4034-4665-2). 48pp. In addition to providing the facts necessary for report writers, this volume emphasizes the features that distinguish West Virginia from its neighbors. (Rev: BL 10/15/03)

1997 Doherty, Craig A., and Katherine M. Doherty. *North Carolina* (5–9). Illus. Series: The Thirteen Colonies. 2005, Facts on File LB $35.00 (0-8160-5412-6). 116pp. Traces the history of North Carolina from the early settlers through 1787, with discussion of the Native American culture and with excerpts from primary documents, maps, and profiles of key individuals. (Rev: SLJ 8/05) [973]

1998 Leese, Jennifer. *Uniquely Maryland* (4–7). Series: State Studies. 2004, Heinemann LB $27.07 (1-4034-4493-5). 48pp. History, industry, tourism, and culture are among the highlights of this survey of Maryland and its characteristics. (Rev: BL 4/1/04) [975.2]

1999 McClellan, Adam, and Martin Wilson. *Uniquely North Carolina* (4–7). Series: Heinemann State Studies. 2004, Heinemann LB $18.95 (1-4034-4653-9). 48pp. In addition to providing the facts necessary for report writers, this volume emphasizes the features that distinguish North Carolina from its neighbors. (Rev: BL 4/1/04)

2000 Owens, Lisa. *Uniquely Missouri* (4–7). Series: Heinemann State Studies. 2004, Heinemann LB $27.07 (1-4034-4495-1). 48pp. In addition to providing the facts necessary for report writers, this volume emphasizes the features that distinguish Missouri from its neighbors. (Rev: BL 4/1/04)

2001 Pobst, Sandy. *Virginia, 1607–1776* (5–8). Illus. Series: Voices from Colonial America. 2005, National Geographic LB $32.90 (0-7922-6771-0). 112pp. A thorough political and social history of early Virginia, with excellent illustrations. (Rev: BL 10/15/05; SLJ 11/05) [975.5]

2002 Sherrow, Victoria. *Uniquely South Carolina* (4–7). Illus. Series: Heinemann State Studies. 2005, Heinemann LB $21.95 (1-4034-4661-X). 48pp. In addition to providing the facts necessary for report writers, this volume emphasizes the features that distinguish South Carolina from its neighbors. (Rev: BL 10/15/03)

2003 Stout, Mary. *Atlanta* (4–7). Illus. Series: Great Cities of the World. 2005, World Almanac LB

$22.50 (0-8368-5042-4). 48pp. Report writers will find useful information on Atlanta's history, culture, lifestyle, and current problems. (Rev: BL 4/15/04)

2004 Wilson, Martin. *Uniquely Alabama* (4–7). Series: Heinemann State Studies. 2004, Heinemann LB $27.07 (1-4034-4485-4). 48pp. In addition to providing the facts necessary for report writers, this volume emphasizes the features that distinguish Alabama from its neighbors. (Rev: BL 4/1/04)

2005 Wilson, Martin. *Uniquely Mississippi* (4–7). Illus. Series: Heinemann State Studies. 2004, Heinemann LB $21.95 (1-4034-4656-3). 48pp. In addition to providing the facts necessary for report writers, this volume emphasizes the features that distinguish Mississippi from its neighbors. (Rev: BL 10/15/03)

SOUTHWEST

2006 Coleman, Wim, and Pat Perrin. *The Alamo* (6–9). Illus. Series: Virtual Field Trips. 2005, Enslow LB $18.95 (0-7660-5221-4). 48pp. An attractive overview of the events that make the Alamo an important historical landmark, with Web links for further research. (Rev: BL 8/05; SLJ 5/05) [976.4]

2007 Corrick, James. *Uniquely Arizona* (4–7). Series: Heinemann State Studies. 2004, Heinemann LB $27.07 (1-4034-4486-2); paper $8.50 (1-4304-4501-X). 48pp. In addition to providing the facts necessary for report writers, this volume emphasizes the features that distinguish Arizona from its neighbors. (Rev: BL 4/1/04)

Philosophy and Religion

Philosophy

2008 Constable, Kate. *The Singer of All Songs* (7–10). Series: Chanters of Tremaris. 2004, Scholastic $16.95 (0-439-55478-0). 304pp. In this impressive fantasy, Calwyn, a novice priestess, is able to control all things cold and uses this power to fight an evil sorcerer. (Rev: BL 2/1/04*; SLJ 4/04; VOYA 4/04)

World Religions and Holidays

General and Miscellaneous

2009 Feiler, Bruce S. *Walking the Bible: An Illustrated Journey for Kids Through the Greatest Stories Ever Told* (5–8). Illus. 2004, HarperCollins LB $17.89 (0-06-051118-4). 112pp. Feiler's interesting descriptions of his travels to biblical sites throughout the Middle East are accompanied by photographs and maps. (Rev: BL 10/1/04; SLJ 11/04) [222]

2010 Gaskins, Pearl Fuyo. *I Believe In . . .: Christian, Jewish, and Muslim Young People Speak About Their Faiths* (7–10). 2004, Cricket $18.95 (0-8126-2713-X). 208pp. Suitable for browsing, this is a collection of interviews with about 100 young adults from diverse religious backgrounds in the Chicago area. (Rev: BCCB 9/04; BL 10/1/04; HB 7–8/04) [200]

2011 *Halloween Howls: Spooky Sounds, Stories and Songs to Scare You Silly* (6–8). 2003, Sourcebooks paper $14.95 (1-4022-0193-1). 179pp. An oversized paperback offers 13 chilling short stories, trivia, games, and decorating tips including selections by Edgar Allan Poe, R. L. Stine, and Bram Stoker; the accompanying CD contains a history of Halloween, songs, eerie sounds, and five of the stories. (Rev: SLJ 6/04)

2012 Hoffman, Nancy. *Sikhism* (6–9). Series: Religions of the World. 2005, Gale LB $28.70 (1-59018-453-X). 128pp. A basic introduction to the beliefs and practices of Sikhism, with a chronology of important events. (Rev: SLJ 2/06) [294.6]

2013 Lottridge, Celia B. *Stories from Adam and Eve to Ezekiel: Retold from the Bible* (4–7). 2004, Groundwood $24.95 (0-88899-490-7). 192pp. Some of the best-loved stories from the Hebrew Bible are engagingly adapted in this attractively illustrated volume. (Rev: BL 10/1/04; SLJ 4/05) [220]

2014 Mason, Claire. *New Religious Movements: The Impact on Our Lives* (6–10). Series: 21st Century Debates. 2003, Raintree LB $28.56 (0-7398-6032-1). 64pp. Zen Buddhists, Hare Krishnas, Mormons, and Scientologists are all included in this discussion of non-mainstream religious movements and cults around the world. (Rev: SLJ 6/04)

2015 Ward, Elaine. *Old Testament Women* (5–10). Series: Art Revelations. 2004, Enchanted Lion $18.95 (1-59270-011-X). 32pp. Large paintings by masters accompany stories about 18 women including Rachel, Ruth, and Bathsheba. (Rev: SLJ 8/04) [224]

2016 Wilkinson, Philip. *Buddhism* (5–8). Illus. 2003, DK $15.99 (0-7894-9833-2). 64pp. An attractive, well-illustrated overview of the teachings and symbols of Buddhism, with information on history, different forms, important sites, and art and artifacts. (Rev: BL 1/1–15/04) [294.3]

Christianity

2017 Barnes, Trevor. *Christianity* (5–8). Series: World Faiths. 2005, Kingfisher paper $6.95 (0-7534-5880-2). 40pp. This volume expands on the earlier *Kingfisher Book of Religions*, looking at the diversity of practices and rituals within the Christian church worldwide. (Rev: SLJ 10/05) [202]

2018 Connolly, Sean. *New Testament Miracles* (5–10). Series: Art Revelations. 2004, Enchanted Lion $18.95 (1-59270-012-8). 32pp. Presents brief retellings of 12 miracles performed by Jesus Christ, each illustrated by a well-known painting by an eminent artist, such as Rembrandt, El Greco, and Tintoretto. (Rev: SLJ 8/04) [226.7]

2019 Lottridge, Celia B. *Stories from the Life of Jesus* (5–7). 2004, Douglas & McIntyre $24.95 (0-88899-497-4). 128pp. Lottridge draws on the first four books of the New Testament for this illustrated collection of stories. (Rev: BL 5/1/04; HB 7–8/04; SLJ 11/04) [232.9]

2020 Pandell, Karen. *Saint Francis Sings to Brother Sun: A Celebration of His Kinship with Nature* (4–7). 2005, Candlewick $18.99 (0-7636-1563-3). 64pp. The story of Saint Francis of Assisi and his unique relationship with nature includes excerpts from the priest's own writings and is enhanced by mixed-media illustrations. (Rev: BL 12/1/05; SLJ 2/06) [271.302]

2021 Self, David. *Christianity* (5–8). Series: Religions of the World. 2005, World Almanac LB $30.00 (0-8368-5866-2). 48pp. A basic introduction to the beliefs and practices of Christianity, with a chronology of important events. (Rev: SLJ 2/06)

2022 Teece, Geoff. *Christianity* (3–7). Illus. Series: Religion in Focus. 2004, Smart Apple Media LB $18.95 (1-58340-465-1). This slim, photo-filled volume introduces the history, beliefs, and practices of Christianity, covering festivals, sacred places, and a list of denominations. Also use *Buddhism* (2004). (Rev: BL 10/1/04) [202]

2023 Visconte, Guido. *Clare and Francis* (4–7). 2004, Eerdmans $20.00 (0-8028-5269-6). 40pp. Eye-catching artwork highlights the inspiring stories of saints Clare and Francis in this picture book for older readers. (Rev: BL 2/1/04*; SLJ 6/04) [270]

Islam

2024 Barnes, Trevor. *Islam* (5–8). Illus. Series: World Faiths. 2005, Kingfisher paper $6.95 (0-7534-5882-9). 40pp. Originally published in 1999 as part of *The Kingfisher Book of Religions: Festivals, Ceremonies, and Beliefs from Around the World*, this 40-page expanded volume provides a wide-ranging overview of Islam and its followers. (Rev: BL 10/1/05; SLJ 10/05) [297]

2025 Conover, Sarah, and Freda Crane. *Beautiful Signs/Ayat Jamilah: A Treasury of Islamic Wisdom for Children and Parents* (5–7). Series: Little Light of Mine. 2004, Eastern Washington Univ. paper $19.95 (0-910055-94-7). 200pp. Muslim folktales, fables, stories from the Koran, and historic tales originate from countries around the world. (Rev: BL 10/15/04; SLJ 8/04) [297.1]

2026 Dudley, William. *Islam* (8–12). Series: Opposing Viewpoints. 2004, Gale LB $26.96 (0-7377-2238-X); paper $17.96 (0-7377-2239-8). 203pp. Opposing perspectives are offered on wide-ranging topics including the compatibility of Islam with democratic ideals; the status of women; conflicts with Western values; and attitudes toward terrorism and violence. (Rev: BL 10/1/04; SLJ 12/04) [297.2]

2027 Egendorf, Laura K., ed. *Islam in America* (7–12). Series: At Issue. 2005, Gale LB $28.70 (0-7377-2727-6). 112pp. Essays cover topics including discrimination against Muslims, the growing popularity of the religion among Hispanic Americans, and the degree of support of terrorism. (Rev: SLJ 2/06) [297]

2028 Einfeld, Jann, ed. *Is Islam a Religion of War or Peace?* (7–9). Series: At Issue. 2005, Gale LB $28.70 (0-7377-3100-4). 108pp. Opposing perspectives on Islam's attitude toward violence are examined in this thought-provoking collection of essays, many of which quote from the Koran in support of their assertions. (Rev: SLJ 11/05) [297]

Judaism

2029 Keene, Michael. *Judaism* (5–8). Series: Religions of the World. 2005, World Almanac LB $30.00 (0-8368-5869-7). 48pp. A basic introduction to the beliefs and practices of Judaism around the world, with a chronology of important events. (Rev: SLJ 2/06) [296]

2030 Kimmel, Eric A. *Wonders and Miracles: A Passover Companion* (4–8). Illus. 2004, Scholastic $18.95 (0-439-07175-5). 144pp. In addition to a description of the holiday and its rituals, Kimmel provides stories, songs, prayers, poems, and recipes. (Rev: BL 2/15/04*; SLJ 2/04) [296.4]

Society and the Individual

Government and Political Science

United Nations and Other International Organizations

2031 Maddocks, Steven. *UNICEF* (5–8). Series: World Watch. 2004, Raintree LB $27.14 (0-7398-6617-6). 48pp. Introduces UNICEF's history, organization, and work on behalf of the world's children; sidebars provide key facts and relevant quotations. (Rev: BL 4/1/04; SLJ 6/04) [362.7]

2032 Ross, Stewart. *United Nations* (5–8). Illus. Series: World Watch. 2004, Raintree LB $18.99 (0-7398-6616-8). 48pp. Ross explains the role of the United Nations as an international watchdog and provides a brief review of its history and organization. (Rev: BL 4/1/04) [341.23]

International Relations, Peace, and War

2033 Bixler, Mark. *The Lost Boys of Sudan: An American Story of the Refugee Experience* (8–12). Illus. 2005, Univ. of Georgia $24.95 (0-8203-2499-X). 288pp. Journalist Bixler tracks the progress of four young men — refugees who were part of the so-called Lost Boys of Sudan — as they adjust to their new lives in America. (Rev: BL 2/1/05) [962.404]

2034 Dalton, Dave. *Refugees and Asylum Seekers* (7–10). Illus. Series: People on the Move. 2005, Heinemann LB $21.95 (1-4034-6961-X). 56pp. A look at the plight of civilians who have been forced from their native lands by war or ethnic cleansing; a poor layout is offset by the personal stories. (Rev: BL 8/05; SLJ 12/05) [305.9]

2035 Dalton, David. *Living in a Refugee Camp: Carbino's Story* (6–9). Illus. Series: Children in Crisis. 2005, World Almanac LB $22.50 (0-8368-5960-X). 48pp. A Sudanese native tells the story of his 14-year exile from his country; background information and photographs add context. (Rev: SLJ 11/05)

2036 Gottfried, Ted. *The Fight for Peace: A History of Antiwar Movements in America* (8–11). Illus. Series: People's History. 2005, Twenty-First Century LB $26.60 (0-7613-2932-3). 136pp. Chronicles the history of American protest movements from the Civil War to the present. (Rev: BL 10/1/05; SLJ 11/05) [303.6]

2037 *Making It Home: Real Life Stories from Children Forced to Flee* (5–8). Illus. 2006, Dial $17.99 (0-8037-3083-7); paper $6.99 (0-14-240455-1). 144pp. The horrific impact of war on children is documented in these first-person accounts, with many photographs, from children who were displaced from their homes in Afghanistan, Bosnia, Burundi, Congo, Iraq, Kosovo, Liberia, and Sudan. (Rev: BL 12/1/05; SLJ 2/06) [305.23]

2038 Newcomb, Rain. *The Master Spy Handbook* (4–7). 2005, Lark $17.95 (1-57990-626-5). 96pp. This guide to the tricks of the trade for spies is presented in the form of a fictionalized first-person narrative by a kid detective. (Rev: BL 1/1–15/06) [327.12]

United States Government and Institutions

General and Miscellaneous

2039 McIntosh, Kenneth, and Marsha McIntosh. *When Religion and Politics Mix: How Matters of*

179

Faith Influence Political Policies (7–10). Illus. Series: Religion and Modern Culture. 2006, Mason Crest LB $22.95 (1-59084-971-X). 112pp. Statistics from the 2004 election provide a basis for this overview of Americans' views on religion and politics. (Rev: BL 4/1/06) [201]

The Constitution

2040 Eck, Kristin. *Drafting the Constitution: Weighing the Evidence to Draw Sound Conclusions* (5–8). Illus. Series: Critical Thinking in American History. 2005, Rosen LB $18.95 (1-4042-0412-1). 48pp. This slim volume offers a review of the issues debated at the Constitutional Convention, plus study questions, a reading list, and a Web site with links to related online resources. (Rev: BL 10/15/05) [342.7302]

2041 Finkelman, Paul. *The Constitution* (4–8). Series: American Documents. 2006, National Geographic LB $23.90 (0-7922-7975-1). 48pp. An unusually attractive introduction to the Constitution, with reproductions, photographs, and profiles of key individuals. (Rev: SLJ 2/06) [342.73]

2042 Friedman, Ian C. *Freedom of Speech and the Press* (7–12). Series: American Rights. 2005, Facts on File $35.00 (0-8160-5662-5). 128pp. Issues relating to the freedoms of speech and the press — in the past, present, and future — are explored in this title. (Rev: SLJ 12/05)

2043 Head, Tom. *Freedom of Religion* (7–10). Illus. Series: American Rights. 2005, Facts on File $35.00 (0-8160-5664-1). 146pp. Examines the significance of freedom of religion as guaranteed by the First Amendment to the Constitution and provides an overview of the role played by religion in America's early history, the Scopes trial, and questions surrounding school prayer. (Rev: BL 10/15/05) [323.44]

2044 Horn, Geoffrey M. *The Bill of Rights and Other Amendments* (5–8). Series: World Almanac Library of American Government. 2004, World Almanac LB $29.26 (0-8368-5475-6). 48pp. A thorough and detailed examination of the process of changing the Constitution and the issues underlying the various amendments. (Rev: SLJ 9/04) [342.73]

2045 Johnson, Terry. *Legal Rights* (7–12). Series: American Rights. 2005, Facts on File $35.00 (0-8160-5665-X). 152pp. A look at the controversial issue of legal rights under the U.S. Constitution, with discussion of government initiatives since September 11, 2001. (Rev: SLJ 12/05)

Federal Government, Its Agencies, and Public Administration

2046 Bausum, Ann. *Our Country's Presidents* (5–8). Illus. 2005, National Geographic LB $45.90 (0-7922-9330-4). 208pp. Full of interesting facts, quotations, and illustrations, this new edition has been extended with information on vice presidents, the Electoral College, and presidential security. (Rev: BL 5/15/05; SLJ 4/05) [973]

2047 Esherick, Joan. *The FDA and Psychiatric Drugs: How a Drug Is Approved* (6–10). Illus. Series: Psychiatric Disorders: Drugs and Psychology for the Mind and Body. 2003, Mason Crest LB $24.95 (1-59084-578-1). 124pp. As well as a clear explanation of the drug approval process, this volume contains information on alternative medicines and an interesting look at how treatment of schizophrenia has advanced over time. (Rev: SLJ 5/04)

2048 Horn, Geoffrey M. *The Presidency* (5–8). Series: World Almanac Library of American Government. 2003, World Almanac LB $26.60 (0-8368-5458-6). 48pp. Information on the first lady, the White House, and key presidents add to the coverage here, which includes primary sources as well as many photographs and statistics. (Rev: SLJ 1/04) [973]

2049 Torr, James D., ed. *Homeland Security* (6–12). Series: At Issue. 2004, Gale LB $27.45 (0-7377-2188-X). 122pp. The creation of this department, its duties, and its possible impact on civil liberties are topics raised in this collection of writings expressing different viewpoints. (Rev: BL 2/15/04) [336]

The Law and the Courts

2050 Anderson, Wayne. *Brown v. Board of Education: The Case Against School Segregation* (5–8). Series: Supreme Court Cases Through Primary Sources. 2004, Rosen LB $29.25 (0-8239-4009-8). 64pp. Primary sources — photographs, police records, newspaper clippings, and court documents — provide details of the case and the narrative discusses the historical and social context. Also use *Plessy v. Ferguson: Legalizing Segregation* (2004). (Rev: SLJ 6/04) [345.73]

2051 Anderson, Wayne. *The Chicago Black Sox Trial: A Primary Source Account* (5–8). Illus. Series: Great Trials of the Twentieth Century. 2003, Rosen LB $31.95 (0-8239-3969-3). 64pp. This is a detailed, readable account of the 1919 Chicago Black Sox scandal and the plot to fix the World Series. (Rev: BL 4/1/04; SLJ 6/04; VOYA 4/04) [796.357]

2052 Burnett, Betty. *The Trial of Julius and Ethel Rosenberg: A Primary Source Account* (5–8). Illus. Series: Great Trials of the Twentieth Century. 2004, Rosen LB $21.95 (0-8239-3976-6). 64pp. Primary sources — photographs, original transcripts, quotations, and so forth — give depth to this compelling account of the complex trial. (Rev: BL 4/1/04; SLJ 10/04)

2053 Crewe, Sabrina, and Michael V. Uschan. *The Scottsboro Case* (4–7). Illus. Series: Events That Shaped America. 2005, Gareth Stevens LB $18.50 (0-8368-3407-0). 32pp. A thorough and thought-provoking look at the infamous Scottsboro case in which nine young African Americans were accused of raping two white women. (Rev: BL 1/1–15/05; SLJ 3/05) [345.73]

2054 Donnelly, Karen. *Cruzan v. Missouri: The Right to Die* (5–7). Illus. Series: Supreme Court Cases Through Primary Sources. 2004, Rosen LB $31.95 (0-8239-4014-4). 64pp. The lengthy legal battle for a patient's right to die is chronicled in this account of the Supreme Court's decision in Cruzan *v.* Missouri. (Rev: BL 6/1–15/04; SLJ 6/04) [344.73]

2055 Fireside, Bryna J. *The Trial of the Police Officers in the Shooting Death of Amadou Diallo: A Headline Court Case* (8–11). Illus. Series: Headline Court Cases. 2004, Enslow LB $19.95 (0-7660-2166-1). 128pp. Covers the trial of four New York City police officers for the 1999 shooting of West African immigrant Amadou Diallo. (Rev: BL 2/1/05) [345.73]

2056 Fridell, Ron. *Capital Punishment* (8–12). Series: Open for Debate. 2003, Benchmark LB $25.95 (0-7614-1587-4). 144pp. Strong illustrations, graphs, and sidebars add to the narrative on the history of the death penalty, the arguments for and against, and ways to make the system more just and humane. (Rev: SLJ 3/04) [346.66]

2057 Gold, Susan Dudley. *Brown v. Board of Education: Separate But Equal?* (7–12). Series: Supreme Court Milestones. 2004, Benchmark LB $25.95 (0-7614-1842-3). 143pp. An overview of the groundbreaking decision, with information on the key individuals involved and on the legal process itself plus human-interest stories that add depth. (Rev: SLJ 1/05) [344.73]

2058 Gold, Susan Dudley. *The Pentagon Papers: National Security or the Right to Know* (7–12). Series: Supreme Court Milestones. 2004, Benchmark LB $25.95 (0-7614-1843-1). 144pp. An easily understood account of the events surrounding the Pentagon Papers case and the high court's decision that blocked the Nixon administration's efforts to keep the papers secret. (Rev: SLJ 1/05) [342.73]

2059 Himton, Kerry. *The Trial of Sacco and Vanzetti: A Primary Source Account* (5–8). Illus. Series: Great Trials of the Twentieth Century. 2004, Rosen LB $21.95 (0-8239-3973-1). 64pp. Primary sources — photographs, original transcripts, quotations, and so forth — give depth to this compelling account of the complex trial. (Rev: BL 4/1/04; SLJ 6/04)

2060 Horn, Geoffrey M. *The Supreme Court* (5–8). Series: World Almanac Library of American Government. 2003, World Almanac LB $26.60 (0-8368-5459-4). 48pp. An excellent introduction to the U.S.

Supreme Court and the important role it plays in interpreting the laws of the land. (Rev: SLJ 1/04)

2061 Hulm, David. *United States v. the Amistad: The Question of Slavery in a Free Country* (6–8). Series: Supreme Court Cases Through Primary Sources. 2004, Rosen LB $29.25 (0-8239-4013-6). 64pp. Using many primary documents, this volume retells the story of the slave revolt aboard the *Amistad* in 1839 and the resulting legal battle that went all the way to the Supreme Court. (Rev: SLJ 6/04) [326]

2062 Jacobs, Thomas A. *They Broke the Law, You Be the Judge: True Cases of Teen Crime* (7–12). 2003, Free Spirit paper $15.95 (1-57542-134-8). 224pp. A former juvenile court judge presents 21 real-life cases involving juveniles, gives the reader the sentencing options, and reveals the actual outcome of each case. (Rev: BL 2/1/04; SLJ 1/04) [345.73]

2063 Koopmans, Andy. *Leopold and Loeb: Teen Killers* (7–12). Series: Famous Trials. 2004, Gale LB $21.96 (1-59018-227-8). 112pp. The story of the famous trial of two privileged boys for the murder of a third, with details of Clarence Darrow's innovative defense strategy. (Rev: SLJ 6/04) [345.73]

2064 Kowalski, Kathiann M. *Lemon v. Kurtzman and the Separation of Church and State Debate* (8–12). Series: Debating Supreme Court Decisions. 2005, Enslow LB $26.60 (0-7660-2391-5). 128pp. This well-documented title examines the Supreme Court's decision in Lemon *v.* Kurtzman and reviews its impact on the doctrine of separation of church and state. (Rev: SLJ 12/05)

2065 Naden, Corinne J., and Rose Blue. *Dred Scott: Person or Property?* (5–8). Illus. Series: Supreme Court Milestones. 2005, Benchmark LB $25.95 (0-7614-1841-5). 144pp. The Supreme Court's 1857 Dred Scott decision, arguably the high court's most misguided ruling ever, is examined in detail. (Rev: BL 2/1/05) [342.7]

2066 Olson, Steven P. *The Trial of John T. Scopes: A Primary Source Account* (5–8). Series: Great Trials of the Twentieth Century. 2004, Rosen LB $29.25 (0-8239-3974-X). 64pp. Primary sources — photographs, original transcripts, quotations, and so forth — give depth to this compelling account of the complex trial. (Rev: BL 4/1/04; SLJ 8/04) [344.73]

2067 Payment, Simone. *Roe v. Wade: The Right to Choose* (5–7). Illus. Series: Supreme Court Cases Through Primary Sources. 2004, Rosen LB $31.95 (0-8239-4012-8). 64pp. Illustrations are used to good effect in this overview of the issues raised in the Supreme Court's landmark decision. (Rev: BL 6/1–15/04; SLJ 6/04) [342.73]

2068 Payment, Simone. *The Trial of Leopold and Loeb: A Primary Source Account* (5–8). Illus. Series: Great Trials of the Twentieth Century. 2004,

Rosen LB $21.95 (0-8239-3970-7). 64pp. Primary sources — photographs, original transcripts, quotations, and so forth — give depth to this compelling account of the complex trial. (Rev: BL 4/1/04; SLJ 6/04; VOYA 4/04)

2069 Roensch, Greg. *The Lindbergh Baby Kidnapping Trial: A Primary Source Account* (5–8). Series: Great Trials of the Twentieth Century. 2004, Rosen LB $29.25 (0-8239-3971-5). 64pp. Primary sources — photographs, original transcripts, handwriting samples, and so forth — give depth to this account of this controversial trial. (Rev: BL 4/1/04; SLJ 8/04) [345.73]

2070 Scheppler, Bill. *The Mississippi Burning Trial: A Primary Source Account* (5–8). Illus. Series: Great Trials of the Twentieth Century. 2004, Rosen LB $21.95 (0-8239-3972-3). 64pp. Primary sources — photographs, original transcripts, quotations, and so forth — give depth to this compelling account of the complex trial. (Rev: BL 4/1/04; SLJ 10/04)

2071 Somervill, Barbara A. *Brown v. Board of Education: The Battle for Equal Education* (5–8). Series: Journey to Freedom. 2005, Child's World LB $28.50 (1-59296-229-7). 40pp. A brief overview of the landmark Supreme Court case that sounded a death knell for school segregation in America. (Rev: SLJ 8/05)

2072 Sonneborn, Liz. *Miranda v. Arizona: The Rights of the Accused* (5–8). Series: Supreme Court Cases Through Primary Sources. 2004, Rosen LB $29.25 (0-8239-4010-1). 64pp. Primary sources — photographs, police records, newspaper clippings, and court documents — provide details of the case and the narrative discusses the historical and social context. (Rev: BL 6/1–15/04; SLJ 6/04) [345.73]

2073 Sorensen, Lita. *The Scottsboro Boys Trial: A Primary Source Account* (5–8). Illus. 2003, Rosen LB $31.95 (0-8239-3975-8). 64pp. Sorensen dissects the sensational Scottsboro Boys rape case in Alabama that attracted media attention from around the globe. (Rev: BL 4/1/04) [345.761]

2074 Telgen, Diane. *Brown v. Board of Education* (8–12). Series: Defining Moments. 2005, Omnigraphics LB $38.00 (0-7808-0775-8). 246pp. An accessible examination of the landmark Supreme Court decision on school segregation, including many interesting sidebar features and chronicling events before and after the ruling, up to the present day. (Rev: SLJ 12/05*)

2075 Torr, James D. *The Patriot Act* (7–12). Series: The Lucent Terrorism Library. 2005, Gale LB $28.70 (1-59018-774-1). 96pp. Torr explores the provisions of this controversial piece of legislation and looks at the ongoing criticisms about its threats to privacy and the Fourth Amendment. (Rev: SLJ 3/06) [345.73]

2076 Wecht, Cyril H., ed. *Crime Scene Investigation: Crack the Case with Real-Life Experts* (8–12). Illus. 2004, Reader's Digest $26.95 (0-7621-0540-2). 192pp. Fans of television's popular *CSI* series will be fascinated by this step-by-step examination of the crime scene investigation process. (Rev: SLJ 4/05)

Politics

ELECTIONS

2077 Goldman, David J. *Presidential Losers* (6–9). Illus. 2004, Lerner LB $28.45 (0-8225-0100-7). 72pp. From Aaron Burr to Al Gore, this account profiles unsuccessful presidential candidates across two centuries of American history. (Rev: BL 4/1/04) [973]

2078 Horn, Geoffrey M. *Political Parties, Interest Groups, and the Media* (5–8). Series: World Almanac Library of American Government. 2004, World Almanac LB $29.26 (0-8368-5478-0). 48pp. An engaging introduction to the world of politics, the importance of money and lobbying, and the role of the press. (Rev: SLJ 9/04) [324]

2079 Marzilli, Alan. *Election Reform* (7–10). Series: Point/Counterpoint. 2003, Chelsea House LB $25.95 (0-7910-7698-9). 123pp. The thorny topics of voter registration, campaign contributions, and political advertising are discussed after an account of the November 2000 Florida recount. (Rev: SLJ 6/04) [324.6]

The Armed Forces

2080 Haney, Eric L. *Inside Delta Force: The Story of America's Elite Counterterrorist Unit* (7–10). 2006, Delacorte LB $17.99 (0-385-90273-5). 192pp. Haney, one of the founding members of Delta Force, offers a fascinating look inside the U.S. Army's elite counterterrorist unit. (Rev: BL 2/1/06; SLJ 3/06) [356]

2081 Zeinert, Karen, and Mary Miller. *The Brave Women of the Gulf Wars: Operation Desert Storm and Operation Iraqi Freedom* (5–8). Illus. Series: Women at War. 2005, Twenty-First Century LB $30.60 (0-7613-2705-3). 112pp. Highlights women's roles in the Persian Gulf military campaigns. (Rev: BL 10/1/05; SLJ 11/05) [956.7]

Citizenship and Civil Rights

General and Miscellaneous

2082 Ellis, Richard J. *To the Flag: The Unlikely History of the Pledge of Allegiance* (7–12). Illus. 2005, Univ. Press of Kansas $29.95 (0-7006-1372-2). 312pp. Traces the history of the Pledge of Allegiance and the flap over two words — "under God" — that were inserted into the pledge nearly 60 years after it was written. (Rev: BL 3/1/05) [323.6]

2083 Grodin, Elissa. *D Is for Democracy: A Citizen's Alphabet* (5–8). 2004, Sleeping Bear $16.95 (1-58536-234-4). 40pp. From "Amendment" to "Zeitgeist," this is an exploration of key concepts, people, places, and things, with the emphasis on the United States. (Rev: BL 1/1–15/05; SLJ 10/04) [320.973]

Civil and Human Rights

2084 Bausum, Ann. *Freedom Riders: John Lewis and Jim Zwerg on the Front Lines of the Civil Rights Movement* (6–9). 2005, National Geographic LB $28.90 (0-7922-4174-6). 80pp. The passion of those involved in the 1961 Freedom Rides is captured in these profiles of two young men — John Lewis and Jim Zwerg — who played key roles in the protests. (Rev: BL 2/1/06*) [323]

2085 Bausum, Ann. *With Courage and Cloth: Winning the Fight for a Woman's Right to Vote* (6–12). 2004, National Geographic $32.90 (0-7922-6996-9). 112pp. A lively, well-illustrated text chronicles the history of the women's suffrage movement in America, focusing in particular on the period between 1913 and 1920 when the more militant National Women's Party, led by Alice Paul, stepped up pressure for women's right to vote. (Rev: BCCB 1/05; BL 10/15/04; SLJ 9/04) [324.6]

2086 Fridell, Ron. *Privacy vs. Security: Your Rights in Conflict* (6–9). Series: Issues in Focus. 2004, Enslow LB $20.95 (0-7660-2161-0). 128pp. The importance of protecting privacy is balanced against the interests of national security, with discussion of many topics from hidden cameras to medical records to airport searches. (Rev: SLJ 9/04) [342.7308]

2087 Gay, Kathlyn. *Cultural Diversity: Conflicts and Challenges: The Ultimate Teen Guide* (7–12). Series: It Happened to Me. 2003, Scarecrow paper $25.95 (0-8108-4805-8). 121pp. Prejudice, stereotypes, and intolerance are among the topics discussed in this overview of the challenges faced and the possible solutions; teens' personal stories add immediacy. (Rev: SLJ 5/04; VOYA 4/04) [305.8]

2088 Hudson, David L., Jr. *Gay Rights* (8–12). Series: Point/Counterpoint. 2004, Chelsea House LB $25.95 (0-7910-8094-3). 114pp. Both sides of the heated debate over gay rights are addressed, including the peripheral issues of military service, rights in the workplace, gay marriage, and adoption rights. (Rev: SLJ 4/05) [305.9]

2089 Kops, Deborah. *Women's Suffrage* (5–8). Illus. Series: People at the Center. 2004, Gale LB $18.96 (1-56711-772-4). 48pp. This brief but fact-filled volume introduces key leaders in the women's suffrage movement in America. (Rev: BL 5/15/04; SLJ 9/04) [324.6]

2090 McKissack, Patricia C., and Arlene Zarembka. *To Establish Justice: Citizenship and the Constitution* (6–10). Illus. 2004, Knopf LB $20.99 (0-679-99308-8). 160pp. Legal decisions regarding the civil rights of various minority groups — Native Americans, slaves, immigrants, women, students, gays and lesbians — are reviewed in light of the mainstream thinking of the time. (Rev: BL 10/15/04; SLJ 10/04; VOYA 10/04) [342.7]

2091 McWhorter, Diane. *Dream of Freedom: The Civil Rights Movement from 1954–1968* (6–8). 2004, Scholastic $19.95 (0-439-57678-4). 160pp. A sweeping, chronological survey of the modern civil rights movement, with personal commentary and many photographs. (Rev: BL 11/15/04*; SLJ 12/04; VOYA 4/05) [323.1]

2092 Mayer, Robert H. *The Civil Rights Act of 1964* (6–12). Series: At Issue in History. 2004, Gale LB $22.96 (0-7377-2304-1); paper $15.96 (0-7377-2305-X). 128pp. The landmark act is described in an introductory overview followed by a collection of essays, speeches, and editorials that provide diverse views about the legislation and its impact on race relations in the United States. (Rev: BL 9/1/04; SLJ 9/04) [342.73]

2093 Morrison, Toni. *Remember: The Journey to School Integration* (5–12). Illus. 2004, Houghton $18.00 (0-618-39740-X). 80pp. With striking archival photographs and a fictionalized narrative based on historical fact, this fascinating book explores the impact of the American struggle for civil rights on the children who were often at its center. (Rev: BL 4/15/04; SLJ 6/04) [379.2]

2094 Nakaya, Andrea C., ed. *Censorship* (7–12). Series: Opposing Viewpoints. 2005, Gale LB $34.95 (0-7377-2925-2); paper $23.70 (0-7377-2926-0). 192pp. This new edition adds thoughtful essays on censorship and free speech as they relate to the press, telemarketing, electronic filtering, spam, and other issues. (Rev: SLJ 9/05) [363.3]

2095 Nakaya, Andrea C., ed. *Civil Liberties and War* (8–11). Illus. Series: Examining Issues Through Political Cartoons. 2005, Gale LB $21.96 (0-7377-2517-6). 78pp. A current hot-button issue — the suspension of civil liberties during wartime — is put into historical perspective in this volume with cartoons dating from the wars as far back as the Civil War. (Rev: BL 2/1/06) [323]

2096 Ojeda, Auriana, ed. *Slavery Today* (6–12). Series: At Issue. 2004, Gale LB $27.45 (0-7377-1613-4). 80pp. The problem of slavery today, particularly in some African countries, is explored in this collection of writings. (Rev: BL 2/15/04; SLJ 7/04) [326]

2097 Sirimarco, Elizabeth. *The Civil Rights Movement* (6–9). Illus. Series: American Voices From. 2004, Benchmark LB $23.95 (0-7614-1697-8). 135pp. Primary source documents and excellent illustrations are accompanied by good introductory text and "Think about This" questions. (Rev: SLJ 2/05) [973]

Immigration

2098 Aykroyd, Clarissa. *Refugees* (8–12). Series: The Changing Face of North America: Immigration Since 1965. 2004, Mason Crest LB $24.95 (1-59084-692-3). 112pp. An overview of the origins of refugees to the United States and Canada, the reasons for their flight from their home countries, and the process they must undergo on arrival. (Rev: SLJ 11/04)

2099 Outman, James L., and Lawrence W. Baker. *U.S. Immigration and Migration Primary Sources* (7–10). Series: Immigration and Migration Reference Library. 2004, Gale $60.00 (0-7876-7669-1). 232pp. Primary source documents — including articles, letters, and Supreme Court rulings — chronicle the history of immigration to and migration within America. (Rev: SLJ 2/05) [304.8]

2100 Roleff, Tamara L., ed. *Immigration* (7–12). Series: Opposing Viewpoints: World History. 2004, Gale LB $33.70 (0-7377-1701-7). 240pp. Pros and cons concerning immigration are presented in this collection of opposing viewpoints. (Rev: BL 2/15/04) [325]

2101 Sherman, Augustus F. *Augustus F. Sherman: Ellis Island Portraits, 1905–1920* (8–12). Illus. 2005, Aperture $40.00 (1-931788-60-X). 160pp. Moving photographs taken by an Ellis Island immigration clerk spotlight would-be immigrants — many of them young people — who were held for further interrogation. (Rev: BL 5/15/05) [779.9]

2102 Staeger, Rob. *Asylees* (8–12). Series: The Changing Face of North America: Immigration Since 1965. 2004, Mason Crest LB $24.95 (1-59084-685-0). 112pp. An overview of asylum seekers in the United States and Canada and the process they must undergo on arrival. Also use *Deported Aliens* (2004). (Rev: SLJ 11/04)

2103 Wills, Chuck. *Destination America: The People and Cultures That Created a Nation* (7–12). Illus. 2005, DK $35.00 (0-7566-1344-2). 284pp. A companion to the PBS series of the same name, this volume examines the waves of immigration that helped to shape the United States into the country it is today. (Rev: BL 12/1/05) [973]

Ethnic Groups and Prejudice

African Americans

2104 Fradin, Judith Bloom, and Dennis Brindell Fradin. *5,000 Miles to Freedom: Ellen and William Craft's Flight from Slavery* (6–9). Illus. 2005, National Geographic LB $29.90 (0-7922-7886-0). 96pp. Ellen and William Craft, a married couple, escaped slavery in Georgia only to find they were in danger again in Boston; this appealing volume documents their adventures, including their flight to England. (Rev: BL 3/15/06) [326.0]

2105 Haley, James, ed. *Reparations for American Slavery* (6–12). Series: At Issue. 2004, Gale LB $27.45 (0-7377-1340-2). 80pp. The arguments for and against the payments or other compensation for the years of slavery to present-day African Americans are the subject of this collection of writings. (Rev: BL 2/15/04) [326]

2106 Horton, James Oliver. *Landmarks of African American History* (8–12). Series: American Landmarks. 2005, Oxford LB $30.00 (0-19-514118-0). 207pp. A tour of 13 historic sites that played a significant role in African American history, with good illustrations and maps. (Rev: SLJ 8/05) [973]

2107 Hudson, Wade. *Powerful Words* (5–9). 2004, Scholastic $19.95 (0-439-40969-1). 192pp. Excerpts from the writings and speeches of both well-known and less-familiar African Americans are accompanied by notes on the context and the writer. (Rev: BL 2/15/04; SLJ 2/04) [081]

2108 Rappaport, Doreen. *Free at Last! Stories and Songs of Emancipation* (4–8). 2004, Candlewick $19.99 (0-7636-1440-8). 64pp. First-hand accounts form the basis of this portrait of the black experience from emancipation to the 1954 Supreme Court decision declaring school segregation illegal. (Rev: BL 2/15/04*; HB 5–6/04; SLJ 2/04) [973]

2109 Sharp, Anne Wallace. *A Dream Deferred: The Jim Crow Era* (7–10). Illus. Series: Lucent Library of Black History. 2005, Gale LB $22.96 (1-59018-700-8). 112pp. An overview of the impact of the Jim Crow laws that stretched from Reconstruction to the Supreme Court's decision in Brown *v.* Board of Education (1954). (Rev: BL 10/15/05) [323.1196]

2110 Summers, Barbara, ed. *Open the Unusual Door: True Life Stories of Challenge, Adventure, and Success by Black Americans* (8–11). 2005, Houghton paper $7.99 (0-618-58531-1). 224pp. Sixteen successful African Americans write about choices they made that changed the direction of their lives. (Rev: BL 1/1–15/06; SLJ 12/05) [920]

Asian Americans

2111 Coleman, Lori. *Vietnamese in America* (4–8). Series: In America. 2004, Lerner LB $27.93 (0-8225-3951-9). 72pp. The reasons for Vietnamese migration to the United States and the life the newcomers find when they arrive are discussed in engaging narrative, with personal stories, notes on key figures, illustrations, and a timeline. Also use *Koreans in America* (2004). (Rev: BL 11/15/04; SLJ 3/05) [973]

2112 Harkrader, Lisa. *South Korea* (5–8). Illus. Series: Top Ten Countries of Recent Immigrants. 2004, Enslow LB $25.26 (0-7660-5181-1). 48pp. Information on South Korea — culture, history, climate, and people — accompanies an explanation of the reasons for migration to the United States and discussion of the contributions of this community; supported by Web links. (Rev: SLJ 3/05) [304]

2113 Oppenheim, Joanne. *Dear Miss Breed: True Stories of the Japanese American Incarceration During World War II and a Librarian Who Made a Difference* (7–10). Illus. 2006, Scholastic $22.99 (0-439-56992-3). 288pp. An affecting portrait of a World War II children's librarian and the incarcerated young Japanese Americans who benefited from her commitment to her profession. (Rev: BL 1/1–15/06*; SLJ 3/06; VOYA 2/06) [940.53]

2114 Teitelbaum, Michael. *Chinese Immigrants* (5–8). Series: Immigration to the United States. 2004, Facts on File $35.00 (0-8160-5687-0). 96pp. After an overview of the reasons underlying immigration in general, this illustrated volume looks at the circumstances of migrants from China, the group's history in the United States, and the contemporary situation, with sidebar features, a timeline, and a glossary. (Rev: SLJ 4/05)

Hispanic Americans

2115 Behnke, Alison. *Mexicans in America* (4–8). Series: In America. 2004, Lerner LB $27.93 (0-8225-3955-1). 80pp. The reasons for Mexican migration to the United States and the life the newcomers find when they arrive are discussed in engaging narrative, with personal stories, notes on key figures, illustrations, and a timeline. (Rev: SLJ 3/05) [304.8]

2116 Taus-Bolstad, Stacy. *Puerto Ricans in America* (5–8). Series: In America. 2004, Lerner LB $27.93 (0-8225-3953-5). 80pp. This overview of Puerto Rican migration to the United States looks at the motivations for moving and explores the lives of the new arrivals and the traditions they maintained. (Rev: BL 11/15/04) [304.8]

2117 Tobar, Héctor. *Translation Nation: Defining a New American Identity in the Spanish Speaking United States* (8–12). 2005, Riverhead $24.95 (1-57322-305-0). 320pp. Tobar, a Pulitzer Prize-winning journalist, explores how the rapidly growing Spanish-speaking population is changing the face of America, presenting his own story (he was born in Los Angeles to Guatemalan immigrants) and the experiences and aspirations of many legal and illegal migrants. (Rev: BL 3/15/05) [305.868]

2118 Worth, Richard. *Mexican Immigrants* (5–8). Series: Immigration to the United States. 2004, Facts on File $35.00 (0-8160-5690-0). 96pp. After an overview of the reasons underlying immigration in general, this illustrated volume looks at the circumstances of migrants from Mexico, the group's history in the United States, and the contemporary situation, with sidebar features, a timeline, and a glossary. Also use *Jewish Immigrants* and *Africans in America* (both 2004). (Rev: SLJ 4/05) [304.8]

Jewish Americans

2119 Rubin, Susan G. *L'Chaim! to Jewish Life in America! Celebrating from 1654 Until Today* (7–9). 2004, Abrams $24.95 (0-8109-5035-9). 176pp. This beautifully illustrated volume chronicles the history of Jews in America with many quotations and personal stories. (Rev: BL 11/1/04; SLJ 1/05; VOYA 2/05) [973]

Other Ethnic Groups

2120 Burgan, Michael. *Italian Immigrants* (5–8). Series: Immigration to the United States. 2004, Facts on File $35.00 (0-8160-5681-1). 96pp. After an overview of the reasons underlying immigration in general, this illustrated volume looks at the circumstances of migrants from Italy, the group's history in the United States, and the contemporary situation, with sidebar features, a timeline, and a glossary. (Rev: SLJ 4/05)

2121 Goldstein, Margaret J. *Irish in America* (5–8). Series: In America. 2004, Lerner LB $27.93 (0-8225-3950-0). 80pp. This overview of Irish migration to the United States looks at the underlying reasons for the exodus and explores the lives of the new arrivals and the traditions they maintained. (Rev: BL 11/15/04) [973]

2122 Howard, Helen. *Living as a Refugee in America: Mohammed's Story* (6–9). Illus. Series: Children in Crisis. 2005, World Almanac $22.50 (0-8368-5959-6). 48pp. This accessible story about Mohammed, an Afghan teenager who fled the Taliban with his family and eventually made his way to the United States, incorporates historical and cultural information plus discussion of such topics as discrimination. (Rev: BL 12/1/05*; SLJ 11/05) [973.086]

2123 Ingram, W. Scott. *Greek Immigrants* (5–8). Series: Immigration to the United States. 2004, Facts on File $35.00 (0-8160-5689-7). 96pp. After an overview of the reasons underlying immigration in general, this illustrated volume looks at the circumstances of migrants from Greece, the group's history in the United States, and the contemporary

situation, with sidebar features, a timeline, and a glossary. Also use *Japanese Immigrants* and *Polish Immigrants* (both 2004). (Rev: BL 4/1/04; HB 3–4/04; SLJ 4/05)

2124 Paulson, Timothy J. *Irish Immigrants* (5–8). Series: Immigration to the United States. 2004, Facts on File $35.00 (0-8160-5682-X). 96pp. After an overview of the reasons underlying immigration in general, this illustrated volume looks at the circumstances of migrants from Ireland, the group's history in the United States, and the contemporary situation, with sidebar features, a timeline, and a glossary. (Rev: SLJ 4/05)

2125 Schur, Joan Brodsky. *The Arabs* (8–11). Illus. Series: Coming to America. 2005, Gale LB $26.96 (0-7377-2148-0). 218pp. With profiles of several famous Arab Americans (including Ralph Nader and Naomi Shihab Nye), this title uses primary and secondary sources to present an overview of Arab Americans, their reasons for migrating, their social mores, and their adaptation to their new country. (Rev: BL 3/15/05; SLJ 3/05) [973]

2126 Testa, Maria. *Something About America* (6–9). 2005, Candlewick $14.99 (0-7636-2528-0). 96pp. In free verse, Testa recounts the poignant story of a young immigrant from Kosovo who was badly burned as she and her family fled their war-torn homeland. (Rev: BL 8/05; SLJ 9/05; VOYA 2/06) [811]

2127 Trumbauer, Lisa. *German Immigrants* (5–8). Series: Immigration to the United States. 2004, Facts on File $35.00 (0-8160-5683-8). 96pp. After an overview of the reasons underlying immigration in general, this illustrated volume looks at the circumstances of migrants from Germany, the group's history in the United States, and the contemporary situation, with sidebar features, a timeline, and a glossary. Also use *Russian Immigrants* (2004). (Rev: SLJ 4/05)

Forms of Dissent

2128 Williams, Mary E., ed. *Is It Unpatriotic to Criticize One's Country?* (7–9). Series: At Issue. 2005, Gale LB $28.70 (0-7377-2396-3); paper $19.95 (0-7377-2397-1). 77pp. Previously published articles offer diverse views on whether criticism of one's country is unpatriotic. (Rev: SLJ 7/05) [323.6]

Social Concerns and Problems

General and Miscellaneous

2129 Gold, Susan Dudley. *Gun Control* (8–12). Series: Open for Debate. 2003, Benchmark LB $25.95 (0-7614-1584-X). 143pp. An evenhanded survey of the gun control controversy, discussing the Second Amendment, history of legislation, school shootings, and the activities of gun makers and dealers. (Rev: SLJ 3/04) [363.3]

2130 Griffin, Starla. *Girl, 13: A Global Snapshot of Generation e* (6–12). 2005, Hylas paper $22.95 (1-59258-112-9). 239pp. Thirteen-year-olds around the world contributed to this volume, answering questions about their views of the world and writing essays about their lives and aspirations. (Rev: SLJ 2/06)

Environmental Issues

General and Miscellaneous

2131 Ballard, Carol. *The Search for Better Conservation* (4–7). Illus. Series: Science Quest. 2005, Gareth Stevens LB $18.50 (0-8368-4553-6). 32pp. A look at how lack of conservation affects us, and what scientists are doing to tackle this problem. (Rev: BL 4/1/05)

2132 Blatt, Harvey. *America's Environmental Report Card: Are We Making the Grade?* (8–12). Illus. 2004, MIT $27.95 (0-262-02572-8). 284pp. From global warming to water pollution, this volume looks at today's burning environmental issues and potential solutions. (Rev: BL 11/1/04) [363.7]

2133 Burnie, David. *Endangered Planet* (4–8). Illus. Series: Kingfisher Knowledge. 2004, Kingfisher $11.95 (0-7534-5776-8). 63pp. This volume looks at how human requirements threaten the flora, fauna, and resources of our planet. (Rev: BL 9/1/04; SLJ 1/05) [333.95]

2134 Ingram, W. Scott. *The Chernobyl Nuclear Disaster* (5–8). Series: Environmental Disasters. 2005, Facts on File $35.00 (0-8160-5755-9). 100pp. Ingram assesses the continuing environmental fallout from the 1986 Chernobyl nuclear disaster. (Rev: SLJ 11/05) [333.79]

2135 Juettner, Bonnie. *Energy* (5–8). Illus. Series: Our Environment. 2004, Gale LB $23.70 (0-7377-1821-8). 48pp. Answers such questions as "How is energy managed?" and "Are we running out of energy?" in four chapters that feature many illustrations and large type. (Rev: SLJ 4/05) [333.79]

2136 Parks, Peggy. *Global Warming* (5–8). Illus. Series: Lucent Library of Science and Technology. 2004, Gale LB $27.45 (1-59018-319-3). 112pp. Explores the controversies surrounding the theory of global warming and the potential consequences of the Earth's rising temperature. (Rev: BL 1/05)

2137 Parks, Peggy J. *Global Warming* (5–8). Illus. Series: Our Environment. 2004, Gale LB $23.70 (0-7377-1822-6). 48pp. Answers such questions as "Caused by humans or caused by nature?" and "What can be done?" in four chapters that feature many illustrations and large type. (Rev: SLJ 4/05) [363.738]

2138 Parry, Ann. *Greenpeace* (5–8). Illus. Series: Humanitarian Organizations. 2005, Chelsea House LB $20.95 (0-7910-8815-4). 32pp. Maps, timelines, factboxes, and color photographs add to this account of Greenpeace's history and mission. (Rev: SLJ 12/05)

2139 Sheehan, Sean. *Greenpeace* (5–8). Series: World Watch. 2004, Raintree LB $27.14 (0-7398-6612-5). 47pp. A thorough review of the sometimes controversial conservationist organization since its founding in 1970, with some graphic photographs. (Rev: BL 4/1/04; SLJ 3/04) [333.7]

Pollution

2140 Bryan, Nichol. *Exxon Valdez: Oil Spill* (4–8). Illus. Series: Environmental Disasters. 2003, World Almanac LB $29.26 (0-8368-5506-X). 48pp. The environmental impact of the 1989 Exxon Valdez oil spill in Alaska's Prince William Sound is thoughtfully explored in this slim volume about the disaster. (Rev: BL 2/1/04; SLJ 3/04) [363.738]

2141 Bryan, Nichol. *Love Canal: Pollution Crisis* (4–8). Illus. Series: Environmental Disasters. 2003, World Almanac LB $29.26 (0-8368-5508-6). 48pp. A look at the dumping of hazardous industrial wastes in upstate New York and the devastating effects on the area's environment. (Rev: BL 2/1/04; SLJ 3/04) [303.738]

2142 Leacock, Elspeth. *The Exxon Valdez Oil Spill* (5–8). Series: Environmental Disasters. 2005, Facts on File $35.00 (0-8160-5754-0). 100pp. A look at the environmental impact of the 1989 *Exxon Valdez* oil spill in Alaska's Prince William Sound. (Rev: SLJ 11/05) [363.7]

Recycling

2143 Hall, Eleanor J. *Recycling* (5–8). Illus. Series: Our Environment. 2004, Gale LB $23.70 (0-7377-1517-0). 48pp. Answers such questions as "What is recycling?" and "What does the future hold?" in four chapters that feature many illustrations and large type. (Rev: SLJ 4/05) [363.72]

Population Issues

General and Miscellaneous

2144 Atkin, S. Beth. *Gunstories: Life-Changing Experiences with Guns* (7–10). Illus. 2006, Harper-Collins LB $17.89 (0-06-052660-2). 256pp. In first-person accounts, teenagers write about their very varied experiences with guns. (Rev: BL 1/1–15/06; SLJ 1/06) [363.33]

2145 Reef, Catherine. *Alone in the World: Orphans and Orphanages in America* (8–11). Illus. 2005, Clarion $18.00 (0-618-35670-3). 144pp. A history of orphanages in America from the early years of the 18th century through their decline in the early 1900s. (Rev: BL 4/1/05; SLJ 6/05; VOYA 10/05) [362.73]

Crime, Gangs, and Prisons

2146 Albrecht, Kat. *The Lost Pet Chronicles: Adventures of a K–9 Cop Turned Pet Detective*

(8–12). 2004, Bloomsbury $23.95 (1-58234-379-9). 224pp. This is a memoir of a former police officer who has become a pet detective and a solver of such crimes as dognapping. (Rev: BL 3/1/04) [363.28]

2147 Balkin, Karen F., ed. *Violence Against Women* (8–12). Series: Current Controversies. 2003, Gale LB $33.70 (0-7377-2041-7); paper $22.45 (0-7377-2042-5). 208pp. Contributors from many walks of life present differing viewpoints on the causes, nature, and extent of violence against women and what can be done to prevent it. (Rev: SLJ 6/04) [362.88]

2148 Barbour, Scott, ed. *Gangs* (8–12). Illus. Series: Introducing Issues with Opposing Viewpoints. 2005, Gale LB $32.45 (0-7377-3221-0). 128pp. Diverse opinions are presented on topics including the reasons why young people join gangs and measures that can be taken to reduce the violence. (Rev: SLJ 1/06) [364.1]

2149 Butterfield, Moira. *Pirates and Smugglers* (5–7). Series: Kingfisher Knowledge. 2005, Kingfisher paper $12.95 (0-7534-5864-0). 64pp. A broad historical survey of outlaws on the high seas, from early smugglers to today's dealers in drugs and exotic animals. (Rev: SLJ 12/05)

2150 Dahl, Michael. *Computer Evidence* (4–8). Illus. Series: Forensic Crime Solvers. 2004, Capstone LB $16.95 (0-7368-2698-X). 32pp. After a story that draws the readers in, Dahl looks at the use of computer evidence in tracking down and convicting criminals. Also use *Poison Evidence* (2004). (Rev: BL 5/1/04)

2151 Dudley, William, and Louise L. Gerdes, eds. *Gangs* (8–12). Series: Opposing Viewpoints. 2005, Gale LB $34.95 (0-7377-2234-7); paper $23.70 (0-7377-2235-5). 206pp. A look at the causes of gang behavior and what can be done to combat the alarming increase in violence. (Rev: SLJ 8/05) [364.1]

2152 Gifford, Clive. *Spies* (5–9). Illus. Series: Kingfisher Knowledge. 2004, Kingfisher LB $11.95 (0-7534-5777-6). 64pp. Stories of notable espionage achievements are included along with brisk facts, plenty of high-interest illustrations, a history of spying, and discussion of the future of this field. (Rev: BL 9/1/04; SLJ 5/05)

2153 Nakaya, Andrea C., ed. *Juvenile Crime* (8–12). Series: Opposing Viewpoints. 2005, Gale LB $34.95 (0-7377-2945-7); paper $23.70 (0-7377-2946-5). 208pp. A collection of diverse opinions on the causes of juvenile crime and on ways to prevent it, to punish or treat offenders, and to improve the juvenile justice system. (Rev: SLJ 1/06) [364.9]

2154 Platt, Richard. *Forensics* (5–10). Illus. Series: Kingfisher Knowledge. 2005, Kingfisher paper $12.95 (0-7534-5862-4). 64pp. This introduction to the use of the forensic sciences in crime investigation is presented in short blocks of text that will make it appealing to reluctant readers. (Rev: SLJ 11/05) [363.2]

2155 Rollins, Barbara B., and Michael Dahl. *Ballistics* (4–7). Series: Edge Books, Forensic Crime Solvers. 2004, Capstone LB $22.60 (0-7368-2421-9). 32pp. Report writers and reluctant readers will be attracted to this brief, concise discussion of the science of ballistics. (Rev: BL 5/1/04; SLJ 8/04) [363.25]

2156 Rollins, Barbara B., and Michael Dahl. *Blood Evidence* (4–8). Illus. Series: Forensic Crime Solvers. 2004, Capstone LB $22.60 (0-7368-2418-9). 32pp. Reluctant readers will be attracted to the gruesome nature of the subject matter and the often lurid presentation of facts. (Rev: BL 5/1/04; SLJ 8/04) [363.25]

2157 Rollins, Barbara B., and Michael Dahl. *Cause of Death* (4–8). Illus. Series: Forensic Crime Solvers. 2004, Capstone LB $22.60 (0-7368-2420-0). 32pp. This look at how crime scene technicians and medical examiners determine cause of death will draw in reluctant readers. (Rev: BL 5/1/04; SLJ 8/04) [614]

2158 Rollins, Barbara B., and Michael Dahl. *Fingerprint Evidence* (4–7). Series: Edge Books, Forensic Crime Solvers. 2004, Capstone LB $22.60 (0-7368-2419-7). 32pp. After a story that draws the readers in, the authors describe the features of fingerprints and discusses their use in solving crimes. (Rev: BL 5/1/04; SLJ 8/04) [363.25]

2159 Schroeder, Andreas. *Scams!* (5–8). Series: True Stories from the Edge. 2004, Annick $18.95 (1-55037-853-8); paper $7.95 (1-55037-852-X). 154pp. Ten stories reveal daring trickery, con jobs, and scams, including the 1938 radio broadcast of *War of the Worlds* that terrified millions of Americans and the baseless claim that a tribe of cavemen had been found living in a remote corner of the Philippines. (Rev: SLJ 8/04) [364.16]

2160 Schroeder, Andreas. *Thieves!* (5–10). Series: True Stories from the Edge. 2005, Annick $18.95 (1-55037-933-X); paper $8.95 (1-55037-932-1). 164pp. Ten world-class crimes are described in compelling detail. (Rev: SLJ 3/06) [364]

2161 Torr, James D., ed. *Guns and Crime* (6–12). Series: At Issue. 2004, Gale LB $27.45 (0-7377-1997-4). 80pp. The relationship between availability of guns and crime is explored in a series of articles and essays that express different viewpoints. (Rev: BL 2/15/04) [363.4]

2162 Yancey, Diane. *Murder* (7–10). Illus. Series: Inside the Crime Lab. 2006, Gale LB $24.96 (1-59018-619-2). 112pp. Readers learn how clues found at a murder scene are analyzed and interpreted to reconstruct what happened; there are references to famous cases, and sidebar features and photographs add interest. (Rev: BL 4/1/06) [363.25]

Poverty, Homelessness, and Hunger

2163 Haugen, David M., and Matthew J. Box, eds. *Poverty* (8–11). Series: Social Issues Firsthand. 2005, Gale LB $22.96 (0-7377-2899-X). 108pp. Wide-ranging essays present the plight of those living in poverty as well as the thoughts of those who are determined to do something about the problem. (Rev: BL 10/15/05) [362.5]

2164 Mason, Paul. *Poverty* (4–7). Illus. Series: Planet Under Pressure. 2006, Heinemann LB $22.00 (1-4034-7743-4). 48pp. A clear presentation of how poverty affects people around the world, with charts, photographs, and profiles. (Rev: BL 4/1/06) [362.5]

Social Action, Social Change, and Futurism

2165 Gay, Kathlyn. *Volunteering: The Ultimate Teen Guide* (8–12). Series: It Happened to Me. 2004, Scarecrow $32.50 (0-8108-4922-4). 127pp. This guide examines a wide range of volunteering opportunities for teenagers, from working with the elderly or the homeless to tutoring to building houses; real-life stories add interest. (Rev: SLJ 4/05; VOYA 4/05) [361.8]

2166 Halpin, Mikki. *It's Your World — If You Don't Like It, Change It: Activism for Teenagers* (7–12). 2004, Simon & Schuster paper $8.99 (0-689-87448-0). 304pp. Covering activism on a wide range of topics — the environment, war, gay rights, women's rights, and so forth — this is a useful guide, providing practical ideas and sensible cautions. (Rev: BL 12/15/04; SLJ 12/04) [305.23]

2167 Karnes, Frances A., and Kristen R. Stephens. *Empowered Girls: A Girl's Guide to Positive Activism, Volunteering, and Philanthropy* (6–12). 2005, Prufrock paper $14.95 (1-59363-163-4). 191pp. A helpful, information-packed guide that will motivate young people to volunteer. (Rev: SLJ 2/06; VOYA 4/06) [361.8]

2168 Marcovitz, Hal. *Teens and Volunteerism* (7–10). Series: The Gallup Youth Survey, Major Issues and Trends. 2005, Mason Crest LB $22.95 (1-59084-877-2). 112pp. An attractive volume documenting Gallup findings on teens' attitudes toward various forms of volunteerism including community service, military service, and activism. (Rev: SLJ 1/06) [361.8]

2169 Shostak, Arthur B., ed. *Futuristics: Looking Ahead* (6–9). Illus. Series: Tackling Tomorrow Today. 2005, Chelsea House LB $27.95 (0-7910-8401-9). 120pp. A collection of thought-provoking essays about the field of futuristics. (Rev: BL 4/1/05) [303.49]

Terrorism

2170 Balkin, Karen F., ed. *The War on Terrorism* (7–12). Illus. Series: Opposing Viewpoints. 2004, Gale LB $33.70 (0-7377-2336-X); paper $22.45 (0-7377-2337-8). 206pp. The 28 essays in this collection present both sides of the ongoing debate over the Bush administration's measures to combat terrorism. (Rev: SLJ 3/05) [973.9]

2171 Bingley, Richard. *Terrorism* (5–9). Series: Face the Facts. 2003, Raintree LB $28.56 (0-7398-6852-7). 56pp. An examination of terrorism, its causes, and the efforts being made to combat it. (Rev: SLJ 4/04) [303.6]

2172 Campbell, Geoffrey. *A Vulnerable America* (7–12). Series: Library of Homeland Security. 2004, Gale LB $27.95 (1-59018-383-5). This book discusses national security, how the government dealt with terrorist attacks in the past, and how 9/11/01 changed intelligence activities. (Rev: BL 4/15/04; SLJ 5/04) [363.3]

2173 Corona, Laurel. *Hunting Down the Terrorists: Declaring War and Policing Global Violations* (7–12). Series: Lucent Library of Homeland Security. 2004, Gale LB $21.96 (1-59018-382-7). 112pp. This account describes international efforts to hunt down terrorists and the cooperative efforts that are emerging. (Rev: BL 5/15/04; SLJ 4/04) [364.1]

2174 Friedman, Lauri S., ed. *How Should the United States Treat Prisoners in the War on Terror?* (7–9). Series: At Issue. 2005, Gale LB $28.70 (0-7377-3113-3); paper $19.95 (0-7377-3114-1). 110pp. Previously published articles examine questions surrounding the Geneva Convention and treatment of detainees in America's war on terror. (Rev: SLJ 7/05)

2175 Katz, Samuel M. *Against All Odds: Counterterrorist Hostage Rescues* (6–12). Series: Terrorist Dossiers. 2004, Lerner LB $26.60 (0-8225-1567-9). 72pp. The notable hostage rescues by antiterrorist groups around the world covered here go back to the early 19th century. (Rev: SLJ 4/05; VOYA 6/05) [364.15]

2176 Katz, Samuel M. *At Any Cost: National Liberation Terrorism* (7–12). Series: Terrorist Dossiers. 2004, Lerner LB $26.60 (0-8225-0949-0). 72pp. This is an excellent introduction to the terrorist groups active today whose cause is the liberation of their homelands. (Rev: BL 3/15/04; SLJ 3/04; VOYA 4/04) [363.2]

2177 Katz, Samuel M. *Jihad: Islamic Fundamentalist Terrorism* (7–12). Illus. Series: Terrorist Dossiers. 2003, Lerner LB $26.60 (0-8225-4031-2). 72pp. A look at Middle East-based terrorist groups, their histories, and present-day activities. (Rev: BL 3/15/04; SLJ 5/04) [303.6]

2178 Katz, Samuel M. *Raging Within: Ideological Terrorism* (7–12). Series: Terrorist Dossiers. 2004, Lerner LB $26.60 (0-8225-4032-0). 72pp. This book examines terrorists whose motivation is based on ideologies and religion. (Rev: BL 3/15/04; SLJ 5/04) [363.2]

2179 Keeley, Jennifer. *Deterring and Investigating Attack* (7–12). Series: Library of Homeland Security. 2004, Gale LB $27.95 (1-59018-374-6). This volume explores the roles played by both the CIA and FBI in counterterrorism and how various kinds of information are found and used. (Rev: BL 4/15/04) [363.32]

2180 Ruschmann, Paul. *The War on Terror* (7–10). Series: Point/Counterpoint. 2005, Chelsea House LB $26.95 (0-7910-8091-9). 134pp. Offers opposing views on terrorism-related topics, including pre-emptive wars, the suspension of human rights, and anti-terror laws. (Rev: SLJ 9/05)

2181 Stewart, Gail B. *Defending the Borders: The Role of Border and Immigration Control* (7–12). Series: Lucent Library of Homeland Security. 2004, Gale LB $21.96 (1-59018-376-2). 112pp. This account presents the difficulties in fighting terrorism and other threats while keeping our borders open. (Rev: BL 5/15/04) [364.1]

2182 Streissguth, Thomas. *Combating the Global Terrorist Threat* (6–8). Illus. Series: American War Library: The War on Terrorism. 2004, Gale LB $21.96 (1-59018-327-4). 112pp. An overview of efforts to combat terrorism in Afghanistan, Iraq, Pakistan, the Philippines, and Saudi Arabia. (Rev: BL 8/04) [973.93]

2183 Torr, James D. *Responding to Attack: Firefighters and Police* (7–12). Series: Lucent Library of Homeland Security. 2004, Gale LB $21.96 (1-59018-375-4). 112pp. This account chronicles the part that the police and firefighters can play in counteracting a terrorist attack. (Rev: BL 5/15/04) [364.1]

2184 Uschan, Michael V. *The Beslan School Siege and Separatist Terrorism* (5–8). Illus. Series: Terrorism in Today's World. 2005, World Almanac LB $22.50 (0-8368-6555-3). 48pp. The deadly 2004 attack on a Russian school by Chechen Muslim terrorists is only the first of several attacks described in this volume on independence movements that use violence. (Rev: BL 4/1/06) [947.5]

2185 Woolf, Alex. *Terrorism: The Impact on Our Lives* (6–10). Series: 21st Century Debates. 2003, Raintree LB $28.56 (0-7398-6034-8). 64pp. From the terror of the French Revolution (when the word first appeared) to the activities of the IRA, Hamas, the PLO, the Tamil Tigers, Basque separatists (ETA), and al Qaeda, this is an overview of terrorism and how it affects us. (Rev: SLJ 6/04)

Economics and Business

General and Miscellaneous

2186 Aaseng, Nathan. *Business Builders in Sweets and Treats* (5–8). Illus. Series: Business Builders. 2005, Oliver LB $24.95 (1-881508-84-6). 160pp. This attractive title examines food companies that succeed through satisfying America's sweet tooth. (Rev: BL 12/1/05) [338.7]

2187 Frisch, Aaron. *The Story of Nike* (6–10). Series: Built for Success. 2003, Smart Apple Media LB $19.95 (1-58340-295-0). 48pp. Traces Nike's development from a small importer to a major internationally recognized brand, with details of successes and setbacks, celebrity endorsements, and advertising campaigns. (Rev: SLJ 7/04) [338.7]

2188 Harman, Hollis Page. *Money $ense for Kids!* 2nd ed. (4–7). Illus. 2004, Barron's paper $10.95 (0-7641-2894-9). 180pp. Explains the basics of money and currency and of earning, saving, and investing, with exercises at the end of each chapter and a "Money Games" section. (Rev: SLJ 11/04) [332.024]

2189 Linecker, Adelia Cellini. *What Color Is Your Piggy Bank? Entrepreneurial Ideas for Self-Starting Kids* (6–8). 2004, Lobster paper $10.95 (1-894222-82-2). 144pp. Suggestions for making money are presented in concise chapters on topics including brainstorming, creating a business plan, advertising, and opening a bank account; tip sheets are provided for common activities such as baby sitting and dog walking. (Rev: BL 6/1–15/04; SLJ 9/04) [650.1]

2190 Richardson, Adele. *The Story of Disney* (6–10). Series: Built for Success. 2003, Smart Apple Media LB $19.95 (1-58340-291-8). 48pp. Traces Disney's development into the major internationally recognized brand it is today, with a biography of Walt Disney, a timeline of important events, discussion of Disney's influence on our lives, and mention of criticism of Disney's liberties with history. (Rev: SLJ 7/04) [384.8]

2191 Schiffman, Stephan. *The Young Entrepreneur's Guide to Business Terms* (7–12). Illus. 2003, Scholastic LB $38.00 (0-531-14665-0). 128pp. A useful, alphabetically arranged guide to business terms and concepts, with feature sidebars. (Rev: BL 1/1–15/04; SLJ 7/04) [650]

2192 Thomas, Keltie. *The Kids Guide to Money Cent$* (4–7). 2004, Kids Can $14.95 (1-55337-389-8); paper $7.95 (1-55337-390-1). 56pp. Readers follow three children — the Money Cent$ Gang — who join together to investigate the ins and outs of banking, credit, investment, and money making; quizzes and examples make the content clear and comic-strip scenes add appeal. (Rev: SLJ 7/04) [332.02]

Money and Trade

2193 January, Brendan. *Globalize It!* (8–12). Illus. 2003, Millbrook LB $26.90 (0-7613-2417-8). 144pp. The continuing advance of globalization and arguments for and against this phenomenon are thoughtfully examined in this accessible overview. (Rev: BL 1/1–15/04; SLJ 5/04) [337]

2194 Kummer, Patricia K. *Currency* (4–8). Series: Inventions That Shaped the World. 2004, Watts LB $29.50 (0-531-12341-3). 80pp. After looking at the nature of currency, this title discusses modern forms and the role of currency in our lives. (Rev: SLJ 2/05) [332.4]

Guidance and Personal Development

Education and Schools

General and Miscellaneous

2195 Bluestein, Jane, and Eric D. Katz. *High School's Not Forever* (8–12). Illus. 2005, Health Communications paper $12.95 (0-7573-0256-4). 302pp. High school students talk about their experiences in high school, covering a range of typical problems plus some of the joys of those years. (Rev: SLJ 1/06) [373.18]

Development of Academic Skills

Writing and Speaking Skills

2196 Nobleman, Marc Tyler. *Extraordinary E-Mails, Letters, and Resumes* (5–8). Series: F. W. Prep. 2005, Watts LB $30.50 (0-531-16759-3). 128pp. Advice for students who want to write effective e-mails, letters, and resumes, with an explanation of the importance of communicating clearly. (Rev: SLJ 1/06) [808]

Academic Guidance

2197 Karnes, Frances A., and Tracy L. Riley. *Competitions for Talented Kids: Win Scholarships, Big Prize Money, and Recognition* (7–10). 2005, Prufrock paper $17.95 (1-59363-156-1). 295pp. More than 140 competitions covering a number of academic subjects, the performing arts, and leadership are listed alphabetically, with brief advice on entering these contests. (Rev: BL 12/1/05) [371.95]

Careers and Occupational Guidance

Careers

General and Miscellaneous

2198 Burns, Monique. *Cool Careers Without College for People Who Love to Make Things Grow* (6–9). Series: Cool Careers Without College. 2004, Rosen LB $30.60 (0-8239-3789-5). 144pp. Explores careers such as landscaper and soil conservationist that do not require college degrees, with application advice and information about activities on the job. (Rev: SLJ 10/04)

2199 Cefrey, Holly. *Archaeologists: Life Digging Up Artifacts* (5–10). Series: Extreme Careers. 2004, Rosen LB $19.95 (0-8239-3963-4). 64pp. This is an introduction to the field of archeology, its problems, its opportunities, and its rewards. (Rev: BL 5/15/04) [930]

2200 Colbert, Judy. *Career Opportunities in the Travel Industry* (8–12). Series: Career Opportunities. 2004, Ferguson $49.50 (0-8160-4864-9). 246pp. A quick overview of the wide number of opportunities in the travel industry, providing an outline of duties, salary ranges, employment outlook, required education and training, and so forth. (Rev: SLJ 7/04) [331.7]

2201 Coon, Nora E. *Teen Dream Jobs: How to Find the Job You Really Want Now!* (8–12). 2004, Beyond Words paper $9.95 (1-58270-093-1). 132pp. Written by a teen, this is a reader-friendly guide that refers teens to online career-choice quizzes, gives advice on job-finding activities, and suggests possible careers and ways to enter them. (Rev: SLJ 6/04)

2202 *Food* (5–9). Series: Discovering Careers for Your Future. 2005, Ferguson $21.95 (0-8160-5848-2). 92pp. Education and training, salaries, and outlook for the field are all covered here along with a description of the kinds of daily activities found in various positions. (Rev: SLJ 1/06)

2203 Greenberger, Robert. *Cool Careers Without College for People Who Love to Drive* (8–12). Series: Cool Careers Without College. 2004, Rosen LB $30.60 (0-8239-3786-0). 144pp. Benefits and disadvantages of this kind of work, education and training, salary outlook, and a description of on-the-job activities are provided for a number of career choices, both working for others and as an entrepreneur. (Rev: SLJ 5/04)

2204 Hinton, Kerry. *Cool Careers Without College for People Who Love Food* (8–12). Series: Cool Careers Without College. 2004, Rosen LB $30.60 (0-8239-3787-9). 144pp. Benefits and disadvantages of this kind of work, education and training, salary outlook, and a description of on-the-job activities are provided for a number of career choices, both working for others and as an entrepreneur. (Rev: SLJ 5/04)

2205 Jackson, Donna M. *ER Vets: Life in an Animal Emergency Room* (5–8). Illus. 2005, Houghton $18.00 (0-618-43663-4). 96pp. With many photos, this is a behind-the-scenes look at life in a veterinary emergency clinic and the frustrations and joys to be found working there. (Rev: BL 11/1/05; SLJ 1/06*) [636.089]

2206 McAlpine, Margaret. *Working in the Fashion Industry* (6–12). Series: My Future Career. 2005, Gareth Stevens LB $26.00 (0-8368-4774-1). 64pp. Seven careers in the field of fashion are highlighted with plenty of good photographs, explanations of a typical day's activities, and "Good Points and Bad Points." (Rev: SLJ 1/06)

2207 McAlpine, Margaret. *Working in the Food Industry* (6–12). Series: My Future Career. 2005, Gareth Stevens LB $26.00 (0-8368-4776-8). 64pp. Seven careers in the food industry are highlighted with plenty of good photographs, explanations of a typical day's activities, and "Good Points and Bad Points." (Rev: SLJ 1/06)

2208 McAlpine, Margaret. *Working with Animals* (6–10). Series: My Future Career. 2005, Gareth Stevens LB $26.00 (0-8368-4240-5). 64pp. In addition to describing various jobs working with animals, McAlpine discusses the best personality type for each task and provides a detailed breakdown of a typical day. (Rev: SLJ 3/05) [636]

2209 McAlpine, Margaret. *Working with Children* (6–10). Series: My Future Career. 2005, Gareth Stevens LB $26.00 (0-8368-4241-3). 64pp. In addition to describing various jobs working with children, McAlpine discusses the best personality type for each one and provides a detailed breakdown of a typical day. (Rev: SLJ 3/05) [362.7]

2210 *Publishing* (5–9). Series: Discovering Careers for Your Future. 2005, Ferguson LB $21.95 (0-8160-5845-8). 92pp. Education and training, salaries, and outlook for the field are all covered here along with a description of the kinds of daily activities found in various positions. (Rev: SLJ 1/06)

2211 Reeves, Diane Lindsey, and Gail Karlitz. *Career Ideas for Teens in Architecture and Construction* (8–12). Illus. Series: Career Ideas for Teens. 2005, Ferguson $40.00 (0-8160-5289-1). 170pp. In addition to details of education requirements, salaries, and so forth, this attractive guide offers interview tips, advice from "real people," and questionnaires. (Rev: SLJ 2/06)

2212 Rosenberg, Aaron. *Cryptologists: Life Making and Breaking Codes* (5–10). Series: Extreme Careers. 2004, Rosen LB $19.95 (0-8239-3965-0). 64pp. After some background material on the history of codes, this volume discusses career opportunities as a cryptologist. (Rev: BL 5/15/04; SLJ 5/90) [410]

2213 Webster, Harriet. *Cool Careers Without College for People Who Love to Work with Children* (8–12). Series: Cool Careers Without College. 2004, Rosen LB $30.60 (0-8239-3792-5). 144pp. Benefits and disadvantages of this kind of work, education and training, salary outlook, and a description of on-the-job activities are provided for a number of career choices, both working for others and as an entrepreneur. (Rev: SLJ 5/04)

2214 Whynott, Douglas. *A Country Practice: Scenes from the Veterinary Life* (7–10). 2004, Farrar $24.00 (0-86547-647-0). 290pp. Covering all aspects of veterinary practice — including finances, staff, and bedside manner — this is an intriguing account of a year in the life of a veterinarian who treats both domestic pets and farm animals. (Rev: BL 11/1/04) [636.089]

Arts, Entertainment, and Sports

2215 *Design*. 2nd ed. (7–12). Series: Careers in Focus. 2005, Ferguson $22.95 (0-8160-5865-2). 188pp. Describes careers in the broad field of design — Including architects, fashion designers, exhibit designers, industrial designers, and toy and game designers. (Rev: SLJ 12/05)

2216 McAlpine, Margaret. *Working in Film and Television* (6–10). Series: My Future Career. 2005, Gareth Stevens LB $26.00 (0-8368-4237-5). 64pp. In addition to describing various jobs in the film and television world, McAlpine discusses the best personality type for each one and provides a detailed breakdown of a typical day. (Rev: SLJ 3/05) [791.43]

2217 McAlpine, Margaret. *Working in Music and Dance* (6–12). Series: My Future Career. 2005, Gareth Stevens LB $26.00 (0-8368-4777-6). 64pp. Seven careers in the fields of music and dance are highlighted with plenty of good photographs, explanations of a typical day's activities, and "Good Points and Bad Points." (Rev: SLJ 1/06)

2218 McLaglen, Mary, et al. *You Can Be a Woman Movie Maker* (4–8). Series: You Can Be a Woman. 2003, Cascade Pass $19.95 (1-880599-64-3); paper $14.95 (1-880599-63-5). 71pp. Three women — a producer, an independent filmmaker, and an executive producer — talk about their jobs, how they got into the movie industry, and what a day on the job is like. Interviews and film clips are on an accompanying DVD. (Rev: SLJ 4/04) [791.43]

2219 *Music* (6–12). 2004, Ferguson LB $22.95 (0-8160-5555-6). 218pp. Describes careers in music, with information on qualifications, working conditions, salaries, opportunities, rewards, and methods of exploring and entering the field. (Rev: SLJ 1/05) [780]

2220 Nathan, Amy. *Meet the Musicians: From Prodigy (or Not) to Pro* (5–8). Illus. 2006, Holt $17.95 (0-8050-7743-X). 156pp. Profiles of members of the New York Philharmonic give readers a good understanding of the different roles of various instruments and the careers of professional musicians. (Rev: BL 3/15/06) [750.92]

2221 Parks, Peggy J. *Musician* (4–7). Illus. Series: Exploring Careers. 2004, Gale LB $18.96 (0-7377-2067-0). 48pp. In addition to a description of the work that musicians (including DJs) do, there is a frank assessment of the opportunities available. (Rev: BL 3/15/04) [780]

2222 Parks, Peggy J. *Writer* (4–7). Illus. Series: Exploring Careers. 2004, Gale LB $18.96 (0-7377-2069-7). 48pp. The ups and downs of a career in writing are frankly discussed in this slim guide. (Rev: BL 3/15/04) [808]

2223 *Radio and Television* (5–9). Series: Discovering Careers for Your Future. 2005, Ferguson LB $21.95 (0-8160-5846-6). 92pp. Education and training, salaries, and outlook for the field are all covered here along with a description of the kinds of daily activities found in various positions. (Rev: SLJ 1/06)

Business

2224 *Advertising and Marketing* (5–9). Series: Discovering Careers for Your Future. 2005, Ferguson $21.95 (0-8160-5847-4). 92pp. Education and training, salaries, and outlook for the field are all covered here along with a description of the kinds of daily activities found in various positions. (Rev: SLJ 1/06)

2225 Giles, M. J. *Young Adult's Guide to a Business Career* (8–12). Illus. 2004, Business Books $14.95 (0-9723714-3-5). 115pp. Full of useful tips, this guide describes more than 25 occupations in business and finance, giving details of benefits and drawbacks, salaries, educational requirements, and so forth. (Rev: SLJ 7/04) [331.7]

2226 Thomason-Carroll, Kristi L. *Young Adult's Guide to Business Communications* (8–12). Illus. 2004, Business Books $14.95 (0-9723714-4-3). 124pp. Full of useful tips, this guide describes the basics required for a job in the business world, including telephone skills, the ability to communicate clearly by letter and e-mail, and proper behavior during meetings. (Rev: SLJ 7/04) [651.7]

Construction and Mechanical Trades

2227 Frew, Katherine. *Plumber* (5–8). Series: Great Jobs. 2004, Children's Pr. LB $20.00 (0-516-24088-9); paper $6.95 (0-516-25935-0). 48pp. This appealing, photo-filled title focuses on the plumbing trade, looking at job requirements, training, and tools, as well as providing a history of the plumbing business and a look at a typical day at work. (Rev: SLJ 7/04) [696]

2228 Overcamp, David. *Electrician* (5–8). Series: Great Jobs. 2004, Children's Pr. LB $20.00 (0-516-24086-2); paper $6.95 (0-516-25924-5). 48pp. This appealing, photo-filled title focuses on the work of an electrician, looking at job requirements, training, and tools, as well as providing a history of the field and a look at a typical day at work. (Rev: SLJ 7/04) [621.3]

2229 Weintraub, Aileen. *Auto Mechanic* (5–8). Series: Great Jobs. 2004, Children's Pr. LB $20.00 (0-516-24090-0); paper $6.95 (0-516-25922-9). 48pp. This appealing, photo-filled title focuses on the work of an auto mechanic, looking at job requirements, training, and tools, as well as provid-

ing a history of the trade and a look at a typical day at work. (Rev: SLJ 7/04) [629.28]

Education and Librarianship

2230 Reeves, Diane Lindsey, and Gail Karlitz. *Career Ideas for Teens in Education and Training* (8–12). Illus. Series: Career Ideas for Teens. 2005, Ferguson $40.00 (0-8160-5295-6). 183pp. In addition to details of education requirements, salaries, and so forth, this attractive guide offers interview tips, advice from "real people," and questionnaires. (Rev: SLJ 2/06)

Law, Police, and Other Society-Oriented Careers

2231 Fine, Jil. *Bomb Squad Specialist* (4–8). Series: Danger Is My Business. 2003, Children's Pr. LB $20.00 (0-516-24340-3); paper $6.95 (0-516-27864-9). 48pp. An illustrated glimpse of the perilous life of a bomb squad member in an age of terrorism, including information on how bombs work and how they are detected and disarmed. (Rev: SLJ 3/04) [363.2]

2232 Greene, Meg. *Careers in the National Guard's Search and Rescue Unit* (5–9). Series: Careers in Search and Rescue Operations. 2003, Rosen LB $26.50 (0-8239-3836-0). 64pp. This account describes the vital role that citizen-soldiers play in the line of defense and tells of the their search and rescue activities during the terrorist attacks of September 11, 2001. (Rev: BL 10/15/03; SLJ 4/04) [335]

2233 Murdico, Suzanne J. *Bomb Squad Experts: Life Defusing Explosive Devices* (5–10). Series: Extreme Careers. 2004, Rosen LB $19.95 (0-8239-3968-5). 64pp. A look at the career opportunities in bomb squads, with material on training, salaries, and working conditions. (Rev: BL 5/15/04) [363]

2234 Roza, Greg. *Careers in the Coast Guard's Search and Rescue Unit* (5–9). Series: Careers in Search and Rescue Operations. 2003, Rosen LB $26.50 (0-8239-3835-2). 64pp. This book covers the search and rescue operations involving the Coast Guard with particular emphasis on their vital role during the September 11, 2001, attacks. (Rev: BL 10/15/03; SLJ 4/04) [355]

Medicine and Health

2235 Reeves, Diane Lindsey, and Gail Karlitz. *Career Ideas for Teens in Health Science* (7–12). Illus. Series: Career Ideas for Teens. 2005, Ferguson $40.00 (0-8160-5290-5). 184pp. In addition to details of education requirements, salaries, and so forth, this attractive guide offers interview tips, advice from "real people," and questionnaires. (Rev: SLJ 2/06) [610.69]

Science and Engineering

2236 Murdico, Suzanne J. *Forensic Scientists: Life Investigating Sudden Death* (5–12). Series: Extreme Careers. 2004, Rosen LB $19.95 (0-8239-3966-9). 64pp. A look at this rapidly growing science and the career opportunities offered. (Rev: BL 5/15/04) [363.2]

Technical and Industrial Careers

2237 Cassedy, Patrice. *Computer Technology* (7–10). Series: Careers for the Twenty-First Century. 2004, Gale LB $27.45 (1-56006-896-5). 112pp. Helpful information about work environment and job satisfaction accompanies the usual material on salary, career prospects, and so forth; the format has less appeal. (Rev: SLJ 11/04) [005]

2238 *Computer and Video Game Design* (7–12). Series: Careers in Focus. 2005, Ferguson $22.95 (0-8160-5850-4). 188pp. Describes the tasks of artists and animators, game designers, packaging designers, technical support specialists, and video game testers. (Rev: SLJ 12/05)

2239 *Computers.* 4th ed. (6–12). Series: Careers in Focus. 2004, Ferguson LB $22.95 (0-8160-5552-1). 188pp. Describes careers in the computer field, with information on qualifications, working conditions, salaries, opportunities, rewards, and methods of exploring and entering the field; a helpful feature is a list of acronyms and identification numbers used in government career indexes. (Rev: SLJ 1/05) [004]

2240 Gerardi, Dave, and Peter Suciu. *Careers in the Computer Game Industry* (6–12). Illus. Series: Careers in the New Economy. 2005, Rosen LB $31.95 (1-4042-0252-8). 144pp. The authors review a wide array of job opportunities in the computer game industry, including designers, testers, graphic artists, animators, and programmers. (Rev: SLJ 10/05) [331.7]

2241 Henderson, Harry. *Career Opportunities in Computers and Cyberspace.* 2nd ed. (8–12). Series: Career Opportunities. 2004, Ferguson $49.50 (0-8160-5094-5). 241pp. A quick overview of the wide number of opportunities in such fields as programming and software development, information systems management, and information science, providing an outline of duties, salary ranges, employment outlook, required education and training, and so forth. (Rev: SLJ 7/04) [004]

2242 McAlpine, Margaret. *Working with Computers* (6–10). Series: My Future Career. 2005, Gareth Stevens LB $26.00 (0-8368-4242-1). 64pp. In addition to describing various jobs working with computers, McAlpine discusses the best personality type for each one and provides a detailed breakdown of a typical day. (Rev: SLJ 3/05) [004]

2243 Thornburg, Linda. *Cool Careers for Girls in Cybersecurity and National Safety* (8–11). Series: Cool Careers for Girls. 2004, Impact $21.95 (1-57023-209-1). 144pp. This volume contains 10 case studies of women who have launched careers dealing with the protection of computer networks and the Internet as well as other high-tech areas. (Rev: BL 3/1/04; SLJ 10/04) [331.7]

Health and the Human Body

Aging and Death

2244 Marzilli, Alan. *Physician-Assisted Suicide* (7–12). Series: Point/Counterpoint. 2003, Chelsea House LB $25.95 (0-7910-7485-4). 112pp. The arguments for and against the right to choose how and when to die, whether medical advice should be necessary, and the implications of medical intervention are all discussed with reference to federal and state laws and court cases. (Rev: SLJ 4/04) [179]

2245 Panno, Joseph. *Aging: Theories and Potential Therapies* (7–12). Illus. Series: The New Biology. 2004, Facts on File $35.00 (0-8160-4951-3). 157pp. In this title from the New Biology series, author Joseph Panno examines various theories about the aging process, as well as methods to stave off the depredations of age. (Rev: SLJ 2/05)

Alcohol, Drugs, and Smoking

2246 Aretha, David. *Cocaine and Crack* (6–9). Illus. Series: Drugs. 2005, Enslow LB $25.26 (0-7660-5276-1). 48pp. Focuses on cocaine and its derivative, crack, examining how they are produced, their effects, and the dangers they pose to users. Also use *Ecstasy and Other Party Drugs* (2005). (Rev: SLJ 6/05) [362.29]

2247 Aretha, David. *Steroids and Other Performance-Enhancing Drugs* (6–9). Illus. Series: MyReportLinks.com. 2005, Enslow LB $18.95 (0-7660-5277-X). 48pp. Explores the dangers of steroids and other performance-enhancing drugs, with password access to Web sites that are regularly monitored. (Rev: BL 6/1–15/05; SLJ 6/05) [362.29]

2248 Deeugenio, Deborah, and Debra Henn. *Diet Pills* (6–9). Illus. Series: Drugs, The Straight Facts. 2005, Chelsea House LB $25.95 (0-7910-8198-2). 120pp. The authors explore the pitfalls of using drugs to lose weight. (Rev: SLJ 11/05)

2249 Elliot-Wright, Susan. *Heroin* (8–10). Series: Health Issues. 2004, Raintree LB $32.79 (0-7398-6894-2). 64pp. This slim volume provides a concise history of heroin and examines the drug's effects on users and its impact on society. (Rev: SLJ 3/05) [363.29]

2250 Fitzhugh, Karla. *Steroids* (7–10). Illus. Series: Health Issues. 2003, Raintree LB $28.56 (0-7398-6426-2). 64pp. An attractive, slim overview of steroids and how they affect the body. (Rev: SLJ 5/04) [362.29]

2251 Fooks, Louie. *The Drug Trade: The Impact on Our Lives* (6–10). Series: 21st Century Debates. 2003, Raintree LB $28.56 (0-7398-6033-X). 64pp. Covers the types of illegal drugs being sold; the reasons why governments find it hard to control their growth/creation, distribution, and sale; the people who take these drugs; and the methods used to move them around the world. (Rev: SLJ 6/04) [362.2]

2252 Gottfried, Ted. *The Facts About Alcohol* (7–12). Series: Drugs. 2004, Benchmark LB $25.95 (0-7614-1805-9). 111pp. A history of alcohol use plus discussion of its effects on the body and impact on society. (Rev: SLJ 3/05) [613.8]

2253 Green, Carl R. *Nicotine and Tobacco* (4–8). Illus. Series: Drugs. 2005, Enslow LB $25.26 (0-7660-5283-4). 48pp. Fictional scenarios are combined with information on the addictive qualities of nicotine and the dangers of smoking and other forms of tobacco use; Web links extend the text. (Rev: SLJ 11/05) [362.2]

2254 Haugen, Hayley Mitchell, ed. *Teen Smoking* (6–12). Series: At Issue. 2004, Gale LB $27.45 (0-7377-1971-0). 80pp. The issues involved in teen smoking, including health and freedom of choice, are explored in this collection of articles, many with different viewpoints. (Rev: BL 2/15/04) [613.85]

2255 Hyde, Margaret O., and John K. Setaro. *Smoking 101: An Overview for Teens* (7–12). 2005, Twenty-First Century LB $26.60 (0-7613-2835-1). 128pp. A nonjudgmental account of the physical effects of smoking, with information on tobacco advertising, the kinds of products marketed, and the industry both in the United States and around the world. (Rev: SLJ 1/06) [362.29]

2256 Kittleson, Mark J., ed. *The Truth About Alcohol* (8–12). Series: Truth About. 2004, Facts on File $29.95 (0-8160-5298-0). 196pp. Discusses the effects and dangers of alcohol use, including binge drinking, alcoholism, unsafe sexual behavior, and impaired driving. (Rev: SLJ 4/05) [613.8]

2257 Laliberte, Michelle. *Marijuana* (6–9). Series: Drugs. 2005, Enslow LB $25.26 (0-7660-5281-8). 48pp. Presents the hard facts about marijuana and its effects on the body, along with links to related online resources. (Rev: SLJ 10/05) [362.29]

2258 Lennard-Brown, Sarah. *Cocaine* (8–10). Series: Health Issues. 2004, Raintree LB $32.79 (0-7398-6893-4). 64pp. A look at the history of cocaine as well as the drug's effects on users and its impact on society. (Rev: SLJ 3/05) [362.29]

2259 Lennard-Brown, Sarah. *Marijuana* (8–10). Series: Health Issues. 2004, Raintree LB $32.79 (0-7398-6896-9). 64pp. Traces the history of marijuana and explores the drug's effects on users and on society. (Rev: SLJ 3/05) [362.29]

2260 Levert, Suzanne. *The Facts About Steroids* (7–12). Illus. Series: Drugs. 2004, Benchmark LB $25.95 (0-7614-1808-3). 96pp. Examines the effects of steroids on users, the health risks, and the laws governing steroid use. (Rev: SLJ 3/05) [362.29]

2261 Lookadoo, Justin. *The Dirt on Drugs: A Dateable Book* (6–10). Illus. Series: The Dirt. 2005, Reveil paper $9.99 (0-8007-5919-2). 112pp. A former Texas probation officer writes frankly about the dangers of drugs. (Rev: SLJ 7/05) [616.8]

2262 McMullin, Jordan, ed. *Marijuana* (6–9). Series: History of Drugs. 2005, Gale LB $26.96 (0-7377-1957-5). 188pp. Excerpts from previously published materials — going back as far as the 16th century — chronicle the history of marijuana, focusing in particular on the controversy surrounding its use in Western society. (Rev: BL 4/1/05) [615]

2263 Menhard, Francha Roffe. *The Facts About Inhalants* (7–12). Series: Drugs. 2004, Benchmark LB $25.95 (0-7614-1809-1). 92pp. Explores the dangers associated with the use of inhalants. (Rev: SLJ 3/05) [362.29]

2264 Olive, M. Foster. *Prescription Pain Relievers* (6–9). Illus. Series: Drugs, The Straight Facts. 2005, Chelsea House LB $25.95 (0-7910-8199-0). 112pp. Describes how drugs work to relieve pain and the growing problems of abuse of such drugs. (Rev: SLJ 11/05) [613.8]

2265 Palenque, Stephanie Maher. *Crack and Cocaine=Busted!* (6–8). Series: Busted! 2005, Enslow LB $31.93 (0-7660-2169-6). 104pp. A useful overview of cocaine and crack and the dangers these drugs pose to individual users and the community at large. (Rev: SLJ 9/05) [362.29]

2266 Shannon, Joyce Brennfleck, ed. *Alcohol Information for Teens: Health Tips About Alcohol and Alcoholism* (7–12). Series: Teen Health. 2005, Omnigraphics $58.00 (0-7808-0741-3). 370pp. Authoritative information about the effects of alcohol on the mind and body and the dangers of alcohol dependency. (Rev: SLJ 7/05) [613.8]

2267 Sheen, Barbara. *Teen Alcoholism* (7–12). Illus. Series: Teen Issues. 2004, Gale LB $21.96 (1-59018-501-3). 112pp. This straightforward examination of teen alcoholism explores the individual and societal impact of the illness and offers a survey of possible treatment programs. (Rev: BL 7/04) [616.86]

Bionics and Transplants

2268 Rosaler, Maxine. *Bionics* (5–9). Series: Science on the Edge. 2003, Gale LB $20.95 (1-56711-784-8). 48pp. This account explores the science of fusing artificial parts with human parts to aid body functions and comments on the controversy surrounding this new science. (Rev: BL 10/15/03; SLJ 3/04) [174]

2269 Schwartz, Tina P. *Organ Transplants: A Survival Guide for the Entire Family: The Ultimate Teen Guide* (7–12). Illus. Series: It Happened to Me. 2005, Scarecrow $36.50 (0-8108-4924-0). 243pp. A clear explanation, in question-and-answer format, of the complex problems relating to medical transplants, with discussion of the hazards and the emotional upheaval to be expected. (Rev: SLJ 10/05) [617.9]

Diseases and Illnesses

2270 Balkin, Karen F., ed. *Food-Borne Illness* (7–12). Series: At Issue. 2004, Gale LB $28.70 (0-7377-1334-8); paper $19.95 (0-7377-1335-6). 80pp. A collection of previously published articles that examine the dangers of food-borne illness and what can be done to protect consumers. (Rev: SLJ 4/05) [615.9]

2271 Barnard, Bryn. *Outbreak! Plagues That Changed History* (5–8). 2005, Crown LB $19.99 (0-375-92986-X). 48pp. Information on microbes and the study of microorganisms precedes details of specific epidemics. (Rev: SLJ 2/06) [614.4]

2272 Bellenir, Karen, ed. *Asthma Information for Teens: Health Tips About Managing Asthma and Related Concerns* (8–12). Illus. Series: Teen Health. 2005, Omnigraphics LB $58.00 (0-7808-0770-7). 386pp. Information-packed but readable, this volume covers all aspects of asthma. (Rev: SLJ 9/05) [616.2]

2273 Bjorklund, Ruth. *Asthma* (4–7). Illus. Series: Health Alert. 2004, Benchmark LB $19.95 (0-7614-1803-2). 64pp. In addition to describing the causes and treatment of asthma, this attractive title opens with a case history and also includes lists of famous people who suffer from the condition. (Rev: SLJ 5/05)

2274 Brill, Marlene Targ. *Alzheimer's Disease* (4–7). Illus. Series: Health Alert. 2004, Benchmark LB $19.95 (0-7614-1799-0). 64pp. In addition to describing the diagnosis and treatment of Alzheimer's disease, this attractive title opens with a case history and also includes lists of famous people who suffer from the condition. (Rev: SLJ 5/05) [362.19]

2275 Bryan, Jenny. *Asthma* (5–10). Illus. Series: Just the Facts. 2004, Heinemann LB $27.07 (1-4034-4599-0). 56pp. A well-organized explanation of asthma, illustrated with numerous color photographs and providing material on how air pollution and smoking are factors in causing or aggravating the disease. (Rev: SLJ 6/04) [616.2]

2276 Bryan, Jenny. *Diabetes* (5–10). Illus. Series: Just the Facts. 2004, Heinemann LB $27.07 (1-4034-4600-8). 56pp. An illustrated overview of the disease, including causes and treatments and the effects of diet and cultural factors. (Rev: SLJ 6/04) [616.4]

2277 Bueche, Shelley. *The Ebola Virus* (4–7). Illus. Series: Parasites. 2003, Gale LB $22.45 (0-7377-1780-7). 32pp. Although it's part of the Parasites series, this book focuses on the Ebola virus, which causes an infectious illness and is found widely in Central Africa. (Rev: BL 3/1/04; SLJ 6/04) [616.9]

2278 Burnfield, Alexander. *Multiple Sclerosis* (5–8). Series: Just the Facts. 2004, Heinemann LB $27.07 (1-4034-4602-4). 56pp. An accessible explanation of multiple sclerosis, its symptoms, treatment, and the efforts being made to find new treatments and a cure. (Rev: SLJ 6/04) [616.8]

2279 Collier, James Lincoln. *Vaccines* (6–10). Series: Great Inventions. 2003, Benchmark LB $25.95 (0-7614-1539-4). 127pp. As well as discussing the development and mechanism of vac-

cines themselves, this well-illustrated volume includes a survey of infectious diseases such as smallpox, cholera, diptheria, influenza, and AIDS. (Rev: SLJ 3/04) [615]

2280 Elliot-Wright, Susan. *Epilepsy* (7–10). Illus. Series: Health Issues. 2003, Raintree LB $28.56 (0-7398-6423-8). 64pp. An attractive, slim overview of epilepsy and how it affects the body and mind. (Rev: SLJ 5/04) [616.8]

2281 Ellis, Deborah. *Our Stories, Our Songs: African Children Talk About AIDS* (6–9). Illus. 2005, Fitzhenry & Whiteside $18.95 (1-55041-913-7). 156pp. First-person accounts from children in Malawi and Zambia whose lives have been touched by AIDS paint a heartbreaking portrait of the devastation wrought by the disease in sub-Saharan Africa. (Rev: BL 10/1/05*; SLJ 11/05*) [362.1]

2282 Favor, Lesli J. *Bacteria* (5–8). Illus. Series: Germs: The Library of Disease-Causing Organisms. 2004, Rosen LB $25.25 (0-8239-4491-3). 48pp. An informative, illustrated discussion of bacteria, covering their discovery, how they survive, and the dangers they pose to humans. (Rev: SLJ 1/05) [616]

2283 Gillie, Oliver. *Cancer* (5–8). Series: Just the Facts. 2004, Heinemann LB $27.07 (1-4034-5144-3). 56pp. Provides accessible explanations of cancer itself, plus the symptoms, diagnosis, and surgery, chemotherapy, and radiation involved in its treatment. (Rev: SLJ 2/05) [616.99]

2284 Gillie, Oliver. *Sickle Cell Disease* (5–8). Series: Just the Facts. 2004, Heinemann LB $27.07 (1-4034-4603-2). 56pp. An examination of sickle cell anemia presented in an accessible style, with coverage of symptoms, treatment, and research. (Rev: SLJ 6/04) [616.1]

2285 Haney, Johannah. *Juvenile Diabetes* (4–7). Illus. Series: Health Alert. 2004, Benchmark LB $19.95 (0-7614-1798-2). 63pp. In addition to describing the treatment and possible complications of juvenile diabetes, this attractive title opens with a case history and also includes lists of famous people who suffer from the condition. (Rev: SLJ 5/05)

2286 Harris, Nancy, ed. *AIDS in Developing Countries* (6–12). Series: At Issue. 2004, Gale LB $27.45 (0-7377-1789-0). 80pp. Through a series of essays that express different points of view, the AIDS situation in countries in Africa, Asia, and South America is explored. (Rev: BL 2/15/04) [616]

2287 Hayhurst, Chris. *E. Coli* (4–7). Series: Epidemics. 2004, Rosen LB $26.50 (0-8239-4201-5). 64pp. A look at the transmission, treatment, and prevention of this bacterium, with an emphasis on the importance of washing hands and food before eating. (Rev: SLJ 8/04) [616.9]

2288 Hirschmann, Kris. *Salmonella* (4–7). Illus. Series: Parasites. 2003, Gale LB $22.45 (0-7377-1785-8). 32pp. This fascinating examination of Salmonella bacteria, responsible for a wide variety of illnesses in the United States and elsewhere, is supplemented with numerous photos and microscopic views of the title bacteria. (Rev: BL 3/1/04) [615.4]

2289 Hyde, Margaret O., and Elizabeth Forsyth. *Diabetes* (4–7). Illus. 2003, Watts LB $25.00 (0-531-12209-3). 96pp. Case studies of young people add to the easy-to-understand coverage of the disease, its different types, causes, symptoms, and popular methods of treatment. (Rev: SLJ 2/04) [616.4]

2290 Landau, Elaine. *Alzheimer's Disease: A Forgotten Life* (7–10). Illus. Series: Health and Human Disease. 2006, Scholastic LB $26.00 (0-531-16755-0). 128pp. Symptoms, diagnosis, treatment, and prognosis are all covered here, plus a question-and-answer "ask the doctor" feature that adds pertinent information. (Rev: BL 12/1/05; SLJ 1/06) [616.8]

2291 Lennard-Brown, Sarah. *Autism* (5–8). Illus. Series: Health Issues. 2003, Raintree LB $28.56 (0-7398-6422-X). 64pp. An in-depth introduction to autism, with attention to the difficulties people with autism face and what is being done to help them. (Rev: SLJ 5/04) [616.89]

2292 Margulies, Phillip. *Creutzfeldt-Jakob Disease* (4–7). Series: Epidemics. 2004, Rosen LB $26.50 (0-8239-4199-X). 64pp. Examines the history and current state of knowledge about this rare disorder that affects the brain and is related to Mad Cow Disease. Also use *West Nile Virus* (2004). (Rev: SLJ 8/04) [616.8]

2293 Margulies, Phillip. *Everything You Need to Know About Rheumatic Fever* (5–8). Series: The Need to Know Library. 2004, Rosen LB $25.25 (0-8239-4509-X). 64pp. After a brief history of the disease and the discovery of its cause, this volume discusses symptoms, treatment, and the concern that the disease may become more prevalent as bacteria develop resistance to antibiotics. (Rev: SLJ 4/05)

2294 Nakaya, Andrea C., ed. *Obesity* (8–12). Series: Opposing Viewpoints. 2005, Gale LB $23.70 (0-7377-3233-4). 203pp. The causes of the soaring rates of obesity are discussed from various viewpoints, as well as who is responsible and what can be done to reduce this health problem. (Rev: SLJ 1/06) [616.3]

2295 Nye, Bill, and Kathleen W. Zoehfeld. *Bill Nye the Science Guy's Great Big Book of Tiny Germs* (4–7). 2005, Hyperion $16.99 (0-7868-0543-9). 48pp. Solid information on bacteria and viruses is presented in an appealing and lively format. (Rev: BL 6/1–15/05; SLJ 7/05) [579]

2296 Panno, Joseph. *Cancer: The Role of Genes, Lifestyle and Environment* (7–12). Illus. Series: The New Biology. 2004, Facts on File $35.00 (0-8160-4950-5). 162pp. In this title from the New Biology series, author Joseph Panno explores the role of genetics, lifestyle choices, and the environment in cancer. (Rev: SLJ 2/05; VOYA 8/04)

2297 Panno, Joseph. *Gene Therapy: Treating Disease by Repairing Genes* (7–12). Illus. Series: The New Biology. 2004, Facts on File $35.00 (0-8160-4948-3). 172pp. The hot-button topic of gene therapy and its implications for the future treatment of diseases and physical injuries are explored in this title from the New Biology series. (Rev: SLJ 2/05)

2298 Peters, Stephanie True. *The Battle Against Polio* (6–10). Illus. Series: Epidemic! 2004, Benchmark LB $29.93 (0-7614-1635-8). 80pp. The history of polio, the toll it took on young lives, and the ultimately successful search for a vaccine are related in a compelling presentation. (Rev: BL 12/15/04; SLJ 2/05) [614.54]

2299 Romano, Amy. *Germ Warfare* (5–8). Illus. Series: Germs: The Library of Disease-Causing Organisms. 2004, Rosen LB $25.25 (0-8239-4493-X). 48pp. An informative, illustrated overview of the history and current status of germ warfare, with discussion of what we can do to protect ourselves. (Rev: SLJ 1/05) [358]

2300 Rosaler, Maxine. *Botulism* (4–7). Series: Epidemics. 2004, Rosen LB $26.50 (0-8239-4197-3). 64pp. A look at outbreaks of botulism and their causes and prevention. (Rev: SLJ 8/04) [614.5]

2301 Routh, Kristina. *Down Syndrome* (5–8). Series: Just the Facts. 2004, Heinemann LB $27.07 (1-4034-5145-1). 56pp. An informative overview of this disease and its diagnosis and treatment, stressing the individuality of children with the syndrome. (Rev: SLJ 2/05) [362.1]

2302 Routh, Kristina. *Meningitis* (5–8). Illus. Series: Just the Facts. 2004, Heinemann LB $27.07 (1-4034-5146-X). 56pp. The symptoms of meningitis are provided along with a thorough explanation of the disease and its diagnosis and treatment. (Rev: SLJ 2/05)

2303 Roy, Jennifer Rozines. *Depression* (4–7). Illus. Series: Health Alert. 2004, Benchmark LB $19.95 (0-7614-1800-8). 64pp. In addition to describing the causes and treatment of depression, this attractive title opens with a case history and also includes lists of famous people who suffer from the condition. (Rev: SLJ 5/05)

2304 Senker, Cath. *World Health Organization* (5–8). Series: World Watch. 2004, Raintree LB $27.14 (0-7398-6614-1). 48pp. The world's health problems and what is being done to combat them are the focus of this somber title, which looks at both the developing world and the wealthiest of nations. (Rev: BL 4/1/04; SLJ 3/04) [362.1]

2305 Silverstein, Alvin, et al. *Cancer: Conquering a Deadly Disease* (8–12). Series: Twenty-First Century Medical Library. 2005, Twenty-First Century LB $27.93 (0-7613-2833-5). 121pp. Using case studies to introduce topics, this is a thorough exploration of new developments in the fight against cancer. (Rev: SLJ 3/06)

2306 Silverstein, Alvin, et al. *The Flu and Pneumonia Update* (5–8). Illus. Series: Disease Update. 2006, Enslow LB $23.95 (0-7660-2480-6). 104pp. Symptoms, treatment, history, and new research are all included in this discussion of flu and pneumonia. (Rev: BL 4/1/06) [616.2]

2307 Viegas, Jennifer. *Parasites* (5–8). Illus. Series: Germs: The Library of Disease-Causing Organisms. 2004, Rosen LB $25.25 (0-8239-4494-8). 48pp. An informative, illustrated discussion of parasites, covering how they survive and the dangers they pose to humans. (Rev: SLJ 1/05) [574.5]

2308 Woolf, Alex. *Death and Disease* (5–8). Series: Medieval Realms. 2004, Gale LB $27.45 (1-59018-533-1). 48pp. Black Death, leprosy, and other diseases are discussed, with their impact on society, and the practice of medicine in general is described. (Rev: BL 4/1/04; SLJ 3/05) [610]

Doctors, Hospitals, and Medicine

2309 Bardhan-Quallen, Sudipta. *Chemotherapy* (8–12). Illus. Series: Great Medical Discoveries. 2004, Gale LB $21.96 (1-56006-926-0). 128pp. An informative history of the use of chemotherapy to treat cancer, with discussion of its efficacy and side effects, and future improvements and alternatives. (Rev: SLJ 8/04)

2310 Casterline, Linda. *Natural-born Killers: A Chapter Book* (3–7). Series: True Tales. 2004, Children's Pr. LB $21.50 (0-516-23725-X). 48pp. Discusses various poisonous plants and animals that have been used in modern medicine to save lives. (Rev: BL 12/1/04; SLJ 2/05) [578.6]

2311 Davis, Sampson, et al. *We Beat the Street: How a Friendship Led to Success* (7–10). 2005, Dutton $16.99 (0-525-47407-2). 128pp. Draper recounts the inspiring story of three young men who grew up in a tough neighborhood of Newark, New Jersey, escaped the mean streets of their childhood, and went on to become doctors. (Rev: BL 4/1/05; SLJ 5/05) [610]

2312 Dawson, Ian. *Renaissance Medicine* (6–9). Illus. Series: History of Medicine. 2005, Enchanted Lion LB $19.95 (1-59270-038-1). 64pp. An informative, well-illustrated overview of medical developments in Europe from the mid-15th to mid-18th centuries. (Rev: BL 4/1/05; SLJ 11/05; VOYA 2/06) [610.9]

2313 de la Bédoyère, Guy. *The Discovery of Penicillin* (6–9). Illus. Series: Milestones in Modern Science. 2005, World Almanac LB $30.00 (0-8368-

5852-2). 48pp. Suitable for reports, this volume provides a good overview of the discovery of penicillin and its impact on public health. Also use *The First Polio Vaccine* (2005). (Rev: SLJ 1/06) [509]

2314 Facklam, Margery, et al. *Modern Medicines: The Discovery and Development of Healing Drugs* (7–12). Series: Science and Technology in Focus. 2004, Facts on File $29.95 (0-8160-4706-5). 208pp. This updated title traces the development of medications from ancient herbal remedies to today's powerful pharmaceuticals, discussing research and testing, the role of the FDA, and the economics of the pharmaceutical industry. (Rev: BL 8/04) [615]

2315 Gilpin, Daniel. *Medicine* (6–9). Illus. Series: History of Invention. 2004, Facts on File $35.00 (0-8160-5442-8). 96pp. A slim introductory overview of advances in medicine from prehistoric times to today, with maps, illustrations, and profiles of key figures. (Rev: SLJ 12/04) [610.9]

2316 Green, Jen. *Medicine* (4–7). Illus. Series: Routes of Science. 2004, Gale LB $23.70 (1-4103-0168-0). 40pp. A look at the history of medicine and the scientific process, with profiles of key individuals and their discoveries, a chronology, and discussion of future advances. (Rev: SLJ 5/05)

2317 Pascoe, Elaine, ed. *Crash: The Body in Crisis* (5–8). Illus. Series: Body Story. 2003, Gale LB $23.70 (1-4103-0062-5). 48pp. Two people are badly hurt in a car crash — he is unconscious, she has a ruptured spleen — and readers accompany them to the emergency room and the operating room as they fight for their lives. (Rev: SLJ 4/04) [617.1]

2318 Tesar, Jeremy. *Stem Cells* (5–9). Illus. Series: Science on the Edge. 2003, Gale $20.95 (1-56711-787-2). 48pp. Clear, accessible text and photographs describe stems cells and present the pros and cons of their use. (Rev: BL 10/15/03; SLJ 2/04) [616]

2319 Townsend, John. *Bedpans, Blood and Bandages: A History of Hospitals* (6–9). Series: A Painful History of Medicine. 2005, Raintree LB $31.36 (1-4109-1334-1). 56pp. The graphic illustrations in sometimes-unsettling history of hospitals from medieval times to the present will attract readers. Other volumes are *Pills, Powders and Potions: A History of Medication* and *Pox, Pus and Plague: A History of Disease and Infection* (both 2005). (Rev: SLJ 7/05) [610]

2320 Townsend, John. *Scalpels, Stitches and Scars: A History of Surgery* (4–7). Illus. Series: A Painful History of Medicine. 2005, Raintree LB $21.95 (1-4109-1332-5). 56pp. Gory it may be but this title conveys accurate facts and the eye-catching illustrations will entice browsers. (Rev: BL 5/15/05; SLJ 7/05) [617]

2321 Woods, Michael, and Mary B. Woods. *The History of Medicine* (5–8). Series: Major Inventions Through History. 2005, Twenty-First Century LB

$26.60 (0-8225-2336-0). 56pp. An attractive look at medical developments through time and their impact on our lives. (Rev: SLJ 1/06) [610]

Genetics

2322 Day, Trevor. *Genetics* (4–7). Illus. Series: Routes of Science. 2004, Gale LB $23.70 (1-4103-0301-2). 40pp. A detailed examination of the development of genetics as a science, with profiles of key individuals and their discoveries, a chronology, and discussion of future advances. (Rev: SLJ 5/05)

2323 de la Bédoyère, Camilla. *The Discovery of DNA* (6–9). Illus. Series: Milestones in Modern Science. 2005, World Almanac LB $30.00 (0-8368-5851-4). 48pp. Suitable for reports, this volume provides a good overview of the discovery of DNA. (Rev: SLJ 1/06) [574.87]

2324 Kafka, Tina. *DNA on Trial* (6–12). Series: Overview. 2004, Gale LB $27.45 (1-59018-337-1). 112pp. Stories of DNA's use in solving criminal cases are accompanied by discussion of the technology's potential flaws and of the process involved in DNA testing. (Rev: SLJ 3/05) [614]

2325 Nardo, Don. *Cloning* (5–9). Illus. Series: Science on the Edge. 2003, Gale $20.95 (1-56711-782-1). 48pp. A concise overview of the techniques involved in cloning and the ways this science can be applied, with a balanced presentation of the pro and con arguments. (Rev: BL 10/15/03; SLJ 2/04) [660.6]

2326 Seiple, Samantha, and Todd Seiple. *Mutants, Clones, and Killer Corn: Unlocking the Secrets of Biotechnology* (6–9). Illus. 2005, Lerner $27.93 (0-8225-4860-7). 112pp. After explaining the basic concepts of genes, DNA, and cloning, the Seiples discuss advances in biotechnology, presenting both sides of controversial techniques. (Rev: BL 6/1–15/05; SLJ 7/05) [660.6]

2327 Taylor, Robert. *Genetics* (5–8). Illus. Series: Lucent Library of Science and Technology. 2004, Gale LB $27.45 (1-59018-103-4). 112pp. Describes the basic scientific principles involved in genetics and discusses practical applications. (Rev: BL 1/05; SLJ 3/04)

2328 Yount, Lisa. *Biotechnology and Genetic Engineering*. Rev. ed. (8–12). Series: Library in a Book. 2004, Facts on File $45.00 (0-8160-5059-7). 316pp. An overview of genetic engineering and biotechnology, with chapters on scientific achievements, ethical concerns, court battles, health issues, and scientific problems. (Rev: SLJ 2/05) [303.48]

Grooming, Personal Appearance, and Dress

2329 Fitzhugh, Karla. *Body Image* (5–9). Series: Health Issues. 2004, Steck-Vaughn LB $32.79 (0-7398-6891-8). Body image and such related issues as cosmetic surgery, piercing, tattooing, eating disorders, and physical culture are examined in attractive text with informative charts and sidebars. (Rev: SLJ 11/05) [155.2]

2330 Graydon, Shari. *In Your Face: The Culture of Beauty and You* (7–12). 2004, Annick paper $14.95 (1-55037-856-2). 176pp. Graydon offers commonsense advice and reassurance to teenagers who may feel overwhelmed by the seemingly ubiquitous message that beauty is all-important. (Rev: BL 12/15/04; SLJ 3/05) [391.6/3]

2331 Libal, Autumn. *Can I Change the Way I Look? A Teen's Guide to the Health Implications of Cosmetic Surgery, Makeovers, and Beyond* (7–12). Illus. Series: The Science of Health. 2005, Mason Crest LB $24.95 (1-59804-843-8). 128pp. Libal clearly lays out the pitfalls of obsessing about body image, as well as the risks involved in piercing, tattooing, eating disorders, cosmetic surgery, and even common cosmetic products. (Rev: SLJ 7/05) [613.4]

2332 Mason, Linda. *Teen Makeup: Looks to Match Your Every Mood* (6–12). Illus. 2004, Watson-Guptill paper $16.95 (0-8230-2980-8). 144pp. A photograph-filled how-to guide to the basics of skin care and makeup. (Rev: SLJ 11/04)

2333 Warrick, Leanne. *Hair Trix for Cool Chix: The Real Girl's Guide to Great Hair* (6–12). 2004, Watson-Guptill paper $9.95 (0-8230-2179-3). 96pp. From quizzes and practical tips to step-by-step directions for different styles and accessories, this is a reader-friendly guide to hair care. (Rev: SLJ 7/04) [391.5]

The Human Body

General and Miscellaneous

2334 Jackson, Donna. *In Your Face: The Facts About Your Features* (5–8). 2004, Viking $17.99 (0-670-03657-9). 48pp. Just about everything one might want to know about faces can be found in this fascinating volume, from study of individual features to ornamentation to face recognition by computer. (Rev: BL 10/15/04; SLJ 11/04) [611]

2335 McNally, Robert Aquinas, ed. *Skin Health Information for Teens: Health Tips About Dermatological Concerns and Skin Cancer Risks* (7–12). Illus. Series: Teen Health. 2003, Omnigraphics $58.00 (0-7808-0446-5). 429pp. Detailed information is provided on health problems and risks including acne, cosmetics, tanning, tattoos, and piercing. (Rev: SLJ 1/04; VOYA 2/04) [616.5]

2336 Parker, Steve. *Allergies* (5–8). Series: Just the Facts. 2004, Heinemann LB $27.07 (1-4034-4598-2). 56pp. A comprehensive and accessible overview of allergies, their causes, symptoms, and treatment. (Rev: SLJ 6/04) [616.97]

2337 Parker, Steve. *Digestion and Reproduction* (6–9). Illus. Series: Understanding the Human Body. 2004, Gareth Stevens LB $24.67 (0-8368-4205-7). 32pp. An attractive format is used to present solid information on the digestive and reproductive systems and the diseases that can affect them. Also use *Heart, Blood, and Lungs* (2004). (Rev: SLJ 4/05) [612]

2338 Pascoe, Elaine, ed. *Out of Control: Brain Function and Immune Reactions* (5–8). Illus. Series: Body Story. 2003, Gale LB $23.70 (1-4103-0063-3). 48pp. This fact-packed book looks first at a baby's brain function, before and after birth, and how its capabilities grow as he learns, then traces the reaction of a young woman's immune system as it copes with a severe allergic reaction to a wasp sting. (Rev: SLJ 4/04) [612.8]

2339 Rosen, Marvin. *Sleep and Dreaming* (6–12). Illus. Series: Gray Matter. 2005, Chelsea House LB $32.95 (0-7910-8639-9). 159pp. Snoring, sleepwalking, and night terrors are among the topics covered in this survey of our sleep processes and our dreams; Freudian and Jungian theories are also addressed. (Rev: SLJ 3/06) [616]

2340 Trueit, Trudi Strain. *Dreams and Sleep* (4–8). Illus. Series: Life Balance. 2004, Watts LB $19.50 (0-531-12260-3); paper $6.95 (0-531-15579-X). 80pp. Discusses why we dream and what dreams mean and gives advice on getting a good night's sleep. (Rev: BL 10/15/03) [616.5]

2341 Walker, Pam, and Elaine Wood. *The Endocrine System* (6–10). Illus. Series: Understanding the Human Body. 2003, Gale LB $27.45 (1-59018-333-9). 96pp. A clear survey of the structure and functions of the endocrine system, discussing the impact of disease and injury and the current and future medical technologies that can help. (Rev: SLJ 2/04) [612.4]

2342 Walker, Richard. *Body* (4–7). Illus. 2005, DK $19.99 (0-7566-1371-X). 96pp. With a spiral binding, acetate overlays, and computer-generated 3-D images, this volume gives an in-depth view of the human body; there is an accompanying CD. (Rev: BL 12/1/05; SLJ 3/06) [611]

2343 Walker, Richard. *Human Body* (5–9). Illus. Series: DK/Google e.guides. 2005, DK $17.99 (0-7566-1009-5). 96pp. This highly illustrated guide introduces readers to the human body and provides

a link to a Web site that serves as a gateway to additional resources. (Rev: SLJ 8/05) [612]

Brain and Nervous System

2344 Newquist, H. P. *The Great Brain Book: An Inside Look at the Inside of Your Head* (5–8). 2005, Scholastic $18.95 (0-439-45895-1). 160pp. The structure of the brain, its inner workings, and the history of our knowledge of this organ are all discussed in detail; interesting anecdotes add to the presentation. (Rev: BL 6/1–15/05; SLJ 9/05) [612.8]

2345 Parker, Steve. *The Brain and Nervous System* (5–9). Illus. Series: Our Bodies. 2004, Raintree LB $19.99 (0-7398-6619-2). 48pp. Details of the human body's brain and nervous system are accompanied by information on keeping them healthy. (Rev: BL 8/04)

2346 Parker, Steve. *Brain, Nerves, and Senses* (6–9). Illus. Series: Understanding the Human Body. 2004, Gareth Stevens LB $24.67 (0-8368-4204-9). 32pp. An attractive format is used to present solid information on the brain and nervous system and the diseases that can affect them. (Rev: SLJ 4/05) [612.8]

2347 Routh, Kristina. *Epilepsy* (5–10). Illus. Series: Just the Facts. 2004, Heinemann LB $27.07 (1-4034-4601-6). 56pp. An overview of epilepsy, with attention to its effect on individuals when it comes to driving, sports, education, and employment. (Rev: SLJ 6/04) [616.8]

2348 Saab, Carl Y. *The Spinal Cord* (6–12). Illus. Series: Gray Matter. 2005, Chelsea House LB $32.95 (0-7910-8511-2). 93pp. Explores the importance of the spinal cord to the whole nervous system and discusses the impact of disorders and injuries. (Rev: SLJ 3/06)

Circulatory System

2349 Parker, Steve. *Heart, Lungs, and Blood* (5–9). Illus. Series: Our Bodies. 2004, Raintree LB $19.99 (0-7398-6621-4). 48pp. Details of the human body's circulatory system are accompanied by information on keeping them healthy. (Rev: BL 8/04) [612.1]

Digestive and Excretory Systems

2350 Parker, Steve. *Digestion* (5–9). Illus. Series: Our Bodies. 2004, Raintree LB $19.99 (0-7398-6620-6). 48pp. Details of the human body's digestive system are accompanied by information on keeping them healthy. (Rev: BL 8/04) [612]

2351 Simon, Seymour. *Guts: Our Digestive System* (5–8). Illus. 2005, HarperCollins LB $16.89 (0-06-054652-2). 32pp. Photographs and straightforward yet fascinating text present the digestive system. (Rev: BL 3/1/05; SLJ 4/05) [612.3]

Musculoskeletal System

2352 Atkins, Jeannine. *Wings and Rockets: The Story of Women in Air and Space* (4–8). 2003, Farrar $17.00 (0-374-38450-9). Katherine Wright, Bessie Coleman, Blanche Stuart Scott, and Amelia Earhart are among those profiled in this book about women who overcame challenges in a male world. (Rev: BL 3/1/04) [920]

2353 Parker, Steve. *The Skeleton and Muscles* (5–9). Illus. Series: Our Bodies. 2004, Raintree LB $28.56 (0-7398-6622-2). 48pp. Details of the human body's skeletal and muscular systems are accompanied by information on keeping them healthy. (Rev: BL 8/04) [612.7]

2354 Parker, Steve. *Skin, Muscles, and Bones* (6–9). Illus. Series: Understanding the Human Body. 2004, Gareth Stevens LB $24.67 (0-8368-4207-3). 32pp. An attractive format is used to present solid information on the musculoskeletal system and the diseases and injuries that can affect it. (Rev: SLJ 4/05) [612.7]

2355 Walker, Pam, and Elaine Wood. *The Skeletal and Muscular System* (6–10). Illus. Series: Understanding the Human Body. 2003, Gale LB $27.45 (1-59018-334-7). 96pp. A clear survey of the structure and functions of the skeleton and muscular system, discussing the impact of disease and injury and the current and future medical technologies that can help. (Rev: SLJ 2/04) [612.7]

Senses

2356 Parker, Steve. *The Senses* (5–9). Illus. Series: Our Bodies. 2004, Raintree LB $19.99 (0-7398-6624-9). 48pp. Details of the human senses are accompanied by information on keeping them healthy. (Rev: BL 8/04) [612]

Hygiene and Physical Fitness

2357 Finestone, Jeanne. *A Girl's Guide to Yoga* (8–11). Illus. Series: Ener-Chi. 2004, Barrons paper $8.95 (0-7641-2839-6). 80pp. Guides readers through a complete hatha yoga session, pointing out the many benefits offered by the practice and illustrating the poses. (Rev: BL 1/1–15/05; VOYA 2/05) [613.7]

2358 Pascoe, Elaine, ed. *Spreading Menace: Salmonella Attack and the Hunger Craving* (5–8). Illus. Series: Body Story. 2003, Gale LB $23.70 (1-4103-0064-1). 48pp. Two stories show how the body can

react to food — Mike is infected with salmonella, and George's hunger is giving him a weight problem. (Rev: SLJ 4/04) [615.9]

Mental Disorders and Emotional Problems

2359 Abeel, Samantha. *My Thirteenth Winter* (7–12). 2003, Scholastic $15.95 (0-439-33904-9). 208pp. Born with a learning disability, Abeel describes how she coped from kindergarten through college. (Rev: BL 2/15/04; SLJ 3/04; VOYA 4/04) [371.92]

2360 Bonnice, Sherry, and Carolyn Hoard. *Drug Therapy and Cognitive Disorders* (6–10). Illus. Series: Psychiatric Disorders: Drugs and Psychology for the Mind and Body. 2003, Mason Crest LB $24.95 (1-59084-562-5). 126pp. Diagrams and charts reinforce the easily read text, which includes discussion of the nature of these disorders and how they are treated plus personal anecdotes from one of the authors. (Rev: SLJ 5/04)

2361 Dendy, Chris A. Zeigler, and Alex Zeigler. *A Bird's-Eye View of Life with ADD and ADHD: Advice from Young Survivors* (5–9). 2003, Cherish the Children paper $19.95 (0-9679911-3-7). 180pp. A guide to ADD and ADHD, written by a dozen teenagers with these disorders with the aim of helping others cope, with advice on succeeding in school, medication, driving, and so forth. (Rev: SLJ 4/04) [618.9]

2362 Kittleson, Mark J., ed. *The Truth About Fear and Depression* (8–12). Series: Truth About. 2004, Facts on File $29.95 (0-8160-5301-4). 164pp. Anxiety and depression are the main focus of this user-friendly volume that describes the causes of these problems, their treatment, individual experiences, and ways to get help. (Rev: SLJ 4/05) [616.85]

2363 Landau, Elaine. *Schizophrenia* (4–8). Illus. Series: Life Balance. 2004, Watts LB $19.50 (0-531-12215-8); paper $6.95 (0-531-16614-7). 80pp. An overview of the causes, symptoms, and treatment of this mental condition, with true stories of sufferers. (Rev: BL 10/15/03)

2364 Libal, Autumn. *Runaway Train: Youth with Emotional Disturbance* (7–12). Illus. Series: Youth with Special Needs. 2004, Mason Crest LB $24.95 (1-59084-732-6). 127pp. The story of a disturbed high school student who resorts to cutting herself is combined with facts about the causes, symptoms, and treatment of severe emotional disturbance. (Rev: SLJ 12/04)

2365 Pigache, Philippa. *ADHD* (4–8). Series: Just the Facts. 2004, Heinemann LB $27.07 (1-4034-5142-7). 56pp. The symptoms, causes, and treatment of attention deficit hyperactivity disorder are described, with discussion of continuing research. (Rev: SLJ 5/05)

2366 Polis, Ben. *Only a Mother Could Love Him: My Life with and Triumph over ADD* (8–12). 2004, Ballantine $22.95 (0-345-47188-1). 208pp. Polis's story of his courageous struggle to overcome attention deficit disorder will resonate with many teens. (Rev: BL 12/1/04) [618.92]

2367 Rashkin, Rachel. *Feeling Better: A Kid's Book About Therapy* (4–8). 2005, Magination paper $8.95 (1-59147-238-5). 48pp. Presented in journal format, this volume uses 12-year-old Maya's experiences with a therapist to offer useful insights into the process and its value. (Rev: SLJ 11/05) [618.92]

2368 Rosaler, Maxine. *Coping with Asperger Syndrome* (6–9). Series: Coping. 2004, Rosen LB $26.50 (0-8239-4482-4). 112pp. This straightforward title provides valuable information on Asperger syndrome and its symptoms and treatment. (Rev: BL 3/1/05; SLJ 12/04) [616.89]

Nutrition and Diet

2369 Ingram, Scott. *Want Fries with That? Obesity and the Supersizing of America* (8–11). Illus. 2005, Scholastic LB $26.00 (0-531-16756-9). 128pp. Examines the relationship between America's burgeoning fast-food business and the country's obesity epidemic. (Rev: BL 11/15/05; SLJ 1/06) [362.196]

2370 Kittleson, Mark J., ed. *The Truth About Eating Disorders* (8–12). Series: Truth About. 2004, Facts on File $29.95 (0-8160-5300-6). 166pp. Causes, diagnosis, and treatment are all covered in this user-friendly guide that looks at emotions along with physical symptoms and does not neglect adolescent males with eating problems. (Rev: SLJ 4/05) [[616.85]

2371 Lawton, Sandra Augustyn, ed. *Eating Disorders Information for Teens: Health Tips About Anorexia, Bulimia, Binge Eating, and Other Eating Disorders* (7–12). Series: Teen Health. 2005, Omnigraphics $58.00 (0-7808-0783-9). 337pp. This title explores all aspects of eating disorders as well as such related topics as body image, nutrition, self-esteem, and athleticism. (Rev: SLJ 12/05; VOYA 4/06)

2372 Moore, Judith. *Fat Girl* (8–12). 2005, Penguin $21.95 (1-59463-009-7). 208pp. An affecting memoir that will resonate with teens and young adults who have struggled with weight problems. (Rev: BL 12/1/04) [362.196]

2373 Schlosser, Eric, and Charles Wilson. *Chew on This: Everything You Don't Want to Know About Fast Food* (6–9). Illus. 2006, Houghton $16.00 (0-618-71031-0). 304pp. An unsettling but informative discussion of fast food and its attractions. (Rev: BL 3/1/06*) [394.1]

Physical Disabilities and Problems

2374 Esherick, Joan. *Breaking Down Barriers: Youth with Physical Challenges* (6–9). Illus. Series: Youth with Special Needs. 2004, Mason Crest LB $24.95 (1-59084-737-7). 127pp. Fiction and fact are interwoven in this presentation of five teens facing physical challenges — amputation, cerebral palsy, spina bifida, muscular dystrophy, and spinal cord injury. (Rev: SLJ 7/04) [362.4]

Reproduction and Child Care

2375 Brynie, Faith Hickman. *101 Questions About Reproduction: Or How 1 + 1 = 3 or 4 or More. . . .* (6–10). 2005, Twenty-First Century LB $27.90 (0-7613-2311-2). 176pp. Information on conception, pregnancy, childbirth, contraception (including a pill for males), abortion, reproductive disorders, and other issues of importance to teens is provided in a question-and-answer format with detailed black-and-white illustrations. (Rev: SLJ 1/06) [612]

2376 MacDonald, Fiona. *The First "Test-Tube Baby,"* (6–12). Illus. Series: Days that Changed the World. 2004, World Almanac LB $21.95 (0-8368-5567-1); paper $11.95 (0-8368-5574-4). 48pp. The science and ethics of in-vitro fertilization are explored in this overview of the 1978 birth of the world's first "test-tube baby." (Rev: BL 4/1/04; SLJ 7/04) [618.1]

2377 Orr, Tamra. *Test Tube Babies* (5–9). Series: Science on the Edge. 2003, Gale LB $20.95 (1-56711-788-0). 48pp. This book discusses in vitro fertilization, and how it has helped many but also caused a great deal of controversy. (Rev: BL 10/15/03; SLJ 3/04) [612]

2378 Parker, Steve. *Reproduction* (5–9). Illus. Series: Our Bodies. 2004, Raintree LB $28.56 (0-7398-6623-0). 48pp. Details of the human body's reproductive organs and how they function are accompanied by information on keeping them healthy. (Rev: BL 8/04) [612.6]

2379 Powers, Meghan, ed. *The Abortion Rights Movement* (8–11). Series: American Social Movements. 2006, Gale LB $27.96 (0-7377-1947-8). 176pp. This collection of 18 articles, speeches, first-person accounts, and interviews lays out the case for abortion. (Rev: BL 2/15/06) [363.46]

Safety and First Aid

2380 Lee, Laura. *100 Most Dangerous Things in Everyday Life and What You Can Do About Them* (8–12). Illus. 2004, Broadway paper $12.95 (0-7679-1716-2). 240pp. The dangers posed by common, everyday objects are explored in accessible, often humorous text and are arranged alphabetically. (Rev: SLJ 1/05) [613.6]

Sex Education and Sexual Identity

2381 Bailey, Jacqui. *Sex, Puberty and All That Stuff: A Guide to Growing Up* (5–10). 2004, Barron's paper $12.95 (0-7641-2992-9). 112pp. In this comprehensive volume full of lighthearted illustrations, Bailey covers the wide range of changes that affect young people, emphasizing the individual's right to choose and the need to resist peer pressure. (Rev: SLJ 1/05) [613.9]

2382 Dickerson, Karle. *On the Spot: Real Girls on Periods, Growing Up, and Finding Your Groove* (4–7). 2005, Adams paper $8.95 (1-59337-215-9). 192pp. The former managing editor of *Teen Magazine* offers upbeat advice on the important physical and emotional changes that pre-adolescent girls can expect. (Rev: BL 2/15/05; SLJ 5/05) [612.6]

2383 Elliot-Wright, Susan. *Puberty* (7–10). Illus. Series: Health Issues. 2003, Raintree LB $28.56 (0-7398-6424-6). 64pp. An attractive, slim overview of puberty and how it affects the body and mind. (Rev: SLJ 5/04) [612]

2384 Feinmann, Jane. *Everything a Girl Needs to Know About Her Periods* (5–9). Illus. 2003, Ronnie Sellers paper $14.95 (1-56906-555-1). 144pp. This useful and reassuring guide to the female body changes of puberty focuses largely on the menstrual cycle. (Rev: BL 2/1/04) [618.083]

2385 Kemp, Kristen. *Healthy Sexuality* (5–10). Illus. Series: Life Balance. 2004, Watts LB $19.50 (0-531-12336-7); paper $6.95 (0-531-16689-9). 80pp. Covering both boys and girls, this easy-to-understand volume looks at physical and emotional changes and provides practical tips on handling difficult decisions and confusing feelings. (Rev: BL 10/15/03; SLJ 4/05)

2386 Marcovitz, Hal. *Teens and Gay Issues* (7–10). Series: The Gallup Youth Survey, Major Issues and Trends. 2005, Mason Crest LB $22.95 (1-59084-873-X). 112pp. An attractive volume documenting Gallup findings on gay teens' attitudes toward coming out, homophobia, the nature/nurture debate, and gay marriage and adoption. (Rev: SLJ 1/06) [305.9]

2387 Movsessian, Shushann. *Puberty Girl* (4–7). Illus. 2005, Allen & Unwin paper $15.95 (1-74114-104-4). 128pp. A frank and friendly guide covering such topics as body changes, conflict resolution, and personal boundaries, as well as the changes that puberty brings in the opposite sex. (Rev: BL 10/15/05; SLJ 10/05; VOYA 10/05) [612.6]

2388 Pascoe, Elaine, ed. *Teen Dreams: The Journey Through Puberty* (5–8). Illus. Series: Body Story. 2003, Gale LB $23.70 (1-4103-0061-7). 48pp. Puberty and the many changes it brings are the topic of this arresting and informative book, seen from the points of view of a teenage boy and girl. (Rev: SLJ 4/04) [612.6]

2389 Rooney, Frances, ed. *Hear Me Out: True Stories of Teens Confronting Homophobia* (8–12). 2005, Second Story paper $9.95 (1-896764-87-8). 197pp. Young people who are volunteers in a Toronto organization called T.E.A.C.H. (Teens Educating and Confronting Homophobia) talk about prejudice they've experienced because of their sexual orientation. (Rev: BL 8/05; SLJ 5/05; VOYA 4/05) [306.76]

Sex Problems (Abuse, Harassment, etc.)

2390 Haley, James, ed. *Date Rape* (6–12). Series: At Issue. 2004, Gale LB $27.45 (0-7377-1569-3). 128pp. Various controversial issues concerning date rape are explored in this collection of essays and magazine articles. (Rev: BL 2/15/04) [362.88]

2391 Lehman, Carolyn. *Strong at the Heart: How It Feels to Heal from Sexual Abuse* (8–11). 2005, Farrar $16.00 (0-374-37282-9). 176pp. First-person accounts reveal the damage caused by sexual abuse and present strategies for healing. (Rev: BL 9/15/05; SLJ 11/05; VOYA 10/05) [362.76]

Human Development and Behavior

Psychology and Human Behavior

General and Miscellaneous

2392 Gross, Michael Joseph. *Starstruck: When a Fan Gets Close to Fame* (8–12). 2005, Bloomsbury $23.95 (1-58234-316-0). 256pp. Gross explores the potent allure of celebrity and the fans who fall under its spell. (Rev: BL 3/1/05) [306.4]

2393 Hernández, Roger K. *Teens and Relationships* (7–10). Series: The Gallup Youth Survey, Major Issues and Trends. 2005, Mason Crest LB $22.95 (1-59084-875-6). 112pp. An attractive volume documenting Gallup findings on teens' attitudes toward parents, divorce, blended families, friendship, and dating the opposite sex. (Rev: SLJ 1/06)

2394 Silverman, Robin L. *Reaching Your Goals* (4–8). Illus. Series: Life Balance. 2004, Watts LB $19.50 (0-531-12342-1); paper $6.95 (0-531-16691-0). 80pp. Practical advice on building self-confidence, making smart decisions, and focusing on achievable goals. (Rev: BL 10/15/03)

2395 Thompson, Kristi Collier. *The Girls' Guide to Dreams* (7–12). 2003, Sterling paper $12.95 (1-4027-0032-6). 128pp. A light and accessible guide to the possible meanings of dreams. (Rev: SLJ 1/04) [154.6]

Emotions and Emotional Behavior

2396 Dennison, Amy, and Allie Dennison. *Our Dad Died: The True Story of Three Kids Whose Lives Changed* (3–7). 2003, Free Spirit paper $9.95 (1-57542-135-6). 107pp. Three young siblings recount their initial reaction to the sudden and unexpected death of their father and how, with support from their mother, they learned to live with this loss. (Rev: SLJ 1/04) [155.9]

2397 Gootman, Marilyn E. *When a Friend Dies: A Book for Teens About Grieving and Healing*. Rev. ed. (6–12). Ed. by Pamela Espeland. 2005, Free Spirit paper $9.95 (1-57542-170-4). 118pp. An updated edition of a guide first published in 1994, this volume offers sound advice and reassurance for teenagers suffering the loss of a friend or peer, including quotes from bereaved teens. (Rev: SLJ 10/05) [155.9]

2398 Myers, Edward. *When Will I Stop Hurting? Teens, Loss, and Grief* (7–12). Series: It Happened to Me. 2004, Scarecrow $34.50 (0-8108-4921-6). 159pp. Firsthand accounts from teens add to this discussion of the stages of grief and of warning signs that should be monitored. (Rev: SLJ 11/04) [155.9]

Etiquette and Manners

2399 Holyoke, Nancy. *A Smart Girl's Guide to Manners* (4–7). 2005, Pleasant paper $9.95 (1-58485-983-0). 120pp. A nice mix of good manners that ranges from introductions to cell phone etiquette to how and when to write real thank-you notes. (Rev: BL 11/1/05; SLJ 1/06; VOYA 12/05) [395]

2400 Post, Peggy, and Cindy Post Senning. *Emily Post's The Guide to Good Manners for Kids* (4–7). Illus. 2004, HarperCollins LB $16.89 (0-06-057197-7). 144pp. A useful guide to good manners, covering such fundamentals as thank-you notes, Internet safety, cell phone etiquette, and table manners. (Rev: BL 1/1–15/05; SLJ 12/04) [395.1]

Intelligence and Thinking

2401 Nikola-Lisa, W. *How We Are Smart* (4–7). 2006, Lee & Low $16.95 (1-58430-254-2). 32pp. A picture book for older readers that looks at different kinds of intelligence, using double-page spreads about 12 famous people to illustrate these concepts. (Rev: BL 4/1/06) [811]

Personal Guidance

2402 Canfield, Jack, and Mark Victor Hansen, comps. *Chicken Soup for the Teenage Soul's The Real Deal: School: Cliques, Classes, Clubs and More* (7–12). Series: Chicken Soup for the Soul. 2005, Health Communications paper $12.95 (0-7573-0255-6). 292pp. Written for teenagers by teenagers, this collection of essays addresses many problems that confront high school students today. (Rev: SLJ 11/05)

2403 Chopra, Deepak. *Fire in the Heart: A Spiritual Guide for Teens* (8–12). 2004, Simon & Schuster $14.95 (0-689-86216-4). 208pp. In this book of spiritual advice for teens, the author uses the device of having a wise old man named Baba give self-help information. (Rev: BL 5/15/04; SLJ 8/04) [204]

2404 Chopra, Deepak. *Teens Ask Deepak: All the Right Questions* (7–10). 2006, Simon & Schuster $12.95 (0-689-86218-0). 208pp. The popular spiritual guru turns his attention to teenage concerns — friendship, success, health, religion, and so forth. (Rev: BL 1/1–15/06; SLJ 1/06) [616]

2405 Crist, James J. *What to Do When You're Scared and Worried: A Guide for Kids* (5–8). 2004, Free Spirit paper $9.95 (1-57542-153-4). 123pp. Reassuring words and sound advice for young people troubled by such diverse issues as school exams, bullies, terrorism, nightmares, monsters, and the dark. (Rev: SLJ 7/04) [152.4]

2406 Desetta, Al. *The Courage to Be Yourself: True Stories by Teens About Cliques, Conflicts, and Overcoming Peer Pressure* (8–11). 2005, Free Spirit paper $13.95 (1-57542-185-2). 160pp. Teens from a wide variety of backgrounds offer personal accounts of how they overcame adversities such as bullying, cliques, prejudice, and peer pressure. (Rev: BL 2/1/06; VOYA 4/06) [305.235]

2407 Drew, Naomi. *The Kids' Guide to Working Out Conflicts: How to Keep Cool, Stay Safe, and Get Along* (6–10). 2004, Free Spirit paper $13.95 (1-57542-150-X). 146pp. Misunderstandings, teasing, bullying, and sexual harassment are all discussed in this guide that includes scenarios and offers strategies for improving self-control plus many quotations from middle school students. (Rev: SLJ 9/04) [303.6]

2408 Hartman, Holly, ed. *Girlwonder: Every Girl's Guide to the Fantastic Feats, Cool Qualities, and Remarkable Abilities of Women and Girls* (4–8). Illus. 2003, Houghton paper $9.95 (0-618-31939-5). 234pp. A browsable look at famous women and their accomplishments, interspersed with informa-

tion and advice on topics ranging from romance to fashion. (Rev: SLJ 5/04) [305.235]

2409 McIntyre, Tom. *The Behavior Survival Guide for Kids: How to Make Good Choices and Stay out of Trouble* (4–7). 2003, Free Spirit paper $12.95 (1-57542-132-1). 167pp. This accessible guide offers concrete suggestions for dealing with behavior disorders and improving relations with teachers, family members, and friends. (Rev: SLJ 1/04) [649]

2410 Paul, Anthea. *Girlosophy: The Breakup Survival Kit* (8–12). 2004, Allen & Unwin paper $11.95 (1-74114-077-3). 224pp. This book, part of a series that gives girls good personal guidance, tells how one can recover from the trauma connected with breakups. (Rev: BL 5/1/04) [646.7]

2411 Peacock, Carol Antoinette. *Death and Dying* (4–8). Illus. Series: Life Balance. 2004, Watts LB $19.50 (0-531-12370-7); paper $6.95 (0-531-16728-3). 80pp. A practical guide to dealing with death and dying, with advice on seeking help when necessary. (Rev: BL 10/15/03)

2412 Piquemal, Michel, and Melissa Daly. *When Life Stinks: How to Deal with Your Bad Moods, Blues, and Depression* (6–10). Series: Sunscreen. 2004, Abrams paper $9.95 (0-8109-4932-6). 112pp. Sensible advice for adolescents suffering from normal anxieties and frustrations and for those who need to recognize that their problems are more deep-seated and professional help is necessary. (Rev: SLJ 4/05) [616.85]

2413 Rutledge, Jill Zimmerman. *Dealing with the Stuff That Makes Life Tough: The 10 Things That Stress Girls Out and How to Cope with Them* (8–10). 2003, Contemporary paper $14.95 (0-07-142326-5). 228pp. Body image, boys, homosexuality, smoking and drinking, divorce — these and other sources of stress are addressed with sensible advice and helpful anecdotes. (Rev: SLJ 1/04)

2414 Tym, Kate, and Penny Worms. *Coping with Your Emotions: A Guide to Taking Control of Your Life* (6–10). Illus. Series: Get Real. 2004, Raintree LB $29.93 (1-4109-0575-6). 48pp. The magazine-style layout, case studies, quizzes, photos, and advice will draw teens to this discussion of issues including depression, peer pressure, love interests, schoolwork, and teacher conflicts. Also use *School Survival: A Guide to Taking Control of Your Life* (2004). (Rev: SLJ 3/05) [646]

2415 Weston, Carol. *For Girls Only: Wise Words, Good Advice* (6–9). 2004, HarperCollins paper $8.99 (0-06-058318-5). 208pp. An update of the earlier edition, adding quotations from contemporary celebrities to the mix that ranges from Aesop and Socrates to Oprah Winfrey and Madonna. (Rev: BL 11/1/04) [305.23]

2416 Williams, Venus, and Serena Williams. *Venus and Serena: Serving from the Hip* (5–8). Illus. 2005,

Houghton paper $14.00 (0-618-57653-3). 144pp. The successful Williams sisters offer practical advice on self-respect, friendship, financial security, and other pertinent topics. (Rev: BL 5/15/05; SLJ 4/05) [796.342]

2417 Winkler, Kathleen. *Bullying: How to Deal with Taunting, Teasing, and Tormenting* (6–10). Series: Issues in Focus Today. 2005, Enslow $31.93 (0-7660-2355-9). 104pp. Including a chapter on girls who bully, this is an accessible look at the problem that draws on discussions with both teens and professionals. (Rev: SLJ 12/05)

2418 Zimmerman, Bill. *100 Things Guys Need to Know* (5–9). 2005, Free Spirit paper $13.95 (1-57542-167-4). Effective graphic design will draw teenage boys into this self-help guide that touches on a wide variety of topics, including body image, dating, school, friendship, and family. (Rev: SLJ 11/05) [305.235]

Social Groups

Family and Family Problems

2419 Bingham, Jane. *Why Do Families Break Up?* (4–8). Series: Exploring Tough Issues. 2004, Raintree LB $29.93 (0-7398-6683-4). 48pp. Every member of the family is considered in this comprehensive examination of divorce and how individuals of different ages cope. (Rev: SLJ 2/05) [306.8]

2420 Haugen, David M., and Matthew J. Box, eds. *Adoption* (8–12). Series: Social Issues Firsthand. 2005, Gale LB $28.70 (0-7377-2881-7). 108pp. Personal accounts from adoptees, birth parents, and adoptive parents give moving perspectives on the process of adoption; gay parents, transracial adoptions, custody battles, and the search for adoptees and birth parents are all covered. (Rev: SLJ 2/06) [362.7]

2421 Lanchon, Anne. *All About Adoption* (6–9). Illus. Series: Sunscreen. 2006, Abrams paper $9.95 (0-8109-9227-2). 104pp. Lanchon offers common-sense advice and reassurance for teens who are adopted. (Rev: BL 4/1/06; SLJ 4/06) [649]

2422 Libal, Joyce. *A House Between Homes: Youth in the Foster Care System* (6–9). Illus. Series: Youth with Special Needs. 2004, Mason Crest LB $24.95 (1-59084-740-7). 127pp. Fiction and fact are interwoven in this presentation of two children in the foster care system, with information on the history of foster care and the current programs offered. (Rev: SLJ 7/04) [362.73]

2423 MacGregor, Cynthia. *Jigsaw Puzzle Family: The Stepkids' Guide to Fitting It Together* (5–8). Series: Rebuilding Books. 2005, Impact paper $12.95 (1-886230-63-3). 128pp. Offers reassuring, practical advice — with an emphasis on talking through problems and seeking solutions — for stepchildren who are having difficulty adjusting to life in a blended family. (Rev: BL 9/1/05; SLJ 10/05) [306.874]

2424 Meyer, Don, ed. *The Sibling Slam Book: What It's Really Like to Have a Brother or Sister with Special Needs* (7–12). 2005, Woodbine paper $15.95 (1-890627-52-6). 152pp. Young people with special-needs siblings share their hopes, joys, fears, frustrations, and triumphs in this slam book. (Rev: SLJ 6/05)

2425 Snow, Judith E. *How It Feels to Have a Gay or Lesbian Parent: A Book by Kids for Kids of All Ages* (5–8). 2004, Haworth $19.95 (1-56023-419-9); paper $12.95 (1-56023-420-2). 110pp. Diverse reflections on what it means to have a gay or lesbian parent come from children, young adults, and adults (up to age 31). (Rev: BL 1/1–15/05; SLJ 10/04) [306.874]

2426 Tym, Kate, and Penny Worms. *Coping with Families: A Guide to Taking Control of Your Life* (5–8). Series: Get Real. 2004, Raintree LB $29.93 (1-4109-0574-8). 48pp. Expert advice and case studies are presented in an appealing format, plus a list of hotline numbers. Also use *Coping with Friends* (2004). (Rev: SLJ 5/05)

Physical and Applied Sciences

General and Miscellaneous

2427 Fradin, Dennis Brindell. *With a Little Luck: Surprising Stories of Amazing Discovery* (6–9). Illus. 2006, Dutton $17.99 (0-525-47196-0). 144pp. Among the 11 serendipitous discoveries described here are Alexander Fleming's accidental invention of penicillin and Jocelyn Bell's discovery of pulsars. (Rev: BL 2/1/06*) [509]

2428 Hakim, Joy. *The Story of Science: Newton at the Center* (7–10). Illus. Series: Smithsonian's Story of Science. 2005, Smithsonian $24.95 (1-58834-161-5). 480pp. In the second volume of the series, Hakim introduces readers to the discoveries of Copernicus, Galileo, Kepler, Newton, and others. (Rev: BL 12/1/05; SLJ 12/05*; VOYA 2/05) [590]

2429 Hoyt, Beth Caldwell, and Erica Ritter. *The Ultimate Girls' Guide to Science: From Backyard Experiments to Winning the Nobel Prize!* (4–8). Illus. 2004, Beyond Words paper $9.95 (1-58270-092-3). 128pp. Designed to pique girls' interest in the study of science, this attractive title offers brief profiles of famous female scientists as well as the major branches of science and also provides instructions for a number of scientific experiments. (Rev: SLJ 8/04) [500]

2430 Krautwurst, Terry. *Night Science for Kids: Exploring the World After Dark* (3–7). 2003, Lark Books $19.95 (1-57990-411-4). 144pp. This beautifully illustrated, large-format guide takes readers out into the night and explores everything from owls' eyes to individual stars. (Rev: BL 12/1/03; SLJ 3/04)

2431 Shields, Carol Diggory. *Brain Juice: Science, Fresh Squeezed!* (4–7). 2003, Handprint $14.95 (1-59354-005-1). 64pp. A humorous, rhyming look at grade-school science with appealing illustrations and useful mnemonic devices. (Rev: SLJ 3/04) [500]

2432 Spangenburg, Ray, and Diane Kit Moser. *The Birth of Science: Ancient Times to 1699.* Rev. ed. (6–10). Illus. Series: The History of Science. 2004, Facts on File $35.00 (0-8160-4851-7). 256pp. A survey of the development of scientific knowledge from ancient times through the seventeenth century, with brief profiles of major scientists plus discussion of discoveries that didn't pan out. Also use *The Rise of Reason: 1700–1799, The Age of Synthesis: 1800–1895, Modern Science: 1896–1945,* and *Science Frontiers: 1946 to the Present* (all 2004). (Rev: SLJ 12/04) [509]

Experiments and Projects

2433 Bardhan-Quallen, Sudipta. *Championship Science Fair Projects: 100 Sure-to-Win Experiments* (5–9). Illus. 2005, Sterling $19.95 (1-4027-1138-7). 208pp. Clearly defined science projects (more than 100 at varying levels of difficulty) are accompanied by lists of materials, illustrations, and extension activities. (Rev: BL 8/05; SLJ 9/05; VOYA 8/05) [507]

2434 Boring, Mel, and Leslie Dendy. *Guinea Pig Scientists: Bold Self-Experimenters in Science and Medicine* (5–9). 2005, Holt $19.95 (0-8050-7316-7). 224pp. Scientists who served as their own guinea pigs — demonstrating their passion for science and often their foolhardiness — are the topic of this appealing volume. (Rev: BL 7/05*; SLJ 7/05*; VOYA 6/05) [616]

2435 *Experiments You Can Do in Your Backyard* (5–8). Illus. Series: Science Experiments. 2003, McGraw-Hill $16.95 (1-57768-624-1). 96pp. The 50-plus backyard experiments and activities outlined in this book come with straightforward instructions and clear explanations of nature and scientific principles. (Rev: SLJ 2/04) [507]

2436 Harris, Elizabeth Snoke. *First Place Science Fair Projects for Inquisitive Kids* (4–7). Illus. 2005, Sterling LB $19.95 (1-57990-493-9). 127pp. Project ideas in biology, chemistry, and physics mostly involve everyday materials and are presented in accessible text with an eight-week schedule and clear photographs. (Rev: SLJ 3/06) [507]

2437 Rhatigan, Joe, and Rain Newcomb. *Prize-Winning Science Fair Projects for Curious Kids* (5–8). Illus. 2004, Lark Books $19.95 (1-57990-478-5). 112pp. Clear graphics and practical tips add to the stimulating text in this guide to science fair projects. (Rev: BL 12/1/04; SLJ 1/05) [507]

2438 Vecchione, Glen. *Blue Ribbon Science Fair Projects* (6–9). Illus. 2006, Sterling $19.95 (1-4027-1073-9). 224pp. Ideas for projects in a wide range of subject areas are clearly presented, with background information, list of materials, hypothesis, steps to take, and so forth. (Rev: BL 2/1/06) [507]

Astronomy and Space Science

General and Miscellaneous

2439 Carruthers, Margaret W. *The Hubble Space Telescope* (5–7). Series: Watts Library. 2003, Watts LB $24.00 (0-531-12279-4). 64pp. Excellent photographs enhance this history of the telescope and explanation of how it works and its importance to our knowledge of space. (Rev: SLJ 2/04) [522]

2440 Garlick, Mark A. *Astronomy: A Visual Guide* (8–12). Illus. 2004, Firefly $29.95 (1-55297-958-X). 304pp. An excellent, photo-filled guide to observing and understanding the nighttime sky. (Rev: BL 10/15/04) [522]

2441 Hope, Terry. *Spacecam: Photographing the Final Frontier from Apollo to Hubble* (6–12). Illus. 2005, F & W $24.99 (0-7153-2164-1). 256pp. Images captured from space — many never before published — offer fantastic views of Earth and beyond. (Rev: BL 12/15/05) [778.35]

2442 Jefferis, David. *Black Holes and Other Bizarre Space Objects* (5–8). Illus. Series: Science Frontiers. 2006, Crabtree LB $25.26 (0-7787-2856-0); paper $8.95 (0-7787-2870-6). 32pp. Double-page spreads with color photographs and informative sidebars explore the life of stars, black holes, gamma-ray bursts, space telescopes, and so forth. (Rev: BL 4/1/06) [523.8]

2443 Macy, Sue. *Are We Alone? Scientists Search for Life in Space* (4–8). Illus. 2004, National Geographic $18.95 (0-7922-6567-X). 96pp. Modern scientific efforts to find extraterrestrial life are discussed along with the popularity of flying saucer, crop circle, and other theories. (Rev: BL 10/1/04; SLJ 12/04*) [001.9]

2444 Orr, Tamra. *The Telescope* (4–8). Series: Inventions That Shaped the World. 2004, Watts LB $29.50 (0-531-12344-8). 80pp. Describes the invention of the telescope, the impact of the knowledge imparted, and future possibilities. (Rev: BL 4/1/04; SLJ 2/05) [522]

2445 Rhatigan, Joe, and Rain Newcomb. *Out-of-This-World Astronomy: 50 Amazing Activities and Projects* (5–8). Illus. 2003, Sterling $19.95 (1-57990-410-6). 128pp. Strong background information adds to the value of this collection of interesting, well-presented activities. (Rev: SLJ 4/04) [520]

Astronautics and Space Exploration

2446 Ackroyd, Peter. *Escape from Earth: Voyages Through Time* (7–10). Illus. Series: Voyages Through Time. 2004, DK $19.99 (0-7566-0171-1). 144pp. Using many colorful photographs and diagrams, this account traces the past history of space travel and possible future developments. (Rev: BL 5/1/04; SLJ 7/04) [387.8]

2447 Barter, James. *Space Stations* (5–8). Illus. Series: Lucent Library of Science and Technology. 2005, Gale LB $26.96 (1-59018-106-9). 112pp. Explores the space stations that have been used for many years as medical laboratories and platforms for space study. (Rev: BL 1/05)

2448 Carlisle, Rodney P. *Exploring Space* (6–10). Series: Discovery and Exploration. 2004, Facts on File $35.00 (0-8160-5265-4). 152pp. The motivations for exploring space are examined in clear, informative text plus photographs, illustrations, and excerpts from primary sources. (Rev: SLJ 12/04) [629.5]

2449 Goldsmith, Mike. *Space* (4–7). Illus. Series: Kingfisher Voyages. 2005, Kingfisher $14.95 (0-7534-5910-8). 60pp. An appealing overview of space exploration, with concise text, good photographs, and a foreword and comments by astronaut Sally Ride. (Rev: BL 10/15/05) [629.45]

2450 Holden, Henry M. *The Tragedy of the Space Shuttle Challenger* (4–8). Illus. Series: Space Flight Adventures and Disasters. 2004, Enslow LB $25.26 (0-7660-5165-X). 48pp. An account of the ill-fated *Challenger* mission, backed up by a list of Web sites that provide additional information. (Rev: BL 10/1/04; SLJ 2/05) [629.5]

2451 Kerrod, Robin. *Dawn of the Space Age* (5–7). Illus. Series: The History of Space Exploration. 2005, World Almanac LB $30.00 (0-8368-5705-4). 48pp. A well-illustrated history of space exploration, from the ideas of Cyrano de Bergerac to the modern Mars probes. Also recommended in this series are *Space Probes*, *Space Shuttles*, and *Space Stations* (all 2004). (Rev: SLJ 3/05) [629.4]

2452 Kupperberg, Paul. *Spy Satellites* (4–8). Illus. Series: Library of Satellites. 2003, Rosen LB $26.50 (0-8239-3854-9). 64pp. The author discusses the history of U.S. spy satellites and how the country has used the information they have gleaned. (Rev: BL 5/15/03; SLJ 1/04) [327.1273]

2453 Mayell, Mark. *Tragedies of Space Exploration* (5–8). Illus. Series: Man-Made Disasters. 2004, Gale LB $21.96 (1-59018-508-0). 112pp. Interesting details add depth to this account that covers not only the *Challenger* and *Columbia* disasters but also several Russian tragedies. (Rev: SLJ 7/04) [363.12]

2454 Tocci, Salvatore. *NASA* (5–7). Illus. Series: Watts Library. 2003, Watts LB $24.00 (0-531-12282-4). 64pp. An accessible introduction to the space agency and its work. (Rev: SLJ 2/04) [629.4]

2455 Vogt, Gregory L. *Disasters in Space Exploration*. Rev. ed. (5–8). 2003, Millbrook LB $25.90 (0-7613-2895-5). 79pp. An illustrated survey of serious accidents that have befallen the U.S. and Soviet space programs, what caused them, and what was learned from them. This revised edition includes the *Columbia* space shuttle disaster of February 2003. (Rev: SLJ 3/04) [363.12]

Comets, Meteors, and Asteroids

2456 Koppes, Steven N. *Killer Rocks from Outer Space: Asteroids, Comets, and Meteorites* (7–10). Illus. 2003, Lerner LB $26.60 (0-8225-2861-4). 112pp. Koppes examines the science and history of planetary impacts by asteroids, comets, and meteorites and looks at steps being taken to protect the Earth from such impacts in the future. (Rev: BL 1/1–15/04; SLJ 3/04) [523.5]

2457 Miller, Ron. *Asteroids, Comets, and Meteors* (7–10). Illus. Series: Worlds Beyond. 2005, Twenty-First Century LB $27.93 (0-7613-2363-5). 80pp.

Using color photographs, vivid paintings, and helpful diagrams, this title introduces readers to asteroids, comets, and meteors. (Rev: SLJ 12/05)

Stars

2458 Asimov, Isaac. *The Life and Death of Stars* (5–8). Illus. Series: Isaac Asimov's 21st Century Library of the Universe. 2005, Gareth Stevens LB $18.50 (0-8368-3967-6). 32pp. A revised, well-illustrated edition of a previously published book, this discusses the birth of stars, profiles different types of stars, and looks at the future of our Sun. Also in this series: *Black Holes, Pulsars, and Quasars*, *The Milky Way and Other Galaxies*, *Our Planetary System*, and *Comets and Meteors* (all 2005). (Rev: BL 3/1/05; SLJ 8/05)

2459 Kerrod, Robin. *The Star Guide: Learn How to Read the Night Sky Star by Star*. 2nd ed. (8–12). Illus. 2005, Wiley $29.95 (0-471-70617-5). 160pp. This guide to identifying heavenly bodies is well organized for novices and includes a removable sky map. (Rev: BL 4/15/05) [523.8]

Sun and the Solar System

2460 Bortolotti, Dan. *Exploring Saturn* (4–8). Illus. 2003, Firefly $19.95 (1-55297-766-8); paper $9.95 (1-55297-765-X). 64pp. This highly visual volume with readable text presents facts about Saturn, explains how and when we acquired this knowledge, and looks at the Cassini-Huygens mission, scheduled to reach the planet in 2004. (Rev: BL 12/1/03; SLJ 5/04) [523.46]

2461 Feinstein, Stephen. *Saturn* (4–7). Illus. Series: Solar System. 2005, Enslow LB $25.26 (0-7660-5304-0). 48pp. Useful for reports, this clearly written title includes links to Web sites for further research. (Rev: SLJ 12/05)

2462 Miller, Ron. *Mars* (7–10). Illus. Series: Worlds Beyond. 2005, Twenty-First Century LB $27.93 (0-7613-2362-7). 96pp. Introduces readers to the planet Mars in a blend of easy-to-understand narrative and colorful space photos. (Rev: SLJ 12/05)

2463 O'Connell, Kim A. *Mercury* (4–7). Illus. Series: Solar System. 2005, Enslow LB $25.26 (0-7660-5209-5). 48pp. A blend of easy-to-understand narrative, vivid color photographs, and links to related online resources introduce Mercury. Also use *Pluto* (2005). (Rev: SLJ 12/05)

2464 Spence, Pam. *Sun Observer's Guide* (7–12). Illus. 2004, Firefly paper $14.95 (1-55297-941-5). 160pp. A useful guide to the sun and the equipment that ensures safe observation of it. (Rev: BL 11/1/04) [522]

Universe

2465 Asimov, Isaac. *The Birth of Our Universe* (5–8). Illus. Series: Isaac Asimov's 21st Century Library of the Universe. 2005, Gareth Stevens LB $18.50 (0-8368-3964-1). 32pp. This is an update of a 1995 edition on the origins of the universe, with illustrations and photographs. (Rev: BL 3/1/05) [523.1]

2466 Fleisher, Paul. *The Big Bang* (5–8). Illus. Series: Great Ideas in Science. 2005, Twenty-First Century LB $27.93 (0-8225-2133-4). 80pp. Stu-

dents with a real interest in science will benefit most from this overview of theories about the creation of the universe, from creation myths onward. (Rev: BL 12/1/05; SLJ 12/05) [523.1]

2467 Miller, Ron. *Stars and Galaxies* (7–10). Illus. Series: Worlds Beyond. 2005, Twenty-First Century LB $27.93 (0-7613-3466-1). 96pp. A comprehensive overview of the universe, discussing theories and facts about neighboring stars and distant galaxies alike, with wonderful NASA photos mixed with original art. (Rev: BL 12/1/05; SLJ 12/05) [523.8]

2468 Villard, Ray, and Lynette Cook. *Infinite Worlds: An Illustrated Voyage to Planets Beyond Our Sun* (8–12). Illus. 2005, Univ. of California $39.95 (0-520-23710-2). 252pp. Using known data, the author and illustrator speculate about the likely appearance of planets in other solar systems. (Rev: BL 6/1–15/05) [523.21]

Biological Sciences

General and Miscellaneous

2469 Fullick, Ann. *Adaptation and Competition* (6–9). Illus. Series: Life Science in Depth. 2006, Heinemann LB $24.00 (1-4034-7518-0). 64pp. Explores living organisms' ability to adapt to a wide array of climates and habitats and how these organisms compete with one another to survive. (Rev: BL 4/1/06) [587.4]

2470 Kelsey, Elin. *Strange New Species: Astonishing Discoveries of Life on Earth* (5–8). Illus. 2005, Maple Tree $24.95 (1-897066-31-7). 96pp. A large-format, well-illustrated introduction to plant and animal classification and to newly discovered species. (Rev: BL 10/15/05; SLJ 2/06) [578]

2471 Panno, Joseph. *Animal Cloning: The Science of Nuclear Transfer* (7–12). Illus. Series: The New Biology. 2004, Facts on File $35.00 (0-8160-4947-5). 164pp. A look at the controversial issue of animal cloning and its scientific implications. (Rev: SLJ 2/05)

2472 Panno, Joseph. *The Cell: Evolution of the First Organism* (7–12). Illus. Series: The New Biology. 2004, Facts on File $35.00 (0-8160-4946-7). 186pp. Reviews theories about life's origin and examines such related topics as cell structure, cell cycle, genes, multi-cellular organisms, and neurons. (Rev: SLJ 2/05)

2473 Walker, Pam, and Elaine Wood. *Ecosystem Science Fair Projects Using Worms, Leaves, Crickets, and Other Stuff* (6–12). Illus. Series: Biology! Best Science Projects. 2005, Enslow LB $26.60 (0-7660-2367-2). 128pp. Biology science projects are clearly presented with background information necessary to full understanding of the underlying principles. (Rev: SLJ 7/05) [570]

Botany

Foods, Farms, and Ranches

GENERAL AND MISCELLANEOUS

2474 *Bound for Glory: America in Color, 1939–43* (8–12). Illus. 2004, Abrams $35.00 (0-8109-4348-4). 192pp. American farm life during the late 1930s and early 1940s is beautifully captured in these color photographs taken under the auspices of the Farm Security Administration, best known for earlier black-and-white collections. (Rev: BL 6/1–15/04) [779]

2475 Bowden, Rob. *Food and Farming* (5–8). Illus. Series: Sustainable World. 2004, Gale LB $23.70 (0-7377-1899-4). 48pp. Bowden looks at conventional methods of farming and at the new focus on sustainable agriculture, providing lots of facts and statistics and highlighting choices we all can make that may improve the future. (Rev: BL 4/15/04; SLJ 10/04) [338]

2476 Eagen, Rachel. *The Biography of Bananas* (4–7). Illus. Series: How Did That Get Here? 2005, Crabtree LB $17.94 (0-7787-2483-2). 32pp. This richly illustrated title offers a wealth of information about the science and business of producing bananas. (Rev: BL 3/1/06) [634]

2477 Jango-Cohen, Judith. *The History of Food* (5–8). Series: Major Inventions Through History. 2005, Twenty-First Century LB $26.60 (0-8225-2484-8). 56pp. Addresses inventions in the food industry such as canning, pasteurization, and genetically modified crops. (Rev: SLJ 2/06)

2478 Webber, Desiree Morrison. *Bone Head: Story of the Longhorn* (4–7). 2003, Eakin $16.95 (1-57168-763-7). 74pp. The longhorn's characteristics and the reasons for its early success but decline with the arrival of the railroad are explored in appealing text and archival photographs. (Rev: SLJ 2/04) [636.2]

Zoology

General and Miscellaneous

2479 Miles, Victoria. *Wild Science: Amazing Encounters Between Animals and the People Who Study Them* (5–8). Series: Scientists in the Field. 2004, Raincoast paper $18.95 (1-55192-618-0). 168pp. This photo-filled volume introduces readers to scientists who study animals and describes memorable moments with animals in the wilderness. (Rev: BL 12/1/04; SLJ 12/04) [591.68]

2480 Wetherbee, Kris, and Rick Wetherbee. *Attracting Birds, Butterflies and Other Winged Wonders to Your Backyard* (8–12). Illus. 2005, Sterling $24.95 (1-57990-594-3). 178pp. From shelter to food and water, this guide provides many suggestions for gardeners and nature watchers. (Rev: BL 8/05) [598]

Amphibians and Reptiles

GENERAL AND MISCELLANEOUS

2481 Dennard, Deborah. *Reptiles* (5–7). Series: Our Wild World. 2004, NorthWord $16.95 (1-55971-880-3). 191pp. A compilation of four shorter books published by NorthWord in 2003, this volume examines the physical characteristics, natural habitat, diet, and behavior of alligators, crocodiles, lizards, snakes, and turtles. (Rev: SLJ 8/04) [597.9]

TORTOISES AND TURTLES

2482 Lockwood, Sophie. *Sea Turtles* (4–7). Illus. Series: World of Reptiles. 2006, Child's World LB $20.95 (1-59296-550-4). 40pp. In addition to the kind of information needed for reports, Lockwood discusses conservation, how scientists track turtles, and the turtle's appearances in folklore and art. (Rev: BL 4/1/06) [597.92]

Animal Behavior

HOMES

2483 Bloom, Steve. *Untamed: Animals Around the World* (4–7). Illus. 2005, Abrams $18.95 (0-8109-5956-9). 75pp. Enthralling photographs of wild animals are accompanied by brief facts and an environmentalist message. (Rev: BL 12/1/05) [636]

Animal Species

GENERAL AND MISCELLANEOUS

2484 Green, Jen, and David Burnie. *Mammal* (5–9). Illus. Series: DK/Google e.guides. 2005, DK $17.99 (0-7566-1139-3). 96pp. This highly illustrated guide introduces readers to the evolution and diversity of mammals and provides a link to a Web site that serves as a gateway to additional resources. (Rev: SLJ 8/05) [599]

2485 Murray, Peter. *Rhinos* (4–7). Series: The World of Mammals. 2005, Child's World LB $29.93 (1-59296-502-4). 40pp. Arresting photographs and engaging text introduce the anatomy, behavior, habitat, and life cycle of the rhinoceros as well as the threats to the animal's survival in the wild. (Rev: SLJ 3/06) [599.72]

APE FAMILY

2486 Green, Carl R. *The Gorilla* (3–7). Series: Endangered and Threatened Animals. 2004, Enslow LB $25.26 (0-7660-5060-2). 48pp. Supplemented by a lengthy list of links to online resources, this overview of the gorilla explores its behavior and physical characteristics, as well as the threats it faces. (Rev: BL 6/1–15/04)

2487 Lockwood, Sophie. *Baboons* (4–7). Series: The World of Mammals. 2005, Child's World LB $29.93 (1-59296-497-4). 40pp. Arresting photographs and engaging text introduce the anatomy, behavior, habitat, and life cycle of the baboon as well as the threats to the animal's survival in the wild. (Rev: SLJ 3/06) [599.8]

2488 Stefoff, Rebecca. *Chimpanzees* (4–7). Illus. Series: AnimalWays. 2003, Benchmark LB $21.95 (0-7614-1579-3). 112pp. A richly illustrated look at chimpanzees, from their physiology to their interaction with humans. (Rev: SLJ 3/04)

BEARS

2489 Lockwood, Sophie. *Polar Bears* (5–8). Illus. Series: World of Mammals. 2005, Child's World LB $20.95 (1-59296-501-6). 40pp. This slim but richly illustrated title looks at polar bears' physical characteristics, behavior, diet, relationship with the Inuit people, and the growing threats to their survival. (Rev: BL 10/15/05) [599.786]

2490 Markle, Sandra. *Polar Bears* (3–7). Series: Animal Predators. 2004, Carolrhoda LB $25.26 (1-57505-730-1). 40pp. Describes the life of a female polar bear in the Arctic — behavior, diet, communication, life cycle, and so forth. (Rev: SLJ 1/05) [599.786]

2491 Montgomery, Sy. *Search for the Golden Moon Bear: Science and Adventure in the Asian Tropics* (5–9). 2004, Houghton $17.00 (0-618-35650-9). 80pp. Nature writer Montgomery describes her search across war-torn Southeast Asia for the elusive golden moon bear. (Rev: BL 12/1/04; SLJ 12/04) [599.78]

CATS (LIONS, TIGERS, ETC.)

2492 Bortolotti, Dan. *Tiger Rescue: Changing the Future for Endangered Wildlife* (3–8). Series: Firefly Animal Rescue. 2003, Firefly LB $19.95 (1-55297-599-1); paper $9.95 (1-55297-558-4). 64pp. A look at how and why tigers are an endangered species and what can be done to help them, with profiles of some of the people involved in the effort. (Rev: BL 1/1–15/04; SLJ 4/04) [333.9]

2493 Gamble, Cyndi. *Leopards: Natural History and Conservation* (7–10). Photos by Rodney Griffiths. Series: WorldLife Library. 2004, Voyageur paper $12.95 (0-89658-656-1). 48pp. Introduces readers to the three leopard species of the world, their habitats, and the threats they face. (Rev: SLJ 4/05) [599.74]

2494 Matignon, Karine Lou. *Tiger, Tiger* (8–12). Illus. 2004, Thames & Hudson $40.00 (0-500-51193-4). 185pp. This informative, photo-filled volume uses *Two Brothers*, the film about two tiger siblings separated at birth, as the base for an exploration of tigers and the historic relationship between the big cats and humans. (Rev: BL 11/1/04) [599.7]

2495 Mills, Stephen. *Tiger* (8–12). Illus. 2004, Firefly paper $24.95 (1-55297-949-0). 168pp. For report writers and general interest, this is an excellent introduction to tigers, their behavior, and the threats they face. (Rev: BL 11/1/04) [599.756]

2496 Seidensticker, John, and Susan Lumpkin. *Cats: Smithsonian Answer Book* (8–12). Illus. 2004, Smithsonian $55.00 (1-58834-125-9); paper $24.95 (1-58834-126-7). 304pp. From the characteristics of the common tabby to the exotic puma, researchers and browsers will find a wealth of information in this book, which is arranged in question-and-answer format and includes many color photographs. (Rev: BL 10/1/04) [599.75]

2497 Sinha, Vivek R. *The Vanishing Tiger* (8–12). Illus. 2004, Trafalgar Square $29.95 (1-84065-441-4). 256pp. A wonderful photographic record of an expedition to locate and photograph India's massive Bengal tiger. (Rev: BL 3/1/04) [599.7]

ELEPHANTS

2498 Morgan, Jody. *Elephant Rescue: Changing the Future for Endangered Wildlife* (4–7). Illus. Series: Firefly Animal Rescue. 2005, Firefly $19.95 (1-55297-595-9); paper $9.95 (1-55297-594-0). 64pp. This photo-filled book documents the many threats facing the world's remaining herds of African and Asian elephants, and discusses elephant physiology, behavior, and habitat. (Rev: BL 2/15/05; SLJ 5/05) [599.67]

MARSUPIALS

2499 Murray, Peter. *Kangaroos* (4–7). Series: The World of Mammals. 2005, Child's World LB $29.93 (1-59296-499-0). 40pp. Arresting photographs and engaging text introduce the anatomy, behavior, habitat, and life cycle of the kangaroo as well as the threats to the animal's survival in the wild. (Rev: SLJ 3/06) [599.2]

PANDAS

2500 Bortolotti, Dan. *Panda Rescue: Changing the Future for Endangered Wildlife* (3–8). Series: Firefly Animal Rescue. 2003, Firefly LB $19.95 (1-55297-598-3); paper $9.95 (1-55297-557-6). 64pp. Threats to the panda's survival and efforts to protect them from extinction are examined in detail, with profiles of some of the key individuals involved. (Rev: BL 1/1–15/04; SLJ 4/04) [599.789]

2501 Croke, Vicki Constantine. *The Lady and the Panda: The True Adventures of the First American Explorer to Bring Back China's Most Exotic Animal* (8–12). Illus. 2005, Random $25.95 (0-375-50783-3). 400pp. The unlikely story of Manhattan socialite Ruth Harkness, who successfully completed her late husband's expedition to capture and bring to America a live giant panda. (Rev: BL 5/1/05) [599.789]

2502 Green, Carl R. *The Giant Panda* (3–7). Series: Endangered and Threatened Animals. 2004, Enslow LB $25.26 (0-7660-5061-0). 48pp. Supplemented by a lengthy list of links to online resources, this overview of the giant panda explores its behavior and physical characteristics, as well as the threats it faces. (Rev: BL 6/1–15/04) [599.789]

Birds

GENERAL AND MISCELLANEOUS

2503 Bateman, Robert. *Bateman's Backyard Birds* (4–7). Illus. 2005, Barrons $14.99 (0-7641-5882-1). 48pp. Wildlife artist Bateman introduces readers to numerous North American species of birds and the joys of birding in this beautifully illustrated guide. (Rev: BL 10/15/05) [598]

2504 Hoose, Phillip M. *The Race to Save the Lord God Bird* (5–8). 2004, Farrar $20.00 (0-374-36173-8). 208pp. The sad tale of the ivory-billed woodpecker's decline is interwoven with discussion of the scientific and sociological implications. (Rev: BL 6/1–15/04; SLJ 9/04) [598.7]

2505 Martin, Gilles. *Birds* (5–8). Illus. 2005, Abrams $18.95 (0-8109-5878-3). 80pp. An oversize book full of color photographs of birds, plus watercolor sketches and brief, quite advanced text that comments on various aspects of the birds. (Rev: BL 5/1/05; SLJ 5/05) [598.22]

BEHAVIOR

2506 Read, Marie. *Secret Lives of Common Birds: Enjoying Bird Behavior Through the Seasons* (8–12). Illus. 2005, Houghton paper $14.95 (0-618-55872-1). 96pp. Beautiful photographs and season-by-season discussion of bird behavior make this satisfying both for browsers and report writers. (Rev: BL 12/15/05) [598.15]

Environmental Protection and Endangered Species

2507 Kendell, Patricia. *WWF* (5–8). Series: World Watch. 2004, Raintree LB $27.14 (0-7398-6615-X). 48pp. Introduces the World Wildlife Fund's history, organization, and work on behalf of the endangered animals; sidebars provide key facts and relevant quotations. (Rev: BL 4/1/04; SLJ 6/04) [333.95]

Insects and Arachnids

GENERAL AND MISCELLANEOUS

2508 Burnie, David. *Insect* (5–9). Illus. Series: DK/Google e.guides. 2005, DK $17.99 (0-7566-1010-9). 96pp. This highly illustrated guide introduces readers to the life cycle, behavior, diet, and habitat of insects and provides a link to a Web site that serves as a gateway to additional resources. (Rev: SLJ 8/05)

2509 Pascoe, Elaine. *Ant Lions and Lacewings* (4–8). Photos by Dwight Kuhn. Series: Nature Close-Up. 2005, Gale LB $18.96 (1-4103-0310-1). 48pp. Eye-catching close-ups illustrate information on these insects' life cycles and eating habits. Also use *Mantids and Their Relatives* (2005). (Rev: SLJ 6/05)

2510 Waldbauer, Gilbert. *Insights from Insects: What Bad Bugs Can Teach Us* (8–12). Illus. 2005, Prometheus paper $18.00 (1-59102-277-0). 260pp. Friend or foe? Waldbauer profiles 20 insects that most humans consider pests and their roles in the natural world. (Rev: BL 3/15/05) [632]

BEES AND WASPS

2511 Buchmann, Stephen, and Banning Repplier. *Letters from the Hive: An Intimate History of Bees, Honey, and Humankind* (8–12). Illus. 2005, Bantam $24.00 (0-553-80375-1). 274pp. A natural history of bees is accompanied by discussion of their importance as pollinators, their relationship with humans, methods of cooking with honey, and the medicinal benefits of honey. (Rev: BL 4/1/05) [638]

BUTTERFLIES, MOTHS, AND CATERPILLARS

2512 Schappert, Phil. *The Last Monarch Butterfly: Conserving the Monarch Butterfly in a Brave New World* (8–12). Illus. 2004, Firefly paper $19.95 (1-55297-969-5). 114pp. The fascinating story of the monarch butterfly and its incredible migrations is told with an emphasis on the threats it faces. (Rev: BL 12/15/04) [595.78]

SPIDERS AND SCORPIONS

2513 Allman, Toney. *From Spider Webs to Man-Made Silk* (4–7). Illus. Series: Imitating Nature. 2005, Gale LB $17.96 (0-7377-3124-9). 48pp. An introduction to scientists' attempts to replicate spider silk in the laboratory. (Rev: BL 10/15/05) [595.4]

2514 Montgomery, Sy. *The Tarantula Scientist* (4–7). Photos by Nic Bishop. Series: Scientists in the Field. 2004, Houghton $18.00 (0-618-14799-3). 80pp. This informative, photo-filled book chronicles the day-to-day field work of arachnologist Sam Marshall as he searches for tarantulas in the French Guianan rain forest. (Rev: BL 3/15/04; HB 7–8/04; SLJ 5/04) [595.4]

Marine and Freshwater Life

GENERAL AND MISCELLANEOUS

2515 Collard, Sneed B. *On the Coral Reefs* (4–7). Illus. Series: Science Adventures. 2005, Marshall Cavendish LB $17.95 (0-7614-1953-5). 48pp. In addition to a profile of a marine biologist who studies fish that eat parasites living on other fish, Collard presents information on scientific research methods and on global warming and other environmental threats. (Rev: BL 2/1/06) [577.7]

2516 Vogel, Carole G. *Ocean Wildlife* (5–9). Series: The Restless Sea. 2003, Watts LB $29.50 (0-531-12324-3); paper $12.95 (0-531-16681-3). 95pp. A thorough examination of marine life, from algae to whales, with an emphasis on those species facing extinction through pollution, overfishing, and other manmade threats. (Rev: SLJ 3/04) [591.77]

CORALS AND JELLYFISH

2517 Walker, Pam, and Elaine Wood. *The Coral Reef* (8–11). Illus. Series: Life in the Seas. 2005, Facts on File $35.00 (0-8160-5703-6). 140pp. An excellent introduction to the world's coral reefs, looking at how they were formed, the creatures that thrive within them, and the threats they face. (Rev: BL 1/1–15/06) [5/8.77]

FISHES

2518 Pascoe, Elaine. *Freshwater Fish* (4–8). Photos by Dwight Kuhn. Series: Nature Close-Up. 2005, Gale LB $18.96 (1-4103-0308-X). 48pp. Eye-catching close-ups illustrate information on the life cycles and eating habits of freshwater fish. (Rev: SLJ 6/05)

SHARKS

2519 Carwardine, Mark. *Shark* (7–12). Illus. 2004, Firefly paper $24.95 (1-55297-948-2). 168pp. Report writers and shark fans will find material of interest here. (Rev: BL 11/1/04) [597.3]

2520 Casey, Susan. *The Devil's Teeth: A True Story of Obsession and Survival Among America's Great White Sharks* (8–12). Illus. 2005, Holt $25.00 (0-8050-7581-X). 304pp. An account of the annual gathering of great white sharks near the Farallon Islands, less than 30 miles west of San Francisco in the Pacific Ocean. (Rev: BL 6/1–15/05) [597.3]

WHALES, DOLPHINS, AND OTHER SEA MAMMALS

2521 Leon, Vicki. *A Raft of Sea Otters: The Playful Life of a Furry Survivor.* 2nd ed. (4–7). Illus. 2005, London Town paper $7.95 (0-9666490-4-4). 48pp. This accessible introduction to the sea otter and its physical characteristics, behavior, diet, habitat, life cycle, and conservation threats is a picture-book-size revision of an earlier edition and contains excellent photographs. (Rev: BL 7/05) [599.7695]

2522 Simmonds, Mark. *Whales and Dolphins of the World* (8–12). Illus. 2005, MIT $29.95 (0-262-19519-4). 160pp. This photo-filled volume introduces readers to the cetaceans — whales, dolphins, and porpoises — and to their relationship with humans. (Rev: BL 3/15/05) [599.5]

Microscopes, Microbiology, and Biotechnology

2523 Farrell, Jeanette. *Invisible Allies: Microbes That Shape Our Lives* (6–9). Illus. 2005, Farrar $17.00 (0-374-33608-3). 176pp. The beneficial role of microbes (in food production, digestion, waste removal, and so forth) is the focus of this engaging title by the author of *Invisible Enemies* (1998). (Rev: BL 4/15/05*; SLJ 5/05; VOYA 8/05) [579]

2524 Rainis, Kenneth G. *Cell and Microbe Science Fair Projects Using Microscopes, Mold, and More* (6–12). Illus. Series: Biology! Best Science Projects. 2005, Enslow LB $26.60 (0-7660-2369-9). 128pp. This introduction to the study of cells and microbes contains step-by-step instructions for a number of related experiments and projects. (Rev: SLJ 9/05) [578]

2525 Thomas, Peggy. *Bacteria and Viruses* (5–8). Illus. Series: Lucent Library of Science and Technology. 2005, Gale LB $26.96 (1-59018-438-6). 112pp. Introduces the scientists who discovered bacteria and viruses and how we fight ones that harm us and attempt to use others to our benefit. (Rev: BL 1/05)

2526 Walker, Richard. *Microscopic Life* (4–8). Illus. Series: Kingfisher Knowledge. 2004, Kingfisher $11.95 (0-7534-5778-4). 63pp. A well-illustrated look at the tiniest living things — bacteria, viruses, mites, fungi, and molds, for example — and how we study them and attempt to use them to our benefit. (Rev: BL 9/1/04; SLJ 1/05) [579]

Pets

CATS

2527 Stefoff, Rebecca. *Cats* (4–7). Series: Animal-Ways. 2003, Benchmark LB $21.95 (0-7614-1577-7). 112pp. A well-illustrated study of cats, their evolution, behavior, and human attitudes toward them. (Rev: SLJ 3/04) [636.8]

DOGS

2528 Fennell, Jan. *The Dog Listener: Learn How to Communicate with Your Dog for Willing Cooperation* (8–12). 2004, HarperResource paper $16.95 (0-06-008946-6). 400pp. This comprehensive guide tells how one can peacefully coexist with one's dog and how successful training can be accomplished without violent behavior. (Rev: BL 1/1–15/04) [636.7]

2529 Gingold, Alfred. *Dog World: And the Humans Who Live There* (8–12). 2005, Broadway $24.00 (0-7679-1661-1). 256pp. A lighthearted look at the wonders of dog ownership. (Rev: BL 2/1/05) [636.7]

2530 Halls, Kelly Milner. *Wild Dogs: Past and Present* (4–7). Illus. 2005, Darby Creek $18.95 (1-58196-027-1). 64pp. A wide-ranging introduction to dogs and their history, with attractive design, many photographs, and lots of factboxes about dogs both wild and domestic. (Rev: BL 12/1/05; SLJ 11/05) [599.77]

2531 Konik, Michael. *Ella in Europe: An American Dog's International Adventures* (8–12). 2005, Delacorte $20.00 (0-385-33851-1). 302pp. Charming stories about travels through Europe with a great dog named Ella. (Rev: BL 12/15/04) [636.7]

2532 Rogers, Katharine M. *First Friend: A History of Dogs and Humans* (8–12). Illus. 2005, St. Martin's $24.95 (0-312-33188-6). 288pp. Examines the millennia-long relationship between dogs and humans; well-selected illustrations add to the coverage. (Rev: BL 8/05) [636.7]

FISHES

2533 Maitre-Alain, Thierry, and Christian Piednoir. *Aquariums: The Complete Guide to Freshwater and Saltwater Aquariums* (8–12). Illus. 2006, Firefly $39.95 (1-55407-085-6). 288pp. A handsome, photo-filled guide to aquariums, with advice on water, equipment, selection of fish, and suitable plants. (Rev: BL 2/1/06) [639.34]

HORSES

2534 Ransford, Sandy. *The Kingfisher Illustrated Horse and Pony Encyclopedia* (4–8). Photos by Bob Langrish. Illus. 2004, Kingfisher $24.95 (0-7534-5781-4). 224pp. After describing the history and various breeds of horses, this comprehensive and highly illustrated volume explains how to care for horses and how to ride them well and safely. (Rev: BL 3/1/05; SLJ 1/05) [636.1]

2535 Richter, Judy. *Riding for Kids* (4–8). 2003, Storey Kids $23.95 (1-58017-511-2); paper $16.95 (1-58017-510-4). 128pp. An introduction to horsemanship, from caring for horses and riding equipment to advice on safety, showing, and jumping. (Rev: BL 1/1–15/04; SLJ 3/04) [798.2]

2536 Stromberg, Tony. *Spirit Horses* (8–12). Illus. 2005, New World Library $40.00 (1-57731-499-9).

168pp. A photographic celebration of horses in a large-format album, accompanied by quotes from diverse sources. (Rev: BL 11/1/05) [636.1]

Zoos, Aquariums, and Animal Care

2537 Balliet, Gay L. *Lions and Tigers and Mares . . . Oh My!* (8–12). 2004, RDR paper $17.95 (1-57143-105-5). 336pp. In humorous, appealing text, the wife of a Pennsylvania veterinarian sheds new light on the day-to-day challenges facing a vet who treats large and exotic animals. (Rev: BL 9/15/04) [636.089]

2538 Brown, Bradford B. *While You're Here, Doc: Farmyard Adventures of a Maine Veterinarian* (8–12). 2006, Tilbury House paper $15.00 (0-88448-279-0). 192pp. Entertaining stories about life as a veterinarian in rural Maine. (Rev: BL 3/15/06) [636.0]

2539 Zoehfeld, Kathleen W. *Wild Lives: A History of the People and Animals of the Bronx Zoo* (4–7). Illus. 2006, Knopf LB $20.99 (0-375-90630-4). 96pp. The colorful history of the Bronx Zoo, which opened in 1899, is presented with many photographs and with discussion of changing trends in zookeeping. (Rev: BL 3/15/06) [590.73747]

Chemistry

2540 Baxter, Roberta. *Chemical Reaction* (4–8). Illus. Series: The Kidhaven Science Library. 2004, Gale LB $23.70 (0-7377-2072-7). 48pp. Clear, concise text, supported by full-color photographs and diagrams, describes many types of reactions — oxidation and photosynthesis, for example — and discusses their uses. (Rev: SLJ 6/05)

2541 Beatty, Richard. *Manganese* (5–8). Illus. Series: The Elements. 2004, Marshall Cavendish LB $17.95 (0-7614-1813-X). 32pp. Easy-to-follow diagrams, fact boxes, and color illustrations accompany an informative text that introduces manganese and its properties, value, and uses. (Rev: BL 12/1/04)

2542 Brandolini, Anita. *Fizz, Bubble and Flash! Element Explorations and Atom Adventures for Hands-On Science Fun!* (4–7). Series: Kids Can! 2003, Williamson paper $12.95 (1-885593-83-X). 127pp. A friendly narrative and cartoon-style drawing present activities that illustrate basic scientific concepts. (Rev: BL 1/1–15/04; SLJ 11/03) [546]

2543 Gardner, Robert. *Chemistry Science Fair Projects Using Acids, Bases, Metals, Salts, and Inorganic Stuff* (7–10). Illus. Series: Chemistry! Best Science Projects. 2004, Enslow LB $26.60 (0-7660-2210-2). 128pp. Experiments and projects that explore various aspects of inorganic chemistry are presented with background information and safety tips. (Rev: SLJ 2/05) [540]

2544 Gardner, Robert. *Chemistry Science Fair Projects Using French Fries, Gumdrops, Soap, and Other Organic Stuff* (7–12). Illus. Series: Chemistry! Best Science Projects. 2004, Enslow LB $26.60 (0-7660-2211-0). 128pp. Progressively more complex experiments and projects explore various aspects of organic chemistry using everyday items. (Rev: SLJ 4/05) [540]

2545 Goodstein, Madeline. *Plastics and Polymers Science Fair Projects: Using Hair Gel, Soda Bottles, and Slimy Stuff* (7–12). Illus. Series: Chemistry! Best Science Projects. 2004, Enslow LB $20.95 (0-7660-2123-8). 128pp. Introduced by a discussion of the concept of polymers and a model of a hydrocarbon chain, subsequent projects build on this knowledge. (Rev: SLJ 7/04) [507]

2546 Goodstein, Madeline. *Water Science Fair Projects: Using Ice Cubes, Super Soakers, and Other Wet Stuff* (7–12). Illus. Series: Chemistry! Best Science Projects. 2004, Enslow LB $20.95 (0-7660-2124-6). 128pp. Projects that use everyday materials teach students about water and its properties. (Rev: SLJ 7/04)

2547 Gray, Leon. *Iodine* (5–8). Series: Elements (Group 7). 2004, Marshall Cavendish $17.95 (0-7614-1812-1). This introduction to iodine examines the importance of this substance to body chemistry, as well as how it was discovered, where it is found, and its physical characteristics. (Rev: BL 12/1/04) [546]

2548 Miller, Ron. *The Elements: What You Really Want to Know* (7–12). 2005, Twenty-First Century LB $29.27 (0-7613-2794-0). 135pp. After historical information and profiles of key scientists, Miller provides information on each element in order of atomic number. (Rev: SLJ 3/06) [540]

2549 Sparrow, Giles. *Nickel* (5–8). Illus. Series: The Elements. 2004, Marshall Cavendish LB $17.95 (0-7614-1811-3). 32pp. Easy-to-follow diagrams, fact boxes, and color illustrations accompany an informative text that introduces nickel and its properties, value, and uses. (Rev: BL 12/1/04)

2550 Watt, Susan. *Mercury* (5–8). Illus. Series: The Elements. 2004, Marshall Cavendish LB $17.95 (0-7614-1814-8). 32pp. Easy-to-follow diagrams, fact boxes, and color illustrations accompany an informative text that introduces mercury and its properties, value, and uses. (Rev: BL 12/1/04)

Geology and Geography

Earth and Geology

2551 Calhoun, Yael. *Earth Science Fair Projects Using Rocks, Minerals, Magnets, Mud, and More* (5–8). Illus. Series: Earth Science! Best Science Projects. 2005, Enslow LB $19.95 (0-7660-2363-X). 128pp. More than 20 geology-related projects are introduced with clear instructions and interesting background information. (Rev: BL 11/1/05) [550]

2552 Gardner, Robert. *Planet Earth Science Fair Projects Using the Moon, Stars, Beach Balls, Frisbees, and Other Far-Out Stuff* (6–12). Illus. Series: Earth Science! Best Science Projects. 2005, Enslow LB $26.60 (0-7660-2362-1). 128pp. Earth science projects are clearly presented with background information necessary to give full understanding of the underlying principles. (Rev: SLJ 7/05) [551]

Earthquakes and Volcanoes

2553 Burleigh, Robert, adapt. *Volcanoes: Journey to the Crater's Edge* (5–9). Photos by Philippe Bourseiller. 2003, Abrams $14.95 (0-8109-4590-8). 75pp. Volcanoes, lava lakes, ash plumes, and other related phenomena are beautifully illustrated in this oversized photoessay. (Rev: BL 1/1–15/04; SLJ 12/03) [550]

2554 Harper, Kristine C. *The Mount St. Helens Volcanic Eruptions* (5–8). Series: Environmental Disasters. 2005, Facts on File $35.00 (0-8160-5757-5). 100pp. The environment impact of Mount St. Helens' eruptions is examined in this title from the Environmental Disasters series. (Rev: SLJ 11/05)

2555 Lindop, Laurie. *Probing Volcanoes* (5–8). Illus. Series: Science on the Edge. 2003, Millbrook LB $26.90 (0-7613-2700-2). 80pp. A lively introduction to the history of volcanoes and eruptions, the scientists who dare to study volcanoes, and techniques for collecting data and forecasting volcanic activity. (Rev: BL 12/1/03; SLJ 1/04) [551.21]

2556 Reed, Jennifer. *Earthquakes: Disaster and Survival, 2005* (4–7). Illus. Series: Disaster and Survival. 2005, Enslow LB $17.95 (0-7660-2381-8). 48pp. Major earthquakes and their effects are detailed in text and personal accounts, with a chapter devoted to the December 2004 Asian tsunami. (Rev: BL 5/1/05; SLJ 10/05) [363.34]

2557 Worth, Richard. *The San Francisco Earthquake* (5–8). Illus. Series: Environmental Disasters. 2005, Facts on File $35.00 (0-8160-5756-7). 100pp. Worth examines how the San Francisco earthquake of 1906 affected the region's environment. (Rev: SLJ 11/05) [363.34]

Physical Geography

Mountains

2558 Tocci, Salvatore. *Alpine Tundra: Life on the Tallest Mountain* (4–7). Series: Biomes and Habitats. 2005, Watts LB $24.50 (0-531-12365-0). 63pp. Introduces the climate, flora, and fauna found high above sea level on the world's highest mountains. Also use *Arctic Tundra: Life at the North Pole* (2005). (Rev: SLJ 7/05) [577.5]

Ponds, Rivers, and Lakes

2559 Castaldo, Nancy. *River Wild: An Activity Guide to North American Rivers* (4–7). Illus. 2006, Chicago Review $14.95 (1-55652-585-0). 150pp. From a general introduction to the water cycle and watersheds, this volume narrows in on specific rivers in North America and the flora and fauna found there, even offering profiles of riverkeepers. (Rev: BL 3/1/06) [372.8991]

2560 Gilpin, Daniel. *The Snake River* (4–8). Illus. Series: Rivers of North America. 2003, Gareth Stevens LB $23.93 (0-8368-3761-4). 32pp. Following the course of the Snake RIver in the Northwestern United States, with attention to the plant and animal life along it and its role in history. (Rev: SLJ 3/04)

2561 Gray, Leon. *The Missouri River* (4–8). Illus. Series: Rivers of North America. 2003, Gareth Stevens LB $23.93 (0-8368-3758-4). 32pp. A trip along the Missouri, the longest river in the United States, from its source to its confluence with the Mississippi, with a look at the history that has been made on its banks. (Rev: SLJ 3/04)

2562 Harris, Tim. *The Mackenzie River* (4–8). Illus. Series: Rivers of North America. 2003, Gareth Stevens LB $23.93 (0-8368-3756-8). 32pp. A visit to the Mackenzie River in Canada's Northwest Territories and the people, plants, and animals who have lived along it. (Rev: SLJ 3/04)

2563 Hawkes, Steve. *The Tennessee River* (4–8). Illus. Series: Rivers of North America. 2003, Gareth Stevens LB $23.93 (0-8368-3763-0). 32pp. A trip along the length of the Tennessee River, with information on its history, natural attributes, and its effect on the people who live along its path. (Rev: SLJ 3/04)

2564 Jackson, Tom. *The Arkansas River* (4–8). Illus. Series: Rivers of North America. 2003, Gareth Stevens LB $23.93 (0-8368-3752-5). 32pp. Tracing the Arkansas River its entire length of nearly 1,500 miles, with coverage of the people who have lived along it over the centuries and its importance to them. (Rev: SLJ 3/04)

2565 Jackson, Tom. *The Ohio River* (4–8). Illus. Series: Rivers of North America. 2003, Gareth Stevens LB $23.93 (0-8368-3759-2). 32pp. Following the Ohio River from Pittsburgh to its confluence with the Mississippi at Cairo, Illinois, with material on the people and places found along its banks. (Rev: SLJ 3/04)

2566 Lambrecht, Bill. *Big Muddy Blues: True Tales and Twisted Politics Along Lewis and Clark's Missouri River* (8–12). Illus. 2005, St. Martin's $25.95 (0-312-32783-8). 352pp. An engaging history of the Missouri and what has happened to its natural flow in the 200 years since the river was first charted by Lewis and Clark. (Rev: BL 3/15/05) [331.91]

Prairies and Grasslands

2567 Collard, Sneed B. *The Prairie Builders: Reconstructing America's Lost Grasslands* (5–8). Illus. 2005, Houghton $17.00 (0-618-39687-X). 72pp. This wide-format look at a project to regenerate tallgrass prairie and populate it with native plants and animals includes excellent photographs. (Rev: BL 6/1–15/05; SLJ 8/05*) [635.9]

2568 Toupin, Laurie Peach. *Life in the Temperate Grasslands* (4–7). Series: Biomes and Habitats. 2005, Watts LB $24.50 (0-531-12385-5). 63pp. Introduces the climatic conditions, plants, and wildlife of the world's temperate grasslands. Also use *Savannas: Life in the Tropical Grasslands* (2005). (Rev: SLJ 7/05) [577.4]

Rocks, Minerals, and Soil

2569 Farndon, John. *Rock and Mineral* (5–9). Illus. Series: DK/Google e.guides. 2005, DK $17.99 (0-7566-1140-7). 96pp. This highly illustrated guide introduces readers to the basics of geology and provides a link to a Web site that serves as a gateway to additional resources. (Rev: SLJ 8/05) [552]

2570 Trueit, Trudi Strain. *Rocks, Gems, and Minerals* (4–7). Series: Watts Library. 2003, Watts LB $24.00 (0-531-12195-X); paper $8.95 (0-531-16241-9). 63pp. This attractive volume introduces readers to rocks, gems, and minerals and examines the natural forces that created them. (Rev: SLJ 1/04) [552]

Mathematics

General and Miscellaneous

2571 Kummer, Patricia K. *The Calendar* (5–8). Illus. Series: Inventions That Shaped the World. 2005, Watts LB $29.50 (0-531-12340-5). 80pp. Traces the development of calendars from prehistoric times, with period and contemporary illustrations, lists of recommended resources, and a calendar. (Rev: BL 5/15/05) [529]

2572 Long, Lynette. *Great Graphs and Sensational Statistics: Games and Activities That Make Math Easy and Fun* (4–7). Illus. 2004, Wiley paper $12.95 (0-471-21060-9). 118pp. The games and activities in this large-format paperback will give new insights into the value of statistics and graphs and how the latter can be used to visually represent the former. (Rev: BL 5/1/04; SLJ 11/04) [372.7]

Mathematical Games and Puzzles

2573 Ball, Johnny. *Go Figure! A Totally Cool Book About Numbers* (4–7). Illus. 2005, DK $15.99 (0-7566-1374-4). 96pp. A fascinating volume for math-minded youngsters and adults, introducing number-related games and puzzles as well as more sophisticated mathematical disciplines, such as chaos theory, fractals, and topology. (Rev: BL 10/15/05; SLJ 1/06) [510]

2574 Zaslavsky, Claudia. *More Math Games and Activities from Around the World* (3–7). Illus. 2003, Chicago Review paper $14.95 (1-55652-501-X). 160pp. More than 70 inventive math games and activities are accompanied by historical background. (Rev: SLJ 1/04) [793.7]

Meteorology

General and Miscellaneous

2575 Staub, Frank. *The Kids' Book of Clouds and Sky* (5–7). Photos by author. Illus. 2004, Sterling $14.95 (0-8069-7879-1). 79pp. Organized in question-and-answer format, this attractively illustrated book provides an overview of clouds and such subjects as lightning and thunder, fog, storms, the atmosphere, and air pollution. (Rev: SLJ 7/04) [551.57]

Storms

2576 Ceban, Bonnie J. *Tornadoes: Disaster and Survival* (4–7). Series: Deadly Disasters. 2005, Enslow LB $23.93 (0-7660-2383-4). 48pp. Explores the science behind tornadoes and offers advice about how to prepare for and survive such natural disasters. (Rev: SLJ 10/05) [551.5]

2577 Cerveny, Randy. *Freaks of the Storm: From Flying Cows to Stealing Thunder* (8–12). Illus. 2006, Thunder's Mouth paper $16.95 (1-56025-801-2). 368pp. Cerveny chronicles bizarre weather phenomena — from fish falling from the sky to chickens plucked bare by hurricane winds — and extremes of heat, cold, rainfall, and so forth. (Rev: BL 12/1/05) [551.5]

2578 Harper, Kristine C. *Hurricane Andrew* (5–8). Series: Environmental Disasters. 2005, Facts on File $35.00 (0-8160-5759-1). 100pp. The impact of 1992's Hurricane Andrew on Florida's wetlands is seen as a warning about the need to be more prepared. (Rev: SLJ 11/05) [551.5]

2579 Lindop, Laurie. *Chasing Tornadoes* (5–8). Illus. Series: Science on the Edge. 2003, Millbrook LB $26.90 (0-7613-2703-7). 80pp. A lively introduction to tornadoes, the scientists who dare to study them, and techniques for collecting data and forecasting tornado activity. (Rev: BL 12/1/03; SLJ 1/04) [551.55]

Water

2580 Parker, Steve. *The Science of Water: Projects and Experiments with Water Science and Power* (4–7). Illus. Series: Tabletop Scientist. 2005, Heinemann LB $27.79 (1-4034-7282-3). 32pp. The 12 experiments and projects in this collection demonstrate the basic scientific properties of water. (Rev: SLJ 12/05)

Weather

2581 Buckley, Bruce, et al. *Weather: A Visual Guide* (8–12). Illus. 2004, Firefly $29.95 (1-55297-957-1). 304pp. Full of color photographs and clear graphics, this informative volume explores the forces that generate weather and the impact of weather extremes. (Rev: BL 10/15/04; SLJ 12/04; VOYA 4/05) [551.5]

2582 Burt, Christopher C. *Extreme Weather: A Guide and Record Book* (8–12). Illus. 2004, Norton paper $24.95 (0-393-32658-6). 304pp. An overview of weather at its worst, this richly illustrated volume contains a wealth of meteorological data on extreme events, including heat, drought, cold, floods, thunderstorms, windstorms, tornadoes, and fog. (Rev: SLJ 2/05) [551.6]

2583 Rupp, Rebecca. *Weather! Watch How Weather Works* (4–8). Illus. 2003, Storey Kids $21.95 (1-58017-469-8); paper $14.95 (1-58017-420-5). 136pp. A well-illustrated and appealing introduction to the science of weather, with numerous experiments and projects. (Rev: SLJ 5/04) [551.6]

2584 *Scholastic Atlas of Weather* (4–7). Illus. 2004, Scholastic $17.95 (0-439-41902-6). 80pp. Full of illustrations, diagrams, and feature sidebars, this volume covers a variety of weather phenomena in attractive, information-packed spreads. (Rev: SLJ 4/05) [551.5]

2585 Wills, Susan, and Steven Wills. *Meteorology: Predicting the Weather* (5–7). Series: Innovators. 2004, Oliver LB $21.95 (1-881508-61-7). 144pp. Introduces seven scientists who have made substantial contributions to the science of meteorology. (Rev: SLJ 7/04) [920]

Oceanography

General and Miscellaneous

2586 Hutchinson, Stephen, and Lawrence E. Hawkins. *Oceans: A Visual Guide* (8–12). Illus. 2005, Firefly $29.95 (1-55407-069-4). 304pp. With dramatic photographs and highly readable text, oceanographers Hutchinson and Hawkins introduce readers to the oceans of the world and the qualities that clearly distinguish one from the other. (Rev: BL 10/15/05; VOYA 4/06) [551.46]

2587 *Scholastic Atlas of Oceans* (4–7). Illus. 2004, Scholastic $18.95 (0-439-56128-0). 96pp. Full of illustrations, diagrams, and feature sidebars, this attractive, information-packed volume looks at the five oceans and five major seas and their marine life and vulnerability to human activities. (Rev: SLJ 4/05) [551.46]

2588 Vogel, Carole G. *Dangerous Crossings* (5–8). Illus. Series: The Restless Sea. 2003, Watts LB $29.50 (0-531-12325-1); paper $12.95 (0-531-16679-1). 79pp. Ranging widely from tales of endurance at sea to pirates and problems created by global warming, this is an arresting account. (Rev: BL 1/1/04; SLJ 1/04) [910.4]

2589 Vogel, Carole G. *Human Impact* (5–9). Series: The Restless Sea. 2003, Watts LB $29.50 (0-531-12323-5); paper $12.95 (0-531-16680-5). 95pp. An examination of how mankind is endangering the sea and its creatures through activities including coastal development, global warming, and oil spills. (Rev: SLJ 3/04) [333.91]

2590 Vogel, Carole G. *Savage Waters* (5–8). Illus. Series: The Restless Sea. 2003, Watts LB $29.50 (0-531-12321-9); paper $12.95 (0-531-16682-1). 79pp. An entertaining and attractive discussion of the origins of the world's oceans and seas and the forces that influence waves, tides, and tsunamis. Also use *Shifting Shores* (2003). (Rev: BL 1/1/04; SLJ 1/04) [551.46]

Underwater Exploration and Sea Disasters

2591 Allen, Judy, et al. *Higher Ground* (5–8). Illus. 2006, Chrysalis paper $8.99 (1-84458-581-6). 156pp. First-person accounts of survivors and rescue workers mixed with fictional treatments based on fact portray the impact on children of the deadly Indian Ocean tsunami of December 2004. (Rev: BL 2/1/06; SLJ 3/06) [363.349]

2592 Stewart, Gail B. *Catastrophe in Southern Asia: The Tsunami of 2004* (5–8). Series: Overview. 2005, Gale LB $28.70 (1-59018-831-4). 112pp. An information-packed review of the tsunami itself, the human costs of the disaster, and the reconstruction efforts. (Rev: SLJ 12/05)

2593 Torres, John A. *Disaster in the Indian Ocean: Tsunami 2004* (5–8). Illus. Series: Monumental Milestones: Great Events of Modern Times. 2005, Mitchell Lane LB $19.95 (1-58415-344-X). 48pp. This slim volume, uneven in its coverage, nonetheless offers a chilling overview of the devastating Indian Ocean tsunami of December 2004 and includes a number of eyewitness accounts. (Rev: BL 10/15/05; SLJ 12/05) [909]

Physics

General and Miscellaneous

2594 Bortz, Fred. *The Quark* (7–10). Illus. Series: The Library of Subatomic Particles. 2004, Rosen LB $26.50 (0-8239-4533-2). 64pp. Suitable for reluctant readers, this is a clear explanation of the quark, featuring large text and many color illustrations. Also recommended in this series are *The Proton*, *The Photon*, and *The Electron* (all 2004). (Rev: SLJ 10/04)

2595 Juettner, Bonnie. *Molecules* (4–8). Illus. 2004, Gale LB $23.70 (0-7377-2076-X). 48pp. Clear, concise text, supported by full-color photographs and diagrams, describes the characteristics of atoms and molecules. (Rev: SLJ 6/05)

2596 Sonneborn, Liz. *Forces in Nature: Understanding Gravitational, Electrical, and Magnetic Force* (7–12). Illus. Series: Library of Physics. 2005, Rosen LB $25.25 (1-4042-0332-X). 48pp. Explores a wide variety of forces, including gravitational, electrical, magnetic, and electromagnetic, using clear narrative with diagrams and photographs. (Rev: SLJ 12/05)

2597 Willett, Edward. *The Basics of Quantum Physics: Understanding the Photoelectric Effect and Line Spectra* (7–12). Illus. Series: Library of Physics. 2005, Rosen LB $25.25 (1-4042-0334-6). 48pp. Examines the nature of light and the atom, key elements in the study of quantum physics, using clear narrative with diagrams and photographs. (Rev: SLJ 12/05)

2598 Woodford, Chris, and Martin Clowes. *Atoms and Molecules* (4–7). Illus. Series: Routes of Science. 2004, Gale LB $23.70 (1-4103-0295-4). 40pp. A detailed examination of the scientific study of atoms and molecules, with profiles of key individuals and their discoveries, a chronology, and discussion of future advances. (Rev: SLJ 5/05)

Energy and Motion

General and Miscellaneous

2599 Bowden, Rob. *Energy* (5–8). Illus. Series: Sustainable World. 2004, Gale LB $23.70 (0-7377-1897-8). 48pp. The present status and possible future uses of sustainable energy sources (such as wind, water, and sun) are covered in succinct and interesting fashion, and energy choices we all can make are introduced. Also use *Cities*, *Environments*, *Transportation*, and *Waste* (all 2004). (Rev: BL 4/15/04) [333.79]

2600 Cruden, Gabriel. *Energy Alternatives* (5–8). Illus. Series: Lucent Library of Science and Technology. 2005, Gale LB $26.96 (1-59018-530-7). 112pp. A look at the importance of finding alternatives to existing energy sources, covering such technologies as solar, wind, and geothermal power. (Rev: BL 1/05)

2601 Gardner, Robert. *Bicycle Science Projects: Physics on Wheels* (6–9). Series: Science Fair Success. 2004, Enslow LB $26.60 (0-7660-1630-7). 112pp. Gardner outlines 22 projects demonstrating physics principles, all of which use the common bicycle as their basic component. (Rev: BL 12/15/04; SLJ 2/05) [531/.6]

2602 Landau, Elaine. *The History of Energy* (5–8). Series: Major Inventions Through History. 2005, Twenty-First Century LB $26.60 (0-8225-3806-7). 56pp. An attractive look at developments through time in the use of various forms of energy (fire, wind, water, coal, steam, oil and gasoline, electricity, and so forth) and their application in transportation and other sectors. (Rev: SLJ 1/06)

2603 Viegas, Jennifer. *Kinetic and Potential Energy: Understanding Changes Within Physical Systems* (7–12). Illus. Series: Library of Physics. 2005, Rosen LB $25.25 (1-4042-0333-8). 48pp. Examines the distinction between potential and kinetic energy, as well as momentum, mechanical energy, and the laws of energy, using clear narrative with diagrams and photographs. (Rev: SLJ 12/05)

2604 Woodford, Chris. *Power and Energy* (6–9). Illus. Series: History of Invention. 2004, Facts on File $35.00 (0-8160-5440-1). 96pp. A slim introductory overview of advances in power and energy from prehistoric times to today, with illustrations, and profiles of key figures. (Rev: SLJ 12/04)

Nuclear Energy

2605 Lüsted, Marcia, and Greg Lusted. *A Nuclear Power Plant* (8–12). Illus. Series: Building History. 2005, Gale LB $27.45 (1-59018-392-4). 112pp. Explores the history of nuclear power generation and considers the arguments for and against the construction of more nuclear power plants in the United States and elsewhere. (Rev: SLJ 6/05) [333.792]

Magnetism and Electricity

2606 Bodanis, David. *Electric Universe: The Shocking True Story of Electricity* (8–12). 2005, Crown $24.00 (1-4000-4550-9). 320pp. The cast of characters involved in harnessing electricity are subjected to rigorous and entertaining scrutiny. (Rev: BL 2/1/05) [537]

2607 Woodford, Chris, and Martin Clowes. *Electricity* (4–7). Illus. 2004, Gale LB $23.70 (1-4103-0165-6). 40pp. A detailed examination of the development of electricity, with profiles of key individuals and their discoveries, a chronology, and discussion of future advances. (Rev: SLJ 5/05)

Sound

2608 Parker, Steve. *The Science of Sound: Projects and Experiments with Music and Sound Waves* (4–7). Illus. Series: Tabletop Scientist. 2005, Heinemann LB $27.79 (1-4034-7281-5). 32pp. The 12 experiments and projects in this collection demonstrate the basic scientific principles of sound waves. (Rev: SLJ 12/05)

Technology and Engineering

General Works and Miscellaneous Industries

2609 Cobb, Vicki. *Fireworks* (4–8). Photos by Michael Gold. Series: Where's the Science Here? 2005, Lerner LB $23.93 (0-7613-2771-1). 48pp. A well-illustrated, engaging text covers the history and science of pyrotechnics; experiments require adult supervision. Also recommended in this series are *Junk Food* and *Sneakers*(both 2005). (Rev: SLJ 2/06)

2610 Crompton, Samuel Willard. *The Printing Press* (7–10). Series: Transforming Power of Technology. 2003, Chelsea House LB $22.95 (0-7910-7451-X). 120pp. This interesting volume explores the impact of the invention of the printing press on literacy and general social and economic conditions. (Rev: SLJ 6/04)

2611 *Fantastic Feats and Failures* (4–8). 2004, Kids Can paper $7.95 (1-55337-634-X). 52pp. Highs and lows of engineering (the Brooklyn Bridge in the first category, for example, and the Tacoma Narrows in the latter) are reviewed in this fascinating large-format book. (Rev: BL 9/15/04) [624.1]

2612 Harrison, Ian. *The Book of Inventions* (8–12). Illus. 2004, National Geographic $30.00 (0-7922-8296-5). 288pp. A photo-filled review of some eclectic and entertaining inventions, including sliced bread and the lava lamp. (Rev: BL 12/1/04) [609]

2613 Kassinger, Ruth G. *Iron and Steel: From Thor's Hammer to the Space Shuttle* (5–7). Illus. Series: Material World. 2003, Millbrook LB $25.90 (0-7613-2111-X). 80pp. The different ways in which humans have used and processed iron and steel through the ages is the focus of this book. (Rev: BL 5/15/03; SLJ 1/04) [669]

2614 Kerrod, Robin. *New Materials: Present Knowledge, Future Trends* (5–9). Illus. Series: 21st Century Science. 2003, Smart Apple Media LB $18.95 (1-58340-353-1). 44pp. Numerous diagrams, photographs, and drawings help to explain the processing of raw materials and the need to conserve our limited resources. (Rev: SLJ 1/04) [620.11]

2615 Landau, Elaine. *The History of Everyday Life* (5–8). Series: Major Inventions Through History. 2005, Twenty-First Century LB $26.60 (0-8225-3808-3). 56pp. Fireplaces, washing machines, and microwave ovens are among the inventions discussed here that have improved our everyday lives. (Rev: SLJ 2/06)

2616 Packard, Mary. *High-Tech Inventions: A Chapter Book* (3–7). Series: True Tales. 2004, Children's Pr. LB $21.50 (0-516-23728-4). 48pp. A clear and attractive look at the history of computers and at new and future developments, such as a cockroach that might be used for search-and-rescue operations. (Rev: SLJ 2/05) [004]

2617 Slavin, Bill. *Transformed: How Everyday Things Are Made* (4–7). Illus. 2005, Kids Can $24.95 (1-55337-179-8). 160pp. A behind-the-scenes look at the manufacturing process for a wide array of everyday products. (Rev: BL 10/15/05; SLJ 1/06) [670]

2618 Woodford, Chris. *Communication and Computers* (6–9). Illus. Series: History of Invention. 2004, Facts on File $35.00 (0-8160-5443-6). 96pp. A slim introductory overview of advances in communications from prehistoric times to today, with maps, illustrations, and profiles of key figures. (Rev: SLJ 12/04)

2619 Woodford, Chris, et al. *Cool Stuff and How It Works* (8–12). Illus. 2005, DK $24.99 (0-7566-1465-1). 256pp. The inner workings of products ranging from the digital camera to the microwave oven are explained in clear text with lots of bright, often high-tech illustrations. (Rev: BL 12/1/05) [600]

2620 Woods, Michael, and Mary B. Woods. *The History of Communication* (5–8). Series: Major Inventions Through History. 2005, Twenty-First Century LB $26.60 (0-8225-3807-3). 56pp. An attractive look at developments through time in methods of communication — the printing press, telephone, radio, television, and the Internet — and the impact on our lives. (Rev: SLJ 1/06) [302.2]

Building and Construction

2621 Dreyer, Francis. *Lighthouses* (4–7). Photos by Philip Plisson. 2005, Abrams $18.95 (0-8109-5958-5). 78pp. A fascinating and strikingly beautiful overview of lighthouses — of the past and present — and of the courage and loneliness of the men and women who tend them. (Rev: BL 1/1–15/06) [387.1]

2622 Gonzales, Doreen. *Seven Wonders of the Modern World* (4–7). Illus. Series: Seven Wonders of the World. 2005, Enslow LB $25.26 (0-7660-5292-3). 48pp. Profiles seven marvels of modern construction, including the Panama Canal, Toronto's CN Tower, and the Empire State Building in New York City; the text is extended by constantly updated links to Web sites. (Rev: SLJ 11/05)

2623 Greene, Meg. *The Eiffel Tower* (5–8). Series: Building World Landmarks. 2004, Gale LB $18.96 (1-56711-315-X). 48pp. The story of the construction of the Eiffel Tower, which when completed in 1899 was the tallest human-made structure in the world. (Rev: SLJ 7/04) [725]

2624 Mann, Elizabeth. *Empire State Building* (3–8). Series: Wonders of the World Books. 2003, Mikaya $19.95 (1-931414-06-8). 48pp. With a four-page foldout, period photographs, and full-color illustrations, this story of the skyscraper's construction will please both browsers and report writers. (Rev: BL 2/1/04; SLJ 4/04) [974.7]

2625 Mattern, Joanne. *The Chunnel* (5–8). Series: Building World Landmarks. 2004, Gale LB $18.96 (1-56711-301-X). 48pp. The story of the long delays and eventual construction of the tunnel under the English Channel, linking England and France, with a focus on the new technology involved. (Rev: SLJ 7/04) [624.1]

2626 Sullivan, George. *Built to Last: Building America's Amazing Bridges, Dams, Tunnels, and Skyscrapers* (5–8). Illus. 2005, Scholastic $18.99 (0-439-51737-0). 128pp. Seventeen marvels of American engineering — including the Erie Canal,

Hoover Dam, Brooklyn Bridge, and Boston's "Big Dig" — are presented in chronological chapters with good illustrations and fact boxes that add historical and technological context. (Rev: BL 12/1/05; SLJ 3/06*) [624]

2627 Yuan, Margaret Speaker. *The Royal Gorge Bridge* (5–8). Series: Building World Landmarks. 2004, Gale LB $18.96 (1-56711-352-4). 48pp. Examines the engineering and construction challenges involved in the 1929 construction of Colorado's Royal Gorge Bridge. (Rev: SLJ 7/04) [624.2]

Clothing, Textiles, and Jewelry

2628 Bell, Alison. *Fearless Fashion* (6–10). Illus. 2005, Lobster paper $14.95 (1-894222-86-5). 64pp. From preppy to punk to goth to boho, this volume analyzes seven hot fashion trends, looks at trends in history, and gives tips on developing one's own style. (Rev: SLJ 3/05) [391]

2629 Kyi, Tanya L. *The Blue Jean Book: The Story Behind the Seams* (6–9). Illus. 2005, Annick $24.95 (1-55037-917-8); paper $12.95 (1-55037-916-X). 78pp. The colorful history of blue jeans — and their cultural and economic impact — is chronicled in this accessible volume. (Rev: BL 11/1/05; SLJ 1/06; VOYA 4/06) [391]

2630 Weaver, Janice. *From Head to Toe: Bound Feet, Bathing Suits, and Other Bizarre and Beautiful Things* (5–8). 2003, Tundra paper $16.95 (0-88776-654-4). 80pp. History and culture are interwoven in this account of fashion fads over the years, mostly in the West. (Rev: SLJ 2/04) [391]

Computers, Automation, and the Internet

2631 Billings, Charlene W., and Sean M. Grady. *Supercomputers: Charting the Future of Cybernetics*. Rev. ed. (8–12). Illus. Series: Science and Technology in Focus. 2004, Facts on File $29.95 (0-8160-4730-8). 228pp. This revised and expanded edition covers the history of computing devices from ancient clay tablets onward and looks forward to the future potential of optical and quantum computers. (Rev: SLJ 6/04) [004.1]

2632 de la Bédoyère, Guy. *The First Computers* (6–9). Illus. Series: Milestones in Modern Science. 2005, World Almanac LB $30.00 (0-8368-5854-9). 48pp. Suitable for reports, this volume provides a good overview of the development of the first computers and the possibilities these offered. (Rev: SLJ 1/06) [004.6]

2633 German, Dave. *Dave Gorman's Googlewhack! Adventure* (8–12). Illus. 2004, Overlook $24.95 (1-58567-614-4). 352pp. Gorman, a British stand-up comic, writes about his global quest to find google-whacks — two-word Google search queries that yield a single, solitary hit — in the process of which he successfully put off writing a contracted novel. (Rev: BL 9/15/04) [910.4]

2634 Gordon, Sherri Mabry. *Downloading Copyrighted Stuff from the Internet: Stealing or Fair Use?* (7–10). Illus. Series: Issues in Focus Today. 2005, Enslow LB $23.95 (0-7660-2164-5). 104pp. In concise, accessible text, Gordon defines fair use and copyright and examines issues involving downloading of text, music, games, and so forth. (Rev: BL 11/1/05; SLJ 11/05) [346.730]

2635 Herumin, Wendy. *Censorship on the Internet: From Filters to Freedom of Speech* (5 Up). Series: Issues in Focus. 2004, Enslow LB $20.95 (0-7660-1946-2). 128pp. A look at the various ways we restrict the free exchange of information over the Internet and the pros and cons of doing so. (Rev: SLJ 4/04) [303.48]

2636 Jones, David. *Mighty Robots: Mechanical Marvels That Fascinate and Frighten* (5–8). Illus. 2006, Annick $24.95 (1-55037-929-1); paper $14.95 (1-55037-928-3). 126pp. Artificial intelligence, mobility, and various robot roles are discussed in this look at the past, present, and future of robots. (Rev: BL 2/1/06) [629.8]

2637 Lindsay, Dave. *Dave's Quick 'n' Easy Web Pages 2: A Guide to Creating Multi-page Web Sites* (6–10). 2004, Erin paper $11.95 (0-9690609-9-8). 122pp. Readers with little prior knowledge will learn such techniques as creating frames and cascading style sheets as this straightforward title introduces concepts clearly with graphics and advice boxes. (Rev: SLJ 11/04) [005.7]

2638 Selfridge, Benjamin, and Peter Selfridge. *A Kid's Guide to Creating Web Pages for Home and School* (5–10). Illus. 2004, Chicago Review paper $19.95 (1-56976-180-9). 110pp. Simple instructions on creating Web pages using HTML are accompanied by helpful illustrations and sample finished pages. (Rev: SLJ 2/05) [005.7]

2639 Thomas, Peggy. *Artificial Intelligence* (5–8). Illus. Series: Lucent Library of Science and Technology. 2005, Gale LB $22.96 (1-59018-437-8). 112pp. An interesting overview of progress in efforts to create machines that can think like humans. (Rev: BL 1/05) [004]

2640 Weber, Sandra. *The Internet* (7–10). Series: Transforming Power of Technology. 2003, Chelsea House LB $22.95 (0-7910-7449-8). 110pp. A look

at the influence of the Internet on areas ranging from the economy to society to health care and at the implications for schools and libraries. (Rev: SLJ 6/04) [004.6]

2641 Whyborny, Sheila. *Virtual Reality* (5–9). Series: Science on the Edge. 2003, Gale LB $20.95 (1-56711-789-9). 48pp. This book examines the use of sophisticated computer technology to create virtual reality and discusses applications in education, engineering, law, medicine, and entertainment. (Rev: BL 10/15/03; SLJ 2/04) [004]

2642 Yount, Lisa. *Virtual Reality* (5–8). Illus. Series: Lucent Library of Science and Technology. 2004, Gale LB $21.96 (1-59018-107-7). 112pp. An interesting exploration of the evolution and potential of virtual reality technology. (Rev: BL 1/1–15/05) [006.8]

Telecommunications

2643 Byers, Ann. *Communications Satellites* (5–9). Series: The Library of Satellites. 2003, Rosen LB $26.50 (0-8239-3851-4). 64pp. From the first important communications satellites launched in 1962, this account traces the growth of this technology and its possible future developments. (Rev: BL 11/15/03; SLJ 1/04) [001.51]

2644 McCormick, Anita Louise. *The Invention of the Telegraph and Telephone* (7–10). Series: In American History. 2004, Enslow LB $20.95 (0-7660-1841-5). 128pp. The story behind these two great inventions and their impact on society are covered in this volume. (Rev: BL 3/15/04) [621]

2645 Maddison, Simon. *Telecoms: Present Knowledge, Future Trends* (5–9). Illus. Series: 21st Century Science. 2003, Smart Apple Media LB $18.95 (1-58340-352-3). 44pp. Numerous diagrams, photographs, and drawings add to this overview of the history of telecommunications and the status of current technology. (Rev: SLJ 1/04) [384]

Television, Motion Pictures, Radio, and Recording

2646 Abraham, Philip. *Television and Movies* (4–7). Illus. Series: American Pop Culture. 2004, Children's Pr. LB $22.00 (0-516-24074-9); paper $6.95 (0-516-25946-6). 48pp. Traces the technological and cultural development of TV and movies in the United States. (Rev: SLJ 1/05)

Transportation

General and Miscellaneous

2647 Herbst, Judith. *The History of Transportation* (5–8). Series: Major Inventions Through History. 2005, Twenty-First Century LB $26.60 (0-8225-2496-1). 56pp. From the wheel to the airplane, technological innovations involving transport have had a profound impact on our lives as shown in this attractive, well-written volume. (Rev: SLJ 2/06) [973]

2648 Sandler, Martin W. *Straphanging in the USA: Trolleys and Subways in American Life* (5–8). Illus. Series: Transportation in America. 2003, Oxford Univ. LB $19.95 (0-19-513229-7). 61pp. An interesting, well-illustrated look at urban transportation since the early 19th century. (Rev: SLJ 1/04) [388.4]

2649 Williams, Harriet. *Road and Rail Transportation* (6–9). Illus. Series: History of Invention. 2004, Facts on File $35.00 (0-8160-5437-1). 96pp. A slim introductory overview of advances in transportation from prehistoric times to today, with maps, illustrations, and profiles of key figures. (Rev: SLJ 12/04) [629]

2650 Woodford, Chris. *Air and Space Travel* (6–9). Illus. Series: History of Invention. 2004, Facts on File $35.00 (0-8160-5436-3). 96pp. A slim introductory overview of advances in aviation and space travel, with illustrations, and profiles of key figures. (Rev: SLJ 12/04)

2651 Woodford, Chris. *Ships and Submarines* (6–9). Illus. Series: History of Invention. 2004, Facts on File $35.00 (0-8160-5439-8). 96pp. A slim introductory overview of advances in waterborne transport from prehistoric times to today, with maps, illustrations, and profiles of key figures. (Rev: SLJ 12/04)

Airplanes, Aeronautics, and Ballooning

2652 Dick, Ron, and Dan Patterson. *Aviation Century: The Early Years* (8–12). Illus. 2003, Boston Mills $39.95 (1-55046-407-8). 240pp. This volume rich in photographs, the first in a projected three-volume set, covers aviation to the 1930s. (Rev: BL 2/1/04) [629.13]

2653 Homan, Lynn M., and Thomas Reilly. *Women Who Fly* (5–8). 2004, Pelican $14.95 (1-58980-160-1). 104pp. Women's efforts to establish a foothold in the male-dominated field of aviation are recounted in this book that is suitable for browsers. (Rev: BL 7/04; SLJ 9/04) [629.13]

2654 Masters, Nancy Robinson. *The Airplane* (4–8). Series: Inventions That Shaped the World. 2004, Watts LB $29.50 (0-531-12360-X). 80pp. An inter-

esting overview of the discovery and development of flight, with discussion of its impact on our lives today and in the future. (Rev: SLJ 2/05) [629.13]

Automobiles and Trucks

2655 Edmonston, Phil, and Maureen Sawa. *Car Smarts: Hot Tips for the Car Crazy* (7–10). Illus. 2003, Tundra paper $15.95 (0-88776-646-3). 80pp. Attractive and lively, this is a large-format compendium of facts and advice about cars — their history, how they work, and their purchase and maintenance. (Rev: BL 4/1/04; SLJ 7/04; VOYA 10/04) [629.222]

Railroads

2656 Weitzman, David. *The John Bull* (4–7). Illus. 2004, Farrar $16.00 (0-374-38037-6). 40pp. The John Bull, one of the first steam locomotives to travel America's rails, was built in England and shipped across the Atlantic in pieces. (Rev: BL 2/15/04; SLJ 3/04) [625.26]

2657 Weitzman, David. *A Subway for New York* (4–7). Illus. 2005, Farrar $17.00 (0-374-37284-5). 40pp. The story behind the early-20th-century construction of New York City's first subway is presented in picture-book format. (Rev: BL 12/1/05; SLJ 2/06) [625.4]

2658 Zimmermann, Karl. *All Aboard! Passenger Trains Around the World* (4–7). Illus. 2006, Boyds Mills $19.95 (1-59078-325-5). 48pp. Photo-filled double-page spreads show the excitement of travel by train and interweave history, geography, commerce, and technology. (Rev: BL 2/15/06) [385]

2659 Zimmermann, Karl. *Steam Locomotives: Whistling, Chugging, Smoking Iron Horses of the Past* (4–8). Illus. 2004, Boyds Mills $19.95 (1-59078-165-1). 48pp. Informative and photo-filled, this is an appealing history of steam engines. (Rev: BL 2/1/04; SLJ 7/04) [625.26]

Ships and Boats

2660 Fine, Jil. *The Whaleship Essex: The True Story of Moby Dick* (5–8). 2003, Children's Pr. LB $20.00 (0-516-24328-4); paper $6.95 (1-516-27872-X). 48pp. In 1820 the whaleship *Essex* sank after being rammed by an enraged sperm whale in the South Pacific, sending its crew of 20 on a nightmare voyage in small boats; this accessible account includes numerous photographs, maps, and other illustrations. (Rev: SLJ 3/04) [910]

2661 Mayell, Hillary. *Shipwrecks* (5–8). Illus. Series: Man-Made Disasters. 2004, Gale LB $21.96 (1-59018-058-5). 112pp. Period photographs enhance the impact of stories of shipwrecks of all kinds — from fishing boats to luxury liners — during the 19th and 20th centuries. (Rev: SLJ 7/04) [910.4]

Weapons, Submarines, and the Armed Forces

2662 Benson, Michael. *The U.S. Marine Corps* (4–7). Illus. Series: U.S. Armed Forces. 2004, Lerner LB $25.26 (0-8225-1648-9). 64pp. Introduces the history of the Marine Corps, followed by information on recruitment, training, and daily life. (Rev: BL 1/05; SLJ 3/05) [359.6]

2663 Byers, Ann. *America's Star Wars Program* (5–7). Series: The Library of Weapons of Mass Destruction. 2005, Rosen LB $26.50 (1-4042-0287-0). 64pp. Photographs and text document the development of 20th-century missiles and America's controversial "Star Wars" strategy. (Rev: SLJ 11/05) [623]

2664 Donovan, Sandy. *The U.S. Air Force* (4–7). Illus. Series: U.S. Armed Forces. 2004, Lerner LB $25.26 (0-8225-1436-2). 64pp. Introduces the history of the Air Force, followed by information on recruitment, training, and daily life. Also use *U.S. Air Force Special Operations* (2004). (Rev: BL 1/05; SLJ 3/05) [358.4]

2665 Egan, Tracie. *Weapons of Mass Destruction and North Korea* (5–7). Series: The Library of Weapons of Mass Destruction. 2005, Rosen LB $26.50 (1-4042-0296-X). 64pp. Explores what the West knows about North Korea's efforts to build stockpiles of biological, chemical, and — potentially — nuclear weapons. (Rev: SLJ 11/05) [623]

2666 Ermey, R. Lee. *Mail Call* (8–12). Illus. 2005, Hyperion paper $17.95 (1-4013-0779-5). 256pp. History Channel personality offers facts and figures about military weaponry, modern warfare, and other military trivia. (Rev: BL 12/15/04) [355.009]

2667 Gifford, Clive. *The Arms Trade* (6–9). Illus. Series: World Issues. 2004, Chrysalis LB $28.50 (1-59389-154-7). 61pp. This thought-provoking title uses a question-and-answer format to examine the dimensions and ethics of the international arms trade. (Rev: BL 1/1–15/05)

2668 Gurstelle, William. *The Art of the Catapult: Build Greek Ballistae, Roman Onagers, English Trebuchets, and More Ancient Artillery* (5 Up). Illus. 2004, Chicago Review paper $14.95 (1-55652-526-5). 172pp. Information on history, physics, and military tactics, plus step-by-step instructions for the construction of 10 working catapults. (Rev: SLJ 11/04) [623.4]

2669 Hasan, Heather. *American Women of the Gulf War* (6–9). Illus. Series: American Women at War. 2004, Rosen LB $21.95 (0-8239-4447-6). 112pp. Profiles women who participated in the Gulf War — as combatants, prisoners, and/or victims — and discusses the restrictions on their daily lives, providing social and historical context. (Rev: BL 10/15/04; SLJ 12/04) [956.704]

2670 Hasan, Tahara. *Anthrax Attacks Around the World* (4–8). Series: Terrorist Attacks. 2003, Rosen LB $26.50 (0-8239-3859-X). 64pp. Examines the use of anthrax as a terrorist weapon and includes accounts of its use in Japan, the Soviet Union, and the United States. (Rev: SLJ 2/04) [303.6]

2671 Herbst, Judith. *The History of Weapons* (5–8). Series: Major Inventions Through History. 2005, Twenty-First Century LB $26.60 (0-8225-3805-9). 56pp. An attractive look at the evolution of weapons from rocks and sticks to today's weapons of mass destruction. (Rev: SLJ 1/06) [623.4]

2672 Hibbert, Adam. *Chemical and Biological Warfare* (5–9). Series: Face the Facts. 2003, Raintree LB $28.56 (0-7398-6847-0). 56pp. Part of a series on international issues, this volume examines the powers and dangers of chemical and biological weapons. (Rev: SLJ 4/04) [358]

2673 Lefkowitz, Arthur. *Bushnell's Submarine: The Best Kept Secret of the American Revolution* (7–10). Illus. 2006, Scholastic $16.99 (0-439-74352-4). 144pp. The little-known story of the *Turtle*, America's first submarine, which was launched during the closing days of the American Revolution. (Rev: BL 2/15/06; SLJ 4/06) [973.3]

2674 Myers, Walter Dean. *USS Constellation: Pride of the American Navy* (4–8). 2004, Holiday House $16.95 (0-8234-1816-2). 86pp. Myers presents the colorful history of the *USS Constellation*, the last of America's all-sail fighting ships, in this volume with extensive illustrations and other materials. (Rev: BL 7/04; HB 7–8/04; SLJ 8/04) [359.8]

2675 Ripley, Tim. *Weapons Technology* (6–9). Illus. Series: History of Invention. 2004, Facts on File $35.00 (0-8160-5438-X). 96pp. A slim introductory overview of advances in weapons from prehistoric times to today, with maps, illustrations, and profiles of key figures. (Rev: SLJ 12/04) [623.4]

2676 Torr, James D., ed. *Weapons of Mass Destruction* (7–10). Series: Opposing Viewpoints. 2004, Gale LB $26.96 (0-7377-2250-9); paper $17.96 (0-7377-2251-7). 207pp. Terrorist attacks using nuclear or biological weapons, the threat from "rogue" nations, U.S. policies regarding its own weapons of mass destruction, and national defense are all discussed in essays introduced by focus questions. (Rev: SLJ 4/05) [355.02]

2677 Walker, Sally M. *Secrets of a Civil War Submarine: Solving the Mysteries of the H. L. Hunley*

(7–10). Illus. 2005, Carolrhoda $17.95 (1-57505-830-8). 64pp. Walker chronicles the story of the Confederate submarine *H. L. Hunley* from its design and construction through its successful attack on the *USS Housatonic* in 1864 to its discovery on the bottom of Charleston Harbor in 1995. (Rev: BL 4/15/05*; SLJ 5/05) [973.7]

2678 Wolny, Philip. *Weapons Satellites* (5–9). Series: The Library of Satellites. 2003, Rosen LB $26.50 (0-8239-3855-7). 64pp. This account explores the growing technology of weapon satellites that are capable of knocking out enemies' satellites, and launching attacks from outer space. (Rev: BL 11/15/03; SLJ 1/04) [629.46]

Recreation and Sports

Crafts, Hobbies, and Pastimes

General and Miscellaneous

2679 Bell, Alison. *Let's Party!* (6–10). Series: What's Your Style? 2005, Lobster paper $14.95 (1-894222-99-7). 64pp. Eight theme parties are suggested, complete with invitations, decorations, food, music, and so forth; particularly useful may be the tips on keeping parents at bay and dealing with crashers. (Rev: SLJ 3/06) [793.2]

2680 Browning, Marie. *Totally Cool Soapmaking for Kids* (4–7). 2004, Sterling $19.95 (1-4027-0641-3). 96pp. Many of the soapmaking projects in this photo-filled guide require adult supervision for at least part, if not all, of the activity. (Rev: BL 8/04) [668]

2681 Bruder, Mikyla. *Button Girl: More than 20 Cute-as-a-Button Projects* (4–7). Photos by Scott M. Nobles. 2005, Chronicle $12.95 (0-8118-4553-2). 64pp. A spiral-bound guide providing 23 ideas for pretty projects — jewelry, belts, and so forth. (Rev: BL 5/1/05) [745.5]

2682 Check, Laura. *Create Your Own Candles: 30 Easy-to-Make Designs* (5–8). 2004, Williamson paper $8.95 (0-8249-8663-6). 61pp. Safety is stressed in this guide to exciting (and complex) candle creations. (Rev: SLJ 11/04) [745.593]

2683 Martin, Laura C. *Recycled Crafts Box* (3–7). Illus. 2004, Storey Kids $19.95 (1-58017-523-6). 96pp. A craft book with an environmental twist, this volume offers great project ideas plus information on recycling and the history of trash. (Rev: BL 3/15/04; SLJ 7/04) [363.72]

2684 Murillo, Kathy Cano. *The Crafty Diva's Lifestyle Makeover: Awesome Ideas to Spice Up Your Life!* (5–12). Illus. 2005, Watson-Guptill paper $12.95 (0-8230-1008-2). 144pp. The Crafty Diva is back with this collection of easy-to-follow instruc-tions for 50 projects that cover everything from room makeovers to fashion accessories. (Rev: SLJ 9/05)

2685 Pensiero, Janet. *Totally Cool Journals, Notebooks and Diaries* (4–8). Illus. 2004, Sterling $19.95 (1-4027-0341-4). 96pp. A well-illustrated primer on designing and creating an artistic personal journal. (Rev: SLJ 6/04) [686]

2686 Rhatigan, Joe, and Rain Newcomb. *Stamp It! 50 Amazing Projects to Make* (3–7). Illus. Series: Lark Kids' Crafts. 2004, Sterling $19.95 (1-57990-504-8). 112pp. Lots of ideas for making stamps out of all sorts of things, from potatoes to cardboard, in a format designed to foster creativity and imagination. (Rev: SLJ 6/04) [761]

2687 Taylor, Terry. *Altered Art: Techniques for Creating Altered Books, Boxes, Cards and More* (8–12). 2004, Lark $19.95 (1-57990-550-1). 144pp. Terry Taylor provides a fascinating introduction into the world of altered art. (Rev: BL 12/15/04; SLJ 4/05)

2688 Torres, Laura. *Best Friends Forever! 199 Projects to Make and Share* (5–8). Illus. 2004, Workman paper $13.95 (0-7611-3274-0). 148pp. Craft ideas that will appeal to young teens — bracelets, key chains, picture frames, and so forth — are clearly explained and organized into chapters such as "Cool Notes" and "Home and School." (Rev: SLJ 2/05) [745.5]

2689 Wagner, Lisa. *Cool Melt and Pour Soap* (4–7). Photos by Kelly Doudna. Illus. Series: Cool Crafts. 2005, ABDO LB $15.95 (1-59197-741-X). 32pp. Coloring, fragrance, and packaging are all covered in this guide to projects using soap. (Rev: SLJ 7/05)

2690 Winters, Eleanor. *Calligraphy for Kids* (6–12). 2004, Sterling $14.95 (1-4027-0664-2). 128pp. Information on basic tools and techniques and the importance of correct posture introduce calligraphy projects. (Rev: BL 12/15/04) [745.6/1]

American Historical Crafts

2691 Anderson, Maxine. *Great Civil War Projects You Can Build Yourself* (7–10). Illus. 2005, Nomad paper $16.95 (0-9749344-1-0). 160pp. Craft projects explore various aspects of life on the Civil War battlefield and home front — making cornbread, a pinhole camera, a rag doll, and so forth. (Rev: BL 11/1/05; SLJ 11/05) [745.5]

Clay Modeling and Ceramics

2692 Belcher, Judy. *Polymer Clay Creative Traditions: Techniques and Projects Inspired by the Fine and Decorative Arts* (8–12). Illus. 2006, Watson-Guptill paper $21.95 (0-8230-4065-8). 144pp. Step-by-step instructions for more than 30 items that can be crafted from polymer clay. (Rev: BL 12/15/05) [745.57]

2693 Scheunemann, Pam. *Cool Clay Projects* (4–7). Photos by Anders Hanson. Illus. Series: Cool Crafts. 2005, ABDO LB $15.95 (1-59197-740-1). 32pp. Clear, step-by-step instructions for a number of clay projects are accompanied by full-color photos and tips about safety. (Rev: SLJ 7/05) [731.4]

Cooking

2694 Bayless, Rick, and Lanie Bayless. *Rick and Lanie's Excellent Kitchen Adventures* (7–12). Photos by Christopher Hirsheimer. 2004, Stewart, Tabori & Chang $29.95 (1-58479-331-7). 231pp. A culinary tour of the world, sampling recipes from almost every continent. (Rev: SLJ 1/05) [641.5]

2695 Behnke, Alison, and Ehramjian Vartkes. *Cooking the Middle Eastern Way* (7–10). Illus. Series: Easy Ethnic Menu Cookbooks. 2005, Lerner LB $25.26 (0-8225-1238-6). 72pp. An introduction to the basics of Middle East cooking plus a number of authentic recipes from the region. (Rev: BL 5/15/05) [641.5956]

2696 Carle, Megan, and Jill Carle. *Teens Cook: How to Cook What You Want to Eat* (7–12). 2004, Ten Speed paper $19.95 (1-58008-584-9). 146pp. A witty and practical cookbook that introduces varied recipes used by teenage siblings Megan and Jill Carle. (Rev: SLJ 10/04; VOYA 12/04) [641]

2697 Dunningham, Rose. *The Greatest Cookies Ever: Dozens of Delicious, Chewy, Chunky, Fun and Foolproof Recipes* (4–8). Photos by Stewart O'Shields. 2005, Sterling $9.95 (1-57990-627-3). 96pp. More than 70 recipes are included in this spiral-bound guide to cookie making, with useful information about measuring, substitutions, types of mixers, and safety. (Rev: SLJ 2/06) [641.8]

2698 Jacques, Brian. *The Redwall Cookbook* (3–7). 2005, Philomel paper $24.99 (0-399-23791-7). 96pp. "Hare's Pawspring Vegetable Soup" and "Savoury Squirrel Bakes" are among the recipes grouped by season and introduced by a tale about preparations for a feast; the recipes themselves are quite complex. (Rev: SLJ 1/06)

2699 Lagasse, Emeril. *Emeril's There's a Chef in My Family! Recipes to Get Everybody Cooking* (5–10). Photos by Quentin Bacon. 2004, Harper-Collins $22.99 (0-06-000439-8). 209pp. Seventy-six recipes are presented with clear instructions that focus on the enjoyment of cooking. (Rev: SLJ 7/04) [641.5]

2700 Locricchio, Matthew. *The Cooking of Greece* (5–10). Photos by Jack McConnell. Illus. Series: Superchef. 2004, Benchmark LB $20.95 (0-7614-1729-X). 80pp. Recipes follow an informative overview of regional cuisines in Greece and the ingredients commonly used. (Rev: SLJ 4/05)

2701 Locricchio, Matthew. *The Cooking of India* (4–8). Photos by Jack McConnell. Illus. Series: Superchef. 2004, Benchmark $20.95 (0-7614-1730-3). 80pp. Clear instructions guide readers through the steps involved in making dishes from various areas of India; fresh ingredients are recommended and safety is emphasized. Also use *The Cooking of Thailand* (2004). (Rev: SLJ 2/05) [641.5954]

2702 MacLeod, Elizabeth. *Bake and Make Amazing Cookies* (3–8). Series: Kids Can Do It! 2004, Kids Can $12.95 (1-55337-631-5); paper $6.95 (1-55337-632-3). 40pp. Organized under headings such as "Holidays" and "Seasons," these are simple recipes for a wide variety of enticing cookies. (Rev: SLJ 2/05) [641.8]

2703 Segan, Francine. *The Philosopher's Kitchen: Recipes from Ancient Greece and Rome for the Modern Cook* (8–12). 2004, Random $35.00 (1-4000-6099-0). 250pp. Food historian Segan updates recipes from ancient Greece and Rome to suit contemporary tastes and injects culture and context with quotes from Hippocrates, Aristotle, and others. (Rev: SLJ 1/05)

2704 Sheen, Barbara. *Foods of Italy* (4–8). Series: A Taste of Culture. 2005, Gale LB $24.95 (0-7377-3034-X). 64pp. Cultural and historical notes add to the simple, traditional recipes provided. Also use *Foods of Mexico* (2005). (Rev: SLJ 2/06) [641]

2705 Vaughan, Jenny, and Penny Beauchamp. *Christmas Foods* (3–7). Series: A World of Recipes. 2004, Heinemann LB $30.00 (1-4034-4697-0). 48pp. Christmas dishes from around the world have straightforward directions and color photographs. (Rev: BL 6/1–15/04) [641.5]

2706 Vaughan, Jenny, and Penny Beauchamp. *Festival Foods* (3–7). Series: World of Recipes. 2004, Heinemann LB $30.00 (1-4034-4699-7). 48pp. The easy-to-follow recipes here focus on dishes for festive occasions worldwide. (Rev: BL 6/1–15/04) [745.594]

2707 Wolke, Robert L. *What Einstein Told His Cook: Further Adventures in Kitchen Science*, vol. 2 (8–12). Illus. 2005, Norton $25.95 (0-393-05963-7). 384pp. Frequently asked culinary questions are answered in this collection of essays on food and food preparation. (Rev: BL 3/15/05) [641.5]

Costume and Jewelry Making, Dress, and Fashion

2708 Haab, Sherri. *Designer Style Handbags: Techniques and Projects for Unique, Fun, and Elegant Designs from Classic to Retro* (7–12). Photos by Dan Haab. 2005, Watson-Guptill paper $19.95 (0-8230-1288-3). 128pp. Projects suitable for every skill level are accompanied by advice on choosing materials and include bags made from objects such as cigar boxes and candy tins as well as a variety of fabrics and yarns. (Rev: SLJ 1/06; VOYA 12/05) [646.4]

2709 Haab, Sherri, and Michelle Haab. *Dangles and Bangles: 25 Funky Accessories to Make and Wear* (6–9). Illus. 2005, Watson-Guptill paper $9.95 (0-8230-0064-8). 96pp. Ideas for stylish accessories are accompanied by guidance on techniques and materials. (Rev: BL 7/05; SLJ 10/05; VOYA 10/05) [745.5]

2710 Newcomb, Rain. *Girls' World Book of Jewelry: 50 Cool Designs to Make* (5–8). Series: Kids Crafts. 2004, Lark Books paper $14.95 (1-57990-473-4). 128pp. Up-to-date designs are accompanied by well-thought-out instructions and advice in this large-format volume. (Rev: BL 12/15/04; SLJ 4/05)

2711 Sadler, Judy Ann. *Hemp Jewelry* (4–7). Illus. Series: Kids Can Do It! 2005, Kids Can $12.95 (1-55337-774-5); paper $6.95 (1-55337-775-3). 40pp. Sixteen projects for boys and girls using hemp, with drawings and photographs to illustrate the steps and the results. (Rev: BL 3/15/05; SLJ 5/05) [746.4]

2712 Scheunemann, Pam. *Cool Beaded Jewelry* (4–7). Photos by Anders Hanson. Illus. Series: Cool Crafts. 2005, ABDO LB $15.95 (1-59197-739-8). 32pp. Step-by-step instructions and full-color photo-

graphs guide the user through beaded jewelry projects. (Rev: SLJ 7/05) [745]

2713 Warrick, Leanne. *Style Trix for Cool Chix: Your One-Stop Guide to Finding the Perfect Look* (7–10). Photos by Shona Wood. Illus. 2005, Watson-Guptill paper $9.95 (0-8230-4940-X). 96pp. A useful collection of tips on shopping, color coordination, closet organization, accessories, and finding clothes that fit. (Rev: SLJ 8/05; VOYA 8/05) [391]

Drawing and Painting

2714 ComicsKey Staff. *How to Draw Kung Fu Comics* (4–8). 2004, ComicsOne paper $19.95 (1-58899-394-9). 160pp. Cheung's instructions on creating architecture and perspective are particularly valuable. (Rev: BL 8/04) [741.5]

2715 Hart, Christopher. *Christopher Hart's Cartoon Studio* (8–12). 2003, Watson-Guptill paper $7.95 (0-8230-0624-7). 48pp. Hart introduces cartoon techniques such as drawing the same characters consistently from different angles. Also use *Christopher Hart's Animation Studio* (2003). (Rev: SLJ 1/04) [741.5]

2716 Hart, Christopher. *Kids Draw Manga* (3–8). Series: Kids Draw. 2004, Watson-Guptill paper $10.95 (0-8230-2623-X). 64pp. For beginners, this is a guide to the basics of manga, showing how to draw a number of characters, poses, and action moves. (Rev: SLJ 9/04) [741.5]

2717 Hinds, Kathryn. *The City* (5–8). Illus. Series: Life in the Renaissance. 2003, Marshall Cavendish LB $20.95 (0-7614-1678-1). 96pp. Using London, Paris, and Florence among the examples, this entry in a four-volume series explores most aspects of daily life within the walled cities of Western Europe during the 15th and 16th centuries. Also use *The Court* (2003). (Rev: BL 2/1/04; SLJ 4/04) [940.1]

2718 Hodge, Anthony. *Drawing* (4–8). Series: Mastering Art. 2004, Stargazer Books LB $.00 (1-932799-01-X). 32pp. Along with basic information on materials, colors, and techniques, this slim volume looks at drawing the human body. Also use *Painting* (2004). (Rev: BL 11/1/04) [741.2]

2719 Nagatomo, Haruno. *Draw Your Own Manga: Beyond the Basics* (7–12). Trans. from Japanese by Françoise White. 2005, Kodansha paper $19.95 (4-7700-2304-9). 111pp. Written and illustrated by Japanese manga artists, this is an entertaining yet professional guide to drawing in this style. (Rev: SLJ 9/05; VOYA 12/04) [741.5]

2720 Okum, David. *Manga Madness* (7–12). Illus. 2004, North Light paper $19.99 (1-58180-534-9). 128pp. This is an excellent guide for would-be cartoonists and *manga* fans with step-by-step directions on how to produce your own art. (Rev: BL 3/15/04) [741.5]

2721 Temple, Kathryn. *Drawing* (5–8). Illus. Series: Art for Kids. 2005, Sterling $17.95 (1-57990-587-0). 112pp. A comprehensive and clearly written guide to equipment and techniques, with useful illustrations and practical exercises at the end of each section. (Rev: BL 5/1/05; SLJ 9/05) [741.2]

Gardening

2722 Klindienst, Patricia. *The Earth Knows My Name: Food, Culture, and Sustainability in the Gardens of Ethnic Americans* (8–12). Illus. 2006, Beacon $26.95 (0-8070-8562-6). 304pp. A tour of 15 American gardens that represent the culture and ethnicity of their immigrant designers. (Rev: BL 4/1/06) [635.09]

Magic Tricks and Optical Illusions

2723 Keable, Ian. *The Big Book of Magic Fun* (5–9). Photos by Steve Tanner. Illus. 2005, Barron's paper $14.99 (0-7641-3222-9). 192pp. Step-by-step instructions, with photographs, are given for 40 tricks plus discussion of suitable props and a history of different kinds of magic and famous performers. (Rev: SLJ 3/06) [793.8]

2724 Mandelberg, Robert. *Mind-Reading Card Tricks* (6–9). 2004, Sterling paper $5.95 (1-4027-0948-X). 95pp. Tricks that convince others that you are reading their minds are explained in detail, with difficulty ratings. (Rev: SLJ 3/05) [795.4]

2725 *Wizardology: The Book of the Secrets of Merlin* (5–8). Illus. 2005, Candlewick $19.99 (0-7636-2895-6). 32pp. This follow-up to *Dragonology* offers a variety of information for wannabe wizards. (Rev: BL 10/15/05)

Paper Crafts

2726 Aimone, Katherine Duncan. *Artful Cards: 60 Fresh and Fabulous Designs* (8–12). Illus. 2005, Sterling $24.95 (1-57990-551-X). 144pp. Suggestions for creating a wide array of greeting cards, tags, and invitations are included in this easy-to-follow guide. (Rev: BL 12/15/05) [745.594]

2727 Nguyen, Duy. *Jungle Animal Origami* (4–12). 2003, Sterling $19.95 (1-4027-0777-0). 96pp. Best suited for paper crafters with fairly advanced skills, this book by master artist Duy Nguyen offers

instructions for creating a menagerie of origami animals. (Rev: BL 12/15/03; SLJ 3/04)

2728 Nguyen, Duy. *Under the Sea Origami* (5–7). Illus. 2005, Sterling $19.95 (1-4027-1541-2). 96pp. Sharks, an octopus, and a sea horse are among the marine animals featured in this origami collection. (Rev: SLJ 4/05) [736]

2729 Prins, M. D. *Paper Galaxy: Out-of-This-World Projects to Cut, Fold, and Paste* (6–9). Illus. 2005, Sterling $19.95 (1-402-72131-5). 128pp. Most of the designs in this volume — sunbursts, stars, meteorites, and so forth — require glue and consist of geometric bases with 3-D attachments. (Rev: BL 12/15/05) [736]

2730 Rhatigan, Joe, and Rain Newcomb. *Paper Fantastic: 50 Creative Projects to Fold, Cut, Glue, Paint and Weave* (3–7). Illus. Series: Lark Kids' Crafts. 2004, Sterling $19.95 (1-57990-476-9). 111pp. Interesting, practical projects feature papier mâché, origami, mosaics, and stamp-making. (Rev: SLJ 6/04) [745]

Photography, Video, and Film Making

2731 Bidner, Jenni. *The Kids' Guide to Digital Photography: How to Shoot, Save, Play with and Print Your Digital Photos* (7–10). Illus. 2004, Sterling $14.95 (1-57990-604-4). 96pp. A user-friendly guide to digital photography and the transfer of the results to the Web and other applications. (Rev: BL 1/1–15/05; SLJ 5/05) [775]

2732 Shulman, Mark, and Hazlitt Korg. *Attack of the Killer Video Book: Tips and Tricks for Young Directors* (5–8). 2004, Annick $24.95 (1-55037-841-4); paper $12.95 (1-55037-840-6). 64pp. Practical advice on all aspects of movie making will be helpful for aspiring directors. (Rev: BL 5/15/04; SLJ 6/04) [778.59]

Sewing and Other Needle Crafts

2733 Bradberry, Sarah. *Kids Knit! Simple Steps to Nifty Projects* (4–8). Photos by Michael Hnatov. 2004, Sterling $14.95 (0-8069-7733-7). 96pp. Simple, clear instructions and illustrations add to the value of this book full of appealing projects. (Rev: BL 12/15/04; SLJ 2/05)

2734 Clewer, Carolyn. *Kids Can Knit: Fun and Easy Projects for Small Knitters* (3–7). 2003, Barron's paper $16.95 (0-7641-2718-7). 128pp. The reader gradually moves from simple techniques to more sophisticated projects. (Rev: BL 12/15/03; SLJ 3/04)

2735 Eckman, Edie. *The Crochet Answer Book: Solutions to Every Problem You'll Ever Face, Answers to Every Question You'll Ever Ask* (7–12). Illus. 2005, Storey paper $12.95 (1-58017-598-8). 400pp. For novice crocheters, this is a well-organized and comprehensive guide. (Rev: BL 12/15/05) [746.43]

2736 Ivarsson, Anna-Stina Linden, et al. *Second-Time Cool: The Art of Chopping Up a Sweater* (7–10). Trans. by Maria Lundin. Illus. 2005, Annick $24.95 (1-55037-911-9); paper $12.95 (1-55037-910-0). 96pp. Adventurous clothes recycling for the ambitious teen with too much old wool lying around. (Rev: BL 1/1–15/06; SLJ 1/06) [646.4]

2737 Nicholas, Kristin, and John Gruen. *Kids' Embroidery: Projects for Kids of All Ages* (3–7). 2004, Stewart, Tabori & Chang $19.95 (1-58479-366-X). 144pp. Step-by-step instructions guide readers through 15 colorful embroidery projects. (Rev: BL 12/15/04)

2738 Okey, Shannon. *Knitgrrl: Learn to Knit with 15 Fun and Funky Projects* (5–8). Photos by Shannon Fagan. Illus. 2005, Watson-Guptill paper $9.95 (0-8230-2618-3). 96pp. Up-to-date designs are shown clearly and explained in detail. (Rev: BL 12/15/05*; SLJ 11/05; VOYA 12/05) [746.43]

2739 Radcliffe, Margaret. *The Knitting Answer Book* (8–12). Illus. 2005, Storey paper $12.95 (1-58017-599-6). 400pp. This well-organized volume introduces newcomers to knitting and also provides expert guidance for longtime knitters. (Rev: BL 12/15/05) [746.43]

2740 Ronci, Kelli. *Kids Crochet: Projects for Kids of All Ages* (4–8). Photos by John Gruen. Illus. 2005, Stewart, Tabori & Chang $19.95 (1-58479-413-5). 128pp. A poncho, a quilt, and a tool pouch are among the 15 crocheting projects presented, which are introduced by detailed coverage of techniques. (Rev: BL 5/15/04; SLJ 6/05) [745.5]

2741 Sadler, Judy Ann. *Embroidery* (4–8). Series: Kids Can Do It! 2004, Kids Can $12.95 (1-55337-

616-1); paper $6.95 (1-55337-617-X). 40pp. In addition to a thorough introduction to embroidery and various stitches, Sadler provides nine projects that progress in difficulty. (Rev: SLJ 8/04) [746.44]

2742 Sadler, Judy Ann. *Simply Sewing* (4–8). Series: Kids Can Do It! 2004, Kids Can $12.95 (1-55337-659-5); paper $6.95 (1-55337-660-9). 48pp. Detailed instructions for 12 projects — a makeup bag and a jeans skirt, for example — follow basic information on sewing by hand and by machine. (Rev: BL 12/15/04; SLJ 11/04)

2743 Sadler, Judy Ann, et al. *The Jumbo Book of Needlecrafts* (4–7). 2005, Kids Can paper $16.95 (1-55337-793-1). 208pp. After advice on getting started, step-by-step directions guide readers through a range of needlecraft projects. (Rev: SLJ 5/05)

2744 Wenger, Jennifer, et al. *Teen Knitting Club: Chill Out and Knit Some Cool Stuff* (5–9). Illus. 2004, Artisan $17.95 (1-57965-244-1). 128pp. Children who already know how to know will derive the most benefit from this collection of 35 appealing projects. (Rev: BL 12/15/04; SLJ 2/05)

Woodworking and Carpentry

2745 Robertson, J. Craig, and Barbara Robertson. *The Kids' Building Workshop: 15 Woodworking Projects for Kids and Parents to Build Together* (3–7). Illus. 2004, Storey Kids $22.95 (1-58017-572-4); paper $12.95 (1-58017-488-4). 136pp. After discussing tools and techniques, 15 projects — a bird house, a stool, for example — are presented in order of increasing difficulty. (Rev: SLJ 2/05) [684]

2746 Schwarz, Renee. *Birdhouses* (4–7). Illus. Series: Kids Can Do It! 2005, Kids Can $12.95 (1-55337-549-1); paper $6.95 (1-55337-550-5). 40pp. Nine different birdhouse projects for children to tackle, with illustrated instructions and photographs of the finished products. (Rev: BL 4/1/05; SLJ 5/05) [690]

Jokes, Puzzles, Riddles, and Word Games

2747 Becker, Helaine. *Funny Business: Clowning Around, Practical Jokes, Cool Comedy, Cartooning, and More. . . .* (5–8). 2005, Maple Tree $21.95 (1-897066-40-6); paper $9.95 (1-897066-41-4). 160pp. Tips on body language, stand-up routines, clowning, and so forth are accompanied by discussion of various types of humor, a self-quiz, and recipes for delights including "Moose Droppings." (Rev: SLJ 1/06) [808.7]

Mysteries, Curiosities, and Controversial Subjects

2748 Allman, Toney. *Werewolves* (4–7). Series: Monsters. 2004, Gale LB $23.70 (0-7377-2620-2). 48pp. An examination of the origins of the werewolf, with references to and illustrations from movie and TV appearances by these monsters. (Rev: SLJ 4/05) [398]

2749 Blackwood, Gary L. *Debatable Deaths* (4–8). Series: Unsolved History. 2005, Benchmark LB $20.95 (0-7614-1888-1). 72pp. Mysterious deaths discussed include those of Tutankhamen, Mozart, Sacagawea, and Meriwether Lewis. Also recommended in this series (both published in 2005) are *Legends or Lies?* (Atlantis, King Arthur, Robin Hood, and so forth) and *Perplexing People* (Anastasia and Billy the Kid, to name just two). (Rev: SLJ 3/06)

2750 Feldman, David, and Kassie Schwan. *Do Elephants Jump? An Imponderables Book* (8–12). Illus. Series: Imponderables. 2004, HarperCollins $19.95 (0-06-053913-5). 352pp. Why *do* elephants jump? Another intriguing — or unexpected — question is answered in this tenth installment in the attention-grabbing series. (Rev: BL 11/1/04) [031]

2751 Holt, David, and Bill Mooney, retel. *The Exploding Toilet: Modern Urban Legends* (7–12). 2004, August House $16.95 (0-87483-754-5); paper $6.95 (0-87483-715-4). 112pp. Amazing, often funny, shocking stories, many of which have appeared on the Internet. (Rev: SLJ 8/04) [398.2]

2752 Johnson, Julie Tallarad. *Teen Psychic: Exploring Your Intuitive Spiritual Powers* (8–12). 2003, Inner Traditions paper $14.95 (0-89281-094-7). 256pp. An introduction to investigating and developing one's intuitive powers, with quizzes, exercises, mediations, and many personal stories from teens. (Rev: BL 1/1–15/04; VOYA 4/04) [131]

2753 Kallen, Stuart A. *Dreams* (4–8). Illus. Series: The Mystery Library. 2004, Gale LB $27.45 (1-59018-288-X). 112pp. In this volume in the Mystery Library, Kallen examines topics including dream science, the interpretation of dreams, and telepathic dreaming. Also use *Ghosts, Possessions and Exorcisms*, and *Shamans* (all 2004). (Rev: BL 5/15/04) [154.6]

2754 Kallen, Stuart A. *Fortune-Telling* (4–8). Illus. Series: Mystery Library. 2004, Gale LB $21.96 (1-59018-289-8). 112pp. This exploration of the history and mystery of fortune-telling separates fact from fiction. (Rev: BL 5/15/04) [133.3]

2755 Miller, Raymond H. *Vampires* (4–7). Series: Monsters. 2004, Gale LB $23.70 (0-7377-2619-9). 48pp. An examination of the origins of the vampire, with references to and illustrations from movie and TV appearances by these monsters. (Rev: SLJ 4/05) [398]

2756 Nardo, Don. *Atlantis* (5–8). Illus. Series: The Mystery Library. 2004, Gale LB $21.96 (1-59018-287-1). 112pp. The author examines whether the ancient story of the lost continent of Atlantis — as described by Plato — could be true. (Rev: BL 5/15/04; SLJ 4/04) [001.94]

2757 Nardo, Don. *Extraterrestrial Life* (4–8). Illus. Series: Mystery Library. 2004, Gale LB $21.96 (1-59018-320-7). 112pp. This overview of encounters with aliens and the search for life elsewhere separates fact from fiction. (Rev: BL 5/15/04) [579.8]

2758 Nardo, Don, and Bradley Steffens. *Medusa* (4–7). Series: Monsters. 2004, Gale LB $23.70 (0-7377-2617-2). 48pp. Describes the mythological personage, telling the story of Perseus killing Medusa, and showing her role in paintings, sculptures, movie stills, and computer games. Also use *Cyclops* (2004). (Rev: SLJ 4/05) [398.2]

2759 *Ripley's Believe It or Not!* (4–7). Illus. 2004, Ripley $25.95 (1-893951-73-1). 256pp. Packed with fascinating trivia and fun for browsing, this appealing volume focuses on weird and amazing facts. (Rev: SLJ 2/05) [031.02]

2760 *Ripley's Believe It or Not! Planet Eccentric!* (6–12). 2005, Ripley $27.95 (1-893951-10-3). 256pp. Weird and wonderful facts in categories such as "Animal Antics" and "All-Consuming" are accompanied by eye-catching photographs. (Rev: SLJ 1/06) [031.02]

2761 Shaw, Maria. *Maria Shaw's Book of Love: Horoscopes, Palmistry, Numbers, Candles, Gemstones and Colors* (8–12). Illus. 2005, Llewellyn paper $14.95 (0-7387-0545-4). 174pp. A lighthearted guide to unscientific methods of predicting the course of true love. (Rev: SLJ 2/05) [133.3]

2762 Slade, Arthur. *Monsterology: Fabulous Lives of the Creepy, the Revolting, and the Undead* (5–8). 2005, Tundra paper $8.95 (0-88776-714-1). 95pp. Dracula, Medusa, Dr. Jekyll/Mr. Hyde, and Sasquatch are among the characters profiled in this entertaining volume, each with a list of loves and hates, favorite saying, and fashion rating. (Rev: SLJ 2/06; VOYA 2/06)

2763 Van Praagh, James. *Looking Beyond: A Teen's Guide to the Spiritual World* (8–12). Illus. 2003, Simon & Schuster paper $12.00 (0-7432-2942-8). 160pp. Psychic Van Praagh tells teens what his contacts with the spirit world have taught him about the meaning of life and what we can do to make the most of it. (Rev: BL 1/1–15/04) [133.9]

Sports and Games

General and Miscellaneous

2764 Blumenthal, Karen. *Let Me Play: The Story of Title IX: The Law That Changed the Future of Girls in America* (6–10). Illus. 2005, Simon & Schuster $17.95 (0-689-85957-0). 160pp. Personal anecdotes, political cartoons, and profiles of female athletes add to the story of the 1972 passage of Title IX, which bans sex discrimination in U.S. schools. (Rev: BL 7/05; SLJ 7/05*) [796]

2765 Glenn, Jim, and Carey Denton. *The Treasury of Family Games: Hundreds of Fun Games for All Ages, Complete with Rules and Strategies* (5–10). Illus. 2003, Reader's Digest $29.95 (0-7621-0431-7). 256pp. Games of every kind are simply explained and illustrated in this compendium, with material on their rules and their history. (Rev: SLJ 6/04) [793]

2766 Housewright, Ed. *Winning Track and Field for Girls* (7–12). 2003, Facts on File $35.00 (0-8160-5231-X). 188pp. A history of women's track is followed by specific information on sprints, hurdles, cross-country, triathlon, and so forth, with details of record holders and quotations from famous athletes; final chapters cover mental and physical preparation. (Rev: SLJ 6/04; VOYA 6/04) [796.42]

2767 Jones, Jen. *Cheer Tryouts: Making the Cut* (3–7). Illus. Series: Snap Books Cheerleading. 2005, Capstone LB $22.60 (0-7368-4361-2). 32pp. The focus here is on preparation — from good nutrition and regular stretching to practicing drills and a good attitude; part of a series that also includes *Cheer Squad: Building Spirit and Getting Along* (2005). (Rev: SLJ 1/06) [791.6]

2768 Kalman, Bobbie, and John Crossingham. *Extreme Sports* (4–8). Series: Extreme Sports No Limits! 2004, Crabtree LB $23.92 (0-7787-1673-2).

32pp. All manner of extreme sports are covered in this overview. (Rev: BL 9/1/04)

2769 King, Daniel. *Games: Learn to Play, Play to Win* (5–8). Illus. 2003, Kingfisher $16.95 (0-7534-5581-1). 64pp. An instructional introduction to 14 board and card games, including cribbage to chess, with appropriate historical background. (Rev: SLJ 5/04) [794]

2770 Porter, David L. *Winning Weight Training for Girls: Fitness and Conditioning for Sports* (7–12). 2003, Facts on File $35.00 (0-8160-5185-2). 205pp. The benefits of weight training for specific sports — basketball, softball, field hockey, and volleyball — are outlined following the basics of safe weight training. (Rev: SLJ 6/04) [613.7]

2771 Shannon, Joyce Brennfleck, ed. *Sports Injuries Information for Teens: Health Tips About Sports Injuries and Injury Prevention* (8–12). Series: Teen Health. 2003, Omnigraphics $58.00 (0-7808-0447-3). 405pp. Basic information on sports injuries and treatment is provided in separate sections on such topics as emergency treatment, common injuries affecting teens, rehabilitation and physical therapy, injury prevention, and sports nutrition. (Rev: SLJ 7/04; VOYA 10/04) [617.1]

2772 Swissler, Becky. *Winning Lacrosse for Girls* (7–12). 2004, Facts on File $35.00 (0-8160-5183-6). 192pp. A clear and detailed introduction to the game of lacrosse, covering its history as well as individual skills and team dynamics. (Rev: SLJ 5/04) [796.34]

2773 Thomas, Keltie. *Blades, Boards and Scooters* (4–8). Illus. Series: Popular Mechanics for Kids Books. 2003, Maple Tree $21.95 (1-894379-45-4). 64pp. Practical information on equipment, maintenance, and safety are accompanied by discussion of the history, science, and culture of these sports. (Rev: BL 2/1/04) [796.2]

2774 Tomlinson, Joe, and Ed Leigh. *Extreme Sports: In Search of the Ultimate Thrill* (8–12). 2004, Firefly $19.95 (1-55297-992-X). 192pp. Explores the full spectrum of extreme sports — on land, in the air, and in or on the water. (Rev: SLJ 4/05; VOYA 10/05)

Automobile Racing

2775 Buckley, James. *NASCAR* (5–8). Illus. Series: Eyewitness Books. 2005, DK LB $19.99 (0-7566-1193-8). 72pp. A visual pleasure for NASCAR fans, full of information about people, places, individual races, engineering advances, and so forth. (Rev: BL 9/1/05) [796.72]

2776 Miller, Timothy, and Steve Milton. *NASCAR Now* (8–12). 2004, Firefly $19.95 (1-55297-829-X). 160pp. Covering the basics of maintenance, safety, and equipment as well as history, scoring, track features, and profiles of key individuals, this well-illustrated guide will suit novices and diehard fans. (Rev: SLJ 1/05) [796.72]

2777 Schaefer, A. R. *The Daytona 500* (4–7). Illus. Series: NASCAR Racing. 2004, Capstone LB $22.60 (0-7368-2423-5). 32pp. This slim volume celebrates one of America's most famous automobile racing venues and some of the illustrious drivers who achieved fame there. (Rev: BL 4/1/04) [790.72]

Baseball

2778 Bissinger, Buzz. *Three Nights in August: Strategy, Heartbreak, and Joy Inside the Heart of a Manager* (8–12). 2005, Houghton $25.00 (0-618-40544-5). 304pp. Bissinger dissects a three-game August 2003 series between baseball's St. Louis Cardinals and Chicago Cubs. (Rev: BL 3/1/05) [796.357]

2779 Bryant, Howard. *Juicing the Game: Drugs, Power, and the Fight for the Soul of Major League Baseball* (8–12). 2005, Viking $24.95 (0-670-03445-2). 424pp. Traces the history of steroid use in professional baseball and the impact on the sport as a whole. (Rev: BL 7/05) [796.357]

2780 Coffey, Michael. *27 Men Out: Baseball's Perfect Games* (8–12). 2004, Atria $25.00 (0-7434-4606-2). 320pp. In the history of major league baseball, there have been only 14 perfect games in which all of the batters struck out. This is an analysis of each of these games. (Rev: BL 3/1/04) [796.357]

2781 January, Brendan. *A Baseball All-Star* (6–8). Illus. Series: The Making of a Champion. 2004, Heinemann LB $29.93 (1-4034-5362-4). 48pp. History, rules, training, and tactics are among the topics discussed, along with information on key players. (Rev: SLJ 3/05) [796.357]

2782 Krasner, Steven. *Play Ball like the Hall of Famers: Tips for Kids from 19 Baseball Greats* (6–9). 2005, Peachtree paper $14.95 (1-56145-339-0). 208pp. Using a question-and-answer format, notable baseball players give advice on different topics — pitching, fielding, base-running, and so forth. (Rev: BL 5/1/05; SLJ 6/05) [796.357]

2783 Mackel, Kathy. *MadCat* (5–8). 2005, HarperCollins LB $16.89 (0-06-054870-3). 192pp. Madelyn Catherine (aka MadCat), catcher on her local girls' fast-pitch softball team, is at the center of this story about sports, team play, and family involvement. (Rev: BL 2/15/05; SLJ 3/05)

2784 Whiting, Robert. *The Meaning of Ichiro: The New Wave from Japan and the Transformation of Our National Pastime* (8–12). Illus. 2004, Warner $25.00 (0-446-53192-8). 320pp. This collection of essays describes the way baseball is viewed and played in Japan as opposed to the United States and also supplies material on such stars as Ichiro. (Rev: BL 4/15/04) [796.357]

Basketball

2785 Ingram, Scott. *A Basketball All-Star* (6–8). Illus. Series: The Making of a Champion. 2004, Heinemann LB $29.93 (1-4034-5363-2). 48pp. History, rules, training, and tactics are among the topics discussed, along with information on key players. (Rev: SLJ 3/05) [796.323]

2786 Klein, Leigh, and Matt Masiero, eds. *My Favorite Moves: Shooting Like the Stars* (6–12). Series: Five Star Basketball. 2003, Wish paper $12.95 (1-930546-58-0). 137pp. Best for readers already familiar with the game, this drill book includes advice from five professional women players. Also use *My Favorite Moves: Making the Big Plays* (2003). (Rev: SLJ 1/04) [796.323]

2787 Lazenby, Roland. *The Show: The Inside Story of the Spectacular Los Angeles Lakers in the Words of Those Who Lived It* (8–12). Illus. 2006, McGraw-Hill $27.95 (0-07-143034-2). 544pp. This excellent volume traces the NBA team's fortunes from its inauspicious beginnings in Minneapolis in the early 1950s through its most recent string of championships. (Rev: BL 11/15/05) [796.323]

2788 Palmer, Chris. *Streetball: All the Ballers, Moves, Slams, and Shine* (8–12). Illus. 2004, Harper Resource paper $16.95 (0-06-072444-7). 224pp. A celebration of urban playground basketball and the talented young people who enjoy it. (Rev: BL 11/15/04) [796.323]

2789 Stewart, Mark. *The NBA Finals* (5–10). Series: Watts History of Sports. 2003, Watts LB $33.50 (0-531-11955-6). 95pp. National Basketball Association finals over more than half a century are detailed year by year, with ample information on the teams and the players. (Rev: SLJ 3/04) [797]

2790 Thomas, Keltie. *How Basketball Works* (5–8). Illus. 2005, Maple Tree $16.95 (1-897066-18-X); paper $6.95 (1-897066-19-8). 64pp. A lively overview of basketball's history, equipment, training, and skills, with interesting anecdotes and factoids. (Rev: BL 5/15/05) [796.323]

2791 Wertheim, L. Jon. *Transition Game: How Hoosiers Went Hip-Hop* (8–12). Illus. 2005, Penguin $23.95 (0-399-15250-4). 256pp. A look at how the game of basketball has changed over the past two decades. (Rev: BL 2/1/05) [796.323]

Bicycling, Motorcycling, etc.

2792 Haduch, Bill. *Go Fly a Bike! The Ultimate Book About Bicycle Fun, Freedom, and Science* (4–8). 2004, Dutton $16.99 (0-525-47024-7). 112pp. Packed with facts and cartoon illustrations, this comprehensive guide covers everything from the history of bicycling to practical tips for bike care and repair. (Rev: BL 2/1/04; SLJ 3/04) [796.6]

2793 Sidwells, Chris. *Complete Bike Book* (8–12). Illus. 2005, DK paper $17.95 (0-7566-1427-9). 240pp. History, technology, training, and maintenance are all covered in this volume for all levels of riders that also includes a stunning section of color photographs. (Rev: BL 9/1/05) [796.6]

Camping, Hiking, Backpacking, and Mountaineering

2794 Kalman, Bobbie, and John Crossingham. *Extreme Climbing* (4–8). Series: Extreme Sports No Limits! 2004, Crabtree LB $23.92 (0-7787-1671-6). 32pp. Explores the full spectrum of climbing sports, looking at the specific challenges of each and offering readers valuable advice about equipment, climbing techniques, locations, and difficulty ratings, as well as profiles of notable climbers. (Rev: BL 9/1/04)

2795 Oxlade, Chris. *Rock Climbing* (4–8). Illus. Series: Extreme Sports. 2003, Lerner LB $22.60 (0-8225-1240-8). 32pp. An appealing introduction to the history, equipment, techniques, safety concerns,

and challenges of this sport. (Rev: BL 3/1/04; SLJ 5/04) [790.52]

2796 Rhatigan, Joe. *The Kids' Guide to Nature Adventures: 80 Great Activities for Exploring the Outdoors* (3–7). 2003, Lark Books paper $17.95 (1-57990-373-8). 128pp. This beautifully illustrated guide is loaded with great ideas for having fun outdoors, including locations ranging from the family's backyard to America's large national parks. (Rev: BL 10/1/03; SLJ 1/04)

Football

2797 Ingram, Scott. *A Football All-Pro* (6–8). Illus. Series: The Making of a Champion. 2004, Heinemann LB $29.93 (1-4034-5364-0). 48pp. History, rules, training, and tactics are among the topics discussed, along with information on key players. (Rev: SLJ 3/05) [796.332]

2798 McDonell, Chris, ed. *The Football Game I'll Never Forget: 100 NFL Stars' Stories* (8–12). Illus. 2004, Firefly paper $24.95 (1-55297-850-8). 224pp. One hundred football stars talk about the games they remember. (Rev: BL 9/1/04; VOYA 4/05) [796.332]

Hockey

2799 Connolly, Helen. *Field Hockey: Rules, Tips, Strategy, and Safety* (4–8). Series: Sports from Coast to Coast. 2005, Rosen LB $26.50 (1-4042-0182-3). 48pp. This title puts the spotlight on field hockey, including a brief history of the sport as well as a look at its rules, equipment, training, and so forth. (Rev: SLJ 10/05)

2800 Kennedy, Mike. *Ice Hockey* (5–7). Series: Watts Library. 2003, Watts LB $24.00 (0-531-12273-5). 64pp. This overview explores the history of the sport, its rules, and styles of play, and provides information on some of the key players. (Rev: SLJ 2/04) [796.962]

Horse Racing and Horsemanship

2801 Kimball, Cheryl. *Horse Showing for Kids* (4–8). Illus. 2004, Storey paper $16.95 (1-58017-501-5). 151pp. A comprehensive guide to showing horses, covering preparations for both horse and rider/handler, plus advice on safety, sportsmanship, and appropriate attire (for animals and humans). (Rev: SLJ 2/05) [798.2]

Martial Arts

2802 Rielly, Robin L. *Karate for Kids* (5–8). Illus. Series: The Martial Arts for Kids. 2004, Tuttle paper $11.95 (0-8048-3534-9). 48pp. After an overview of the history of karate, this appealing volume with clear illustrations looks at the moves, rules and etiquette, uniform and belts, and so forth. (Rev: BL 9/1/04; SLJ 2/05) [796.815]

Olympic Games

2803 Coffey, Wayne. *The Boys of Winter: The Untold Story of a Coach, a Dream, and the 1980 U.S. Olympic Hockey Team* (8–12). Illus. 2005, Crown $23.95 (1-4000-4765-X). 320pp. In this inspiring look back at the 1980 Winter Olympics victory of the U.S. men's hockey team, sportswriter Coffey introduces readers to the players and coach who pulled off this miracle on ice. (Rev: BL 11/15/04; SLJ 5/05) [796.962]

2804 Gifford, Clive. *Summer Olympics: The Definitive Guide to the World's Greatest Sports Celebration* (4–8). Illus. 2004, Kingfisher $12.95 (0-7534-5693-1). 80pp. An attractively illustrated overview of the history of the games with information on the individual sports, plus coverage of training, key athletes, important records, and so forth. (Rev: SLJ 8/04) [796.48]

2805 Macy, Sue. *Freeze Frame: A Photographic History of the Winter Olympics* (6–9). Illus. 2005, National Geographic $18.95 (0-7922-7887-9). 96pp. A vivid overview of the Winter Games, looking at the various events and the challenges of these winter sports. (Rev: BL 12/15/05; SLJ 2/06) [796.98]

2806 Macy, Sue. *Swifter, Higher, Stronger: A Photographic History of the Summer Olympics* (6–10). 2004, National Geographic $18.95 (0-7922-6667-6). 96pp. Full of photographs and fascinating trivia, this volume covers the history of the games through the Sydney Games of 2000 and discusses controversies, sportsmanship, and the opening up of the games to women. (Rev: BCCB 7–8/04; BL 7/04; SLJ 6/04) [796.4]

2807 Middleton, Haydn. *Modern Olympics* (4–8). Series: The Olympics. 2003, Heinemann LB $16.95 (1-4034-4677-6). 32pp. A concise look at the modern games, with many illustrations, graphics, and sidebars, plus discussion of terrorism incidents, drug use, the choice of host cities, and the Paralympics. (Rev: SLJ 5/04) [796.48]

Running and Jogging

2808 Griffis, Molly Levite. *The Great American Bunion Derby* (5–10). 2003, Eakin $15.95 (1-57168-801-3); paper $9.95 (1-57168-810-2). 87pp. The story of a poor part-Cherokee farm boy who joined a marathon run across the United States in the late 1920s and won the $25,000 top prize. (Rev: BL 1/1–15/04; SLJ 3/04) [796.42]

Sailing, Boating, and Canoeing

2809 Heller, Peter. *Hell or High Water* (8–12). 2004, Rodale $24.95 (1-57954-872-5). 336pp. Heller chronicles the 2002 conquest of Tibet's Tsangpo River by an elite kayaking team and discusses the attractions of this dangerous sport. (Rev: BL 9/15/04) [797.122]

Skateboarding

2810 Badillo, Steve, and Doug Werner. *Skateboarding: Book of Tricks* (7–12). 2003, Tracks paper $12.95 (1-884654-19-3). 176pp. Basic and advanced moves are well illustrated in black-and-white photographs although Badillo is shown without protective gear. (Rev: SLJ 5/04) [796.2]

Skiing and Snowboarding

2811 Barr, Matt, and Chris Moran. *Snowboarding* (4–8). Illus. Series: Extreme Sports. 2003, Lerner LB $22.60 (0-8225-1242-4). 32pp. An appealing introduction to the history, equipment, techniques, safety concerns, and stars of this increasingly popular sport. (Rev: BL 3/1/04; SLJ 5/04; VOYA 6/04) [790.9]

Soccer

2812 Stewart, Mark. *The World Cup* (5–10). Series: The Watts History of Sports. 2003, Watts LB $33.50 (0-531-11957-2). 96pp. An overview of the international soccer championship that takes place every four years, this volume, which will be useful for reports, starts with the 1930 games and includes information on teams and players. (Rev: SLJ 3/04) [796.3]

Surfing, Water Skiing, and Other Water Sports

2813 Egan, Tracie. *Water Polo: Rules, Tips, Strategy, and Safety* (4–8). Series: Sports from Coast to Coast. 2005, Rosen LB $26.50 (1-4042-0186-6). 48pp. Introduces readers to the sport of water polo, along with its rules, training, and equipment. (Rev: SLJ 10/05)

2814 Lake, Sanoe, and Steven Jarrett. *Surfer Girl* (8–11). Illus. 2005, Little, Brown paper $12.99 (0-316-11015-9). 144pp. Designed especially for girls, this witty, easy-to-understand guide to surfing pro-

vides a brief history of the sport as well as helpful advice on equipment, techniques, and safety. (Rev: BCCB 7–8/05; BL 5/15/05; SLJ 7/05) [797.3]

2815 Lourie, Peter. *First Dive to Shark Dive* (5–8). Illus. 2006, Boyds Mills $17.95 (1-59078-068-X). 48pp. This attractive, interesting photoessay documents a 12-year-old girl's introduction to scuba diving among sharks. (Rev: BL 2/15/06) [797.2]

Volleyball

2816 Giddens, Sandra, and Owen Giddens. *Volleyball: Rules, Tips, Strategy, and Safety* (4–8). Series: Sports from Coast to Coast. 2005, Rosen LB $26.50 (1-4042-0185-8). 48pp. Introduces the sport of volleyball — including its rules, equipment, and strategies. (Rev: SLJ 10/05) [796.32]

Author Index

Authors are arranged alphabetically by last name. Authors' and joint authors' names are followed by book titles — which are also arranged alphabetically — and the text entry number. Book titles may refer to those that appear as a main entry or as an internal entry mentioned in the text. Fiction titles are indicated by (F) following the entry number.

Title Index

This index contains both main entry and internal titles cited in the entries. References are to entry numbers, not page numbers. All fiction titles are indicated by (F), following the entry number.

Subject/Grade Level Index

All entries are listed by subject and then according to grade level suitability (see the key at the foot of pages for grade level designations). Subjects are arranged alphabetically and subject heads may be subdivided into nonfiction (e.g., "Africa") and fiction (e.g. "Africa — Fiction"). References to entries are by entry number, not page number.

IJ = Upper Elementary/Lower Middle School; J = Middle School/Junior High; JS = Junior High/Senior High

IJ = Upper Elementary/Lower Middle School; J = Middle School/Junior High; JS = Junior High/Senior High

IJ = Upper Elementary/Lower Middle School; J = Middle School/Junior High; JS = Junior High/Senior High

Automobile racing
See also NASCAR
IJ: 2777

**Automobile racing —
Biography**
IJ: 1453

Automobile racing — Fiction
J: 990

Automobile travel — Fiction
J: 56, 192, 835

Automobiles
J: 2655

Automobiles — Biography
IJ: 1404

Automobiles — Fiction
JS: 229

Avi
IJ: 1199 J: 2650

Aviation
See also Airplanes
J: 2650

Aviation — Biography
JS: 1399

Aviation — History
IJ: 2653 JS: 1399

Azerbaijan
JS: 1807

Aztecs
See also Mexico — History
IJ: 1642 J: 1830

B

Baboons
IJ: 2487

Bach, Johann Sebastian
JS: 1258

Bacteria
IJ: 2282, 2288, 2295, 2525

Baker, Alia Muhammad
IJ: 1534

Baker, Ella
JS: 1295

Balanchine, George
J: 1268 JS: 1267

Balboa, Vasco Nunez de
IJ: 1151

Ballet
IJ: 1585, 1587–88 JS: 1586

Ballet — Biography
J: 1268 JS: 1267

Ballet — Fiction
IJ: 661 J: 568

Bananas
IJ: 2476

Bangladesh
JS: 1766

Barton, Clara
IJ: 1384

Baseball
IJ: 2781 J: 2782 JS: 2778–80

Baseball — Biography
IJ: 1451, 1454–56, 1458 JS: 1457,
1538

Baseball — Fiction
IJ: 217, 419–20, 984, 992, 999
J: 994, 1003

Baseball — History
IJ: 1451, 2051

Baseball — Japan
JS: 2784

Basketball
IJ: 2785, 2790 J: 2789 JS: 2786,
2788, 2791

Basketball — Biography
IJ: 1459, 1461 JS: 1460, 1462

Basketball — Fiction
IJ: 991, 995, 997, 1001 J: 982, 988

Basketball — Poetry
IJ: 1060

Bates, Daisy
JS: 1296

Battles (military)
See also specific battles, e.g.,
Alamo, Battle of the
IJ: 1899 JS: 1608

Bay of Pigs
JS: 1840 J: 2491

Bears
See also specific types, e.g., Polar
bears
J: 2491

Bears — Fiction
J: 16

Beauty — Fiction
JS: 235

Beauty contests — Fiction
JS: 853

Beckham, David
JS: 1468

Beckwourth, James
IJ: 1535

Bees
JS: 2511

Behavioral problems
IJ: 2409

Beijing, China
IJ: 1755

Bell, Alexander Graham
IJ: 1403

Ben-Gurion, David
J: 1817

Bengal tigers
JS: 2497

Benjamin of Tudela — Fiction
IJ: 620

Benz, Karl
IJ: 1404

Berlin, Germany
IJ: 1796

Berlin Wall
IJ: 1799

Berlioz, Hector
IJ: 1259

Bethune, Mary McLeod
IJ: 1297

Bible — Geography
IJ: 2009

Bible stories
IJ: 2013, 2019 J: 2015, 2018
JS: 29

Bicycle racing — Biography
IJ: 1466 JS: 1467

Bicycles
IJ: 2792 JS: 2793

Big Bang theory
IJ: 2466 J: 2043 JS: 2042

Bill of Rights (U.S.)
See also Constitution (U.S.)
J: 2043 JS: 2042

Billy the Kid — Fiction
J: 735

Bin Laden, Osama
JS: 1491

Bioethics
J: 2268

Biography — Collective
IJ: 1288, 1486 J: 1167, 1392, 1398,
1484 JS: 1171, 1292, 1393, 1395,
1399, 1474

Biography — General
IJ: 1479

Biology
J: 2469

**Biology — Experiments and
projects**
JS: 2473

Bionics
J: 2268

Biotechnology
J: 2326 JS: 2297, 2328, 2471

Bioterrorism
IJ: 2299

IJ = Upper Elementary/Lower Middle School; J = Middle School/Junior High; JS = Junior High/Senior High

IJ = Upper Elementary/Lower Middle School; J = Middle School/Junior High; JS = Junior High/Senior High

IJ = Upper Elementary/Lower Middle School; J = Middle School/Junior High; JS = Junior High/Senior High

IJ = Upper Elementary/Lower Middle School; J = Middle School/Junior High; JS = Junior High/Senior High

IJ = Upper Elementary/Lower Middle School; J = Middle School/Junior High; JS = Junior High/Senior High

Date rape
See also Rape
JS: 2390

Dating (social)
J: 2393

Dating (social) — Fiction
J: 125, 261, 269–70, 305, 337
JS: 238

da Vinci, Leonardo
IJ: 1177–78, 1416

da Vinci, Leonardo — Fiction
J: 494

Davis, Miles
IJ: 1270

Death
IJ: 202, 2054, 2396, 2411

Death — Fiction
IJ: 71, 175, 820 **J:** 184, 223, 533,
643 **JS:** 162, 212, 239, 244, 246,
286, 301

Death penalty
JS: 2056

**Declaration of Independence
(U.S.)**
IJ: 1373

Degas, Edgar — Fiction
J: 668

Delaware (state)
IJ: 1985

Delaware (state) — History
IJ: 1894–95

Delhi, India
IJ: 1765

Democratic Party — History
IJ: 1945

Deported aliens
JS: 2102

Depression, Great
IJ: 1953–54 **J:** 1956

Depression, Great — Fiction
IJ: 754, 760 **J:** 739, 759 **JS:** 756

Depression (mental state)
IJ: 2303 **J:** 2412 **JS:** 1542, 2362

**Depression (mental state) —
Fiction**
J: 199

Design
See Clothing and dress; Fashion
design

Design — Careers
JS: 2215 **JS:** 541

Detectives — Fiction
See also Mystery stories — Fiction
JS: 541

Diabetes
IJ: 2285, 2289 **J:** 2276

Diabetes — Fiction
IJ: 996

Diaries
See also Journals
IJ: 1255 **J:** 1546 **JS:** 1824

Diaries — Fiction
IJ: 104, 164, 692, 755 **J:** 118, 209,
220, 693, 733, 842–43, 862–63, 1094

Dickens, Charles
IJ: 1208 **J:** 1207

Dickinson, Emily
J: 1209 **JS:** 1122, 1210

Dictators — Biography
JS: 1501

Diet and dieting
JS: 2369

Diet pills
J: 2248

Digestive system
IJ: 2351 **J:** 2337, 2350

Dinesen, Isak
JS: 1211 **JS:** 1599

Dinosaurs
See also Fossils; Paleontology;
Prehistoric animals
JS: 1599

Dinosaurs — Humor
JS: 1110

Disasters
IJ: 1619

Diseases and illness
See also Medicine; and specific
diseases, e.g., AIDS
IJ: 1679, 2277, 2288 **J:** 2279
JS: 2297

Diseases and illness — Fiction
IJ: 177 **JS:** 762

Diseases and illness — History
J: 2319

Disney (firm)
J: 2190

Divorce
IJ: 2419

Divorce — Fiction
IJ: 43, 99, 189

DNA
J: 2323 **JS:** 2324

Doctors — Biography
J: 2311

Dogs
See also individual types, e.g.,
Guide dogs; Sled dogs
IJ: 2530 **JS:** 2528–29, 2531

Dogs — Fiction
IJ: 26, 328 **J:** 792 **JS:** 24

Dogs — History
JS: 2532

Dollhouses — Fiction
IJ: 823

Dolphins
JS: 2522

Domestic violence — Fiction
J: 190

Dominican Americans
IJ: 1841

Down syndrome
IJ: 2301

Dragons — Fiction
IJ: 383, 392, 428, 555 **J:** 393, 532
JS: 481

Drake, Sir Francis
JS: 1511

Drake, Sir Francis — Fiction
J: 662

Drama
IJ: 1596

Drawing and painting
See also Art; Crafts
IJ: 2714, 2716, 2718, 2721
JS: 1553, 2719

Dreams and dreaming
IJ: 2340, 2753 **JS:** 2339, 2395

**Dreams and dreaming —
Fiction**
IJ: 457

Dred Scott Case
IJ: 2065 **J:** 1915

Dred Scott Case — Fiction
JS: 718

Dress
See Clothing and dress

Driving — Careers
JS: 2203

Droughts — Fiction
IJ: 757

Drugs and drug abuse
See also specific drugs, e.g.,
Cocaine
IJ: 2265 **J:** 2047, 2246–47, 2251,
2261, 2264, 2360

**Drugs and drug abuse —
Fiction**
J: 196, 249 **JS:** 345

**Drugs and drug abuse —
History**
J: 2319

Duncan, Tim
IJ: 1459

Dust Bowl
IJ: 1953 **JS:** 1958

Dylan, Bob
JS: 1271

IJ = Upper Elementary/Lower Middle School; J = Middle School/Junior High; JS = Junior High/Senior High

E

E. coli
IJ: 2287

Earhart, Amelia
JS: 1155

Earth
JS: 1616, 2441

Earth science — Experiments and projects
JS: 2552

Earthquakes
IJ: 2556

East Africa
JS: 1738

Easter — Poetry
IJ: 1040

Eastern Europe
J: 1808

Eastern Europe — History
IJ: 1723

Eating disorders
JS: 2370–71

Eating disorders — Fiction
J: 222

Ecology and environment
See also Pollution
IJ: 1731, 1756, 1758, 1762, 2133, 2135, 2138, 2143, 2504, 2554, 2578, 2599–600 J: 2589 JS: 2132, 2296, 2510

Ecology and environment — Biography
IJ: 1438

Ecology and environment — Fiction
IJ: 79

Economics and business
JS: 2191, 2193, 2226

Economics and business — Careers
JS: 2225

Economics and business — History
J: 1678

Ecstasy (drug)
J: 2246

Edison, Thomas Alva
IJ: 1419 J: 2764

Education
See also High schools; Schools
J: 2764

Education — Careers
JS: 2230

Education — History
IJ: 1686

Egypt
IJ: 1655, 1813

Egypt — Art
J: 1652

Egypt — Biography
IJ: 1490 J: 1488

Egypt — Crafts
J: 1652

Egypt — History
See also Pyramids
IJ: 1649, 1653, 1655 J: 1551, 1647, 1652, 1810 JS: 1648, 1650, 1811

Eichmann, Adolf
J: 1693

Eiffel Tower
IJ: 2623

Einstein, Albert
IJ: 1420, 1422 JS: 1421

Eleanor of Aquitaine
J: 1512

Elections (U.S.)
J: 2077, 2079 JS: 1913, 1963

Elections (U.S.) — Fiction
J: 124

Electricians — Careers
IJ: 2228

Electricity
IJ: 2607 JS: 2606

Electricity — Biography
JS: 1445

Electronic mail — Fiction
IJ: 164 JS: 951

Elements
JS: 2548

Elephants
IJ: 2498

Elion, Gertrude
IJ: 1423

Elizabeth I, Queen of England
IJ: 1513

Elizabeth I, Queen of England — Fiction
IJ: 684

Elizabethan England — Fiction
J: 673 JS: 650

Ellis Island
IJ: 1946 JS: 2101

Emancipation Proclamation
IJ: 1916, 1921

Emotional problems
JS: 2364

Emotional problems — Biography
JS: 2359

Emotional problems — Fiction
J: 97 JS: 262

Empire State Building
IJ: 2624

Endangered species
IJ: 2492 JS: 2512

Endocrine system
J: 2341

Energy (physics)
IJ: 2135 J: 2604 JS: 2603

Energy (physics) — History
IJ: 2602

Energy (sources)
See also Geothermal energy, Nuclear energy, Solar energy
IJ: 2600

Engineering
See Technology and engineering

England — Biography
IJ: 1513 JS: 1197, 1468

England — Fiction
IJ: 231, 644, 656–57, 680, 689, 821 J: 107–8, 125, 197, 305, 311, 334, 465, 613, 617, 643, 646, 653, 665, 674–75, 681, 687, 845, 854, 870, 936 JS: 113, 225, 247, 872, 915 JS: 2392

Entertainment industry
See Motion pictures; Television; Theater

Entomology
JS: 2510

Environment
See Ecology and environment

Epidemics
IJ: 2271

Epilepsy
J: 2280, 2347

Escapes
J: 1623

Essays
J: 1112 JS: 1113

Estonia
J: 1806 J: 2034

Ethnic cleansing
See also Genocide
J: 2034

Ethnic groups
See also see specific groups, e.g., African Americans; Hispanic Americans

Etiquette
IJ: 2399–400

IJ = Upper Elementary/Lower Middle School; J = Middle School/Junior High; JS = Junior High/Senior High

Etymology
IJ: 1127

Europe
IJ: 1786

Europe — Fiction
JS: 85

European Community
JS: 1788

Evolution
JS: 1601–3, 2472

Evolution — Biography
IJ: 1417 J: 1418

Evolution — Trials
IJ: 2066

Ex-convicts — Fiction
JS: 87

Experiments
See as subdivision of other
subjects, e.g., Astronomy —
Experiments and projects

Explorers
See Adventurers and explorers

**Extrasensory perception —
Fiction**
JS: 769

Extraterrestrial life
IJ: 2443, 2757

Extreme sports
IJ: 2768, 2794 JS: 2774, 2809

***Exxon Valdez* oil spill**
IJ: 2140, 2142

F

Faces
IJ: 2334

Fairy tales
IJ: 1086 JS: 1090

Fairy tales — Fiction
IJ: 468, 1080 J: 1081

Family life
J: 2393

Family life — Fiction
IJ: 72, 96, 120, 172, 738, 823, 850,
927 J: 92, 106, 192, 197, 290, 322,
336, 932 JS: 45, 75, 113, 132, 289

Family problems
See also specific problems, e.g.,
Divorce
IJ: 202, 2426 JS: 2372

Family problems — Fiction
IJ: 38, 40, 48, 62, 66, 73, 76–77, 109,
164, 166–67, 171, 175, 177, 180–81,
187, 198, 200–1, 210–11, 213,
216–17, 231, 260, 265, 339, 676, 754,
989 J: 39, 46, 50, 65, 74, 82, 84,

101, 121, 125, 133, 174, 178, 188,
190–91, 194–96, 199, 204–5, 209,
214, 240, 294, 329, 341, 681, 687,
982 JS: 60, 83, 105, 127, 162, 169,
176, 185, 207–8, 212, 248, 259, 267,
624, 756, 872, 1002

Family violence
See Domestic violence; Violence

Fantasy — Fiction
IJ: 351, 354, 356–57, 363–65, 370,
375–76, 381, 383, 386, 388, 391–92,
397, 401, 403, 405, 407, 409, 414–17,
419–21, 425, 428, 431, 439–41, 443,
447–50, 457, 461, 468–69, 471–73,
475–79, 482, 484–85, 488, 492, 497,
499, 506–8, 510–11, 515, 519–24,
526, 530, 585, 794–97, 800, 807–10,
812, 814, 816, 820, 825–26, 834, 869,
920, 958 J: 27, 353, 361–62, 366,
372–74, 377–79, 382, 385, 387, 389,
394–95, 398–99, 402, 404, 406, 408,
411–13, 418, 423–24, 426–27, 429,
432–33, 435–38, 442, 445, 453–54,
456, 458–59, 463–65, 467, 474, 483,
486, 491, 493–96, 502–4, 513, 518,
525, 528–29, 531–33, 554, 565, 587,
643, 647, 703, 806, 2008 JS: 352,
358, 360, 367–69, 371, 380, 390, 396,
400, 410, 422, 430, 434, 444, 451–52,
460, 466, 470, 481, 487, 489–90, 498,
501, 509, 512, 514, 516–17, 547, 576,
582–83, 603, 837, 861, 1021

Fantasy — Short stories
J: 1018 JS: 462

Farm workers — Biography
IJ: 1299

Farms and farm life — Fiction
IJ: 52, 698 J: 102, 764

Farms and farm life — History
JS: 2474

Fashion
J: 2628, 2713

Fashion — Fiction
J: 114

Fashion — History
IJ: 2630

Fashion design — Biography
JS: 1408

Fashion industry — Careers
JS: 2206

Fast food
IJ: 2609

Father-daughter relationships
JS: 1533

**Father-daughter relationships
— Fiction**
IJ: 679

**Father-son relationships —
Fiction**
IJ: 177, 679 J: 41–42, 89, 647, 926
JS: 162, 985

Fathers — Fiction
IJ: 166, 846

**Federal Bureau of Investigation
(U.S.)**
IJ: 1363

**Federal Bureau of Investigation
(U.S.) — Fiction**
JS: 917

Fencing — Fiction
J: 305

Fermi, Enrico
JS: 1424

Field hockey
IJ: 2799

Firefighters
JS: 2183

Fires — History
J: 1617

Fires — Poetry
IJ: 1048

Fireworks
IJ: 2609

First aid
See Safety

First Ladies (U.S.)
See Presidents (U.S.) — Wives —
Biography

Fish
See also different species of fish,
e.g., Sharks
IJ: 2515, 2518

Fish — Pets
JS: 2533

Fishing — Fiction
J: 183 JS: 5

Fitzgerald, F. Scott
IJ: 1212 J: 1213

Fleischman, Sid
J: 1214

Florida
IJ: 2578

Florida — Fiction
IJ: 79, 757 J: 205 JS: 726

Folk art
JS: 1577

Folk singers — Biography
JS: 1271

Folk tales
See Folklore

Folklore
See also Mythology; and specific
countries and regions, e.g., China
— Folklore; and specific topics,
e.g., Birds — Folklore
IJ: 826, 1083–84, 1088, 1091–92,
2025 JS: 1082

IJ = Upper Elementary/Lower Middle School; J = Middle School/Junior High; JS = Junior High/Senior High

Folklore — Africa
JS: 1087

Folklore — Celtic
JS: 1095

Folklore — Mesopotamia
JS: 1097

Food
IJ: 2358, 2477 J: 2373 JS: 2707

Food — Fiction
J: 870–71

Food — History
IJ: 2186

Food and Drug Administration
J: 2047

Food industry — Careers
J: 2202 JS: 2204, 2207

Food poisoning
JS: 2270

Football
IJ: 2797

Football — Fiction
IJ: 993 J: 102, 1004 JS: 983,
985–86

Force (physics)
JS: 2596

Forensic anthropology
J: 1425

Forensic sciences
IJ: 2150, 2155–58 J: 2154, 2162
JS: 2076

Forensic sciences — Biography
J: 1425

Forensic sciences — Careers
J: 2236

Forensic sciences — Fiction
J: 922

Fortifications
IJ: 1624

Fortune telling
IJ: 2754

Fossils
J: 1600 J: 2422

Foster care
See also Adoption; Family
  problems
J: 2422

Foster care — Fiction
IJ: 339 J: 209, 900

Fox, Paula
IJ: 1215

France — Biography
IJ: 1175 JS: 1524

France — Fiction
IJ: 23, 661 J: 668, 774

France, Diane
J: 1425

Francis of Assisi, Saint
IJ: 2020

Frank, Anne
IJ: 1515–16, 1713 J: 1514, 1517

Franklin, Benjamin
J: 1358–59

Freedom of speech
JS: 2042

Freedom of the press
JS: 2042

French Revolution
JS: 1524, 1793

Friendship
J: 2393

Friendship — Fiction
IJ: 38, 48, 71, 81, 103–4, 109, 115,
120, 140, 156, 216, 243, 263, 299,
333, 698, 753, 772, 874, 899 J: 37,
46, 58, 65, 68, 84, 93–94, 97, 101,
106, 197, 264, 266, 269–70, 274, 285,
293, 302, 307, 322, 330, 337, 341,
350, 749, 780, 866, 932, 938, 990
JS: 35, 57, 80, 147, 218, 225, 233,
238, 244, 248, 251, 268, 279, 281,
318, 569, 595, 655, 666, 726, 782,
985

Frontier life (U.S.) — Biography
IJ: 1362

Frontier life (U.S.) — Fiction
IJ: 704, 731 J: 733 JS: 727

Frontier life (U.S.) — Women
IJ: 1937

Fung, Inez
J: 1426

Future — Fiction
J: 384 JS: 509

Futurism
J: 2169

G

Gabon — Animals
JS: 1748

Galileo
IJ: 1427 J: 1428

Gambling — Fiction
J: 188, 253

Games
See also Sports
IJ: 2769 J: 2765

Gandhi, Mahatma
IJ: 1495 J: 1493 JS: 1494

Ganges River
IJ: 1762

Gangs
JS: 2148, 2151

Gangs — Fiction
IJ: 99 J: 350

Gardens and gardening
JS: 2480, 2722

Garvey, Marcus
J: 1300–1

Gates, Henry Louis, Jr.
JS: 1387

Gay rights
JS: 2088

Gay youth
JS: 2389

Gay youth — Fiction
JS: 326

Gays
See Gay rights; Gay youth;
  Homosexuality; Lesbians

Gehrig, Lou
IJ: 1455

Gehry, Frank
J: 1179

Gems
IJ: 2570

Gender roles — Fiction
JS: 227 JS: 2297, 2328, 2471

Gene therapy
See Genetic engineering

Genetic engineering
See also Clones and cloning
JS: 2297, 2328, 2471

Genetic engineering — Fiction
IJ: 977

Genetics
IJ: 2322, 2327 JS: 2296–97, 2328,
2471

Genetics — Biography
IJ: 1435

Genetics — Fiction
JS: 913

Genghis Khan
JS: 1496 J: 1739

Genocide
See also Ethnic cleansing
J: 1739

Geography
IJ: 1598, 1613, 1622 J: 1628
JS: 1620–21

Geography — Poetry
IJ: 1046

Geology
See also Rocks and minerals
IJ: 1610 J: 2569

IJ = Upper Elementary/Lower Middle School; J = Middle School/Junior High; JS = Junior High/Senior High

IJ = Upper Elementary/Lower Middle School; J = Middle School/Junior High; JS = Junior High/Senior High

Harlem Renaissance
JS: 1955

Hawaii
IJ: 1992

Hawk, Tony
JS: 1470

Hawking, Stephen
J: 1430

**Hawthorne, Nathaniel —
Criticism**
J: 1118

Hayslip, Le Ly
IJ: 1388

Health and health care
IJ: 2304, 2358

**Health and health care —
Careers**
JS: 2235

Hemingway, Ernest
IJ: 1217 JS: 1120

Henson, Matthew
IJ: 1156–57

Heroes and heroism
IJ: 1281 JS: 1143

Heroes and heroism — Poetry
IJ: 1050

**Heroes and heroism — Short
stories**
J: 1022

Heroin
J: 2249

Herzl, Theodor
J: 1817

Hiawatha
J: 1879

Hickok, Wild Bill
IJ: 1362

High schools
JS: 2195, 2402

High schools — Fiction
J: 94, 123, 152, 160, 199, 214, 236,
249, 261, 295, 312, 316, 321, 335,
347, 543, 942, 950, 987 JS: 49, 67,
147, 157, 255, 257, 279, 286, 289,
292, 298, 300, 306, 325, 331, 805,
818, 838, 847, 948, 983

Hiking
IJ: 2796

Himalayas — Fiction
JS: 2

Himmler, Heinrich
JS: 1519

Hiroshima, Japan
JS: 1706

Hiroshima, Japan — History
JS: 1696 JS: 2117

Hispanic Americans
See also specific groups, e.g.,
Mexican Americans
JS: 2117

**Hispanic Americans —
Biography**
IJ: 1158, 1276, 1299 JS: 1292

Hispanic Americans — Fiction
IJ: 134, 309 J: 78, 135, 142, 149
JS: 137

Hispanic Americans — Poetry
JS: 1067

Historic sites (U.S.)
JS: 2106

History
See also under specific countries
and continents, e.g., Africa —
History; and historical eras and
events, e.g., Ancient history;
World War I
IJ: 1607, 1618

Hitler, Adolf
J: 1520

HIV (virus) — Fiction
J: 142 JS: 225

Holidays — Cookbooks
IJ: 2705–6

Holocaust
IJ: 1709, 1713–14 J: 1693–94,
1697, 1702 JS: 1700

Holocaust — Biography
IJ: 1515–16, 1531, 1539 J: 1514,
1517

Holocaust — Fiction
IJ: 659 J: 773 JS: 567

Holocaust — Memoirs
J: 1711

Holy Land — History
J: 1815

**Homeland Security,
Department of**
JS: 2049, 2172, 2179

Homeless people — Fiction
JS: 267, 324

Homer
IJ: 1218

Homosexuality
See also Gay rights; Gay youth;
Lesbians
IJ: 2425 J: 2386 JS: 2389

Homosexuality — Fiction
J: 266, 272, 282 JS: 132, 280, 317,
952

Honeybees
JS: 2511

Hook, Captain
J: 4

Hoover, Herbert
IJ: 1322

Hoover, J. Edgar
IJ: 1363

Hopkins, Lee Bennett
IJ: 1219

Horror — Fiction
See also Supernatural — Fiction;
and specific supernatural beings,
e.g., Ghosts
IJ: 798–99, 810 J: 33, 374, 806
JS: 830

Horseback riding
IJ: 2534–35

Horseback riding — Fiction
J: 129

Horses
IJ: 2534–35, 2801 JS: 2536

Horses — Fiction
IJ: 25, 654, 1008

Horses — Poetry
JS: 1043

Horses — Short stories
IJ: 1019

Hospitals — History
J: 2319

Hostages
JS: 2175

House of Representatives (U.S.)
See United States — Government
and politics

Houston, Sam
IJ: 1364

Hubble, Edwin
J: 1431

Hubble space telescope
IJ: 2439

Hughes, Langston
JS: 1220

Human body
See also specific parts and systems
of the human body, e.g.,
Circulatory system
IJ: 2317, 2342 J: 2343 J: 1694,
2180

Human rights
See also Civil rights
J: 1694, 2180

Human rights — Biography
J: 1528 JS: 1483

Humor and satire
IJ: 844 JS: 1110, 1113, 2633

Humorous poetry
See Poetry — Humorous

Humorous stories — Fiction
IJ: 79, 165, 313, 414, 455, 549, 645,
821, 836, 839, 844, 846, 850, 856,

IJ = Upper Elementary/Lower Middle School; J = Middle School/Junior High; JS = Junior High/Senior High

859, 867–69, 874 **J:** 39, 102, 119, 194, 258, 295, 303, 835, 840–43, 845, 849, 851–52, 854, 858, 860, 862–66, 870–71, 873 **JS:** 277, 838, 847–48, 853, 855, 857, 861, 872, 945

Hurricane Andrew
IJ: 2578

Hussein, Saddam
J: 1722 **JS:** 1497

I

Ice climbing
IJ: 2794

Ice hockey
IJ: 2800 **JS:** 2803

Ice hockey — Biography
IJ: 1463

Ice hockey — Fiction
IJ: 989, 996

Ichiro (baseball player)
JS: 2784

Illegal aliens — Fiction
J: 343

Illness
See Diseases and illness

Imaginary animals — Fiction
IJ: 355, 455

Immigration
J: 1835 **JS:** 2100, 2102

Immigration — Fiction
IJ: 140

Immigration (U.S.)
IJ: 1216, 1545, 1841, 2112, 2114, 2118, 2120, 2123–24, 2127 **J:** 2122, 2126 **JS:** 2033

Immigration (U.S.) — Fiction
IJ: 145–46, 148, 153, 752 **J:** 69, 343, 744, 747

Immigration (U.S.) — History
IJ: 1946 **J:** 2099 **JS:** 2101, 2103

Immune system
IJ: 2338

Impressionism (art)
IJ: 1056

In vitro fertilization
J: 2377

Incas
IJ: 1843 **J:** 1830, 1846

Independence National Historical Park
IJ: 1990

India
IJ: 1763–64

India — Art
IJ: 1568

India — Biography
IJ: 1495 **J:** 1493 **JS:** 1494

India — Cookbooks
IJ: 2701

India — Fiction
JS: 308, 637

India — History
IJ: 1638, 1640, 1753

Indian (Asian) Americans — Fiction
IJ: 189

Indians of North America
See Native Americans and specific Indian tribes, e.g., Apache Indians

Indonesia
IJ: 2593

Indonesia — Fiction
JS: 346

Industry — Biography
J: 1407

Influenza
IJ: 2306

Inhalants
JS: 2263

Inline skating
IJ: 2773

Insects
See also names of specific insects, e.g., Butterflies and moths
IJ: 2509 **J:** 2508 **JS:** 2510

Intelligence
IJ: 2401

International organizations
IJ: 2507

International relations
JS: 2193

Internet
See also World Wide Web
IJ: 2635 **J:** 2634, 2640, 2645
JS: 2633

Interpersonal relations — Fiction
J: 63

Inuit — Fiction
IJ: 20 **J:** 742

Inventions
See Inventors and inventions; and specific inventions, e.g., Telephones

Inventors and inventions
See also specific inventions, e.g., Telephones
IJ: 2477, 2615, 2647 **J:** 2610
JS: 1633, 2612

Inventors and inventions — Biography
IJ: 1177–78, 1403, 1419, 1449
J: 1394 **JS:** 1397, 1445

Inventors and inventions — Fiction
IJ: 1404

Inventors and inventions — History
IJ: 1400 **J:** 2427

Investing (business)
IJ: 2188

Iodine
IJ: 2547

Iran
IJ: 1827 **JS:** 1825

Iran-Iraq War
JS: 1825

Iraq
See also Iran-Iraq War; Operation Iraqi Freedom; Gulf War (1991)
IJ: 1826 **J:** 1722 **JS:** 1721, 1828–29

Iraq — Biography
IJ: 1534 **JS:** 1497

Iraq — History
J: 1716

Ireland — Biography
J: 1528

Ireland — Fiction
IJ: 654 **JS:** 470

Ireland — Folklore
IJ: 1091

Ireland — Poetry
IJ: 1091

Irish Americans
IJ: 1216, 2121, 2124

Iron — History
IJ: 2613

Iroquois Indians — History
J: 1879

Islam
IJ: 2024–25 **J:** 1675, 2028
JS: 2026–27

Islam — Art
IJ: 1567

Islam — History
JS: 1766, 1782, 1804–5, 1807

Islam — Terrorism
JS: 2177

Islamic fundamentalism — Fiction
JS: 346

Israel
J: 1809

IJ = Upper Elementary/Lower Middle School; J = Middle School/Junior High; JS = Junior High/Senior High

J

K

IJ = Upper Elementary/Lower Middle School; J = Middle School/Junior High; JS = Junior High/Senior High

IJ = Upper Elementary/Lower Middle School; J = Middle School/Junior High; JS = Junior High/Senior High

IJ = Upper Elementary/Lower Middle School; J = Middle School/Junior High; JS = Junior High/Senior High

IJ = Upper Elementary/Lower Middle School; J = Middle School/Junior High; JS = Junior High/Senior High

IJ = Upper Elementary/Lower Middle School; J = Middle School/Junior High; JS = Junior High/Senior High

IJ = Upper Elementary/Lower Middle School; J = Middle School/Junior High; JS = Junior High/Senior High

IJ = Upper Elementary/Lower Middle School; J = Middle School/Junior High; JS = Junior High/Senior High

IJ = Upper Elementary/Lower Middle School; J = Middle School/Junior High; JS = Junior High/Senior High

IJ = Upper Elementary/Lower Middle School; J = Middle School/Junior High; JS = Junior High/Senior High

S

Sachar, Louis
J: 1239

Saddam Hussein
See Hussein, Saddam

Safety
JS: 2380

St. Helena — Fiction
J: 677

St. Louis World's Fair, 1904
IJ: 1944

Saints
IJ: 2023

San Francisco — Fiction
J: 749

San Francisco earthquake
IJ: 2557

Satellites
J: 2643

SATs — Fiction
JS: 67

Saturn (planet)
IJ: 2460–61

Saving (business)
IJ: 2188

Scandinavia
See Norway; Vikings

Scandinavia — Mythology
IJ: 1108 JS: 1109

Schizophrenia
IJ: 2363

Scholarships
J: 2197

Schools
See also Boarding schools;
Education; High schools
IJ: 1386 J: 2414

Schools — Fiction
IJ: 51, 64, 66, 70, 104, 115, 126, 130,
231, 250, 260, 263, 320, 542, 548,
555, 645, 856, 867, 874, 880, 989
J: 59, 74, 101, 106, 119, 135, 254,
256, 258, 311, 628, 702, 713, 884
JS: 248, 872

Schools — Poetry
IJ: 1039

Schools — Segregation
IJ: 2071 J: 2093 JS: 2057, 2074

Schools — Violence — Fiction
J: 342 JS: 301

Schulz, Charles M.
IJ: 1190

Schwarzenegger, Arnold
IJ: 1380–81

Schwarzkopf, Norman
J: 1382

Science
See also branches of science, e.g.,
Chemistry
IJ: 2429, 2431

Science — Biography
IJ: 1411, 1416, 1420, 1423, 1440,
1505 J: 1406, 1413–15, 1418, 1426,
1428, 1433, 1439, 1448 JS: 1393,
1395, 1401, 1412, 1442

Science — Careers
IJ: 2479, 2514

**Science — Experiments and
projects**
See also under specific branches of
science, e.g., Astronomy —
Experiments and projects
IJ: 1419, 2429, 2435–37 J: 2433,
2438

Science — History
J: 1615, 2427–28, 2432

Science — Renaissance
J: 2428

Science — Research
J: 2434

Science fairs
IJ: 2437, 2551 J: 2433, 2438, 2543
JS: 2473, 2524, 2544, 2552

Science fairs — Fiction
J: 873

Science fiction
IJ: 962–64, 967, 976–79 J: 884,
953, 955, 959–60, 968–70, 973, 975,
981 JS: 540, 608–9, 954, 956, 961,
965–66, 974, 980

Science fiction — Short stories
J: 1018

Science projects
See Science — Experiments and
projects

Scopes trial (1925)
IJ: 2066

Scopes trial (1925) — Fiction
J: 758

Scotland — Fiction
IJ: 414, 977 J: 125, 221, 649, 665,
936 JS: 671, 857

Scuba diving
IJ: 2815

Sea otters
IJ: 2521

Sea stories — Fiction
IJ: 13 J: 12, 670

Sea turtles
IJ: 2482

Seafaring — Fiction
J: 646

Seas
See also Oceans
IJ: 2587

Segregation (U.S.) — Biography
IJ: 1307

Segregation (U.S.) — Fiction
IJ: 941 JS: 761

Self-confidence — Fiction
IJ: 232

Self-image — Fiction
J: 230, 273 JS: 226

Selkirk, Alexander
IJ: 1163

Senate (U.S.)
IJ: 1375 J: 1368

Senses
J: 2356

September 11, 2001
See also Terrorism
IJ: 1961 J: 1425, 2232, 2234

September 11, 2001 — Fiction
J: 78 JS: 346

Sewing
See also Needlecrafts
IJ: 2742–43

Sex — Fiction
J: 303 JS: 338

Sex roles
JS: 2389

Sex roles — Fiction
J: 41 JS: 247

Sexual abuse
JS: 2391

Sexual abuse — Fiction
IJ: 62, 265 J: 59 JS: 163

Shackleton, Sir Ernest
JS: 1164

**Shackleton, Sir Ernest —
Fiction**
J: 10

Shakespeare, William
IJ: 1241, 1552 J: 1242 JS: 1121

**Shakespeare, William —
Adaptations**
J: 1035

Shakespeare, William — Fiction
J: 673 JS: 650

Shakespeare, William — Plays
IJ: 1032–33 J: 1031

Shanghai, China
IJ: 1761

Sharks
IJ: 2815 JS: 2519–20

Sharks — Biography
J: 1469

IJ = Upper Elementary/Lower Middle School; J = Middle School/Junior High; JS = Junior High/Senior High

IJ = Upper Elementary/Lower Middle School; J = Middle School/Junior High; JS = Junior High/Senior High

IJ = Upper Elementary/Lower Middle School; J = Middle School/Junior High; JS = Junior High/Senior High

IJ = Upper Elementary/Lower Middle School; J = Middle School/Junior High; JS = Junior High/Senior High

IJ = Upper Elementary/Lower Middle School; J = Middle School/Junior High; JS = Junior High/Senior High

IJ = Upper Elementary/Lower Middle School; J = Middle School/Junior High; JS = Junior High/Senior High

IJ = Upper Elementary/Lower Middle School; J = Middle School/Junior High; JS = Junior High/Senior High

About the Authors

JOHN T. GILLESPIE, renowned authority in children's literature, is the author of more than 30 books on collection development. In addition to the other volumes in the Best Books series (*Best Books for Children* and *Best Books for High School Readers*), he is also the author of *Teenplots, Classic Teenplots, The Newbery Companion: Booktalk and Related Materials for Newbery Medal and Honor Books,* and *The Children's and Young Adult Literature Handbook: A Research and Reference Guide.*

CATHERINE BARR is the coauthor of other volumes in the Best Books series (*Best Books for Children* and *Best Books for High School Readers*) and of *Popular Series Fiction for K–6 Readers, Popular Series Fiction for Middle School and Teen Readers*, and *High/Low Handbook: Best Books and Web Sites for Reluctant Teen Readers, 4th Edition.*